EXPLORERS OF AUSTRALIA

EXPLORERS
OF
AUSTRALIA

GEOFFREY BADGER

KANGAROO PRESS

EXPLORERS OF AUSTRALIA

First published in Australia in 2001 by Kangaroo Press
an imprint of Simon & Schuster (Australia) Pty Limited
20 Barcoo Street, East Roseville NSW 2069

A Viacom Company
Sydney New York London Toronto Tokyo Singapore

National Library of Australia
Cataloguing-in-Publication data:

Badger, G. M. (Geoffrey Malcolm), 1916–
Explorers of Australia
Includes index.
ISBN 0 73180 878 9
1. Explorers – Australia. 2. Australia – History – To 1788. 3. Australia –
History – 1788–1900. 4. Australia – Discovery and exploration. I. Title
919.404

Set in Bembo 10.5/13.5
Printed by Griffin Press, Adelaide

10 9 8 7 6 5 4 3 2 1

CONTENTS

ACKNOWLEDGMENTS

Many friends and colleagues, scientific and other, have helped me in many ways during the preparation of this book. Some have provided specific information; others have read one or more of the draft chapters and have invariably made helpful comments. Other friends have helped in the selection and or provision of suitable illustrations; or have allowed me to use some of their own photographs.

I should particularly like to mention Dr Rowland Twidale, Dr Jennifer Bourne and Dr Elizabeth Campbell – all of whom read and commented on the draft chapters. Instructor Commander Oscar Jones, Anthony Sturt (since deceased), Stephen Jeffries, Associate Professor John Earl, Dr Ivan Jarrett, Dr Robert Culver, Arthur Robinson, Associate Professor J. Brand-Miller, Kenneth Price, W. A. R. Richardson, Warren Bonython, Phillip Jones, Terry Sim, Gavin Walkley, Colin Pardoe, Dr Chris Watts, K. T. Borrow, Mrs Joan Donald, Graeme Pretty, David Mack, Bernard Basedow, J. A Bennett, Julian Holland, Bruce Macdonald (since deceased), Ralph Middenway, Archie McArthur, Professor Geoffrey Sharman, Dr Brian Coote, Zoë Bowan, Dr Max Day, Dr John Calaby, Geraldine Triffitt, Sylvia Carr, Graeme Henderson, Dick Kimber, Dick Bland and Anthony Brown also provided information of the greatest interest. Deborah Hagger prepared the splendid maps illustrating the routes taken by some of the explorers. Denis Sitters has made a major contribution to the production of the book and I am most grateful for his help.

Last but not least I should like to thank the many librarians who helped. In particular, thanks to Valerie Sitters, librarian of the Royal Geographical Society of South Australia, whose knowledge of the literature of exploration is second to none. I should also like to thank Sylvia Carr of the National Library of Australia, Gerald Hayes of the State Library of Victoria, Susan Woodburn of the Barr Smith Library of the University of Adelaide, and Valmai Hankel of the State Library of South Australia. All these librarians have a great knowledge of the literature of exploration and I thank them all for their help.

The manuscript was almost complete by August 1999 when I became ill. It was necessary for me to have a couple of operations and, in this interval (and afterwards), Dr Rowland Twidale, Dr Jennifer Bourne and Dr Elizabeth Campbell agreed to format the typescript. I am most grateful to all of them.

PREFACE

This book is concerned with the early maritime and overland explorers of Australia. It does not attempt to describe the work of all the explorers of note over the years – because these numbered well over a hundred. I have had to restrict my coverage to the early years and to those I think have made the most important contributions. Moreover, I have had a special interest in the navigational and nutritional aspects of their journeys. I do not suppose that everyone will entirely agree with my selection; there will always be scholars who would like to press the claims of others, and rightly so.

It must also be remembered that exploration has been a continuing process and did not cease at the conclusion of the nineteenth century. For example, considerable exploration of the northern coast of Australia was carried out during World War II. New techniques have been developed. In the early days, mariners could determine the latitude of their position, but the longitude had to be estimated using the speed of the ship and the course and the time following that course. On land, explorers could determine only the latitude – using an artificial horizon. Here again, however, they had to estimate their longitude by estimating their distance travelled in a certain direction by, for example, counting the number of paces taken by the navigator's horse. Captain Cook was the first maritime explorer of Australia to use the recently discovered method of lunar distances to determine his longitude. Indeed, Cook was the first maritime explorer to use the chronometer to determine longitude. Nowadays,

the explorer can obtain latitude and longitude by pressing a button on a hand-held instrument.

Other techniques have been developed to obtain information that could not have been obtained a few years ago. The depth of the sea measurements made aboard *Endeavour* were obtained by using a lead and line. Developments in World Wars I and II led to the introduction of ultrasonic devices to measure and record the depth of water under the ship, and to locate submarines under the surface of the sea. These devices are known as SONAR – from sound navigation and ranging. More recently the Australian Defence and Technology Organisation, in conjunction with BHP and the Royal Australian Navy, has developed an airborne laser system which gives a three-dimensional perspective of sections of the Great Barrier Reef. It is now possible to obtain a 'picture' of the reef structure where Captain Bligh and the eighteen loyal survivors of the mutiny on the *Bounty* found an 'opening' (now known as the Bligh Boat Entrance) and so avoided destruction. Incidentally, Bligh had been aiming for Providential Channel that had been discovered by Cook in August 1770. This channel is only 15 nautical miles to the north of the entrance which he did find – a remarkable feat of maritime navigation after sailing for 2400 nautical miles from the position where he and his men had been cast adrift in an open boat. This new technique has also been used to obtain a perspective of the reef where *Pandora* was wrecked.[1]

Most of the work of the maritime and overland

explorers of Australia was carried out towards the end of the eighteenth century and during the first half of the nineteenth century – using what we now regard as old-fashioned techniques of navigation. Many of the explorers were British – but not all. The Dutch dominated the early years of maritime exploration and named the country 'New Holland'. French maritime explorers later made major contributions and several German overland explorers were pre-eminent in this field. The British and French made significant maritime discoveries. Nevertheless, Australia was colonised by the British, and this colonisation was one of the major contributions to the expansion of the British Empire. Nowadays, people tend to forget the contributions, and emphasise the drive for overlordship, wealth, and expansion for its own sake. However as Lawrence James has written:[2]

> What matters most today is that the British Empire transformed the world. What it has now

become is in considerable part the consequence of three hundred years of British overseas expansion. The present day demography, economy and political life of North America and much of Asia, the Middle East, Africa and the Pacific owes much to former British rule and influence. English is the most widely spoken global language, and the governance, everyday lives and habits of mind of hundreds of millions of men and women have been shaped by prolonged contact with Britain and its values.

This is not just a British view. Charles McKenna, from New York City, has written in *Time*:[3]

> the British may seem to be stereotypically aloof, superior and uncompromising, but wherever they went they performed better than their predecessors and successors. They brought democracy, made a better civilisation for people, and fostered in their subjects the cultural values of the British people: strength of character, integrity, discipline and above all incorruptibility.

1

THE OPENING OF THE WORLD

THE EARLY YEARS

Even in ancient times there was limited and sporadic contact between Europe and Asia. Merchants from several countries travelled overland by a caravan route – known as the 'silk road' – to bring silk, spices and other Asian goods into the homes of wealthy Europeans. Spices were especially important. At that time there was no satisfactory method by which meat could be kept fresh, and spices were the only means of disguising the unsavoury taste of meat that was more than a few days old. European goods were taken to Asia on the return voyage. It was a long and difficult journey, and Asia remained 'the mysterious East' – known to only a few. The situation changed at the end of the thirteenth century, with the publication of the book we now know as *The Travels of Marco Polo*.

Marco Polo's father, Nicolo, and his uncle, Maffeo Polo, both Venetian merchants, had visited Asia between 1260 and 1269. In 1271 they embarked on a second caravan journey to China, this time accompanied by Marco, who was then a young man aged seventeen. Marco Polo spent the next twenty years in the service of Kublai Khan – the Great Khan of the Mongols who was a direct descendant of the first Great Khan, Genghis. Marco Polo travelled extensively in China and many of the adjacent countries during this time. In due course he, his father and his uncle returned to Venice by ship through the Strait of Malacca, arriving home in 1292.

It was not long, however, before Marco Polo became involved in one of the frequent wars between the city–states in Italy, and he had the misfortune to be captured and thrown into jail as a prisoner of war. There he met Rustichello of Pisa, who was a writer. Rustichello recorded Marco Polo's accounts of his travels and published these in a book *Divisament dou Monde* ('Description of the World'). The book was an immediate success and was translated and published in many different countries.

The account of Marco Polo's travels and adventures greatly stimulated European interest in the East. The descriptions of the great wealth to be found in India, China and Japan, and neighbouring countries, were particularly stimulating to merchants whose desire to engage in trade with the East became compelling. The book contains frequent references to the abundance of gold, precious stones, porcelain and other desirable goods. Of the Great Khan's palace, for example, the author stated:[1]

> The palace itself has a very high roof. Inside, the walls of the halls and chambers are all covered with gold and silver and decorated with pictures of dragons and birds and horsemen and various breeds of beasts and scenes of battle. The ceiling is similarly adorned, so that there is nothing to be seen anywhere but gold and pictures.

And of the city of Khan-balik (Beijing) he wrote:[2]

> You may take it for a fact that more precious and costly wares are imported into Khan-balik than any other city in the world. Let me give you particulars. All the treasures that come from India – precious stones, pearls, and other rarities – are brought here ... It is a fact that every day more than 1000 cart-loads of silk enter the city; for much cloth of gold and silk is woven here.

The Travels also provides a description of the use of coal. It was evidently a surprise to Marco Polo – despite the fact that coal was already being used for heating in England:[3]

> Let me tell you next of stones that burn like logs. It is a fact that throughout the province of Cathay there is a sort of black stone, which is dug out of the veins in the hillsides and burns like logs. These stones keep a fire going better than wood.

Some of the accounts given by Marco Polo of the wonders of the East were disbelieved by many educated Europeans. Nevertheless the fact remains that, as the prologue to *The Travels* claims:[4]

> Since God first created man, no Christian, Pagan, Tartar, Indian, or person of any other race has explored every part of the world as thoroughly as Marco Polo, nor seen so many of its wonders.

Merchants and others remained sceptical, but they hoped that the riches described by Marco Polo would indeed prove to be real and that they could share some of this wealth. The desire to trade with the East stimulated mariners to consider the possibility of finding a sea route from Europe to Asia – by sailing around the foot of Africa to the East, by sailing westwards across the Atlantic Ocean, or by sailing to the north and then eastwards along the northern coast of Europe and Asia. It took some years to achieve but, in the end, two routes were discovered. Dutch, Portuguese, Spanish, British and French ships then began to trade in the Indies. The maritime discovery of the continent we now know as Australia then became a matter of time.

CHRISTOPHER COLUMBUS

Two Genoese brothers, Ugolino and Guido Vivaldi, were apparently the first to attempt to reach the Orient by sea – but it is not clear whether they proposed to sail by a western or eastern route. Their expedition sailed in 1291 but, unfortunately their fate has never been determined.

The first mariner known to have sailed westwards in an attempt to reach the Orient was Christopher Columbus (as his name is rendered in English-speaking countries). Columbus was born and christened Cristoforo Colombo in the city–state of Genoa in 1451 and, as he wrote to the King and Queen of Spain in 1501:[5]

> I went to sea at a very early age and have continued to do so until today. The art of navigation inclines those who follow it to desire to know the secrets of this world. I have been involved in it for over forty years.

During his early years as a mariner Columbus acquired a knowledge of the prevailing winds in the Mediterranean Sea and the Atlantic Ocean. It seems that he visited several of the islands in the eastern waters of the Atlantic and that he also visited England, and possibly even Iceland. For about ten years he was based in Portugal, during which time he endeavoured to persuade the King, João II (anglicised as John II), to finance an expedition that was to sail westwards until it reached Cathay and Cipangu (China and Japan). This had become the passionate ambition of Columbus. However, he failed to persuade the Portuguese King, and went to Spain – where he was known as Cristóbal Colón. He obtained an audience with the joint monarchs of Spain, Fernando and Isabel (or Ysabel) – known as Ferdinand and Isabella in English-speaking countries.[6] There was considerable delay during which time the advisers to the royal court examined the proposed project. In the end, despite negative advice, Ferdinand and Isabella approved the voyage and agreed to provide a major share of the cost.[7]

Columbus sailed from the Spanish port of Palos on 3 August 1492. He had three ships – the *Santa María* (the flagship, carrying forty men), the *Pinta* (with twenty-six men) and the *Niña* (with twenty-four men). The *Pinta* and *Niña* are more properly described as *caravels*, whereas the *Santa María* was a *nao* (a ship).

To take advantage of the prevailing winds – which had been recognised by Arab navigators in the Arabian Sea and Indian Ocean, and of which he had personal experience in the Mediterranean – Columbus first sailed south-west to the Canary Islands, which had been occupied by Spain in 1431. The fleet took on provisions and then set a westerly course for the Orient. Four weeks later Columbus saw a number of small land-birds flying from the north to the south-west. He altered course to west-south-west and, on 12 October 1492, they reached an inhabited island that Columbus named San Salvador – but which was known to its inhabitants as Guanahini. In later years this island became known as Watling Island – after the English buccaneer who used it as his headquarters. However, in 1926, it was officially renamed San Salvador. The identification of this island as the island named San Salvador (after the Saviour) by Columbus is still controversial. It has also been claimed that Samana Cay (a few miles to the south-east of Watling Island) is the San Salvador of Columbus.[8]

Columbus spent some time in the Caribbean Sea and discovered Cuba and Hispaniola – where the *Santa María* struck a sandbank and was wrecked. Columbus arranged for thirty-nine men to remain on Hispaniola and then prepared to return to Spain by a more northerly route than that sailed on the outward voyage. Columbus, now in the *Niña*, called at Lisbon for repairs, and then returned to Palos. The *Pinta* had first called at Bayona, on the west coast of Spain and then sailed for Palos. Columbus had discovered a New World – but he believed, and always continued to believe, that he had discovered islands not far from Cipangu (Japan).

Columbus had kept a journal during the voyage and, on his return, he handed this to Ferdinand and Isabella – who arranged for a copy to be made. Unfortunately, both the original and the copy have disappeared. An abstract of the journal had, however, been prepared by a Dominican historian, Bartolomé de las Casas, and this has been published in a number of different translations.[9] Even in this abstract there are frequent references in the journal to his desire to find gold, precious stones and spices. He wrote:[10]

> It is true that, if I arrive anywhere where there is gold or spices in quantity, I shall wait until I have collected as much as I am able. Accordingly I do nothing but go forward in the hope of finding these.

There is no doubt that it was *The Travels of Marco Polo* that had kindled the ambition of Columbus to find gold and spices in the Orient. Columbus owned a copy of the book and this copy still exists. Columbus had made numerous annotations in the margins – particularly in those parts of the book that referred to the great riches to be found in the East.

Columbus made three further voyages to the New World – soon to be called America, after the explorer Amerigo Vespucci, and it is he who is usually given the credit for its discovery. However, there is solid evidence that the Vikings had sailed across the North Atlantic, and arrived at North America, several hundred years before Columbus. A few Vikings even settled there for a time; but their discovery made little impact. In contrast, in the years following the voyage led by Columbus 'explorers, soldiers of fortune, missionaries, and settlers continued to stream across the Atlantic, in the wake of Columbus.'[11]

Columbus had seen new lands on each of his four voyages and, on his fourth voyage, he had discovered the southernmost part of the continent of North America. However, even by the time of Columbus's second voyage '...caravels were shuttling between Cádiz and Española [Hispaniola] with trade goods, initiating the famous *carrera de Indias* that maintained regular trade across the Atlantic for over three centuries.'[12]

The discovery of America was a mixed blessing. The crews of the three ships brought smallpox and several other diseases to the West Indies. Smallpox soon spread from Columbus's base, Hispaniola, to Cuba and Mexico. As Zvi Dor-Ner and W. G. Scheller have pointed out, smallpox reached Peru five years before Francisco Pizarro, with 600 men, sacked and conquered the Inca capital of Cuzco in 1533. The deadly European diseases followed established trade routes throughout the Caribbean islands – even those not yet visited by Spaniards – and onto the North American mainland. There, according to many scholars, introduced diseases might have drastically reduced native populations in advance of the arrival of English and French explorers and settlers.[13]

Over the next three centuries it seems that the native population was reduced from about thirty million to 'just over one and a half million' by smallpox and other introduced diseases.[14] Moreover, many of the Indians became slaves, and some were forcibly taken back to Spain. The decimation of the Indian population led to the introduction of slaves from Africa.

It is generally supposed that the spread of disease was not, however, a one-way problem. Many of the crews in Columbus's ships are alleged to have contracted syphilis following intercourse with the Indian women and, in this way, the malady was introduced to Spain. By 1495 it had been recorded in France, Germany, and Switzerland and, during the following year, it appeared in Holland and Greece. The first outbreaks were recorded in the Middle East and India in 1498,[15] and it reached Canton, in China, in 1503.

But this conventional view has been challenged. Palaeopathological evidence is interpreted by some to indicate that the disease was rife in Europe long before Columbus. Until fifty years ago there was no effective treatment for syphilis – much less a cure. Unchecked it leaves characteristic markings on bone – for example, 'worm-eaten' patterns and sclerotic healing – and such signs have been recognised on skeletal remains from settlements in southern Italy and France dating from the third to sixth centuries AD, and from mediaeval Scottish cemeteries.[16]

PORTUGUESE EXPLORERS

Portugal, under the guidance of Dom Henrique – the third son of King João I and his English-born Queen Philippa – had already established a substantial sphere of interest on the western coast of Africa, an interest that was much greater than that of Spain in this area. In English-speaking countries Dom Henrique is known as Prince Henry the Navigator, and the King is known as John I. Spain now sought to ensure that the New World remained Spanish. Ferdinand and Isabella communicated this view to the Portuguese King, and sent envoys to the Pope to seek his agreement. Pope Alexander VI was a member of a prominent family in Aragón. He agreed and, in his Bull of 4 May 1493, he fixed a north–south line of demarcation – 100 leagues west of the Azores. East of this line was to be the Portuguese sphere of interest, and all land to the west of this line was to belong to Spain. In 1494, however, after discussions between Portugal and Spain, the line of demarcation was moved, and set at 370 leagues west of the Azores and Cape Verde. This agreement, known as the Treaty of Tordesillas, endorsed Spain's claims to most of the islands adjacent to the continents of North and South America – except for the eastern 'bulge' of South America, which was later to become the Portuguese-speaking country of Brazil.[17]

It was all very well to establish this line of demarcation but, at that time, it was not possible to determine distances at sea and, even more significantly, it was not possible to determine longitude.

Thus, it was not possible to determine exactly where the Tordesillas line was located – either in the western hemisphere (in the Americas) or on the other side of the world. This became important when the islands of the East Indies were discovered. Were the Spice Islands, for example, in the Portuguese sphere of interest, or in the Spanish?

Portuguese mariners and merchants had already extended their trading posts southwards along the western coast of Africa and, probably in early summer 1487, Bartolemew Dias – with two caravels and a store ship – reached and rounded the southern extremity of Africa. He reached a prominent headland, which he named Cabo Tormentoso (Cape of Storms), and then turned towards the east to anchor in a bay now known as Mosselbaai. Sailing eastwards again, he came to the bay where Port Elizabeth now stands. There is no doubt that he had reached and passed the southernmost point of the continent of Africa and that the riches of the East Indies were almost within reach. Cabo Tormentoso was soon renamed Cabo de Boa Esperança – Cape of Good Hope – by Dias.[18]

King Manuel succeeded to the throne of Portugal in 1495. He was determined to continue the search for a sea route to the Indies. He decided to appoint Vasco da Gama to lead the definitive expedition to the East. Gama's date of birth is not accurately known but it seems that he was, at the time, still younger than forty years of age. Four ships were commissioned, and Gama took command of the flagship, *São Gabriel*. The fleet sailed from Lisbon on 8 July 1497 and, after calling at St Helena Bay, arrived at the mouth of the Quelimane River. By this time many members of the crew were seriously ill with scurvy – now known to be due to a deficiency of vitamin C. However, at this location, it was possible to obtain fresh water and supplies of fresh food, to reverse the onset of the ailment. Gama then sailed further north along the coast and called at Moçambique (Mozambique), Mombasa, and then Malindi, before setting a course to the north-east

across the Arabian Sea – a sea that had been sailed by Arab mariners for centuries. He arrived at Calicut, on the western coast of India, on 18 May 1498. He had succeeded in finding a route to the riches of the Indies.[19]

In the meantime, the Spaniards had not been idle. At this time, and in the early years of the sixteenth century, Spanish mariners and conquistadors were engaged in extending knowledge of the New World. In September 1513 Vasco Nuñez de Balboa, with a few compatriots, crossed the Isthmus of Panama (Darien) – becoming the first Europeans to sight the eastern shores of the ocean that was to be later named the Pacific Ocean. Then, as Hammond Innes has written:[20]

> On September 25 Balboa is supposed to have waded into the waters of the Pacific, waving his drawn sword and claiming the ocean for his emperor. It is here, on the shores of the great South Sea – the Mar del Sur – that he is also supposed to have been given more precise information about the fabulous golden land to the south and to have been shown Indian drawings of a strange camel-like creature, the llama.

It was now clear that yet another ocean would need to be crossed before the riches of the Orient could be won, and no one knew just how large or small this ocean would prove to be – mainly because of the continuing inability to determine longitude accurately. The Portuguese were already exploiting the eastern route to the Indies that had been pioneered by Vasco da Gama in 1498. Indeed, King Manuel had appointed Dom Francisco de Almeida as his first viceroy in the Indies in 1505 and, shortly afterwards, Almeida had assembled a fleet of twenty-two ships and had sailed for the East. Almeida had appointed to his staff a young man named Fernão Magalhaes – who came to be known as Ferdinand Magellan in English-speaking countries, and who was to play a major role in delineating the geography of the southern Pacific Ocean and adjacent areas.[21]

Magellan had been born in Portugal in about 1480, and had served for a few years as a page in the Portuguese court. He had later been appointed as an officer in the King's marine department and, in this capacity, he had learnt how to outfit the ships that were sent out on long voyages of exploration. He was destined to spend some years in the Indies and, by the time he returned to Portugal, he had a good knowledge of the spices and other useful products to be found there.

On his arrival in the Indies Almeida established good relations with the local rulers and was able to obtain permission to occupy additional bases – such that Portuguese expansion in the Indies could continue. The second viceroy, Dom Affonso de Albuquerque, who succeeded Almeida in 1509, took a much more aggressive approach. Indeed, as Roditi has stated, Albuquerque ' ... by a series of atrocious acts of piracy and of bombardments and massacres of the civilian populations of whole cities that his troops sacked ... inspired terror throughout Asia'.[22]

Goa, on the western coast of India, with an excellent and easily defended harbour, was captured in 1510 and became the Portuguese capital of the Indies. It remained a Portuguese state until it was occupied by Indian troops in 1961 and was incorporated into the Republic of India in 1962.

Albuquerque continued his aggression. Malabar, Sri Lanka (Ceylon) and Malacca were soon captured. He also encouraged Portuguese ships to venture even further to the East – to the islands of what is now Indonesia. In 1526 Portuguese ships reached New Guinea – so named because of a supposed resemblance to Guinea in western Africa. Even before this, however, in 1513, the first Portuguese ship reached Macao on the coast of China and, within a few years, this became a centre of trade between Portugal and China. Nagasaki, in Japan, was first visited by a Portuguese ship in 1571 and, until the Portuguese were expelled in 1639, this too became a centre of trade.

The Portuguese had created an empire that brought them great wealth, but the search for wealth had become an end in itself. As a later viceroy to the Indies wrote in 1548:'The Portuguese entered India with the sword in one hand and the Crucifix in the other; finding much gold they laid aside the Crucifix to fill their pockets.'[23]

Despite Portugal's success, there were many who still believed that a western route to the Orient should be further investigated. A ship could possibly be constructed on the shores of the newly discovered ocean, but this procedure would have the disadvantage that most of the materials would have to be carried overland, across the isthmus – from the Atlantic Ocean side. A sea route from the Atlantic Ocean into the newly discovered ocean was clearly to be preferred. However, this did not seem possible because, at that time, the South American continent was believed to be joined to a great land mass surrounding the South Pole. The only alternative was to find a strait between the two oceans. Optimists believed that such a strait had to exist. Ferdinand Magellan was just such an optimist.

Magellan decided to seek financial support from the Portuguese King for an expedition to examine again the possibility of finding a western route from Europe to the Indies. He made little progress. After all, the Portuguese already had a route to the Indies, and it was very profitable. Why should they seek another route? Magellan was frustrated by his lack of support in Portugal and decided to move to Spain to further his dream. This was in 1517 – soon after Carlos I had inherited the Spanish throne. A little later Carlos was elected emperor of the Holy Roman Empire and became Carlos V – or Charles V in English-speaking countries. He accepted Magellan's proposal that Magellan sail westwards to the Orient, and preparations for the voyage proceeded.

Magellan was given the command of five small ships for this purpose and he himself took command of the *Trinidad*. Great attention was given to the stores and provisions to be put on board the five ships. Magellan's training – as a young man in the Portuguese King's marine department – must have been valuable. There were many items that might be required to effect any necessary repairs to the ships. There were arms and munitions to protect the fleet from hostile peoples in the countries to be visited. Considerable quantities of dried meat, wine, vinegar, garlic, raisins, biscuit and other foodstuffs were put on board. Seven cows and three pigs were included – two of the cows going to the *Trinidad*. There were hammers, knives, spades, lanterns and other hardware. There was also a good supply of the instruments necessary for navigation – hour-glasses, compasses, wooden quadrants, metal astrolabes and a number of charts. Many goods thought to be suitable for trade or barter were also selected and placed on board the ships.[24]

The fleet sailed from San Lúcar de Barrameda, the port of Seville, on 20 September 1519 and set a course for the Canary Islands. From there the ships sailed for South America.[25] The crews were comprised of 237 men – of whom nearly half were Spaniards; the others being Basques, Italians, French, Greeks, Flemish, Irish and one Englishman. Most of the captains were Spaniards and they resented being under the command of a native of Portugal. One man is of special interest. He was Antonio Pigafetta, a young man from Vicenza, northern Italy, who was a knight of Rhodes. He sailed in the *Trinidad* as a supernumerary and became the official historian of the voyage. Indeed, the account that he wrote is the major source of information about the voyage.[26]

Magellan aimed to examine every inlet on the eastern coast of South America – in case it proved to be the entrance to a strait. He sailed into the estuary of the River Plate, for example; but he soon realised that the freshness of the water indicated that he was sailing on a river.

The voyage was not without serious incident. The ships reached San Julián Bay in March 1520,

and Magellan decided to winter there before sailing further south. It was here, at San Julián Bay, that he suppressed a mutiny with exceptional severity. One mutinous captain was beheaded and then quartered. Juan de Cartagena (another captain) and a priest were put ashore on Patagonia – and left to starve to death. One ship, *San Antonio*, deserted, and another, *Santiago*, was wrecked. However, Magellan did find a strait – which Pigafetta described:[27]

> After going and setting course to the fifty-second degree toward the said Antarctic Pole, on the festival of the eleven thousand Virgins, we found by a miracle, a strait [the entrance to] which we called the Cape of the Eleven Thousand Virgins.

The cape at the entrance to the strait is still known as Cabo Virgenes, and its position is 52° 20' S. The strait is known as the Strait of Magellan – but Magellan had named it the Strait of Patagonia. They saw smoke on the hills to the south of the strait, and Magellan therefore named this land Tierra del Fuego.

Three of his ships, *Trinidad*, *Concepción* and *Victoria*, sailed through the strait and into the ocean. The calm weather at this time prompted Magellan to name it the Pacific Ocean. It was 28 November 1520. The ships sailed northwards to reach a warmer climate, and then turned to the north-west to reach the Orient. Two small islands were sighted, but it was impossible to anchor with safety to obtain fresh food and water. Eventually, however, the fleet arrived at the Ladrones (Guam) where Magellan was able to obtain fresh food for the first time since entering the Pacific Ocean. The crews had had a fearful time during the crossing – because they were starving and suffering from scurvy. Most of the men were too weak to work the ship. Magellan sailed on, and it was not until Sunday 7 April 1521 that the ships were able to sail into a harbour at Cebu in the Philippines. The crossing of the Pacific Ocean had taken more than four months. The sailing master in the *Trinidad* estimated that they had sailed 60 or 70 leagues a day. He had been able to determine the latitude with acceptable accuracy – but his estimate of the longitude at Cebu was more than 55 degrees in error.[28]

During their stay at Cebu, Magellan was foolish enough to become involved in a tribal war that required an attack on the neighbouring small island of Mactan. This was a disaster and Magellan, and many of his men, were killed. The survivors resolved to continue the voyage westwards – back to Spain. In view of their losses, the *Concepción* had to be scuttled. Not long afterwards, the *Trinidad* became unseaworthy and, when she and *Victoria* reached the Moluccas, *Trinidad* was abandoned. The *Victoria* reached Ternate, where she obtained a large cargo of spices, and then continued on her way to Spain under the command of the Basque captain, Juan Sebastian del Cano.[29] The sole surviving ship arrived at San Lúcar on 6 September 1522, and del Cano wrote to the King:[30]

To the King's most Exalted Majesty:

Your Most Exalted Majesty should know that we, eighteen men only, have reached here with one ship of the five which Your Majesty despatched to find the Spiceries under the command of Hernando de Magellanes of glorious memory.

It was nearly three years since the fleet of five ships had sailed from San Lúcar. A further thirteen members of the expedition arrived safely in Seville some time later. They had been imprisoned by the Portuguese at the Cape Verde Islands. A further four or five survivors from *Trinidad* also arrived later. In human terms it was a tragedy, but no other expedition has ever contributed so much to the opening of the New World and few have contributed so much to the advance of world trade. It should also be noted that *Victoria's* cargo of spices was:[31]

... sold in Seville for ten thousand times what it had cost in the distant Moluccas, in fact for a sum sufficient to cover all. the expenses of Magellan's whole fleet for three years and even to leave a profit

to the King of Spain and to Magellan's other financial backers.

The *Victoria* was therefore the first ship ever to circumnavigate the world, and the first to demonstrate that the world is much larger than had been supposed. Magellan had shown that the Pacific Ocean is of such vast dimensions that further attempts to reach the Spice Islands by a westerly route from Europe would be of little value. Nevertheless, once Spanish ships were sailing into the Pacific Ocean it became possible for them to sail between the Isthmus of Panama and the Philippines, and for goods to be carried overland to the shores of the Atlantic Ocean – and thence, by ship, to Europe. The trading vessels in the Pacific Ocean, known as 'Manila Galleons', ferried vast amounts of rich cargo and were prime prizes. Many were intercepted by English mariners – such as Anson and Drake.[32]

The enormous financial success of the Portuguese ventures in the Indies soon persuaded kings, and the mariners of other European nations, to send ships, soldiers and officials to this part of the world. Francis Drake, in the *Golden Hind*, visited the Moluccas in 1579 after crossing the Pacific Ocean, and saw for himself the great possibilities for lucrative trade. In the meantime he loaded 6 tonnes of cloves – which he knew would bring a high price back in England. A few years later, in December 1600, Queen Elizabeth gave the East India Company a charter.

The Dutch were also very active. The first Dutch ship arrived in Jakarta in 1606 and, in the next seven years, sixty-five Dutch ships visited the area. The Dutch established a base at Bantam, on the north coast of Java. But, in 1618, Jan Pieterszoon Coen conquered Jakarta which, with a new name – Batavia – became the headquarters for Dutch interests. The name has since reverted to Jakarta. Anthonie van Diemen became governor-general of the Dutch possessions in the Indies in 1636 and, under his direction, Malacca was captured from the

Portuguese. In 1824, it was to be ceded to Britain. The Portuguese were also driven from Ceylon by the Dutch, and the Dutch gave way to the British in 1796. Ceylon later became an independent republic, and reverted to its ancient name, Sri Lanka (Resplendent Island).

French mariners also came to the Indies. For many years there were French outposts in India, for example. These included Pondichéry, Chanernagore, Karikal, Mahé and Yanoan. Similarly, French interest in Laos and in Vietnam from the seventeenth century led to a French protectorate in Laos and the establishment of the French colonies of Tonkin, Annam and Cochin-China.

With Portuguese, Dutch, English and French vessels operating in South-East Asian waters, and with Macassan and Chinese ships sailing in the same general area, the time was opportune for a first sighting of Australia – already inhabited by many different tribes of dark-skinned people.

2

NAVIGATION AT SEA AND ON LAND

NAVIGATION AT SEA

Whether on land or at sea, early travellers used the Sun and the stars, and the prevailing winds, to indicate direction. The North Pole star, Polaris, was of particular value. Nevertheless, direction-finding remained hazardous until the invention of the magnetic compass. It is generally accepted that the early Chinese, Arabs, Greeks and Romans were all aware of the existence of the naturally occurring magnetic iron ore known as lodestone. They also knew that a suitably suspended iron needle that had been magnetised by contact with lodestone would align itself in a north–south direction. The first magnetic compass was constructed in this way; but it is uncertain who ought to be credited with the discovery. It is known, however, that magnetic compasses were used by European mariners at least as early as the twelfth century.

In its early forms, the compass consisted of a magnetised iron needle supported by a vertical brass pin in such a way that the needle was free to take up a reasonably steady north–south position. A circular compass card – marked to indicate eight points – was placed under the suspended needle. The eight points of the compass were based on the direction of the eight prevailing winds common in the Mediterranean. The tramontano, or north wind, was marked with a 'T', which later became a fleur-de-lis and, for many years, the fleur-de-lis was the

symbol for north on magnetic compasses. The east, the direction of the Holy Land, was marked with a cross. The compass was usually contained in a wooden bowl which, on board ship, was secured on top of a wooden column in front of the helmsman. This wooden column was first known as the 'bittacle' (supposedly after the Portuguese word *bitacolo*), and later became the binnacle.

From about the fourteenth century the compass card was marked in thirty-two points – each of which was named with reference to the four cardinal points: north, south, east and west. Steering directions were given in such terms as north-east, nor'-nor'-east, and east-nor'-east. One of the first skills required of an apprentice seaman was how to 'box the compass' – that is, to recite the thirty-two points of the compass in proper sequence. The compass card also came to be marked in degrees. The division of a circle into 360 degrees originated with the ancient Babylonians but was not adopted until the second century AD – by the Greek astronomer Ptolemy. So north-east meant north 45° east, and nor'-nor'-east meant north 22½° east, and east-nor'-east meant north 67½° east. There were other changes from time to time. It was found better to attach several magnetic needles, in parallel, to the underside of the compass card – which, itself, was suspended on the pivot pin. Other changes included covering the bowl containing the compass needle with glass, and mounting the bowl on

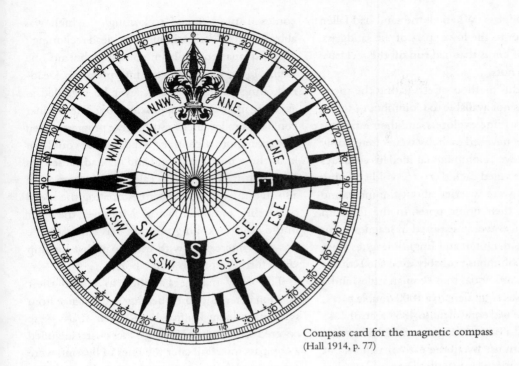

Compass card for the magnetic compass
(Hall 1914, p. 77)

gimbals – a device to offset the pitch and roll of the ship. Still later, in the mid nineteenth century, the bowl was filled with alcohol to dampen its movements.[1]

The gyro compass, developed from the gyroscope, became a standard fitting in all large ships from the early twentieth century, but a magnetic compass was usually retained as a stand-by. The gyro compass is graduated in 360 degrees – such that north 45° east is 045°, and north 45° west is 315°.

However, at the time of Columbus, Magellan and other early maritime explorers, the magnetic compass was a clumsy and relatively unreliable instrument. The magnetic needle could lose its magnetism, and it was not unusual to carry a number of spares, and a stock of lodestone to re-magnetise needles. Nevertheless, once the magnetic compass had been developed for use at sea, it became possible for a mariner to steer a course out of sight of land and return home on a reciprocal course. The distance covered had to be estimated from the speed

of the ship and the time. The time was determined using a half-hour or hour sandglass – these instruments often being made by the famed Venetian glassblowers.

The speed of the ship was more difficult to determine. At first it was estimated by experienced guesswork. Later, speed was estimated by throwing a floating object over the bow of the ship – and noting how long it took to reach the stern. The length of the ship was known, and the time was estimated from chants (of known duration) by the sailors. The speed of the ship was then calculated – and hence the distance travelled in a given time. This method was gradually improved. For example, it became customary for a log, often in the shape of a quadrant, or of a fish – which was attached by three short pieces of rope to the log-line – to be thrown over the stern of the ship, and the line paid out. This line was marked at constant interval with a series of knots in the form of pieces of cord worked between the strands. The time was measured by a small sandglass. When all the sand had fallen from the upper to the lower part of the sandglass, the number of knots that had run off the reel gave the speed in knots.

However, this method of estimating the speed of the ship was not available to Columbus or to the other early maritime explorers, and their estimates of the distances travelled each day were often grossly in error. Moreover, Columbus falsified his estimates of the distance sailed each day – to avoid alarming his men, who were worried about the increasing distance from their home ports. In the fifteenth century, distances were measured in leagues – but Spanish, Roman, Dutch and English leagues were all different. Columbus probably used the Roman league, which was equal to 4 Roman miles, and a Roman mile was equivalent to a 1000 double paces. A Roman mile was equivalent to 4850 feet, or 1.48 kilometres, and a Roman league to 5.92 kilometres. Leagues were in use by all the early mariners, but the nautical mile eventually superseded that measure. A nautical mile is defined as one minute of arc (one-sixtieth of a degree) measured along a meridian. In other words, if a mariner in the northern hemisphere sails due north for 60 nautical miles his latitude will be one degree greater than before. However, the Earth is not a perfect sphere – it is, for example, flattened at the poles – so the nautical mile is somewhat shorter at the equator than at high latitudes. For many years the nautical mile was taken, for practical purposes, to have an average length of 6080 feet, or 1.853 kilometres. The International Nautical Mile is now defined as being 1.852 kilometres, or 6076 feet, and the league, as used in earlier times, is usually taken as being 3.2 nautical miles.

To calculate the distance travelled in each twenty-four hours, the mariner needed to know the speed of his ship. Then, knowing the course or courses steered, he obtained a rough estimate of the ship's position. This was known as a 'dead-reckoning' position. It is commonly believed that this phrase

comes from 'deduced reckoning' – which was abbreviated to 'ded reckoning', or 'dead reckoning'. This explanation has been contested, but no one seems able to suggest a better interpretation. Dead-reckoning positions could never be regarded as anything more than an approximation. The mariner could make allowance for the zigzag progress caused by tacking into a contrary wind, but he could not know how much the wind and sea had caused his ship to drift. To upset his calculations, there were also steering errors, errors in estimating the speed of the ship, and other factors. Moreover, the error in the dead-reckoning position was cumulative – this error increasing with every day that his ship sailed further from his home port.

The early mariners tended to record their position in terms of their bearing and distance from some prominent landmark, and their charts were covered with lines of bearing. Later charts included a compass rose. Still later the lines of bearing were omitted and the compass rose became pre-eminent. The long-continued reliance on lines of bearing is perhaps surprising because Hipparchus, the Greek philosopher, had introduced the concept of latitude and longitude in the second century BC, and Ptolemy had sought to apply these concepts from about AD 150.[2] It was not until 1409, however, that Ptolemy's works were translated from Greek into Latin – and thus became available to a greater number of educated people. It was Prince Henry the Navigator (the Infante Dom Henrique of Portugal) who encouraged the systematic use of measurements of latitude as an aid to navigation. But, in Henry's time, there was no scientific method for the determination of longitude.

The latitude of any position on the Earth is its angular distance from the equator. Angular distances are measured in degrees – each degree being divided into 60 minutes of arc (or 60'). In turn, each minute of arc is divided into 60 seconds of arc (or 60"). The equator defines latitude 0°, the poles are at latitude 90° (north or south), and a position that is midway has a latitude of 45° (north or south). All positions having the same latitude are said to lie on that parallel – that is on a line parallel to the equator.

The longitude of any position on the Earth is the angular distance of the meridian through that place and the meridian through a selected reference point and the poles. Ptolemy chose the meridian through the Peak of Tenerife (in the Canary Islands) as the prime or reference meridian – because this was the most westerly land known at that time – and this later received support from Cardinal Richelieu. It was widely used by navigators of many different countries, and it is of interest that the map of the world prepared by Johann Matthius Hase, published in 1746, used this as the prime meridian. The Old World lies to the east of this meridian and the New World to the west.[3]

However, the meridian through the Peak of Tenerife was not universally used. Different navigators used the meridians through Lisbon, or Madrid, or London, or (since 1768) Greenwich. It was not until 1884 that the meridian through the transit telescope at the royal observatory at Greenwich was chosen – by international agreement – as the prime meridian. Even then the French continued to use the meridian through Paris as the prime meridian for some years – but eventually they too adopted the Greenwich meridian. The meridian through the Paris observatory is 2° 20' 12" to the east of the Greenwich meridian. For many years now it has been customary to identify any position on the Earth by its latitude and longitude.

The determination of longitude at sea proved to be an intractable problem. For many centuries, estimates of longitude were often hundreds of leagues (or hundreds of nautical miles) in error – mainly because the distance between meridians at the equator was unknown. The first satisfactory method for the determination of longitude was known as 'the method of lunar distances'. This involved an observation of the angle between the Moon and the Sun, or between the Moon and one

of the prominent stars. Even then it was not practicable at sea until the publication of the *Nautical Almanac* by the Greenwich observatory. This almanac, first available in 1766 for the year 1767, included the calculated lunar distances for Greenwich – from which the mariner could convert his own observation of the lunar distance to determine his own longitude. Captain James Cook, on his voyage to the Pacific Ocean in 1768, was the first explorer to use this method. However, within a short time, the development of accurate timekeepers – which could be relied on to indicate Greenwich Mean Time – made it possible to determine longitude much more readily. Captain Cook used an accurate timekeeper, or chronometer, on his second and third voyages to the Pacific Ocean – in addition to the method of lunar distances. Cook's chronometer, or 'marine timekeeper' as he called it, was a large watch, 15.2 centimetres in diameter. It was made by Larcum Kendall in 1769 and was a copy of John Harrison's fourth timekeeper – which eventually won the prize of £20 000 offered to the person who could design and build a clock that would keep Greenwich time sufficiently accurately for it to be used to determine longitude at sea (see below). For example, if the mariner observed the Sun at its highest point (that is, at noon), and the clock registered 1100, he knew that he was 15° to the east of the Greenwich meridian – that is, his longitude was 15° 00' E. It was some years before Harrison received the full amount of the prize, and even then it was awarded only after the personal intervention of the King. An amount of £20 000 was a fortune in those days. A measure of its bounty can be appreciated by the fact that, at the time, the astronomer royal, Flamsteed, received a salary of £100 per annum, and was personally liable to pay for the (Greenwich) observatory's instruments![4]

The invention of methods to determine longitude at sea was of enormous importance. However, the practice of navigation at sea had also been greatly improved by the invention, by Gerard Mercator in 1569, of a method for representing the Earth on a flat sheet of paper. Charts prepared using the Mercator Projection show all the meridians parallel to one another – so that a straight line between two positions on the chart represents the course to be steered when sailing from A to B. As a consequence of the distortion introduced by parallel meridians, the latitude scale is more and more elongated with increasing latitude. The distance between two positions on the chart can, however, be measured with dividers from the latitude scale adjacent to the two positions. This distance, in nautical miles, is thus obtained – knowing that one degree of latitude is equivalent to 60 nautical miles.

The advantages of the Mercator Projection were such that it was soon in universal use by mariners. The first map of the world using the Mercator Projection was published in 1568, and it remains one of the most important maps ever devised.

The next problem was to devise methods for the determination of the latitude and longitude of any position on the Earth's surface. As far as the mariner is concerned, the Earth appears to be at the centre of the universe, and the Sun, Moon, planets and stars all appear to be part of an enormous sphere, called the celestial sphere, which surrounds the Earth – or so it appears. The Earth rotates on its north–south axis from west to east – such that heavenly bodies appear to rise in the east and set in the west. Further, if the axis of rotation of the Earth is projected in both directions, it intersects the celestial sphere at points known as the North Celestial Pole and the South Celestial Pole.

The heavenly bodies – the Sun, the Moon, the planets and the stars – have always been a help to mariners (including the early Polynesians, the ancient Chinese and the Europeans) in their attempts to find their way. Mariners everywhere soon became familiar with the heavenly bodies that appeared to pass directly overhead at their home ports. They also noted that, when they sailed to the north, these same heavenly bodies no longer passed directly overhead, but were seen to the south of the ship. Conversely, a mariner sailing southwards noticed that these same heavenly bodies became progressively lower in the northern sky.

As far as the mariner is concerned he *appears* to be on the top of the world. The position directly above him on the celestial sphere is his zenith, and the North Celestial Pole (or the South Celestial Pole if he is in the southern hemisphere) is at an angle above the horizon that is equal to his latitude. Polaris, the North Pole Star, happens to be close to the North Celestial Pole in the heavens, and *appears* to rotate about the pole as the Earth rotates. Early European mariners were therefore able to determine their latitude quickly, if only approximately, by measuring its altitude – that is, its angle of elevation above the horizon. In the fifteenth century, Polaris appeared to rotate about the North Celestial Pole about 3½ degrees from the pole and, for an accurate determination of latitude, this had to be taken into account. In any 24-hour period there are two occasions when Polaris is at exactly the same altitude as the North Celestial Pole. If possible, observations of the altitude should be taken at one of these times. Unfortunately, the mariner could take an observation only when he could see both Polaris and the horizon. In other words, he had to take his sight during twilight. In practice, the mariner took his sight at twilight and then used a correction, plus or minus, depending on the position of an adjacent group of stars relative to Polaris. Simple rules were devised using the positions of the stars in the Little Bear relative to Polaris. For example, when the Guards are in the south, Polaris is three degrees above the North Celestial Pole but, when the Guards are in the north, Polaris is three degrees below the Pole.[5] Nowadays, because the Earth's axis slowly precesses, Polaris is less than one degree from the North Celestial Pole.[6]

Polaris, being so close to the North Celestial

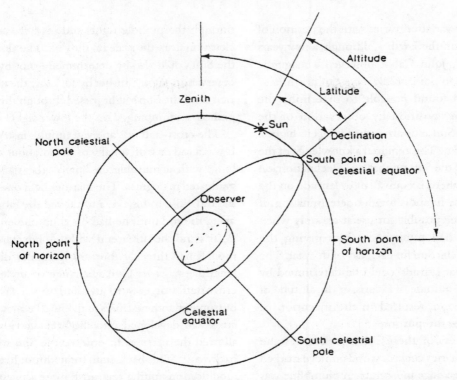

Schematic diagram to illustrate the method of calculating latitude used by early European navigators. (Badger 1988, pp 25–26)

Pole in the heavens, is an excellent indicator of north, and became a device to check the accuracy of magnetic compasses. It was well known to the very early mariners that the magnetic compass does not point to true north (that is, in the direction of the North Geographical Pole), but to the magnetic North Pole. This can, in some periods, differ from true north by several degrees. The difference is known as magnetic variation. In the fifteenth century it was found that magnetic compasses exhibit an easterly variation when in the Mediterranean or in the eastern waters of the Atlantic Ocean. However, as Columbus sailed westwards on his first voyage it was noticed that the magnetic variation became westerly. This change in magnetic variation caused alarm among the crew who, like all mariners at that time, were unaware that magnetic variation changes with the position of observation on the Earth.

According to the *Journal of Christopher Columbus*:[7]

The pilots took the north, marking it, and they found that the needles declined north-west a full point; and the sailors were alarmed and depressed, and they did not say why. When the admiral noticed this, he gave orders that they should mark the north again at dawn, and they found that the needles were true. The explanation was that the star appears to change its position and not the needles.

According to another account:[8]

He also noted that in the evening the needles varied a whole point, while at dawn they pointed directly to the pole star. This fact greatly disquieted and confused the pilots, until he told them its cause was the circle described by the pole star about the pole. This explanation partly allayed their fears, for these variations on a voyage into such strange and distant regions made them very apprehensive.

It seems that Columbus was the first to discover

that magnetic variation varies with the position of the observer on the Earth – although, a few years later in 1497, John Cabot observed a magnetic variation of two points (22½°) west of north.[9]

It was also found possible to determine the latitude of any position by observation of the altitude of the Sun at noon – when it is at its highest point for the day. This required a knowledge of the declination of the Sun on that day. Declination, on the celestial sphere, is equivalent to latitude on the Earth, and this method for the determination of latitude became possible for use at sea only when astronomers had published tables giving the declination of the Sun for each day of the year. The knowledge that latitude could be determined by measuring the altitude of Polaris, or the altitude of the Sun at noon, resulted in the invention of instruments for this purpose.

The simplest of these instruments was the quadrant – a quarter circle of wood or metal marked along its curved edge in degrees. A plumbline was suspended from the intersection of the two straight edges to indicate the vertical position. The altitude of Polaris was then measured on the graduated scale after lining up the sights on one of the straight edges with the star. An advantage of this instrument was that it did not require the simultaneous observation of the horizon.

The astrolabe was a more accurate instrument which became widely used at sea, but which (in a more complicated form) was extensively used by astronomers.[10] It was named from the Greek words *astron* (star) and *lambano* (take). It was a star-taker, for finding the altitude of a heavenly body – again without having to view the horizon. In its simplest form, it was a flat disc or ring of brass, graduated in degrees, with an arm capable of being rotated around the ring and which was provided with pinhole sights. It was held vertically – and was often heavier on the side opposite the suspension point to facilitate this – by suspension from a thumb or forefinger, and the mariner then observed Polaris

through the pinhole sights and read the angle of elevation from the scale on the disc. The altitude of the Sun could also be determined – not by direct observation of the Sun, but by adjusting the movable arm until the Sun's light passed through the upper pinhole and impinged on the lower sight.

The cross-staff was an even simpler instrument. It was a rod or staff, usually of wood, about a metre long, with a movable crosspiece, the staff being graduated in degrees. The mariner held one end of the rod close to his eye, and moved the crosspiece along the rod until he had lined up one end with Polaris and the other end with the horizon. Later models had three or four crosspieces of different lengths – to cover a greater range of angles. The cross-staff was easy to use and was a favourite instrument with mariners in the middle ages.[11] The cross-staff developed into the back-staff – which allowed the mariner to observe the Sun with his back to it. The back-staff went through various modifications until it was much more accurate than the astrolabe.

Nevertheless, the back-staff was soon discarded when Hadley's octant was invented. This instrument – which could be used to measure angles up to 90 degrees with great accuracy – was later modified so that it became a sextant capable of measuring angles to 120 degrees.[12] With the octant and with the sextant, it became possible to determine latitude with increased accuracy.

The principle of the sextant (and also of the octant) is illustrated opposite. In both instruments the Sun is viewed after double reflection (and through dark glass), and the angle of elevation is twice the angle between the mirrors. The arms of the frame of the octant were 45 degrees apart and measured angles up to 90 degrees. The arms of the frame of the sextant are 60 degrees apart, and this instrument measures angles to 120 degrees (130 degrees in some instruments) – this being necessary for observations of the lunar distance. The octant was often referred to as Hadley's quadrant

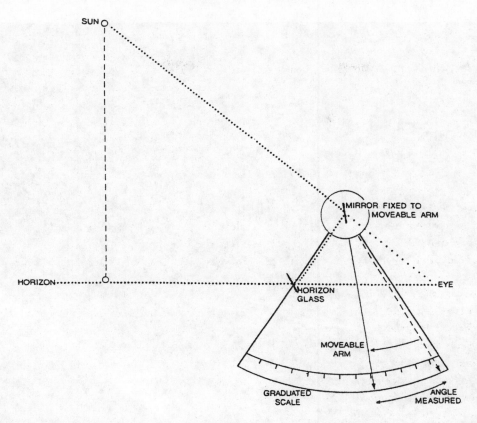

Diagrammatic sketch illustrating the principle of the sextant; this instrument was developed in England by Captain John Campbell, Royal Navy, to meet the need for an instrument to measure the altitude of the Sun and also to measure the angle between the Sun and the Moon and hence to determine the longitude of the observer. (Geoffrey Badger)

(because it measured angles to 90 degrees), but it is less confusing to call it an octant (because the frame extends through 45 degrees).[13]

On his first voyage, Columbus certainly used a quadrant (the quarter circle of wood or metal), and possibly also used an astrolabe. He also had several magnetic compasses. Magellan's fleet was supplied with a dozen compasses and also with a number of spare needles. They had twenty-one wooden quadrants, six metal astrolabes, and one wooden astrolabe. They also had eighteen hour-glasses.[14] However, Columbus and Magellan had no telescopes, no accurate method for measuring the speed of the ship (and hence the distance run), and no method for determining the longitude.

Longitude was an insoluble problem in the fifteenth century, and no one knew the size of the Earth. Eratosthenes (circa 276–192 BC) had demonstrated the principle whereby the circumference of the planet could be measured, and his result was remarkably good for the time – because his errors cancelled out. But the precise instrumentation required for this and other surveying procedures was not available until many centuries later. Some attempt had been made to measure the distance between degrees of latitude, but there was no information about the distance between degrees of longitude at the equator. In fact, the circumference of the Earth is much greater than either Columbus or Magellan had imagined.

In 1768, less than three centuries after the first voyage of Columbus, Captain James Cook sailed

Mitchell's sextant was made by R. B. Mate of 'Mathematical, Optical and Philosophical Instruments Wholesale, Retail and for Exportation' of 17 Poultry, London, about 1830; it is housed, with various lenses, in a cedar box 55 x 55 centimetres; it weighs 24 kilograms. (Reproduced with permission of the National Library of Australia, where it is preserved)

from Plymouth in the *Endeavour* bound for Tahiti for the observation of the Transit of Venus – the passage of the planet Venus across the face of the Sun. Cook had several reflecting telescopes and ordinary telescopes. He also had an astronomical quadrant of one-foot radius, and a brass sextant made by Jesse Ramsden. He had greatly improved magnetic compasses, a magnetic dip needle, and a pendulum clock (for use on land). The *Nautical Almanac* for 1768 had been published, and he probably had copies of the 1769 edition, and even a manuscript copy, or proofs, of the 1770 edition. The method of lunar distances for the determination of longitude had recently been invented,

and tables to facilitate this were included in the almanac. As noted above, on his second voyage Cook also carried an accurate timekeeper. Maritime navigation had been transformed by these advances – and Cook was able to set new standards in exploration.

The search for a method for the determination of longitude at sea had been a long and difficult one. It was in 1675 that King Charles II had resolved to build a 'small observatory within our park at Greenwich ... to a design by Sir Christopher Wren' and had appointed John Flamsteed as the astronomer royal. The paramount object of this new observatory was to devise a method for the determination of longitude at sea. The Board of Longitude was established in 1714. The Greenwich observatory was responsible for the publication of tables that enabled longitude to be determined after the observer had measured the lunar distance – that is, the angle between the Moon and the Sun, or between the Moon and one of the prominent stars. The board was also responsible for promoting the quest for a timekeeper, or chronometer, capable of keeping Greenwich Mean Time very accurately over a period of months, or even a couple of years.[15]

It had long been recognised, however, that longitude and time are intimately connected. The Earth rotates once every twenty-four hours, and it therefore rotates 15 degrees every hour. If the Sun is due south of the Greenwich observatory, and is at its maximum height, it is 'apparent noon' at Greenwich. However, the Earth does not move along its ecliptic at a constant speed and, for astronomical purposes, a 'Mean Sun' is imagined. When the Mean Sun is due south of the Greenwich observatory, it is noon in Greenwich Mean Time. If it can be shown that the Mean Sun crosses the meridian through a place to the west of Greenwich exactly one hour after this same event at Greenwich, then that place must have a longitude 15 degrees west of Greenwich. The problem of longitude therefore resolves into a problem of determining how the time at any place differs from the time at Greenwich.

This can be done if a timekeeper can be constructed that would keep Greenwich Mean Time, at sea, for months on end. It can also be done by comparison of the Local Mean Time of an event (such as an eclipse) with the calculated time for the same event at Greenwich. Further, the measurement of the angular distance between the Sun, or one of the bright stars, and the Moon, at a known Local Mean Time, could be compared with angular distances for a series of times (say every three hours) calculated by astronomers at the Greenwich observatory. By this means, longitude of the obser-

vation site could be obtained. In other words, the angular distance between the Moon and the Sun (or between the Moon and a selected bright star) could be using a natural astronomical clock keeping Greenwich Mean Time.

These two methods required considerable research before they could be perfected. The first method required the construction of an accurate timekeeper or chronometer – and this was first achieved by John Harrison. But it was not long before other skilled technicians were producing marine chronometers – notably John Arnold and Thomas Earnshaw in Britain, and Pierre le Roy and Ferdinand Berthoud in France. The method of lunar distances required the preparation of accurate tables setting out the Moon's movements in a form suitable for ships' officers to use. This task was made easier by the work of the German astronomer Tobias Mayer, and was followed by important contributions by James Bradley and Nevil Maskelyne – the third and fifth astronomers royal, respectively, at the royal observatory at Greenwich. The necessary tables for the use of the lunar distance method were included in the first *Nautical Almanac* – published in 1766 for the 1767 year.[16]

NAVIGATION OVER LAND

The principles of navigation during expeditions over land are not very different from those methods used at sea – but some procedures require modification.

The major direction-finding instrument on land is still the magnetic compass. It cannot be mounted on a binnacle, of course, and it usually has to be held in the hand, and used even when riding a horse or a camel. The prismatic compass – invented by Charles Schmalcalder in 1812 – is a particularly useful modification. The compass needle was mounted as in a marine compass – with a printed or engraved card. It was fitted with an object-vane that could be folded down on the face of the glass

The sextant used by Captain Sturt, and carried in a leather container over his shoulder, on his expedition to central Australia; this sextant was also used during the construction of the overland telegraph from Adelaide to Darwin, and is preserved in the Museum of Australian Surveying, National Surveyors House, Canberra. (Consulting Surveyors Australia)

when not in use. It was also fitted with an eye-vane carrying a reflecting prism – so that the mountain peak (or other target object) and the degree scale could be seen simultaneously. The prism usually had both the horizontal and vertical faces convex to give a magnified image of the graduations.[17]

As with marine navigation the distance travelled each day had to be determined in one way or another so that a new dead-reckoning position could be obtained. A variety of techniques has been used by explorers. Of course, the distances travelled in a day by walking, or by riding a horse or camel, were far less than those travelled by ship. After all, explorers by land had to stop for meals and for sleep; but ships continued for twenty-four hours. A ship, with a good wind, might travel two or three hundred miles in twenty-four hours. In the eighteenth and nineteenth centuries, explorers on land might travel about 10 or 20 (or perhaps even 30) statute miles in a day. A 20 per cent error in the distance travelled by land would be, say, 5 statute miles. A 20 per cent error in estimating the distance made in a twenty-four-hour day by a ship would be about 50 nautical miles. And, after ten days, this error could well be 500 nautical miles.

The distance travelled by a ship has long been estimated from the speed of the ship (measured by the 'log and line'), and the time. The distance travelled on land has often been estimated by 'experienced guesswork' – or by some relatively non-technical method for estimating the distance. One early Australian explorer estimated his distance travelled by counting the number of paces taken by his horse. He placed a supply of beads, or of some similar object, in one of his waistcoat pockets. After each hundred paces he transferred one bead to the waistcoat pocket on the other side – and so on throughout the day. He estimated 950 paces to the statute mile.[18] Alternatively, the explorer could reckon that, if he maintained a steady average pace of 30 inches (about 80 centimetres), he would progress 3 statute miles in an hour.

A few explorers, the botanist–explorer Allan Cunningham for example, have used a 'measuring wheel' to measure the distances travelled. These instruments – known as odometers, hodometers or waywisers – consisted of a wheel, with a handle attached, which was pushed by one of the party as they travelled. Each revolution on the wheel would be recorded by a device mounted on the handle –

which would also convert the number of revolutions into distances travelled.[19] The most accurate method, however, was to use a Gunter Chain.[20]

> The Gunter Chain was a 'chain' [20.1 metres] in length and divided into 100 links. Made of thick iron wire, each (straight) link was looped at the ends, and each connected to the next by three oval rings. Brass handles with swivel joints formed the ends of the chain.

Charles Sturt and Thomas Mitchell frequently used the chain in their explorations. On one occasion, for example, Sturt wrote that the ' ... length of the chain-line to the flag-staff was 70¾ miles which with the 61 we had measured from the Depot made 131¾ miles in all'.[21]

The normal method for determining the latitude on a land expedition has been to use the sextant and the Sun – but with one important difference. There is no satisfactory horizon on land as there is at sea, and it is necessary therefore to use an artificial horizon. The reflection of the Sun from a pool of mercury is observed with a sextant and a double reflection of the Sun is superimposed upon it by moving the index arm until the two images coincide. The angle thus obtained has to be divided by two to give the Sun's altitude. Special devices were made to hold the mercury – these devices being protected as much as possible from the wind or from any vibration. (Indeed, the rippling effect on the mercury, caused by traffic, prevents the satisfactory use of the artificial horizon in busy cities today.) On suitable occasions it is possible to use a pool of water as the reflecting medium – but water is perhaps even more susceptible to rippling than mercury.[22]

The great advantages of mercury as the artificial horizon are that it automatically takes up a horizontal position, and that it provides a good reflecting surface. In windy conditions it might be necessary to use a black glass mirror in a brass mount – with three levelling screws and a spirit level. The reflecting surface must, of course, be completely horizontal. Such a device was available from

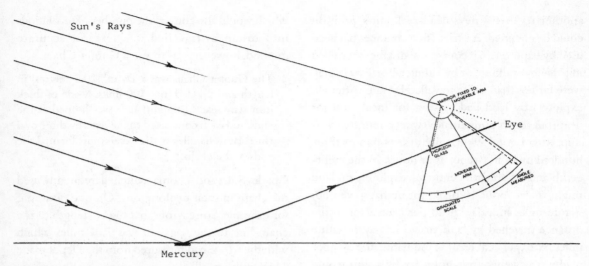

Diagrammatic sketch illustrating the use of an artificial horizon when there is no natural horizontal horizon. (Geoffrey Badger)

Artificial horizon showing container for the mercury and device for protecting the mercury, from dust and ripples during the observation. (Royal Geographical Society of South Australia)

Troughton & Simms in the mid nineteenth century, and it is interesting to note that Wills – the surveyor and astronomer with the Burke and Wills expedition – possessed such an artificial horizon device.[23] His notes explain his method of use:

In making these astronomical observations a Mercurial or Water Horizon, without any shade or cover has been used, whenever the weather has been such as to admit of so doing, when however it has been so windy as to prevent the use of either of these a Plain Glass Horizon (Ordinance Pattern) by Troughton and Simms has been used. This horizon is adjusted by the assistance of a glass spirit level one side of which [is] planar and rests on the surface of the mirror. The level is divided from the centre towards each end, the value of a part of division being thirty seven seconds of arc. It has been carefully checked and examined at the Flagstaff Observatory. The mirror has also been carefully examined and its correction rated by means of a great number of Circummeridian altitudes taken at the above mentioned national Observatory, the horizon having been placed with its marked end alternately towards and from the observer. From these the errors were found to keep well within the limits of Observation, except when the reflection was obtained from near the edge of the mirror when it will sometimes make a difference of more than one minute in altitude.

In using the Horizon it is levelled as nearly as possible and the spirit level left on the side of the mirror in order that any change in the position may be immediately perceived. As soon as the altitudes have been taken the level is read off from the centre towards each end, the end towards the object observed being registered – plus, and that towards the observer – minus. The Level is then raised from the mirror reversed and again registered, that end of the level which may hapen [sic] to be towards the observer being always registered – minus. Now if the value in seconds of arc corresponding to the mean difference between the + & – readings, be applied by addition or subtraction, according to its sign, to the unreduced reading of the sextant we ought to obtain the unreduced

double altitude of the object as observed by reflection from a perfectly level surface; but in windy weather it is seldom possible to keep the mirror free from dust even for a few seconds and this so interferes with the readings of the spirit level that altitudes taken with this horizon cannot be depended on within one minute of arc.

This detailed account indicates that navigation on land was just as difficult, if not more difficult, than navigation at sea. Of course, the maritime explorer also had to use an artificial horizon for the determination of latitude on land. Cook used this procedure on occasion on islands in the Pacific. So also did the Russian explorers who visited the eastern coast of Australia in the early years of the nineteenth century. It seems that Rossiiskii and another navigator in *Suvorov*, Joseph de Silvier, 'had an encounter with a group of five Aboriginals by Benelong's Point. The Aboriginals were curious and friendly, and were entertained by Russian sextants and an "artificial horizon".' Further, to ' ... prevent their damaging a good chronometer, Rossiiskii offered them his watch, which they duly broke'.[24]

The theodolite is an extremely accurate instrument for the measurement of angles from a position on land. It has a small telescope which is attached in such a way that it can move on two graduated circles – one horizontal and the other vertical. It is mounted on a sturdy tripod, with adjustable legs, and is fitted with a spirit level to ensure that, by appropriate adjustment, the horizontal circle does indeed lie in the horizontal plane. It can be used for the determination of the altitude of the Sun or of a number of stars – and therefore for determination of the latitude of that position. It can also be used for the determination of the angles of bearing of different features on the landscape and, in conjunction with a 'base-line' of known length, for the determination of the distance of mountains or other features. However, for a nineteenth-century explorer, a theodolite was a heavy and awkward instrument to transport.

PREPARING THE CHARTS AND MAPS

When preparing a chart, the maritime explorers usually sailed as close as possible to the coastline of the unexplored country as the safety of the ship allowed. To ensure this safety it was necessary always to keep a sharp lookout for rocks, reefs and other obstructions, and to take frequent soundings to determine the depth of water under the ship. The course of the ship – with changes demanded by the shape of the coast, and the requirements of tacking – was plotted to scale on the chart, together with a representation of the coastline, with points, bays, hills and other features.

To add a feature to the chart – be it a hill, a cape, a bay, or even a prominent tree – it was necessary to take the bearing of the feature from at least two positions on the ship's track. To achieve greater accuracy, multiple bearings of each feature were necessary.

To achieve the best results, overland explorers set off from a position for which the latitude and longitude had been determined with precision. They took bearings of all the prominent features in or around the direction in which they proposed to travel. It was necessary to estimate their distance travelled and, for this purpose, they counted the number of paces taken by their horses – or some

Theodolite used by Captain Charles Sturt; donated to the Charles Sturt 1828–31 Memorial Museum Trust, 1983, by Mrs Bond, a daughter of Bernard Ingleby. (K.T. Borrow)

similar method. To achieve greater accuracy, they measured the distance using a Gunter Chain. Having reached a convenient position some distance from the starting position, bearings were taken of all the prominent features that they had observed from the starting point. Bearings were also taken of other features on either side of the route that they proposed to travel. This procedure was repeated indefinitely as they returned, by a different route, to their original starting point. Thomas Mitchell was a master of this technique, and his maps are surveyor's models.

3

THE FIRST SIGHTINGS OF AUSTRALIA

ARRIVAL OF THE ABORIGINAL PEOPLE

The Aboriginal people of Australia are thought to have arrived from the north – possibly in a number of migratory waves – beginning at least 60 000 years ago. Aboriginal remains have been dated as about that age at Lake Mungo, in western New South Wales and, given its location distant from the northern shore of the continent, this is a minimum age for the Aboriginal invasion.[1] It is frequently suggested that they arrived by land – because for much of that time the level of the sea was much lower than it is today, such that the inner parts of the continental shelf were exposed around the continents and land bridges connected many land masses which are now separated by water. If the Aboriginal people did arrive by land they could have done so only during an ice age – when the level of the sea was low. During glacial periods of the last 100 000 years, Papua New Guinea was connected to the Australian mainland, as was the island of Tasmania. On the other side of the world, the British Isles were connected to the mainland of Europe.[2]

However, as Flood has pointed out, at no time during the last three million years has there been a complete and continuous land bridge between the Asian and Australian continents and, assuming that the ancestral Aborigines originated in an immediate

sense in South-East Asia, 'the first migrants could not have walked to Australia, but must have come across the sea'.[3] They must have arrived by rafts or canoes, and Papua New Guinea might well have been an intermediate landfall. The highland people of Papua New Guinea have many alleles, or 'markers', in their leucocyte antigen system that are similar to those found in Australian Aborigines today.[4]

It is necessary to ask whether a bamboo raft could possibly make the journey from, say, one of the islands north of Australia, to the north coast of Australia. To examine this:[5]

> An experimental bamboo raft based on contemporary ethnographic rafts in South China was built (in two hours) and sailed by Alan Thorne, who found it 'surprisingly easy to steer' and achieved a speed of four to five knots. Data from this raft voyage were used to set up a computer simulation experiment, which showed that during the monsoon nearly every raft (without sails) blown away from the coast of Timor would end up on the Australian coast sooner or later, most within a week or ten days. These results were obtained at present sea level; at times of much lower sea level 'it appeared literally impossible for such a raft to miss Australia'.

The absence of Asian animals in Australia has also been cited as evidence that there has long been a significant water barrier between Asia and Australia. But there is one animal, the dingo, that is of

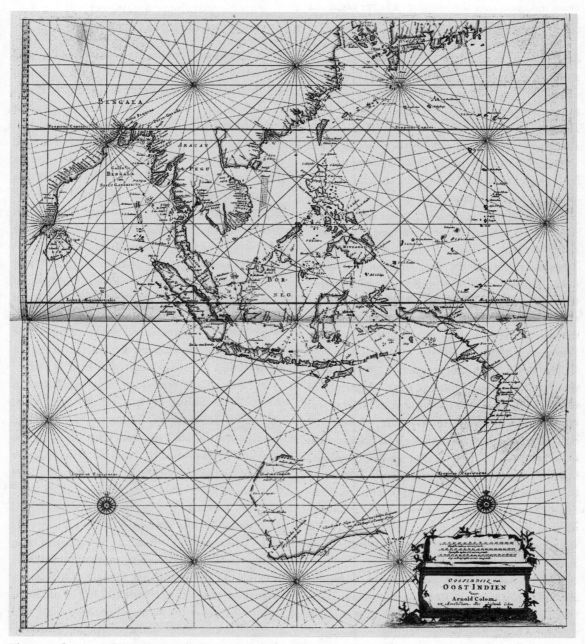

This map from c. 1658 shows Dutch discoveries of the west coast of Australia and in the Gulf Carpentaria. (Royal Geographical Society of South Australia)

Asian origin. It was introduced about 3500 years ago, probably by 'Asian seafarers who landed on the north coast to trade'. These seafarers doubtless carried the dingoes as a source of fresh food during their absence from their home countries. On arrival in Australia some of these dingoes were released, or escaped, and, over the years, spread over vast tracts of northern Australia and became a significant pest.[6]

The Australian dingo, *Canis familiaris dingo*, is descended from the Asian wolf, and is a rapacious animal that has proved to be difficult to control. It often scavenges alone but belongs to 'socially integrated packs'. Dingoes have a variety of prey, and they harass and kill sheep and cattle. But they also attack introduced pests – such as the rabbit and feral pig. A barrier fence, 5309 kilometres long, has been constructed to prevent the dingo from expanding further south into more pastoral land. The dingo did not reach Tasmania – being unable to cross Bass Strait which attained its present configuration about 11 000 years ago. The Tasmanian tiger, the thylacine, and the Tasmanian devil, a carnivorous marsupial, *Sarcophilus harrisii*, were still found in Tasmania when the Europeans arrived – but they had been exterminated by the dingoes on the Australian mainland by the time of European settlement.

The Aboriginal people reached every part of Australia, including Tasmania, but with the rise of sea level following the last ice age, the Tasmanian Aborigines became isolated, and developed separately from those on the mainland. For example, it has been claimed that the Tasmanian Aborigines lost the technique of making fire after their isolation but, as Flood has pointed out:[7] 'The only evidence for this is that Robinson never observed anyone making fire because fire-sticks were always carried. An argument based on flimsy negative evidence is always suspect.'

The Aboriginal tribes on continental Australia also developed in relative isolation from one another, and spoke many different languages. It is thought that there might have been 250 different languages at one stage – but many have disappeared over the years. Even so, it has been suggested that in 1800 there were more different languages spoken in Australia than in Europe.[8]

DID THE CHINESE DISCOVER AUSTRALIA?

The Chinese were great seafarers and certainly sailed to the East Indies, to the east coast of Africa, and to the Persian Gulf. Chinese ships reached Malaysia as early as the fourth century. China's greatest maritime explorer was, undoubtedly, Cheng-Ho. A Muslim of Mongol ancestry, Cheng-Ho carried out his first voyage of exploration in 1405 – under the patronage of the Emperor Ch'eng-tsu. His seventh voyage, in 1431–33, took him through the Straits of Malacca to Sri Lanka, India and the Persian Gulf – with subsidiary voyages from India to the east coast of Africa and to the Red Sea.[9]

In this connection it is to be noted that Marco Polo returned to Venice via the Persian Gulf after his long sojourn in China.[10] It would be surprising if no early Chinese ship ever approached within sight of the coast of Australia, and there are said to be Chinese manuscripts that report such contacts – but evidence in a European language is hard to find.

In 1802, when Flinders was at Sweers Island, in the Wellesley Group in the Gulf of Carpentaria, one of his crew carved the name of their ship, *Investigator*, in the trunk of a tree on the island. When John Lort Stokes visited the same island in the *Beagle* in 1841, he discovered the inscription, and added the name of his own ship. Later visitors added other names. However, in 1887, a severe cyclone damaged the tree and, soon afterwards, it was decided to remove the trunk to a museum in Brisbane. The multitude of inscriptions now on the tree, many of which were difficult to decipher, led to various suggestions that some were of Chinese or of Dutch origin. However, in a careful study, Stubbs and Saenger 'found no evidence to corroborate such claims'. Nevertheless, as Rolls has written:[11]

There are unproven, unprovable, but not irrational suggestions, that Zheng He [Cheng-Ho] travelled to Australia. It is more than likely that Chinese vessels did have early contact with northern

Australia, either by design or by accident. The Chinese traded with Timor from early times and it is only 650 kilometres from Darwin. They traded with West New Guinea and that is even closer. Perhaps they made early trips to Australia for bêche-de-mer (trepang). Carbon dating of sites where the trepang was cooked gave readings of 1200 and 1400 AD among the expected dates of two hundred years ago. Aborigines tell tales of people with golden skins who once came to fish for trepang.

In 1879 a team of Chinese workmen – preparing the ground for a road not far from Darwin, under the supervision of William Strawbridge, a government official – unearthed a carved Chinese figurine. The figurine was found at a depth of about 1 metre and was firmly wedged between the roots of a large banyan tree. It had apparently been buried for a very long time. Strawbridge described it as made 'of a kind of jade, now very hard and polished'. He soon sold it to Thomas Worsnop, the town clerk of Adelaide, for 5 guineas.[12] Tindale, the noted ethnologist, identified it as a representation of Shou Lao, a deification of Lao Tzu, the Taoist immortal who was born about 604 BC. Tindale described it as 'pale green'. Various estimates of the age of the figurine have been made. Davidson suggested that it dates from the period between the ninth and early eleventh century AD; and Tindale thought that it belonged to the T'ang Dynasty (AD 618–906). Fitzgerald dated it to the Ming Dynasty (AD 1368–1644) – probably fourteenth century.[13]

By this time the figurine was being widely regarded as physical proof that the Chinese had landed on Australian shores. However, more recent determinations of the age of the figurine favour its age as being early nineteenth century. It has also been shown that the carving is not in jade or soapstone, but is pinite – a rock that has often been used for carving small to medium-sized objects. It is preserved in the Powerhouse Museum, Sydney.[14] It is now clear that the figurine is no more than a curio, and that it provides no evidence for the early presence of Chinese mariners on Australian soil.

VISITS BY THE MACASSANS

There is no doubt, however, that the Macassans (Macassarese, often wrongly referred to as Malays) made yearly contact with the northern shores of Australia. As Warner has stated:[15]

> The Malays [Macassans], from a very early date, made yearly voyages down through the East Indian Islands and through the Arafura Sea to the northern coast of Australia. Their prows [praus, or proas] sailed into many harbours and river mouths that indent the coast from the Victoria River, which flows into the Indian Ocean in West Australia, to the southern limits of the Gulf of Carpentaria in the east.

These were fishing expeditions for the harvesting of trepang (sea-slugs, sea-worms or bêche-de-mer) for sale to the Chinese. They also engaged in trade (for pearls and pearl shell and turtle shell) with the Australian Aboriginal people living in the northern parts of the country. This fishing and bartering was continuing at the time of Matthew Flinders' circumnavigation of Australia in the *Investigator* early in the nineteenth century. In December 1802, for example, Flinders visited the Sir Edward Pellew group of islands in the Gulf of Carpentaria. Here he found evidence of occupation by 'some foreign people'. He noticed pieces of earthen jars, remains of blue cotton trousers, and other objects. 'What puzzled me most', he wrote:[16]

> ... was a collection of stones piled together in a line, resembling a low wall, with short lines running perpendiculary at the back, dividing the space into compartments. In each of these were the remains of a charcoal fire, and all the wood near at hand had been cut down.

Flinders also saw evidence of foreign occupation in Caledon Bay, in the Gulf of Carpentaria. A little later, in February 1803, he came across six Malay [Macassan] praus fishing for trepang. These Macassans were under the command of a man named Pobassoo. According to Pobassoo sixty praus 'carrying one thousand men, had left Macassar ... upon an expedition to this coast'.[17] In April 1803, Baudin also made contact with some Macassan praus near Cassini Island in the Bonaparte Archipelago. Dumont d'Urville later reported that he too had seen Macassans – this time in Raffles Bay, in 1839.[18] More recently, attention has been drawn to evidence of the early presence of Macassans on Groote Eylandt in the Gulf of Carpentaria – in the form of large kitchen middens of shells, pearl-shell clippings, remains of drying ovens, and graves.[19]

The frequent visits of Macassan fishermen to the northern shores of Australia are also confirmed by the influence of the Macassans on the canoes made by the Aboriginal people. The Australian Aborigines had long made rather primitive canoes from sheets of bark roughly tied into the desired shape. They lacked adequate tools and were therefore unable to make dug-out canoes – unlike the Macassans who, during their visits to the north-west coast of Australia, traded such primitive boats for pearls, tortoise shell or trepang. As Davidson has written:[20]

> The modern use of the dugout canoe in northern Australia is definitely known to be the result of Malay [Macassan] influence. These people for at least a century and a half, and probably an unknown but considerable period of time before that have visited the coast of Arnhem Land, and undoubtedly other points of the Northern Territory coast, in search of trepang and other commodities for trading in the East Indies ... and even taught the art of manufacturing this type of craft to some of the Australians.

Thus the evidence for Macassan contacts with northern Australia is overwhelming, and suggests that they began to visit Australian waters in the period from about 1650 to 1750.[21]

ARRIVAL OF THE EUROPEANS

There is a possibility, and even a probability, that European ships might have made unrecorded sightings, and landings, on the Australian coast as they searched for further opportunities for trade or plunder. There is particular interest in the wreck of a ship found on the shore near Warrnambool by European settlers in 1836. That stretch of coast has seen so many wrecks that it is known as the 'shipwreck coast'. According to the local Aboriginal people who were questioned soon after the wreck was discovered, it had been there for a very long time. The wreck was sighted by White settlers in 1843, 1846, 1847, 1850, 1870, 1877 and, most recently, in 1880, when 'she was sanded over for the ninth time in the memory of white men'.[22] There can be no doubt that the wreck existed; but it has not now been seen for well over a hundred years. A very large reward has been offered for its rediscovery – but to no avail.

The ship was described as being constructed from a hard wood which was 'dark like mahogany'. It became known as the 'Mahogany Ship'.[23] Its origin has given rise to much speculation. Perhaps it was a Dutch vessel – on her way from Cape Town to Batavia – that failed to alter course to the north before reaching the longitude of Australia? After all, the *Gulden Zeepaard* sailed from the Netherlands in 1626 and sailed halfway across the southern coast of Australia (and discovered the Nuyts Archipelago) before turning back and reaching Batavia in 1627 (see below). Perhaps another Dutch vessel sailed even further eastwards until she was wrecked on the 'shipwreck coast'.[24]

It has also been suggested that the Mahogany Ship was the wreck of the Spanish caravel *San Lesmes*. This vessel, of 81.3 tonnes (80 tons), was captained by Francisco de Hozes, and sailed from La Corunna, in Galicia (Spain), in July 1525. She was a member of a fleet of seven Spanish ships under the command of Garcia Jofre de Loaysia which had been instructed to follow up the discoveries made by the Basque Captain Juan Sebastian del Cano in the *Victoria* – the sole surviving ship of Magellan's fleet. Del Cano was appointed second-in-command of the new fleet. Four ships successfully sailed through the Straits of Magellan – but they then experienced a severe four-day gale and became scattered. *San Lesmes* was never heard of again. Roger Hervé has examined the records and has concluded that the *San Lesmes* survived the gale and sailed across the Pacific Ocean to reach New Zealand and then on to the southern coast of Australia where she was wrecked on the 'shipwreck coast' and became the Mahogany Ship.[25] If this is so, it might also explain the presence of the old Spanish helmet that was discovered in Wellington Harbour in 1906.

Robert Langdon, however, has developed a theory that the *San Lesmes* survived the gale and sailed to the north-west into the Pacific Ocean and was wrecked on an atoll to the east of Tahiti. He has also suggested that the crew survived and intermarried with Polynesian women. Langdon drew attention to some facts which seemed to support his view.[26]

It is idle to speculate further. Portuguese mariners might well have sighted the west coast of Australia on their way to and from Timor. Even more interesting, however, is the possibility that the Portuguese and/or the Spanish mariners might have explored the east coast of Australia many years before Captain Cook's voyage in the *Endeavour*. Central to a discussion of this possibility are the Dieppe Maps – which were the 'products of a flourishing school of navigation and cartography established at Dieppe to meet the expanding maritime interests of France'.[27] One of these, the 'Dauphin Map' (so called because it was probably prepared for the Dauphin, afterwards Henry II), has also been referred to as the 'Harleian Map' because it came into the possession of Edward Harley, Earl of Oxford. It dates from about the middle of the sixteenth century, and is attributed to the school of Pierre Desceliers. This map was acquired by Sir Joseph Banks who presented it to the British Museum in 1790. Other Dieppe Maps are by Jean Rotz, Guillaume de Testu and Nicolas Desliens. Most of the Dieppe Maps contain inscriptions or place names in 'French, Portuguese and Gallicised Portuguese, while the language of a few is not immediately identifiable'.[28] It seems that these and other Dieppe Maps:[29]

> ... are world maps [mappemondes] or atlas sheets and none of them is directed specifically to Australia. Nevertheless, they embody a continental outline south of the East Indies which, in such a location, could be no other land; but in shape is so unlike reality as to create great controversy as to whether such delineation is factual or conjectural.

In the Dauphin Map, the land mass to the south of the East Indies is inscribed 'Iave La Grande' – a French translation of Marco Polo's 'Java Major', or the Portuguese version, 'Jaua maior'; in other words, 'Java' in today's charts.

The Dieppe Maps have long attracted the attention of cartographers and historians. In 1883 the state libraries in Adelaide, Melbourne and Sydney obtained large reproductions of three of the Dieppe Maps and engaged George Collingridge, an expert in six languages, to interpret the inscriptions on the maps.[30] Collingridge became completely engrossed in this subject and he published his magnum opus, *The Discovery of Australia*, in 1895.[31] He claimed to have 'read every book, and examined every map, of real importance to the question, which had been produced in English, French, Spanish, Portuguese, Italian and Dutch'.[32] He recognised that the maps must have been prepared by the Dieppe cartographers and copyists from a number of manuscript charts – most of them of Portuguese origin. Indeed, it is 'the presence of Portuguese names on the landmass, very roughly in the position of Australia, that has been the prime reason for the Portuguese "discovery" claim'.[33] Collingridge concluded that the Portuguese had been the first to discover the east coast of Australia. But, as Richardson has pointed out:[34]

> ...no surviving Portuguese sixteenth-century chart shows any trace of land in that area, and there are no records whatsoever of any voyage along any part of the Australian coastline before 1606.

Collingridge's view that the Portuguese were the first to sail along the eastern coast of Australia failed to gain immediate acceptance. But opinion shifted towards acceptance of the theory in 1977 with the publication of McIntyre's *The Secret Discovery of Australia*. FitzGerald's *La Grande* (1984) also supported Collingridge's view, and was influential because FitzGerald was known to be a professional cartographer. However, it remains to be proved whether the Portuguese did or did not sail along the east coast.[35]

Many early attempts were made to equate features on the Dieppe Maps with capes or bays on a modern map, and to equate the names or inscriptions on the Dieppe Maps with an identified location on the Australian coast. Thus, *coste dangereuse* was 'identified' with the Great Barrier Reef – despite the fact that there are hundreds of dangerous coasts in the world. Similarly, *coste des herbiages* (coast of pastures) was 'identified' with Botany Bay. It has even been suggested that Cook chose the name Botany Bay because it has a similar (but not identical) meaning to an inscription on the Dauphin Map (which Banks had with him). In fact, Cook's journal makes it quite clear that he chose 'Botany Bay' because of the wealth of botanical specimens discovered there by Banks and Solander: 'The great quantity of New Plants &ca Mr Banks and Dr Solander collected in this place occasioned my giving it the name of *Botany Bay*.'[36] Various alterations in Cook's journal make it clear that he first considered 'Sting Rays Harbour', then 'Botanist Harbour', 'Botanist Bay', and then 'Botany Bay'.

It is notoriously difficult to equate features on early maps with 'similar' features on a modern map.

How 'similar' must it be before it is 'the same'? Similarities being 'looked for' are too readily accepted as fact. The large eastern projection at the southern end of Java La Grande, and named *cap de fremose*, is perhaps the most difficult to 'identify' with any feature on a modern map. Different authors have attempted to identify this with Cape Howe, with the southern, and with the north-eastern tips of Tasmania, and with the East Cape of the North Island of New Zealand.[37]

FitzGerald, in *Java La Grande*:[38]

> ... attributes chart errors [in the Dieppe Maps] to inherent deficiencies in navigational instruments and techniques of that era and to cartographic mis-assembly of the navigator's charts. He rejects any concept of deliberate falsification of global positioning for the purposes of concealment from or of misleading other powers. He rejects dependence on hearsay, and does not attribute the chart distortion to projection factors or lack of them. The ultimate analysis of chart data depends almost entirely on detail delineation of features, their sequence, and resolution by comparative cartography.

FitzGerald believed that he identified features, and sequences of features, that convinced him that 'Java La Grande' in the Dieppe Maps represents Australia. But is this definitive, or are there any facts which indicate the contrary?

In the sixteenth century, Portuguese mariners were able to determine latitude within about 1 degree, but longitude could not be determined at all. Only an 'educated guess' could be obtained from the captain's estimate of the eastward or westward distance sailed since the last known longitude. The east coast of Java La Grande is about 20 degrees to the west of the east coast of Australia. Many of those features on the east coast of Java La Grande – which have supposedly been 'identified' with features on the Australian coast – are about 10 degrees of latitude in error. Many of the manuscript charts used to prepare the Dieppe Maps doubtless had no latitude or longitude scales, and it would be only too easy, accidentally, to transfer a coastline to the wrong latitude and longitude. Misinformation supplied by mariners could also lead to errors in the maps. For instance, seamen frequently plotted on maps and charts coastlines that they had never even seen. The transfer of a coastline from the northern hemisphere to the southern has occurred in maps quite independent of the Dieppe Maps. For example, Cipangu (Japan) appears in the southern hemisphere in several, and Guam (first discovered by Magellan) is transferred to the southern hemisphere in others. It would be easy for a copyist to repeat or introduce such errors.[39]

It must also be remembered that no language had consistent spelling norms in the sixteenth century. The first English dictionary was that prepared by Samuel Johnson and published in 1755. Moreover, the copyists were:[40]

> ... incredibly careless ... especially when dealing with unfamiliar material ... place-names on maps and charts were miscopied, misplaced, translated, frequently incorrectly, and transliterated, in other words, adapted to the pronunciation and spelling habits of another language. Long names got divided, for reasons of space, the separate sections later being attached to different features; adjacent words were amalgamated ...

and so on. The interpretation of the inscriptions on the Dieppe Maps undoubtedly requires the expertise of an historical linguist with considerable experience of sixteenth-century handwriting and a detailed understanding of the history of the period.

On the western coast of the Dauphin Map there is a feature given the name (as interpreted by Collingridge) 'Quabesegmesce, or Quabe se quiesce as it should read'. McIntyre wrote the name as Quabe segmesse, and FitzGerald rendered it as Quabesegmesce (and 'identified' it with Cape Bougainville on the north-west coast of Australia).[41] Richardson made a close re-examination and suggested that it is Quabesequiesce or Quabesequieste. Quabeb (Dutch) or

Quabes (an Elizabethan misspelling) are alternative renderings of the word cubeb which is the name of a spice which grew only in Sunda — the western districts of Java. It was further suggested that the remainder of the word had originally consisted of two Portuguese words, aqui esta, which means 'is here'. As Richardson asked: 'what was an inscription concerning an exclusively Sundanese spice doing on a map of "Australia"?' Further, he concludes that the:[42]

> ... west coast of Jave-la-Grande was evidently not Australia's west coast, but a copy of an early, rough, Portuguese sketch chart of part of Java's south-west coast on a completely different scale from the world map into which the French had incorrectly introduced it.

If this is accepted, the east coast of Java La Grande is even less likely to represent the east coast of Australia. In other words, the Dieppe Maps do not confirm the presence of Portuguese mariners on the east coast of Australia many years before Cook. This does not necessarily mean that no European ship ever reached the eastern coast of Australia before Cook.

It is of some interest, however, that there are a few Aboriginal paintings of a ship, possibly a caravel, in a cave on Flinders Island, in Princess Charlotte Bay, off the Queensland coast. It is not known when these paintings were executed; but they certainly do not represent early Aboriginal boats.[43]

It must be concluded: 'Despite frequent claims, nourished on imagination and abetted by ingenuity, there is no surviving evidence for contacts by European or Asian seafarers with Australia and its Aboriginal inhabitants before 1606.'[44]

The Portuguese mariners were not the only ones to seek their fortunes in the East Indies. The first Dutch ship arrived in Jakarta (Batavia) in 1596 and the Vereenigde Oost Indische Compagne (the Dutch United East India Company) was established in 1602. This company is usually known as the VOC. Within a few years, Dutch ships were searching for further opportunities for profitable trade. In 1606, one such search was commanded by Willem Jansz in the *Duyfken* (Little Dove). He sailed eastwards along the southern coast of New Guinea, and then entered the Gulf of Carpentaria (which was named after Pieter de Carpentier, the governor-general of the Dutch East Indies). Jansz examined the eastern coast of the Gulf (that is, the western coast of Cape York Peninsula) as far as Cape Keerweer (Turn again) – which is some distance to the south of Duyfken Point. This was the first authenticated sighting of the Australian coast by a European mariner.

The Gulf of Carpentaria was also entered by Jan Carstensz in the *Pera*, and by Willem van Colster in the *Arnhem* in 1623, but Tasman and Visscher's voyage in 1644 was the first to obtain a rough idea of the gulf's nature. Abel Tasman was the commander of this expedition and Franchoys Visscher was the chief pilot. They had three ships – *Limmen*, *Zeemeeuw* and *Bracq* – and explored the eastern, southern and western coasts of the gulf. But they were evidently some distance from the coast – because they regarded many of the islands in the gulf as part of the mainland. Groote Eylandt (Great Island) was the exception. This had first been observed from the *Arnhem*. Tasman sailed between the island and the mainland, and it was he who named it Groote Eylandt.[45] He also outlined the western shores of the gulf, and much of the northern coastline of Australia.

Jansz was unlucky, however, because the new country did not look promising for trade. Moreover, as Sharp has commented: 'The *Duyfken* thus traversed some 200 miles [320 kilometres] of Australian coastline without discovering Torres Strait.'[46] That honour belongs to Luis Vaez de Torres who, in the *San Pedrico*, sailed westwards through Torres Strait in September 1606 – only a few months after *Duyfken* had been in the vicinity).[47]

The *San Pedrico* (the Almiranta), with Torres in command, was one of the three ships under the command of Fernandez de Queirós – the others being the *San Pedro y San Pablo* (the Capitana), captained by Queirós himself, and the much smaller tender, or launch, *Los Tres Reyes*. The object of this expedition – which sailed from Callao, in Peru, in December 1605 – was to find a suitable site for a Spanish settlement in the South Pacific Ocean. The three ships arrived at the northernmost island of Vanuatu (formerly the New Hebrides) – which Queirós named Austrialia del Espíritu Santo. He thought it must be part of the unknown, but 'predicted', southern continent – predicted because there had to be a balance for the known land masses of the northern hemisphere.[48] The ships became separated, and Queirós decided to return to America. The other two ships had to fend for themselves. The captain of *Los Tres Reyes*, Pedro Bernam de Cermeño, moved to the *San Pedrico* as chief pilot (with Torres remaining in command) and Gaspar Gonzalez Gómez became captain of *Los Tres Reyes*. They decided to sail westwards and to attempt to reach the Philippines via the south coast of the island of New Guinea.

There has been considerable controversy about the route taken, but it seems likely that the two ships did indeed hug the south coast of New Guinea for the greater part of their voyage. However, this was not always possible – because of the shallow water, and the many islands, reefs and rocks to the north of Cape York. It was necessary to sail to the south-west to avoid these hazards. Brett Hilder, after a thorough study, concluded that the ships sailed between Cape York and Prince of Wales Island – through Endeavour Strait. If this was so, they must have been in sight of Cape York Peninsula for two or three days – but without knowing that it is part of a continent. They turned to the north-west, regained the southern coast of New Guinea, and eventually reached Manila in the Philippines on 22 May 1607. The existence of Torres Strait did not, however, become generally known for many years.[49]

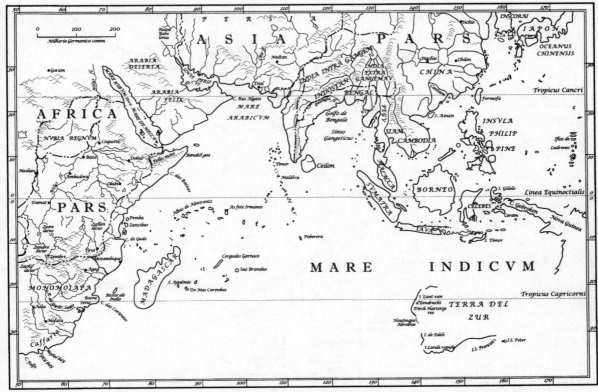

Map of Indian Ocean. Neither Tasman's 1640s voyages nor those of the *Arnhem* around the Gulf of Carpentaria in 1623 are included. (After 'Mar di India 1650' drawn by Johannes Janssonius. pp 82–83 in Clancy and Richardson, 1988)

THE DUTCH MARINERS

The rapid expansion of Dutch interests in the Indies led to the discovery of the western coast of Australia and to the first confirmed landing on the continent. Ships sailing from Holland were instructed to call at the Cape of Good Hope and then to take advantage of the prevailing westerly winds to make good progress towards the east – before setting a direct course for Bantam, the company's head-quarters in Java. In 1616 Dirk Hartog, in the *Eendraght*, followed this procedure and came to an island, Dirk Hartog Island, just off the coast of the Australian mainland in a latitude of about 25½° S. With a party of men he went ashore and attached an inscribed pewter plate to a post to commemorate his visit. The English translation of the inscription is as follows:[50]

> On 25 October there arrived here the ship Endraght of Amsterdam, Supercargo Gillis Mie-bais of Liege, skipper Dirck Hatichs of Amsterdam. On 27th do. she set sail again for Bantam. Suncargo Jan Stins; upper steersman Pieter Doores of Bil. In the year 1616.

The dinner plates used by ships' officers in the Middle Ages were commonly made of pewter, and it seems likely that the pewter plate used for the above inscription was one of these. For example, many pewter plates were recovered from the wreck of the *Mary Rose*,[51] a British man-o'-war wrecked

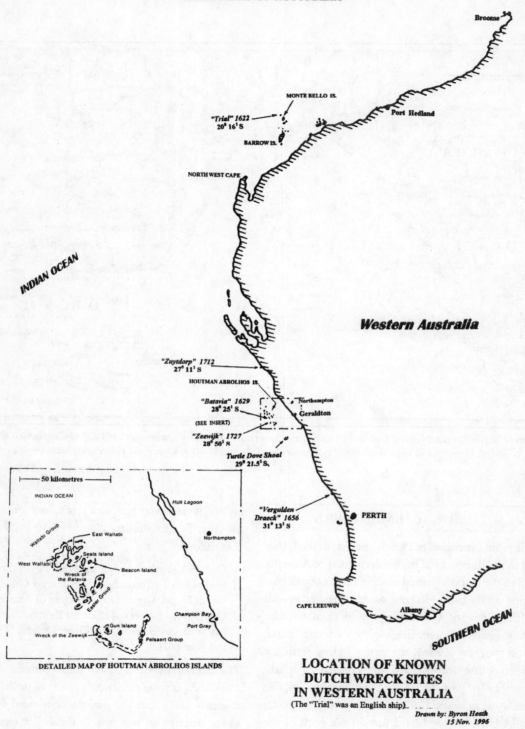

Broome

MONTE BELLO IS.

"Trial" 1622
20° 16' S

Port Hedland

BARROW IS.

NORTH WEST CAPE

INDIAN OCEAN

Western Australia

"Zuytdorp" 1712
27° 11' S

HOUTMAN ABROLHOS IS.

"Batavia" 1629
28° 25' S

Northampton
Geraldton

(SEE INSERT)

"Zeewijk" 1727
28° 50' S

Turtle Dove Shoal
29° 21.5' S,

"Vergulden
Draeck" 1656
31° 13' S

PERTH

CAPE LEEUWIN

Albany

SOUTHERN OCEAN

Detailed map of Houtman Abrolhos Islands

50 kilometres

INDIAN OCEAN

Hutt Lagoon

Wallabi Group

East Wallabi

Seals Island

West Wallabi

Wreck of
the Batavia

Beacon Island

Northampton

Easter Group

Champion Bay

Port Grey

Gun Island

Wreck of the Zeewijk

Pelsaert Group

DETAILED MAP OF HOUTMAN ABROLHOS ISLANDS

LOCATION OF KNOWN
DUTCH WRECK SITES
IN WESTERN AUSTRALIA
(The "Trial" was an English ship).

Drawn by: Byron Heath
15 Nov. 1996

Dutch sea voyages and location of known Dutch wreck sites in Western Australia.

in the Solent, off the south coast of England in 1545, and raised from the seafloor in the 1980s.

The *Leeuwin* (Lioness) evidently followed the same procedure as the *Eendraght* in making as much use as possible of the prevailing westerly wind in the Indian Ocean before turning northwards towards Batavia. However, the *Leeuwin* (the captain's name is not known) was further south than the *Eendraght* and approached the south-western extremity of New Holland in March 1622. This became known as Land van de Leeuwin. The cape was formally named Cape Leeuwin by Matthew Flinders on 6 December 1801, and he named the adjacent bay Flinders Bay.[52]

Another Dutch discovery was made on the northernmost coast – where the *Arnhem*, under Willem Joosten van Colster, touched 'the north-eastern extremity of Arnhem Land and the Wessel Islands in April–May 1623'.[53]

With other ships in company, the *Gulden Zeepaard* (Golden Seahorse) – with Pieter Nuijts (or Nuyts) a high official of the VOC, and with François Thijssen as captain – also took advantage of the prevailing westerlies on her voyage from the Cape of Good Hope. The ships sailed in relatively high southern latitudes and, with no method for the determination of longitude, reached as far east as about 133½° E, and discovered the Nuyts Archipelago. But, by this time, the *Gulden Zeepaard* was alone. She arrived safely at Batavia in April 1627. However, Heeres has suggested that this was a deliberate voyage of exploration – and not an accidental discovery.[54]

Many other Dutch ships en route from the Cape of Good Hope to Batavia also made sightings of the west coast of Australia. These included the *Zeewolf* (1618), the *Mauritius* (1618), the *Dordrecht* and *Amsterdam* (1619), and the *Batavia* and *Sardam* (1629). The *Dordrecht* and *Amsterdam* were under the overall control of Frederik de Houtman, a senior official of the VOC, with the (non-maritime) title of 'commandeur'. The skippers were Rever Jans-

zoon van Buiksloot and Maarten Corneliszoon, respectively. Houtman later reported that they sailed from Table Bay on 8 June 1619 and that, after sailing eastwards for an estimated 4000 miles [6437 kilometres], they turned towards the north. On 29 July they came upon 'low land unexpectedly'. Houtman added that 'it is low broken land with reefs round it, and we could see no high land or mainland so that these banks should be avoided, for it lies very treacherously to ships'.[55] These reefs and islands, about 60 kilometres to the west of present-day Geraldton, became known as Houtman Abrolhos – from the Portuguese words *abre* and *olhos*, meaning 'open eyes'. This was a common Portuguese maritime term for a reef – especially a coral one. The term was adopted by other maritime nations and appears on numerous sixteenth-century and seventeenth-century charts to indicate a potential danger.[56]

The *Batavia* of 612 tonnes, sailed from Amsterdam on 29 October 1628 on her maiden voyage, bound for Batavia (now Jakarta) in the then Dutch East Indies. More than 300 sailors, soldiers, merchants and women were on board this ship – which was the pride of the VOC. The senior official on board was commandeur Francisco Pelsaert, an 'uppermerchant' who was returning to Batavia after a visit to Amsterdam. As the senior official he was in charge of the considerable amount of treasure on board. Jeronimus Cornelisz was the 'under-merchant' – the second-most senior company official. The skipper was Adriaen Jacobsz, and Gijsbert Bastiaensz was the predikant (chaplain). Pelsaert kept a journal which records many of the events, and Bastiaensz also wrote an account of the time spent on the Abrolhos.[57]

About two hours before daybreak on 4 June, despite Houtman's warning, and with experienced skipper Jacobsz on watch, *Batavia* struck the Abrolhos and soon became a wreck. Many of the passengers and crew were taken to an adjacent island, but this had no water and other islands had to be investigated and occupied. Pelsaert and Jacobsz, with a few men, set off in an open boat for the mainland – but they failed to find any water. Pelsaert therefore set off for Java to seek help – with Jacobsz as navigator. They arrived at Batavia on the evening of 7 July 1629 and, on the following day, Pelsaert saw the governor-general, Jan Pieterszoon Coen. The governor-in-council decided to send Pelsaert in the yacht *Sardam* to rescue the survivors. Pelsaert set off on 15 July and arrived at the Abrolhos on 17 September. In the meantime, Jeronimus Cornelisz had made himself dictator and had mounted a campaign of tyranny – during which many of the survivors were murdered in cold blood. Some survivors had moved to the north to Wallabi Island, where fresh water was available and where there were 'jumping rabbits' (wallabies). These survivors had built some stone huts and walls – the first European-type structures on Australian soil.

Pelsaert's first task was to identify Cornelisz and the other murderers and mutineers. Many were tortured to obtain confessions and were then hanged or put to death in many horrible and cruel ways. Two young men, regarded as guilty, were spared and were marooned on the mainland. They might have survived by living with the Aboriginal people.

Other Dutch ships must also have sighted the western coast of Australia over the next century or so, and a few were wrecked on that coast – *Vergulde Draech* (1656), *Zuytorp* (1712) and *Zeewyk* (1727), for example. Just a few kilometres to the south of Dirk Hartog Island, there is evidence of just such a wreck – the rotting mast from a Dutch ship, a stockade of crude construction using local stone, a seventeenth-century musket ball, and a graveyard with skulls and bones of Aboriginal people (and possibly a few Dutchmen).[58]

Willem de Vlamingh is of special interest. He arrived at the western coast in 1696 in *Geelvinck*. In the ship's boat he explored the Swan River (where Perth now stands) for about 50 kilometres. Moreover, he discovered a small island about 20 kilometres to the north-west of the mouth of the Swan River. He landed on this island on New Year's Eve and was intrigued by the presence of many small animals which he described as 'a kind of rat as big as a common cat, whose dung is found in abundance over all the island'. He was not the first European to see these animals – Samuel Volkersen, another Dutch officer, had observed them in 1658. It was Vlamingh, however, who named the island *Rotte Nest* ('Rat's Nest') – hence the present Rottnest Island. The rat-like animals on this island are marsupials and are known as quokkas. Today, they show no fear of humans, and live in harmony with the many tourists who visit the island.[59] Further north, the *Geelvinck* came to Dirk Hartog Island. It was now 1697 and, when Willem de Vlamingh landed, he discovered the inscribed pewter plate that Hartog had affixed to a wooden post in 1616. Vlamingh decided to take this plate to Batavia, and then to forward it to the Netherlands. He replaced the original plate with another inscribed pewter plate – which repeated the original inscription and added details of his own visit. The English translation is as follows:[60]

> On 4th February 1697 arrived here the vessel Geelvinck of Amsterdam, Commander and skipper, Willem de Vlamingh of Vielandt ... Our fleet set sail from here to continue exploring the Southern Land, on the way to Batavia.

The Vlamingh Plate was, in turn, discovered in 1801 by a member of the crew of the *Naturaliste* – who took it to Captain Hamelin. Hamelin had it remounted on a new post. However, in 1818, Louis de Freycinet, in the *Uranie*, decided to take it back to France:[61]

> Believing that such a rare plate might again be swallowed up by sands, or else run the risk of being taken away and destroyed by some careless sailor, I felt that its correct place was in one of these great scientific depositories which offer to the historian such rich and precious documents. I planned therefore, to place it in the collections of the

Academie royale des inscriptions et belles–lettres de l'Institut de France, and this I had the honour of doing ... on 23 March 1821.

Towards the end of the nineteenth century, the French government, in response to an Australian enquiry, admitted that the whereabouts of the Vlamingh Plate was unknown. However, in 1940, the plate was found in a cupboard in the Museum of Humanity and, in 1947, it was presented to the Australian government. It is now preserved in the Western Australian Maritime Museum, in Fremantle. The original Hartog Plate is preserved in the Rijksmuseum, in Amsterdam.

The Dutch authorities had continued to take an interest in the area to the south of the known extent of New Guinea and, as early as 1623, Jan Carstensz in *Pera* made some discoveries on the western coast of Cape York Peninsula. Willem Joosten van Colster, in the *Arnhem*, discovered the Wessel Islands and a part of what is now known as Arnhem Land. He also sighted Groote Eylandt.

The many Dutch discoveries were all included on a map constructed by Hessel Gerritsz about 1630. Gerritsz was the cartographer to the Vereenigde Oost-Indische Compagnie. It can hardly be claimed, however, that these Dutch discoveries resulted from a serious program of maritime exploration. However, in 1642 and in 1644, two important voyages of exploration were carried out by order of Anthonie van Diemen, the governor-general of the VOC. These two voyages were under the command of Abel Janszoon Tasman, with Franchoijs Jacobszoon Visscher as chief pilot.

Tasman was an experienced and trusted skipper in the company and he was aged about thirty-nine when he sailed from Batavia on 14 August 1642 in the *Heemskerck* – with the *Zeehaen* in company. Visscher, who also sailed in the *Heemskerck*, was an experienced pilot, having already visited Cambodia and Japan. The two ships first sailed to Mauritius – which was then a Dutch possession – and from that island Tasman took advantage of the prevailing

westerly winds to sail eastwards at a latitude between about 45° to 50° S. On the afternoon of 24 November 1642 they approached land. On the following day they estimated their position to be 42° 30' S, 163° 50' E. Tasman and Visscher were calculating their longitude east of the Peak of Tenerife which, as Tasman wrote in his journal, was 'at present in use by everyone' as the prime meridian.[62] As the Peak of Tenerife is 16° 39' to the west of Greenwich, Tasman's estimate of the longitude was 147° 11' E (of Greenwich) – which is 2 degrees in error. Cape Sorell, near the landfall, is at 42° 12' S, 145° 12' E – at the entrance to Macquarie Harbour on the west coast. Tasman's journal summarised their success:[63]

> This land is the first land in the South Sea that we sighted; unknown to any European people, we have given this land the name of Anthoony van Diemenlandt, in honour of the Hon. Governor General, our highest authority, who first sent us out to make these discoveries.

The latitude and longitude of the landfall, as determined by Tasman and Visscher, must be regarded as reasonably good for the times. The Pole Star, Polaris, is not visible from the southern hemisphere, and latitude must have been determined by observation of the Sun at noon. The subsequent calculation required a knowledge of the Sun's declination – as published in tables provided by astronomers. However, there was no method for the determination of longitude by observation, and this must have been obtained by Tasman and Visscher from their estimate of the distance travelled since leaving Mauritius. This distance travelled could never be much better than an informed guess. The two mountains visible from the discovery position were named Mt Heemskerck and Mt Zeehaen, after the two ships, by Matthew Flinders in 1798. However, Tasman's estimates of his latitude and longitude were not always in such good agreement with modern determinations. When he arrived in Mauritius on 5 August 1642, at the beginning of

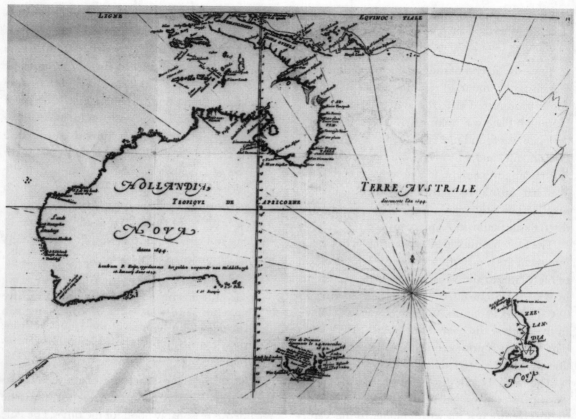

Map of *Terre Australe*, showing Dutch discoveries to 1644, including Van Diemen's Land and the west coast of New Zealand. (Royal Geographical Society of South Australia)

his voyage of exploration, he estimated that he was in latitude 20° S and longitude 83° 48' E (of Tenerife Peak). The position of Port Louis, the main port of Mauritius, is at 20° 10' S and 57' 30' E (of Greenwich), or 74° 09' E (of Tenerife Peak). In other words his longitude was about 9 degrees in error after sailing from Batavia to Mauritius.[64]

Tasman followed the coast of the newly discovered land to the south-east, and then to the north-east. During this time, crew members made a number of landings without, however, seeing any of the inhabitants. The presence of the inhabitants was presumed — because they observed smoke in the distance. Some footprints of 'certain animals' were also observed. One such landing was recorded in Tasman's journal for 2 December 1642. On this

occasion armed men from both ships landed at an inlet to obtain water and other necessities. The journal continues:[65]

About three hours before nightfall, the boats returned, bringing samples of different vegetables which our sailors had seen growing there in abundance (not unlike those they had seen growing at the Cape of Good Hope) and suitable to use as herbs, together with one with long leaves and a brackish taste not unlike sea-parsley.

Van Diemen's Land was not identified as an island until Matthew Flinders and George Bass, in the *Norfolk*, passed through Bass Strait and succeeded in circumnavigating the island in 1798.[66]

When Tasman left the shores of Van Diemen's Land he continued on an easterly course until he reached the previously unknown islands of New Zealand, where he met some of the inhabitants – the Mâori. He then sailed nor'-nor'-east and discovered the islands of the Tongan Group. Further northwards he discovered the Fiji Islands, Ontong Java and New Ireland. He returned to Batavia in June 1643 via the northern coast of New Guinea.

Six months later Tasman and Visscher set off again, this time with three ships – the *Limmen*, the *Zeemeeuw* and the *Bracq*. The main object of this new voyage was to seek a passage into the Pacific Ocean. The company's instructions continued:[67]

> But if (as probable) the land of Nova Guinea, is joined to the Southland without any channels, and therefore one land, you shall be able conveniently to sail along, and fully discover, the north coast of the same from the 17 as far as 22 degrees, with the south east trade wind ...

In the event, the three ships called at Macassar, Ambon and Banda before arriving at the coast of New Guinea. They sailed along the coast towards the east – but failed to find Torres Strait. The strait had actually been discovered by Torres forty years before, but there had been no publication about it and the Dutch were unaware of it. Tasman's ships explored the eastern and western shores of the Gulf of Carpentaria instead, and named Groote Eylandt (which Flinders later circumnavigated). They then sailed westwards along the northern coast of Australia. They continued until they reached a point not far from present-day Port Hedland, and then returned to Batavia – where Tasman's description of the country failed to excite the interest of the VOC. Nevertheless, Tasman had carried out a significant exploration of the northern coast of Australia and had made many important discoveries.

The Dutch mariners had succeeded in exploring the southern coast of Australia as far as the Nuyts Archipelago, and the western coast as far north as Shark Bay. The north-western coast remained unexplored until the arrival of William Dampier.

DAMPIER

William Dampier was born in Somerset, England. He was baptised on 5 September 1651 (Gregorian calendar) and was probably born a day or so before this. He went to sea in 1669, sailed to France and to Newfoundland and, in 1672, served in the Anglo-Dutch War. Dampier then went to the West Indies where he served as a privateer, operating against Spain 'which at the time was still England's cold war enemy'.[68] It should be noted that privateers were not outlawed until 1856.

Dampier returned to England in 1678 for a time, but then went back to the West Indies. He served in a number of ships before joining the *Revenge*, which was under the command of Captain Davis. He then transferred to the *Cygnet*, with Captain Swan in command.[69]

Cygnet had been engaged on privateering activities near the western coast of South America. With Dampier as a member of the crew, she sailed to Guam and then to Mindanao, in the Philippines, where she remained for several months. By this time the crew had become divided. Those who had money (including the captain) lived ashore. Those who had little or no money lived aboard. They were tired of the long and tedious voyage, and wished to take advantage of the easterly monsoon to take them to the Indies. Those on board effectively mutinied against Captain Swan – who refused to come on board. 'So we left Captain Swan and about 36 Men ashore in the City, and six or eight who ran away; and about 16 we had buried there,' wrote Dampier.[70] Captain Reed then took over the command.

According to Dampier's account 'we fell in with the Land of New Holland' at 16° 50' S on 15 January 1688. They were not far from Cape Leveque – which is at 16° 25' S, 122° 55' E (of Greenwich) – at the mouth of King Sound, in the north of Western Australia. They sailed northwards along the coast and reached a point that was later (1821) named Swan Point by Phillip Parker King in the belief that Captain Swan was still in charge of the *Cygnet* when she visited these coasts. The adjacent bay is Karrakatta Bay, and it was, almost certainly, the place where the *Cygnet* was beached for careening. King believed that the *Cygnet* had been beached in Cygnet Bay (which he named) – a short distance to the south.[71] The present-day Cygnet Bay is only a part of the original Cygnet Bay. Phillip Parker King also named the many islands in the vicinity the Buccaneer Archipelago in memory of the men of the *Cygnet*. One of the islands in the archipelago, the present Cockatoo Island, contained a rich body of iron ore which was, for some years, mined by the Australian company, Broken Hill Proprietary Limited. The island is now a resort, and the views of the archipelago are magnificent.

During the careening, the men had an opportunity to visit the shore where they were able to meet some of the local Aboriginal people. Dampier wrote in his journal:[72]

> They are people of good stature, but thin and leane, I judge from want of food. They are black, yett I believe their haires would be long if it was comed out, but for want of combs it is matted up like a negroes hair. They have, all that I saw, two front teeth of their upper jaw wanting, both men, women and children.

When the cleaning of the ship's hull was complete, the *Cygnet* sailed – and made for the Nicobar Islands, in the Bay of Bengal (Andaman Sea). On arrival there Dampier took an early opportunity to desert. He could no longer stand the abandoned lifestyle of the crew. He eventually managed to return to England in September 1691 – when he was aged thirty-nine. He busied himself writing an account of his adventures, and his book was published in 1697 as *A New Voyage Round the World*. Dampier's book was an instant success. It was a well-written account, with perceptive observations on the people, plants and animals that he had encountered during his travels. A second

edition was published during the same year, and a third edition in 1698. Two more editions were published before Dampier died in 1715, and further editions followed from time to time. It was translated into Dutch, French and German – and these editions were also successful. His book was 'different' in that it gave a new 'scientific' description of the world.

The book soon came to the attention of the Board of the Admiralty, and to the fellows of the Royal Society. As a result, Dampier was given the command of a naval ship, HMS *Roebuck*, and was instructed to carry out a scientific voyage of exploration of New Holland and New Guinea. *Roebuck* mounted twelve guns and carried a crew of fifty men – but they were a mixed lot, with some being naval men and others being civilian sailors. Unfortunately, this led to discord and the *Roebuck* was not a happy ship during her voyage. She was provisioned for twenty months and sailed from The Downs on Saturday 14 January 1699. *Roebuck* called at Tenerife 'where I intended to take in some Wine and Brandy for my Voyage'.[73] She also called at the Cape Verde Islands before setting out for Bahia (now Salvador), in Brazil, to refresh the crew and to take on supplies. Dampier explained:[74]

> Beside the refreshing and furnishing my Men, I aim'd also at the inuring them gradually and by Intervals to the Fatigues that were to be expected in the Remainder of the Voyage, which was to be in a part of the World they were altogether Strangers to; none of them, except two young Men, having ever cross'd the Line.

Roebuck crossed the equator on 10 March and arrived in sight of Brazil on 23 March 1699. She sailed into the harbour of Bahia a few days later.

Dampier was clearly fascinated by Bahia and by the surrounding country. He mentioned the town's forts, the churches, the Jesuits college, the nunnery, the gardens, the merchants, the items imported and exported, the vegetables, the crops, the trees – and everything else that caught his eye. The fruit was of special interest. He mentioned the three or four sorts of oranges, limes, pomegranates, plantains, grapes, custard-apples and many others – but 'Mango's are yet but rare here.'[75] He mentioned the various animals: horses, cattle, sheep, goats, rabbits, hogs, leopards, tigers, foxes, monkeys, alligators, lizards, toads, frogs – and 'a sort of amphibious Creatures called ... in English Water-Dogs'.[76] He went on to describe the many shell fish, and the fish.

Roebuck spent about a month at Bahia, not only to refresh the crew and to take on water, but also to have: 'the better Opportunity to compose the Disorders among my Crew: Which, as I have before related, were grown to so great a Heighth'.[77] *Roebuck*, well stocked with oranges and other useful foodstuffs, sailed from Bahia on 23 April 1699. Dampier aimed to sail eastwards some distance to the south of the Cape of Good Hope, and to arrive at the western coast of New Holland. During this time at sea he observed the many sea-birds and the whales, and other items of interest. He also studied the magnetic variation as they moved to the east. He took the necessary readings every couple of days and was surprised at the magnitude of the variation as shown by the magnetic compass.

Not far from the Cape of Good Hope, on 3 June, they met another English ship, the *Antelope* – which was on her way to the Bay of Bengal. Dampier went aboard to exchange courtesies and, upon leaving, was presented with a fine package of useful foodstuffs. In exchange, he gave them some oatmeal 'which they wanted'.

On 15 July, Dampier could tell that his ship was approaching land, and he knew that every care would have to be taken to avoid the Houtman Abrolhos – a hazard to navigation more especially as the position of the shoals was then known only approximately. Soundings were taken with the lead and line and, by changing his course at frequent intervals Dampier was able to avoid them. They began to look for a suitable harbour on the coast where they could lie in safely. Then, as Dampier wrote:[78]

> The 6th of August [1699] in the Morning we saw an Opening in the Land, and we ran into it, and anchored in 7 and a half Fathom-water, 2 Miles from the Shore, clean Sand. It was somewhat difficult getting in here, by Reason of many Shoals we met with: But I sent my Boat sounding before me. The Mouth of this Sound, which I call'd Shark's Bay, lies in about 25 deg. S. Lat.

The *Roebuck* had entered Shark Bay (as it is now known) on 7 August and, although fresh water was not found, it was possible to eat a variety of foodstuffs. Dampier recorded that the guanos (lizards) he observed provided very good meat:[79]

> And I have often eaten of them with Pleasure, but tho' I have eaten of Snakes, Crocodiles and Allegators and many Creatures that look frightfully enough, and there are but a few I should have been afraid to eat of, if prest by Hunger, yet I think my Stomach would scarce have serv'd to venture upon these N. Holland Guano's [sic], both the Looks and the Smell of them being so offensive.

Dampier anchored at three different sites while *Roebuck* was in Shark Bay and, on 14 August, they sailed out of the bay and towards the north. They passed, but apparently did not enter, Roebuck Bay. It is a shallow bay – especially at low tide. The Dampier Creek flows into the bay, and the only relatively deep water at low tide is provided by the course of this creek. Broome, famous for its pearling industry, is situated on the northern shores of Roebuck Bay. The town was named after Sir Frederick Napier Broome, who was appointed the governor of Western Australia in 1883. Further north, in what was later named the Dampier Archipelago, Dampier landed on an island that he named Rosemary Island (because one of the shrubs on the island was 'just like Rosemary'). However, due to an error by the French explorer Louis de Freycinet, the island labelled 'Rosemary' in modern maps is not identical with the island on which

Dampier landed. It seems that he landed on an island a little to the south-east, and which is named East Lewis Island.[80] It is south-east of the island which is known as Rosemary Island on present-day maps. Dampier reported:[81]

> Some of the other Shrubs had blue and yellow Flowers; and we found 2 Sorts of a creeping Vine that runs along on the Ground, having very thick broad Leaves, and the Blossom like a Bean Blossom, but much larger, and of a deep red Colour, looking very beautiful.

Dampier had seen what we now know as 'Sturt's desert pea' on East Lewis Island. Many years later Edward John Eyre also saw this spectacular plant, *Clianthus formosus*, on the early stages of his expedition from Spencer Gulf to King George Sound in Western Australia, and Sturt and his companions saw the brilliant red flowers of this plant during the early stages of their expedition to search for an inland sea.

Dampier had spent about five weeks following the western coast of New Holland 'without finding any good water, or any convenient place to clean the ship', as he had hoped.[82] He had made many observations on the country and on the fauna and flora, and many on the magnetic variation — observations of great value to mariners sailing in relatively uncharted waters. Some of the botanical specimens he collected, those from Shark Bay, for example, are still preserved in the herbarium at Oxford, and have been identified by A. S. George.[83] By this time, however, some of his men had

developed scurvy 'which was likely to increase upon them and disable them, and was promoted by the brackish Water they took in last for boiling their Oatmeal'.[84] On 8 September, therefore, he set sail for Timor, and arrived on 22 September. From there, Dampier sailed to the northern coast of New Ireland, then to the southern coast of New Britain and then, in a north-westerly direction, along the northern coast of Papua New Guinea. Dampier then began the voyage home. The *Roebuck* arrived at the Cape of Good Hope on 30 December 1700, and reached Ascension Island on 21 February 1701. The next day it was found that the *Roebuck* was leaking badly, and all efforts to save the ship were fruitless.

The *Roebuck* sank on 24 February. The officers and men managed to set up a camp ashore. Then, on 3 April, four naval ships arrived at the island, and the officers and men were taken aboard for a passage home to England. As Spencer has written:[85]

> Dampier's resolve to persevere and his resourcefulness in carrying out a demanding voyage with a small and reluctant crew, no first lieutenant, an unreliable master, an incompetent carpenter and a rapidly deteriorating ship, was no small achievement.

Dampier wrote an account of his voyage, and it was published under the title *A Voyage to New Holland*. The first part was published in 1703, and the second in 1709. The two parts were combined in one volume in 1729. It was a great success and there have been numerous editions.

4

THE MARITIME EXPLORATION – PREPARING THE CHARTS

THE EARLY YEARS

The history of the discovery of Australia is similar in some ways to that of America in that the first to land on its shores are not always regarded as the discoverers. Leif Ericsson and his men landed on North American shores nearly 500 years before Columbus. But it was not until after Columbus's voyage that European settlements were established – and Columbus is usually regarded as the discoverer of America. Similarly, several Dutch mariners had seen, and roughly charted, the western and south-western coasts of Australia, and Dampier had explored part of the north-western coast. Little more happened, however, until the Englishman, James Cook, sailed northwards along the eastern coast of the island continent in the *Endeavour*, and produced a preliminary chart of this coastline.

Lieutenant James Cook, Royal Navy (RN), had been given the command of *Endeavour* in May 1768, and had been instructed to proceed to the island of Tahiti in the Pacific Ocean to be one of the observers of the Transit of Venus – the passage of the planet Venus across the face of the Sun. The other observer was to be Charles Green – an astronomer from the royal observatory at Greenwich. This transit had been predicted to occur on 3 June 1769 and the data obtained at Tahiti was to be used to calculate the distance of the Earth from the Sun. Joseph Banks, a wealthy young man with a keen interest in botany, requested and obtained permission to join the expedition and to take with him, at his own expense, several scientists and artists who would carry out botanical and other scientific studies. First among these was Daniel Carl Solander – who had studied under Carl Linnaeus, the famous professor of botany at Uppsala. Also to be included were: Solander's assistant, Herman Diedrich Spöring; a botanical draughtsman, Sydney Parkinson; and a general artist, Alexander Buchan.

The expedition was well equipped – not only to make the observation of the Transit of Venus, but also to determine latitude and longitude with some precision. This was essential, not only for the calculation of the distance of the Earth from the Sun, but also for the geographical discoveries which were confidently expected during the voyage. Cook was supplied with a quality sextant – an instrument recently developed from the octant (which had been in use for some years). A nautical almanac, with its tables of astronomical information for the coming year, had just been produced by Nevil Maskelyne and his astronomers at Greenwich. Cook was supplied with copies of this publication for 1768, 1769 and 1770 – either in a printed form or in manuscript. This publication included the information required for the determination of the longitude using the observed angle between the Moon and the Sun, or between the Moon and one of the prominent stars.

It was known that longitude could also be determined with the help of a chronometer keeping the same time as that on the meridian at Greenwich. A few chronometers had been constructed in England and in France at this time, but they were still under examination for their accuracy in 1768 and Cook had no chronometer on this voyage.

The *Endeavour* sailed from Plymouth on 25 August 1768 bound for Rio de Janeiro, then southwards to Cape Horn and into the Pacific Ocean. The ship arrived at Tahiti on 13 April 1769 – in good time to make the necessary arrangements for the observation of the transit on the predicted date. Everything went well, the weather was fine, and the results of the observation were eventually reported in the *Transactions* of the Royal Society. After the observations were completed Cook opened his sealed orders regarding the return voyage.

Cook was instructed to sail southwards from Tahiti as far as 40° S. He reached this latitude on 2 September 1769 and, because he had not discovered a southern continent, he then sailed westwards – seeking to find the land that Tasman had discovered in 1642, and had named 'New Zeland'. The *Endeavour* reached Poverty Bay on the eastern coast of New Zealand on 6 October 1769. Cook circumnavigated both islands of New Zealand and then sailed from Cape Farewell in a north-westerly direction until, at six o'clock on the morning of 20 April 1770 – or 19 April by 'ship-time' (in which each day begins at noon and ends at noon the following day) – land was sighted by Lieutenant Zachary Hicks, who was the officer of the watch. Cook immediately came on deck and decided to continue on the same course until the ship was closer to the land. Two hours later the *Endeavour* altered course to the north-east, and Cook named 'the southernmost point of land we had in sight' Point Hicks – 'because Lieutenant Hicks was the first who discovered this land'.[1] Unfortunately, in 1843 the same point was named Cape Everard (in honour of Sir Everard Home,

the senior naval officer on the Australian station) by Captain Stokes of the *Beagle* – and it remains so named.

Proceeding further to the north-east Cook named Cape Howe – after Earl Howe, who was one of the lords of the Admiralty at the time that the *Endeavour* left England. Cook then set a more northerly course to follow the direction of the coastline. He named a 'pretty high mountain' Mount Dromedary, then Bateman Bay after the captain of *Northumberland* when Cook was the master of that ship. Cape St George was discovered on St George's Day. Then, near the site of present-day Bulli, a few Aboriginal people were seen on the shore. Cook, Banks and Solander went in one of the boats to see if they could talk with these people and they took Tupia (a young man from Tahiti) with them in the hope that he would be able to understand their language (as he had done with the Mâori in New Zealand). However, the Aborigines disappeared into the woods as soon as the boat neared the shore. In the event, the surf was so violent that it was deemed too dangerous to attempt a landing at that time. The following morning Cook discovered:[2]

> ... a Bay which appeard to be tollerably well shelterd from all winds into which I resolved to go with the Ship and with this view sent the Master in the Pinnace to sound the entrance while we kept turning up with the Ship haveing the wind right out.

The *Endeavour* sailed into the bay and Cook noted that Aboriginal men, women, and children, as well as a few primitive huts, were to be seen on both points of the entrance. He later named the northern point Cape Banks, and the southern one, Point Solander. Cook hoped to be able to speak with the Aborigines – and he, Banks, Solander and Tupia took a boat to the shore. Most of the Aborigines retired into the woods, but two men seemed determined to oppose their landing. Cook fired a couple of shots between them, and then landed without incident. It seems that Isaac Smith, one of the oarsmen, was the first Englishman to land on Australian soil. Cook gave some beads to the Aboriginal children, and he examined the three canoes on the beach which were:[3]

> ... the worst I think I ever saw, they were about 12 or 14 feet long made of one peice of the bark of a tree drawn or tied up at each end and in the middle kept open by means of peices of sticks by way of Thwarts.

Their time in the bay was full of interest and there were ample opportunities to obtain fresh food. In the cove on the north side of the bay they caught more than 130 kilograms of fish and, on several occasions, they noted the presence of oysters and of large stingrays. Two stingrays that were caught weighed nearly 300 kilograms. Indeed, Cook first thought of naming the bay 'Stingray Bay' – and this name appears on some of the manuscript charts. Banks and Solander were so fascinated by the great variety of the plants on shore that Cook then considered naming it 'Botanist Bay'. In the end, he named it Botany Bay.[4] Cook described the nature of the country and mentioned the many birds to be seen. He could not converse with the Aboriginal people, but his comments are of interest:[5]

> The Natives do not appear to be numberous neither do they seem to live in large bodies but dispers'd in small parties along by the water side; those I saw were about as tall as Europeans, of a very dark brown colour but not black nor had they wooly frizled hair, but black and lank much like ours. No sort of cloathing or ornaments were ever seen by any of us upon any one of them or in or about any of their hutts, from which I conclude that they never wear any. Some we saw had their faces and bodies painted with a sort of white paint or Pigment.

On the morning of Sunday 6 May Cook weighed anchor, left Botany Bay, and sailed northwards along the coast. About 16 kilometres to the north they were abreast of another bay or harbour – which Cook named Port Jackson after a secretary of the Admiralty. As he sailed further northwards Cook named Point Stephens, Cape Hawke and Cape Byron. The last was named after Commodore Byron who had sailed the *Dolphin* around the world in 1764–65. Keppel Bay was named after Augustus Keppel who had sailed around the world in the *Centurion* with Commodore Anson. Cape Capricorn was so named because it is on the Tropic of Capricorn. The beautiful Whitsunday Passage was discovered 'on the Day the Church commemorates that Festival'. The Cumberland Islands were named after the Duke of Cumberland, the younger brother of George III; and Cape Gloucester was named after the Duke of Gloucester, another brother of George III. Cape Sandwich was named after the Earl of Sandwich – a friend of Banks who had served as First Lord of the Admiralty. Trinity Bay was named after the day it was discovered, and Cape Tribulation 'because here begun all our troubles'.[6]

On the evening of 10 June (according to the civil calendar, or 11 June according to ship-time), the *Endeavour* was sailing northwards with a man heaving the lead to measure the depth of water beneath the ship. This was the usual procedure when sailing close to land. There did not seem to be any danger, however, because depths averaged between 14 and 21 fathoms. The measured depths were then 12, 10, and 8 fathoms. Cook was just about to order the ship to come about when the depth increased again, and he thought that the danger had been avoided. Some time later, however, the measured depth was 17 fathoms and, before the lead could be heaved again, the ship struck a section of the Great Barrier Reef, and stuck fast.

The ship had struck at about high tide and, when immediate steps to free the ship failed, attention was directed to the next high tide – which would occur about twelve hours later. The ship was lightened as much as possible by jettisoning six of the guns and sundry other items – such as decayed

Captain Cook discovered the Whitsunday Passage between the east coast and the Cumberland Islands on Whit Sunday, 3 June 1770. (Geoffrey Badger)

stores and ballast. However, the next high tide, at eleven o'clock the next morning, was about half a metre lower than the previous high tide. The only thing to do was to continue to lighten the ship and to wait for the next evening high tide. This time, the ship was freed from the reef. She had been holed, and emergency arrangements were made to stem the entry of the sea while Cook searched for a place to beach the ship to enable repairs to be undertaken. Cook sent the master ahead, with two boats, to check the depth of the water and to search for a suitable place. One possible bay, named Weary Bay by Cook, was deemed too shallow for the *Endeavour*, and the search continued. In due course the ship was beached on the banks of a river, soon to be named Endeavour River, and the town that was eventually built there was named Cooktown. Cook was justly proud of both his officers and men and wrote in his journal:[7]

> ...no men ever behaved better than they have done on this occasion, animated by the beheavour of every gentleman on board, every man seem'd to have a just sence of the danger we were in and exerted himself to the very utmost.

The *Endeavour* had been holed near the bow, but a large piece of coral had become fixed in the hole and this must have reduced the amount of water that entered the hull. Repair work took seven weeks and, during this time, Cook carried out an investigation on the rise and fall of the tides at that location. He was able to demonstrate that, with the spring tides, the evening tides rose 2.7 metres (9 feet) whereas the morning tide rose only 2.1 metres (7 feet), and that the low water preceding the evening tide fell considerably lower than the one preceding the morning tide. Cook later published a summary of his observations in the *Philosophical Transactions* of the Royal Society.[8]

Banks and Solander were also busily engaged examining the plants and collecting botanical specimens for subsequent study. Sydney Parkinson was preparing drawings of the specimens, and many of these were later published in *Banks' Florilegium*.[9] Banks and Solander (and many of the crew) also took an interest in the animal life. There were several sightings of kangaroos. Two adult specimens, and one juvenile specimen, were eventually taken for examination. The first adult specimen, weighing about 17 kilograms (38 pounds), has since been identified as an Eastern Wallaroo, *Macropus robustus*. The second specimen was a very large kangaroo weighing 38 kilograms (84 pounds), and this has since been identified as an Eastern Grey Kangaroo, *Macropus giganteus*.[10] A few Aborigines visited the site and were given presents. But they tried to run off with two turtles, and this soured relations between them and the crew.

The *Endeavour* was repaired and ready for sea on 4 August and continued her voyage towards the East Indies. Cook anchored near an island a short distance from the Endeavour River and then climbed the highest hill to choose the best route through the reefs. While there he came across some large lizards and he therefore named the island Lizard Island. Cook continued the running survey of the coast and, on 21 August, observed and named Cape York – the most northerly point on the continent. He then had to sail the ship through the maze of shoals and islands. Boats were sent ahead, and he climbed a hill on an adjacent island.

Having 'satisfied my self of the great Probabillity of a Passage, thro' which I intend going with the Ship, and therefore may land no more upon this Eastern coast of *New Holland*', he took possession of the whole of the eastern coast in the name of King George III – and named the island Possession Island. He gave the entire area he had discovered the name 'New South Wales.[11]

Some native people were observed on the islands to the north of Cape York. They were naked, like those on the mainland but, unlike the people he had observed on the mainland, they had bows and arrows, and some had on 'pretty large breast plates' made of shells. Cook noted 'that this was a thing as well as the Bow and Arrows we had not seen before'.[12] These were Torres Strait Islanders – who are Melanesians. Cook's route through the maze of islands became known as Endeavour Strait, and is still shown as such on the charts. But it is but one of several passages through the strait.

Cook successfully navigated the *Endeavour* through Endeavour Strait and arrived safely at Batavia (Jakarta), where further repairs were effected. Many of the officers and men succumbed to the diseases that were prevalent there, and several died. As soon as the repairs had been completed, the *Endeavour* sailed for England via the Cape of Good Hope – and arrived in the Downs on 13 July 1771.

It had been one of the greatest and most successful maritime expeditions ever made – not least because Cook had produced an excellent chart of the eastern coast of Australia, from Point Hicks in the south to Cape York in the north. There were, of course, some details that would have to be settled by later explorers. He had not sailed into Port Jackson, for example, and he did not determine whether Van Diemen's Land was an island (as he believed probable) or whether (as had long been supposed) it was joined to the mainland.[13]

COOK'S ACHIEVEMENTS

Although Cook is chiefly remembered for his discovery of the eastern coastline of Australia – a discovery that resulted in the establishment of colony, first at Botany Bay and then at Port Jackson – his real contributions were many and varied.

First, James Cook and Charles Green (the astronomer in *Endeavour*) determined the latitude and longitude of their observatory, Fort Venus, in

Tahiti, with great precision. The latitude was obtained from twenty-one meridian altitudes of the Sun and twenty-seven observations of stars. These gave a mean of 17° 29' 15" S. During Cook's second voyage, his two astronomers — Wales and Bayly — again determined the latitude of the observatory and obtained 17° 29' 13" S — a difference of about 65 metres.[14] Cook and Green also determined the longitude of the Fort Venus Observatory by fifty-seven observations of the lunar distance. These gave a mean of 149° 32' 30" W.[15] Cook's journal gave the longitude as 149° 30' W — close to the value that is accepted today (149° 29' W).[16] The accuracy of these observations far exceeded the general run of determinations of latitude and longitude in the eighteenth century.

Second, Cook had been one of the three observers of the Transit of Venus at Tahiti — the others being Charles Green and Daniel Solander. The results of all the observations of the transit gave the distance of the Sun from the Earth.[17] Although this distance has been more accurately obtained in the twentieth century, the work of Cook, Green and Solander — using eighteenth-century instruments — was as good as could be expected.

Third, it can be argued that Cook's most enduring contribution to maritime exploration was his demonstration that the age-old disease of ocean mariners, scurvy, could be prevented. Vasco da Gama seems to have been the first to describe the devastating effects of scurvy. In his voyage of exploration beyond the Cape of Good Hope he lost 100 of his 160 men to this disease. Magellan's men also suffered severely during their long voyage across the Pacific Ocean, and there were many deaths. Scurvy had decimated the crews of Anson's ships during his voyage to the Pacific Ocean (to harass the Spanish ships) in 1740–41. Anson's own ship, the *Centurion*, left England with about 500 men but, by the time she arrived at the island of Juan Fernandez, off the west coast of Chile, only 200 remained alive. The crews of the *Gloucester* and

of the *Tryal* suffered similarly — indeed the captain of *Tryal* reported to Anson at Juan Fernandez that only he and the lieutenant and three men were fit enough to work the ship. On these early voyages, the disease was recognised by the fact that the gums began to bleed, the teeth became loose, the breath became foul, and the legs and feet became covered with purple patches due to haemorrhages under the skin. Moreover, the disease was 'usually attended with a strange dejection of the spirits, and with shiverings, tremblings, and a disposition to be seized with the most dreadful terrors on the slightest accident'.[19]

The cause of the disease was unknown but, over the years, it was variously attributed to foggy weather, to the shortage of fresh drinking water on board ship, to overindulgence in tobacco, to laziness, or to the fact that seamen had to live on salt meat, 'biscuit' and beer or spirits. Lord Nelson refused to eat salt meat at sea because he thought it caused scurvy. With regard to 'biscuit', Banks was to write in his journal that 'Our bread indeed is but indifferent, occasioned by the quantity of Vermin that are in it, I have often seen hundreds nay thousands shaken out of a single bisket'.[20]

In 1747, a Royal Navy surgeon, James Lind, carried out the first controlled dietetic experiment on record on a number of patients suffering from scurvy. He divided the patients into pairs and treated each pair with one or other of a series of possible remedies. The only treatment of any value was found to be the administration of citrus fruit — the two patients to whom the citrus fruit was given soon becoming well again. The reason for this was unknown. Indeed, it was sometimes suggested that the beneficial effect of citrus fruit might be due to acidity — despite the fact that Lind had found that vinegar has no beneficial effect on patients with scurvy. Unfortunately little notice was taken of Lind's findings.[21] Only a few years later, during the Seven Years War (1756–63), 130 000 British seamen alone died of scurvy, and the seafarers of other nationalities also continued to be afflicted by this readily avoidable disease.

Cook observed the effects of scurvy in July 1756 – the first year of the war – when he joined the *Eagle* at Plymouth. The captain, Hugh Palliser, had to land 130 of his seamen because they were too ill with scurvy. Soon afterwards, Cook was appointed master of the *Pembroke* – which was part of the fleet that had been ordered to attack Louisbourg. But so many members of the crew were ill with scurvy that she had to put into Halifax to allow them to recover – a small delay that resulted in *Pembroke's* not arriving at Louisbourg until four days after the attack began.[22] Cook remained with the *Pembroke*, in the Quebec basin, until 1762, and he then spent five years surveying Newfoundland.

The *Endeavour* was supplied with a number of supposed remedies for scurvy – which Cook was asked to evaluate. These supposed remedies included sauerkraut, salted cabbage, portable soup, malt and 'rob of oranges' (partially dehydrated orange juice). All were included in the diet of both officers and men. Cook was to report that the rob of oranges had little or no effect on the disease. In view of Lind's finding, this was unexpected. But scurvy was later shown to be caused by a deficiency of vitamin C in the diet, and most of the vitamin C in the orange juice was destroyed during the dehydration process. Cook found that sauerkraut is effective in reducing the incidence of scurvy – and it is now known to contain vitamin C. Portable soup was simply a dehydrated broth and could not have contained any vitamin C – but Cook added various wild 'greens' to the soup, and this procedure doubtless provided some vitamin C. Indeed, Cook's main contribution to the prevention of scurvy was his insistence that fruit and wild vegetables should be collected and added to the diet, and this procedure was further promoted during his second and third voyages. Cook wrote:[23]

We came to few places where either the art of man or nature did not afford some sort of refreshment or other, either of the animal or vegetable kind. It was my first care to procure what could be met with of either by every means in my power, and to oblige our people to make use thereof, both by my example and authority.

The attitude of the seamen to these additions to their diet is of interest. Alexander Home, who sailed on Cook's third voyage to the Pacific Ocean, wrote that 'it was the Custom of Our Crews to Eat almost Every Herb plant Root and kinds of Fruit they Could Possibly Light [upon] with [out] the Least Inquirey or Hesitation' – but grumbling all the time. They wished 'for gods Sake that he [Cook] Might be Obledged to Eat such Damned Stuff Mixed with his Broth as Long as he Lived. Yet for all that there were None so Ignorant as Not to know how Right a thing it was'.[24] In this connection it is of interest that Thomas Perry, who sailed on Cook's second voyage, wrote a song:[25]

We were all hearty seamen no cold did we fear
And we have from all sickness entirely kept clear
Thanks be to the Captain he has proved so good
Amongst all the Islands to give us fresh food.
And when to old England my Brave Boys we arrive
We will tip off a Bottle to make us alive
We will toast Capt. Cook with a loud song all round
Because that he has the South Continent found.

Cook's decision to use wild vegetables and fruit whenever possible was dramatically successful – so much so that the Royal Society presented him with its prestigious Copley Medal. His lecture to the fellows of the society included the following:[26]

The *Resolution* performed a voyage of three years and eighteen days, through all climates from 52° North to 71° South, with the loss of only one man by disease, and who died of a complicated and lingering illness, without any mixture of scurvy. Two others were unfortunately drowned, and one killed by a fall; so that of the whole number with which I set out from England I lost only four.

Cook used this method of living off the land on all three of his voyages. The health record of the first voyage was, however, marred by many of his men contracting dysentery and malaria at Batavia (Jakarta) – resulting in a number of deaths. On his third voyage Cook called at Kerguelen Island in the southern Indian Ocean where, on his instruction, the men collected a quantity of the Kerguelen cabbage, and this was added to the soup. It is now known as *Pringlea antiscorbutica*. William Anderson, surgeon on the *Resolution*, named it *Pringlea* in honour of Sir John Pringle, the president of the Royal Society. The heart leaves of this cabbage have been found to contain 155 milligrams of vitamin C per 100 grams.[27]

Cook's methods for avoiding scurvy were clearly successful, but no one understood why they were successful – and this might explain why other explorers, both maritime and overland, were slow to adopt his procedures. The French expeditions led by D'Entrecasteaux and by Baudin suffered severely from scurvy. Baudin avoided calling at the Cape of Good Hope where, thanks to the East India Company, fruit and vegetables were readily available. The cause of scurvy was still not understood and theories were many and various. In 1910, when Captain Scott led his party over Antarctica, it was thought that scurvy resulted from eating tainted meat. Their rations included biscuits, pemmican, butter, cocoa, sugar and tea – but no foods containing vitamin C. As a result, 'it seems certain that Scott and other members of his party were suffering from scurvy in the weeks before their death.'[28] Moreover, Douglas Mawson's expedition to Antarctica in 1911 carried no provisions containing vitamin C.

Vitamins were not isolated and identified until the twentieth century. Vitamin C was originally isolated from the adrenal cortex of cattle by Albert Szent-Györgyi in 1928, but he did not recognise it as a vitamin. Charles Glen King later obtained it from cabbages, and recognised it as vitamin C. It was named ascorbic acid from the Greek for 'no scurvy'.

ARRIVAL OF THE FIRST FLEET

The *Endeavour* had returned safely to England in July 1771 with news of the discovery of the eastern coast of New Holland. Then, as now, British gaols were full to overflowing, and it was soon decided to transport a substantial number of felons and to establish a convict settlement overseas. On the recommendation of Sir Joseph Banks, Botany Bay was selected for the proposed settlement. A fleet of ships was assembled – later to be known as the 'First Fleet'. A storeship named *Berwick* was selected to be the flagship, and was renamed HMS *Sirius*. *Sirius* had a displacement of 624 tonnes and was fitted with twenty guns. An old brig-rigged sloop of 173 tonnes and eight guns became HMS *Supply* and was ordered to escort the fleet of three storeships – which were loaded with provisions and other stores reckoned to be sufficient to maintain the proposed colony for about two years. These ships, together with the six transports carrying the male and female convicts, made up the fleet.[29]

Arthur Phillip, a post-captain in the Royal Navy, was appointed the commander-in-chief of the fleet, and governor of the proposed penal colony. He received his commission on 12 October 1786. Another post-captain, John Hunter, was appointed 'second captain' of *Sirius* – so that Phillip could be relieved of many of the routine duties. Lieutenant Henry Ball, RN, was appointed to the command of the armed tender *Supply*.[30]

There were 565 male and 192 female convicts, and eighteen children. The 'major part of the prisoners were mechanics and husbandmen, selected on purpose by order of the government'.[31] There were 212 marines – 210 of whom were volunteers. Captain-Lieutenant Watkin Tench, who commanded a company of marines, wrote a famous book describing the voyage and the first couple of years at the settlement. The marines were not entitled to be called '*Royal* Marines' at that time – the prefix being officially granted on

29 April 1802 by George III 'in consideration of the very meritorious services of the Marines during the late war'.[32]

The fleet sailed from Portsmouth on Sunday 13 May 1787, and reached Tenerife on 3 June. The ships proceeded to Rio de Janeiro, and then to the Cape of Good Hope – where Captain Phillip shifted his pennant from *Sirius* to *Supply*. The fleet was then divided, and *Supply* and other selected ships continued without waiting for the slowest ship. Phillip's object was to sail as quickly as possible for Botany Bay so that some work could be undertaken there in readiness for the arrival of the remainder of the fleet. *Supply* arrived at Botany Bay on 18 January 1788 and, by ten o'clock on the morning of 20 January, the whole fleet was at anchor in the bay. As Tench wrote in his journal:[33]

> Thus, after a passage of exactly thirty-six weeks from Portsmouth, we happily effected our arduous undertaking with such a train of unexpected blessings as hardly ever attended a fleet in a like predicament. Of 212 marines we lost only one; and of 775 convicts put on board in England, but twenty-four perished in our route. To what cause are we to attribute this unhoped for success? I wish I could answer to the liberal manner in which government supplied the expedition. But when the reader is told that some of the necessary articles allowed to ships on a common passage to the West Indies were withheld from us ... his surprise will redouble at the result of the voyage.

Governor Phillip soon decided that Botany Bay had some deficiencies as a site for a new settlement. The bay was too exposed to the westerlies and the south-westerlies, it was too shallow, and the soil did not seem satisfactory for agricultural purposes. He decided to take three boats, with a few officers (including Captain Hunter and Second Lieutenant Philip Gidley King) to examine the 'Bay or Harbour' that Cook had observed (without, however, entering it) 3 leagues to the north of Botany Bay. Cook had named it Port Jackson.

Phillip was soon convinced that Port Jackson was a much more suitable site for the settlement than Botany Bay, and the whole fleet was ordered to prepare to move to Port Jackson. Tench wrote that the '... thoughts of removal banished sleep'; and he 'rose at the first dawn of the morning'. He heard from a sergeant 'who ran down almost breathless to the cabin' where Tench was dressing, 'that a ship was seen off the harbour's mouth'. Tench 'flew upon deck' and had hardly set foot there when he heard the cry 'another sail'. It turned out that they were the French ships *Boussole* and *Astrolabe* on a voyage of discovery, under the command of the Comte de la Pérouse. A British officer was sent to assist them to enter the bay.[34] Next morning, 25 January 1788, Phillip set off in *Supply* for Port Jackson. The other ships in the fleet were to follow, but were delayed by adverse winds. *Supply* sailed into Port Jackson, and Phillip later reported to the British government, describing the harbour as:[35]

> ... the finest harbour in the world, in which a thousand sail of the line may ride in the utmost security ... The different coves were examined with all possible expedition. I fixed on the one that had the best spring of water, and in which the ships can anchor so close to the shore that at very small expence quays may be made at which the largest ships may unload.

Governor Phillip named this cove 'Sydney Cove' after Viscount Sydney who, as a member of the Pitt government (secretary of state for the Colonies), had appointed him to the command of the fleet. As Phillip wrote in his report to London: 'This cove, which I honoured with the name of Sydney, is about a quarter of a mile across at the entrance, and half a mile in length'.[36]

On Saturday 26 January 1788, Governor Phillip, with a suitable party, went ashore at Sydney Cove and raised the Union Flag (of England and Scotland). They then toasted the King, then the Queen, then the Prince of Wales, and then drank to 'The Success of the Colony'.

The other ships of the fleet left Botany Bay on 26 January and, as Tench has recorded:[37]

Our passage to Port Jackson took up but few hours, and these were spent far from unpleasantly. The evening was bright, and the prospect before us such as might justify sanguine expectation. Having passed between the capes which form the entrance, we found ourselves in a port superior, in extent and excellency, to all we had seen before. We continued to run up the harbour about four miles [actually about 6 miles], in a westerly direction, enjoying the luxuriant prospect of its shores, covered with trees to the water's edge, among which many Indians [the Aborigines] were frequently seen, till we arrived at a small snug cove on the southern side, on which banks the plan of our operation was destined to commence.

The formal annexation of New South Wales did not take place until 7 February 1788. This was done despite the fact that Cook had taken possession of the whole of the eastern part of New Holland, under the name New South Wales, on 22 August 1770. The chaplain of the fleet was able to conduct divine service, in the presence of the marines and the convicts, on Sunday 27 January. Work to establish the settlement was begun. The unloading of the ships was pushed forward as quickly as possible, and efforts were made to clear the ground for the tents and future buildings. 'The provost-martial with his men was ordered to patrol the country around, and the convicts informed that the severest punishment would be inflicted on transgressors.'[38] Not long afterwards, one of the prisoners, convicted of striking a marine, received 150 lashes, and another prisoner, having committed a petty theft, 'was sent to a small barren island [Pinchgut?] and kept there on bread and water only, for a week'.[39] Another man, found guilty of stealing provisions, was hanged in the presence of the marines and the convicts.[40] Some time later a convict was detected in a garden stealing potatoes. 'He was ordered to receive three hundred lashes immediately, to be chained for six months to two other criminals who were thus

fettered for former offences, and to have his allowance of flour stopped for six months.' Tench added that 'such was the melancholy length to which we were compelled to stretch our penal system'.[41]

Such massive punishments were not confined to the convicts, however. Surgeon-General John White recorded:[42]

Two men of the *Sirius* were brought before the criminal court and tried for assaulting and beating, in a cruel manner, another man belonging to the same vessel, while employed on an island appropriated by the governor to the use of the ship. They were sentenced to receive five hundred lashes each, but could not undergo the whole of that punishment, as, like most of the persons in the colony, they were much afflicted with the scurvy.

The construction of the settlement proceeded slowly; but there were some worries. When Cook had explored the east coast he had seen very few Aborigines, but the members of the First Fleet saw several groups – even on their way into Port Jackson.

'Both sexes,' wrote Tench, 'and those of all ages, are invariably found naked.' He added:[43]

To cultivation of the ground they are utter strangers, and wholly depend for food on the few fruits they gather, the roots they dig up in the swamps, and the fish they pick up along the shore or contrive to strike from their canoes with spears.

The colonists regarded the Aborigines as 'savages', and it was some time before they realised that the local people had a number of skills that were totally absent in Europeans. The Aborigines had learnt how to straighten the long shafts of wood that they required for their spears – by using steam and by manipulation with their hands. They affixed a number of barbs to the ends of their spears to ensure severe wounds, if not death, to their target animal or enemy. Tench recorded:[44]

On first setting foot in the country we were inclined to hold the spears of the natives very cheap. Fatal experience has, however, convinced us that the wound inflicted by this weapon is not a trivial one, and that the skill of the Indians [the Aboriginal people] in throwing it as far from despicable.

Moreover, it was not unusual for a spear to pass entirely through the thickest part of the body.

The Aboriginal people had also invented the woomera for throwing their spears, and the boomerang – a very versatile weapon. Their huts were of extremely simple construction, and:[45]

> ... the canoes in which they fish are as despicable as their huts, being nothing more than a large piece of bark tied up at both ends with vines. Their dexterous management of them, added to the swiftness with which they paddle and the boldness that leads them several miles in the open sea are, nevertheless, highly deserving of admiration.

The bark canoe 'tied up at both ends' was not found everywhere in Australia, however. The explorers were later to find that, in some places, the Aborigines used a large piece of bark as a raft; and that at least one tribe used the bark fitted to a frame.

The Aboriginal people did not welcome the invaders and there were some conflicts. Flannery has pointed out that, by December 1790, the Aboriginal people had killed or seriously wounded seventeen of the colonists, and that Governor Arthur Phillip was one of those seriously wounded.[46] Phillip ordered that there should be no retaliation, and did not report the incident to London. In retrospect, it is surprising that the number of casualties was so small – after all, the convicts and marines were invading the country that the Aborigines regarded as theirs. Governor Phillip tried hard to encourage friendship between the races, and he himself became friendly with well-known Aboriginal people Arabanoo, Bennelong and Colbee. This clearly helped to reduce bloodshed.

Another difficulty in the early days of the colony was caused by disease – particularly dysentery, but also smallpox. There was an outbreak of smallpox some months after the arrival of the First Fleet.

Where had this originated? There had been no cases of smallpox during the voyage from England to Sydney Cove. Perhaps it was introduced by the French sailors in the ships under the command of La Pérouse? This did not seem likely for, as Tench wrote: 'Let it be remembered that they [the French ships] had now been departed more than a year and we had never heard of its existence on board of them.'[47]

There were many deaths from smallpox among the Aboriginal people – including Arabanoo, the governor's friend. The disease was new to Australia and the Aboriginal people had no resistance. Indeed, the governor reported to Lord Sydney that groups of Aboriginal people had been found dead on the harbour foreshores. As Rienits has explained:[48]

> White [the surgeon-general] ascertained that the cause was smallpox, so virulent in its onslaught that within a few weeks, according to Bennelong, who had himself survived an attack, it had reduced the aboriginal population in the Sydney area by about half.

A hospital was built on the west side of Sydney Cove, and the sick were cared for – but there was little that could be done. The origin of this disease in Australia remained a mystery for many years. Nowadays, it is generally thought that the disease was introduced by the Macassans – who had doubtless been infected by the Europeans in the East Indies, and who made annual visits to the northern coasts of Australia to obtain trepang – and that the smallpox was passed from Aboriginal tribe to tribe over most of the country.

There is little doubt, however, that tuberculosis was introduced to Australia by the Europeans. Nicolas Baudin, the captain of the French expedition that departed from Le Havre in October 1800, suffered from tuberculosis and died of the disease on the way back to France. François Péron, the zoologist and anthropologist, had also contracted tuberculosis, and died of the disease not long after his return to France.

Scurvy was also a problem in the early days of the colony. In his report to London dated 15 May 1788 (just over three months after the arrival of the First Fleet) Governor Phillip reported to London that the 'people were healthy when landed, but the scurvy has, for some time, appeared amongst them, and now rages in a most extraordinary manner'. He added that '... most of the people are affected, and near two hundred rendered incapable of doing any work.'[49] The medical officer, Surgeon-General White, wrote that scurvy:[50]

... has now risen to a most alarming height, without any possibility of checking it until some vegetables can be raised, which, from the season of the year, cannot take place for many months. And even then I am apprehensive that there will not be a sufficiency produced, such are the labour and difficulty which attend the clearing of the ground.

Apart from disease, and the possibility of a major attack by the Aboriginal people, the main problem was the impending shortage of provisions in the settlement. Although the transports had been loaded with a quantity of food calculated to be sufficient to last for two years, much of it was rotten by the time it arrived at Sydney Cove. Indeed as Milford has written:[51]

There can be little room for doubt that much of the food which was taken on board the various vessels of the fleet was unfit for human consumption long before the eight months of the voyage had elapsed, and therefore, was quite useless before two years had been completed.

The transports which had arrived in January 1788 were not scheduled to remain at the settlement and could not be used to obtain additional food. They began their return to England in July. Tench wrote:[52]

The departure ... had long been impatiently expected, and had filled us with anxiety to communicate to our friends an account of our situation, describing the progress of improvement and the probability of success or failure in our enterprise. That men should judge very oppositely on so doubtful and precarious an event will hardly surprise.

A little later he wrote that it 'was impossible to behold without emotion the departure of the ships. On their speedy arrival in England perhaps hinged our fate, by hastening our supplies to us.'[53]

The situation was becoming worse every day. *Sirius* and *Supply*, the only ships remaining, were sent to search for turtles or other supplies – without much success. Some of the convicts were transported to Norfolk Island to relieve the settlement at Sydney Cove – but *Sirius* was wrecked on that Island. *Supply* was sent to the East Indies to obtain food, and the governor decided to cut the daily rations for every member of the Sydney Cove settlement.

No ship had entered the harbour since their arrival at Sydney Cove but, on the evening of 3 June 1790, the arrival of a ship was signalled. Tench ran to a hill where, with 'the assistance of a pocket-glass' his 'hopes were realised'. He added that 'my next door neighbour, a brother officer, was with me, but we could not speak. We wrung each other by the hand, with eyes and hearts overflowing.'[54] Soon afterwards, Tench was able to join the governor in his boat. They went towards the ship and:[55]

As we proceeded, the object of our hopes soon appeared: a large ship with English colours flying, working in between the heads which form the entrance to the harbour.

She was the *Lady Juliana*, with a cargo of provisions and 225 female convicts on board. She had left Plymouth eleven months before. Other ships arrived over the next few days.[56] The settlement could now rest easy and proceed with its development.

It was necessary to survey the country in the vicinity of the settlement and, for this purpose, they needed a focal point – an observatory. The First Fleet had been supplied with a number of navigational instruments by the Board of Longitude in London. These instruments had been used with good effect during the voyage out, and were now to be used on land. The observatory was built on the western shore of Sydney Cove 'at a small distance from the encampment' and one of its first tasks was to determine its position with as much precision as possible. 'The latitude of the Observatory, from the result of more than three hundred observations', was found to be 33° 52' 30" S, and the longitude to be 151° 16' 30" E (of Greenwich). The South Head of the harbour was found to be at 33° 51' S, and the North Head 33° 49' 45" S.[57]

Exploration of the surrounding country had begun long before this, however. Phillip wrote in his dispatches home:[58]

> The 2d of March I went with a long-boat and cutter to examine the broken land mentioned by Captain Cook, about eight miles to the northward of Port Jackson. We slept in the boat that night within a rocky point, in the north-west part of the bay (which is very extensive), as the natives tho' very friendly, appeared to be numerous ...

Indeed, within a few weeks of landing, the governor and his party had discovered Broken Bay and the Hawkesbury River to the north of Port Jackson. This river was named after Lord Hawkesbury – the president of Trade and Plantations, in London. Pittwater was so called after the British prime minister. A site for agricultural development was found about 25 kilometres to the west of Sydney Cove. It was named Rose Hill but, on 4 June 1791 (the King's birthday), it was renamed Parramatta – the name used by the Aboriginal people.[59]

VANCOUVER

George Vancouver was the next English explorer to visit the Australian coast. He had served on Cook's second and third voyages and, in December 1790, he was promoted to the rank of commander, given the command of two ships, the *Discovery* and the *Chatham*, and instructed to explore the western coast of North America in the hope that a passage would be found from the Pacific Ocean to the Atlantic Ocean. *Discovery* was a relatively new vessel, but carried the same name as that used by Cook on his third voyage. As usual with expeditions into the Pacific Ocean, Joseph Banks had considerable influence with the Admiralty, and recommended the appointment of Archibald Menzies as the naturalist. Lieutenant William Broughton was appointed captain of *Chatham*.

Vancouver sailed from Falmouth on 1 April 1791 and made for the Cape of Good Hope. He then sailed eastwards on a latitude of 35° S, to 'the S.W. side of New Holland'. Very little was known about this coastline and he considered this to be 'a real blot in geography'.[60] Therefore, on making his landfall, he sailed along the southern coast naming the principal features – Chatham Island, Cape Howe 'in honor of that noble earl', Bald Head, Michaelmas Island and Seal Island. Eclipse Island was named to commemorate an eclipse of the Sun which was seen on 28 September. Vancouver then discovered an excellent harbour which he named King George III Sound (now King George Sound) and Princess Royal Harbour, it 'being the anniversary of her Royal Highness'. He surveyed the bay and determined the latitude and longitude of their anchorage with as much precision as possible. The latitude was determined from nine meridian altitudes of the Sun – taken by four different observers using different quadrants – and found to be 35° 05' 30" S. The longitude was determined from twenty-five sets (of lunar distances of the Sun and prominent stars) taken before their arrival at the anchorage, eight sets taken at anchor, and fifty-two sets taken after leaving the anchorage. All these were adjusted to the position of the anchorage – making eighty-five sets in all. Each set was of six observed distances – so there were 510 observations in all. These observations gave a mean figure of 118° 14' 13" E for the longitude. Each ship also

The beautiful harbours of Albany on King George Sound in south-western Australia, discovered by Vancouver in 1791, and later visited by Flinders, Baudin and Phillip Parker King; and settled by Major Lockyer and party in 1826–27. (Geoffrey Badger)

had a chronometer. The *Discovery* had been issued with K3, made by Kendall; *Chatham* had Arnold 82. The K3, corrected for its error as found at the Cape of Good Hope, gave the longitude as 118° 23' 00" E. Using Arnold 82, similarly corrected, gave 117° 38' 30" E.[61] The correct figure was probably about 117° 57' E. During their stay in the sound, Menzies was able to study the country and the plants and animal life.[62] He climbed a mountain to obtain a better view, 'and was entranced by the number and variety of the plants and shrubs, many of which were in full bloom'.[63]

Vancouver had no time for further investigation of the southern coast – much as he would have liked to pursue it; his orders were to examine the north-west coast of North America. So he soon turned to the south-east, skirted the southernmost point of Van Diemen's Land and made for Dusky Sound in New Zealand, and then for North America.

D'ENTRECASTEAUX

Earlier, in August 1785, an important French expedition to the Pacific Ocean had left Brest under the command of Jean-François de Galup, Comte de la Pérouse. There were two ships in that expedition – the *Boussole* (French for compass) and the *Astrolabe* – and they carried a number of distinguished French savants who were to study the countries visited, the plants and the animal life. The expedition had called at Conception Bay in South America, Easter Island, Maui, Port des Français in North America, the eastern coast of China, then Samoa, and arrived at Botany Bay on 26 January 1788 – five days after the First Fleet had arrived there. Early in February, La Pérouse sailed from Botany Bay to the north-east. Nothing further was heard of the expedition. Had the ships been wrecked and the passengers and crew drowned? Had they been killed by savages?

The French government decided to send a further expedition to determine the fate of La Pérouse and his companions and chose Antoine-Raymond-Joseph de Bruni d'Entrecasteaux (then aged fifty-two) to lead the search. D'Entrecasteaux was given the command of two ships, the *Recherche* and the *Espérance*, and this expedition also carried a number of French savants who were determined to make significant contributions to science. The ships sailed from Brest on 29 September 1791 for Cape Town. After a month in Cape Town, the ships sailed again and headed for Adventure Bay in Van Diemen's Land. D'Entrecasteaux was acting on information that seemed to suggest that La Pérouse might have been wrecked in the Admiralty Islands and decided to sail there via Van Diemen's Land. In the event, owing to an incorrect report of a compass bearing, they entered a new bay which d'Entrecasteaux promptly named Recherche Bay. Boats were sent to explore the neighbouring waters and they discovered a channel that was named D'Entrecasteaux Channel. The large island to the east was named Bruni Island (now North and South Bruny Islands). Adventure Bay was found to be situated on the north-eastern side of (South) Bruni Island. D'Entrecasteaux sailed from Van Diemen's Land on 28 May 1792 for New Caledonia, then the Solomon Islands, New Ireland and the Admiralty Islands. He could find no indication that La Pérouse had visited there. He then sailed to Amboina and entered the Indian Ocean.

He sailed southwards at some distance from the western coast of what was still known as New Holland, and arrived at Cape Leeuwin. Soon afterwards he came to a point of land which was named Pointe D'Entrecasteaux. Sailing further eastwards they found a group of dangerous islands during a storm and hastily retreated into a bay for shelter. The islands were named the Recherche Archipelago, and the bay in which they sheltered was named Espérance. The town of Esperance was later established on the coast. The prominent cape

at the eastern entrance of the bay was named Cape Le Grand after the young officer, *enseigne* Le Grand, who had been sent to the masthead and whose observations had guided the ships through a deep-water passage into the bay. The small island at the western entrance to the bay was named Ile de l'Observatoire.[64] The position of Esperance was determined to be 33° 55' 17" S, 119° 27' 14" E (of Paris). Because Paris is 2° 20' 14" to the east of Greenwich, their longitude was 121° 47' 28" E (of Greenwich). Modern determinations give the position as 33° 49' S, 121° 52" E.

D'Entrecasteaux was anxious to survey the entire southern coast of New Holland but he was forced, by the ship's severe shortage of water, to leave the coast and to make for Recherche Bay, at the entrance to the D'Entrecasteaux Channel – where water would be readily available. He reached the bay on 21 January 1791 and, soon afterwards, visited Adventure Bay – where he discovered the apple trees that Bligh had planted during his stay there during his second breadfruit voyage.

D'Entrecasteaux then sailed for New Zealand, Tonga and other islands in the western Pacific, looking for clues to the disappearance of La Pérouse – but without success. He then decided to make for Batavia. By this time many of the crew members were suffering from scurvy and dysentery, and D'Entrecasteaux himself was ill with both diseases. He died on 20 July 1798. The official account of his voyage was written by Elisabeth-Paul-Edouard de Rossel who, when aged twenty-four, had embarked as second lieutenant of the *Recherche*.[65]

The mystery of the disappearance of La Pérouse and his ships, the *Boussole* and the *Astrolabe*, was not solved until 8 September 1827 when Peter Dillon, an Irish trader, found a number of relics – undoubtedly of French origin – on the island of Vanikoro. Another French captain, Dumont d'Urville, visited Hobart on his third voyage into the Pacific Ocean (the last two under his own command), and it was there that he learnt of Dillon's finds. He immediately sailed to Vanikoro where he was able to confirm that the two ships commanded by La Pérouse had been wrecked on the adjacent coral reefs. Dumont d'Urville had a monument erected and, on 14 March 1828, this monument to the memory of La Pérouse and his companions was inaugurated with suitable ceremony.

In the meantime the penal settlement at Port Jackson was expanding into a substantial colony – with a small naval and military garrison, and with a number of free settlers. Moreover, there was a body of opinion favouring further exploration. Matthew Flinders and George Bass were notable figures in this movement.

FLINDERS AND BASS

Matthew Flinders was a midshipman on the *Reliance*, which sailed for Port Jackson in January 1795. He had previously served as a midshipman on the *Providence*, on Captain Bligh's second breadfruit voyage. George Bass was the surgeon on the *Reliance*. John Hunter, who was about to take up his position as the second governor of the colony (succeeding Governor Phillip), sailed in the same ship. Flinders and Bass were both keen to take part in the further exploration of New South Wales. Bass, for example, had written that he had an ambition to explore 'more of the country than any of his predecessors in the colony' and that he was 'anxious to procure new and rare specimens of subjects in natural history'.[66] With this in mind he obtained a small boat – about 2.5 metres (8 feet) long, and with a beam of 1.5 metres (5 feet) – which he named *Tom Thumb*, and brought it to Port Jackson aboard the *Reliance*.

A few weeks after their arrival in Port Jackson, Bass and Flinders took the *Tom Thumb* into Botany Bay and explored the Georges River, which flows into the bay. They reported to the governor so favourably about the land they examined that Hunter visited the area himself and soon established a settlement called Bankstown. They made other brief expeditions and, in December 1797, Governor Hunter agreed to provide Bass with a whaleboat and six sailors (most of whom were from the *Reliance*) so that he could examine the southern coast to the west of Point Hicks (which is to the west of Cape Howe). Bass was an amateur explorer, of course, but 'he was something more than a dashing amateur in this field',[67] and his crew was composed of experienced sailors. One of them, John Thistle, later became master on the *Investigator* under the command of Matthew Flinders. The whaleboat left Port Jackson on 3 December 1797, carrying provisions for six weeks. Bass reached Cape Howe on 20 December and then proceeded westwards along the coast. He discovered Wilson's Promontory and, a few days later, discovered Westernport Bay before reversing his course to return to Port Jackson. He did not *prove* the existence of a strait on this expedition, but the mountainous seas that the whaleboat experienced suggested that this was very probable.

The matter had to be determined unequivocally. In October 1798, accompanied by Bass, Matthew Flinders, now a lieutenant in command of the brig *Norfolk*, set out to sail through the strait. They had a crew of eight men. They sailed past Cape Barren Island and Clarke Island, and discovered Port Dalrymple, on the north coast of Tasmania (where George Town now stands). Continuing westwards they rounded a headland and sailed southwards along the western coast. They entered the Derwent Estuary and spent several days there before completing their circumnavigation of the island and returning to Sydney. At the suggestion of Flinders, with the approval of the governor, the newly discovered strait was named Bass Strait.[68] The account of this expedition, written by Matthew Flinders, was first published in 1801 and was dedicated to Sir Joseph Banks. It contains many comments designed to assist the mariner sailing in these waters.

Flinders had not been able to obtain a chronometer for use on this voyage and he therefore warned future ships' captains that his longitudes should be treated with caution. He also pointed out:[69]

> ... that I can by no means answer for there being no rocks or islands in the middle of the strait; or indeed in any of the blank places, except a few miles on each side of the day track. Islands and rocks must be expected to be fallen in with in other places; it therefore behoves every man who has the charge of a ship here, to run with caution in the day; and if he does run during a moonlight night, it should be under working sail, and with the best look-out. But with every advantage it would be hazardous to run before the wind in the night.

Flinders had added significantly to knowledge of the Australian coastline. He was later to make an even greater contribution.

GRANT

The news of the discovery of Bass Strait took some months to reach London – where an expedition was being planned for a ship to sail eastwards along the south coast of New Holland and, in this way, to determine whether Van Diemen's Land is an island or is part of the continent. For this purpose, it was decided to build a brig of sixty tonnes which was to be fitted with retractable keels to facilitate sailing close to the coast on surveying expeditions. This was a new invention of Captain John Schank, RN. The brig was built at Deptford, England in 1799 and was named the *Lady Nelson* – after the wife of Horatio Nelson. In August of the previous year Nelson had won a decisive victory over the French fleet at Aboukir Bay, and had become Baron Nelson of the Nile, and a popular hero. Lieutenant James Grant (who was a personal friend of Captain Schank) was appointed to command the brig – which was provisioned for fifteen men for nine months, and with water for six months. The *Lady Nelson* was 'hauled out of Deadman's Dock in the River' on 13 January 1800 and sailed for Portsmouth and then for the Cape of Good Hope and for Port Jackson.[70] Some repairs had to be undertaken at the cape as a result of the severity of the weather that the brig had experienced. New keels were made under Grant's direction – and these proved to be far better than those originally fitted. The caulking of the deck had also been defective because the builders had used putty instead of oakum. This fault was also rectified.[71]

The *Lady Nelson* arrived off the eastern end of the south coast of present-day South Australia on 3 December 1800, and Grant named the two mountains then in sight Mt Schank (also Schanck), after the inventor of the retractable keel, and Mt Gambier, after the naval officer who became the admiral who commanded the British fleet at the second Battle of Copenhagen in 1807. Two capes were also named. Cape Banks was named for Sir Joseph Banks, and Cape Northumberland was named after the Duke of Northumberland (to whom Grant dedicated his narrative).

As he sailed eastwards along the southern coast Grant named capes Bridgewater, Nelson, Solicitor (or Sir William Grant's Cape), Otway (originally Cape Albany Otway, after a senior official at the Admiralty) and Patton. He also named Portland Bay, and Lady Julia Percy Island. Then, seventy-one days after leaving the Cape of Good Hope, Grant sailed the *Lady Nelson* through the heads of Port Jackson and into 'an excellent harbour, perhaps, one of the finest in the known world'.[72] Grant was not the first to discover Bass Strait, but he was the first to sail *eastwards* through the strait. He reflected with much pleasure that he had conducted his little vessel safely out – which many judged impracticable, both in England and at the Cape of Good Hope – without any damage in rigging, masts or spars. He had also fulfilled the Duke of Portland's orders to search for a passage through these straits.

He added that many able officers and seamen

This type of bark canoe was used by the Aboriginal people in eastern Australia; the illustration is taken from Lieutenant James Grant's book 'The Narrative of a Voyage of Discovery', published in 1803. (Royal Geographical Society of South Australia)

had thought it 'too hazardous an attempt in running down the land in such high southern latitude ... and where I might, from the long range of coast, not be able to extricate myself'.[73] Moreover, whereas Flinders and Bass had discovered the northern coast of Van Diemen's Land, Grant had discovered much of the southern coast of present-day Victoria. Two ships, the Harbinger and the Margaret, had closely followed the Lady Nelson through the strait. Captain Black of Harbinger confirmed many of Grant's observations and, in addition, he discovered an island – which he named King Island after Philip Gidley King, the governor of New South Wales.

The Lady Nelson arrived at Sydney Cove on 31 August 1800, and the men were discharged – having completed their contract. The original plan had been for Matthew Flinders to take over the command for a major exploration of the coasts of Australia, but Flinders had returned to England and would shortly be given the command of another vessel for this purpose. The original plan, as far as Grant was concerned, was that he would take command of the armed vessel, Supply, already in New South Wales waters; but Grant found that she was laid up as a hulk and was unfit for sea. With King's agreement, Grant again took command of Lady Nelson. However, because the governor had no such instructions from the Admiralty, Grant had to be content with 'Colonial Pay' rather than that of a lieutenant in the Royal Navy. Fortunately, Grant's loss was later rectified by the secretary of state for the Colonies.

His new appointment was dated from 1 January

1801. Only two members of the original crew signed on under the new conditions – presumably because the pay was much less than the prevailing rate for merchant seamen. The other members of the crew were convicts, and Grant wrote: 'Amongst the convicts that entered I found some of the most dissatisfied, idle and worthless characters.'[74] In addition, Ensign Francis Barrallier, of the New South Wales Corps, was appointed as the surveyor, to prepare the charts, and George Caley was engaged for 'the express purpose of collecting plants'.

Barrallier had been born in France, probably in Toulon, in 1773. He was a French royalist and, together with his father and two brothers, he had been evacuated (along with thousands of other royalists) from Toulon by the Royal Navy following the attack on that city by Napoléon, the rising star of the French Revolution. The Barrallier family went to England where the father, an engineer, found ready employment. Francis Barrallier was more difficult to place, but he had the good fortune to meet Charles Greville, a nephew of the Duke of Portland (who administered the Colonial Office). Greville, with the support of the Duke of Portland, arranged for Francis Barrallier to be given a passage to Sydney – where it was expected that he would soon obtain an appointment, probably in the New South Wales Corps.

George Caley had been born in Yorkshire on 10 June 1770. He became a self-taught botanist – so much so that he attracted the favourable attention of Sir Joseph Banks, who arranged for him to be given passage to Sydney. These two young men, Barrallier and Caley, were to make significant contributions to the advancement of the colony. They sailed from Portsmouth on 26 November 1799 and reached Port Jackson on 15 April 1800. Philip Gidley King and Mrs King travelled in the same ship. King had been appointed to succeed John Hunter as governor of the colony. Also on board were fifty women convicts, and a substantial quantity of stores required to maintain the infant settlement. On arrival, Barrallier's first employment was apparently to design an orphanage, but he was commissioned as an ensign in the New South Wales Corps on 2 July 1800. Nevertheless he was able to take part, as surveyor, in exploring expeditions to Bass Strait, the Hunter River and the Blue Mountains.[75]

Caley set up his home at Parramatta, some distance from the major settlement, and was soon busy collecting botanical and other specimens. During his ten years in the colony Caley 'named and described 750 plant species in the Port Jackson area, 82 at the Hunter River, 22 on Norfolk Island and 71 at Hobart', and 'he collected nearly 700 bird skins.' In 1805 he collected and named 'Caley's Grevillea', *Grevillea caleyi*.[76]

Caley was not always an easy companion. Indeed, Joseph Banks wrote that 'had he been born a gentleman he would have been shot long ago in a duel.' He was, however, a great friend of the Aboriginal people. As Currey has stated: 'He treated the Aborigines with unfailing kindness, and became so attached to his own native black-tracker [Moowat'tin] that he took him back to England with him.'[77]

Governor King decided that the *Lady Nelson*, with Grant in command, would be used to obtain further information about the Australian coastline, and particularly about the coast to the south of Port Jackson. Initially, it was decided to explore Jervis Bay – the bay that had been by-passed by Cook 'as we had the wind it was not in my power to look into it and the appearence was not favourable enough to induce me to loose time in beating up to it.' It had been named Jervis Bay (after Admiral Sir John Jervis) by Lieutenant Richard Bowen in 1791.[78] The idea was that the *Lady Nelson* would be accompanied by a small sloop, the *Bee*, as she sailed southwards along the coast. But the sloop proved to be so unseaworthy that she returned to Port Jackson. Grant continued, however, and took the *Lady Nelson* into Jervis Bay – which he found to be large and commodious, suitable for the shelter of many ships. During their stay of three days Grant and Barrallier surveyed the bay, and Caley went off to collect plant specimens. Grant also had an opportunity to meet some of the local Aboriginal people.

Grant then sailed for Cape Howe and proceeded along the southern coast to Wilson's Promontory, and then to Western Port, where the *Lady Nelson* remained for thirty-three days to allow Barrallier to prepare a chart of the harbour and its islands, and Caley to collect more plant specimens. While there, the second mate, Bowen, found a native canoe, which he brought to Grant.

Grant noted:[79]

This canoe differed from any before seen, as it was framed with timber, and instead of being tied together at the ends was left open, the space being afterwards filled with grass worked up with strong clay.

Grant named many of the local features in and around Western Port – although some names have not survived. He named the more southerly large island Snapper Island from a supposed likeness to a snapper's head – but this later became Phillip Island. The French expedition under the command of Baudin had named it 'Ile des Anglais', and the northerly large island 'Ile des Françis' – and this remains French Island. A small island to the east of Phillip Island was named Churchill Island by Grant, and this name also remains on modern maps. It was here that Grant planted a garden with a variety of seeds of useful vegetables, the stones of peaches and nectarines, and the kernels of several different kinds of apples. Some of these seeds had been given to Grant by John Churchill of Devon, and some by Captain Schank.[80] A small island to the north-west of French Island was named Barrallier Island – after the surveyor who was responsible for much of the surveying work.

Grant had intended to sail further westwards along the coast, but the weather became more and more tempestuous and he decided to return to Port

Jackson – which the *Lady Nelson* reached safely on 14 May 1801. Then, in June, Grant, again in the *Lady Nelson*, was sent northwards to examine the mouth of the Hunter River in the vicinity of which coal had recently been discovered. Not long afterwards, on 31 August, Grant asked permission to return to England, and this was approved. He sailed in November and arrived back in England in the following April. It is often stated that Grant was no 'scientific navigator' and that he himself believed that he should seek other employment. There is no doubt, however, that he was an excellent seaman, and that he fully recognised the advantages of the retractable keel. There is also little doubt that he was ill-used by the system, and that he was disappointed that 'no offers were made to me to stay behind'.[81]

The command of the *Lady Nelson* was then given to Lieutenant John Murray, and Governor King asked him to continue the exploration of the northern coast of Bass Strait to the west of Western Port – that is, from Cape Schank[82] (at the tip of the Mornington Peninsula) to Cape Otway. Murray sailed on 12 November 1801 and arrived at Western Port on 7 December. He remained there for nearly a month because of bad weather. He found the garden that Grant had planted on Churchill Island to be thriving – and some of the grain was used to feed some swans. Murray left the shelter of Western Port, turned westwards at Cape Schank and, following the coast, observed the entrance to a substantial bay. He examined the bay from the masthead and decided that the weather was too rough to attempt a passage through the headlands at that time. He therefore continued his voyage towards the west. Weeks later the *Lady Nelson* returned to Western Port. From there, Murray sent a launch, with six men, to enter the new bay. This preliminary excursion was sufficiently satisfactory to encourage Murray to sail the *Lady Nelson* into the bay on 15 February 1802. He named it Port King and took possession in a ceremony at which the Union Jack was flown. It was the first time that the Union Jack had been flown in a ceremony to take possession of any part of the British Empire.[83] In 1770 Cook had used the Union Flag of England and Scotland when he took possession of the whole of the eastern part of New Holland but, by 1802, Ireland, England and Scotland had been brought under the same monarch.

Philip Gidley King, who was governor of New South Wales from 1800 to 1806, decided not to endorse the name chosen by Murray, and named it Port Phillip Bay – after the first governor, Arthur Phillip, who was now an admiral. Within a few years a settlement had been established at the head of Port Phillip Bay and, in 1837, this was named Melbourne (after the British prime minister) by General Sir Richard Bourke, who was governor of New South Wales from 1831 to 1837.

5

A MAJOR FRENCH EXPEDITION

PLANNING AND PREPARATION

The La Pérouse and d'Entrecasteaux expeditions had made important geographical and scientific discoveries, and informed French citizens believed that a further French voyage of exploration to the South Seas should be undertaken. For example, it was clearly necessary to complete the exploration of the coastline of New Holland. Nicolas-Thomas Baudin was determined to undertake such an expedition and, in 1798, he submitted a plan for consideration by Pierre Forfait, the minister of Marine. Baudin was well qualified to command such an expedition. He had served in merchant and in naval ships, and had the necessary experience. He had already made several voyages to collect botanical, zoological and mineralogical specimens, and had developed a personal interest in natural history. Indeed, he was friendly with many of the great naturalists of the time – including Lamarck, Lacépède, Cuvier and Humboldt. He had corresponded with Antoine-Louis de Jussieu, and even with Sir Joseph Banks. Alexander von Humboldt was invited to join the proposed expedition but, after consideration, he declined.

The minister submitted Baudin's proposal to the Institut National for advice, and a committee of distinguished men was appointed in 1804 to consider it. A revised version of Baudin's plan was prepared. It was submitted to Napoléon and, after revision and refinement, it was approved. It was to be an expedition for geographical and scientific discovery and not for political or strategic purposes. Although many had contributed to the scheme, there is no doubt that Baudin was 'the true instigator' of the *Voyage aux Terres Australes*.[1]

Baudin was given two ships, the *Géographe* and the *Naturaliste* – names which emphasised the purposes of the expedition. His instructions were written by Charles-Pierre-Claret de Fleurieu, and are reproduced in Baudin's journal. Fleurieu had a detailed knowledge of voyages of exploration, having written an account of French expeditions carried out during the years 1768 and 1769, and his book, published anonymously, remains a valuable reference.[2]

Baudin took command of the *Géographe*, with the rank of *capitaine de vaisseau* (post-captain), and the command of the *Naturaliste* was given to Jacques-Félix-Emmanuel Hamelin with the rank of *capitaine de frégate* (commander). Alexandre Le Bas de Sainte-Croix was second-in-command of the *Géographe*, and junior officers included Pierre-Guillaume Gicquel des Touches, Henri de Freycinet and Hyacinthe de Bougainville (the son of Louis-Antoine de Bougainville). Junior officers in the *Naturaliste* included Pierre-Bernard Milius, Louis de Freycinet (the brother of Henri de Freycinet) and Jacques de St Cricq.

Considerable attention was given to the selection

of the navigational instruments. One astronomical clock was provided, and four chronometers. Two chronometers, B31 and B38 – which had been made by the Swiss clockmaker Ferdinand Berthoud, who spent most of his life in France – went to the *Géographe*. Another two chronometers, B27 and B35 (also made by Berthoud) went to the *Naturaliste*. There was also a 'deck' chronometer – one that could be checked against the main chronometers and used on deck, so that the main chronometers did not have to be disturbed. The expedition was also provided with two sextants (one of which had been used by Captain Cook), and four reflecting circles (devices invented by French astronomers to serve the same purpose as the sextant). Four artificial horizons, for use on land, were also supplied. The expedition had six barometers, eight magnetic dip needles, four hygrometers, one precision balance and sundry other items.[3]

Baudin's ships were issued with a vast array of goods for use as gifts or for barter with the indigenous people whom they expected to encounter. These goods included silk ribbon, cotton ribbon, silver braid, assorted pins and needles, and a thousand fish hooks. Each ship carried 500 wooden-handled knives, 200 horn-handled knives, 100 sheath knives, and 100 pairs of scissors. Also included were 42 gross of buttons, 500 rings 'for the fingers', and 100 'for the feet'. Each ship also had 125 German mirrors for use as gifts. The two captains were provided with copies of every available chart of New Holland and of the adjacent countries, and with copies of books relating to earlier expeditions to these areas.[4]

The scientists who were to travel in the two ships were appointed on the recommendation of a committee of the *institut* and approved by the First Consul (Napoléon). Baudin had no say in their selection. Twenty-two scientists (and artists) were appointed and were distributed between the two ships. There were three botanists, five zoologists, two mineralogists, five gardeners, two astronomers, two hydrographers and three artists. According to François Péron, he received the fifth place among the zoologists 'from the recommendation of several illustrious and learned characters'.[5]

Finally, it was necessary to obtain a passport from the British government to ensure that this geographical and scientific expedition would be free to carry out its work without hindrance from British ships – even though a state of war existed between the two countries. The Peace of Amiens between Britain and France was signed in 1802, but neither Baudin nor Flinders knew this at the time. In any case, war broke out again in 1803. A passport was soon provided.[6] Indeed, Joseph Banks wrote that the passport had been granted 'without a moment's hesitation'.[7]

THE EXPEDITION BEGINS

The *Géographe* and the *Naturaliste* sailed from Le Havre on 19 October 1800. Baudin was aged forty-six. The ships called at Tenerife as required by their instructions, and then made for Ile de France (Mauritius) without calling at the Cape of Good Hope. They arrived at Port North-West (Port Louis) on 15 March 1801 – five months after leaving their home port. It had been an unusually long and very tedious voyage and there had been several acrimonious disputes. By that time, there was a growing lack of confidence in Baudin as the leader of the expedition. There were twenty-two scientists and artists in the two ships – most of whom had little work to do until they reached land. There were so many of them that they tended to interfere with the smooth running of the ships. Moreover, they did not enjoy the life on board ship. They were bored.

When the ships arrived at Ile de France, Baudin was able to report to the minister that 'he had not a single sick man aboard either corvette', and this is confirmed by other written comments.[8] Nevertheless the level of dissatisfaction among the junior officers, the artists and the scientists was so great that several claimed to be too sick to continue – and forty sailors deserted. Some of them were rounded up and a few new hands were recruited. But the losses were important – for example, two of the five zoologists and all three artists left the expedition. Moreover, the authorities at Ile de France were singularly unhelpful. It was not a happy beginning. Two of the assistant gunners were found to be accomplished artists, however, and they now became the official artists for the expedition. The two ships sailed from Ile de France on 25 April 1801, bound for the south-west coast of New Holland – soon to be named Cape Leeuwin by Matthew Flinders. The scientists and artists at that time were:

Astronomer	Pierre-François Bernier
Horticulturist	Anselme Riedlé (who had previously sailed with Baudin on a botanical expedition to the West Indies)
Botanist	Jean-Baptiste-Louis-Claude Lescenault
Hydrographers	Charles-Pierre Boulanger and Pierre Faure
Mineralogists	Louis Depuch and Joseph-Charles Bailly
Zoologists	René Maugé (who had also sailed with Baudin on a previous expedition) and Stanislas Levillain; François Péron
Gardeners	Antoine Sautier and Antoine Guichenot
Artists	Charles-Alexandre Lesueur and Nicolas-Martin Petit

Many of these men were still in their early twenties. Lesueur was twenty-two when he joined the expedition, Petit was twenty-three, Faure was twenty-three, and Boullanger was a little older – at twenty-nine.

According to his instructions, Baudin was supposed to leave the Ile de France by 15 February 'at the very latest' and sail direct to the D'Entre-casteaux Channel in Van Diemen's Land and arrive there by the end of March – so that he could carry out his exploration of the east coast before the winter. Baudin was already two months behind schedule and quite unable to reach the D' Entre-casteaux Channel by the planned date. Moreover, he wanted to replenish his stores – which had been seriously depleted during the long voyage to the Ile de France, and which he was unable to obtain at the French colony. The state of his provisions can be illustrated by the fact that, as Péron has reported:[9]

> We were scarcely under sail, when we were informed by our commander, that from that time we should have but half a pound of new bread once in ten days; that instead of the allowance of wine, we should have three-sixteenths of a bottle of bad rum of the Ile de France, bought at a low price in that colony; and that the biscuit and salt provisions should be our general food.

In these circumstances, Baudin decided to sail along the 34-degree parallel until he reached Cape Leeuwin, and then turn northwards and make for Kupang in Timor. He reached the vicinity of Cape Leeuwin on 15 May, turned northwards, and soon observed a cape that he named Cape Naturaliste. Immediately afterwards he sailed into a fine bay that he named Géographe Bay, and where he anchored on 30 May 1801 – enabling a few people, including Péron, to go ashore. Péron was now in his element and enjoyed the opportunity to study the local Aboriginal people, the plants, animals and the land. He wrote a report (which has not been published) and central to this report:[10]

> ... was a description of the local aboriginal tribe. He recorded their physical appearance in detail, strength, culture, weapons, language and vocabulary. He found the tribe to have a strong territorial attachment to a limited area of land in the region of the river.

Indeed, Péron seems to have 'conceived a new science which he called Anthropology'.[11]

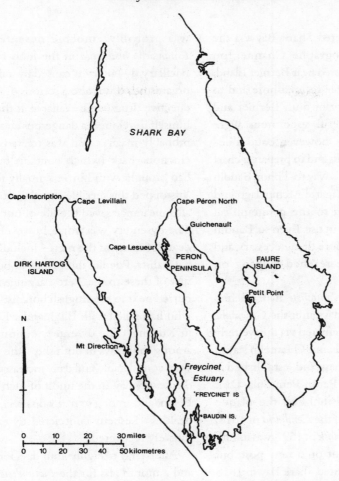

SHARK BAY

Cape Inscription

Cape Levillain

Cape Péron North

Guichenault

Cape Lesueur

DIRK HARTOG
ISLAND

PERON
PENINSULA

FAURE
ISLAND

Petit Point

N

Mt Direction

Freycinet
Estuary

FREYCINET IS

BAUDIN IS.

```
0    10    20    30 miles
0  10  20  30  40  50 kilometres
```

Map of Shark Bay indicating the predominantly French place names

Unfortunately, a seaman named Vasse was drowned when the ship's boat was returning to the ship, and the river that had been traversed by the shore party was named the Vasse River. It is near present-day Busselton.

Baudin intended to make a running survey of the western coast of New Holland as they sailed towards Timor and thought it prudent to select two rendezvous in case the ships became separated. The first rendezvous was to be Rottnest Island, a few nautical miles west of the Swan River – the island that the Dutch mariner Willem de Vlamingh had visited and named in 1696. The second rendezvous was to be at Shark Bay, which François Alesno Comte de St Allouarn, in the *Gros Ventre*, had visited in March 1772, but which Dampier had discovered and named in 1699. In the event, Baudin's two ships did become separated in a gale. The *Naturaliste* arrived at Rottnest Island on 14 June and anchored to await the *Géographe*. During this time parties were sent to examine Rottnest and the adjacent islands – which Louis de Freycinet was later to name Iles Louis Napoléon.[12] The *Géographe* approached Rottnest Island on 18 June but failed to see the *Naturaliste*, and sailed past. Hamelin then made sail for Shark Bay – the second rendezvous. But, by the time he reached the bay, the *Géographe* had sailed for Timor.

The *Géographe* had entered Shark Bay via the easterly channel, the Géographe Channel, on 27 June 1801, and had anchored near Bernier Island. The scientists were then able to go ashore and to examine the natural history of both Bernier and Dorre islands. Many useful specimens were collected. After two weeks, however, Baudin decided to continue northwards and to prepare a chart of the north-west coast on his way to Timor. Baudin reached and named the Bonaparte Archipelago, and many of the names given to the geographical features at that time are still in use. Even so, Baudin did not want to delay any more than necessary, and pressed on to Timor. He reached Kupang on 23 August 1801.

In the meantime, the *Naturaliste* had reached Shark Bay on 16 July (two days after the *Géographe* had sailed from the bay) and entered via the westerly channel – the Naturaliste Channel. Hamelin stayed for seven weeks in the bay and established a temporary observatory on Péron Peninsula. Dirk Hartog Island was also visited and the plaque commemorating the visits of the *Eendracht* in 1616, and of Vlamingh in the *Geelvinck* in 1697, was found. Hamelin had the plaque put on a new post; but when Louis de Freycinet visited Shark Bay in 1818 he removed it and took it back to Paris for the *institut*. While at Shark Bay the young Ensign Jacques de St Cricq carried out sixty lunar distance observations to determine the longitude for comparison with that obtained by using the chronometer. In this way he was able to determine the present error of the chronometer.[13]

THE VISIT TO KUPANG

The *Naturaliste* sailed for Timor and arrived there on 21 September 1801. The *Géographe* had been anchored there for a month. Their stay at Kupang was a disaster. Sickness was rife. Many members of the expedition were affected by dysentery – the cause of which was not understood at that time. It was probably amoebic dysentery, caused by *Entamoeba histolytica* in the local food and water. Bacillary dysentery is caused by a different microorganism and was also a serious disease because no effective drugs were available at that time. Baudin himself developed 'a dangerous ataxic fever'. It was probably malaria, and was treated by Péron with cinchona bark (which contains quinine) that he had brought with him, essentially for his own use. 'It stopped this terrible fever,' wrote Péron, 'and in all appearance saved the life of our commander.'[14] The dysentery was worse, however, and led to the death of many of the men – including some of the naturalists. Riedlé, the principal botanist, was the first of these to die. Péron arranged for him to be buried next to the English botanist, David Nelson, who had sailed with Bligh and who had also died in Kupang. 'The dysentery continued its ravages among the crews of both ships, the number of sick were considerable, and daily increased, some of them died every day. In the midst of such sorrow', wrote Péron, 'and among so many disasters, I was in perfect health.'[15] Lesueur contracted dysentery but, fortunately, recovered.

After a stay of eighty-four days for the *Géographe*, and a month less for the *Naturaliste*, the two ships sailed from Kupang on 13 November 1801. They sailed well into the Indian Ocean, turned in the vicinity of Cape Leeuwin and made for the D'Entrecasteaux Channel in Van Diemen's Land. The deaths continued during this voyage. There were eleven in all – six from dysentery, two from dysentery and fever combined, and two from fever. The eleventh death was apparently due to a liver complaint.[16] Many more men were still on the sick list.

The coast of Van Diemen's Land was sighted on the morning of 13 January 1802, and the two ships turned into the D'Entrecasteaux Channel and anchored in the bay now known as Great Taylor Bay (which Baudin referred to as 'Great Cove') near Partridge Island off the west coast of South Bruny

Island. On the following day, Baudin arranged for his longboat to investigate Port Cygnet and the Huon River – the command being given to Henri de Freycinet, with written instructions. Freycinet was asked to 'find some swans for us' and 'if you should meet any natives, which is very likely, you are absolutely forbidden to commit a single act of hostility towards them' unless lives were at stake.[17] The naturalists were to be given their first opportunity – Péron, Guichenot and Lesueur were among those who would go with him.

VAN DIEMEN'S LAND

It was a productive period both for the officers and for the naturalists. Péron, in particular, was able to conduct some very important studies on the nature of the indigenous people, and Petit and Lesueur prepared a number of drawings of the natives and of the environment. Many new plants and birds were examined, and specimens collected. After a few days, however, Baudin decided to sail further up the channel and to anchor in North West Bay. Accessible fresh water was found in the river that flowed into this bay, but it proved to be more difficult to obtain than expected, and was of rather poor quality. Henri de Freycinet led a party up the Derwent somewhat further than d'Entrecasteaux's men had explored. Faure led a party to explore Frederick Henry Bay – which Beautemps-Beaupré, during the d'Entrecasteaux expedition, had called North Bay – and Pitt Water. He was also able to show that the so-called 'Tasman Island' is, in fact, a peninsula.

In February, Baudin moved his ships again and anchored to the west of Maria Island. Four boat parties were then instructed to survey the land in the vicinity of Maria Island. Tasman's 'Schouten Islands' was found to be a single island. Maria Island itself was surveyed by Boullanger. Louis de Freycinet discovered and charted Prosser Bay – where Orford now stands. Henri de Freycinet led his party to the

south and surveyed the bay now known as Blackmans Bay. During this time Maugé died – after having been seriously ill since Kupang. Baudin regarded him as one of his few friends. He could neither read nor write but was a skilled collector.[18]

The ships spent nine days at the Maria Island anchorage, before sailing on 27 February 1802. When the *Géographe* reached the vicinity of Cape Tourville (at 42° 07' S, 148° 21' E), Baudin decided to send a boat to survey the coast, and gave instructions to Charles-Pierre Boullanger to carry out this work. The boat was to be under the command of Midshipman Maurouard, but Boullanger was given written instructions to keep the *Géographe* in sight. Six seamen were to man the boat. Maurouard was instructed to return to the ship at nightfall. In the event, however, the boat was out of sight in a very short time and failed to return at night – despite the ship's rockets and lights. Both ships searched for the boat with no success and, even worse, the two ships became separated. Baudin himself was so sick he could not leave his bunk for several days – during which time Henri de Freycinet was responsible for the ship and reported to Baudin in writing.

A southward search for the boat was unsuccessful and a northern search was instituted – also without success. An English schooner in the vicinity was approached to take part in the search but her captain was unwilling to delay his hunt for seals. Baudin proceeded to Banks Strait and then to Waterhouse Island off the north coast, but the *Naturaliste* was not sighted. Indeed, it was not until 6 December – after the *Géographe*'s stay and refit at Port Jackson – that the sister ship rejoined Baudin, at Elephant Bay, on the east coast of King Island (see Chapter 8). The only good news was that an eclipse of the moon had been observed and that this had given them their longitude – and hence an estimate of the errors of the chronometers.[19] On this occasion they had to use the Greenwich meridian as the prime meridian because, in the French almanac, 'somebody' had transcribed the times for the phases of the moon 'but has forgotten to reduce them to the Paris meridian'.[20] As for Waterhouse Island, Baudin wrote that he was convinced that it was named Waterhouse Island 'because the English who visited it must have had a lot of rain there'.[21]

EXPLORING THE COAST OF THE MAINLAND

Baudin commenced his survey of the southern coast of the mainland at Wilson's Promontory. He had been provided with a copy of the chart which had been prepared by Flinders incorporating data from Bass's survey of this coast in a whaleboat. Bass had had no navigational instruments other than a compass, and his survey was, therefore, only an approximation. Moreover, the chart supplied to Baudin in France did not include data from James Grant's voyage, west to east, in *Lady Nelson*. Grant's passage through Bass Strait had been accomplished in December 1800 – a few weeks after Baudin had sailed from France.

Sailing further westwards, Baudin recognised the entrance to Western Port, but failed to see the less obvious opening leading to Port Phillip Bay. Still further to the west he observed Cape Desaix (Cape Otway), Ile Fouteroy (Lady Julia Percy Island), Cape Duquesne (Cape Bridgewater) and Cape Rabelais (Cape Lannes).[22]

The *Géographe* then sailed further westwards and, on 8 April, another ship was seen in the distance. At first, Baudin thought that she must be the *Naturaliste*; but this was soon found to be incorrect. Baudin's journal continues:[23]

Finally, at five o'clock, when we were both able to see each other clearly, this ship made a signal which we did not understand and so did not answer. She then ran up the English flag and shortened sail. We, for our part, hoisted the national flag, and I braced sharp up to draw alongside her. As they spoke [to] us first, they asked what the ship was. I replied that she was French. Then they asked if

Captain Baudin was her commander. I was very surprised not only at the question, but at hearing myself named as well. When I said yes, the English ship brought to.

The English ship was, of course, the *Investigator* – with Matthew Flinders in command. Flinders knew that the Baudin expedition had sailed from France in October 1800, but there is no way that Baudin could have learnt that Flinders had sailed from England nine months after him. The two ships hove to, and Flinders and Robert Brown – the *Investigator*'s naturalist, who knew a little French – took a boat over to the *Géographe* for a friendly discussion. Horner has emphasised that only these three men were present and that accounts of the discussion by Péron and by the young Bougainville are not eye-witness accounts.[24] Flinders and Brown returned to the *Investigator*, but revisited the *Géographe* early the next morning. It seems that Flinders described his discovery of Kangaroo Island and of the two gulfs on the south coast of the mainland, and gave an account of his examination of the Nuyts Archipelago. Baudin described his discoveries on the eastern and northern coasts of Van Diemen's Land and referred to the 100 boxes of natural history and other specimens that had been collected. He showed them many of the drawings that had been executed by Lesueur and by Petit. It is also clear that Flinders gave Baudin 'several charts published by Arrowsmith' since Baudin's departure from France.

The two ships then separated. Baudin continued to sail towards the west and Flinders to the east. Baudin soon sighted Kangaroo Island – which was later named Ile Decrès in the official account of his voyage. Baudin spent three days in Gulf St Vincent, which was named Golfe Joséphine in the published account of his expedition. He also made a brief examination of Spencer Gulf, which was likewise given another name – Golfe Napoléon – in the 1811 published account. Baudin then sailed to the Nuyts Archipelago and wrote in his journal that 'to judge from what we have seen of them, are scarcely worth the trouble that we took over them'.[25] He continued sailing westwards, and reached the cape that d'Entrecasteaux had named Cape Adieu. It was here that Baudin decided to abandon the exploration of the southern coast to seek fresh food and water.

On 6 May 1802 Baudin wrote in his journal:[26]

Everybody was longing for a rest, and in point of fact we all needed one. We had no more wood … our water-supply could not last long … Scurvy, which was beginning to get a hold on several members of the crew, was what worried me most, but I nevertheless persisted in my resolution to pass around the western side of St. Peter islands …

A few days later he wrote:[27]

… the weakness of my crew, which now consisted of only thirty men for the handling of the ship, our pressing need for firewood, the shortness of the days, and a host of other private considerations all decided me to abandon the coast and make first for the D'Entrecasteaux Channel, where the anchorage is good, and from there to proceed to Port Jackson.

The *Géographe* arrived at the south of Bruny Island on 20 May, but the mist prevented the ship from entering D'Entrecasteaux Channel and Baudin decided to anchor in Adventure Bay. Boats were sent to cut firewood, to catch fish and to enable the scientists to carry out their studies. Water was found to be abundant and so were fish. Some ate so much fish that they had indigestion.[28] The *Géographe* sailed from Adventure Bay on 22 May and, a few days later, Baudin recorded that he had twenty men on the sick list out of a total of seventy-five – a number that included the naturalists and other scientists. They approached Port Jackson on 17 June and, as it was a *Journal de Mer*, Baudin ceased writing his account on this day and did not resume until 17 November when the *Géographe* sailed from Port Jackson.

It is clear from the official account of the voyage, written by François Péron,[29] that the passage from Van Diemen's Land to Port Jackson was a nightmare. The weather was extremely stormy and 'the number of our sick increased every hour; and every day we had to commit some of our unfortunate companions to the deep.' In the second week of June 'the stormy weather was incessant.' However, on 17 June a ship approached them. She had left Port Jackson two days before and brought the pleasing news that the *Naturaliste* had been at anchor there but had gone out again in search of the *Géographe*. She also reported that the longboat that had been 'lost' on the eastern coast of Van Diemen's Land had been found by an English brig, the *Harrington*, at the eastern end of Banks Strait – and that the men were now safely aboard the *Naturaliste*. The third piece of news was that the *Investigator* was at anchor at Port Jackson.

It took several days for the *Géographe* to tack into the harbour. The task was made even more difficult because, according to Péron, only four men, including a midshipman, were capable of working the ship – 'what ravages had been made amongst us by the scurvy'.[30] Péron also quoted from an account written by their 'second doctor', Taillefer:[31]

Everything conspired to overwhelm our sick; having for food only rotting meat, biscuits eaten by worms and weavils, a very small provision of stale and infected water, realizing themselves deprived of the most effective means of recovery, crowded together in a small ship, victims of the sea and the winds and far from any port of call, their state of health deteriorated from day to day. On their bodies appeared tumours covered by black scabs; all over their skin, at the base of the hairs, were small round purplish spots. Their joints stiffened and the flexor muscles seemed to shrink and so held their limbs half-flexed.

One could imagine nothing more repulsive than the appearance of their faces: to the leaden colour common to patients suffering from scurvy were added swollen gums protruding from the mouth and showing dead patches and more ulcers. The sick exhaled a fetid breath which when breathed in seemed to attack the very centre of life. How many times in bringing them a doctor's care did I not feel my courage fail me! In spite of their weak state, moreover, these unfortunate souls remained in full possession of their mental faculties, which only permitted them to feel more acutely the hopelessness of their situation ...

It was 20 June when the *Géographe* arrived at Sydney Cove and there can be no doubt that the men were in a critical condition. Flinders observed the approach of the *Géographe* and wrote: 'It was grievous to see the miserable condition to which the officers and crew were reduced by scurvy, there being not more ... than twelve men capable of doing their duty.'[32] On arrival, the sick were soon transferred to the hospital. Péron later wrote:[33]

Two more men died the day after the ship had anchored; but all the rest recovered so rapidly, as to strike us with astonishment; not one of those who had been landed died, and in a few days, those who were actually on the brink of the grave, recovered their health. We were, in short, lost in wonder at the magical effect of the country and the vegetables upon a disorder, to counteract which, all the medicines on board ship, all the most active operations, and energetic attentions, had proven fruitless.

Péron blamed Baudin for the scurvy, stating that Baudin 'despised the liberal orders of government in this respect', and that 'he disdained all the instructions that had been given to him in Europe.'[34] It must be remembered, however, that the cause of scurvy was not known to the government, nor to Péron, nor to Baudin.

The governor, Philip Gidley King, immediately arranged for the ship's officers and men to receive all possible help, food and medical attention. Baudin later wrote an open letter to the French authorities at the Ile de France, and at Réunion, to let them know how well the British had helped his expedition – in the hope that all French officials would provide similar help to any British ship in distress:[41]

Whatever the duties of hospitality may be, Governor King has given the whole of Europe the example of a benevolence which should be known, and which I take pleasure in publishing.

He went on to say:

On our arrival at Port Jackson the stock of wheat there was very limited and that for the future very uncertain. The arrival of 170 men was not a happy circumstance at the time, yet we were well received; and when our present and future wants were known, they were supplied by shortening part of the daily ration allowed to the inhabitants and the garrison of the colony. The Governor first gave the example. Through those means, which do so great honour to the humane feelings of him who put them into motion, we have enjoyed a favour which we would perhaps have experienced much difficulty in finding anywhere else.

It might also be noted, however, that when the *Investigator* had arrived at Port Jackson on 9 May 1802, Flinders was pleased to report:[35]

... there was not a single individual on board who was not upon deck working the ship into harbour; and ... the officers and crew were, generally speaking, in better health than on the day we sailed from Spithead, and not in less good spirits.

The contrast with the *Géographe* is striking, and must be attributed to the facts that the *Investigator* had not called at Kupang, and that Flinders made good use of lime juice and of wild vegetables whenever possible.

The absence of the *Naturaliste* was a worry, however, because Hamelin had lost sight of the *Géographe* as long ago as 8 March 1802. In the meantime the *Naturaliste* had sailed to Banks Strait – and it was there that Hamelin met the *Harrington*. Maurouard, Boullanger and the six men rowed the *Géographe*'s boat over to the *Naturaliste*.[36] The *Naturaliste* had then visited Cape Portland, Waterhouse Island, Wilson's Promontory and Western Port. The two main islands in Western Port were named Ile des Français (which was circumnavigated) and Ile des Anglais. Hamelin then sailed to Cape Howe and to Port Jackson – where he arrived on 26 April 1802. He was well received by the governor and other authorities, but stocks of salt meat were low in the colony – the salt pork was imported from Tahiti! Hamelin decided to make one further foray to search for the *Géographe* and, if he failed, to sail to Ile de France (Mauritius). As Horner has remarked: 'There is an uncharacteristic air of desperation about Hamelin's decision to leave Port Jackson.'[37]

In the event, Hamelin's attempt to sail westwards through Bass Strait was frustrated by strong westerly winds, and his attempt to sail around the south coast of Van Diemen's Land was likewise frustrated. He therefore returned to Port Jackson where the *Géographe* was still at anchor. Boullanger, Maurouard and the six seamen were at last able to rejoin their ship. Flinders, Baudin and Hamelin now had an opportunity to have friendly discussions about their explorations. Flinders hosted a dinner aboard the *Investigator* and invited Baudin, Hamelin, Péron and some others. Colonel William Paterson, of the New South Wales Corps, and lieutenant-governor of the colony, attended. Baudin became very friendly with the governor, Philip Gidley King. He also had an opportunity to meet George Bass, who was now a maritime trader, and, from him, he was able to purchase 4500 kilograms (10 000 pounds) of salt pork for the *Géographe* and *Naturaliste*.[38]

The importation of salt pork from Tahiti into Port Jackson began about the turn of the century, but the first shipment of *live* hogs had been in April 1793, when eight were landed. The official trade in salt pork from Tahiti, with the encouragement of Governor King, began with the naval ship *Porpoise* – which landed 14 000 kilograms (31 000 pounds) of Tahitian salt pork in October 1801. Thereafter, merchant ships carried out the trade. Indeed, 'King undertook to provide casks and purchase all pork brought to Sydney at 6d per lb.' However, 'if sufficient casks could not be supplied, Bass and

Bishop were permitted to obtain an additional supply themselves and sell all pork shipped in them as a private speculation.'[39] Baudin also seems to have purchased a few live pigs in Port Jackson – presumably also from Bass. If so, they must have been 'Polynesian' pigs – which are much smaller than those in Europe.

Both ships were cleaned and repaired and made ready for sea again. In addition, Baudin decided to send the *Naturaliste* back to France with many of the boxes of specimens that had been collected, and with all the men he considered unsuitable, or who had not lived up to expectations. Those of uncertain health would also sail in the *Naturaliste*. Baudin also decided to purchase a newly completed schooner of thirty tonnes that could be used close inshore for preparing the charts. Baudin named the schooner *Casuarina*, and gave Louis de Freycinet the command – with Léon Brévedent, and fourteen men. Hamelin then had fifty-nine officers and men – but five were now invalids. All the scientific staff were now accommodated in the *Géographe*. The *Naturaliste* carried seventy tubs of live plants, four live kangaroos, two black swans, two dingoes, several emus and parrots, and a goose from Waterhouse Island. It also carried a number of bottles of lime juice – as did the *Géographe*.[40]

Baudin's three ships made for the north-west of Van Diemen's Land. The *Casuarina* explored the Hunter Islands and the *Géographe* anchored in Sea Elephant Bay on the eastern coast of King Island. During this time the hydrographer, Pierre Faure, circumnavigated King Island. When the time came to farewell the *Naturaliste*, Baudin went aboard to examine the condition of the plants, and to dine with Hamelin and give him a fond farewell. As Baudin wrote:[41]

After dinner I took leave of Captain Hamelin and wished him a good journey ... I sent Citizen Depuch [Louis Depuch, mineralogist] two sheep, twelve hens and one pig from my store, to contribute, with Captain Hamelin's help, to his having fresh food for as long as possible on the voyage, for his health was poor.

In the meantime, the governor had learnt from some of his officers that the French officers had gossiped about their desire to see a French settlement in Van Diemen's Land. King was very disturbed to learn this, and immediately arranged for the colonial schooner *Cumberland* to sail to King Island, where Baudin's ships were likely to be found, and to hand Baudin a letter emphasising the fact that Van Diemen's Land was a British possession. King's letter began:[42]

> You are acquainted with my intention to establish a settlement in the South; however it has been hastened by information communicated to me immediately after your departure. This information is to the effect that the French wish to set up an establishment in Storm Bay Passage [D'Entrecasteaux Channel] or in the area known as Frederik Hendrik Bay. It is also said that these are your orders from the French Republic.

No senior officer was available to command the *Cumberland* on this important mission and Charles Robbins, a midshipman, was appointed acting lieutenant and given the command. Charles Grimes, the surveyor-general, was asked to accompany him. Three marines were added to the ship's complement. Surprisingly, the *Cumberland* did manage to locate Baudin's ships off King Island and Lieutenant Robbins made a point of planting 'His Majesty's colours' close to the French tents 'and kept them flying during the time that the French ships stayed there'.[43]

It was a clumsy attempt by Governor King to make sure that the French government could not expect to establish their own colonies in this region. King knew that Hamelin would report this in Paris. Baudin wrote a personal reply to the governor:[44]

> I have never been able to conceive that there was justice or even fairness on the part of Europeans in seizing, in the name of their governments, a land seen for the first time, when it is inhabited by men who have not always deserved the title of savages or cannibals that has been freely given them; whereas they were still only children of nature and just as little civilized as your Scotch Highlanders or our Breton peasants, etc. who, if they do not eat their fellow-men, are nevertheless just as objectionable ... I have no knowledge of the claims which the French Government may have upon Van Diemen's Land, or of its designs for the future; but I think that its title will not be any better founded than yours.

Baudin's stay at King Island was, however, a happy one for naturalists. Péron especially was fascinated by the enormous sea elephants. In the meantime, Freycinet, with the expert contribution of the hydrographer Charles-Pierre Boullanger, carried out a detailed survey of the Hunter Islands. They were able to improve the chart which Flinders had prepared a few years before, but on which Flinders had spent less than a quarter of the time spent by the *Casuarina*.[45]

BAUDIN ON THE SOUTHERN COAST

The *Géographe* and *Casuarina* then sailed for Kangaroo Island. Flinders had surveyed the northern coast, but the southern coast had not been examined, and this was now carried out by Baudin. When the official account of the expedition came to be published, the geographical features on both the northern and southern coasts were all given French names. On 10 January 1803 the *Casuarina*, again with Boullanger on board, set off to examine the two gulfs which Flinders had surveyed. Baudin instructed Freycinet to pay particular attention to the western coasts of the gulfs, and to Port Lincoln.[46]

In the meantime, Baudin was adding to the menagerie of Australian animals on board the *Géographe*. He had obtained some emus, a very tame kangaroo and a few wombats, from a sealer at King Island. He also obtained a number of live kangaroos and emus at Kangaroo Island. All of these animals were destined for gardens or museums in France and, although there were some deaths, many survived and reached France. Several of those that died during the voyage were skinned, and the hides and bones preserved. The interesting thing is that the King Island emus, the Kangaroo Island emus and the emus from the mainland were of different species. The ordinary emu of the mainland is *Dromaius novahollandiae* – which has a height of about 1.9 metres, and a height at the shoulder of about 1.2 metres. The King Island emu, *Dromaius ater*, had a height of about 0.86 metres, and height of the shoulder of about 0.66 metres. Moreover, the plumage of this species was much darker than that of the mainland emu. These emus became known as 'Black Emus' or 'Dwarf Emus'. The Kangaroo Island emu, now named *Dromaius baudinianus*, was of intermediate height, about 1.16 metres, with a shoulder height of 0.78 metres – but the plumage was not dark. The King Island emus and the Kangaroo Island emus are now extinct, and the only evidence of their existence is held in the preserved specimens – all obtained by the Baudin expedition, and now in the Musée National d'Histoire Naturelle in Paris.[47]

Having taken all these animals on board and many natural history specimens, Baudin prepared for departure. But before doing so he 'had a rooster and two hens put ashore at the place where the water is collected. On this beach I likewise left a boar and a sow to multiply and possibly be of use to future navigators in these regions.'[48] The pigs, presumably Polynesian pigs obtained in Port Jackson from Bass, multiplied and became wild pigs – but they died out in the early 1880s. It is not known whether the fowls survived. Possibly they were killed by the large lizard, *Varanus varius*.[49] The bay where the pigs and fowls were released was called Anse des Sources (Spring Cove) by the French – but the colloquial name, Hog Bay, bestowed by an island trader, Captain W. A. Meredith, has become established.[50]

Hog Bay is adjacent to present-day Penneshaw.

'Frenchman's Rock' – a rock with an inscription carved by a member of the Baudin expedition – is now preserved in the Kangaroo Island Gateway Visitors Information Centre, at Penneshaw. The inscription reads: 'expedition de decouverte par le Commendant Baudin, sur le Géographe, 1803'.

The *Casuarina* had not yet returned from Freycinet's survey of the two gulfs and Baudin decided to sail and hope that Freycinet would catch up. Soon after the *Géographe* had made sail, however, the *Casuarina* was sighted but, owing to some mix-up, the two ships again became separated, and they sailed independently to Nuyts Archipelago. They did not meet there either. The *Casuarina* was very short of water, and Freycinet was compelled to sail as quickly as possible for King George Sound. But Baudin, in the *Géographe*, visited Streaky Bay before sailing to the Nuyts Archipelago, and there surveyed the coast – where some features are still known by the names bestowed by the French expedition.[51] The *Casuarina* reached King George Sound on 13 February – her water almost totally expended – and was beached in Princess Royal Harbour. The *Géographe* arrived at King George Sound on 17 February and anchored in the outer harbour to the west of Bald Head.[52]

The stay in King George Sound was productive in many ways. Both ships were able to take on an ample supply of wood and water, there was an opportunity to wash clothes and to clean the decks. The north arm of the sound, Oyster Harbour, was surveyed by hydrographer Pierre Faure, and the stream flowing into it (Kalgan River, Rivière des Françaises) was also examined. Baudin sent *aspirant* (midshipman) Joseph Ransonnet, in the longboat with supplies for ten days, to examine the mainland to the east of the sound. Ransonnet discovered a useful bay – which was named Port des Deux Peoples (now Two People Bay). The name derives from the fact that it was there that Ransonnet met the American sealer *Union*, under the command of Captain Pendleton. The *Union* sailed for Kangaroo

Island where Pendleton built a forty-tonne schooner at a spot which became known as American River.[53] The main achievement of the Ransonnet expedition, however, was that they made contact with the local Aboriginal people. The meeting was friendly, and presents were exchanged. The Aborigines were naked and the three older men (there were five in all) 'had large black beards, filed teeth and pierced nostrils, and red earth smeared on their bodies'.[54] Unfortunately, Péron was not in Ransonnet's party.

King George Sound was also notable for the large number of plants collected by the naturalists. Baudin wrote: 'the gardener had collected more than one hundred and fifty species of plant during his stay ashore and had sixty-eight pots of growing ones. This was work and not wit.'[55] He could not resist adding that Péron 'our observer of mankind' and Leschenault 'will have composed sixty pages of writing which, for a different reason, will be all wit and no work'.[56]

The two ships sailed from King George Sound on 1 March 1803. Baudin's main object now was to reach and to survey the Gulf of Carpentaria. But first he was anxious to check the positions of the St Allouarn Islands (near Cape Leeuwin), Rottnest Island, Shark Bay and North West Cape. After completing the first two tasks, Baudin sailed to Shark Bay – where the *Géographe* dropped anchor near the Péron Peninsula. The captain of the *Casuarina* was instructed to chart the Naturaliste Channel. A party from the *Géographe* attempted to land on the peninsula, but an aggressive party of Aborigines made it clear that they were not welcome, and the boat retreated. Next day the engineer, François Ronsard, led an armed party ashore, but the Aborigines had abandoned their camp – fortunately for everyone. Péron obtained permission to go ashore with *enseigne* Bonnefoi and a party of seamen – the main object being to collect salt so that the fish caught in the bay could be preserved. Petit and Guichenot were also in the party and Péron

(described by Baudin as 'the most thoughtless and most wanting in foresight of everyone aboard'[57]) persuaded Petit and Guichenot to cross the island (without informing Bonnefoi). They became lost, had no food or water, met some hostile Aborigines, but eventually found their way back. They had walked slowly *towards* the party of Aborigines who did not attempt to prevent their further progress. After this display of courage they returned to the ship in a very sorry state – exhausted, famished and dehydrated. The sole benefit of their expedition was a collection of shells.[58]

The two ships sailed from Shark Bay on 23 March and made for the North West Cape. On their earlier visit, Bernier had determined its position as 21° 31' 31" S; 114° 10' E (of Greenwich). The new determinations gave 21° 37' S; 114° 18' E.[59] Modern determinations are 21° 47' S; 114° 10' E (of Greenwich).

Baudin then sailed for the Bonaparte Archipelago and, on 24 April, sent a boat party to examine Cassini Island. Guichenot was the only naturalist able to take part and to spend a night on the island. During their return they sighted four praus. They were part of a fleet of praus from Macassar intent on catching bêche-de-mer, or sea-cucumbers, for the Chinese market.[60]

TO KUPANG AGAIN

On 28 April, as they approached Kupang, Baudin recorded that one of the chronometers, no. 31, had stopped, for no known reason. Baudin interrupted his journal at this point and resumed when the ships departed from Kupang. The men were in reasonably good health at this time. For the last month he had issued a ration of 'lemon juice and syrup mixed with water', and this could have been the 'lime' juice that he had obtained at Port Jackson. Baudin himself, however, was showing signs of tuberculosis. Two weeks previously he had several days of weakness and an 'almost continuous chest cough'.[61]

Baudin's journal resumed on 3 June – the day the ships departed from Kupang – and recorded the latitude and longitude of Fort Concordia in Kupang Bay as 10° 09' 55" S, 123° 50' E (of Greenwich). The longitude had been determined by the method of lunar distances and by using the chronometers – corrected for their errors since leaving France.[62] Their stay at Kupang was not as disastrous as their previous visit – although the doctor reported 'that many of the crew had gone down with venereal diseases'. Bernier now had a fever, and Petit was also ill. Indeed, two days later, the 23-year-old Bernier died. Baudin himself had his third bout of spitting blood.[63]

On 7 July, Baudin wrote that he had haemorrhaged badly and that he became so weak that he had to take to his bed. But he 'did not find much relief there'. Several of the animals were also sick. Moreover twenty of the men were now ill – 'several with dysentery, the others unfit for duty because of serious venereal diseases contracted at Timor'. The *Casuarina* could not keep up with the *Géographe*. Everything seemed to be going wrong. At this time Baudin decided to abandon the projected exploration of the Gulf of Carpentaria, and to make for the Ile de France.[64]

ILE DE FRANCE

The *Géographe* arrived at Ile de France on 7 August 1803, and the *Casuarina* reached the island twelve days later. The sick were transferred to the hospital, and the *Casuarina* was paid off. Baudin died on 16 September, and the local authorities decided to appoint Pierre Bernard Milius – formerly first lieutenant in the *Naturaliste* under Hamelin – as commander of the expedition. Milius had been sick and had been discharged at Port Jackson. He had travelled to Ile de France in a merchant ship. Under his command, the *Géographe* departed on 16 December, called at the Cape of Good Hope, and arrived at Lorient in France on 25 March 1804.

Péron, now the acknowledged leader of the scientists, was given the task of writing the official account of the voyage, and he completed a substantial section before his sickness led him to return to his native Cérilly – where he died of tuberculosis on 14 December 1810. His official account did not once mention Baudin by name. Moreover, Napoléon's decree – authorising publication at government expense – also failed to mention Baudin's name.[65]

THE SUCCESS AND FAILURE OF THE BAUDIN EXPEDITION

There had been great expectations of the Baudin expedition to New Holland. In the event, however, the *Géographe* and *Naturaliste* had been plagued with sickness – so much so that the successes tend to be forgotten.

It had taken far too long for the ships to reach the shores of New Holland, and so little attention had been paid to the need to obtain fresh fruit and vegetables that scurvy was beginning to make its appearance – even if it was not yet lethal. The need to sail to Kupang in Timor for fresh food and water was unfortunate because so many men contracted dysentery from the local water. The causes of scurvy, and dysentery, were completely unknown at the beginning of the nineteenth century. Indeed, microorganisms of any kind had not then been recognised. It was known, however, that the mortality from dysentery in that era was about fifty per cent, or even more. Dysentery, contracted in Timor, was responsible for the majority of the deaths among the members of the expedition.

However, as Faivre has pointed out, 'not one man fell victim to a native spear or club' and 'no Australian native blood was spilt.'[66] This includes the Aboriginal people from Van Diemen's Land. Yet, thirty years later, the original population of about 2000 had been reduced to about 200 – and these were rounded up and transported to Flinders

Island. The Aboriginal people, in what is now known as Tasmania, are now extinct. The Baudin expedition has provided us with the most extensive and sympathetic account of these people.[67]

There is no doubt that Baudin and his officers made significant geographical discoveries, particularly on the eastern and south-eastern coasts of Van Diemen's Land, but also on the northern coast of the same island, on the southern coast of eastern Australia, and on the north-western coast of Australia. There is also no doubt that there were significant discoveries in the fields of natural history and in anthropology. Péron is often credited with coining the name 'anthropology' and he, helped by the artists, showed how interesting this subject can be. As Ernest Scott has written:[68]

> It is probably safe to say that no expedition, French or English, that ever came down to Australasian waters, added so much that was new to the world's scientific knowledge, or accumulated so much material, as did this one whose chief naturalist was François Péron.

The number of animals and birds successfully taken to France illustrates this, and the vast number of natural history specimens still preserved in France attests to the energy and diligence of the savants who accompanied Baudin – even if Baudin was rather scornful.

BAUDIN THE MAN

Baudin is something of an enigma. He was totally dedicated to the expedition, but his relationship with the scientists and with his officers left much to be desired. Instead of helping and encouraging his younger officers, he seemed to concentrate on fault-finding and on committing these (often trivial) faults to paper so that they would become known

to ministers and others back in France. Most young officers were given written orders and, regardless of the circumstances, these orders had to be obeyed in every detail. Failure to do so would often result in a written reprimand and a note in his *Journal de Mer*. The result was that few if any of the young officers looked up to Baudin. After Baudin died, Midshipman Charles Baudin (no relation) wrote that 'he was universally detested'.[69] The engineer, François-Michael Ronsard, summed up Baudin as follows:[70]

> Unfortunately, Mr Baudin has not enough consideration for his officers; it can be seen in his whole conduct from the first day of the expedition to the last, and he has always seized with avidity opportunities to humiliate them.

Another weapon frequently used by Baudin was sarcasm. When the *Naturaliste* was about to leave Port Jackson to return to France, Baudin arranged a dinner for her captain, Emmanuel Hamelin. Baudin recorded:[71]

> I had the pleasure of seeing only one of his [Hamelin's] officers, and even then I think he would not have appeared if Captain Hamelin had not invited him to dine with us. As I left, I had them thanked for their politeness and told that I was very happy to have no farewells to make to them.

As another example of Baudin's comments, the following can be quoted. He wrote that the scientists: 'all returned [from King Island] at about nine o'clock, except for M. Péron, who seeing nothing but molluscs at every step, had amused himself by missing the first boat.'[72] Nevertheless Baudin did know his business as a seaman and navigator, and his expedition achieved much more than the French government of that period gave him credit.

6

FLINDERS AND THE *INVESTIGATOR*

PREPARATIONS FOR AN EXPLORATION

Matthew Flinders left Sydney in the *Reliance* on 3 March 1800 to return to England. He arrived at Portsmouth on 26 August and, a few days later, he sent a letter to Joseph Banks seeking his support for a new expedition to complete the exploration of the coast of New Holland. 'The interests of geography and of natural history in general, and of the British nation in particular,' he wrote, 'seem to require, that this only remaining considerable part of the globe should be thoroughly explored.' He added that the *Lady Nelson* alone would not be sufficient and that she needed to be joined by a larger vessel. He went on to say that if his late discoveries in New Holland 'should so far meet approbation as to induce the execution of it to be committed to me, I should enter upon it with that zeal which I hope has hitherto characterized my services'.[1] Banks was a man of considerable influence in government circles in England. He was a member of the landed gentry, and was a confidant of the King. He had sailed with Cook on his voyage to Tahiti, and to New Zealand and New Holland, and was regarded as being extremely knowledgeable on matters connected with the Pacific Ocean. He had been created a baronet in 1781 and, in 1778, had become the president of the Royal Society – 'the most learned society in the world'.[2] He was to remain president until his death in 1820.

Banks invited Flinders to call on him at his London house, in Soho Square, and the interview was clearly a success because Banks immediately supported the proposed expedition. It was approved by Earl Spencer, the First Lord of the Admiralty, and then by the King.[3] Five days after Banks had written to invite Flinders to call on him, the Admiralty chose the three-masted *Xenophon* for the task, and three weeks later the Navy Board was instructed to provision her for overseas service for six months. After a further two weeks she was renamed *Investigator*,[4] and the secretary of the Navy (Evan Nepean) signed the papers appointing Flinders as lieutenant in command on 19 January 1801. He was promoted to the rank of commander on 16 February.

Flinders was a Lincolnshire man and had lived not far from Banks' estate, Revesby Abbey, near Boston, in the same county. He selected Robert Fowler, another Lincolnshire man, as his first lieutenant, and his younger brother, Samuel, as second lieutenant. John Franklin, another officer from Lincolnshire (and one to achieve great fame in later years) was appointed one of the eight midshipmen and master's mates. John Thistle was appointed master, Hugh Bell as surgeon, and Robert Purdie as assistant surgeon.[5] Six civilians (plus four boys 'to keep their cabins clean') were added to the ship's complement. The first was an astronomer, John Crosley, who was selected by the Board of Longitude. The other five were all selected by Banks

– who had been informed by the secretary of the Admiralty, that 'Any proposal you may make will be approved. The whole is left entirely to your decision.'[6]

Banks selected Robert Brown as the naturalist. Brown was an army surgeon who had a special interest in botany, and who was already known to Banks. Ferdinand Bauer was appointed as botanical draughtsman. William Westall, aged only twenty, was selected to serve as landscape and figure painter. Peter Good, an experienced gardener, was appointed to assist the naturalist. Mineralogical matters were in the hands of John Allen, a practical miner, who was instructed to 'take specimens of all rocks, and particularly of all mineral veins he meets with and bring them home'.[7] The civilian members of the *Investigator* were not all regarded as having equal status. Banks suggested that the astronomer and the naturalist might mess with the officers, the two artists with the midshipmen, and the gardener and the miner with the warrant officers – namely the boatswain, gunner, carpenter and master at arms.[8]

The Navy Board issued Flinders with a set of astronomical and surveying instruments – many of which were supplied by the London instrument-maker Edward Troughton. There was a 23-centimetre sextant by Jesse Ramsden, for example, and three sextants of 20-centimetre radius by Troughton 'the latter being made in 1801, expressly for the voyage'.[9] A Ramsden universal theodolite was also provided. There were telescopes, pocket compasses, an azimuth compass, a surveyor's chain, thermometers, two artificial horizons, drawing instruments, magnets and even three pedometers (for counting the number of paces on land, and so estimating the distance travelled). The astronomer, Crosley, was also supplied with several chronometers – for use in determining longitude. Two of these were made by Thomas Earnshaw (numbered 543 and 520),[10] and two by John Arnold (numbered 176 and 82) – both London instrument-makers. Arnold also

supplied a watch (numbered 1736) for use during expeditions on land or on rivers. The reason for using two instrument-makers was to compare the accuracy and reliability of their chronometers on a prolonged voyage – and this was done. (Later, when the *Investigator* reached Port Jackson, Flinders was to take the opportunity to send back the two Arnold chronometers to the astronomer royal at Greenwich – because both had stopped. However, the two Earnshaw chronometers performed well.[11])

The Navy Board supplied Flinders with copies of a number of books describing earlier voyages to the South Seas, and Joseph Banks presented a set of the third edition of the *Encyclopaedia Britannica*. The *Investigator* was issued with copies of every chart in the Admiralty that related to New Holland. In addition, Flinders was provided with a large number of different items – intended as presents for native people, or for barter. There were 50 axes and 300 hatchets, for example, and 500 pocket knives, 300 scissors, 500 mirrors, 200 strings of beads, 100 pairs of ear rings, and 200 rings of different sizes.[12]

This was not all, however. It was desirable to obtain a passport, or a certificate of safe conduct, from the French government. Only a few months ago the French expedition of two ships *Géographe* and *Naturaliste*, under the command of Nicolas-Thomas Baudin, had obtained such a certificate from the British government to facilitate their voyage to New Holland and return. This had been done at the suggestion of Joseph Banks. In view of this, Flinders urged the Admiralty to write to Prime Minister Addington and to the Foreign Office – suggesting that an approach be made to France to obtain a passport for the *Investigator* on her voyage of discovery to New Holland. The Admiralty made the approach to the French government but, at first, supplied insufficient detail. Nevertheless a passport for the *Investigator* was obtained on 23 June 1801,[13] and Flinders was directed 'to act in all respects towards French ships as if the two countries were not at war'.[14]

THE VOYAGE

When all was ready, the *Investigator* sailed from Spithead on 18 July 1801 – bound for Cape Town. Flinders began 'very early to put in execution the beneficial plan, first practised and made known by the great captain Cook' to maintain the health of his men.[15] The lower deck, and the cockpits, were cleared, washed and aired every fine day and, on wet days, they were cleaned and aired without washing. On Sunday and Thursday mornings the ship's company was mustered 'clean shaved and dressed', and on fine evenings they were encouraged to dance to the fife and drum. The main health hazard at sea was scurvy – which had so often swept through a crew during long sea voyages. Flinders was supplied with lime juice to combat the scurvy and, in the tropics, the men were supplied with this together with some sugar (which has no antiscorbutic properties). At higher latitudes they were given sauerkraut, and some vinegar (which is also without antiscorbutic properties). Nevertheless, when the *Investigator* arrived at the Cape of Good Hope, Flinders recorded that 'we had not a single person in the sick list, both officers and men being fully in as good health, as when we sailed from Spithead.'[16]

The *Investigator* arrived at False Bay (Cape Town) on 16 October, and anchored in Simon's Bay at the north-western part of False Bay. Seven Royal Navy ships were at anchor there. Flinders called on the vice-admiral and, after showing his orders, was given every help in obtaining supplies and also tradesmen to give his ship a 'thorough caulking'. During his time there Flinders exchanged four members of the crew for a similar number from other Royal Navy ships – one midshipman (Nathaniel Bell) wished to return to England and was succeeded by another; and John Crosley also retired from the expedition owing to sickness, probably chronic sea-sickness. His departure was a great loss. Flinders would now have to carry out a larger proportion of the astronomical observations. Moreover, Crosley took with him his personal chronometer – Earnshaw 465 – which Flinders considered the most reliable of all the chronometers. Before he left, however, Crosley was able to check the accuracy of all the timekeepers. The longitude of Cape Town had been determined some years before by Charles Mason, using the Transit of Venus, and this figure was adjusted by 2' 00" to give the longitude on the shore of Simon's Bay. Each of the *Investigator*'s chronometers was then used to determine the longitude – and the result compared with that obtained by Mason. Earnshaw's 543 was found to be the most accurate, but Arnold's 82 was found to be so erratic as not to be worth using. This particular study was carried out by Crosley over seven days, and was continued by Flinders for a further five days.[17] The scientists also had not been idle during their stay in False Bay. They 'were almost constantly on shore upon the search; and their collections, intended for examination on the next passage, were tolerably ample'. They climbed Table Mountain and had been delighted 'to find the richest treasures of the English green house, profusely scattered over the sides and summits of these barren hills'.[18]

Flinders sailed from False Bay on 4 November 1801 – after a stay of eighteen days. He set a course for the south-western coast of New Holland (otherwise known as *Terra Australis*) and, after thirty-two days, the coast was sighted. On the following day he named Cape Leeuwin 'as being the south-western, and most projecting part of Leeuwin's Land'. This cape had previously been known as 'the largest *Ile St Alouarn* of d'Entrecasteaux'.[19] Flinders followed the land to the south-east, and observed Point d'Entrecasteaux – 'one of the most remarkable projections on this coast'.[20] Not far away were some rocks that George Vancouver, in the *Discovery* accompanied by the *Chatham*, had sighted in 1791, and named Point Chatham.[21] Flinders continued to sail eastwards along the coast, being careful to ensure that the breakers on the shore were visible from the deck. In this way he hoped that 'no river or opening could escape being seen'. When this was not possible he was 'commonly at the mast head with a glass'. He hauled off from the coast at night but 'every precaution was taken to come in with the same point in the morning, as soon after daylight as practicable.'[22]

The *Investigator* entered King George III Sound (now abbreviated to King George Sound) on 8 December 1801. This fine harbour had been discovered and named by Vancouver in 1791, and Flinders used a copy of the chart that Vancouver had prepared and was able to enter the sound without difficulty. Flinders wanted to spend some time in this sheltered harbour – to effect some repairs to the sails and to the rigging. In addition, the scientists were keen to examine the local fauna and flora, and other matters of interest.

In the meantime, Flinders himself was to undertake a detailed survey of the sound and determine the latitude and longitude with as much precision as possible. He used the chronometers to determine the longitude, but he also made thirty-one separate observations of the lunar distance (the angle between the Moon and the Sun, or between the Moon and one of the prominent stars) to obtain the longitude for comparison with the value obtained using the chronometer. The latitude was determined on shore using a Ramsden universal theodolite so that an artificial horizon was not needed. The lunar distance method for the determination of longitude had been devised before a reasonably accurate clock, or chronometer, had been developed for use at sea. The method was not easy. It involved considerable calculation and, for this reason, it was more often used in harbour when time was not a problem. It has been pointed out that the latitude determinations by Flinders are usually correct to within a mile (often much less) and that his longitudes, determined using a chronometer, usually had a westerly error –

indicating that his chronometer had a more or less constant error.[23]

The time spent at anchor in King George Sound was exciting for the scientists. Robert Brown and Peter Good collected specimens of 500 species during this period.[24] Moreover, all the scientific people and several of the officers went on expeditions to examine the country – to view the fauna, and to meet the Aboriginal inhabitants. Flinders reported that the Aboriginal men of the King George Sound area do not 'extract one of the upper front teeth at the age of puberty, as is generally practised at Port Jackson', and that 'they do not make use of the woomera, or throwing stick.'[25]

The *Investigator* sailed from the sound on 5 January 1802 and, a few days later, found herself in a maze of small islands during a storm. These islands had been named the Recherche Archipelago by d'Entrecasteaux. Flinders noted that d'Entrecasteaux 'had mostly skirted round the archipelago' which was 'a sufficient reason for me to attempt passing through the middle, if the weather did not make the experiment too dangerous'. It was dangerous and, in the late afternoon, the ship was still in the labyrinth of islands and rocks. Flinders decided to make for the mainland and, at seven o'clock, they entered a small sandy bay. 'The critical circumstance under which this place was discovered,' wrote Flinders, 'induced me to give it the name of Lucky Bay.'[26] This bay, which still carries the name given by Flinders, is a few kilometres to the east of Cape Le Grand and north of Mondrain Island.

When the *Investigator* was safely anchored in Lucky Bay, opportunities were taken to make astronomical observations ashore, and the scientists were also able to examine the country. The master was sent to examine the coast towards the east and returned with a list of further islands that would have to be avoided. Fowler and Thistle also went to Mondrain Island and noted the seals and the 'small kanguroos [wallabies] of a species different from any I had seen before'. Robert Brown made an excursion to Cape Le Grand.

The *Investigator* sailed from Lucky Bay on 14 January and arrived at Ile du Milieu, Middle Island and Goose Island – almost due south of Cap Aride (Cape Arid). It was clear that the French explorers had pioneered the exploration of this area and Flinders recorded his praise of Beautemps Beaupré, of the *Recherche*, who had drawn their charts.[27] The *Investigator* continued to follow the coastline to the north-east, and the next point seen was named Point Culver. Fifty nautical miles further to the north-east, Point Dover was named. On 27 January Flinders reached the head of the Great Australian Bight and reckoned its latitude to be 31° 29' S and longitude 131° 10' E. D'Entrecasteaux had also reached the head of the bight and gave slightly different figures for latitude and longitude.[28]

Shortly after this d'Entrecasteaux had left the coast and headed for Van Diemen's Land, but Flinders continued to follow the coast and arrived at a bay that he named Fowler's Bay (now Fowlers Bay) after his first lieutenant. Not long afterwards, he named Point Bell and the Purdie Islands and noted that 'it would be dangerous to pass between them'. He next visited Nuyts Archipelago. The first group he named the Isles of St Francis 'in the persuasion that the central one is that named St. Francis by Nuyts'. Here they observed sooty petrels, penguins and wallabies. A party of men went ashore at dusk and collected enough petrels 'to give four birds to every man in the ship'.[29] He named Petrel Bay. The islands found to the north-east of St Francis were identified as 'the Isles of St Peter in Nuyts chart' (the chart prepared by Hessel Gerritsz showing the Dutch discoveries up to the year 1628).

Matthew Flinders named Cape Westall after William Westall, the landscape figure artist on the *Investigator*. (Geoffrey Badger)

Flinders summarised his findings as follows:[30]

> Besides the nine Isles of St. Francis and two of St. Peter, and several distinct rocks and patches of reef, it [the Nuyts Archipelago] contains Sinclair's four Rocks, Purdie's Isles, Lound's Isle, Lacy's and Evans' Islands, Franklin's Isles, and Olive's Island; all of which are named after young officers of the *Investigator*.

Lacy, or Lacey, was the midshipman who joined at Cape Town following the retirement of Nathaniel Bell.

As Flinders sailed further along the coast to the south-east he named features after his officers and scientists, and some after senior Admiralty officials or after the nature of the feature. Point Brown was named after the botanist, Streaky Bay because it looked 'streaky', Cape Bauer after the botanical artist, Point Westall after the landscape artist, Cape Radstock after Lord Radstock, Anxious Bay because Flinders was anxious, Flinders Island after his second lieutenant, Point Sir Isaac and Coffin Bay after Admiral Sir Isaac Coffin 'who, when resident commissioner at Sheerness, had taken so zealous a part in the outfit of the *Investigator*', and Whidbey's Isles 'after my worthy friend the former master-attendant at Sheerness'. Point Avoid was named because it was considered dangerous.[31] The northern point of Coffin Bay was named Point Drummond after Captain Alan Drummond of the Navy, and Cape Wiles was named after 'a worthy friend at Liguanes, in Jamaica'.[32] The *Investigator* sailed between the mainland and a small island (afterwards named Williams Island) to the south and, a little later, Flinders wrote:[33]

> A tide from the north-eastward, apparently the ebb, ran more than one mile an hour; which was the more remarkable from no set of tide, worthy to be noticed, having hitherto been observed upon this coast. No land could be seen in the direction from whence it came, and these circumstances, with the trending of the coast to the north, did not fail to excite many conjectures. Large rivers, deep inlets, inland seas, and passages into the Gulph of Carpentaria, were terms frequently used in our conversations of this evening; and the prospect of making an interesting discovery, seemed to have infused new life and vigour into every man in the ship.

Flinders and Thistle went ashore on the land to the east and satisfied themselves that it was an island – which Flinders named Thistle Island. It was approaching dusk and Thistle was sent with a party of men to the mainland to find a suitable place to anchor, and to locate some fresh water. In the meantime Flinders completed the observations needed for the determination of their position. The beach at the north end of Thistle Island was found to be 34° 56' S and 136° 03.5' E. The latter figure was determined using the chronometers corrected for their errors, and was confirmed by thirty sets of lunar distance observations.

At dusk Thistle was observed returning to the ship in the cutter but, half an hour later, it had not arrived and Lieutenant Fowler took a boat 'to see what might have happened'. It seems that the cutter had been overturned by the 'rippling of tide' and that all its occupants had been drowned. Flinders named the southern cape 'Cape Catastrophe'. Taylor Island was named after the midshipman who was with Thistle. Two officers and six men had been lost. One of the men was named Williams and, as already mentioned, Flinders named the island close to Cape Catastrophe, Williams Island.[34]

Flinders was deeply moved by the loss of these men. 'Mr Thistle', he wrote, 'was truly a valuable man, as a seaman, an officer, and a good member of society', and he added 'From his merit and prudent conduct, he was promoted before the mast to be a midshipman, and afterwards a master in his Majesty's service.' Taylor 'was a young officer who promised fair to become an ornament to the service, as he was to society by the amiability of his manners and temper'. Flinders also noted that all six of the seamen who lost their lives had volunteered for the service. Apart from anything else 'this diminution of our force was heavily felt.'[35]

Five other small islands near Cape Catastrophe were named after the five seamen who were lost. A small cove was named Memory Cove, and an engraved copper plate was erected there. Soon afterwards Flinders discovered a new inlet. The cape at its entrance was named Cape Donington, the bay was named Port Lincoln, and other features were named Boston Bay, Boston Island and Louth Bay – his native Lincolnshire was clearly in Flinders' mind at this time!

Flinders spent some time in the Port Lincoln area, filling the ship's casks with fresh water, and taking astronomical observations and surveying. On 4 March he observed a solar eclipse with a refracting telescope of 117 centimetres (46 inches) focus. This eclipse had been predicted for this day in the *Nautical Almanac*. On another occasion, on Boston Island, he wanted to measure a base line so that bearings of prominent features from each end of the base line could be used to determine their positions. Flinders went to the south-east end of the island and established a pendulum to swing half seconds. It was a musket ball suspended with twine and was 24.9 centimetres (9.8 inches) from the fixed end of the twine to the centre of the musket ball. He had arranged for a cannon to be fired from the ship at given times. Then: 'From the instant that the flash of the first gun was perceived, to the time of hearing the report, I counted eighty-five vibrations of the pendulum, and the same with two succeeding guns.' Knowing the speed of sound, the base-line was found to be 8.01 geographic [nautical] miles of 1847 metres (6060 feet) (at that latitude).[36] The latitude of their tents at Port Lincoln, from four meridian observations of the Sun, using an artificial horizon, was found to be 34° 48' 25" S. The longitude, from thirty sets of lunar distances, was found to be 135° 44' 51" E. From these results Cape Donington was found to be at 34° 44' S, 135° 56.5' E.[37] A modern determination places Port Lincoln at 34° 44' S, 135° 52' E.

The *Investigator* sailed from Port Lincoln on 6 March 1802, and came to a cluster of small islands that Flinders named the Sir Joseph Banks Group. The largest was named Reevesby Island after the Banks estate, Revesby Abbey, but the island seems to have retained the spelling used by Flinders.[38] The ship followed the coastline to the north-east and, two days later, Flinders decided that they were in a gulf – but was still hoping that it would terminate with a river of some importance. A mountain to the north-east was named Mt Brown after the botanist and one, more to the north, was named Mt Arden, after Flinders' great grandmother. Brown, Bauer and Westall, with a few attendants, set off to climb Mt Brown. They had to walk 24 kilometres (fifteen miles) to the foot of the mountain, but gained the top in the late afternoon and had to spend the night on the summit without water. However, they returned safely.[39] The mountains were later named the Flinders Ranges by the governor of South Australia. Flinders noticed signs that Aboriginal people lived in the area – but he did not have the good fortune to meet any.

The *Investigator* was anchored towards the head of the gulf and Flinders, accompanied by the surgeon, Hugh Bell, went forward in the cutter. They made five landings in the gulf, and the positions have all been identified by Cooper.[40] The gulf was found to terminate in mud flats – which was disappointing. As there was nothing further to detain Flinders at the head of the gulf, he decided to sail southwards along its eastern coast. It might be noted, however, that a town was later established near the head of the gulf, and that the wool obtained from the adjacent farms was shipped from there. The township was named Port Augusta after Lady (Augusta) Young – the wife of the governor of the colony, Sir Henry Young – in the early 1850s.

Sailing southwards, Flinders named Point Riley and Point Pearce, after two officials at the Admiralty. The bay near the base of the gulf, where the coastline bears west, was named Hardwicke Bay 'after the noble earl of that name'. Flinders named Spencer Gulf after Lord Spencer, who presided over the Board of Admiralty when the voyage was planned, and the cape at the foot of the gulf was named Cape Spencer. Three islands to the south of this cape were named the Althorpe Islands after a parish in Lincolnshire.[41]

Early signs of rough weather persuaded Flinders to leave the coast and to sail towards the south – where some land was to be seen. On the next morning the ship approached the land, and Point Marsden was named after the Second Secretary to the Admiralty and, towards the east, Nepean Bay after the First Secretary, Sir Evan Nepean. It was now too late to go ashore 'but every glass in the ship was pointed there ... Several black lumps, like rocks were pretended to have been seen in motion by some of the young gentlemen, which caused the force of their imagination to be much admired.' Next morning, on going ashore, Flinders observed many dark-brown kangaroos – but there were no signs of Aborigines. Thirty-one kangaroos were killed and their tameness also confirmed the absence of humans. The whole ship's company was employed all afternoon skinning and preparing the kangaroos for a real feast 'after four months privation from almost any fresh provisions'. 'In gratitude for so seasonable a supply,' wrote Flinders, 'I called this southern land Kanguroo Island' (now Kangaroo Island).[42]

Flinders took care to take bearings of any features that he could see, and it was at this time that he observed a mountain to the north-east and named it Mt Lofty. He also observed and named Cape Jervis – after the family name of Admiral the Earl of St Vincent. Flinders determined the latitude near his landing, using an artificial horizon, to be 35° 43' S. The longitude, using the chronometers, was 137° 58' 31" E.

Flinders sailed from Kangaroo Island on 24 March and headed north-west to renew his running survey of the south coast – a survey that had been interrupted by the bad weather that had caused him to leave Cape Spencer. The sea between the mainland and Kangaroo Island was named Investigator Strait. It was soon clear that they had discovered a new gulf, and Mt Lofty was clearly visible. Flinders sailed northwards and went ashore at the head of the gulf with the naturalist – to examine the country. Flinders named it the Gulf of St Vincent after the Earl of St Vincent, and the land between the two gulfs was named Yorke Peninsula after Charles Phillip Yorke who later became Lord Hardwicke and First Lord of the Admiralty. Flinders now returned to Kangaroo Island for a time and named Pelican Lagoon (which later became American River) where a good supply of wood, and a few more kangaroos, were obtained. Sailing eastwards he named Backstairs Passage, because 'it forms a private entrance, as it were, to the two Gulphs.'[43]

THE MEETING WITH BAUDIN

In the late afternoon of 8 April 1802, a ship was sighted, and Flinders immediately cleared for action and remained at the ready until it was clear that she was a French vessel carrying a passport from the British Admiralty. Flinders went aboard the French ship, which was the *Géographe*, under the command of Baudin (see Chapter 5). Because Flinders did not understand French, he took Robert Brown with him. Baudin explained that he had examined the south and east coasts of Van Diemen's Land and parts of Bass Strait. He was rather critical of the chart that had been prepared by Bass, and had not appreciated that Bass had carried out his preliminary investigation using an open boat and without instruments to determine the latitude and longitude. Flinders offered to bring him a copy of a chart prepared since that made by Bass, and the next morning they continued their discussions, which were mainly in English. Flinders named the bay Encounter Bay – and both ships proceeded on their way.

THE VICTORIAN COAST

Flinders continued to sail to the south-east until he entered Bass Strait. He made a brief examination of the north coast of King Island and then turned northwards. Before long he saw:[44]

> ... a small opening, with breaking water across it ... although the entrance seemed to be very narrow, and there were in it strong ripplings like breakers, I was induced to steer in at half past one; the ship being close upon a wind and every man ready for tacking at a moment's warning.

He added:[45]

> The extensive harbour we had thus unexpectedly found I supposed must be Western Port, although the narrowness of the entrance did by no means correspond with the width given to it by Mr. Bass. It was the information of captain Baudin, who had coasted along from thence with fine weather, and had found no inlet of any kind, which induced this supposition ... This, however, was not Western Port, as we found next morning.

Flinders thought that he had made a new discovery but, when he arrived at Port Jackson, he learnt that the bay had been discovered ten weeks before by Lieutenant John Murray in the *Lady Nelson*, and had been named Port Phillip. The *Investigator* entered Port Jackson on 8 May 1802 with, as already mentioned, everyone in good health. She remained there for twelve weeks – during which time the ship was cleaned, refitted, and reprovisioned. Nine convicts were recruited as crew members on the promise of conditional or absolute pardons if they gave good service. It had always been intended that the *Lady Nelson* would now join the *Investigator* in the further exploration of the coastline, and the two ships sailed from Port Jackson on 22 July 1802 – with Lieutenant John Murray as captain of the *Lady Nelson*, but with Flinders in overall command.

EXPLORING THE NORTHERN COAST

The main object was to survey the northern coast of the continent – but until they reached the north they had an opportunity to review and to add detail to the chart of the eastern coast as prepared by Cook in the *Endeavour* some years before. Flinders found that many of Cook's longitude determinations were about 15–35 nautical miles in error. This has led to the suggestion that Flinders was a better navigator than Cook. It has also been claimed that Bligh was a superior navigator. Whitehouse, for example, has claimed that 'Bligh's Cape York was 16 miles [26 kilometres] to the east of the true position while Cook's was 60 miles [97 kilometres] west.'[46] However, it is not reasonable to compare Cook's determinations with those of later navigators using more modern techniques. Cook had no chronometer on his first voyage when he discovered the eastern coast of Australia. He pioneered the use of the chronometer on his second and third voyages into the Pacific Ocean. Moreover, except when he was anchored in Botany Bay and when beached on the banks of Endeavour River, Cook was making a running survey – which meant that he could not take a large number of duplicate observations. In this context it might be mentioned that, when the *Investigator* was anchored at Sydney Cove, Flinders determined the longitude by averaging the results of forty-four sets of lunar distance observations – from which he obtained a longitude of 151° 11' 49" E. The latitude was found to be 33° 51' 45.6" S.[47]

Flinders had been issued with four chronometers. By the time that he reached Port Jackson two had stopped, and he made arrangements for them to be returned to the astronomer royal. He was expecting to receive Kendall's K3 chronometer – an instrument that had been used on Cook's third voyage, and also by Vancouver.[48] It was to be delivered to him by James Inman, the chief author of *Inman's Tables* – for use by those making astronomical observations for navigational purposes. Inman had not arrived at Sydney Cove by the time that the *Investigator* and the *Lady Nelson* departed for the northern coast. He had expected to join the *Investigator* as the astronomer, but this never eventuated. Flinders did not receive this chronometer (K3) until he arrived back at Sydney Cove with his ship in an unseaworthy condition.

The *Investigator* and the *Lady Nelson* sailed northwards inside the Great Barrier Reef, and Flinders was able to add some detail to Cook's first chart of the coastline – particularly between present-day Rockhampton and Mackay. The problem that soon faced them was to find a way through the reef to reach the open sea before altering course to pass through Torres Strait. The *Lady Nelson* was unfortunate in that she did strike the reef and, to be on the safe side, Flinders decided to send her back to Port Jackson. The *Investigator*, however, found an opening in the reef and sailed northwards until she reached the latitude of Torres Strait. Flinders then sailed almost due west, and chose a passage between Wednesday Island (so named by Captain Bligh during his launch voyage in 1789) and Prince of Wales Island. This is now known as Flinders Passage. He then passed through the Prince of Wales Passage and turned southwards to enter the Gulf of Carpentaria – a gulf that had been discovered by Willem Jansz in 1606 (see Chapter 3).

Flinders, in the *Investigator*, entered the Gulf of Carpentaria on 3 November 1802 – about 150 years after the Dutch explorers – and he carried a copy of the rough chart that had been prepared by them. He sailed southwards close to the eastern coast of the gulf – preparing a more detailed chart. He had an additional matter on his mind. The *Investigator* had not been regarded as a particularly good vessel when she was assigned to Flinders, but ships were in great demand during the war with France and this was the only ship that could be spared. Flinders obtained evidence that the ship was

even worse than he had thought. On 17 October 1802 he recorded:[49]

> In Torres Strait, when running with a fresh side wind, the ship had leaked to the amount of ten inches of water per hour, and in some hours the carpenters had reported as much as fourteen; but no anchorage, adapted to the purpose of caulking the bends had presented itself ...

It seemed likely, however, that he would find a suitable anchorage somewhere in the gulf, and he made a careful examination of the coast with this end in view. He recognised some of the features marked on old Dutch charts – the Batavia River and Cape Keerweer,[50] for example – but he also found several errors. Near the head of the gulf, Flinders discovered a group of islands that the Dutch had regarded as part of the mainland. The Dutch had also named a river on the southern coast of the gulf, the Maatsuyker, or Maet Suÿker – as shown on the Thevenot chart. But Flinders could not identify a river in this position. The Nicholson, Albert and Leichhardt rivers are further to the east. Flinders named the group of islands the Wellesley Islands – after the Marquess of Wellesley, the governor-general of India. (Much later, after his release from confinement at Ile de France, he named the largest island of the group Bentinck Island – after Lord William Bentinck who was governor of Madras and who had intervened on Flinders' behalf with the French authorities.) There was another island, however, to the south-east of Bentinck Island, and Flinders selected this island to land, and to careen the ship on its shore. He had to select a name for this island and, because he had concluded that there was no Maatsuyker River entering the gulf, he considered transferring this name to the island to the south-east of Bentinck. This would seem to be appropriate as Maatsuyker was the member of the Batavia Council who had signed Tasman's instructions; but Flinders knew that this name had already been given to some islands to the south of Tasmania. He therefore decided to name it after another member of the Batavia Council – Salamon Sweers.

As briefly mentioned in Chapter 3, Flinders landed on Sweers Island, as did many of his crew, and it was here that they attempted to repair the ship's most serious faults. The state of the ship was found to be so bad that Flinders asked his two very experienced warrant officers – the master and the carpenter – to carry out a detailed examination of the state of the ship. It soon became clear that many of her timbers were rotten and that 'in a strong gale … the ship would hardly escape foundering; so that we think she is totally unfit to encounter much bad weather.' They added:[51]

From the state to which the ship now seems to be advanced, it is our joint opinion, that in twelve months there will be scarcely a sound timber in her; but that if she remains in fine weather and happens no accident, she may run six months longer without much risk.

Flinders was gravely worried by this report, which seemed to indicate that he would not be able to complete the survey of the Australian coastline, but he wrote:[52]

Laying aside the two great questions, our safety and the completions of the voyage, for the present, I have determined to go on in the examination of this gulph, if the north west monsoon does not prove too great an hindrance, and afterwards to act as the rising circumstances shall most seem to require.

Notwithstanding the worry about the state of the ship the officers and crew seem to have enjoyed their brief time on Sweers Island.[53] Flinders arranged to cut the name of the ship into the trunk of a tree to record their stay. The *Investigator* sailed from Sweers Island on 1 December 1802 and steered north-west, still following the coastline of the gulf, and came to another group of islands that had also been shown as part of the mainland in the early Dutch charts. Flinders later named this group 'in complement to the distinguished officer of the British navy, whose earnest endeavours to relieve me from oppression in a subsequent part of the voyage demand my gratitude'.[54] He named this 'cluster of islands' the 'Sir Edward Pellew's Group' after Admiral Sir Edward Pellew, who was commander-in-chief in the East Indies.

The largest island in this group had been seen by Tasman and named Cape Vanderlin – believing it to be part of the mainland. It is now Vanderlin Island. Further to the north-west, Flinders was able to prove that the 'cabo de maria' (Cape Maria) of the Dutch explorers is also an island. Still further north, Flinders circumnavigated Groote Eylandt. He also named and examined Chasm Island, which 'lies one mile and a half from a low point of Groote Eylandt, where the shore trends southward and seemed to form a bay, into which I proposed to conduct the ship'.[55] Flinders went ashore on Chasm Island with a few officers and men and, during their examination of the island they came upon a number of caves 'upon the walls of which I found rude drawings, made with charcoal and something like red paint upon the white ground of the rock. These drawings represented porpoises, turtle, kanguroos, and a human hand.'[56] This discovery was of very great interest as these were 'the first pictographs reported in Australia'.[57] It has since been shown that there are more than 2400 rock paintings on Groote Eylandt and Chasm Island. Many of these paintings are of fishing groups using both bark and dug-out canoes. Indeed, fishing has been found to be the 'principal subject depicted throughout the 45 galleries'. It is further of interest that the paintings depict 'hafted stone axes of Aboriginal type, and metal axes of both Indonesian and European types'.[58]

Flinders was to meet some Macassan visitors to the northern coast of Australia soon after this discovery. Flinders went on to complete his exploration of the coast of the gulf and, although he had missed the mouths of several rivers – which reach the sea via broad mud flats – it was clear that the gulf provides no entrance to the interior of *Terra Australis*. Not long afterwards, on 17 February 1803, they saw a canoe full of men and Flinders sent his brother to investigate. It was soon found that they had come upon a fleet of Macassan praus that was fishing for trepang for sale to China. These Macassan praus were sailing vessels with one outrigger. As Flinders wrote:[59]

> We learned that they were prows [praus] from Macassar, and the six Malay commanders shortly came on board in a canoe. It happened fortunately that my cook was a Malay, and through his means I was able to communicate with them. The chief of the six prows was a short, elderly man, named Pobassoo.

Flinders made them a number of gifts and named the area Malay Road. A nearby island was named Pobassoo Island.[60] Baudin had also come across a similar fleet of Macassan praus, and had managed to establish friendly terms with them. As already mentioned (page 29), the Macassans had been visiting Australian waters on fishing expeditions for several centuries.

HEALTH PROBLEMS

Flinders was now well aware that scurvy had become a problem. Indeed the surgeon reported that twenty-two men were showing symptoms of scurvy – 'spongy gums and livid sores on the legs' – and a few of these were unable to carry out normal duties. The ship's surgeon wrote that they had sailed from England more than nineteen months ago and that they had very little opportunity to obtain a varied diet. Even at Port Jackson 'the ships company had it not in their power to procure any animal food, and but few vegetables ... For the last eight months, we have had no refreshments but what chance threw in our way, and fruit and vegetables, the best antiscorbutics, formed no part of what was procured.'[61] Flinders himself had signs of scurvy – 'a lameness in both feet from incorrigible scorbutic

ulcers render me unable to go about any longer in boats, or to the mast head of the ship.'[62] He decided to sail first to Kupang – where he could send one of his officers to England to seek a new ship from the Admiralty to continue the survey – and then sail to Port Jackson. Before he arrived at Kupang, however, he found that many of the bottles of lime juice he had obtained at Port Jackson had broken – presumably from the pressure caused by natural fermentation. It was disappointing because Flinders had conserved a supply for the run to Port Jackson.

The *Investigator* arrived at Kupang on 31 March – but this was a disappointment. There was no suitable ship by which he could send an officer back to England to report to the Admiralty. Moreover, he found that very little food was available. Worst of all, however, many men went down with dysentery. Two men, including the Malay cook, deserted. Nevertheless Flinders carried out a search for the 'Trial Rocks' – which were supposed to be in the vicinity of Timor. He was able to show that they did not exist.

The increasing incidence of sickness, however, led to the decision to make all haste to Port Jackson. The *Investigator* reached Cape Leeuwin on 13 May. At this time there were fourteen men on the sick list.[63] Soon afterwards, the boatswain, Charles Douglas, died of 'fever and dysentery'. Several deaths followed as they raced towards Port Jackson, and the number on the sick list increased to eighteen. Two more men died just outside Port Jackson and were buried at sea. The *Investigator* came to anchor in the harbour on 9 June and eleven men were transferred to the hospital on shore. Peter Good the gardener, was too ill to move – and he died soon afterwards.[64] There were three more deaths, but the remainder recovered. The loss of Peter Good, was a serious one for the scientific work of the expedition. The record shows that he introduced 116 species of Australian plants to Kew Gardens, and 'all the best and rarest plants from that country, now at Kew, have his name attached to them.'[65]

THE END OF THE VOYAGE

At Port Jackson the *Investigator* was condemned as unfit for exploration. The Flinders expedition was effectively over and James Inman – who had come to Sydney with the chronometer K3, and who had expected to be the astronomer on the last part of the voyage – had no alternative but to seek a passage back to England. Flinders was determined to return to England himself and to seek another ship in which he could continue the examination of the Australian coastline. He therefore took passage, with some of his officers and men, in the *Porpoise* – accompanied by the *Bridgewater* and the *Cato*. The *Porpoise* and *Cato* were unfortunately wrecked on what became known as 'Wreck Reef' off the coast of Queensland, and the survivors set up camp on the sandbank, hoping for rescue. Flinders, with a few men, took the ship's cutter and sailed back to Sydney Cove to seek help. The governor reacted swiftly and sent two merchant ships to rescue the survivors. Flinders was given command of a 30-tonne vessel, the *Cumberland*, which he sailed to Wreck Reef to make sure the survivors were safely aboard the merchant ships, and then set off to sail to England to seek a ship to continue his exploration.

He called at Kupang and then sailed for the Cape of Good Hope, but decided to stop at Ile de France for food and water, and to effect some repairs – confident that his passport from the French government would ensure good treatment at this island. Unfortunately, the passport referred to the *Investigator* and not to the *Cumberland*, and this aroused suspicion that Flinders was seeking information on the island's defences. He was interned and held prisoner for seven years. He was eventually released, having signed a parole, and obtained a passage to the Cape of Good Hope. He arrived at Spithead on 24 October 1810, 'exactly four months and ten days after leaving Port Louis'[66] and 'absent from England nine years and three months, and nearly four years and a half without intelligence from any of my connexions'.[67]

7

PHILLIP PARKER KING
AND THE NORTHERN COASTS

When the charts prepared during the Baudin and Flinders expeditions were eventually published it was clear that almost the whole of the Australian coastline had been explored – but not quite all. Baudin had visited parts of the western coast, and had 'skirted the islands which front the North-West Coast, without landing upon, and indeed scarcely seeing, any part of the mainland'.[1] Flinders had intended to examine the northern and north-western coasts, but had been prevented from doing so by the fact that the *Investigator* had become unseaworthy. The colonial secretary (Earl Bathurst) felt that the exploration should be extended and Lieutenant Phillip Parker King, Royal Navy (RN), was selected to command the new expedition.

King had been born on Norfolk Island on 2 December 1791. His father, Captain Philip Gidley King, RN, was the superintendent of the settlement there, and later became the third governor of New South Wales – from 1800 to 1806. The young King was named after his two godfathers – Arthur Phillip, and Captain John Parker (of HMS *Gorgon*, which had arrived at Sydney Cove on 21 September 1791).[2]

The letter from the Admiralty to Lieutenant Phillip Parker King made the object of the proposed expedition clear:[3]

The principal object of your mission is to examine the hitherto unexplored Coasts of New South Wales, from Arnhem Bay, near the western entrance

of the Gulf of Carpentaria, westward and southward as far as the North-West Cape; including the opening, or deep bay called Van Diemen's Bay, and a cluster of islands called Rosemary Islands, and the inlets behind them, which should be minutely examined: and, indeed, all gulfs and openings should be the objects of particular attention, as the chief motive for your survey is to discover whether there be any river on that part of the coast likely to lead to an interior navigation into this great continent.

The same letter also mentioned that 'two young gentlemen' – Frederick Bedwell, 'a passed mate', and John Septimus Roe, 'an unpassed mate' – had been appointed 'to assist you in the care and use of the time-keepers and instruments' and 'to follow your orders'. A few days later King received a letter from Earl Bathurst which instructed him to receive on board Allan Cunningham – 'botanist now in New South Wales, who has received the orders of Sir Joseph Banks to attend you'. Cunningham had arrived at Port Jackson on 20 December 1816, when he was aged twenty-five. He was under instructions from Sir Joseph Banks and had travelled to Australia after spending some time botanising in Brazil. During the voyage he took the opportunity to learn the principles of navigation and how to take astronomical sights. Cunningham was entirely devoted to the advancement of botany. Everything he had done was in this cause. He had benefited from the support of Sir Joseph Banks and he was grateful. When he learnt Joseph Banks had died he found a letter from Banks waiting for him:[4]

I write you a short note because I am not well. I know of nothing more to say than that I entirely approve of the whole of your conduct, as does our worthy friend Aiton.

Cunningham was very deeply moved by this and in his next letter home he wrote:[5]

... it is the word of a dying nobleman, whose liberality had fallen alike on the just and unjust, whose kindness none of us can any more experience; and if, from a sight of it, I can from time to time call up the courteous spirit of its illustrious writer, to regulate my own frame of mind in the 'jostlings of the world', literally I shall be a happy man.

The kindness of Joseph Banks in writing to Cunningham as he did is even more notable when it is remembered that, during the last few years of his life, Banks was grossly overweight and in constant pain from gout. However, as Patrick O'Brian has written: 'in spite of his heavy, bull-like appearance and an expression that had by now taken on the cast of habitual pain or the expectation of pain, [Banks] was an unusually affectionate man.'[6]

In the custom of the day the earl completed his letter to the young lieutenant with 'I have the honour to be, Sir, Your most obedient, humble servant, Bathurst'.[7] King accepted this assignment with enthusiasm. He was supplied with a few books and other items to improve his background knowledge. First among these was Matthew Flinders' book, A Voyage to Terra Australis. He was also supplied with a copy of François Péron's account of the Baudin voyage and with a copy of John Arrowsmith's chart of the Indian and Pacific oceans. He was confident that he would be able to add considerable detail to the known outline of Australia (as it was now referred to, following the suggestion of Matthew Flinders).

King, his wife Harriet (née Lethbridge), and the two master's mates, Roe and Bedwell, travelled to Gravesend and embarked in the merchantman Dick,

which, with two other ships, had been hired by the government to convey the 74th Regiment to New South Wales. The Dick sailed on 13 February 1817 and, 199 days later, on 3 September 1817, came safely to anchor at Sydney Cove.

KING'S FIRST VOYAGE OF EXPLORATION

The governor, Lachlan Macquarie, had been instructed to provide King with a suitable vessel to carry out the proposed exploration, and to complete the work begun by Flinders. Two ships were available. One was the Lady Nelson, which had earlier been used for exploration, but which had been used as a collier for the last ten years. The other had recently been launched, but drew too much water and 'was in every other way unsuitable for my purpose', wrote King.[8] Fortunately, the Mermaid, an almost new cutter of 86 tonnes, arrived in Port Jackson from India. She was about 17 metres (56 feet) in length and, even when deep-laden, did not draw more than 2.75 metres (9 feet). She was clearly superior to the Lady Nelson – which, in any case, would require a major refit. The Mermaid was therefore purchased by the New South Wales government for use on the proposed exploration of the north and north-west coasts.

King sailed from Port Jackson on 22 December 1817. The two master's mates were with him, as was the botanist, Allan Cunningham. There were twelve seamen, two boys and an Aborigine named Bungaree (Bongaree, or Boongaree), who had earlier sailed with Flinders in the Norfolk. At that time of the year the north-westerly monsoon blows over the northern seas, and King therefore decided to sail to Bass Strait, and then westerly, intending to turn northwards when the Mermaid reached Cape Leeuwin. King touched at the Recherche Archipelago, and also spent several days at King George Sound – where he arrived on 20 January 1818. Cunningham was especially delighted with the plants that he found there, but King and the other officers were disappointed that they were unable to see any of the local Aboriginal people – despite the fact that they found evidence of their presence.

When King sailed from the sound he made for Cape Leeuwin. It was an uncomfortable passage, however, because nearly everyone in the ship had fever and diarrhoea. King believed that this epidemic was the result of overindulgence in shellfish during their time in the sound. The *Mermaid* turned to the north after passing Cape Leeuwin, and King set a course far from land to give everyone time to recover from the suspected food poisoning. When he reached the approximate latitude of the North West Cape, King set a course for the land, and hoped accurately to determine the position of the cape. Baudin had recorded a latitude of 21° 36' S. King recorded a latitude of 21° 48' 35" S; a modern determination gave its position as 21° 47' S, 114° 10' E. As the *Mermaid* approached the North-West Cape, King decided to continue towards the east and found himself in a bay or gulf. He carried out a survey of this gulf and decided to name it Exmouth Gulf after Viscount Exmouth who, as Admiral Sir Edward Pellew, had been King's commanding officer in the Napoleonic War.[9] King was not impressed by the adjacent country, however. 'The soil' he wrote, 'if such it can be called, is composed of red quartzose sand; but on the hills it contained also a small portion of earth, which gave it a strong resemblance to brick-dust.' [10]

The *Mermaid* sailed from Exmouth Gulf on 22 February 1818 and continued in a north-easterly direction through a maze of small islands. Later, a more impressive group of islands, which had been named the Dampier Archipelago, was encountered. King sought to identify Dampier's Rosemary Island and concluded that Dampier had actually landed on Malus Island. King explained that, from the direction in which Dampier saw it, Rosemary Island

appears to be joined to Malus Island – which would justify Dampier's conclusion that it was 'an island five or six leagues in length, and one in breadth'.[11] Nevertheless, King was incorrect in his deduction. It has now been established that Dampier landed on East Lewis Island – a little further south. Cook had named Endeavour Strait after his ship; and Flinders had named Investigator Strait. King decided to name the strait immediately south of East Lewis Island the Mermaid Strait, and it appears as such on the Admiralty chart published after his voyage.

It was in Mermaid Strait that King had an opportunity to meet the local Aboriginal people – but they spoke a language quite unlike that spoken by Bungaree, and he had to make do with sign language and presents. The island in Mermaid Strait where King met the Aborigines was named Interview Island, and the group of islands in the strait the Intercourse Islands.[12] King was fascinated with the Dampier Archipelago. He gave the name Courtenay Head to the north-eastern cape of Baudin's Malus Island, and the island further to the north became Gidley Island. Further to the east, the *Mermaid* anchored overnight near Depuch Island – which the French had originally named Ile des Amiraux. King did not examine it, however, and did not see the Aboriginal art for which the site is now well known.

The *Mermaid* sailed from Depuch Island on 6 March 1818,[13] and made for an area that the French had named the Géographe Shoals. He located this area and determined the latitude and longitude – but his longitude was not as accurate as is desirable for marking a hazard on a chart. King recorded 20° 16' 45" S, 118° 18' E; but a modern determination gave 20° 16' S, 117° 55' E.[14] King now decided to make a detour – to locate the reef that had been discovered by Captain Sir Josias Rowley in HMS *Imperieuse* in 1800. This was a substantial detour but the reef was located 'just before sunset on 14 March'[15] and King was able to examine the reef on the following day. He determined its position to be 17° 31' 24" S, 118° 50' 30" E – which was reasonably accurate bearing in mind that his chronometer had not been checked since King George Sound.[16] A modern determination gave 17° 35' S, 118° 55' E.[17] To the north-east of this shoal (which is known as Imperieuse Reef) King investigated two further shoals. The closer one he named Clerke Reef – after the whaler captain who first reported its existence. The further reef he named after the *Mermaid*, and the three together became Rowley's Shoals – after the naval captain who discovered the southernmost one.

The westerly monsoon was now nearly over and King prepared to sail out of sight of land, to Arnhem Bay (which has a longitude of 136° 10' E) and, from there, to sail westwards while making a running survey of the coast. However, as Hordern has pointed out:[18]

King's plan to sail to Arnhem Bay, on the tail of the north-west monsoon came to an end two hundred miles short of it when the wind swung against him. He conceded defeat with the comment 'the westerly monsoon is over and will not permit me to reach Arnhem Bay'.

There was no alternative and he decided to reverse his course when he was close to a small point of land just over two degrees of longitude to the west of Arnhem Bay which he named Braithwaite Point – after Admiral R. Braithwaite. He sailed westwards and soon discovered and named South Goulburn and North Goulburn Islands (named in honour of Henry Goulburn, the under-secretary of state for the Colonies). The strait between South Goulburn Island and the mainland was named Macquarie Strait, and the hills to the south, on the mainland, became Wellington Range. A small island in Macquarie Strait was named after Dr Sims, the editor of the *Botanical Magazine*, at the request of Allan Cunningham, who found the plants there of special interest.[19]

At this time King was concerned about the aggressive nature of the local Aborigines, and by the Macassans in their praus – who were also inclined to want to attack the explorers. At one stage there was a fleet of fifteen praus. However, King managed to avoid a serious conflict and continued to sail westwards. He discovered and named Croker Island after John Croker, the First Secretary at the Admiralty. Soon afterwards, the *Mermaid* approached a splendid peninsula – which King promptly named the Cobourg Peninsula after HRH Prince Leopold of Saxe Cobourg.[20] Even more important, however, was his discovery of the great expanse of sheltered water – which he named Port Essington after Vice-Admiral Sir William Essington, who had been instrumental in obtaining a pension for King's mother after the death of his father, Philip Gidley King.[21]

King then examined (as his instructions required) Van Diemen Gulf. He found an opening, which turned out to be the mouth of a river, but with a sandbar at the entrance. King, Cunningham, and Roe took a whale boat up the river for 58 kilometres (36 miles), but King was not impressed by the country which was:[22]

... a low level plain, the monotony of which was occasionally relieved by a few wooded hills, and some groups of trees, among which the palm tree was conspicuous, and tended in a triffling degree to improve the view, which, to say the best of it, was unvaried and heavy.

The river was also disappointing – because it soon became very shallow. Its main interest was that it contained many crocodiles – which King believed to be alligators. He therefore named it the Alligator River. Continuing, King sailed to the south-west and soon found the mouth of another river, and this time there was no bar. King, with Roe and Cunningham, again set off to explore this new river in the whale boat. When they were 64 kilometres (40 miles) from its mouth, the river was still 140 metres (150 yards) wide – but the depth was only 4.6 metres. It was clearly useless as a waterway into the centre of the continent – even for small vessels such as the *Mermaid*.[23] This river also had many crocodiles swimming about. It was clear that the earlier discovery should be renamed the East Alligator River and that the new discovery should be named the South Alligator River. King continued to explore the gulf to the west and discovered yet another river teeming with crocodiles, which he named the West Alligator River.

The *Mermaid* sailed from Van Diemen Gulf on 13 May 1818 via the Dundas Strait (which Pieter Pieterszoon had discovered in 1636) and then sailed towards the west along the coast of what we now know as Melville Island. During this time he named Lethbridge Bay after his father-in-law, Christopher Lethbridge. Further to the west he named Apsley Bay. During his passage along the coast he believed that he was sailing along the northern coast of the continent of Australia. After all, the *Chart of Terra Australis*, which Flinders had published, showed Cape Van Diemen on the northern coast of the continent. As he progressed to the west, King discovered an opening at the southern end of Apsley Bay and he naturally believed – or hoped – that he had discovered the long-sought-for river which would lead him into the heart of the continent. He sailed into this opening and then southwards in what he named Apsley Strait. He soon found, however, that this was not a river leading him into the centre of the continent – but a strait, dividing two islands which are entirely separate from continental Australia. The larger island was named Melville Island after the First Lord of the Admiralty. The smaller one was named Bathurst Island after the secretary of state for the Colonies – who had ordered the exploration of these coasts. The strait to the south of Melville Island became Clarence Strait – after the Duke of Clarence, who later became King William IV. Cape Van Diemen was then recognised as the north-western cape of Melville Island.[24]

King circumnavigated Bathurst Island and had several opportunities to meet some of the Aboriginal people of both islands. They are the Tiwi people – who differ significantly from the Aboriginal people on the adjacent mainland. By this time the ship's provisions were almost exhausted and, as King wrote, 'we had only a sufficiency of bread to carry us back to Port Jackson, although we had been all the voyage upon a reduced allowance'.[25] Drinking water was also a problem as a number of casks were found to be empty, and some had been made from staves of salt-provision casks. King therefore had no alternative – the ship would have to proceed to Kupang, in Timor, to obtain meat, vegetables, firewood and water. Kupang was not a large settlement at that time. King's *Narrative* has a footnote to the effect that de Freycinet had estimated the population to be 1500 – of whom 1000 were slaves and 300 were Chinese. King was able to purchase most of the provisions he required, but he was dismayed at the prices – 'a small mountain sheep, weighing from twelve to twenty pounds, cost five shillings' and 'fowls were from four-pence to five-pence each'; and he had 'much difficulty for want of money'.[26]

As soon as the provisioning was completed, the *Mermaid* sailed again for the north-west coast. But, on the way, King wanted to search for Tryal Rocks. In 1622, the *Tryal* had been wrecked on some uncharted rocks in latitude 20° 10' S, 'somewhere west of Java' – and the survivors had reached Batavia by boat. These uncharted rocks had been a worry to mariners ever since. King began his search for Tryal Rocks and, when the lookout reported a breaker, he thought that he had located them. But no further foam appeared and King concluded that the lookout had seen the spout of a whale. He marked the spot 'doubtful' on his chart. King did not know that, only five months before the *Mermaid* arrived in the vicinity, Lieutenant Ritchie, in the *Greyhound*, had discovered some rocks that he had named Ritchie's Reef. Much later, in 1935, it was shown that Ritchie's Reef and Tryal Rocks are one and the same.

On 20 June they came in sight of land. The French explorer Freycinet had seen land in this position and had concluded that it was part of the continent, but King was able to prove that it is an island. He named it Barrow Island after John Barrow – 'one of the Secretaries of the Admiralty'.[27]

By this time, several members of the crew of the *Mermaid* had contracted dysentery, as a result of their stay in Timor, and 'at one time the disease wore a very alarming appearance.' In Bass Strait one of the patients later died[28] and King decided that his voyage of exploration was over. From Bass Strait he set course to Port Jackson and anchored safely in Sydney Cove on 29 July 1818. The *Mermaid* had been absent from Port Jackson for thirty-one weeks and three days. With the help of the two master's mates, Roe and Bedwell, and other members of the crew, King had:[29]

> ... discovered Exmouth Gulf, explored Dampier's Archipelago, Van Diemen's Bay and a large extent of Australia's unknown coast. He had found some promising harbours, determined the insularity of Bathurst and Melville islands and gained considerable information concerning the Aboriginals and the Malays.

In addition, Allan Cunningham, the botanist, had made a collection of 300 plants and seeds. King had also discovered the East, South and West Alligator rivers, and Port Essington.[30] King did not discover Port Darwin, however. It was discovered in 1839 by Lieutenant John Lort Stokes in the *Beagle* – who named it after the great naturalist Charles Darwin. Stokes also discovered and named the Victoria River, and explored it far upstream.[31]

MACQUARIE HARBOUR

The *Mermaid* was now in need of a thorough refit. She had been taking in far too much water, and many fittings needed replacement or repair. Most of this work was supervised by the master's mates – Roe and Bedwell. While the work was in progress

King transferred to his home, Rosehill Cottage, in Parramatta, where he busied himself writing his narrative and perfecting his charts. By the time that the refit was concluded, the year 1818 was drawing to a close. King was anxious to return to the north-west coast, but he knew that the weather in the tropics at that time of the year would be unsuitable for exploration. He needed a project that could occupy the *Mermaid* for a few months. The charting of Macquarie Harbour on the western coast of Van Diemen's Land was such a task.

The harbour had been discovered in 1815 by a young whaling captain, James Kelly, but it was desirable to prepare a detailed chart of it, and particularly of the entrance to the harbour – which became known as Hell's Gates.[32] Phillip King and the *Mermaid* left Port Jackson in December 1818,[33] surveyed the west coast of Van Diemen's Land, including Macquarie Harbour, and returned to Port Jackson in mid February 1819.

KING'S SECOND VOYAGE TO THE NORTH-WEST

King now planned to complete the exploration of the northern and north-western coast of Australia which he (and Flinders before him) had begun. Governor Macquarie supported King's project, but also wished him to survey Port Macquarie during his passage to the north. Port Macquarie – 440 kilometres to the north of Port Jackson, and at the mouth of the Hastings River – had been discovered by Surveyor-General John Oxley. Oxley had travelled inland, hoping to find the fabled 'inland sea', but had been defeated by the Macquarie Marshes. John Oxley and the *Lady Nelson* were added to the expedition, but were required to return to Port Jackson after King and Oxley had evaluated the suitability of Port Macquarie as the site for a further convict settlement. Their report was favourable, and a penal settlement was soon established there. Oxley's association with Port Macquarie is commemorated by the Oxley Highway which runs westerly and then north-westerly from Port Macquarie to join the New England Highway.

The *Mermaid* sailed from Port Macquarie on 21 May 1819, and arrived at Cape Conway, at the entrance to the Whitsunday Passage, on 9 June. King, Cunningham, and Roe landed on the coast a short distance to the north of this cape to take meridional observations. The *Mermaid* continued northwards through the Whitsunday Passage, and Cook's chart was refined. Further north, near Goold Island,[34] a few Aboriginal men approached the *Mermaid* in small canoes which were 'generally too small for two people'.[35] In the evening the officers returned the compliment and visited the Aboriginal settlement. The tribe consisted of fifteen males — two of whom 'were old and decrepit, and one of these was reduced to a perfect skeleton by ulcerated sores on his legs, that had eaten away the flesh, and left large portions of the bone bare'.[36] King also noted that 'no teeth were deficient in their jaws'.

During this passage to the north, Allan Cunningham continued to study the plants, and to collect suitable specimens. He also observed that the Aboriginal people used ovens that were similar to those used by the natives of Tahiti.[37] On 26 June, in the vicinity of Cook's Weary Bay, south of the modern Cooktown, Bedwell found a canoe 'which, being hollowed out of the trunk of a tree, was very different construction to any we had before seen'. It was 6.4 metres (21 feet) long, and was fitted with an outrigger. It was quite unlike any of the simple bark 'canoes' usually used by the Aboriginal people of Australia — but was doubtless similar to those used by the Macassans.[38] If so, how did it come to be so far south?

On 27 June 1819 the *Mermaid* arrived at the mouth of the Endeavour River and by noon:[39]

> ... she was secured to the shore, within ten feet of a steep beach on the south side of the entrance; in all probability the very same spot that Captain Cook landed his stores upon forty-nine years ago.

King wanted his men to start work on the construction of a whale boat — using the spare frame that had been supplied for this purpose. But, before doing so, he took the precaution of burning the nearby grass. He was aware that, when Cook was at Endeavour River, the local Aborigines had set fire to the grass near the *Endeavour* 'in a fit of rage, at not being allowed to take away some turtles that were lying on the ship's deck'.[40] It seems likely that the Aborigines thought that they owned the land and that the turtles also belonged to them. In the event, many of the *Endeavour*'s stores and sails had been destroyed. King knew that he would have to keep his eyes open for trouble with these Aborigines. As he recorded, 'every thing was done by our people to amuse and keep them in good humour.'[41] Cunningham was also a worry to King — because he liked to go off on his own to collect botanical specimens. Before long, King had assigned a man to go with Cunningham as a safety measure, and when the master's mate, Roe, was asked to explore Endeavour River using the ship's boat, Cunningham went with him.

The *Mermaid* put to sea again on 12 July 1818, and King took the opportunity to explore Princess Charlotte Bay and the Flinders group of islands — which had been discovered and named in 1815 by Lieutenant Charles Jeffreys, RN, when sailing, inside the Great Barrier Reef, from Port Jackson to Ceylon, in the armed brig *Kangaroo*.[42] Still further north, King had to negotiate the hazardous Torres Strait. Flinders had sailed north of Wednesday Island and north of Hammond Island. However, because certain soundings had not been recorded — between Mount Adolphus Island (which is at 10° 38' S, 142° 39' E) and Wednesday Island (that is, in the Adolphus Channel) — King decided to take the same route and to remedy this omission. However, before doing so, he circumnavigated Mount Adolphus Island in the ship's boat. He then set a course for the north-east point of Wednesday Island. As the ship approached this island they 'narrowly escaped striking upon some rocks, two of which were seen about fifty yards off our lee bow'.[43]

After reaching the north-east point of Wednesday Island the *Mermaid* sailed westwards along its northern coast, and along the northern coast of Hammond Island, and arrived safely at Goode Island where, in attempting to anchor, the bower anchor was broken. King recorded that it was 'badly wrought' and 'made in Port Jackson'.[44] This was the second of his bower anchors to break. The *Mermaid* sailed westwards to Booby Island – which King described as 'a mere rock, the retreat of boobies and turtles'. He added that this island 'was so entirely covered with the excrement of birds, that it had the appearance of being white-washed'.[45] The island had been named by Cook, and the same name had been used by Bligh.

King was now safely through Torres Strait, and he had effectively confirmed Flinders' belief that a ship under sail might readily reduce the sailing time from the Pacific to India by four to six weeks.[46] However, he conceded that it involved sailing in hazardous seas and through what became known as the 'Prince of Wales Channel'.

From Booby Island, King set a course across the Gulf of Carpentaria to Cape Arnhem, and was now determined to complete his survey of the northern coast of Arnhem Land. After crossing the gulf, King recorded that 'no incident occurred of sufficient interest to be worth recording.'[47] On 27 July 1819 the *Mermaid* arrived at the Wessel Islands – discovered in 1623 by van Colster in the *Arnhem*. The *Mermaid* sailed down the western coast of the most northerly island of the group and, at noon, reached the opening through which Flinders had sailed further to the west in the *Cumberland*. King named this Cumberland Strait. He continued to sail to the south-west and discovered a group of islands to the south and west of the Wessel Islands. The strait between these two groups of islands was named Brown Strait 'after my friend, Robert Brown, Esq., the profound botanist' of the Flinders voyage.[48]

Sailing on, the *Mermaid* arrived at a bay that King named Castlereagh Bay after Viscount Castlereagh – who was the secretary of state for the Foreign Department. With some difficulty, King avoided the hazards in this bay and, shortly afterwards, observed the mouth of a river. It looked promising, and King, with Bedwell and Cunningham, and a suitable crew, took off to examine the river. It was disappointing, however. They were not impressed by the country that they saw. The Aboriginal people whom they encountered were clearly unfriendly and, worst of all, mosquitoes were present in large numbers.[49] Nevertheless, King named it the Liverpool River after Lord Liverpool – the secretary of the Treasury. King and his party explored the river for 65 kilometres upstream, and found that it was infested with crocodiles:[50]

> Upon seeing these monsters, we congratulated ourselves on our escape, for had we known of their existence in this river before we passed the night on its bank, the danger of being surprised by the natives, and the stings of the mosquitoes, would have dwindled into insignificance, in comparison with the presence of such voracious animals.

The *Mermaid* now sailed westwards along the northern coast and came to a bay, the north-western point of which was recognised as Braithwaite Point – the point where, in the previous year, King had commenced his exploration to the west. King therefore named it Junction Bay – but he did not explore it because he was convinced that, as no great river entered it,[51] it could be of no great interest. The *Mermaid* sailed on and reached South Goulburn Island on 7 August, and again anchored in South-West Bay.[52]

By this time the expedition was very short of water and King went on shore 'to examine whether water could be obtained'.[53] They were successful and 'a basin was dug to receive the water that drained through the cliffs; but from the advanced state of the dry season, it did not flow in half the quantity that it did last year.' But when Bedwell, with a watering party, went to the shore the next morning, he found that the tide had reached the hole 'and spoilt what had been collected during the night.' With perseverance, they were able to collect some water fit to drink – but the Aborigines pelted them with large stones and dispersed only when muskets were fired over their heads.[54] A few days later Bedwell went to the adjacent Sims Island – which King had named. Bedwell's object was to obtain a few turtles, but he came upon a grave – the burial site for a Macassan who had visited this coast. The nature of the grave suggested that the dead man had been of some importance. Bedwell noticed that some of the bones of the body had been removed, and King later wrote in his narrative:[55]

> I cannot account for the absence of many of the bones of the skeleton, unless the natives are cannibals, of which we have hitherto neither had proofs, nor entertained the least suspicion; dogs or birds may certainly have carried them off, or the natives themselves may have removed them as trophies.

By this time most of those on board the *Mermaid* were suffering from the humid heat. Cunningham was suffering from 'jaundice', 'loss of blood' and 'laxative medicines'. As he wrote: 'I now present myself to my messmates a saffron dyed being with a "green and yellow melancholy" depicted on my sallow countenance.'[56] Cunningham was by no means the only man on the sick list, however. A few weeks later, on 30 September 1819, King recorded:[57]

> We were now very weak-handed; three men, besides Mr. Bedwell who was still an invalid, being ill, considerably reduced our strength; insomuch that being underweigh night and day, with only one spare man of the watch to relieve the mast-head look-out, the lead, and the helm, there was great reason to fear the fatigue would very much increase the number of complaints. Since leaving Port Jackson we had never been free from sickness, but it was confined principally to two or three

individuals, who were not able to endure the very great heat.

The *Mermaid* sailed from the Goulburn Islands on 18 August 1819 and, on the following day, passed Port Essington. King sailed westwards along the northern coast of Melville Island, and then south-wards along the coast of Bathurst Island. By so doing, King missed seeing the gulf (Port Darwin) where the city of Darwin now stands. On 1 September the *Mermaid* reached the vicinity of Péron Island – so named by Baudin. The peak of Péron Island was found (by the French) to be in a longitude of 127° 34' 36" E, and King's longitude for this feature differed by only 6' 24". King was able to show, however, that Péron Island is two islands – Péron Island North and Péron Island South.[58] The bay to the south and east of the two islands was named Anson Bay – after Lord Anson. Further south, the French explorers had reported the existence of the Barthelemy Islands – but Baudin must have been too far from the shore because King found that they are not islands, but hills. He therefore renamed them the Barthelemy Hills.[59] On 29 September they named Cambridge Gulf in honour of HRH the Viceroy of Hanover.[60]

By 1 October 1819 the *Mermaid* had reached that part of the north-west coast which 'excepting a few of the islands that front it, the French expedition did not see'; but King's satisfaction with their progress was dulled by the fact that they were 'rapidly consuming' their stock of water 'without any prospect of finding a supply at this season'.[61] Nevertheless they continued, and discovered the Eclipse Islands – which were so named because there was an eclipse of the Moon that evening. To the south of these islands they named Vansittart Bay (after the chancellor of the exchequer). Roe and Cunningham explored this bay on 12 October, and as King wrote:[62]

> During the absence of the boat, the state of our provisions and water was examined, on both of which, as we had anticipated, the rats had made

considerable havoc; two of the casks were quite empty, from holes gnawed by these animals to get at the water.

The amount of water remaining was sufficient for two weeks only. Moreover, several of the crew had developed scurvy.[63] Nevertheless, they continued through a maze of islands towards the Bonaparte Archipelago. According to King, 'the plan given by M. de Freycinet [who drew the charts of the Baudin voyage] of this Archipelago is so defective, that many of his islands could not be recognised.' King went on to say that 'In the space between Cape Bougain-ville and Cape Voltaire, which was named the Admiralty Gulf, we have given the positions of at least forty islands or islets.'[64]

On the next day King decided to abandon the exploration of the archipelago and to make for the Dutch East Indies, and then to return to Port Jackson. No water was to be had at Savu, so King sailed for Kupang in Timor, where a few days sufficed to provide the *Mermaid* with food and water. King sailed from Kupang on 9 November and the *Mermaid* reached Lady Julia Percy Island (off Port-land, Victoria) on 27 December. King wrote that this island 'is incorrectly laid down in Captain Flinders' chart owing to the very unfavourable weather which he experienced in passing this part of the coast'.[65] The *Mermaid* entered Bass Strait on the afternoon of 2 January 1820, and arrived at Port Jackson on 'the morning of the 12th, having been absent thirty-five weeks, and four days'.[66] King went on to write:[67]

> The result of our proceedings during this voyage, has been the survey of 540 miles of the northern coast, in addition to the 500 that were previously examined. Besides which we had made a running survey of that portion of the east coast, that is situated between the Percy Isles and Torres Strait; a distance of 900 miles; the detailed survey of which had never before been made, for Captain Cook merely examined it in a cursory manner as he passed up the coast. The opportunity, therefore, was not lost of making such observations on our voyage as enabled me to present to the public a route

towards Torres Strait infinitely preferable on every account to the dangerous navigation without the reefs, which has hitherto been chiefly used.

Before the *Mermaid* could leave Port Jackson on her third voyage it was necessary to fit a new copper bottom and to effect a few other repairs. It was also hoped to destroy the many rats and cockroaches that infested the ship. After the coppering had been completed the ship was 'immersed in water for several days' in the expectation that the pests would be destroyed.[68] Many of them probably were destroyed, but the problem was not solved. Even before they sailed from Port Jackson the ship was again infested with rats and, when the *Mermaid* reached a warmer climate, the many cockroach eggs in the recesses and cracks in the timbers were hatched – and the ship was again infested.

KING'S THIRD VOYAGE TO THE NORTH-WEST

Only two crew members elected to continue in the *Mermaid* and it was nearly a month before a new crew could be signed on. The good news, however, was that James Hunter, a naval surgeon, had volunteered his services. The *Mermaid* sailed from Port Jackson on 14 June 1820, but ran into a severe gale and suffered so much damage that she had to return to port. Repairs were made and she sailed again on 13 July and followed the coast towards the north. King and some officers and men were able to make a number of landings to meet groups of Aboriginal people. The *Mermaid* arrived at the mouth of the Endeavour River, where King was able to meet another group of Aborigines. He prepared a brief vocabulary to compare with that which Cook had obtained at the same location. King also took the opportunity to determine the latitude and longitude of this site with as much precision as possible. His results were 15° 27' 04" S, 145° 10' 40" E. Modern determinations give 15° 28' S, 145° 15" E.[69]

Continuing, the *Mermaid* sailed northwards in Princess Charlotte Bay, and entered Torres Strait. King decided to sail through Endeavour Strait (Cook's route) and anchored for the night at Possession Island. Next day he sailed to Booby Island where they obtained a number of turtles and about 1000 eggs. Further west he came to Braithwaite Point, then South Goulburn Island, and then to Bonaparte Archipelago. Montague Sound, to the south of the Bonaparte Archipelago, was named after Robert Montague, Admiral of the White,[70] at the request of the ship's doctor. Further south, the Roe River (which flows into Prince Frederic Harbour) was named after the father of King's junior officer. Prince Frederic Harbour and York Sound (to the north-west of Prince Frederic Harbour) were named after the Duke of York.[71] Modern maps give Frederic as Frederick.

It seems that the ship's bottom had been damaged during the early part of this voyage because, at Booby Island, the *Mermaid* was found to be 'leaky'. The leak became progressively worse and, by mid September, it was clear that the *Mermaid* would have to be beached – that is, careened – for repairs to be undertaken. The problem now was to find a suitable beach. King recorded that 'the beaches in York Sound and Prince Frederic's Harbour were too steep' to be used. But, after a search, King found a convenient place 'at the bottom of the port in which we had anchored' and they then landed 'on the sandy beach of a bay which, to my inexpressible satisfaction, was found in every way suitable for the object we had in view'.[72] King referred to this bay as Careening Bay. He determined its position to be 15° 06' 18" S, 125° 11' 24" E,[73] and he prepared an excellent sketch of the bay, with the *Mermaid* beached on the sand.

The *Mermaid* was beached in such a position that she could be floated at a high spring tide – and the repairs were carried out. On 5 October 'after two ineffectual attempts to heave the cutter off the ground, she floated; and, by the 8th, everything

being embarked, we made preparations to quit this place.'[74]

King returned to Port Jackson so that the ship could be properly inspected and, when the *Mermaid* was laid up on the beach at Sydney Cove, it was found that the ship's bottom was so damaged that only the copper sheathing had ensured their safe return. Governor Macquarie decided to purchase another vessel to allow King to complete his exploration of the coast. A suitable vessel, of 170 tonnes, built of teak, was accordingly purchased and named the *Bathurst*, and officers and crew were appointed. Frederick Bedwell and John Roe continued as master's mates and assistant surveyors, and Perceval Baskerville, a midshipman, was added to the complement. Hunter, the doctor on the previous voyage, was no longer available, but Andrew Montgomery, who had recently arrived after serving as medical officer in a convict ship, was appointed. Allan Cunningham was again appointed botanist-collector. A further twenty-one men and five boys completed the crew. In addition, there was an Aboriginal volunteer, Bundell, who succeeded Bungaree.

The *Bathurst* sailed from Port Jackson on 26 May 1821, and was accompanied by the *Dick*, a merchant ship on her way to Batavia (Jakarta). Three days later a young girl, aged fourteen, was found to be a stowaway in the *Bathurst*. It was not possible to put her ashore and she had to continue with the expedition.

On their way to the north, the ships anchored at Clack Island – an island in the Flinders Group in Princess Charlotte Bay. It was here that Cunningham discovered a cave 'upon the roof and sides of which some curious drawings were observed ... They represented tolerable figures of sharks, porpoises, turtles, lizards ... trepang, star-fish, clubs, canoes, water gourds, and some quadrupeds.' King added:[75]

As this is the first specimen of Australian taste in the fine arts that we have detected in these voyages,

Phillip Parker King was given the command of the *Mermaid* to explore 'that part of the coast of New Holland ... not surveyed or examined by the late Captain Flinders'; reproduced from King 1827, vol. 1. (Royal Geographical Society of South Australia)

it became me to make a particular observation thereon: Captain Flinders had discovered figures on Chasm Island, in the Gulf of Carpentaria, formed with a burnt stick; but this performance, exceeding a hundred and fifty figures, which must have occupied much time, appears to be one step nearer refinement than those simply executed with a piece of charred wood.

On 1 July the *Bathurst* sailed past Cape York, rounded the northern shores of Wednesday Island, passed Booby Island and made for Cape Wessel. On 8 July, Cape Van Diemen was sighted. Letters to England were taken on board the *Dick* – which parted company on her way home. The *Bathurst* then sailed to Careening Bay – that is, to the site where they had repaired the *Mermaid* – and anchored almost a kilometre (about half a mile) from the beach. King and others then explored the area and, in particular, examined the Prince Regent River (which flows into St George Basin). This area

is now known as the Prince Regent Native Reserve and is designated as a 'World Biosphere Reserve'. It has a large population of saltwater crocodiles. The carvings on the trunk of a large boab tree on the shore of Careening Bay – made by members of the *Mermaid* – are still to be seen.[76] During the exploration of this area a party went to Hanover Bay, a few kilometres west of Careening Bay, and examined the adjacent land. During this expedition an Aboriginal man speared the doctor, Andrew Montgomery. Although the spear penetrated for nearly 8 centimetres, he was out of danger in a few days. King reported that the Aboriginal men in the Hanover Bay area did not have one of their front teeth knocked out as had been observed of the Aboriginal people living further east.[77]

At this time the wind 'blew constantly from the S.W., or from some other southern direction, and caused our progress to be very slow and tedious'. Moreover, he wrote:[78]

... our water was also nearly expended, and our provisions, generally, were in a very bad state; besides which, the want of a second anchor was so much felt, that we dared not venture into any difficulty where the appearance of the place invited a particular investigation.

King decided that the best plan would be to sail the *Bathurst* to Mauritius for extensive repairs. This island was now a British colony, after its French occupation for many years. After twenty-five days she arrived at Port Louis on 22 September 1821. The refit completed, the *Bathurst* sailed on 15 November and made for King George Sound. On this occasion King had no difficulty in finding the Aboriginal people of this district and he examined their weapons and studied the local language. He later wrote that the 'natives of King George Sound are the only Indians that we have seen clothed; and these wear a mantle of Kangaroo Skin over their bodies, leaving the right arm free.' He added that, generally speaking, the Aborigines of Australia 'justly despise' articles of clothing 'on account of the warmth of their climate'; but:[79]

... at King George's Sound they were happy to receive any thing which they could use as clothing. The demand, however, at this place is only of late date; for Captain Flinders found all his presents to these people thrown away, and left upon the bushes near his tents.

There was one further coast that King especially wished to explore. 'Swan River and Rottnest Island,' he wrote, 'had been already carefully examined by the French; but from the latter island to the North-West Cape, with the exception of Shark's Bay, they saw very little of the coast.'[80] So he sailed to Rottnest Island to begin a survey of this neglected coast and anchored there on 13 January 1822. Rottnest Island had first been described in 1658 by Samuel Volckerts – a Dutch skipper from Batavia.[81] Some years later, in 1696, it was seen, and named 'Rottnest', by the Dutch explorer Willem de Vlamingh – the captain of the *Geelvinck*.[82]

King then sailed to the Houtman Abrolhos, and to the mainland coast, and then northwards to Shark Bay. The ship was immediately surrounded by sharks 'which at once impressed us with the propriety of Dampier's nomenclature'.[83] The following morning a party landed at Cape Inscription – the northernmost point of Dirk Hartog Island. They were eager to examine the 'interesting memorials' that had been nailed to a post there (the Dirk Hartog and Vlamingh plates). They found 'to our great mortification, that they had been removed.' The *Bathurst* remained in Shark Bay for a few days, during which they were able to catch fish. They then sailed, and 'passed outside' Dorre and Bernier islands and continued northwards, naming suitable features. Cunningham persuaded Captain King to name Point Anderson after William Anderson of the Apothecaries Garden at Chelsea (London). It is now one of the features of the Ningaloo Marine Park. King then sailed to Barrow Island, and to the Montebello Islands, and then north-eastward to Cape Lévèque – so named by Baudin after Pierre Lévèque, the French hydrographer. Turning to the south, King came to Cygnet Bay and to a point that he named 'after my friend Mr Cunningham, to whose indefatigable zeal the scientific world is considerably indebted for the very extensive and valuable botanical collection that has been formed on this voyage'.[84] The next day Master's Mate Roe obtained an 'indifferent meridian altitude' to give a latitude of 16° 40' 18" S. It was an extremely hot day; but the meridian altitude was not very indifferent.[85] Modern determinations place Cape Cunningham at 16° 42' S, 123° 08' E. The weather became 'so unfavourable for our doing any good upon the coast, as well as increasing the danger of navigating among reefs and islands, where the tides were so strong' that King 'very unwillingly determined upon leaving the coast, and returning immediately to Port Jackson'.[86]

King sailed southwards, turned at Cape Leeuwin and passed through Bass Strait to Cape Howe. There, the *Bathurst* fell in with a merchant brig on her way from Port Jackson to Van Diemen's Land – from which they learnt that King had been elevated to the rank of commander and that the two master's mates – Bedwell and Roe – had been promoted to lieutenant. The *Bathurst* arrived at Sydney Cove on 25 April 1822, after an absence, on this expedition, of 344 days.[87]

THE EXPLORER AND THE MAN

Phillip Parker King made a major contribution to the elucidation of the Australian coastline, and deserves to be better recognised. Many Australians have never heard of him, but Geoffrey Ingleton has referred to him as 'the greatest of the early Australian marine surveyors', and has expressed the view that King's charts, 'although not numerous, were of a quality not attained by any previous navigator in the Pacific'.[88] He seems to have been more appreciated by the English than by the Australians of the time. He was nominated for fellowship of the Royal Society by eighteen sponsors, and was elected on 26 February 1824. A few weeks later he was elected to the Linnaean Society. It is to be noted that King's ships had a remarkably good health record for the time – 'two deaths in six years'. And 'he never did stain his record with the blood of Aboriginals.'[89]

In view of King's record as an explorer it is remarkable that, until recently, there has been no full-length biography of Phillip Parker King – a deficiency that has been remedied by the publication of *King of the Australian Coast* by Marsden Hordern, who commanded a Royal Australian Navy patrol boat during World War II, and who has personal experience of New Guinea waters.

At the conclusion of his last exploration of the north-west coast, King received his orders from the

Admiralty to return to England with the *Bathurst*. Before he could do so, however, it was necessary to carry out a number of repairs to his ship. It was 25 September before the *Bathurst* sailed, and the prevailing stormy weather to the north of Port Jackson persuaded him to set a course via Van Diemen's Land. This was fortunate because he was able to improve the charts of the coast as prepared by Flinders, d'Entrecasteaux and Baudin. King then sailed westwards, called at King George Sound, and at the Cape of Good Hope, and arrived at Plymouth Sound on 23 April 1823. He had been on overseas duty for more than six years. He died in 1856 as a rear admiral.

Two of King's men deserve special mention. John Septimus Roe, King's 'zealous and diligent assistant' was later appointed the first surveyor-general of Western Australia, and he 'held the post for forty-two years'. His contributions were such that, when he died in 1878, he was given a public funeral.[90] Allan Cunningham continued his work as a botanical explorer and was 'held in the highest regard by men as distinguished as Robert Brown in England and Phillip Parker King in Australia'.[91]

It must not be supposed, however, that the survey of the Australian coastline was now complete. Many later coastal surveyors have added to the information gathered by the early explorers, and the coastal surveys will never be finished.

In contrast, the exploration of inland Australia had hardly begun. But King was confident that it would be achieved. He wrote:[92]

> The examination of its vast interior can only be performed by degrees: want of navigable rivers will naturally impede such a task, but all these difficulties will be gradually overcome by the indefatigable zeal of our countrymen, of whose researches in all parts of the world the present times teem with such numerous examples.

8

THE BREAKOUT –
EXPLORING THE LAND

By about 1810 the outlines of the Australian continent had been determined and roughly charted. Many considerable features had been missed by the maritime surveyors – Cambridge Gulf and the Victoria River for example – but the configuration of the coastline had been established. By contrast, little was known of the land either adjacent to the sea or inland. The refinement of coastal charts continued to the present day, and is still in train. But, from early in the nineteenth century, explorers turned away from the coast and towards the interior.

In part, this reflected natural curiosity. In part, it reflected a realisation that land communications between coastal centres would be needed. But inland exploration was also driven by the search for pastoral and agricultural land, for forest resources and for minerals.

THE BREAKOUT FROM SYDNEY

The *Supply*, with Governor Phillip, had entered Port Jackson on Friday 25 January 1788 and had anchored in Sydney Cove – which Phillip had selected as the site for the settlement during his reconnaissance of Port Jackson a few days before. They had raised the Union Flag (of England and Scotland) at first light on Saturday 26 January 1788. The struggle to create a new colony, with convicts and free colonists, now began in earnest.[1]

Apart from fish and edible molluscs, there was little local food to be had because native animals – such as kangaroos and emus – were not considered suitable, and the early settlers knew little of other sources of 'bush tucker'. But the provisions brought from Britain by the store-ships were sufficient to feed everyone for some time. These provisions included 44 sheep, 32 hogs, 5 rabbits,[2] 4 cows, 1 bull, 291 poultry of various kinds, 448 barrels of flour, 80 bushels of seed wheat and 20 barrels of seed barley. There were 8000 fish hooks and a host of other items.[3] It was to be many years, however, before the colony could expect to be self-supporting. It was clearly necessary for houses and other buildings to be constructed without delay. And it was also essential to establish vegetable gardens, orchards and farms with all possible speed.

Grazing land was available on the coastal plain within easy distance of the settlement at Sydney Cove but, as the colony expanded, it would become necessary to find additional land that would be suitable for sheep and cattle farms. The mountain range – about 60 kilometres to the west of the settlement – was an enormous barrier to western expansion. This range often seemed to be covered by a blue haze – caused by the eucalyptus oil evaporated from the leaves of the eucalyptus trees – and, for this reason, early settlers referred to this range as the 'Blue Mountains', a name soon accepted by everyone.

Following his circumnavigation of the continent Matthew Flinders wrote:[4]

The interior of this new region, in extent nearly equal to all Europe, strongly excited the curiosity of geographers and naturalists; and the more so as, ten years after the establishment of a British Colony at Port Jackson on the east coast, and the repeated effort of some enterprising individuals, no part of it beyond 30 leagues from the coast had been seen by a European. Various conjectures were entertained upon the probable consistence of this extensive space. Was it a vast desert? Was it occupied by an immense lake – a second Caspian Sea, or by a Mediterranean to which existed a navigable entrance in some part of the coasts hitherto unexplored?

The influential Sir Joseph Banks certainly thought that there *must* be rivers. He wrote to the Colonial Office in May 1798: 'It is impossible to conceive that such a body of land, as large as all Europe, does not produce vast rivers, capable of being navigated into the heart of the interior.'[5]

Several attempts had been made to find a route over the mountains to find rivers and good pasture, however:[6]

All early attempts to get beyond the great western wall were defeated by the peculiarly broken, precipitous and irregular character of the region where deep gorges cut across every ridge, and every stream was a succession of waterfalls.

In May 1788 only twenty-nine sheep were left; but the number was soon increased by further importations, and by newly born lambs. By 1805 there were over 16 000 sheep in the colony and, in 1813, there were 50 000. That year was an extremely dry one, 'the grass was nearly all destroyed, and the water failed.' Moreover, 'the horned cattle suffered severly from this drought, and died in great numbers.'[7] The discovery of a route over the mountains, and additional grazing land, was urgent.

On 11 May 1813 Gregory Blaxland (a pioneer farmer), William Lawson (a lieutenant in the Royal Veteran Company) and William Charles Wentworth (son of the colonial surgeon, and soon to be a prominent politician) set off – determined to conquer the Blue Mountains. They took with them four servants, five dogs and four horses, which were loaded with provisions.[8] They found a feasible route and discovered rich grazing land. On the way, Lawson carved his initials in the trunk of a tree, and what is said to be the stump of this tree is still to be seen not far from the present-day town of Katoomba.

Governor Macquarie then asked George Evans, the assistant surveyor-general, to survey the route for a road. This he did – and proceeded even further into the plains beyond the mountains. He reported that the land would be excellent for grazing. Evans discovered and named the Lachlan River and the Macquarie River. He reported to the governor that '12 Men might clear a good road in 3 Months for a Cart to travel over the Mountains and make the descent of them so easy that it might be drove down in safety.'[9] The road was built and, in April 1815, Governor Macquarie and his wife, together with several members of his staff – a surgeon, two army officers, an artist, John Oxley (surveyor-general), James Meeham (deputy surveyor-general) and George Evans (deputy surveyor of lands) – travelled over the Blue Mountains by this road. Macquarie personally selected the site for a new township – which he named Bathurst, after Earl Bathurst, the colonial secretary.

THE SEARCH FOR GRAZING LAND

Oxley was impressed by the discoveries that had been made by George Evans and was anxious to expand on them. Under orders from the governor he organised his first expedition. He was provided with two lightweight boats, horses and a suitable array of navigational instruments – a sextant, an artificial horizon, a small theodolite, a pocket chronometer, an odometer to measure the distance travelled, and a pocket compass. George Evans was appointed second-in-command, Allan Cunningham as king's botanist, Charles Fraser as colonial botanist, and William Parr as mineralogist. They, together with eight others, constituted the party.[10]

The Oxley expedition left Sydney on 6 April 1817 and made for Bathurst. From there, Oxley went to the Lachlan River and followed its general direction. He left the river for a time to avoid being trapped in low country by the rising water, but returned as soon as this danger passed. He again followed the general direction of the river until it terminated in impenetrable marshes. He then retraced his course back along the river as far as the Goobothery Range – where he took a more northerly route until he reached the Macquarie River. This was followed to the south-east – that is, upstream – until they arrived back in Bathurst.[11]

Oxley had been greatly impressed by some of the country that he had seen. On 23 April, for example, he wrote: 'I never saw a country better adapted for the grazing of all kinds of stock than we passed over this day.' However, Oxley had also found many disappointing areas – 'we proceeded to the north north-west, our course taking us over a broken barren country; the hills composed of rocks and small stones, the valleys and flats of sand.'[12] Oxley had, however, discovered a 'beautiful fertile valley' – which he named Wellington Valley. It is at the junction of the Bell and Macquarie rivers. A convict settlement was established there in 1823, but this was abandoned in 1830 – after which Wellington soon became a prosperous town.

The expedition had made contact with Aboriginal people on several occasions and Oxley was surprised by the differences between the tribes. Some were always naked; some 'were covered with cloaks made of opossum skins'. With one group, 'the front tooth in the upper row was wanting in them all.'[13] On another occasion Oxley observed 'that the loss of the upper front tooth is not common to every tribe, as several of these men retained it, although others were without it.'[14] He added that 'the wearing of a stick, or bone, through the cartilage of the nose, appeared common to them all.' The languages of these Aboriginal people differed markedly from that among the Aborigines in the area nearer Port Jackson.[15]

As for Allan Cunningham, he was able to report to Banks that he had collected more than 400 herbarium specimens, and about 150 packets of seeds. On his return to Port Jackson, Cunningham received a letter from Banks instructing him to join Phillip Parker King's voyage of exploration to the north-west coast – which he did (see Chapter 7).[16]

Another expedition was needed to trace the course of the Macquarie River – and it was hoped that this would lead to an inland sea. John Oxley was again chosen to lead it and he was to be supported by George Evans, John Harries (a surgeon) and Charles Fraser (the colonial botanist). Twelve men were selected to accompany them and they were to be provided with eighteen horses and two boats. A depot was established in the Wellington Valley – about 145 kilometres west of Bathurst – and the expedition left this depot on 5 June 1818. They made good progress down the river but, on 3 July, Oxley realised that the Macquarie River, like the Lachlan, ended in an impenetrable morass – the Macquarie Marshes. He wrote:[17]

> Although there had been no previous change in the breadth, depth, and rapidity of the stream for several miles, and I was sanguine in my expectations of soon entering the long sought for Australian sea, it all at once eluded our further pursuit by spreading on every point from north-west to north-east, among the ocean of reeds which surrounded us, still running with the same rapidity as before.

A few days later Oxley sent a small party under the command of Evans to explore to the north-east. They returned ten days later having discovered a substantial river that Evans had named the Castlereagh River – after Lord Castlereagh. Oxley decided to return on an easterly course to the coast. He soon agreed that the 'Castlereagh River is certainly a stream of great magnitude', and as the party travelled they had to cross a number of other streams. He recorded: 'Numerous fine streams, running northerly, watered a rich and beautiful country.' All originated on the western side of the mountains and flowed inland.[18] On his return journey, Oxley had to cross the mountains about 80 kilometres inland, and he then followed a river flowing to the coast. He called this the Hastings River after the Marquess of Hastings – the then governor-general of India. Oxley found that it enters a fine bay which he named Port Macquarie. He spent some little time examining the port before heading southwards. They arrived at Port Stephens – where Evans and a party of three men went by boat to Newcastle. From there a boat was sent to transfer Oxley and the remainder of the expedition back to Port Jackson.[19] Phillip Parker King and John Oxley carried out additional surveys in the area in 1819.

In the meantime, the settlement at Sydney Cove continued to expand, and more and more free settlers were arriving. In these circumstances the governor, Sir Thomas Brisbane, decided that it would be desirable to move some of the hardened criminals among the convicts further from the main settlement. He therefore instructed John Oxley to engage a small party and to sail, in the *Mermaid* ('the same one which had been under the command of Captain King on her voyage around New Holland'[20]) to the north and to select a suitable site for a new penal settlement. The *Mermaid* – with Oxley, Lieutenant James Stirling (an army officer) and John Uniacke (surprisingly, 'the Superintendent of Distilleries'), together with an Aboriginal man named Bowen – sailed from Port Jackson on 21 October 1823.[21] Oxley examined Port Curtis (the harbour for present-day Gladstone), but thought it unsuitable for a convict settlement and sailed southwards to examine other sites. They reached Moreton Bay, to the west of Moreton Island, on 29 November 1823. Moreton Bay had been seen

and named by Captain Cook, and had also been seen by Captain Flinders. Indeed, the *Mermaid* anchored in the bay '150 yards off the shore in the exact place where twenty-four years previously Matthew Flinders had brought the *Norfolk* to an anchorage'.[22]

Flinders had landed on Bribie Island, to the west of his anchorage, and met the Aboriginal people who lived there. Soon after the *Mermaid* had anchored, Oxley 'observed a number of natives running along the beach towards the vessel. The foremost one appeared very much lighter in colour than the rest. We took him for a half-caste.'[23] They were astounded when he hailed them in English. 'We immediately went on shore and were received by the poor man with a breathless joy, that almost deprived him of utterance.' His name was Thomas Pamphlet. He was a convict and he had left Sydney on 21 March 1823 in an open boat with three convict companions – intending to go to the 'Five Islands' for cedar. However, they had experienced a severe gale and had been blown out of sight of land. One of his companions had died of thirst. The others reached Moreton Island where their boat was wrecked. They had been kindly treated by the local Aborigines and, at the time Oxley arrived, Pamphlet was naked and painted with black and red pigments in the native fashion. One of the other convicts, John Finnegan, was away with the tribe, hunting – but he soon returned. The third convict, Parsons, had begun to walk to the north because he presumed Sydney Cove to be in that direction. He was wrong, however. They had been blown off their course and Sydney Cove was to the south. It was not long before he decided to return to Moreton Bay.[24]

Pamphlet and Finnegan told Oxley of the existence of a major river on the mainland to the south-west – a river that flowed into Moreton Bay. Oxley, Stirling and Finnegan, in the whaler, rowed to the mouth of the river on 2 December 1823 – and then up-river for 32 kilometres, and a further

48 kilometres on the following day. When Oxley returned to Sydney he was able to report to the governor that he had discovered the largest river on the east coast and that he had named it the Brisbane River.

The convicts, however, had to resume their imprisonment. The story of Finnegan and Pamphlet was written up by John Uniacke – and this accompanied his official report to the governor.[25]

In September 1825, Governor Brisbane sent the *Mermaid*, with Major Edmund Lockyer (who had recently arrived with the 57th Regiment), to explore the Brisbane River – and he navigated it for a 150 kilometres. Lockyer was one of the many explorers who maintained good relations with the Aboriginal people. Towards the end of his exploration he noted in his journal that the '... attachment of these people to their dogs is worthy of notice', and he added:[26]

I was very anxious to get one of the wild native breed of a black colour, a very handsome puppy, which one of the men had in his arms. I offered a small axe for it. His companions urged him to take it, and he was about to do so, when the animal licked his face, which settled the business; he shook his head, determined to keep him. I tried him afterwards with handkerchiefs of glaring colours, but it would not do; he would not part with his dog. I gave him, however, the axe and the handkerchief.

In the following year Brisbane decided to send a party of soldiers and convicts to establish a settlement at King George Sound – a harbour that had been discovered by George Vancouver in the *Discovery* in 1791, visited by Matthew Flinders in the *Investigator* in 1801, by Baudin (with the *Géographe* and *Casuarina*) in 1803, by Phillip Parker King (in the *Mermaid*) in 1818, and by Dumont d'Urville (in the *Astrolabe*) in 1825. Lockyer was selected to command this expedition and he sailed in the brig *Amity* in November and reached the sound on Christmas Day 1826. The new settlement

was named Frederick's Town – in honour of the Duke of York and Albany, whose given name was Frederick. However, the settlers soon called it Albany.[27] The western part of Australia – the old 'New Holland' – was formally annexed on 21 January 1827, Lockyer's birthday.

Allan Cunningham now emerged as an explorer in his own right. He had taken part in Oxley's expeditions and he had sailed with Phillip Parker King on all four voyages. In the interval he had collected specimens in New South Wales and in Van Diemen's Land. Indeed, Cunningham:[28]

... had worked through a great range of latitudes and a wide variety of plant communities – in the tropical forests of north-eastern Australia and Timor, on the arid coasts of western Australia and among the mangrove swamps of the north, in the rain-forests of the Illawarra, the rugged bush of western Van Diemen's Land and the sub-tropical hills of Mauritius.

Sir Thomas Macdougall Brisbane – a Scottish soldier who had served under Wellington, and who had a deep interest in astronomy – had become the governor of New South Wales in 1821. He encouraged Cunningham in his desire to lead his own expeditions. Cunningham set off from Parramatta in March 1823 for Bathurst, and then went to Wellington Valley. From there he made a number of forays into the surrounding country. Sir Ralph Darling became governor in 1825, and he also encouraged Cunningham. He was to explore beyond the northern limit of Oxley's discoveries as far as Moreton Bay. Cunningham set out from 'an extensive and valuable estate' on an upper branch (Pages Creek) of the Hunter River with six men and eleven horses 'of which eight were the property of the Crown'. He was provided with a sextant 'of superior construction', a pocket chronometer, a pocket compass, an odometer 'or improved perambulator' and a mountain barometer (for determining heights above sea level). He also had an artificial horizon.[29]

Before leaving the station he determined its position to be 32° 06' 37" S, 150° 57' 15" E, and obtained its height above sea level. Cunningham continued to the north along the eastern edge of the Liverpool Plains. Further to the north they crossed a river that was named Mitchell River, and then another, named Buddle River. Here, for the first time, they saw a few Aborigines. Still further north they came to a considerable stream which received the name Dumaresq River – in honour of the family with which the governor 'is so intimately connected'. Cunningham reached the river system not far from present-day Yetman, and this part of the river system is now called the Macintyre River. The Dumaresq of today flows into the Macintyre some kilometres to the north-west of Yetman.[30] Cunningham had named the present-day Dumaresq 'Macintyre's Brook'. A little further on he came to some excellent and extensive rolling plains which, bearing in mind the rolling topography of the Chalk Downs of south-eastern England, he promptly named the 'Darling Downs'.

In July 1828, Cunningham led a party from Brisbane to the south-west, to 'Cunningham's Gap' in the Great Dividing Range, and to the Darling Downs – an expedition that greatly enhanced the commercial value of his initial discovery of this first-class farming land.[31]

Governor Brisbane had also been anxious to investigate the possibility of establishing a settlement at Westernport on the south coast. He wanted to send unrepentant convicts further from Sydney, and he also wanted to forestall the French whom he suspected of having designs on that area. After all, the French explorers had surveyed Westernport and had named one of the islands there 'Ile des Français'. Brisbane invited Hamilton Hume to find an overland route to Westernport.

Hume had been born in Australia on 19 June 1797 and was the first 'colonial-born' explorer of distinction. Indeed: 'In the eight years between 1814 and 1822 this young currency [i.e. Australian-born]

lad, unskilled in the techniques of navigation and survey, was either the leader or the pivot of thirteen expeditions, into the unknown interior.' The *Sydney Gazette* referred to him as 'The Australian Tourist'.[32] Hume accepted the assignment. William Hovell, an English sea captain (eleven years older than Hume) 'who is capable of taking observations', was anxious to accompany Hume on a cost-share basis – and this was agreed.[33]

They set off from Hume's station at Lake George on 2 October 1824, crossed the Yass Plains, crossed the Murrumbidgee River (which was then in flood), and came to an unknown river. Hovell wrote in his journal: 'This I name Hume's River, he being the first that saw it'.[34] Some years later it was realised that the 'Hume River' is one of the major headwaters of Sturt's Murray River.

On 16 December they reached the southern coast and believed themselves to be at Westernport. In fact, they had arrived at what is now known as Corio Bay – the western part of Port Phillip Bay. This is the site of present-day Geelong – a city that takes its name from the Aboriginal word 'Jillong' meaning 'a swampy plain' or 'a white seabird'.[35] Their mistake was recognised in 1826 when another expedition, which included Hovell, was sent to occupy Westernport. Hovell immediately recognised that it was not the coast that he and Hume had reached. He went westwards to Port Phillip Bay and soon recognised the place where he and Hume had arrived in 1824.[36]

Hovell's journal does not explain why they had been so off-course. It seldom mentions any astronomical observations – one of the few being those taken on 14 October, not long after they had started. He records that he found 'lat. by Ant. 34 deg 48 min. S; by double altitude, 34 deg. 51 min; by Ant. 140 deg. 21 min.'[37]

Notwithstanding the navigational errors of the Hume and Hovell expedition, their journey helped to open the south coast for settlement. Moreover, Hamilton Hume was an excellent bushman who had a good rapport with the Aboriginal people. Some years later (1918) the then chief protector of Aborigines in Melbourne wrote that Hume had:[38]

> ...made the first overland journey to Geelong, Port Phillip, an undertaking in those days of no ordinary character. The natives were exceedingly friendly and invited him to go to a white man at Indented Head, since ascertained to be Buckley, the individual who lived thirty years with the natives. Mr. Hume said he never had occasion to pull a trigger in self defence against a black – he always treated them kindly.

The later exploration of the Port Phillip Bay area was due to Charles Grimes – who also contributed to the exploration of Van Diemen's Land. Grimes had been born in England in 1772 and had arrived at Port Jackson on either 21 or 22 September 1791. He was, for a time, surveyor on Norfolk Island but, in 1801, was appointed acting surveyor of New South Wales, succeeding Augustus Theodore Atl who had arrived with the First Fleet. Grimes, at the request of Governor Philip King, set off from Port Jackson in the *Cumberland* to search for the site of a new penal settlement. His exploration party included Dr McCallum (a surgeon), James Meeham (a surveyor) and James Flemming ('a man in whom the Governor had great confidence'). Flemming wrote the journal of the expedition – which includes an account of the discovery of the river (later named the Yarra) that made the establishment of a settlement at the head of the bay possible:[39]

> The most eligible place for a settlement that I have seen is on the Freshwater River. In several places there are small tracts of good land, but they are without wood or water. I have every reason to think that there is not often so great a scarcity of water as at present from the appearance of the herbage. The country in general is excellent pasture and thin of timber, which is mostly low and crooked. In most places there is fine clay for bricks, and abundance of stone. I am of opinion that the timber is better both in quality and size further up the country, as

> I saw some what is called ash on the banks of the Freshwater River, and the hills appear to be clothed with wood. As to the quantity of good land at the different places, I shall be better able to describe when I am favoured with a sight of a chart, as I have not been permitted to see one since I came out. There is great plenty of fish in Port King. The country in general is newly burnt.

Free settlers were always looking for good farming land and John Batman, of Launceston, was one of these. As Ernest Scott wrote:[40]

> John Batman, a man of dogged perseverance, fond of adventure, fixed his gaze steadily on the mainland to the north of Bass Strait, interest in which was increased when the story of Messrs. Hume and Hovell's overland journey was published. In 1834 he joined a syndicate of fifteen Launceston men who found the money for sending out a small expedition to examine Port Phillip.

Batman was entranced with the land near the head of Port Phillip Bay. He examined the river that Charles Grimes had named the Freshwater River. He then wrote in his notebook:[41]

> The boat went up the large river I have spoken of, which comes from the east, and I am glad to state about six miles up found the river all good water and very deep. This will be the place for a village.

This was the same river that Charles Grimes had named Freshwater River. It was later renamed the 'Yarra River' by John Wedge – the assistant surveyor-general of Van Diemen's Land, and one of Batman's associates – after learning that the Aboriginal people called it the 'yarra yarra', believed to mean 'always flowing'.[42] The 'village' was named Melbourne in 1837 by Governor Bourke – after Lord Melbourne, the British prime minister.

STRZELECKI

Many of the early explorers of south-eastern Australia had been searching for major rivers that would facilitate transport into the interior, and

Paul Edmund de Strzelecki, aged seventy-seven; Strzelecki was born in Poland and became famous for his discovery of Australia's highest mountain (2228 metres), which he named Mount Kosciuszko after the Polish patriot Tadeusz Kosciuszko. (Royal Geographical Society of South Australia)

would provide adequate water for the further development of the sheep and cattle industries. Coal had been discovered in the vicinity of present-day Newcastle by escaped convicts in 1791, and also by Lieutenant John Shortland in 1797 – but there had been little attempt to investigate the geology and mineral potential of the country. Strzelecki attempted to overcome this lack of information, and was the first to explore the highlands of south-eastern Australia.

Paul Edmund de Strzelecki was unusual in many respects. He was born at Gluszyna, near Poznan in western Poland (which was then part of Prussia), on 20 July 1797. His parents were aristocrats, but without a title, and apparently with limited

resources. As the *Australian Dictionary of Biography* puts it, he was 'the son of poor gentry, without land or title'.[43] It seems that Strzelecki attended more than one university for a time, and that he became interested in geology and mineralogy – but the details are obscure. He travelled widely in England, Scotland, North America and South America. According to Kaluski:[44]

Two of Strzelecki's long sea voyages were facilitated by invitations from the British navy to join its ships. On the voyage from Chile up the South American coast he was the guest of Captain George Grey of HMS *Cleopatra*, and on his Pacific cruise he accompanied Captain Russell Elliot of HMS *Fly*.

Even so, it is not clear how he financed his many

journeys. He also sailed northwards along the western coast of North America, visited a number of Pacific Islands – including Hawaii and New Zealand – and arrived in Sydney in April 1839.[45] During all this time he seems to have been referred to as 'Count' Strzelecki. There is no evidence that he called himself 'Count' at this time, but he might have done little to 'deny the title that his breeding and bearing suggested to people'.[46]

At Sydney, Strzelecki wrote in his journal:[47]

I cannot cease asking myself, am I really in the capital of that 'Botany Bay' which has been represented as 'The Community of Felons', as 'the most demoralised colony known in the history of nations', as 'a possession which adds a tarnish rather than a lustre to the British Crown' ... The evening I effected my disembarkment in Sydney, I did it with all imaginable precaution, leaving my watch and purse behind me, and arming myself with a stick; being resolved to encounter inevitable and imminent dangers with the least possible risk!

I found, however, on that night, in the streets of Sydney, a decency and a quiet which I have never witnessed in other ports of the United Kingdom. No drunkenness, no sailors' quarrels, no appearance of prostitution, were to be seen.

Strzelecki was fortunate – for many crimes were committed by convicts and others during the early days of the colony. Strzelecki was clearly a man of great charm, and he settled into the life of Australia without difficulty. He became the friend and confidant of many of the most prominent and influential citizens – Wentworth and James Macarthur, for example. He also became friend and confidant to the governor of New South Wales, Sir George Gipps, the previous governor, Philip Gidley King, and the lieutenant-governor of Tasmania, Sir John Franklin.

Strzelecki undertook a number of field trips, or explorations, to study the geology and mineral potential of New South Wales – and he did find indications of mineral wealth. He found specks of gold in the Wellington district. On 26 October 1839

he wrote to his friend James Macarthur:[48]

I have specimens of excellent coal, some of fine serpentine, with asbestos, curious native alum, and brown hepatite, fossil bones and plants, which I digged out from Boree and Wellington Caves, but particularly a specimen of native silver, in horn-blende rock, and gold in specks in silicate [sand?].

He mentioned the existence of a gold field to Sir George Gipps, 'who requested me to keep the matter secret for fear of serious consequences which, considering the condition and population of the colony, were to be apprehended'. Strzelecki added: 'Of course I complied with this request.' But he did mention it in confidence to several friends.[49] Even so a report of the find was included in extracts from his journal which were published in the *Sydney Herald* of 19 August 1841.

Strzelecki was not the first to discover gold in Australia. It seems that, in February 1823, James McBrian had discovered gold in the Fish River – which had been discovered and named by George Evans in 1813 when surveying the first road over the Blue Mountains. These and other discoveries of small amounts were not widely publicised. The discovery by Edward Hammond Hargraves in 1851 was different. He and his co-workers, William Tom and John Lister, obtained over 100 grams of gold in April of that year at a site near Bathurst – that Hargraves promptly named 'Ophir' after the biblical city of gold. A report of this discovery appeared in the *Sydney Morning Herald* of 5 May. Ten days later there were 300 diggers at the site.[50] The governor had been correct in his expectation that the discovery of gold, when publicised, would lead to disruption!

Strzelecki is usually remembered for his expeditions to the Australian Alps, to Gippsland and to Tasmania. The expedition to the Australian Alps was largely financed by James Macarthur – a wealthy grazier. Strzelecki, Macarthur and their party – and a young man named James Riley (a protégé of Macarthur), two convict servants and an Aborigine named Charlie Tarra from the Goulburn Plain – left their respective homes, but it is not clear where exactly they joined forces. A 'local' Aborigine, Jacky, was later added to the party. They had several horses, but Strzelecki preferred to travel on foot so that his instruments would not be damaged. After crossing the Murrumbidgee River they were in unexplored country and Strzelecki carried out a survey 'of the predominent characteristic features of the country, partly trigonometrically, partly astronomically'.[51] For this purpose he had a number of surveying instruments:[52]

> Schmalcalder's [Schumder's] three and a half inches reflecting compass in conjunction with a clinometer (which supplied remarkably well the place of a theodolite) determined the trigonometric part of the survey. A chronometer, a full size sextant and artificial horizon, that of latitude, longitude and azimuth observations.

The map showing the country travelled after leaving the Murrumbidgee River was later handed to the government of New South Wales. The most important discovery was that of the highest mountain in Australia – which Strzelecki named after the Polish patriot and general, Thaddeus Kosciuszko. As Strzelecki wrote:[53]

> The particular configuration of this eminence struck me so forcibly by the similarity it bears to a tumulus elevated in Krakow over the tomb of the patriot Kosciuszko, that, although in a foreign country on foreign ground, but amongst a free people, who appreciate freedom and its votaries, I could not refrain from giving it the name of Mount Kosciuszko.

It must be admitted, however, that many of the positions he determined were not as accurate as they might have been. His chronometer might well have been more than a few seconds in error, and he might not have been experienced in determining latitude and longitude. Nevertheless he did bring back very useful information. He discovered the ranges in southern Victoria which are named after

him. He also examined Gippsland. He was not the first to visit this area, but it was Strzelecki who named it Gipps Land (now Gippsland) after his friend the governor, Sir George Gipps. Strzelecki then went on to Melbourne, where he arrived on 28 May 1840 and where he spent several weeks before sailing from Port Phillip to Launceston.

Strzelecki spent several months exploring Tasmania and, in the summer of 1842, he explored the islands in Bass Strait. He climbed the highest peak on Flinders Island – the hills of which were later named Strzelecki Peaks by Captain John Lort Stokes of the *Beagle*. The national park there also bears Strzelecki's name. The Strzelecki Creek, which occasionally flows through the Strzelecki Desert in South Australia, was so named by Charles Sturt in 1845. The gravel road from Queensland through Innamincka to South Australia is known as the Strzelecki Track.

Strzelecki sailed from Launceston on 29 September 1842 and arrived at Port Jackson on 2 October. On 22 April 1843, four years after his arrival in Australia, he left Sydney and returned to England. Sir John Franklin had also returned to England and, on 1 November 1844 he wrote to Strzelecki:[54]

My dear Strelecki [sic]

We hope to find you disengaged tomorrow and that you will dine with us at six and you will meet our excellent friend Robert Brown.

You must not say no, if you are disengaged. We expect to leave town [London] next week for a short time.

Yours faithfully
John Franklin

In 1845 Strzelecki published his book on the *Physical Description of New South Wales and Van Diemen's Land* – dedicated to Franklin. Franklin was just about to depart on his expedition to explore the Arctic, and Strzelecki extended 'most warm and cordial wishes for the success of that important

Expedition which in a few days will leave the shores of England under your command'. Included as a frontispiece to the book was a reduced version (reduced by the famous map-maker, J. Arrowsmith) of Strzelecki's 'Map of New South Wales & Van Diemen's Land'.[55]

In 1846 Strzelecki published a small book, *Gold and Silver*, which (successfully) disputed the common view that Hargraves was the first discoverer of gold in Australia. Nevertheless, the parliament in New South Wales had rewarded Hargraves with £10 000.

Strzelecki became a British subject in 1845 and he was commended by parliament for his work during the Irish famine. He was also made a companion of the Order of the Bath (CB). In 1846 he was awarded the Gold Founder's Medal of the Royal Geographical Society 'for exploration in the south-eastern portion of Australia'. He was knighted (KCMG) in 1869. He died of cancer in 1873.[56]

9

EXPANSION OF THE COLONY TO VAN DIEMEN'S LAND

While the early exploration of the mainland had been going on, Van Diemen's Land had been explored and settled. Strzelecki had explored the highlands, but he had been preceded by several notable travellers.

It will be recalled that Baudin, in the *Géographe*, had sailed from Port Jackson on 18 November 1802 and had made for Elephant Bay on the eastern coast of King Island – where the *Naturaliste*, and the colonial-built schooner *Casuarina*, joined them on 6 December. Three days later the *Naturaliste* sailed for France – with many boxes of scientific specimens and with the officers and men in poor health – while the *Géographe* and *Casuarina* then continued the exploration of the southern coast of the continent. Soon after the *Géographe* had sailed from Port Jackson, Philip Gidley King learnt from his officers that a few French officers had expressed the hope that France should establish a French settlement on Van Diemen's Land – especially as French mariners had contributed so largely to the exploration of the coast. The Baudin expedition had, of course, been designed to undertake scientific and geographical studies but it is not surprising that some of the French officers would have liked to see a French settlement on Van Diemen's Land. No evidence seems to have come to light, however, to suggest that Napoléon himself, or his government, had any such thoughts.

Governor King was greatly disturbed when it was suggested that the French might wish to establish their own settlement. After all, Captain Cook had taken possession of the whole of eastern New Holland in the name of the British King. And Governor Phillip, on 26 January 1788, had repeated this claim. The last thing that Governor King wanted was a foreign power in Van Diemen's Land – especially on its northern coast and northern islands. He decided to dispatch the *Cumberland*, a schooner of 30 tonnes, under the command of a young officer, to find Baudin and to give him a letter that would emphasise that the whole of Van Diemen's Land was British. The young officer did find Baudin and delivered King's letter. He also set up camp close to that of Baudin and made a point of flying the British flag.

However, Governor King realised that he would have to do more than this. He would have to establish a settlement, or preferably two settlements, on Van Diemen's Land. A young naval officer, Lieutenant John Bowen, had arrived at Port Jackson on 11 March 1803 and, a few days later, he volunteered to lead a small group of soldiers, settlers and convicts – to establish a settlement on Van Diemen's Land. The governor accepted his offer and instructed him to establish the first settlement at Risdon Cove – which had been discovered and named in 1793 by Lieutenant John Hayes during a voyage under the auspices of the British East India Company. Risdon is on the eastern banks of the

Derwent River. Lieutenant Bowen made two un-successful attempts to sail from Port Jackson – both frustrated by bad weather – but his third attempt was successful. In September 1803 the *Lady Nelson* and the *Albion* arrived at Risdon Cove with nine soldiers, four settlers and thirty-five convicts – of whom at least three were women.[1]

A few weeks later, in October 1803, Lieutenant-Colonel David Collins arrived at Port Phillip Bay from England, with two ships – the *Calcutta* and the *Ocean* – with instructions to establish another settlement. He brought nearly 300 convicts plus a guard of marines and other staff. Possible sites for a settlement were investigated (including the site where the city of Melbourne now stands), but Collins was not impressed. He petitioned the governor for permission to move the settlement to Risdon Cove, on the Derwent River, in Van Diemen's Land. (It might be added, in parentheses, that Collins Street in Melbourne is named after Lieutenant-Colonel Collins.)

So Collins moved his expedition to the Risdon Cove settlement. But he soon realised that this site had some disadvantages, and he decided to move the entire settlement to the western banks of the Derwent River – about 10 kilometres to the south of Risdon Cove. Bowen had suggested that the settlement be named Hobart in honour of Robert, Lord Hobart, the secretary of state for War and the Colonies under Prime Minister Henry Addington (who had succeeded William Pitt the Younger in March 1801). In fact, it became known as Hobart Town, and it was not until 1891 that it became 'Hobart'. It was a good site for a new settlement. It has a deep-water harbour, and Mt Wellington (then called 'Table Mountain'), with a height of 1271 metres, in the background. The harbour was a decided advantage – because it was hoped to use Hobart Town as a base for whaling. Hobart Town prospered and gradually attracted many free settlers.

The administration was anxious to increase the number of settlements in Van Diemen's Land – for reasons that had nothing to do with the French. First, it was thought desirable to have several small convict settlements rather than one large one at Port Jackson – thus reducing the danger of a mass revolt which the military might not be able to contain. Second, it was desirable to employ the convicts on work that would advance the prosperity of the colony – by growing vegetables and cereal crops, for example, but also for harvesting wood for housing, and even for ship-building. It was already known that some areas in Van Diemen's Land were heavily wooded, and the possibility of developing a timber industry seemed attractive.

The opportunity to obtain valuable timber was enhanced following the discovery of Macquarie Harbour in 1815. A young whaling captain named James Kelly decided to explore the coasts of Van Diemen's Land in a whaleboat with a crew of four men. It was 'a voyage which those familiar with those latitudes had considered the greatest folly'.[2] They left Hobart Town in mid December 1815, discovered Port Davey on the south-west coast, and then made an even more important discovery – that of Macquarie Harbour, which James Kelly named after Governor Lachlan Macquarie. He named the river which flows into the harbour the Gordon River – after James Gordon of Pittwater, who had loaned him the whaleboat. The inlet at the southern end of Macquarie Harbour was named Birch Inlet – after a friend in Hobart Town – and Sarah Island was named after Mrs Birch.[3] Of Sarah Island it was later stated that this 'region is lashed with tempests; the sky is cloudy, and the rain falls more frequently than elsewhere'.[4]

The shores of Macquarie Harbour were (and still are) covered with a wilderness of magnificent trees (Huon pine), and shrubs. Even today it is almost impossible to land on the shore from an open boat. The lieutenant-governor, Colonel William Sorell, decided that Sarah Island would be a satisfactory site for the establishment of a penal colony and 'as a place of punishment for the worst class of criminals'.[5] It would also help towards the establishment of a timber industry for the benefit of the colony. Convicts were sent there from 1821 until 1833 – when it was closed and the prisoners transferred to Port Arthur. Fortunately, Sarah Island had proved too expensive to maintain and was too isolated.

It was an age when the treatment of convicts was brutal. Minor offences attracted severe punishment. The punishments for robbery or other offences were very severe. For example, in Port Jackson, during the evening of the King's birthday celebrations, a young convict named Samuel Peyton broke into an officer's marquee with intent to commit a robbery. He was convicted at his trial and sentenced to death and was executed the following day. On the night before his execution he was able to write to his 'dear and honoured mother' back in Britain:[6]

Banish from your memory all my former indiscretions, and let the cheering hope of a happy meeting hereafter, console you for my loss. Sincerely penitent for my sins; sensible of the justice of my conviction and sentence, and firmly relying on the merits of a Blessed Redeemer, I am at perfect peace with all mankind, and trust I shall yet experience that peace, which this world cannot give.

He signed the letter 'Your unhappy dying son, Samuel Peyton'.

But even in such a climate of cruelty Sarah Island had become notorious for sadism. Flogging was frequently used as punishment for relatively minor offences – apparently in the mistaken belief that this would tame the convicts into submission. Some prisoners were forced to endure solitary confinement for up to a month. There were more than 180 escape attempts, but little if any food was available in the bush for escaped convicts, and many

Hell's Gates – the entrance to Macquarie Harbour and to the convict settlement on Sarah Island. (Geoffrey Badger)

escapers died of starvation. Some escaped convicts resorted to cannibalism. Such was the reputation of Sarah Island that the entrance to Macquarie Harbour became known as 'Hell's Gates'.

The life of a convict was vividly described in one of the classics of Australian literature – *For The Term of His Natural Life*, by Marcus Clarke. For example:[7]

> Is it possible to imagine, even for a moment, what an innocent man, gifted with ambition and disgusts, endowed with power to love and to respect, must have suffered during one week of such punishment? We ordinary men, leading ordinary lives – walking, riding, laughing, marrying and giving in marriage – can form no notion of such misery as this. Some dim ideas we may have about the sweetness of liberty and the loathing that evil company inspires; but that is all. We know that we were chained and degraded, fed like dogs, employed as beasts of burden, driven to our daily toil with threats and blows, and herded with wretches among whom all that savoured of decency and manliness was an open mock and scorn, we would – what? Die, perhaps, or go mad. But we do not know, and can never know, how unutterably loathsome life must become when shared with such beings as those who dragged the tree trunks to the banks of the Gordon, and toiled, blaspheming in their irons, on the dismal sandpit of Sarah Island.

A report on Sarah Island was submitted on 22 May 1824. In 1827, Captain J. Butler of the 40th Regiment submitted a further report to the lieutenant-governor, Colonel George Arthur.[8]

It is interesting to enquire whether the convicts sent to Sarah Island were evil, incorrigible men and women. Butler has published extracts from the convict records of ten men who were sent to Sarah Island.[9] At this time those who committed major crimes in the British Isles were sentenced to the gallows. Those who were found guilty of more minor offences were sent to prison, or were transported. Butler recorded that one of the Sarah Island convicts was transported for stealing a handkerchief. Another was transported for larceny (street robbery) – and so on. The treatment to which they were subjected in the convict establishments did not subdue them – it brutalised them. The opening of the penal settlement at Port Arthur in 1830 led to the closure of Sarah Island, and it soon became a complete ruin. Port Arthur was named after Colonel George Arthur. He had been appointed lieutenant-governor in May 1824, and was subordinate to the governor of New South Wales. In November 1825 Van Diemen's Land became a separate colony and Colonel Arthur became independent. However he still retained the title of lieutenant-governor.

Sir John Franklin (who, as a midshipman, had sailed with Matthew Flinders on the *Investigator*) later became the lieutenant-governor of Van Diemen's Land and undertook an overland journey from Hobart Town to Sarah Island to inspect the ruins of the convict settlement on the island. He had with him his wife, Lady Franklin, some members of his staff and a few friends. Lady Franklin was carried for much of the time in a palanquin – 'a boxlike litter borne by means of poles resting on men's shoulders'.[10] The Franklins did inspect the decaying settlement on Sarah Island, and spent some time in Macquarie Harbour. They did not have an easy time in the vicinity, however, as the following quotations from the journal of the expedition indicate:[11]

> Like Plymouth, the locality of Macquarie Harbour is somewhat of the moistest, rain being said to fall three days out of four ...
>
> A night of unmitigated severity, blowing hard, and raining in torrents ...
>
> Another tempestuous night has past, and another lowering day has dawned.

Yet another settlement in Van Diemen's Land needs to be mentioned. The war between Britain and France had been interrupted by the Peace of Amiens but, in May 1803, war was again declared between the two countries. In Port Jackson, and in

London, there were concerns that the French might carry the war into Australian waters and seek to occupy Van Diemen's Land. The British government ordered Governor King to establish a settlement on the northern coast of Van Diemen's Land as an added protection for Bass Strait. The actual dispatch reads rather strangely:[12]

> It appears to be advisable that a part of the establishment now at Norfolk Island should be removed, together with a proportion of the settlers and convicts, to Port Dalrymple, the advantageous position of which, upon the southern coast of Van Diemen's Land [presumably he meant 'the southern coast of Bass Strait'] and near the eastern [?] entrance of Bass' Streights, renders it, in a political view, peculiarly necessary that a settlement should be formed there, and, as far as the reports of those who have visited that coast can be depended upon, it is strongly recommended by the nature of the soil and the goodness of the climate.

Port Dalrymple had been named by Bass and Flinders – after the distinguished British hydrographer and cartographer Alexander Dalrymple. Lieutenant-Colonel William Paterson, of the New South Wales Corps, was appointed to the command of the expedition, and to be the lieutenant-governor of the new settlement. Three officers and sixty-four non-commissioned officers and men were to accompany him. Seventy-four convicts constituted the labour force. One settler joined the group, and there were a few officials – 146 in all.[13] They embarked in HMS *Buffalo* and the schooners *Francis* and *Integrity*.

The *Buffalo* arrived at the mouth of the river which Paterson named the Tamar – in honour of Governor King, who had been born at Launceston on the Tamar River in south-western England. The other two ships arrived a few days later. Paterson established the settlement near present-day George Town, but he soon found this to be less than satisfactory and moved the settlement to the western arm of the Tamar River – and named it York Town. He was constrained by the desire of the British

government to provide a settlement near the northern coast to discourage the French from trying to establish a colony. However, as York Town still proved to be less than satisfactory, he moved the colony to a site where the North Esk and South Esk rivers join the Tamar. This was in March 1806. At first he had in mind to name it Patersonia, but thought better of it, and named it Launceston – after the town in Devon. More convicts arrived, especially from Norfolk Island, and sheep and cattle were imported from Calcutta (but there were many deaths in transit). Launceston became the 'senior' settlement in northern Van Diemen's Land.[14]

Early in 1807, however, Paterson became increasingly concerned at the rapidly diminishing stocks of food and of other supplies in his area of command. The people in Launceston were living under near-famine conditions. He decided to send a small party of men overland from Launceston to Hobart Town in the hope that the southern settlement would be able to help those in the north. No such overland journey had previously been attempted. Paterson appointed Thomas Laycock, a lieutenant in the New South Wales Corps, to lead a party of four men, with provisions for three weeks, to Hobart Town. They set off on 3 February 1807, and Laycock's brief account of their journey has been published in the *Historical Records of New South Wales*. They crossed the South Esk River and came to the Lake River, which they followed for some kilometres. When the river turned towards the east, they had to negotiate the mountains. This was the most difficult part of the journey, as his report indicates:[15]

> On the 6th I proceeded in a south direction about three miles down the side of the mountains into a large plain. The best proof of the difficulty of our passage is that it took me more than five hours to go the three miles.

On the 9th they made good progress and, on the 11th, they reached the settlement – only to find that Hobart Town was also suffering a famine and unable to help the northern settlement. However, Laycock reported:[16]

> Nothing could exceed the kind attention I personally received from Lieut.-Governor Collins and all the officers at the Derwent during my stay of four days at the settlement, nor was there anything for myself or party that was not most liberally supplied for our journey back.

Laycock and his men made the return journey to the north in less than a week and 'arrived at Launceston at about 10 o'clock in the morning' of 22 February 1807. It is said that he was rewarded for his efforts with the present of a cow 'then greatly prized because of the shortage of food and livestock'.[17]

The second man to lead a party from Launceston to Hobart Town was Charles Grimes,[18] who was earlier concerned with the investigation of the Port Phillip Bay area (see Chapter 8) and who, in March 1807, had been sent to Van Diemen's Land.

Thus, the outlines and major features of the island that is Van Diemen's Land were soon determined, settlements established, and the threat of French colonisation quietly repelled. Van Diemen's Land was the first of the Australian colonies to be given self-government. This was in 1855 and, in 1856, the colony decided to change its name – to honour her discoverer, Abel Janszoon Tasman, rather than Anthony Van Diemen, the governor-general of the Dutch East Indies, who had authorised Tasman's expedition. In 1856, Van Diemen's Land became the independent self-governing colony Tasmania.

10

CHARLES STURT
AND THE MURRAY–DARLING BASIN

Charles Sturt was born in Bengal, India, on 28 April 1795. His father, Napier Sturt, was a puisne judge in the service of the East India Company. His mother, Jeannette (née Wilson), 'a girl of no great fortune', was the daughter of a physician in Bath. In 1799 it was decided to send Charles and his elder sister to England where they would be cared for by relatives during their school years. They did not see their parents again for ten years. Charles spent some years at Astbury, in Cheshire, two years at Harrow, and a further year under a private tutor near Cambridge. By this time it was necessary to choose a career, and the army was selected. With the assistance of an aunt, who used her acquaintance with the Prince Regent, an appointment was facilitated. Charles Sturt was gazetted as an ensign in the 39th Regiment of Foot (later called the Dorsetshire Regiment) on 9 September 1813.[1]

Sturt found army life full of interest. His regiment was stationed in England for the first few months of his service but, in mid 1814, it was sent to Canada. When Napoléon escaped from Elba in March 1815, the 39th Regiment was shipped to France but arrived too late to take part in the Battle of Waterloo. Sturt spent over three years with the army of occupation in France and, during this time, he apparently learnt the elements of surveying. He was then posted to Ireland. He seems to have been a good but not spectacular officer.

In the British Army of the early nineteenth century, any officer without private means was severely disadvantaged. Sturt was never a pauper but he certainly had an inferiority complex regarding his lack of money in comparison with many of his brother officers. His parents had limited means and had also made some bad investments. It seemed that Charles Sturt was destined to have a small estate – so that the education of his children, and their proper placement in employment, became a continuing worry. Years later he wrote to Sir Ralph Darling (who had served as governor of New South Wales):[2]

> I may yet live to make up by personal exertion for want of Fortune and may elevate myself to that position amongst my friends in England from which my limited means have hitherto kept me.

Sturt's perceived need to 'elevate' himself was a driving force throughout his career. He was not promoted to the rank of lieutenant until April 1823, when he was nearly twenty-eight years of age, and he was promoted to captain in December 1825.

In 1826 Sturt was ordered to lead a detachment from his regiment which would escort convicts to the penal settlement at Port Jackson. Late in that year they sailed from England on the *Mariner* for New South Wales.[3]

Sturt embarked for New South Wales 'with strong prejudices against it', as he later confessed but, when the *Mariner* reached her destination, he was fascinated by all he saw:[4]

Captain Charles Sturt, aged fifty-four; portrait by John Crossland. (Art Gallery of South Australia)

It was with feelings peculiar to the occasion, that I gazed for the first time on the bold cliffs at the entrance of Port Jackson, as our vessel neared them, and speculated on the probable character of the landscape they hid; and I am free to confess, that I did not anticipate any thing equal to the scene which presented itself both to my sight and my judgment, as we sailed up the noble and extensive basin we had entered, towards the seat of government. A single glance was sufficient to tell me that the hills upon the southern shore of the port, the outlines of which were broken by houses and spires, must have been covered with the same dense and gloomy wood which abounded every where else. The contrast was indeed very great – the improvement singularly striking ... The cornfield and the orchard have supplemented the wild grass and the brush; a flourishing town stands over the ruins of the forest; the lowing of herds has succeeded the wild whoop of the savage; and the stillness of that once desert shore is now broken by the sound of the bugle and the busy hum of commerce.

Sturt's fascination with Australia continued throughout his life. He had 'strong feelings in its favour' and 'a deep feeling of interest in its prosperity'.[5]

Soon after the arrival of the *Mariner* Sturt paid his official call on the governor of the colony, Lieutenant General Ralph Darling, who had succeeded General Sir Thomas Brisbane in 1825. Darling (who was later knighted and, later still, became a general) took an immediate liking to Sturt and looked on him as a man he could trust.[6] Sturt was soon appointed Darling's private secretary and, in this capacity, was privy to all the problems of the colony. He realised that there would now be little opportunity to advance his military career; but the need to explore the inland river systems was apparent to all, and Sturt believed that this was a field in which he could make a valuable and timely contribution.

Sturt became more and more interested in the idea of becoming an explorer and was fascinated by the theory that the known westward-flowing rivers terminated in an inland sea. This theory had been supported by John Oxley, and also by Allan Cunningham. Oxley had followed the Lachlan and Macquarie rivers for some distance towards the west in 1817 and 1818; but it had been a very wet season and he had been prevented from following the Macquarie River any further by a large area of marshland. Darling thought that, in a dry season, the riddle could be solved and he decided to give Sturt an opportunity to ascertain whether the

Macquarie did, in fact, flow into an inland sea. Darling had ample opportunity to discuss his ideas with Sturt and, in September 1828, he instructed him to organise an expedition 'for the purpose of exploring the interior of New Holland' and, specifically, 'to endeavour to determine the fate of the Macquarie River, by tracing it as far as possible beyond the point to which Mr. Oxley went, and by pushing westward ... to ascertain if there be any high lands in that direction ...'.[7] The public announcement of this decision caused something of a stir. The new surveyor-general, Thomas Mitchell, was incensed that he had been passed over, and wrote to the *Sydney Monitor* asking 'what qualifications has the Captain [Sturt], either as a scientific or practical traveller, to justify this appointment?' He might well ask. But, in the event, Darling's appointment of Sturt was commendable. Nevertheless, Mitchell became Sturt's most spiteful enemy.[8]

Sturt knew the elements of surveying but he was no professional. Sturt included an appendix to the published account of his first expedition which listed the stores provided to him by the government.[9] Only two of the items listed could be regarded as of use in surveying – a 'boat compass' and a 'telescope'. Nevertheless, there is no doubt that he had a 'plain theodolite' – which he took with him on both his first and second expeditions. Later this 'plain theodolite' came into the possession of Bernard Ingleby, who lent it to the Art Gallery of South Australia – where it was exhibited for many years, with a legend indicating that it had been used by Sturt on his 1828 and 1831 expeditions. In 1983, Mrs Bond, daughter of Bernard Ingleby, donated it to the Charles Sturt Memorial Museum Trust Inc., and it is one of the exhibits at Sturt House, Grange, a suburb of Adelaide (see page 24).

Hamilton Hume was appointed second-in-command of the expedition. He had already had considerable experience of exploration – indeed, he had been the leader of the Hume and Hovell

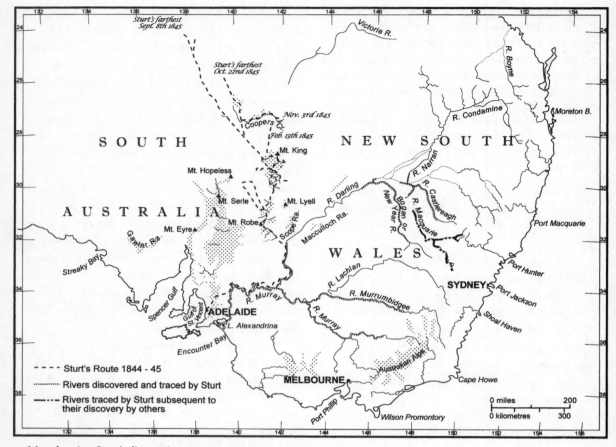

Map showing Sturt's discoveries. (reproduced from Sturt 1849, facing p. 5)

expedition to the south coast of Australia. There is some confusion about the number and names of the other members of the expedition. Darling had authorised Sturt to take two soldiers and eight convicts – but the list of names provided by Sturt included eleven convicts. Two or three of these might have been intended as couriers who would not continue beyond a certain point. Hopkinson and Fraser were the two soldiers. 'John' Harris was Sturt's batman – but Sturt did not mention him by name in his account of the expedition. Harris's real given name was Joseph. He had been Sturt's batman, or 'body servant' back in Ireland and had apparently 'begged to go with Sturt to Australia'.[10]

The detailed arrangements for the expedition

were completed early in November and, on 10 November 1828, Sturt and the other members of his party set off for Wellington, then the most distant settlement north-west of Sydney – where the expedition was mustered. They set off, with horses and bullocks, a lightweight boat and a boat carriage. Sturt had hoped to persuade one of the Wellington Aborigines to travel with him as a guide, but 'they were too lazy to wander far from their own district, and too fond of Maxwell's beef to leave it for a precarious bush subsistence.'[11] However, the expedition followed the Macquarie River and, from time to time, they met other tribes. Occasionally, Sturt obtained the services of an Aborigine as a guide. He was particularly impressed by one young man – Botheri. Sturt wrote that this young man 'acted as interpreter, and, by his facetious manner, contrived to keep the whole of us in a fit of laughter as we moved along'.[12] The Macquarie River diminished in volume as they continued, but they made good progress – despite the summer heat. On one occasion it was nearly 54 degrees Celsius (129 degrees Fahrenheit) in the shade at 2 p.m. Two of the men suffered from overexposure to the sun, and another had an attack of dysentery. Before long they reached the fringe of the marshes where Oxley had had to abandon his search. Sturt succeeded in locating Oxley's camp; and wrote that Oxley 'saw the river when it was overflowing its banks; on the present occasion it had scarcely sufficient water to support a current.'[13]

Progress now became very difficult; but it was essential that they determine the extent of the marshes and elucidate the further course of the river. Sturt and Hume, each with two men, set out on a number of separate scouting expeditions which, however, soon became urgent searches for drinking water. After one of these scouting expeditions Sturt wrote:[14]

We returned to camp, after a vain search for water, and were really at a loss what direction next to pursue ... The circumstance of there having been natives in the neighbourhood, of whom we had seen so few traces of late, assured me that water was at hand, but in what direction it was impossible to guess. As the path we had observed was leading northerly, we took up that course, and had not proceeded more than a mile upon it, when we suddenly found ourselves on the bank of a noble river ... The channel of the river was from seventy to eighty yards [seventy metres] broad, and enclosed an unbroken sheet of water, evidently very deep, and literally covered with pelicans and other wild fowl. Our surprise and delight may be better imagined than described.

It was 2 February 1829, and Sturt's first major discovery, which he named the Darling River 'as a lasting memorial of the respect I bear the

governor'.[16] But the delight of the members of the expedition turned to disappointment when the water was found too salty to drink.

Some Aboriginal people were found living not far from the river and, although they were frightened by the appearance of white people and of the horses, they recovered soon enough. The expedition then set off to follow the river downstream – but following the river was so difficult that they turned away for a time. They returned to the river banks and found that 'Its water was still salt, and from the increased number of wild fowl and pelicans upon it, as well as from the general flatness of the country, I certainly thought we were rapidly approaching some inland sea.'[15] Sturt found occasional supplies of fresh water but, eventually, he had to admit that 'the last pond ... was now eighteen miles behind us.' A few days later the absence of fresh water was critical and he decided to abandon 'the further pursuit of the river though it was with extreme reluctance that I did so'.

Sturt estimated that he had first seen the Darling River at 29° 37' S, 145° 33' E, and that he had traced it downstream for about 100 kilometres. It is now generally accepted that he first saw the Darling River near present-day Bourke – the position of which is 30° 09' S, 141° 55' E.[17]

However, this was not the only discovery by this expedition. They had made scouting excursions in several directions to determine the extent of the Macquarie Marshes, and to examine the neighbouring country. They had crossed a small river (later to be known as the Bogan) flowing northwards. They had followed the course of the Castlereagh River (first discovered by Evans in 1817). Sturt reported that despite the fact that it had a wide channel 'there was not a drop of water in it'. There was no water in it for a distance of 72 kilometres.[18] The channel of the Castlereagh River was found to reach the Darling River at a point 145 kilometres upstream of Sturt's first discovery of it. The Darling River 'seemed to roll on, totally heedless of such a tributary'.[19] Sturt and Hume confirmed the confluence of the Macquarie and Darling rivers.[20] The general picture, but perhaps not all the detail, was now clear – the Macquarie, Bogan and Castlereagh rivers are tributaries of the Darling. Sturt had justified Darling's selection to command the expedition to clarify the river system to the north-west. He had not had any serious difficulties with the local Aboriginal people, and the expedition arrived back at Wellington on 21 March 1829 'without the loss of a single man or beast'.[21] They returned to Sydney where Sturt rejoined his regiment.

THE MURRAY RIVER AND LAKE ALEXANDRINA

Sturt had been unable to trace the Darling River for any great distance and had not been able to determine whether it flows into an inland sea or the ocean. He had, however, established that it flows towards the south-west. A further expedition would be needed to examine the country in that direction. It seemed likely that the Murrumbidgee River – which had been discovered by Charles Throsby in 1821 and which had been crossed by Hume and Hovell on their expedition to the south coast – might also flow into the Darling River. This possibility needed investigation. In September 1829 Sturt received the governor's instruction to make necessary preparations for a second expedition.

Sturt invited Hamilton Hume to accompany him again – but Hume had to decline this invitation because his harvest was approaching. Sturt therefore engaged George Macleay, the son of the colonial secretary in Sydney. Sturt also arranged for his batman, Harris, and for the two soldiers from his regiment – Hopkinson and Fraser, who had accompanied him on his earlier expedition – to join the new venture. In addition, he engaged Joseph Clayton – a convict who was a skilled carpenter – and eight other convicts. A good carpenter was

required because Sturt had decided to build a prefabricated whaler, about 8 metres (about thirty feet) long, and to carry this overland until they reached the Murrumbidgee River. It would then be re-assembled. Moreover, in view of the likely difficulty of finding potable water en route, it was decided to include among the many stores a still for the distillation of brackish water. The expedition was supplied with drays to carry the food and equipment and set off from Sydney on 3 November 1829. They made for Brownlow Hill, the Macleay property, where George Macleay was scheduled to join them.

Sturt described the scene:[22]

> My servant Harris, who had shared my wanderings and had continued in my service for eighteen years, led the advance, with his companion Hopkinson. Nearly abreast of them the eccentric Fraser stalked along wholly lost in thought ... He had a gun over his shoulder, and his double shot belt as full as it could be of shot ... Some dogs Mr. Maxwell had kindly sent me followed close at his heels, as if they knew his interest in them, and they really seemed as if they were about to exchange their late confinement for the freedom of the woods. The whole of these formed a kind of advanced guard. At some distance in the rear the drays moved slowly along, in one of which rode the black boy mentioned in my previous volume, and behind them followed the pack animals. Robert Harris, whom I had appointed to superintend the animals [including the small flock of sheep] generally, kept his place near the horses, and the heavy Clayton, my carpenter, brought up the rear.

The 'black boy', an invited but unofficial member of the expedition, was evidently Botheri who had served for a time as a guide on Sturt's first expedition.[23] On the present expedition Botheri travelled with them until 22 December when Sturt recorded that 'my black boy deserted me.' He added that 'I was not surprised at his doing so ... he was far too cunning for our purpose.'[24]

The expedition travelled via Liverpool and

arrived at Brownlow Hill – where George Macleay joined them and assumed his role as second-in-command. Three days later they crossed the Goulburn Plains and visited several properties – including that owned by Hamilton Hume. This was on the banks of the Lorn River, a branch of the Lachlan River. They passed a number of other properties and, at last, reached the Murrumbidgee River (which Sturt wrote as 'Morumbidgee') 'whose waters, foaming among rocks, or circling in eddies, gave early promise of a reckless course'.[25] They were then not far from present-day Gundagai. They followed the course of the river for a time and then crossed it, using a rope ferry and a punt made by fixing some tarpaulins on an oblong frame. Continuing, they averaged about 20 kilometres a day.

From time to time they met groups of Aboriginal people – one of whom recalled seeing a party of White men, many years earlier, in the same area. It seems likely that they were members of Oxley's party.

A few days later, they came to some marshy ground which was reminiscent of the Macquarie Marshes. Sturt and Macleay crossed the river again – to investigate. They were soon convinced that the marsh was caused by the Lachlan River flowing into the Murrumbidgee. Beyond this confluence they found that the Murrumbidgee became a rapidly flowing river. Sturt decided that it was now time to take to their whaler, and to dispense with the drays. They established a camp by the river and, under the expert guidance of Clayton, the whaler was assembled.[26] They also built a skiff, about half the size of the whaler, using the local timber. The two boats were painted and ready for use in seven days.

It had always been accepted that it would be impossible to accommodate all the members of the expedition in the two boats and Sturt therefore had to decide who would continue down the river and who would become a member of the 'Base Party'. After much thought Sturt decided that the 'Boat Party' was to include: Charles Sturt, George Macleay, Harris (soldier, batman), Fraser (soldier), Hopkinson (soldier), John McNamee (convict, labourer), William Mulholland (convict, labourer) and Joseph Clayton (convict, carpenter). The 'Base Party' was to be comprised of: Robert Harris (convict), Michael Shaw (convict, bullock driver), William Littlewood (convict), Thomas Hall (convict, ploughman, and shepherd), Peter Moreton (convict) and Peter Whelan (convict).[27] The base party was ordered to remain by the river for a week after the boats had departed, and then to return to Goulburn Plains.

On 7 January 1830 the two boats were launched and loaded. All the flour, the tea and the tobacco went into the whaler, and the meat casks, still and carpenter's tools went into the skiff. They then set off down the Murrumbidgee.[28] Both boats experienced difficulty with submerged logs. The skiff was holed and sank, but was recovered and repaired. Most of the stores were also saved, but it was later found that water had entered the meat casks and 'the greater part of the provisions had got spoiled'.[29] The whaler was holed on another occasion, but this too was repaired.

Then, on 14 January: 'At 3 p.m., Hopkinson called out that we were approaching a junction, and in less than a minute afterwards, we were hurried into a broad and noble river.'[30] Sturt was fond of using the adjective 'noble' but, on this occasion, he was well justified. The new river had a width of about 100 metres, with a depth of from 4 to 6 metres, and was flowing at 2½ knots.[31] It was a larger river than any that had been discovered in New South Wales. They continued down this waterway and observed that, before long, it was joined by another, which was reckoned to be the Darling River – the Murrumbidgee and the Darling both flowed into the newly discovered 'noble' river. Sturt decided to name the new river the Murray River as a compliment to 'the distinguished officer,

Sir George Murray, who then presided over the colonial department'.[32] Sturt placed the junction of the Murray and Darling rivers at 34° 03' S, 140° 56' E, but he added: 'I must remark, however, that the lunars I took on this occasion, were not satisfactory and that there is, probably, an error, though not a material one, in the calculation.'[33] Present-day Wentworth – which lies at the junction of these rivers – has a latitude of 34° 06' S, and a longitude of 141° 55' E.

Not long afterwards, when Sturt was indisposed, George Macleay offered to wind the chronometer but, being inexperienced, managed to break the spring.

Sturt has been criticised for not taking a fair share in the daily rowing down the river – although he did take turns on the return journey against the current.[34] The truth is, however, that he had other things to do. Both before and after the accident with the chronometer, Sturt recorded every bend in the river by a compass reading. 'The bearings of the angles as they opened,' he wrote, 'were regularly marked by me, so that not a single winding or course of the Murray is omitted in the large chart.'[35]

From time to time, groups of Aborigines gathered on the banks of the river and appeared to be determined to attack Sturt and his companions and to prevent their progress down the river – but the tolerance exercised by both Sturt and Macleay managed to prevent a major conflict. After they had passed the present North West Bend, the Aboriginal men, women and children were observed to be horribly diseased. Sturt wrote:[36]

It would disgust my readers were I to describe the miserable state of disease and infirmity to which these tribes were reduced ... the most violent cutaneous eruptions, and glandular affections, absolutely raged through the whole of them; yet we could not escape from the persecuting examination of our persons that curiosity prompted them in some measure to insist upon.

A few of them were blind.

It seems that these Aboriginal people were suffering from smallpox. It is thought that this disease was first introduced by the Macassans who had annually visited the northern shores of Australia for many years to collect trepang. As far as is known, there was no case of smallpox on the First Fleet itself – but there was an epidemic of smallpox among the Aborigines of Port Jackson a year after first settlement.[37] The disease seems to have been carried from tribe to tribe over a period. Indeed, Cleland refers to a later introduction which 'unquestionably spread as far as the Great Bight'.[38] It has been established that there were three epidemics of smallpox in Aboriginal Australia between 1788 and 1870. The first was on the east coast, at Port Jackson and elsewhere in 1789; the second was between 1829 and 1831; and the third was in the 1860s on the north-west coast and inland.[39]

Sturt did not immediately identify the disease as smallpox but, in 1838, when he was overlanding cattle to South Australia, he saw the results of the disease. He wrote:[40]

We were joined by parties [of Aborigines] from different quarters, that when united form a considerable body of athletic and well proportioned men ... I observed many of them as if pitted by the Small Pox, so it would appear the disease which was enjoying such fearful effect upon them when I was on the Banks of the Darling in 1828 and of the Hume [Murray] in 1829 had been universal. It must have committed dreadful havoc amongst them, since on this journey I did not see hundreds to the thousands I saw on my former Expeditions.

It has been suggested that the Aborigines were also the victims of venereal syphilis and that it was introduced to the Aboriginal population on the south coast and Murray mouth by the sealers and whalers who had been active in that area since about 1806.[41]

Thirty-three days after leaving their base camp on the Murrumbidgee River, Sturt and his companions arrived at the termination of the Murray

This view of the Murray River below Moorundie is reminiscent of that recorded in Sturt's watercolour, reproduced as a colour plate in this volume. (Geoffrey Badger)

River – a beautiful lake that Sturt named Lake Alexandrina (after the Princess of that name who later became Queen Victoria) on 9 February 1830. Sturt wrote that they could see the mountain ranges stretching from south to north, and a peak that he first identified as Mt Lofty (named by Matthew Flinders), but later corrected to Mt Barker (which had not been named at the time it was seen by Sturt).

Sturt and his party were not the first Europeans to sight Lake Alexandrina. It had been visited by sealers from Van Diemen's Land at least fifteen months before Sturt sailed over its waters in February 1830.[42] These sealers were presumably the first Europeans to discover the lake.

However, the lake was a disappointment in one respect. It was soon apparent that its exit to the Southern Ocean would not normally be navigable by even medium-sized vessels. On 12 February Sturt, Macleay and Fraser descended the westerly,

or Goolwa, channel, walked across the sand hummocks to the sea, and then headed easterly along the beach until they reached the mouth of the river and the lake.[43]

In the height of summer very little, if any, water flows from the river into the sea. There was clearly no chance that Sturt and his companions could be picked up by any vessel sent from Sydney to find them, and the only course open to them was to retreat up the river against the current. The men were already very tired and their rations had been reduced almost to starvation level. Sturt and Macleay now took their share of the rowing – bearing in mind that four oars were now necessary rather than the two that sufficed on their way down the river. They used a sail whenever there was a suitable wind – but it was exhausting work. The return journey, up the river, took four days longer than the passage downstream.[44] They were all near starvation and completely exhausted when they reached the site of the base on the Murrumbidgee River. It was deserted. Two men were sent off to Goulburn to alert the base party and a week later supplies arrived for them all.

The return journey up the river had been little short of a nightmare. But there were some consolations – not the least of which was that, despite a few threatening situations with Aboriginal people on the banks of the river, no one had been killed or even injured. Sturt's account of his expedition is almost free of anecdotes, but one incident deserves mention. Sturt wrote that on one occasion he had just thrown himself on his bed and had scarcely lain down for five minutes when Harris called out:[45]

'The blacks are close to me, sir; shall I fire at them?'
'How far are they?' Sturt asked.
'Within ten yards, sir'.
'Then fire', said Sturt, and Harris immediately did so. Macleay and Sturt jumped up and joined Harris.
'Well, Harris', said Sturt, 'did you kill your man?'
'No, sir', said Harris, 'I thought you would repent it, so I fired between the two'.

Sturt's second expedition returned safely to Sydney on 25 May 1830 – seven months after their departure.

Sturt submitted his report to Governor Darling – who recognised the importance of the discoveries made. He arranged for Captain Collet Barker to lead a further expedition to explore the environs of Lake Alexandrina and the eastern shores of St Vincent Gulf. Barker noted a mountain not far from Mt Lofty, and Sturt later decided it should be named Mt Barker. Unfortunately, Barker, when alone, was speared by three Aboriginal men, and his body thrown into the sea.

Sturt's contribution to the exploration and development of Australia was second to none. He had discovered the Murray–Darling River system – which is now known to be the greatest and most important in the continent. It drains about one million square kilometres, or one-seventh of Australia. Moreover:[46]

The Basin supports one-quarter of the nation's cattle and dairy farms, about one-half of the sheep, lambs and cropland, and almost three-quarters of its irrigated land.

11

THOMAS LIVINGSTON MITCHELL – THE SURVEYOR-GENERAL

Thomas Livingston Mitchell was born at Craigend, Strathclyde, Scotland, on 15 June 1792. His father was John Mitchell and his mother was Janet, née Wilson. It might also be noted that he was the grandson of Alexander Mitchell and Alisa Mitchell, née Livingston. Some authors give Thomas Mitchell's second given name as Livingstone, but it seems likely that Thomas Mitchell's parents wanted to commemorate the grandmother.[1]

Very little is known of Mitchell's early life, or of his family. However, it seems that he was well educated and that he was commissioned as a second lieutenant in the First Battalion of the 95th Regiment of Foot in July 1811 when he was nineteen years of age, and that he served in the Iberian Peninsula, where Wellington had already had some successes against the French. In May 1812 Mitchell was seconded to the staff of General Sir George Murray, the quartermaster-general under Wellington. From that time Mitchell was 'busy on field work, surveying, and general topographical intelligence'. He was promoted to the rank of lieutenant on 16 September 1812.[2]

Wellington continued to make progress against the French in the Iberian Peninsula, and in Russia. Napoléon was forced to retreat from Moscow and was defeated by the allies at the Battle of the Nations in 1813. Napoléon abdicated soon afterwards and was exiled to Elba. He escaped from Elba, however, and raised an army – but was decisively defeated

by Wellington and the allied armies at the Battle of Waterloo on 18 June 1815. Mitchell, to his everlasting regret, was still on staff duties in the Peninsula and was not with his regiment at this great battle, being occupied with his maps of the peninsular battles.

In June 1818 Mitchell married Mary Blunt, the daughter of General Richard Blunt. However, with the defeat of Napoléon, British expenditure on the armed forces was greatly reduced and, in December 1818, Mitchell was placed on half-pay – only six months or so after his marriage. Had the war continued he would not have been financially embarrassed, but it was now clear that he would have to seek other employment, in the meantime continuing to work on his maps of the peninsular battles. In 1825 he was promoted to the rank of captain and, in September 1826, he became a major – but still on half-pay. In accordance with the custom of the time he wrote letters to titled men of eminence seeking their support and patronage in his search for suitable employment. Prominent among these was General Sir George Murray, his commanding officer during the Peninsular War. Such was the power of patronage that Murray arranged for Mitchell to be interviewed by Robert Hay, the permanent under-secretary at the Colonial Office.[3]

In that era the procedures followed by the Colonial Office left a good deal to be desired, as the following contemporary account indicates:[4]

> Mr. Hay, the intelligent, patriotic, and urbane under-secretary, has not, I believe, ever been in the colonies, nor am I aware of any clerk in the Colonial Office who had even been out of Europe: nay more the very agents appointed by the secretary of state to represent the colonies in England, have never, so far as I can ascertain, with very few exceptions, crossed the Channel! Let any unprejudiced man ask himself how can our colonies be well managed under such a system.

On 29 January 1827 Under-Secretary Robert William Hay (who was under-secretary from 1825 to 1836) was able to tell Mitchell that the secretary of state for the Colonies, Earl Bathurst, had approved his appointment as deputy surveyor-general in New South Wales, and that he would be appointed surveyor-general when the incumbent, John Oxley, died. Oxley was already very ill and was expected to die within a short time. Hay also told Mitchell that he would be free to write private letters to him about his life and difficulties after his arrival in Sydney. Mitchell was to take full advantage of this permission, more especially to criticise the governor, Lieutenant-General Sir Ralph Darling.

This was an extraordinary arrangement, and it has been examined by D. M. Young:[5]

> Hay instituted a dubious practice by encouraging lesser colonial officials to write to him privately; thus he received and acknowledged unofficial reports on colonial governors, a practice that was subversive of the trust traditionally reposed in those officials.

However, Young went on to say: 'There was no deep dark purpose in this. To him [Hay] the colonial civil service in its many branches was like a club with whose members he kept in touch by means of personal letters.' Nevertheless, James Stephen 'when he became Permanent Undersecretary, very properly, took steps to suppress such letters'.[6] Mitchell's official letter of appointment was dated 7 February and he was later asked to ensure that

he, and his family, would be on board the convict ship *Prince Regent* on 17 May 1827. They were given the exclusive use of the 'Great Cabin' at a cost of £200. The ship did not sail at once, however, and Mitchell spent the next few days buying articles (such as a double-barrelled gun with bayonet),[7] that would be useful to him or his family in New South Wales.

The *Prince Regent* weighed anchor on Sunday 10 June and moved further out before anchoring again. The next morning they sailed, and arrived at Sydney on Sunday 27 September 1827 – only four months after Captain Charles Sturt. Sydney was still essentially a penal settlement. The total White population of the colony was then about 50 000, many of whom were either convicts or emancipists – that is, convicts who had served their sentence or who had been pardoned by the governor. There were a few 'free' settlers, and their number was increasing. Some of these were already wealthy and powerful. Many free settlers had become pastoralists, or squatters, and used convict labour to develop their properties. They also tended to argue that the emancipists should not be regarded as free settlers but should provide a pool of cheap labour. Those who held this view were regarded as 'exclusives'. A few service personnel and a few civil servants made up the rest of the population.

As the number of free settlers increased so did the demand for grazing land for sheep and cattle. In 1788 there were only twenty-nine sheep in the colony. A few additional sheep were imported over the next few years and, by 1805, the number had multiplied to 16 500 and, by 1813, to 50 000. In 1821 they totalled 290 000, and there were further increases over the next few years. Cattle numbers were also increasing.[8]

The free settlers who intended to become farmers or pastoralists had to select their land – which then had to be surveyed by the surveyor-general and his staff. But this work lagged behind the occupation of the land – to the irritation of the settlers. Before Mitchell's arrival the government had appointed three commissioners in addition to Surveyor-General John Oxley – who was the chief commissioner. In 1827 Oxley was so ill that Mitchell was immediately made acting surveyor-general, and he was confirmed as surveyor-general when Oxley died two months later. The commission made little progress, however, and was disbanded in 1830 when the surveying of New South Wales became the responsibility of the surveyor-general.

Mitchell was convinced that a trigonometrical survey of the entire colony should be undertaken as a foundation for the surveying of individual farms or pastoral leases, and he set about this work. He proposed that in accord with the 'King's Instructions', the colony should be divided into sixteen counties. A medium county, he decided, would measure 40 miles (64.36 kilometres) square and thus contain 1600 square miles (4146 square kilometres). A medium parish would be 25 square miles (64.75 square kilometres), and there would be sixty-four parishes in each county. Moreover, according to his instructions, natural divisions formed by rivers or other landmarks should be used as boundaries whenever possible. It was clear that many years would be required to carry out the survey.[9]

Mitchell was also anxious to achieve fame as an explorer. Oxley had carried out a number of explorations while he was surveyor-general, and Mitchell saw no reason for his being denied the opportunity to do likewise. On 30 September 1828 he wrote a confidential letter (that is, without the knowledge of Governor Darling) to the permanent under-secretary at the Colonial Office, Robert Hay:[10]

I now avail myself of the permission you gave me to write, for I now feel the necessity for your support ... I am persuaded that you can never hear of anything creditable done by me under Governor Darling ... I embarked for this country with the prospect of succeeding Mr Oxley in exploring the interior and surveying the physical geography of this Colony, but have hitherto been disappointed in all those prospects which induced me to accept an appointment here. An officer on full pay [Captain Sturt] of a regiment here (who never travelled anywhere) is to be sent to explore the interior, while the Governor wishes the joint Commissioners of Survey and Valuation (who are not surveyors) to conduct a survey of the Colony! It being arranged that I should not leave Sydney. Many people believe that all this is intended to make me resign in favour of Captain [William] Dumaresq.

There were three Dumaresq brothers – Edward, Henry and William – and they were brothers-in-law of Governor Darling. All three had been appointed to positions of authority in the five months that Darling had been in office.[11] Darling had recommended William Dumaresq for appointment to the Surveyor-General's Department; but this recommendation had not been approved by the Colonial Office in London.[12] Mitchell claimed that Charles Sturt was also a relative of the governor. However, as Cumpston has written: 'Mitchell must have known that Sturt was not, in any degree of relationship, a relative of Darling.'[13]

Darling and Mitchell were mutually antagonistic. This is clear from a personal letter that Darling wrote to Hay on 28 March 1831:[14]

You will judge of my disposition towards him by my private letter to you of 6 June 1829. At that time I looked upon him as a hard-working, rude, ill-tempered fellow who quarelled with everyone, and who, I may add, is still as much detested as ever by those who have any business to transact with him.

Anxious to get the business of the Government done, I was willing to make any sacrifice, and he was allowed to snarl and growl unheeded, until at last his insolence became intolerable.

In the meantime there had been some changes in London. Sir George Murray had been appointed in 1828 but had ceased to be the secretary of state for the colonies in November 1830 and was succeeded by Viscount Goderich. It was Goderich who, on 15 March 1831, wrote to Darling to dismiss him from the position of governor and to recall him to London. Darling had not yet received this letter when he wrote to Goderich on 27 April 1831 to request that Major Mitchell be dismissed from the civil service! Even worse, as far as Darling was concerned, Goderich later wrote to the new governor of New South Wales, General Sir Richard Bourke, to instruct him that, in future, expeditions for the purpose of exploration should be carried out by the surveyor-general himself, or by his officers 'as, in this way, considerable expense would be saved'.[15] It would seem that Mitchell had triumphed! Nevertheless, Goderich wrote to Sir Richard Bourke:[16]

> I cannot approve of the line of conduct which he [Mitchell] has pursued towards the local Government under the administration of your Predecessor, whose views, however different from those conceived by Major Mitchell himself, or contrary to what he considered to be the spirit of the King's instructions, it was, nevertheless, his duty to carry into effect.

Darling left the colony on 22 October 1831 and Colonel Patrick Lindesay became the acting governor until the arrival of Sir Richard Bourke on 31 December 1831.

Mitchell was delighted that Lindesay had been appointed – for his relationship with Governor Darling was then at an all-time low. He was even more pleased when Lindesay agreed to authorise him to proceed on an expedition to explore the inland in order to confirm or otherwise some persistent reports of a large river flowing to the north-west. These reports had been enhanced by the account given by a convict named George Clarke, alias 'the Barber'. Clarke had escaped from custody, had disguised himself as an Aborigine by painting himself black, and had been living with Aboriginal people to the north of the settled

districts. He became a bushranger, stealing cattle. Mitchell described bushrangers as a '*sub-genus* in the order *banditti*, which, happily, can no longer exist, except in places inaccessible to the mounted police'.[17]

Clarke was recaptured and, under interrogation, he had claimed that he had seen the great river which the Aborigines called the 'Kindur'. Clarke gave impressive details about the river and about the Aboriginal people who lived in its locality. There were serious doubts about his story, but it seemed prudent to investigate it because, if true, the Kindur could well be of immense importance to the colony. Mitchell wrote that the acting governor, 'with due regard to the responsibility which my office seemed to impose upon me, as successor to Mr. Oxley, at once accepted my proffered services to conduct a party into the interior'.[18]

MITCHELL'S SEARCH FOR THE KINDUR

Mitchell set about organising his first expedition as an explorer without delay. He wanted to be able to return to Sydney before the arrival of the new governor. He briefed the staff of the Survey Department on the duties that they would be required to undertake during his absence, and he 'collected in haste a few articles of personal equipment'. 'Little time remained,' he wrote, 'for me to look at the sextants, theodolite, and other instruments necessary for the exploratory journey.' He selected 'the best men I could find' from among the convicts, and he also chose Heneage Finch, surveyor, and G. B. White, assistant surveyor, to accompany him.[19] The main party, under the command of Heneage Finch, left Sydney two weeks before Mitchell – who began this enterprise on Thursday 24 November 1831.

Mitchell and White spent the first night near Parramatta at the home of John Macarthur, where they were shown 'the first olive tree ever planted in

Australia'.[20] The next morning, James Macarthur accompanied Mitchell for a few kilometres to see him on his way. Later, Mitchell spent the night at Blaxland's property at Broke – which Mitchell had previously named in honour of one of his friends from the Peninsular War.

The complete party was assembled at the rendezvous on Foy Brook on 28 November, and set off two days later. In addition to the surveyors there were fifteen convicts. Burnett was a carpenter, who was convicted and transported for poaching – having been 'too fond of shooting game, his only cause of trouble'. The second carpenter was Robert Whiting, and Mitchell noted approvingly that he had been a soldier in the Guards. Four men were described as sailors, three as bullock drivers, one was a blacksmith, one was a groom and one – James Souter – was a medical assistant. There were two servants. One was Anthony Brown, who was Mitchell's servant. He was to go on all four of Mitchell's expeditions. The second was Henry Dawkins, and he was attached to Surveyor White. The medical assistant was unqualified, of course, but skilful – and attracted the prefix of 'doctor'. There were two carts and three drays, several pack horses and two canvas boats. They were provided with eight muskets, six pistols and a few rockets. On 8 December Mitchell was able to engage an Aboriginal man, named Jemmy, as a guide who soon proved his worth. However, Jemmy did not wish to leave his tribal territory and, when he retired from the expedition, Mitchell appointed another guide – this one being known as 'Mister Brown'.

They were now about to leave the settled areas and to enter country that was unknown – except that Oxley had visited some parts of it.[21] In the meantime they had crossed the Hunter River near Singleton and proceeded 'along the road leading to the pass in the Liverpool Range'.[22] They camped 'beside a small water-course near Muscle Brook [Muswellbrook]' and, two days later, came to a farm being worked by a Scottish 'free settler' who, having established his farm, was eagerly awaiting the arrival of his numerous family. Shortly afterwards a mounted policeman arrived and delivered a letter from the acting governor to Mitchell. Its purpose was to alert Mitchell to the fact that the convict George Clarke had managed to saw off his irons and had escaped from the prison at Bathurst and might cause trouble by arousing the Aboriginal people.

A few days later Mitchell began to ascend the Liverpool Range and, at this time, they came upon some distressed Aborigines who were suffering from 'a virulent kind of small-pox'.[23] They could not do much to help them. They gave them a few medicines, which they appreciated, and continued on their way.

Mitchell had been recording the positions of the prominent features by the process of triangulation, but this method depends on the existence of 'prominent features' and, in the absence of such features, he realised that he would have to depend on his chronometer for the determination of longitude.[24] Nevertheless, they proceeded 'over a perfectly level surface' and reached the bank of the Namoi River. They followed this river for some time and came upon a large stockyard which, the local Aboriginal people indicated, belonged to the convict–bushranger George Clarke. This was clearly 'Clarke's territory' and the stockyard was used to contain the cattle that he was accustomed to stealing.

Clarke had indicated that the large river was to be found further to the north-east beyond the mountains. He had also stated that the big river that was being sought by Mitchell was the first water to be met with after crossing the range. Mitchell managed to travel around the mountain range and did, indeed, come upon a river that flowed towards the west. But it was not the Kindur. It was the Gwydir River – which flows into the Barwon (which joins the Darling River). Allan Cunningham had discovered the Gwydir River in 1827 and named it after a Welsh peer.[25] The supposed Kindur

River was said to flow to the north-west; this one, as Mitchell showed, did not.

On 27 February, on the return journey, Mitchell wrote that 'Scurvy now began to affect the party.' They endeavoured to counteract the progress of the disease by 'plentiful issues of lime juice' but, because this was not fresh, much of its vitamin C had probably been lost. They also used some 'portable vegetable soups'. They do not seem to have tried eating any of the native fruit. Indeed, in January, when near the Gwydir River, Mitchell reported that they found a species of cucumber 'about the size of a plum, the flower being of a purple colour'. He added that it was very bitter and that 'Mr White and I peppered it, and washed the slices with vinegar, and then chewed it, but neither of us had the courage to swallow it.'[26]

It might be added that one native cucumber, Cucumis melo ssp. agrestis I, has been shown to contain a small amount of vitamin C, and that another 'bush cucumber', Mucia sp., has been shown to contain 20 milligrams per 100 grams of vitamin C.[27] Moreover, Frank Badman has written:[28]

When I worked in south-west Queensland in the 1960s I can remember collecting and eating the fruit of this plant, after first rubbing off the white 'bloom' on the skin, as a cure to 'Barcoo rot', which I believe is a mild form of scurvy and which was common amongst bush workers at that time. The symptoms were sores on the hands and fingers which oozed pus and took a very long time to heal up.

Mitchell was able to clarify the river systems in the general area, and the main purpose of the expedition had been achieved — there was no Kindur. He had proved that if any large river did exist it must be as far north of 29° S. 'All the rivers south of that parallel,' he wrote, 'and which had been described by the Barber as falling into such a river as the Kindur, have been ascertained to belong wholly to the basin of the Darling.'[29]

When Mitchell arrived back in Sydney, Clarke was again in custody — and Mitchell managed to cross-examine him. At the conclusion of this encounter Mitchell was quite satisfied that Clarke had never been beyond the range, and had never seen the Gwydir nor, of course, the Kindur. It was not wholly a wasted effort, however. Sheep and cattle stations were soon being established in the country that Mitchell had explored.

MITCHELL'S EXPLORATION OF THE DARLING RIVER

The Darling River had been discovered and named by Charles Sturt — but he had not had the resources to follow it for more than a few kilometres. On his second expedition Sturt had explored the Murrumbidgee—Murray river system and had observed a major river, which he tentatively identified as the Darling River, flowing into the Murray River (at Wentworth). The greater part of the Darling River remained to be explored and the authorities in London believed that this should be remedied, without undue delay, by Mitchell and his survey department.

The load of routine work to be undertaken by the survey department was such that Mitchell decided to defer the departure of his second expedition until 1835. In the meantime he arranged for the construction of two light whalers, and a cart to carry them, one inside the other. They were to be suspended on canvas. This was carried out and the experiment was a great success.

Richard Cunningham (the brother of Allan Cunningham) was appointed botanist to the expedition, and a young assistant surveyor from the survey department, James (or John) Larmer, was selected to accompany Mitchell. Alexander Burnett, a carpenter from Mitchell's first expedition, was appointed overseer, and twenty others were selected. Nine of these men (including Burnett) had served on Mitchell's first expedition. When all was ready the main party left Parramatta on 9 March 1835.

In addition to the boat carriage, there were seven carts, and a number of pack-horses and bullocks. They also took with them two 'mountain barometers', which were carried by two men – this being their main duty when the party was on the move.

Mitchell set off from Sydney on 31 March and, on arrival at Parramatta, he obtained the loan of 'a good chronometer' from the observatory there. He crossed the Hawkesbury and entered the county of Cook 'so named by me, in considering that its lofty summits must have been the first land, that met the eye of the celebrated navigator, on his first approach to the eastern coast'. To cross the mountains he used the 'pass of Queen Victoria, named by me after the youthful Princess'. He arrived at the rendezvous at Boree, just west of Orange, using 'an entirely new road, opened in a new direction, first recommended by me in 1827'.[30]

Mitchell, and the two men carrying his mountain barometers and his theodolite, climbed the adjacent Mt Canobolas – said to be the highest peak between the Blue Mountains and the Indian Ocean.[31] Its name is derived from two Aboriginal words – 'coona' meaning 'shoulder', and 'booloo' meaning 'two'. This referred to its two peaks. Mitchell determined its height to be 1359 metres (4462 feet). Modern determinations give the height as 1397 metres (4583 feet) above sea level.[32] Mitchell wanted to use this peak as a prominent feature in his proposed triangulation survey. Indeed, a few days later he wrote that with Cunningham, and three men to carry his theodolite, sextant and barometer, he climbed another peak and took the bearings of all visible peaks – including that of Mt Canobolas.[33] In this way he was able to extend his survey westwards.

A few days later, on 17 April, Mitchell was told that 'Mr Cunningham was missing.' Occasional absences of Cunningham were not uncommon as he endeavoured to find the most interesting plants. However, 'as he had left the party early in the day,

in order to join me [Mitchell] it was evident ... that he had gone astray.' He was still missing that night and shots were fired and the bugle sounded in the hope that he would find his way to the camp, 'but poor Mr. Cunningham came not.'[34] They followed his tracks for many kilometres and found Cunningham's horse dead. They also found his handkerchief, and a part of his coat. It was later established by Lieutenant W. Zouch of the Mounted Police that Cunningham had been murdered by Aborigines.[35]

There was nothing for it but to proceed along the banks of the Bogan River and continue to hope. At this time Mitchell observed the procedure followed by the Aboriginal people when water was not available – 'they dug up the roots [of trees] for the sake of drinking the sap.' This procedure is described in the chapter on the explorations by Edward Eyre (Chapter 12). From time to time they were guided by Aborigines. There were some difficulties, but they were able to make steady progress. It was a very special day when, climbing a hill, Mitchell came across several stumps of trees which had clearly been cut down with an axe. 'I was thus satisfied,' he wrote, 'that this was the hill on which Captain Sturt's party burnt the trees, when a man was missing.'[36]

As they approached the position of the Darling River, the main problem was that it would prove to be salty, as Sturt had reported. However, when they arrived, Mitchell 'was agreeably surprised, on descending the steep bank, to find the taste perfectly sweet'.[37] Evidently, the rainfall over the country, which drains into the Darling, had been much greater than in the year of Sturt's discovery.

The next step was to prepare a camp and to set it up in such a way that it could be readily defended in case of an attack by the local Aboriginal people. They built a stockade with logs and named it Fort Bourke, after the governor. Soon afterwards they did have a visit from a number of Aborigines who, however, had no hostile intentions. Most of them had had smallpox (which Mitchell attributed to 'bad water'), and he thought the women were 'hideous'. The males (but not the young boy who was with them) had lost the right front tooth.

Mitchell had surveyed the Bogan River nearly from its sources to its junction with the Darling River. It was a substantial achievement; but they now had to follow the Darling River. The Aboriginal people had resumed their normal occupations. Indeed, one Aboriginal man 'while passing down the river to-day on a piece of bark, perceived Mr. Larmer [the assistant surveyor] fishing, upon which he approached the river bank and after throwing to him a fish he had caught, continued in his frail *bark* to float down the stream'. Mitchell added that 'This was a most prepossessing act of kindness'.[38]

Mitchell hoped to examine the Darling River using the two boats that they had brought with them. They began to do so, but the obstructions in the river caused so much trouble that they returned to Fort Bourke. Mitchell then set out with four men on horseback on a scouting expedition and, having obtained some idea of the lie of the land, returned to Fort Bourke again. The entire party then set off to follow the Darling River. Before long they came upon the remains of a large hut 'in the construction of which an axe had been used' – suggesting that Europeans had visited the vicinity. A few kilometres further on they came to a dry watercourse and it occurred to Mitchell 'that this might be the one, at the mouth of which, Mr. Hume [the second-in-command of the Sturt expedition] had cut his name'.[39] The overseer, Burnett, and the 'doctor', Souter, were therefore sent to follow the dry watercourse to the Darling – and they found the large gum tree in which Hamilton Hume had carved his initials, 'H. H.' These letters were found to be about 12 centimetres in height and had evidently been carved with a tomahawk.

From time to time, as they proceeded down the river, they met groups of Aborigines – and had an opportunity to observe their living conditions. On one occasion, for example, they examined a number

of permanent huts on each side of the river. These were large enough to accommodate as many as fifteen people, and the walls were about 30 centimetres thick. Mitchell wrote that these indicated that this tribe had peaceful habits 'for where the natives are often at war, such habitations could neither be permanent nor safe'. The following morning this group of Aborigines, seventeen in number, hailed them from the woods. Mitchell and Burnett advanced towards them and did their best to communicate. Their chief sat in the middle of the front row and, at the conclusion of the interview, Mitchell presented him with a greyhound pup and a tomahawk. The chief had not seen a tomahawk before and its uses had to be demonstrated.[40]

A few days later, however, they met an antagonistic Aboriginal man with a boy. Both of them 'threw up dust' at the intruders 'in a clever way, with their toes'.[41] More Aboriginal people joined them and began spitting at the White invaders. It was clear enough that the Aborigines wanted them to leave. Mitchell wrote that 'The difference in disposition between tribes not very remote from each other was often striking. We had left, at only three days' journey behind us, natives as kind and civil as any I had met with; and I was rather at a loss now to understand, how they could exist so near fiends like these.'[42]

Mitchell took opportunities to examine the surrounding country whenever possible – and he named a number of features. On one such occasion he 'named the first hill beyond the Darling, ever ascended by any European, after my friend Mr. Murchisson [Murchison; Sir Roderick Impey Murchison], a gentleman who has so greatly advanced the science of geology'.[43] It is a relatively small hill, with a height of 201 metres. When he returned to camp after this excursion Mitchell was pleased to find that 'no natives had visited the camp during my absence'.[44] However, on one occasion, the blacksmith was busy at his forge when a party of Aboriginal people arrived – and the Aborigines took the opportunity to steal everything that they could. In contrast, another group of friendly Aborigines helped to round up the cattle. The men in this latter group all retained both front teeth and, as Mitchell put it: 'The difference between the conduct of these harmless people, and that of those we had last seen, was very striking.'[45] On average, however, the antagonism of the Aboriginal people to the explorers seemed to increase the further south they went. 'We wanted nothing, asked for nothing' wrote Mitchell, 'on the contrary, we gave them presents of articles the most desirable to them; and they beset us as keenly and with as little remorse as wild beasts seek their prey.'[46] Mitchell began to regret that they had given so many presents to so many of the Aborigines. 'It was evident now,' he wrote, 'how injudicious we had been in giving these savages presents; had we not done so, we should not have been so much importuned by them.'[47]

It now seemed certain that the Darling River was the same as that which Sturt had seen, joining the Murray River. It had been followed for about 480 kilometres, and Mitchell had arrived at a series of lakes that he named Laidley's Ponds – but this name is no longer used. The settlement there is now known by the Aboriginal word 'Menindee' – and the largest lake is known as Menindee Lake.

It seemed that the continuation of the survey 'was scarcely an object worth the peril to attend it' because they could hardly proceed 'without re-peated conflicts'. Moreover, some of the men were now showing symptoms of scurvy, and one of these was now an invalid. Another man had dysentery and was also an invalid.[48]

Mitchell and his companions therefore set off to return to Fort Bourke. They encountered the 'spitting' Aboriginal people again, and excessively demanding Aborigines wanting tomahawks and the like. However, Mitchell was able to add to his survey. He named Mt Macpherson – after the collector of internal revenue at Sydney. They returned to Fort Bourke with an increased knowledge of Aboriginal behaviour, so much so that Mitchell wrote:[49]

It was evident, that our presents had the worst effect, for although they were given with every demonstration of good will on our part, the gifts only seemed to awaken on theirs, a desire to destroy us, and to take all we had.

They still had to travel overland to Sydney, and sickness was increasing. Robert Whiting, who had been an invalid at the time they were near Menindee, was now described as having 'black scurvy' and was becoming weaker every day. His teeth were dropping out. Another man, Johnston, was also described as having 'black scurvy' which was partly attributed to the rancidity of the salt pork – but it can now be safely stated that he was suffering from a deficiency of vitamin C. On their return to the settled districts the men suffering from scurvy were soon restored to health.[50]

12

EDWARD JOHN EYRE
AND THE DESERT COUNTRY

Edward John Eyre was born at Whipsnade, Bedfordshire, on 5 August 1815. He was educated at 'endowed' schools in Lincolnshire and appeared to be destined for a career in the army. Indeed, his 'name was put down in the Commander-in-Chief's List for the purchase of a commission and the purchase money was lodged with the army agents'. However, on the advice of his father, who was a clergyman, he decided to emigrate to Australia, and his parents gave him £400 to enable him to begin his new life there. 'I felt sure,' he later wrote, 'that I should do well and hoped that perhaps in a few years I might return to my native country with a fortune.'[1] He took passage on the *Ellen* – which sailed from the Downs on 17 October 1832. Eyre was aged seventeen at the time. The *Ellen* reached Hobart on 2 March 1833 and, by a fortunate chance, Captain and Mrs Edward Dumaresq, who had been serving in Van Diemen's Land, boarded the vessel for passage to Sydney.

Edward Dumaresq was the younger brother of the wealthy pastoralist Henry Dumaresq. They (and another brother) were brothers-in-law to Governor Sir Ralph Darling. The *Ellen* docked at Sydney Cove on 28 March, and it was not long before Eyre had an opportunity to meet Henry Dumaresq – who invited him to visit his station, St Heliers, on the Hunter River. During his visit there Eyre was advised to obtain experience of the land by working with an established settler. Eyre accepted this advice

and moved to William Bell's Cheshunt Park – 40 kilometres from St Heliers. There he learnt how to raise sheep and cattle. Before long Eyre purchased, sight unseen, his own sheep station – 'Woodlands', on the Molonglo Plains (near present-day Canberra) – and bought 400 ten-month-old lambs to stock it. Once he had stock he was assigned six convicts to assist him. It seems certain that the man he appointed as overseer, John Baxter, was one of these convicts on assignment.[2] Yet Eyre was not entirely happy. He had trouble with disease in the sheep and, although for a time he was in partnership with John Morphy (his favourite companion on the *Ellen*), there were other financial problems.

The colony was expanding and new settlements had been established at Port Phillip (which was named Melbourne in honour of the British prime minister, in 1837) and on Gulf St Vincent (named Adelaide after Queen Adelaide, the consort of King William IV, in 1836). Eyre became attracted to the possibility of earning money by 'overlanding' sheep and cattle to these new areas. The word 'overlander' had not yet been coined – although, within a few years, it became widely used.[3] Eyre was not the first to overland stock to Port Phillip. Joseph Hawdon, John Gardiner and John Hepburn were the first. Indeed, Hawdon arrived in Melbourne at the end of his *second* overlanding soon after Eyre. Eyre regarded him as 'the most active, enterprising and indefatigable of all the Australian colonists'.[4]

Eyre went to Sydney to assemble stores and stock and to hire the men he needed. It was on this occasion that he met Charles Sturt for the first time, and they became life-long friends. Eyre arranged with Robert Campbell, a wealthy pastoralist, to overland some of his stock (and borrowed £500) from Campbell's son, Charles. Eyre also received a gift of £150 'from a dear and kind aunt in England'. He sold 'Woodlands' at a good profit, but retained the use of it for a further year. Eyre returned to the Molonglo district to obtain additional stock, and again went to Sydney to finalise his affairs. However, all was ready at 'Woodlands' by 1 April 1837, and the overlanding to Port Phillip began. Eyre's men had all become drunk the night before and they 'were fit for nothing in the morning', so they made only about 5 kilometres (three miles) that day.[5]

They travelled in two divisions. In the first division Eyre had an English couple, a shepherd, a watchman, a cart and horse, and the 414 sheep. In the second division he had three drays, seventy-eight head of cattle, his overseer (John Baxter), eight men and a 'gentleman' by the name of Elliott. They reached the Yass Plains on 13 April and Eyre arrived at the Murrumbidgee River at Gundagai on 17 April. On 27 April, by some happy chance, George Macleay 'came up with the party' and spent a night with them before moving on. Macleay was the man who had accompanied Sturt down the Murrumbidgee River and the Murray River – so it was a happy meeting. Crossing of the Murrumbidgee River caused problems and it was 6 May before all the animals and men were across. They had travelled 200 kilometres from Molonglo.

They continued southwards, reached the Ovens River on 16 June and, on 28 June, arrived at the Goulburn River. In this vicinity Eyre met a party travelling under the leadership of William Yaldwyn. They had two young Aboriginal boys with them. They were about eight years old, had 'come with some man from the Murray' and had remained with Yaldwyn's drays 'when he crossed the Goulburn'.

Because no one knew what to do with them, Eyre attached them to his own party.[6] One was called Cootachah (and nicknamed Yarry); the other was Joshuing. Eyre became very fond of those two spirited young boys and his special interest in Aboriginal people seems to have originated with them. Moreover, they were useful both as trackers and as interpreters.

As the overlanders approached the Port Phillip district, Eyre rode on ahead to select a suitable camping site. The remainder of his party, with the stock, arrived two weeks later, on 2 August 1837, a few days before Eyre's twenty-second birthday. It had been a very successful overlanding. They had covered the 756 kilometres (470 miles) in thirteen weeks. Of the original 414 sheep, there were now 400 – but 86 lambs had been born. Eyre sold his stock and made a handsome profit.[7]

There was no regular shipping service from Melbourne to Port Jackson in those days, but there were occasional ships from Melbourne to Launceston, and passage to Port Jackson could be obtained from Hobart. Eyre, Baxter and the two Aboriginal boys – together with two Australian dogs, presumably dingo-crosses – took passage to Launceston. Baxter and the dogs set off to walk to Hobart. Eyre and the two Aboriginal boys had boarded the mail coach for Hobart on 25 September.[8] Eyre spent several days in Hobart, waiting for a passage to Port Jackson, and he recorded:[9]

I took the black boys to the theatre where they attracted a good deal of attention and were loaded with fruits and sweet things given to them by one person or another. They did not seem to care about the performance, and in truth it was execrable. On another day I took them to see the troops parade with which, and especially with the band, they were highly delighted. They, too, were themselves the wonder and admiration of the surrounding crowd, as well as of the officers who gathered round as soon as the parade was over and gave the boys various little presents of one kind or another.

There were no Van Diemen's Land Aborigines to be seen in Hobart at that time. Most of the few remaining had been rounded up and re-settled on Flinders Island – where, unhappily, they soon died out.

On 4 October Eyre, Baxter and the two Aboriginal boys embarked on a small vessel for passage to Sydney. It was a boring voyage relieved only by the sight of many whales. They entered Port Jackson on 11 October and there received news of the death of King William and the accession of Queen Victoria.

Eyre wanted to repeat his successful overlanding by taking cattle and sheep to Adelaide. As he wrote in his *Autobiographical Narrative* soon after his arrival back in Sydney Cove:[10]

> I was most anxious to be the first to arrive in South Australia from Sydney – as yet no one had made the attempt. The distance was so much greater than to Port Phillip, the country so totally unoccupied and for the most part so entirely unknown, whilst the natives likely to be met with in so long a journey would probably be numerous and very troublesome. Hitherto, therefore, the expedition had appeared of too hazardous a nature for anyone to undertake it.

Unfortunately Joseph Hawdon had also decided to overland cattle to Adelaide and had already sent his cattle to the Murray. Nevertheless Eyre made his arrangements as rapidly as possible. Robert Campbell agreed to supply the cattle from his station at Limestone Plains. Baxter went off to settle his affairs – his wife had died during the overlanding to Port Phillip, and he was to join the expedition when this work was completed. Men were hired without difficulty. Sturt instructed Eyre on the use of a sextant and an artificial horizon – to determine the latitude.

They set off from Sydney on 8 November and, on the 28th, reached Campbell's farm at Limestone Plains – but the cattle had to be rounded up at his Snowy River Station. Eyre's second overlanding expedition left Limestone Plains on 21 December. He had 300 head of cattle, a few sheep to kill for meat on the way, eight horses, the two Aboriginal boys and another, named Unmallie, from Gundaroo. He had six men plus Baxter – who joined the expedition on 15 January, bringing sixty cattle of his own.[11] In the meantime, the overlanders had crossed the Murrumbidgee River and had been overtaken by a man on horseback:[12]

> ... carrying the first mail of the recently established overland post between Sydney and Melbourne, for the conveyance of which my friend Mr. Joseph Hawdon was the contractor. His horse was knocked up and he did not know what to do, so I lent him one of mine which he brought back to us on his return when repassing our party at the Murray eight days afterwards.

By coincidence, at the same time that Eyre met the Sydney–Melbourne mailman, Hawdon, on his way to join his own overlanding expedition, was riding with the same mailman.[13]

Eyre had examined the available maps of the country between Limestone Plains and Adelaide, and had also consulted Sturt. He chose a route that he thought would bring him to Adelaide before Hawdon. However, it proved to be too difficult, and he had to abandon it in favour of a route near the Murray River. Waterhouse has elucidated the situation:[14]

> The heart of the problem was that Major Mitchell's map of his 1836 journey, which formed the basis for later maps, was inaccurate. Mitchell simply mistook the identity of streams he encountered. When he crossed a stream near present-day Swan Hill, he thought it was the Goulburn, found and named by Hume and Hovell in 1824. But it was really the Marraboor River, a billabong connecting the true Loddon and the Murray. Later he crossed another stream, which remained unnamed, and a few days later recrossed it, without recognising it, and called this section the 'Yarraine', today's Loddon. To compound the problem, Mitchell also thought that the Yarrayne was the Goulburn not

realising that this latter river was a hundred miles further east. Leaving the Yarrayne, Mitchell proceeded west and crossed the stream called the Loddon but which is now known as Korong Creek.

Hawdon and Bonney followed the Goulburn River upstream, looking for the bridge that Mitchell said he had constructed over it. He had, in fact, built it over the Yarrayne. Hawdon and Bonney searched the Goulburn until it entered the Murray, and finding no bridge, turned west, crossed the Yarrayne, which ironically was almost dry, and then followed the Murray River to Adelaide.

Faulty maps were not the only difficulty faced by Eyre. Some of the men who had been hired to assist the overlanding to Adelaide were distressed by the conditions and wanted to proceed to Port Phillip rather than to Adelaide – citing the shortage of tobacco as their chief complaint. Eyre could not agree and, on 6 May 1838, five of his men defected (without pay) and it seems that they took the Aboriginal boy, Joshuing, with them. They did find their way to Port Phillip where they reported that 'Eyre had perished.'[15]

The net effect of all this was to delay Eyre. Hawdon and Bonney reached Adelaide in late March 1838, whereas Eyre did not arrive until 12 July. Eyre was well received in Adelaide, but it was Hawdon and Bonney who had been greeted with a grand public dinner as the first overlanders. Eyre did celebrate, however, for it was his twenty-third birthday on 5 August 1838.

Two weeks later, news arrived in Adelaide that Captain Charles Sturt and Captain John Finnis and their party, who were overlanding cattle to Adelaide, were near North West Bend on the Murray River, and that they were seriously short of supplies. The next morning, Eyre, with two companions and Cootachah, set off with a variety of foodstuffs to help them. Eyre soon found Sturt and his companions. The supply situation was remedied and a few days later Eyre and Sturt were able to ride into Adelaide together.[16]

Sturt had had some trouble with hostile Aboriginal people on his overlanding expedition. One of his men had been wounded by an Aboriginal spear, but Sturt had managed to restrain his companions. Two years before, Mitchell's exploration party had encountered Aborigines who had been 'demonstrating' against the passage of intruders through their territory – but had not actually attacked the travellers. Nevertheless, the explorers had shot and killed seven Aborigines, and wounded four others. That incident, and others like it, had increased the hostility of the Aborigines when they came upon the white intruders.[17]

Eyre managed to sell all his stock in Adelaide, and made a good profit for Robert Campbell and himself. He returned to Sydney by ship, arrived on 2 October, and immediately began to organise another overlanding expedition – again in cooperation with Robert Campbell and his son, Charles. Twelve days later, all was ready to proceed to Limestone Plains. His party included two 'gentlemen', ten men, two Aboriginal boys – Cootachah and Unmallie – and himself. This time he was to overland about a thousand sheep in addition to about six hundred cattle – and he was to travel by the river route. He took two drays and two carts to carry the supplies, and there were ten horses and a few working oxen. He had not won the race to be the first to overland cattle to Adelaide, but he was determined to be the first to overland *sheep*.

Unmallie did not continue as a member of the expedition. He apparently had a disagreement with one of the men and left to return to his own district. But when Eyre came to the Murrumbidgee River, he managed to recruit another Aboriginal boy, Neramberein, who soon received the nickname 'Joey'. They completed the 1537 kilometres (955 miles) to Adelaide in twenty-one weeks. No shots had been fired at Aboriginal people. They arrived at the outskirts of Adelaide on 12 March 1839. The cattle, sheep and working oxen were all sold for a profit of £4000 – half of which went to Eyre, and the other half to Campbell.[18]

Having felt the excitement of travelling over little-known country, Eyre now wanted to become an explorer. His friendship with Charles Sturt doubtless played a part in the development of this ambition. Eyre decided to mount his own expedition, at his own expense, to explore the country to the north of the settlement at Adelaide. No one had yet travelled more than 130 kilometres (eighty miles) or so north. Beyond that the country was completely unknown, and Eyre hoped to remedy this situation.

Eyre set off on 1 May 1839 accompanied by his overseer, John Baxter, two men, the two Aboriginal boys – Cootachah and Neramberein – a dray, a cart, ten horses, three dogs, eight sheep (to kill for food) and other supplies for a period of two months.[19] As they travelled northwards Eyre named the Broughton River – after William Grant Broughton, the bishop of Australia, whom Eyre had met in Hobart on Eyre's arrival in Australia, and with whom he had got on very well. Eyre also named Crystal Brook – because the water there was so clear. It is interesting that the Aboriginal people called it 'mercowie' – meaning clear water. He named Campbell Range after his overlanding partner. Eyre also named Mt Remarkable. Still further north he came to Mt Arden, which Flinders had seen and named after his grandfather. Not far from Mt Arden, Eyre found a creek with good water and decided to establish a depot there – hence Depot Creek.

Eyre then set off, with one of the Aboriginal boys, to examine the country to the west and north. It was all country unknown to Europeans except that Robert Brown – the botanist on board the *Investigator* – and a couple of companions had climbed Mt Brown (named by Flinders). Eyre climbed a mountain (that was later named Mt Eyre by Governor Gawler) and noted the almost barren plains and the harsh nature of the Flinders Ranges.

Eyre also observed a glittering white area to the west — that he was later to find was a vast salt pan. He was hoping to find good land for grazing, but saw land that was covered with saltbush and bluebush, and was bitterly disappointed. However, as Dutton has explained:[20]

> Eyre was ... not to know that sheep will thrive on saltbush in country where there is maybe a rainfall of no more than seven inches [18 centimetres] a year and not a blade of grass is seen, as long as there is water from dams or bores.

Baxter carried out a reconnaissance to the south-west, and also found relatively barren country. Eyre and Baxter then went on foot for 56 kilometres (thirty-five miles) to examine the sandy country to the west. It was enough. Their supplies were almost exhausted and they had no alternative but to turn back towards Adelaide. Eyre decided to proceed towards the Murray River and they reached the vicinity of North West Bend without difficulty. Following the river, they came to Moorundie (near present-day Blanchetown). Eyre was greatly attracted by Moorundie and he was later to live in this area for several years. Eyre continued to follow the river until just before Lake Alexandrina – where he decided to travel overland to Adelaide. All went well except that, as Eyre recorded, 'my careless driver upset his dray into a water hole, nearly killing the horse and spoiling everything in the dray – amongst other things unfortunately, was my chronometer.'[21] The chronometer was needed for the determination of longitude and its loss explains why although Eyre's account makes frequent reference to the determination of latitude – using both the Sun and several stars – but there are no references to the longitude.[22]

Eyre's appetite for exploration had increased and, after a little more than a month back in Adelaide, he was ready to set out on another expedition – this time to explore what is now known as the Eyre Peninsula. He sailed from Adelaide, with his party, on 8 July 1839 – bound for Port Lincoln. He left Port Lincoln by land on 5 August to explore the coast to the north-west. Water was hard to find but he did find a good spring under a hill – which he promptly named Mt Hope. Further north-west they came to Streaky Bay, where water was readily available, and Eyre established a depot there. Eyre and one of the Aboriginal boys then set off to examine the country to the west. They went just beyond Point Bell – which Flinders had named after his surgeon, Hugh Bell. Water was nowhere to be found and it was necessary to turn back to the Streaky Bay depot. Eyre had expected that the vessel carrying additional supplies would have arrived at Streaky Bay by this time, but there was no sign of it and, in the absence of other information, Eyre decided to make for Adelaide by travelling eastwards towards the head of Spencer Gulf, and then southwards. Eyre was again disappointed. The country was relatively barren but, as Dutton explained:[23]

> Actually this country is now well settled, and grows crops as well as carrying sheep, but even with modern techniques of soil improvement and water conservation the land has to be handled carefully and not overstocked or too heavily cropped.

It was on this journey, in September 1839, that Eyre named Gawler Range (after the governor), Mt Sturt (after his friend Charles Sturt) and Baxter Range, now Baxter Hills (after his overseer). It was also on this journey, on 22 September 1839, that Eyre observed the beautiful and striking flowers of *Clianthus formosus* – commonly known as Sturt's desert pea because Sturt observed it flowering in profusion on his 1844–45 expedition to central Australia. Eyre wrote:[24]

> Today I found a most splendid creeping plant in flower, growing in between the ranges, it was quite new to me, and very beautiful; the leaf was like that of a vetch [*Vicia sativa*] but larger, the flower bright scarlet, with a rich purple centre, shaped like a half globe with the convex side outwards; it

is winged, and something like a sweet pea in shape, the flowers hung pendant upon long slender stalks, very similar to those of sweet peas, and in the greatest profusion; altogether it was one of the prettiest and richest looking flowers I have seen in Australia.

Robert Brown, the distinguished botanist, who wrote the botanical appendix to Sturt's account of his expedition to central Australia, described it as 'one of the greatest ornaments of the desert regions of the interior of Australia'.[25]

Eyre reached his old depot at Mt Arden and then took an opportunity to ride north with one of the Aboriginal boys. He was able to confirm that the white area that he had seen on his earlier expedition was, in fact, a salt lake. He named it Lake Torrens after Colonel Robert Torrens. Baxter examined the country to the east; but neither Eyre nor Baxter found any 'good' country. They returned to Adelaide on 15 October 1839. Three and a half months later, on 30 January 1840, Eyre set sail for Albany, King George Sound, with 1450 sheep and lambs and 70 cattle – all of which he hoped to sell for a good price. He was unable to sell his stock at Albany and had to overland them to Perth – where he obtained a satisfactory price.

While in Perth, Eyre met the captain of the *Beagle*, Commander J. C. Wickham, and Lieutenant Lort Stokes. The *Beagle* was anchored off Fremantle having sailed along the north coast of Australia. Wickham had discovered Port Darwin, which he had named after Charles Darwin, who had sailed in the *Beagle* in 1835 and 1836. He had also discovered two major rivers – the Adelaide River which he had examined upstream for 64 kilometres (forty miles), and the Victoria River, which he had traced for 130 kilometres (eighty miles). Eyre was greatly impressed by this information. It seemed to indicate that the 'North' and the 'Centre' should be further explored in the hope of making discoveries of benefit to the Australian colonies.

Eyre returned to Adelaide by ship in May 1840

to find that everyone was talking about the need to explore the country between Port Lincoln and Albany. Eyre was in two minds about this proposal – as he indicated in an article that he published in the *South Australian Register* of 23 May 1840:[26]

In a geographical point of view it will be exceedingly interesting to know the character of the intervening country between this colony [South Australia] and theirs [Western Australia], and to unfold the secrets hidden by those lofty, and singular cliffs at the head of the Great Bight, and so far, it might be practicable – since it is possible that a light party might, in a favourable season, force their way across.

But he also thought:

As regards the transit of stock, however, my own conviction is that it is quite impracticable. The vast extent of desert country to the westward – the scarcity of grass – the denseness of the scrub – and the all but total absence of water, even in the most favourable seasons, are in themselves, sufficient bars to the transit of stock, even to a distance we are already acquainted with. I would rather, therefore, turn the public attention to the Northward, as being the most probable point from which discoveries of importance may be made.

Eyre offered to lead an expedition northwards into the interior, and to make a substantial contribution to the cost. He was confident that he had the necessary knowledge and experience to undertake the proposed exploration. As he later wrote:[27]

For eight years the author had been resident in Australia, during which he had visited many of the located parts of New South Wales, Port Phillip, South Australia, and Van Diemen's Land. In the years 1836, 1837, 1838, 1839 and 1840 he had conducted expeditions across from Liverpool Plains in New South Wales to the county of Murray, from Sydney to Port Phillip, from Port Phillip to Adelaide, and from King George's Sound to Swan River, besides undertaking several explorations towards the interior, both from Port Lincoln and from Adelaide.

Eyre persuaded the governor to support his proposed expedition to the north rather than the one to the west and, when Charles Sturt publicly supported Eyre's view, the battle was won. An Exploration Committee was established to make the necessary arrangements. This was, at first, chaired by Captain Edward Frome (the surveyor-general), and then by Charles Sturt. On 1 June 1840 Eyre began to organise his party. He engaged Edward Bate Scott, 'an active, intelligent and steady young friend, who had already been [on] a voyage with me to Western Australia' as a 'companion in the journey'.[28] John Baxter, Eyre's overseer, was also to be a member, of course, and was to join the party when it reached Eyre's station on the Light River (just north of Gawler). Two additional men were to drive the drays – one, John Houston, was to join immediately, and the other, Robert McRobert, was to join when they reached Eyre's station. The two Aboriginal boys, Neramberein (Joey) and Coota-chah (Yarry), were also to be members. In addition, Captain Frome seconded his personal servant, Corporal Coles, to the expedition. Coles had served in Grey's expedition exploring the north-west coast and was a wheelwright by trade – so he would be useful.[29] There were to be thirteen horses and forty sheep, plus stores for three months. In addition, arrangements were made for the colonial cutter, *Waterwitch*, to sail to the head of Spencer Gulf with additional stores.[30] Eyre also received 'donations of books and instruments' from his 'many friends'.[31]

The expedition had a good send-off at Government House on 18 June 1840 – the twenty-fifth anniversary of the Battle of Waterloo in which the governor, as Colonel Gawler, had taken a distinguished part. 'May a similar glorious success attend the present undertaking,' he said. The drays set off in advance and, at the conclusion of the ceremonies, Eyre, Scott, Neramberein and Coota-chah left Government House on horseback. They 'dashed over the bridge and up the hill in North Adelaide' and made for the Para River where they were to spend the first night.[32] They then moved on to Gawler, and then further north 'through some very fine country, the verdant and beautiful herbage of which, at this season of the year, formed a carpet of rich and luxuriant vegetation' to arrive at Eyre's station on the Light River.[33] Eyre took an opportunity to observe the latitude to be 34° 15' 56" S and, more importantly, to re-arrange the loads in the drays and ensure that all articles, including the firearms, were secured. Various items from Eyre's station were added, and an extra cart provided for carrying the instruments and the tents. They departed from the station on 23 June and reached Eyre's former base at Depot Creek near Mt Arden on 3 July. The supplies carried by the *Waterwitch* were now collected and carried to the depot.

From his earlier expedition Eyre knew that 'the farther the advance to the north, the more dreary and desolate the appearance of the country became, and the greater was the difficulty, both of finding and of obtaining access to either water or grass. The interception of the singular basin of Lake Torrens, which I had discovered formed a barrier to the westward.'[34] He believed, however, that the Flinders Ranges would be 'the stepping stone to the interior ... because in its recesses alone could I hope to obtain water and grass for my party'.[35] Accordingly, while the stores were being transported from the *Waterwitch* to Mt Arden, Eyre, with one of the Aboriginal boys, set off to the north to locate another possible depot.

He passed Mt Eyre (which he had seen in May 1839 and which had been named by Governor Gawler) and arrived at Lake Torrens. It was covered with salt but, underneath this, it was muddy; it was impossible to walk on it for any great distance. He climbed a hill to examine the surrounding country and named it Mt Deception. No water could be seen from its summit and it now became imperative to find a source of water. He moved to the south. Lake Torrens was now visible to the west and Mt Deception to the north-west. He followed a little

rocky gully and, to his surprise and joy, 'discovered a small but deep pool of water in a hole of the rock; upon sounding the depth, I found it would last us some time, and that I might safely bring my party thus far'.[36] He named this place Depot Pool. Soon afterwards it rained and there were pools of water everywhere. Eyre determined the latitude to be 30° 55' S.

Eyre spent some time exploring this area and then returned to the depot at Mt Arden – where work was proceeding steadily. Scott had already made a collection of botanical and geological specimens. All was now ready to move the party forward to Depot Pool.

Soon after their arrival there, Eyre decided that he would again reconnoitre northwards. On 2 August 1840, therefore, with one of the Aboriginal boys, and one of the men, he set off on horseback, with a pack-horse loaded with water, and reached an eminence that he named Termination Hill. The man in charge of the pack-horse now returned to Depot Pool. Eyre continued to examine the country but returned to Depot Pool on 7 August. Before long he was again on a reconnaissance – this time to the north-west. He was accompanied by one of the men driving a dray loaded with 250 litres (65 gallons) of water, and with the other Aboriginal boy. After travelling 80 kilometres (50 miles) they buried a can containing 45 litres (12 gallons) of water, and the dray was then sent back to the depot. Eyre and the Aboriginal boy continued for a further 80 kilometres and came to what he thought to be an extension of Lake Torrens – where the water was crystal clear but very salty. 'This water, however, was not continuous':[37]

... a little further on, the channel again became dry, as it increased in width in its approach to the main lake, the bed of which, near its shores, was also dry. From a high bank which I ascended, I had a full view of the lake stretching away to the north-east as far as the eye could reach, apparently about thirty miles [48 kilometres] broad, and still seeming to be bounded on its western shores by a low bridge, or table land, beyond which nothing could be seen. No hills were visible any where, nor was there the least vegetation of any kind.

Eyre 'retreated from the dismal scene'. He, and the Aboriginal boy, had no alternative. They returned to the buried water and then to his Depot Pool. In fact, Eyre had discovered what is now called Lake Eyre South.

Water was again a problem and various searches were undertaken. On one such excursion, Eyre and Scott observed a high peak and Eyre named it Mt Scott. But the search for water was paramount, and they would soon have to abandon their Depot Pool. Eyre still wanted to journey westwards to Lake Torrens and wrote:[38]

I had already visited its basin at points fully 150 miles [241 kilometres] apart, viz. in about 29° 10' S latitude, and in 31° 30' S. I had also traced its course from various heights in the Flinders range, from which it was distinctly visible, and in my mind, had not the slightest doubt that it was one continuous and connected basin.

However, the lake was not visible 'to the north of west' from the hills near the depot and he set out, again with an Aboriginal boy, to examine this area. He traced the course of the lake north-westerly for 16 kilometres (10 miles) and satisfied himself that 'it was part of the same vast basin I had seen so much further to the north'.[39] They returned safely to Depot Pool on 24 August, having crossed, going and returning, 160 kilometres (100 miles) of desert. During the last three days the horses had had nothing to eat or drink. The next day they broke camp and moved to the north-east and were fortunate to discover Mundy Creek – which Eyre named after Alfred Mundy, the colonial secretary of South Australia.[40] Eyre also discovered and named the Burr River, Mt Serle and Frome River. On 27 August Eyre set out to climb Mt Serle, and he wrote:[41]

At length, however, having overcome all difficulties we stood upon the summit of the mountain. Our view was then extensive and final. At one glance I saw the realization of my worst forbodings; and the termination of the expedition of which I had the command. Lake Torrens now faced us to the east, whilst on every side we were hemmed in by a barrier which we could never hope to pass.

Eyre determined the latitude, by the meridian altitude of Altair, to be 30° 18' 30" S. Further to the north-east he saw 'the last of the hills to the eastward' and named it Mt Distance 'for it deceived us greatly as to the distance we were from it'.[42] The next day, 2 September, they climbed Mt Distance, and then moved to another peak that Eyre named Mt Hopeless (which has a height of 126 metres). They climbed it 'and cheerless and hopeless indeed was the prospect before us'.[43] The 'lake' was now visible to the north and to the east and Eyre believed it to be a continuation of Lake Torrens 'commencing near the head of Spencer's Gulf, and following the course of Flinders range (bending round its northern extreme to the southward)'.[44] In other words, Eyre believed that the Lake Torrens basin extended to the north, then turned to the east and then southwards, making a continuous horseshoe-like depression. In the map accompanying Eyre's *Journals of Expeditions of Discovery*, drawn by John Arrowsmith, the horseshoe is clearly shown, with the annotation 'Appears to be a Continuation of Lake Torrens as seen from the hills'. There is a further comment:[45]

The Country between the Lake and the hills appears to consist of low barren stony Plains washed smooth and even by the action of water and in many places covered by salsolaceous plants but otherwise destitute of vegetation, interspersed among the plains are fragments of steep sided table lands from 50 to 300 ft elevation composed chiefly of chalk. No timber and but few bushes.

We now know that Eyre was mistaken and that the country to the west, north and east of the Flinders Ranges has a number of *separate* salt lakes

The north-west coast of Australia is a mass of islands and inlets. The Buccaneer Archipelago was so named by Phillip Parker King in 1821 in memory of William Dampier, who first visited this area in the *Cygnet* in 1688. (Geoffrey Badger)

The quokka, *Setonix brachyurus*, was first described by early Dutch explorer Willem de Vlamingh. He thought it resembled a large rat, so named the island where they were discovered 'Rottnest Island'. The quokka used to be found on the mainland, in the south-western corner of Western Australia, but few remain there now. (Geoffrey Badger)

The cape at the south-western corner of Australia was first sighted by men of the *Leeuwin* (Lioness) in 1622 and the coastline in the vicinity was labelled Leeuwinlandt on some early maps. The name of the captain is unknown. In 1802 Matthew Flinders passed this way during his circumnavigation of Australia and named this cape Cape Leeuwin. A lighthouse was later built on the cape and completed in 1895. (Geoffrey Badger)

The mouth of the Murray River is almost invisible from the sea, and both Flinders and Baudin failed to discover it when they visited Encounter Bay in 1802. (South Australian Tourism Commission)

Sturt's Desert Pea, *Clianthus formosus*, near Port Hedland, was first mentioned by Dampier. He observed it on an island he named Rosemary Island (now South Lewis Island). (Geoffrey Badger)

The dense rain forest on the shores of Macquarie Harbour. James Kelly was the first European to visit the harbour. He and his four companions spent three days exploring the waterway in a small whaleboat. (Geoffrey Badger)

The junction of the Darling (foreground) and Murray rivers visited by Charles Sturt and party in January 1830. (Geoffrey Badger)

A watercolour prepared by Charles Sturt during his exploration of the Murray River. The cliffs on the western side indicate that it was painted when he had reached the lower reaches of the river. The painting was discovered during conservation work at the Bodlian Library at Oxford when a backing sheet was removed from one of Sturt's maps. (Rhodes House Library, Ms. Austr.)

The edge of the Nullarbor Plain – scene of the epic journey across the south of the continent completed by Edward Eyre and Wylie, a young Aboriginal man, in 1840–41. (Moira Heath)

Sand ridges and ranges in the Simpson Desert, south-east of Alice Springs. Charles Sturt's search for an inland sea ended when he reached the edge of this desert in 1845. (C. R. Twidale)

'Chaining over the sand hills to Lake Torrens', 1846, by S. T. Gill, based on a drawing by Charles Sturt. (National Library of Australia)

At Depot Glen, Sturt observed the cinnamon-coloured ground thrush, *Cinclosoma cinnamoneus*. It was, according to Gould, the only new species procured during Sturt's Central Australian Expedition. (Reproduced from John Gould, 1848, Vol. 4, Plate 6.)

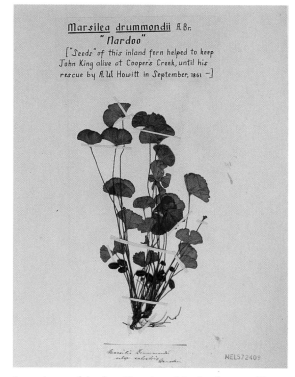

A specimen of the fern-like plant, *Marsilea drummondii*, that became the chief source of food for Burke, Wills and King. It was known to the Aborigines as 'nardoo'. (Collection of the National Herbarium of Victoria, Royal Botanic Gardens, Victoria)

'The Dig Tree' – the most famous coolibah tree in Australia at the site of the Burke and Wills camp on Cooper Creek. (Geoffrey Badger)

Blanche Cup mound spring and Hamilton Hill (an 'extinct' mound spring) discovered by Major Peter Warburton in 1858. Such springs were of great importance in the development of the pastoral industry in the arid zones. (Courtesy of WMC (Olympic Dam Corporation) and the photographer, D. Niejalke)

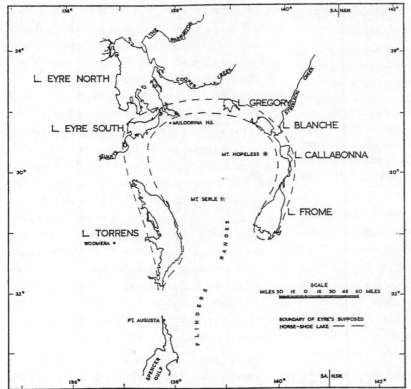

As Eyre travelled northwards he observed what he thought was a horseshoe-shaped lake that would impede his progress; this map published in Black 1963: 'Looking at a present-day map, it can be seen how Eyre had been led astray in his deductions by looking at the country from a distance, his view distorted by heat and mirage.' (Royal Geographical Society of South Australia and Black)

– notably lakes Torrens, Eyre South, Gregory, Blanche, Callabonna and Frome, roughly in a horseshoe like configuration.[46] The country to the north, north-east and east of Mt Hopeless is now known as the Strzelecki Desert.

It was a bitter disappointment to Eyre – who failed to find good farming land and rivers leading to the northern coast of Australia. He decided to abandon the exploration of the inland and move to examine the country between Spencer Gulf and King George Sound in the west. After all, an expedition in this direction had been favoured by many people in Adelaide before he, Eyre, had advocated the primary need to explore to the north.

Eyre moved his party to the Mt Arden depot on 12 September, and then travelled westwards for about 80 kilometres (fifty miles) and camped near a spring in Baxter Range. He then divided his party. On 17 September, Baxter, with two men,

one of the Aboriginal boys, two drays, seven horses, and the remaining sheep, set off westwards, about 420 kilometres (260 miles) towards Streaky Bay – where they were to await the arrival of the second party. This was to consist of Eyre, Scott, one man and the other Aboriginal boy. This party was to have one dray – carrying 150 litres (forty gallons) of water – and five horses, and would obtain supplies at Port Lincoln before continuing to Streaky Bay. This party also left Baxter Range on 17 September and travelled southwards along what is now known as Eyre Peninsula towards Port Lincoln. Water continued to be a problem – so much so that Eyre sent Scott and the other members of his party back to Baxter Range to fill all their water casks and return. In the meantime he would remain alone to continue his journal, to draw the maps, and make some astronomical observations. He had taken the altitude of Vega to determine the latitude (which he found to be 32° 03' 23" S); and then:[47]

> ... leaving my artificial horizon on the ground outside whilst I remained in the tent waiting until Altair came to the meridian, I then took my sextant and went out to observe this star also; but upon putting down my hand to take hold of the horizon glass in order to wipe the dew off, my fingers went into the quicksilver – the horizon glass was gone, and also the piece of canvas I had put on the ground to lie down upon whilst observing so low an altitude as that of Vega.

It was clear that he was surrounded by Aboriginal people – Eyre called them 'my sable friends' – who had also stolen a spade, a parcel of horse shoes, an axe and sundry other things during the half hour he had been in the tent. It seems that they must have seen the dray depart and then waited until dark to rob him, 'and daringly and effectually had they done it'.[48] Scott and the other members of Eyre's party returned with the dray and the casks of water on the evening of 21 September. The following morning they again set off to the south-west and, owing to the sharp eyes of the Aboriginal boy, they found what Eyre named 'Refuge Rocks', (now also known as Secret Rock) with its 'many holes with water in them', and a spring of pure water. Eyre determined the latitude on 23 September, by the Sun's meridian altitude, to be 33° 11' 12" S, but the altitude of Altair at night gave 33° 10' 06" S, and he settled for the mean of these, namely, 33° 10' 39" S, as the position of the spring.[49] They left Refuge Rocks on 25 September, travelling south-west and, at night, Eyre determined the latitude by the altitude of à Cygnus to be 33° 18' 34" S. The next night their latitude, from the altitude of à Aquilae, was 33° 31' S; at noon the next day it was 33° 34' 25" S.[50]

A few days later, on 1 October, Eyre's party arrived at a cattle station which was owned by Charles Driver and managed by C. C. Dutton. They were warmly welcomed and enjoyed the milk, butter and other items that had been missing from their diet. Moreover, Eyre managed to buy a Timor pony for £25. Eyre also took the opportunity to determine the latitude by taking the altitude of à Aquilae. He found it to be 34° 21' 20" S.[51]

The party reached the outskirts of Port Lincoln on 4 October, and Eyre and Scott walked into the town the next day. Eyre then took an opportunity to write a report to the Exploration Committee back in Adelaide. He advised that the route that they had followed from Baxter Range to Port Lincoln would be perfectly practicable for the movement of stock in the winter months, and he had no doubt that 'when the country becomes better known, the present track might be considerably improved upon, and grass and water obtained in greater abundance.' His evaluation of the country he had passed through was adverse. It was 'a low barren country, densely covered by brush'; but Dutton has explained:[52]

> Eyre Peninsula has never been easy country, but it grows a great deal of wheat, oats and barley, and supports a vast number of sheep, as well as its mineral and fishing industries. Eyre was opening up better country than he knew.

Eyre was disappointed to find that little in the way of provisions could be obtained in Port Lincoln. Scott therefore volunteered to go to Adelaide by boat to obtain the supplies necessary for the journey to the west. He also took Eyre's interim reports to the governor and to the chairman of the Exploration Committee. His other task was to recruit a suitable replacement for Robert McRobert – whose work had not been satisfactory. Scott was also asked to try to locate Wylie, the young Aboriginal man from King George Sound, who had come to Adelaide, with Eyre, in the previous May. Scott returned in the colonial cutter *Waterwitch*, on 22 October. He had engaged Thomas Costelow, a member of Eyre's earlier expedition, as the replacement for McRobert, but Wylie had not been available because he was then up-country.

Eyre had not yet decided definitely to overland as far as King George Sound. He had suggested to the Exploration Committee that he would travel to Streaky Bay and might then attempt a northern thrust into the inland. But, in the event, this proved to be impracticable and he did continue towards the sound.

Eyre's party set off from Port Lincoln for Streaky Bay on 26 October. On 31 October, Eyre arrived at Lake Newland – 'a large salt-water lake, with numerous fine and strong springs of excellent water, bubbling up almost in the middle of the salt'. They had travelled 19 kilometres (twelve miles) from Lake Newland and had camped by a lagoon that had been 'seen by Flinders from the masthead'. Eyre recorded its latitude as 33° 14' 36" S.[53]

At this period Eyre was determining the latitude almost every day. He was using a sextant, with an artificial horizon. Nowhere, however, does he record a longitude by observation. It will be recalled that, towards the end of his preliminary expedition, near Lake Alexandrina, his chronometer was ruined when a loaded dray was driven into a water hole. Chronometers were not readily available in the colony at that time and it seems likely that he was unable to obtain one for use on this expedition. As a matter of fact, he does not record how he estimated his distance travelled as he proceeded westwards towards King George Sound, and does not give estimates of his dead-reckoning positions. It seems likely that he monitored his progress by reference to Flinders' chart of the coast – a copy of which he carried with him.

Eyre's party arrived safely at Streaky Bay on 3 November and found Baxter's party in good health and spirits after accomplishing the journey from Baxter Range without difficulty. They had followed the tracks made by Eyre when travelling in the reverse direction – from Streaky Bay to Mt Arden – in 1839. While waiting for Eyre to arrive from Port Lincoln, Baxter's men had been enjoying the oysters that they found there in abundance. The two parties had been separated for nearly seven weeks without any communication.

It was now necessary for the entire expedition to move to the north-west in their attempt to reach the head of the Bight, and beyond. The *Waterwitch* was still available and her master was asked to land a cask of drinking water a little higher up the bay and another at Smoky Bay. The cutter would also take much of the expedition's heavy equipment and stores as far as Fowlers Bay – named by Flinders after his first lieutenant, Robert Fowler. They set off on 6 November. The following day the axes were constantly at work in advance of the drays, clearing a passage 'through this dreadful country' for about 27 kilometres (17 miles) before they came to an open plain, where they managed to find a natural well of water – but it was 'choked up with sand and dirt'.[54] On the next day they again had to clear the dense scrub to allow the passage of the drays, and they arrived at Smoky Bay on the afternoon of 8 November, the horses by then being 'quite exhausted'. The *Waterwitch* had already arrived and landed a cask of water – but it was not sufficient. They found some by digging in the sand to a depth of about 5 metres (fifteen feet). It was rather salty but the horses and sheep drank it. The expedition had now arrived in the vicinity of the Nuyts Archipelago and Eyre was able to take a bearing of

Eyre's water hole; at this spot, Baxter, after crossing the peninsula from Port Augusta, waited in dire anxiety to rejoin his leader, Edward John Eyre, who had ridden from Mount Arden via Port Lincoln.

St Peter Island.[55] The *Waterwitch* then sailed to the north-western point of Denial Bay – so named by Flinders because it had raised his hopes of finding an entrance to the inland. The *Waterwitch* again landed water for the use of the expedition.

It was here that they were visited by a group of Aboriginal people who 'soon became very friendly'. Eyre noted that the men had all been circumcised and, in addition, had undergone an operation (which was not explained) to reduce fertility. One of the members of this group, 'an intelligent cheerful old man' was persuaded to accompany Eyre as a guide. His name was Wilguldy, and Eyre had him mounted on a horse 'to the great admiration and envy of his fellows'. A couple of days later, further west, he led Eyre to a place where water was procured by digging down about a metre.[56]

Eyre believed that the Aborigines were generally friendly, and were seldom aggressive unless provoked by aggressive actions by the intruders. As he wrote:[57]

> I shall be borne out, I think, by facts when I state that the Aborigines of this country have seldom been guilty of wanton or unprovoked outrages, or committed acts of rapine or bloodshed, without some strongly existing cause, or under the influence of feelings that would have weighed in the same degree with Europeans in similar circumstances.

The expedition continued westwards and arrived at Fowlers Bay. When he walked on the shores of the bay, Eyre 'found them literally strewed in all directions with the bones and carcases of whales'. He added that 'scarcely a single [English] vessel fished any where off these coasts, which are entirely monopolised by the French and Americans, who come in great numbers … there cannot, I think, be less than three hundred foreign vessels annually whaling off the coasts'.[58]

All the stores were now removed from the *Waterwitch* – which then moved to a more secure anchorage on the western side of Denial Bay. Once

a depot had been established, Eyre and Neramberein set off on 22 November on a reconnaissance – the main object of which was to locate water for use when the main party moved forward. The search was so unsuccessful that the 'unfortunate horses were again obliged to be tied up [at night] for the second time without either grass or water'.[59] Eyre decided that he must return to the depot at Fowlers Bay as speedily as possible. Indeed, one of the horses became so completely exhausted that Eyre tied him to a bush with the intention of returning later with food and water to collect him. They arrived back at the depot on 25 November and, the next morning, Baxter, Cootachah and one of the men set off with a cask of water on a dray to find and succour the exhausted horse. With care and attention the horse recovered 'but miserably reduced in condition'.[60]

Eyre and Neramberein set off again on 28 November, determined to conquer the desert. Eyre had arranged for John Houston to precede them in the dray, with 265 litres (70 gallons) of water. A party of Aboriginal people joined them for a time; but they became bored and dropped off 'one or two at a time, until only three remained'.[61] By this time, however, it was clear that their reserves of water would be quite insufficient. The horses were already becoming distressed. Something had to be done or they would all perish. Eyre decided to leave the dray in the care of Houston, with sufficient water for him and for the horse, and to set off, with Neramberein, to retrace their steps for 40 kilometres (25 miles) to the sandhills where they knew that water could be obtained. They arrived late at night, watered the horses, and then took them 2½ kilometres to get some grass for them.[62]

Two days later Eyre and Neramberein began their return trek to the dray, and arrived late in the afternoon. They found that Houston had finished his water, and that the mare looked 'weak and wretched'. Both recovered somewhat as soon as they had drunk sufficiently. A party of Aborigines now gathered around the dray and indicated that no water was to be found in that area. Eyre thought that the Aboriginal people were carrying their own supplies of water in skins and that they must be finding small quantities in the 'hollows of the gum shrub' (deposited by rain), or from 'the long lateral roots of the same tree'.[63]

It is well known that the Aborigines who lived in the desert areas of Australia were highly skilled in the art of finding water. It is not so generally known, however, that they could obtain water from the roots of what were called 'water trees'. It has been claimed that the 'mallee, needle-bush, currajong, casuarina, mulga, acacia, and young growth of gum are the best of the "water-trees", storing up supplies in root and stem, the root being most often the source of supply in our arid regions'.[64] The procedure seems to have been as follows:[65]

A native goes up to a water-tree and tries the ground at from 4 ft. to 5 ft. from the stem, or, if guided by a 'bulge' or a 'crack' ... finds the root at once. If the ground is hard the soil is usually scooped away from over the root with his wooden shovel, until it has been bared all along its length. If the soil is loose he drives his yamstick, or spear-point, into the ground, prises the root up, and thus breaks it off near the stem. Then, dropping the spear or stick, he grasps the root with both hands, and, straddling its bed, shakes and pulls up the root to its point. Then, breaking it into lengths of 18 in. to 3 ft., he sets the pieces on end against the trunk, standing them in a coolamin or a wallaby-skin bag, or in a trough formed from the bark stripped from the roots, by which bark-guttering it is conducted into his water-vessel.

The red mallees or mallee trees (*Eucalyptus oleosa*) of the western coast of South Australia 'always have water-roots', and it has been claimed: 'Gallons of water may be obtained from their roots.'[66]

Towards the end of March, Eyre saw the process performed for the first time. The Aboriginal people selected a large healthy-looking tree growing in a hollow or flat between two ridges, and then probed to find the lateral roots. Once located the root was broken next to the tree and run out for 6–9 metres (20–30 feet). The bark was then peeled off and the root broken into pieces 15–20 centimetres (6–8 inches) long. [67]

They are then sucked, or shaken over a piece of bark, or stuck up together in the bark upon their ends, and water is slowly discharged from them; if shaken it comes out like a shower of very fine rain ... The quantity of water contained in a good root, would probably fill two-thirds of a pint. I saw my own boys get one-third of a pint out in this way in about a quarter of an hour, and they were by no means adepts at the practice, having never been compelled to resort to it from necessity.

Eyre now wanted the whole party to retreat to the water, because the horses 'were completely fagged out and could take the dray no further'. He decided to bury the baggage and to leave the dray to be collected later, but the Aboriginal people were camped alongside and Eyre knew that if they observed where the stores were buried they would dig them all up and souvenir everything as soon as he departed. A whole day went by before the Aborigines departed, and the baggage was then buried. A large fire was made over the place where the goods were concealed 'and no trace remained of the earth being disturbed.'[68] They then set off towards the water, but three of the horses were unable to complete the journey and were abandoned until Eyre could reach the water again and return to try and revive them. Unfortunately, all three died.[69]

When Eyre reached the water he sent a man back to Fowlers Bay to ask Baxter to send five fresh horses, two men and more provisions. When they arrived, Eyre and Neramberein, followed later by the two men, set off to recover the buried baggage and the dray. When they arrived at their old site Eyre searched the surrounding country for water, but did not 'observe the slightest indications of the existence of water, although the traces of natives were numerous and recent'.[70] He did, however, notice many fragments of the tree roots which they had clearly used to obtain water. Having again buried a few things that they might require when they would be in that area again, Eyre and his companions set off again for the Fowlers Bay depot. Eyre and Neramberein arrived on 15 December. The two men, with the dray, arrived on the following day:[71]

... being the last detachment of the party engaged in this most unfortunate expedition, which had occupied so much time and caused such severe and fatal loss, independently of its not accomplishing the object for which it was undertaken.

Eyre clearly had to revise his plans. There were no harbours west of Fowlers Bay within easy reach, and he realised that he could not rely on the *Waterwitch* to carry his major stores while the overland party walked or rode. He decided to take only one dray and to reduce the number of men in the overland party. Corporal Coles and John Houston were therefore sent on board the cutter to return to Adelaide. One of the drays and some of the sheep were likewise put on board. Many of the stores were buried so that they could be recovered later. Finally, the depot was moved a few kilometres so that the horses would have a reasonable quantity of grass.

On 30 December Eyre set off on another attempt to conquer the desert and to reach the head of the Bight. He took Baxter and Neramberein, both on horseback, and Costelow, to drive a three-horse dray. Scott and Cootachah, and all the remaining sheep, were to stay at the depot. As they progressed, the absence of water was a continuing problem but, on 7 January 1841, they came upon 'a native pathway, and following it under the hummocks of the coast for eight miles, lost it at some bare sand–drifts, close to the head of the Great Bight, where we had at last arrived, after our many former ineffectual attempts'.[72] They searched from one sandhill to another until they came upon four Aborigines camped 'by a hole dug for water in the sand'. Finding that Eyre wished them no harm they became friendly and offered Eyre's party some fruit 'of which they had a few quarts on a piece of bark'.[73]

One of the surprising things about Eyre's expedition is that neither he nor the other members seem to have developed scurvy. Perhaps this fruit is the answer? Perhaps they were often able to supplement their diet with this fruit – assuming, of course, that it contains vitamin C. According to Eyre:[74]

This fruit grows upon a low brambly-looking bush, upon the sand-hills or in the flats, where the soil is of a saline nature. It is found also in the plains bordering upon the lower parts of the Murrumbidgee, but in much greater abundance along the whole line of the coast to the westward. The berry is oblong, about the shape and size of an English sloe, is very pulpy and juicy, and has a small pyramidal stone in the centre, which is very hard and somewhat indented. When ripe it is a dark purple, a clear red, or a bright yellow, for there are varieties. The purple is the best flavoured, but all are somewhat saline in taste. To the natives these berries are an important article of food at this season of the year [January], and to obtain them and the fruit of the mesembryanthemum, they go to a great distance, far away from water.

Eyre could not have known that this fruit would prevent scurvy because the cause of scurvy was not known. Nevertheless, these berries might well have prevented the onset of the disease in the members of his party. This was not the only occasion that Eyre refers to the eating of wild fruit.[75]

The country in the vicinity of the head of the Bight was known to Aboriginal people as 'Yeerkumban kauwe'.[76] Eyre and his party left Yeerkumban kauwe on 10 January and proceeded further westwards. They:[77]

... passed through an open level tract of country, of from three to four hundred feet in elevation, and terminating seawards abruptly, in bold and overhanging cliffs, which had been remarked by Captain Flinders, but which upon our nearer approach, presented nothing very remarkable in appearance, being only the sudden termination of a perfectly level country, with its outer face washed, steep and precipitous, by the unceasing lash of the southern ocean.

On 11 January Eyre decided that he had accomplished all that he had expected to do on this excursion, and began the long trek back to the depot where Scott 'complained bitterly of having been left alone for so long'. This was on 16 January. Two days later Baxter joined them, after rescuing two jaded horses, and they then moved to Fowlers Bay.

A few days after their arrival at Fowlers Bay the *Hero* arrived – the *Waterwitch* having proved so leaky as to be unsafe for service on a wild coast. She carried English and colonial mail, and also Wylie – the Aboriginal man from King George Sound whom Eyre had been seeking for some time, especially as he would be able to interpret the language spoken by the indigenous people of the west. Further, there was a fine kangaroo dog – a present to Eyre from his friend Sturt.[78] The *Hero* could not be used as a supply ship beyond the western boundary of South Australia – because this was against regulations – and it was therefore necessary to plan for the definitive expedition to be pursued without her assistance. Eyre decided that the party to go to the west would have to be a small one. It would consist of Eyre, Baxter, and the three young Aborigines – Neramberein (Joey), Cootachah (Yarry) and Wylie. Scott and the others would have to return to Adelaide in the *Hero*. As for those who would travel westwards, 'the bridge was broken down behind us,' wrote Eyre, 'and we must succeed in reaching King George's Sound, or perish; no middle course remained.'[79]

They set off on 25 February – five people with nine horses, one Timor pony, one foal (born at Streaky Bay), and six sheep. They experienced the usual difficulty – water – and arrived at the head of the Bight on 2 March. On the following day there was a sandstorm. They were compelled to live among the sandhills because that was the only place where water could be obtained (by digging); but that meant that the sand penetrated their hair, their eyes, their clothes and their provisions. On 8 March Eyre wrote that there 'was no perceptible inclination of the country in any direction, the level land ran to the very borders of the sea, where it abruptly terminated, forming the steep and precipitous cliffs'.[80] Eyre was following the practice whereby he and one of the Aboriginal boys (on this occasion Cootachah) went ahead with the sheep, while Baxter and the others followed with the pack-horses.

On 10 March Eyre wrote that his horses had been four days without water and now he and the boy had exhausted their supply. They had left the sheep, in a rough and ready enclosure, with a note to Baxter, and pushed on. However, 24 kilometres (15 miles) after they had abandoned the sheep, they came to a native pathway – but they were twice unable to follow it, and remained on the high ground. They came to another 'well beaten native pathway' and followed it to the beach and to some white sand drifts. 'Upon turning into these to search for water, we were fortunate enough to strike the very place where the natives had dug little wells; and thus on the fifth day of our sufferings, we were again blessed with abundance of water'.[81]

Near the coast, drinkable water can sometimes be obtained a couple of metres or more under sand dunes in what are known as 'soakages'. Sand is porous and permeable, and the occasional rain which falls in desert regions can migrate under the sandhills towards the sea. Soakages are formed when the sandhills have an impermeable base (clay, calcrete, bedrock) which causes the water to accumulate and, unless the water is polluted by sea spray, it is potable.[82]

On the next day, 12 March, Eyre and Cootachah

rode back to meet Baxter and his party, and to recover the sheep, which were even further back. That night, the whole party was together 'after having passed over one hundred and thirty-five miles of desert country, without a drop of water in its whole extent, and at a season of the year the most unfavourable for such an undertaking'.[83] The animals had suffered. The sheep had been six days without water and the horses had been five days, and 'both had been almost wholly without food for the greater part of the time.'[84]

They continued westwards but their situation became worse and worse. The Aboriginal people whom they had met near the head of the Bight had told them that there were two places where water could be obtained by digging in the sand – but, so far, they had found only one. The second must be still further to the west – but how far west? Eyre decided to bury most of their equipment, clothes, firearms, and a variety of other things

(including a copy of Sturt's book on his two expeditions). From now on Eyre, Baxter and Wylie would walk, the two Aboriginal boys would ride, and the other horses would carry the remaining stores. Two days later, however, the horses were so weak that the boys had to walk also, and the Timor pony had to be abandoned 'to a miserable and certain death'.[85]

On 29 March their last drop of water had been consumed but, on the following morning, Eyre took a sponge and collected a quart of water from the dew. The Aboriginal boys did the same with a handful of grass. Later in the same day they came to 'the high drifts of sand we were looking for so anxiously'. They began digging and found water at a depth of about 2 metres (6 feet) 'on the seventh day of our distress, and after we had travelled one hundred and sixty miles [260 kilometres] since we had left the last water'.[86] A few days later Eyre and Wylie set off eastwards to recover some of the stores

Eyre Highway, looking west, near Nullarbor; the sign warns about camels, wombats and kangaroos. (Moira Heath)

that had been buried, and returned with the most important items. Their food supplies were dangerously low, but they were able to kill an occasional stingray. One of the horses collapsed, and Eyre had it killed for food. Thin slices of the meat were dipped in salt water and hung up to dry. A few days later, however, Eyre and Baxter both suffered from dysentery.

Everything now began to fall apart. Baxter grew despondent. He now despaired of ever reaching King George Sound and tried to persuade Eyre to return to Fowlers Bay. The Aborigines in the party also despaired. Indeed, two of them, Wylie and Neramberein, deserted on 22 April. But, a few days later, they returned to Eyre's camp because they found so little food. Eyre broke camp on 27 April and the party again set off for the west. On the following night Eyre took the first watch and, around 10.30 p.m., while inspecting the horses, he heard the report of a gun some distance away. Soon afterwards Wylie ran up, and the two of them went in that direction and found Baxter 'in the last agonies of death'.[87] The two Aboriginal boys were nowhere to be seen and Eyre concluded that they had been stealing food and other items prior to deserting and making their own way back to the east. He thought that Baxter must have heard them and surprised the boys, who then fired at him. Eyre questioned Wylie, who denied all knowledge of the proposed robbery and desertion; but Eyre's impression was:[88]

> ... that Wylie had agreed with the other two to rob the camp and leave us; that he had been cognisant of all their proceedings and preparations, but that when, upon the eve of their departure, the overseer had unexpectedly awoke and been murdered, he was shocked and frightened at the deed, and instead of accompanying them, had run down to meet me.

Eyre and Wylie did their best to cover Baxter's body and again set off for the west – in an endeavour to complete their journey. In more recent times, a memorial has been constructed to mark the position where Baxter was killed. Dutton has suggested that this is the 'loneliest monument in the world'.[89]

The absence of water continued to be a major problem, and it was not until 3 May that they came to a 'native road' that led them to some sand drifts where, to their great 'joy and relief', they found a place where Aboriginal people had dug for water. 'Thus,' wrote Eyre, 'at twelve o'clock on the seventh day since leaving the last depot, we were again encamped at water, after having crossed 150 miles [240 kilometres] of a rocky, barren, and scrubby table land.'[90]

They pushed on again. They killed another horse for food. They both suffered from indigestion, and were becoming lethargic. Nevertheless they were making progress and were approaching Cape Arid. It was at this time they found an abundance of water from the rain. It was 'the first time we had ever been able to do so on our whole journey without making use of the spade and bucket'.[91] Soon afterwards they came to 'the first permanent fresh water we had found on the surface since we commenced our journey from Fowlers Bay'[92] – a distance of nearly 1130 kilometres (700 miles). Eyre was now aiming for Lucky Bay, so named by Flinders, and it would then be almost 500 kilometres (300 miles) to King George Sound. Their food was now almost exhausted and it was about this time that they began to eat the root of the broad flag-reed – which Eyre described as 'an excellent and nutritious article of food. This root being dug up, and roasted in hot ashes, yields a great quantity of a mealy farinaceous powder interspersed among the fibres.'[93]

As they approached Thistle Cove they noticed two boats and then saw a ship at anchor. A boat soon left the ship for the shore, and Eyre and Wylie were greeted with great kindness by the captain, Captain Rossiter – an Englishman who was in charge of a French whaler with an American name: *Mississippi*. They were invited on board, were well fed, and were able to relax. No one spoke English except the captain. Eyre took an opportunity to walk to Thistle Cove and back, but otherwise they both relaxed. On one occasion Eyre noticed a group of Aboriginal people on the beach and arranged for two of them to come on board. The important thing was that Wylie understood their language: Eyre and Wylie were clearly within reach of King George Sound![94]

On 15 June, Eyre and Wylie said farewell to the kind-hearted people on the *Mississippi*. They had been given so much that the horses had to be used as pack-horses and Eyre and Wylie had to walk. A few days later it was the anniversary of their departure from Adelaide and 'two lone wanderers only remained to attempt its conclusion.' They pushed on and on, often through heavy rain, and arrived on the outskirts of the settlement at King George Sound. It was necessary to cross a river and the horses were left to fend for themselves while Eyre and Wylie continued into the town in the pouring rain. Their arrival was greeted with rapturous joy – they had long been given up for lost. Eyre wrote:[95]

> It was an interesting and touching sight to witness the meeting between Wylie and his friends. Affection's strongest ties could not have produced a more affecting and melting scene – the wordless weeping pleasure, too deep for utterance, with which he was embraced by his relatives, the cordial and hearty reception given him by his friends, the joyous greeting bestowed upon him by all, might well have put to the blush those heartless calumniators, who, branding the savage as the creature only of unbridled passions, deny to him any of those better feelings and affections which are implanted in the breast of all mankind, and which nature has not denied to any colour or to any race.

Eyre's account of his expedition is illustrated by a drawing, by J. Neil, of their arrival at King George Sound.[96] It shows them with two horses. However, as has been pointed out by Uren and Stephens in *Waterless Horizons*, 'the facts are inaccurately

depicted as the horses were left behind when Eyre and Wylie were within easy distance of Albany'.[97]

Wylie was to remain at the Sound, and Eyre arranged for him to receive a weekly allowance of provisions. Eyre himself boarded the *Truelove*, which was about to sail, and which arrived in Adelaide on 26 July 1841. He had been absent for a year and twenty-six days.

Eyre had discovered 'no important rivers', 'no fertile regions' and 'no noble ranges ... from which are washed the debris that might form a rich and fertile district beneath them'. 'On the contrary,' he pointed out, 'all has been arid and barren in the extreme.'[98] As an example of courage and endurance, however, Eyre's explorations of the desert country of Australia are extreme. Lake Eyre was named for him, the Eyre Peninsula commemorates his work, and the Eyre Highway – now linking Adelaide and Perth – likewise commemorates his endeavours.

Eyre did not immediately publish the account of his expeditions. He was known to be a friend of the Aboriginal people and as such, was asked by the governor, Captain George Grey:[99]

> ... to undertake the task of re-establishing peace and amicable relations with the numerous tribes of the Murray River, and its neighbourhood, whose daring and successful outrages in 1841, had caused very great losses to, and created serious apprehensions among the Colonists.

Eyre accepted the task and took up residence at Moorundie, on the Murray River (not far from present-day Blanchetown). From September 1841 to November 1844 he was engaged as resident magistrate of the Murray District and as 'Protector of Aborigines'. He was later to write:[100]

> During the whole of the three years I was Resident at Moorunde [Moorundie], not a single case of serious injury or aggression ever took place on the part of the natives against Europeans; and a district, once considered the wildest and most dangerous, was when I left it in November 1844, looked upon

as one of the most peaceable and orderly in the province.

Eyre left Adelaide in the *Symmetry* on 20 December 1844 to return to England – having previously written, through the governor, to Lord Stanley, requesting an appointment in any of the colonies. He took with him the young son of Tenberry (his favourite Aboriginal man at Moorundie), and another Aboriginal boy, to be educated in England. He seems to have written most of his *Journals of Expedition of Discovery into Central Australia, and Overland from Adelaide to King George's Sound* during the voyage, and it was published in two volumes in 1845. Volume 2 included a substantial account of the 'Manners and Customs of the Aborigines of Australia'. His explorations were recognised by the award of the Gold Medal (Founder's Medal) of the Royal Geographical Society in 1843 'for his enterprising and extensive explorations in Australia, under circumstances of peculiar difficulty'.

Eyre later received appointments in New Zealand, St Vincent and Antigua, and in Jamaica – where he had to endure a particularly unpleasant insurrection. But, as they say, that is another story.[101]

13

STURT'S SEARCH FOR AN INLAND SEA

After his successful exploration of the Murray–Darling River system, Sturt returned to Sydney and resumed his military and other duties. The penal colony at Norfolk Island was within the command of Governor Darling and, before long, Sturt was required to take his turn as commander of the garrison there. After this unpleasant duty he again returned to Sydney – where he began to notice his failing eyesight. Sturt attributed his problem to 'the effect of exposure and anxiety of mind in the prosecution of geographical researches',[1] but this does not seem likely. He sought, and obtained, leave to return to England for treatment. When he arrived at Gravesend in August 1832 he was totally blind and had to be led ashore. Sturt was given a prolonged course of treatment with a herbal medicine, sarsaparilla, which is now known to contain vitamin C. He was totally blind for four months and then his eyesight gradually improved; but it never fully recovered. The fact that his eyesight did improve under the treatment suggests that he had a functional disorder.[2]

His impaired eyesight made him ineligible for further promotion in the army and he therefore decided to resign. He spent much of his remaining time in England completing the account of his two expeditions; and this was published in two volumes in 1833.[3] In February 1834 he wrote to the Colonial Office to recommend a site for the establishment of a settlement in South Australia. This site was approved and soon became the township of Adelaide.[4]

In September of the same year he married Charlotte Greene and, soon afterwards, they sailed for Sydney. Sturt became a primary producer for a time but, in 1838, he decided to take a party, with a herd of cattle, overland from New South Wales to South Australia along the line of the Murray River. Overlanding from New South Wales to the newly established province of South Australia had been pioneered in 1837 by Joseph Hawdon and Charles Bonney.[5] At that time there were nearly 20 000 sheep in the province – sheep that had been imported, principally from Van Diemen's Land 'and which appeared to thrive uncommonly well'. There were more than 1000 cattle and 2000 horses.[6] Within the next eighteen months a further 5000 cattle and about a 150 000 sheep had been 'overlanded'.[7] Of these, Eyre had brought about 300 head of cattle and Sturt had added a further 340.

During his overlanding Sturt was able to confirm that the Hume River, discovered and named by Hume and Hovell some years before, is the headwater of the Murray. Sturt later described the Hume River as 'a noble and beautiful stream'; and he added:[8]

> When I named the Murray I was in a great measure ignorant of the other rivers with which it is connected. But if my knowledge then had been as

extensive as it now is, I shall still have considered myself justified in adopting the usage of other travellers, and in giving a name to that river down which and up which I have toiled for more than 4000 miles ... I want not to usurp an inch of ground or of water over which I have not passed.

Not long afterwards, Sturt and his wife moved to Adelaide where he became a civil servant – a station that held few attractions for Sturt. He had wanted to explore the lower reaches of the Darling River as far as its confluence with the Murray River. Thomas Mitchell, the surveyor-general of New South Wales, had explored the upper reaches of the Darling and its lower reaches in 1836. Moreover, in 1839, Edward John Eyre had led an expedition towards the north of South Australia but, discouraged by what he found in the Lake Torrens basin, he went to Port Lincoln, whence he 'proceeded along the line of the south coast to Fowler's Bay, the western limit of the province of South Australia'. The next year Eyre had made a further attempt to penetrate to the centre and later established the startling fact that 'there is not a single watercourse to be found on the South coast of Australia, from Port Lincoln to King George's Sound, a distance of more than 1500 miles.'[9]

Sturt had long accepted the hypothesis that there 'must' be an inland sea somewhere in central Australia – despite the acknowledged fact that there are 'large tracts of desert country'.[10] He also believed that Australia had once been an archipelago and that some of the 'apparently boundless plains' that had already been discovered had once been covered by the sea. In this respect his views have been proved correct.[11] On one occasion, when he descended from the Blue Mountains 'into a level and depressed interior' he had found that it was so level that 'an altitude of the sun, taken on the horizon ... approximated very nearly to the truth. The circumference of that horizon was unbroken, save where an isolated hill rose above it, and looked like an island in the ocean.'[12]

Sturt was adamant. He wished to lead another expedition, this time into the centre of Australia, in an attempt to find the expected inland sea. So, in January 1843, Sturt wrote to Lord Stanley, now the secretary of state for the Colonies, offering to lead such an expedition. At the same time he wrote to Sir Ralph Darling in the hope that Darling would support the proposal. Stanley received a supporting letter from Darling, and he also had the advice of Sir John Barrow. In the end Stanley approved a modified proposal:[13]

What Captain Sturt will understand as *absolutely prohibited* is any attempt to conduct his party through the tropical regions to the northward, so as to reach the mouths of any of the great rivers ... The present expedition will be limited in its object, to ascertaining the existence and character of a supposed chain of hills, or a succession of separate hills, trending down from N.E. to S.W., and forming a great natural division of the continent; to examining what rivers take their source in those mountains.

Stanley criticised Sturt's proposed route via the Murray and Darling rivers as being too indirect, and favoured one starting from Mt Arden, on the 138° E meridian, and just north of Spencer Gulf. Fortunately, he added: 'I do not wish this to be taken as an absolute injunction, because I am aware that there may be local causes' why the route proposed by Sturt was to be preferred. There *were* good reasons for Sturt's proposed route – the exploration of the major rivers – and he determined to follow it.[14] Preparations for the expedition began as soon as approval had been received from London. Stores had to be accumulated, and the men who were to travel with Sturt had to be selected.

It was no easy task to select the men – because there were over 300 applications. James Poole, a red-headed Irishman, was appointed second-in-command, John Harris Browne as medical officer, and John McDouall Stuart as draughtsman. These were the 'officers' and would be addressed as 'Mister'.

Louis Piesse was appointed storekeeper, with a rank akin to a non-commissioned officer. Daniel Brock, a Devonshire man and a dedicated Methodist, was appointed as 'a spare hand, to look after the fire arms' and to skin birds preparatory to mounting for future study. Robert Flood, who had served as head stockman on Sturt's 'overlanding' to Adelaide, was again appointed head stockman. David Morgan was to look after the horses, and John Kirby the sheep. Foulkes, Jones, Turpin, Lewis and Mack were appointed as bullock drivers. An Aboriginal man from Adelaide – Tampanang (nicknamed 'Bob') – was also selected. In addition, two Aboriginal men, Camboli and Nadbuck, joined the expedition at Moorundie, but only for a part of the journey.[15]

Navigational and other instruments had to be obtained from England, and there were some disappointments. One sextant arrived in excellent condition, but the other had glasses that 'were not clear'. There were two artificial horizons, three prismatic compasses and a barometer. The last, however, had been badly packed and was broken on arrival. Sturt managed to make a barometer with a tube obtained from the surveyor-general, but this was broken during the journey to Moorundie. He also obtained an 'excellent house barometer' and two 'brewer's thermometers'. Sturt proposed to use the variation in the boiling point of water to estimate heights above or below sea level. The thermometers required for measuring the ambient temperature had also been obtained from England; but they were graduated only to 127 degrees Fahrenheit (53 degrees Celsius), and were unsuitable for measuring the high temperatures that occur in central Australia.[16] One broke in its case, and another 'burst' when set in the shade on a very hot day during the expedition.

There is no mention of chronometers at this point in Sturt's *Narrative*, but his *Daily Journal* mentions his chronometers (in the plural) and, on 9 January 1845, Sturt records that his 'chronometer suddenly stopped, owing to one of the small screws

of the balance wheel having worked almost out'. Daniel Brock also mentions Sturt's chronometers in his journal.[17]

The sextant was a relatively unknown instrument to most of the officers. On one occasion Sturt recorded that 'neither Mr Poole nor Mr Browne had as yet acquired the proper use of the sextant.' But, a few days later, he wrote: 'Both Mr Poole and Mr Browne practised with the sextant, with indefatigable zeal and perseverance.'[18] Brock, always a critic, wrote:[19]

> Poole scarcely knows how to take an observation, and Captain Sturt is near sighted, and cannot scarcely discern a planet; the Doctor [Browne] is called upon occasionally to use the instrument, but he does not profess to be able to read the instrument.

Sturt's sextant (see page 20) was made of brass and had been built by B. D. W. Nairne – the mathematical instrument-maker at 20 Cornhill, London. It was slightly smaller than the sextant then used by the Royal Navy at sea – being only 11.5 centimetres from the top of the frame to the bottom of the graduated scale – and, unlike the usual sextants, it had no handle. It had two shades for use when observing the Sun, and was graduated to read to 160 degrees Fahrenheit (71 degrees Celsius). A leather carrying-case for the sextant was made by J. A. Holden & Co. – a saddler located in King William Street, Adelaide.[20] Some years later Sturt presented the sextant to William Trevett Dalwood and, presumably at this time, it was engraved and dated: 'Capt. Sturt 1844'. The same sextant was used during the construction of the overland telegraph from Adelaide to Darwin in 1870. It is now preserved in the Museum of Australian Surveying in Canberra.

Sturt decided to take live sheep with the expedition, rather than carry a supply of salt beef – because fresh meat was thought to prevent the onset of scurvy. Sturt had also taken live sheep with him on the overland leg of his second expedition (the discovery of the Murray River), and he thought it desirable to repeat the experiment. Nevertheless Sturt added four hundredweight (about 200 kilograms) of bacon to his stores – just in case. In the event, some of the bacon eventually returned with Sturt at the conclusion of the expedition and it was still in good condition. Sturt and Browne were both hesitant to eat it – fearing the onset of scurvy. Sturt reported that the sheep 'proved a very valuable supply, and most probably prevented the men from suffering, as their officers did, from that fearful malady the scurvy'.[21] But this could not have been the reason – because scurvy results only from an absence of vitamin C in the diet.

Sturt had decided that the expedition would depart from Adelaide on Saturday 10 August 1844. A public breakfast was organised to farewell the explorers and a good attendance was expected. Organised settlement in South Australia had begun in 1836, and the population – all free settlers, no convicts – had steadily increased. Moreover, in South Australia in 1844, there were 450 000 sheep, and more than 7600 hectares of wheat under cultivation.[22] The departure scene was well recorded by the well-known artist S. T. Gill, and the main body of the party did indeed depart on that day. However, as Sturt wrote in his *Daily Journal*: 'Morgan with the Horse Team and five Drays left Adelaide after the Public Breakfast, and encamped for the night on the Dry Creek.' Sturt added that 'after riding with about two hundred gentlemen to the same place', he had turned off the main road, and 'returned to my residence at Grange to breathe awhile from the confusion and anxiety of the last few weeks'.[23] Daniel Brock also wrote that 'after the breakfast, I went home to take farewell of my wife and boy'.[24] John Browne, the medical officer, arrived in Adelaide only on 12 August. 'After breakfast', on the morning of 15 August, Sturt 'took leave of my kind and excellent friend Mr. Cooper' and left Adelaide, in the company of James Poole and John Browne,[25] determined to overtake the main party on its way to Moorundie on the Murray River.

Apart from the men, the expedition included eleven horses, thirty-two bullocks, five drays, a horse dray, a boat, 200 sheep, four kangaroo dogs, and two sheep dogs.[26] When Sturt arrived at Moorundie he was met by Edward Eyre. Sturt wrote that Eyre had no:[27]

> ... feeling of jealousy that my services had been accepted on a field in which he had so much distinguished himself, and on which he so ardently desired to venture again ... his efforts to assist us were ceaseless as they were disinterested.

It was Eyre who persuaded the two Aboriginal men – Camboli (nicknamed 'Jacky') and Nadbuck – to accompany the expedition as far as Laidley's Ponds on the Darling River. According to Brock they were 'two fine muscular fellows'. Sturt also thought they were 'two fine specimens of Australian Aborigines'. He regarded Nadbuck as 'a perfect politician' and as 'quite a ladies man'.[28]

Aboriginal people had been in possession of the land near Moorundie (meaning 'sand' or 'sandy') and at many other sites near the Murray River, for very many years.[29] A brief account of their language was written only a few years after the first European contact.[30] Another significant Aboriginal settlement – twenty-nine kilometres (eighteen miles) south from Moorundie – had been in occupation thousands of years ago. It was known as Ngaut Ngaut, and the site retains this name. But for some years after the arrival of the Europeans it was known as Devon Downs. At this site it is possible to see ancient fireplace middens, and a number of carvings on the wall and roof of a stone shelter. Ngaut Ngaut was the site of the first archaeological 'dig' in Australia. Bones and stone implements were discovered and identified. The weapons found included basalt axes, adzes (formed by fixing with gum a discoidal flint to the end of a stick about 50–75 centimetres (20–30 inches) in length), spears, spear throwers, waddies and shields.[31]

In October 1841 Edward John Eyre had been appointed 'Protector of Aborigines' and had been given responsibility for the welfare of the river Aboriginal people and for making sure there was no conflict between them and the many 'over-landers' who were bringing sheep and cattle from New South Wales to the developing area near the Gulf of St Vincent. He had visited Moorundie during one of his expeditions and decided to make it 'the centre of his operations, although it was far removed from the area of conflict'.[32] Also in October 1841 the government announced that a small village 'will be laid out' at Moorundie and that it would be named Sturt – 'after the enterprising discoverer of the noble river upon which it is situated'. The price of each allotment with a river frontage was set at £12; allotments without a river frontage were to be sold for £8.[33]

At first, Eyre was the only European man living in the area but, before long, he was joined by a few workmen, police and army personnel. Eventually the European population reached a total of forty-three.[34] Eyre built a small house for himself; and other buildings were constructed for use by the police and the military. As protector of Aborigines, Eyre supervised a monthly issue of blankets and flour to the Aboriginal people and 'very great mobs of blacks used to come, even from near the Darling.'[35] Eyre was also anxious to establish an area where cereals, vegetables and fruit trees could be cultivated. In December 1842 he was visited by James Hawker (and F. Dutton and George Hawker) who wrote that 'with assistance of several natives' Eyre had cleared about 'half an acre of ground and sown it with wheat'. He added that the 'rise of the river caused a soakage of the ground where the wheat was sown. It grew to a height of over 6 ft. [2 metres], with tremendous heads, well filled with grain, and on Christmas Eve we all set to work and reaped it.' Hawker also added:[36]

Eyre was delighted with his experiment ... To keep the water back he proposed making sluice dams across some small creeks through which large bodies of water flowed into the flat, and by doing this regulate the quantity which would be required for irrigation, and also when the river was falling keep back a sufficient supply for all purposes. Eyre's scheme was excellent, but from unforeseen circumstances it utterly failed ... Shortly after Christmas the three of us accompanied Eyre to the different localities in which he proposed to make dams, and we were impressed with the idea that his scheme was simple and could be easily carried out.

This was the first attempt to use the water of the Murray River for irrigation. Eyre's dams were destroyed by flood waters and this, presumably, was the 'unforeseen circumstances' mentioned by Hawker.

Eyre decided to accompany Sturt for a time because he wished (in his capacity as protector of Aborigines) to distribute a number of blankets to the Aborigines whom they met. The Aboriginal people in that area wore no clothes and it was often cold – especially at night. They travelled via Lake Bonney and Lake Victoria – the circumference of each being measured using the 'chains'. According to Sturt 'Lake Bonney ... is an insignificant sheet of water about twelve miles in circumference', but Lake Victoria is 'a much finer sheet of water ... being 25 miles [40 kilometres] in circumference'.[37] They came to the anabranch of the Darling River and followed it for a short distance but, when the water diminished, they moved eastwards to the river itself – which they then followed. On one occasion Sturt dismounted and had 'well nigh trodden on an enormous snake'. It was just about to strike when Sturt drew the sabre (which Eyre had lent him) and 'swept' the snake's head from its body![38]

From time to time they met groups of Aboriginal people with whom they established good relations, but Sturt was always careful to arrange their camp in such a way that a surprise attack could be prevented.[39] He added:[40]

Although I was always disposed to be kind to the natives, I still felt it right to shew them that they were not to be unruly. Neither is it without great satisfaction that I look back to the intercourse I have had with these people, from the fact of my never having had occasion to raise my arm in hostility against them.

Sturt also took a great interest in the Aborigines whom he encountered and often recorded comments regarding differences in colour, whether or not the men had been circumcised, and whether or not one of the front teeth had been removed. Whenever possible he encouraged a member of the local tribe to accompany his party as a guide. 'There can be no doubt', he wrote, 'that the Australian aboriginal is strongly susceptible of kindness, as has been abundantly proved to me, and to the influence of such feeling I undoubtedly owe my life.'[41]

The journey up the Darling took longer than expected and Sturt decided that, to be on the safe side, he would reduce the weekly ration of flour to each man from 45 kilograms to 36 (10 pounds to 8). This decision attracted the scorn of Brock who attributed the reduction to 'a great want of judgement in selecting the stores'.[42]

As the time came for Eyre (and the two Aboriginal men) to leave to return to Moorundie, Sturt recorded his appreciation of the man who had become a close friend:[43]

> I know of no one who had greater claims on Her Majesty's Government for the good he has done on the Murray. He has done more to soften the natives on its banks than all the missionaries and protectors would effect in a thousand years.

The expedition arrived at the place that Mitchell had named Laidley's Ponds (now Menindee) on 10 October 1844 only to find it dry.[44] Sturt's written orders had made no reference to the possibility of finding an inland sea – but this hope was always in his mind. The trouble was that he had very few clues as to its probable location – if it existed. He took note of the migration paths of birds and, bearing these in mind, he had written to Lord Stanley:[45]

If a line be drawn from Latitude 29 deg 30 min. and longitude 144 deg [near Bourke] to the N.W. and another from Mt Arden [north of Spencer Gulf] due north, they would meet a little to the northward of the tropics and there, my Lord, I will be bound to say a fine country will one day or other be discovered.

Sturt imagined that, where the two lines meet, the birds would be congregating around the inland sea.[46] It is now known, however, that the migration paths of birds in Australia are seldom permanent and that they have very little evidential value. Sturt had little alternative but to arrange for small parties to reconnoitre in several different directions as the expedition moved forward. Their initial base was at Lake Cawndilla (south-west of Menindee). Poole and Stuart set off to examine the ranges to the north and reported back that they had seen what they thought was a large body of water, which, however, was a mirage![47] Sturt, Browne, Flood, Morgan and Topar (an Aborigine from the local tribe) then set off, found a dry creek bed (Stephen Creek), and followed this. The adjacent hills were named the Stanley Barrier Range after Lord Stanley – but are now known as the Main Barrier Range.

As they descended to the west they observed a 'carpet' of *Clianthus formosus* – now known as Sturt's desert pea (see colour plates). Sturt wrote that 'we saw that beautiful flower the *Clianthus formosus* in splendid blossom on the plains. It was growing amidst barrenness and decay, but its long runners were covered with flowers that gave a crimson tint to the ground.'[48] However, Sturt was not the first to observe the *Clianthus formosus*. William Dampier had collected specimens of the plant and, for a time, it was named *Clianthus dampieri*.[49] It had also been observed by Eyre.[50] It became the floral emblem of South Australia in November 1961.

Another small party – this time of Poole, Browne and Morgan – set off towards the supposed position of Eyre's boomerang-like Lake Torrens. But they did not find it at the expected position.[51] In fact, they were close to the connecting channel between Lake Frome and Lake Callabonna, and were only about 64 kilometres (about forty miles) from Eyre's Mt Hopeless. Brock recorded in his journal:[52]

> Mr. Poole and the Doctor returned but had experienced disappointment; they found what they suppose the lake to be a mere mud hole – liquid mud, unfit for use ... it has been altogether a failure.

While they were away Sturt rode about 160 kilometres (a hundred miles) to the east – but found the country there even worse.[53]

Sturt now decided that he must move to the north rather than to the north-west – and sent Flood and Mack ahead to look for water. They returned a few days later with good news. They had located a large creek about 100 kilometres (sixty miles) to the north. The whole expedition then moved to this creek – which was named Flood Creek – where another temporary base was established.[54] Poole and Browne were again sent off, this time to the nor-nor-east, and Flood was sent to look for water at the base of the hills. Sturt thought very highly of Flood and found 'it a great consolation to have a man of such utility with me'. He added:[55]

> Yet this man with the instinct of a Native in the bush, careful to a degree with the animals, of great judgement, much indeed beyond his station, and of the coolest courage, when in Adelaide is a Drunkard, and has consequently a bad reputation, but out of reach of temptation there is not a better conducted or more anxious or a more faithful follower to be found. He came with me from New South Wales with Cattle and was the only man who stood by my side in front of the Natives, and only wanted my orders to obey them. I believe Flood to be personally attached to me.

From the base camp at Flood Creek, Poole and Browne were sent north on another scouting expedition. They climbed Mt Arrowsmith and proceeded further to the north-east towards present-day Tibooburra.

In the meantime Sturt, Stuart and Flood reconnoitred to the east and reached the Noontherungie Range. They could see even further towards the east and Sturt was convinced that there was 'not a drop of water on its barren surface'.[56] Poole and Browne returned to the Flood Creek camp on the afternoon of Christmas Day with the news that they had discovered numerous creeks about 80 kilometres to the north. Sturt decided to move the party to that area. In the meantime, however, several of the men were complaining of disordered bowels, and of sore eyes. Poole was very unwell and Sturt's eyes were even weaker than usual. Nevertheless, he was able to establish a temporary camp near present-day Milparinka on 11 January, and the usual scouting expeditions to surrounding areas were organised. Sturt, Browne, Flood and Cowley searched to the north. Poole and Stuart followed up a nearby creek and returned to say that they had found abundant water only a short distance away. This spot was to become their base camp on 27 January 1845 and was named Depot Glen.[57] Sturt wrote that 'Providence had guided us to the only spot, in that wide-spread desert, where our wants could have been permanently supplied'.[58] The position of Depot Glen was determined by astronomical observation to be 29° 40' 14" S, 141° 30' 41" E.[59] Mt Hopeless bore nor'-nor'-west – about 40 kilometres distant.

AT DEPOT GLEN

They arrived at Depot Glen in the height of summer and with little chance of rain for several months. It was too risky to move forward unless water could first be located to the north. There was no alternative – they would have to remain at Depot Glen until rain came. They did not move from the depot until 17 July and there were wearisome months of near-idleness. There were several excursions into the surrounding country to add detail to the map – which was largely prepared by the draughtsman, John McDouall Stuart. They were also able to make occasional contact with the local Aboriginal people, who 'spoke a language totally different from the river tribes'. Sturt recorded that the males had all been circumcised and 'all but one' had had the right front tooth of the upper jaw removed.[60]

On another occasion, Sturt met a group of Aborigines whose language 'was a mixture between that of the river and hill tribes'.[61] He again recorded that all the males, excepting one, had been circumcised. 'The single exception had the left fore-tooth of his upper jaw extracted, and I therefore concluded that he belonged to a different tribe.'[62]

The weather was often excessively hot. On one occasion the temperature rose to 55 degrees Celsius (132 degrees Fahrenheit) in the shade – the temperature in the sun being 69 degrees Celsius (157 degrees Fahrenheit).[63] To provide some relief from the heat Sturt decided to construct an underground room, where it would be possible for the officers to work (on the maps, for example) in greater comfort. The room was duly excavated, lined, and then covered with brush wood mixed with mud – after which the soil that had been excavated was thrown over it. It was 2.1 metres (7 feet) deep, 4.9 metres (16 feet) wide and 3.7 metres (12 feet) long. Not surprisingly, 'the thing ... caused a deal of grumbling' among the men who had to excavate the room.[64] It was of some help, however. The temperature in the underground room was found to be 4 degrees Celsius (7–8 degrees Fahrenheit) cooler than the outside air.[65] The mean outside temperatures in the shade, for the months of December, January and February, were 38, 40, and 38 degrees Celsius (101, 104 and 101 degrees Fahrenheit), respectively.

Sturt observed:[66]

Under its effects every screw in our boxes had been drawn, and the horn handles of our instruments, as well as our combs, were split into fine laminae. The lead dropped out of our pencils, our signal rockets were entirely spoiled; our hair as well as the wool on the sheep, ceased to grow, and our nails had become as brittle as glass. The flour lost more than eight per cent of its original weight, and the other provisions in a still greater proportion. The bran in which our bacon had been packed, was perfectly saturated, and weighed almost as heavy as the meat; we were obliged to bury our wax candles; a bottle of citric acid in Mr. Browne's box became fluid, and escaping, burnt a quantity of his linen; and we found it difficult to write or draw, so rapidly did the fluid dry in our pens and brushes.

The harsh conditions and the restricted diet (damper, mutton, bacon and tea) led to a deterioration in the health of both officers and men. Sturt noted that the officers were worse than the men, and he attributed this to the fact that the officers had so often been away from the depot and had had to eat bacon – rather than the fresh mutton available to the men at Depot Glen. In his *Weekly Journal* Sturt wrote:[67]

About this time ... both Mr Poole, Mr Browne and myself began to feel the effects of scurvy ... We had swelled gums, taste as of copper in the mouth and violent headaches, and I had what perhaps did me good, constant but not profuse bleeding at the nose.

Poole began to suffer great pain, and 'all his skin along the muscles turned black, and large pieces of spongy flesh hung from the roof of his mouth, which was in such a state that he could hardly eat.'[68] On 26 March Poole 'took to his bed, and never rose from it again ... he was at once reduced to perfect helplessness'.[69] Poole requested that he be carried into the underground room for greater comfort – but his health continued to deteriorate.

Early in June Sturt decided to send Poole back to Adelaide, but he knew that it would be folly to begin the journey until the weather broke. Sturt and the others could not move far either. Never-theless, anticipating that the rain would soon come, he had already arranged for Stuart and six of the men to 'chain' the direction in which he proposed to move as soon as it became practicable.

The drought broke on 12 July, and Poole and the other members of the returning party – with Piesse in command – left Depot Glen on 14 July. They had not gone far before it was noticed that Poole was sinking fast and, with only brief warning, he died – probably following an internal haemorrhage. Sturt decided that Poole would be buried at Depot Glen, and he arranged for all members of the expedition to return there for the funeral.[70]

We buried Mr Poole under a Grevillia that stood close to our underground room; his initials, and the year, are cut in it above the grave, 'J. P. 1845', and he now sleeps in the desert.

RECONNAISSANCES FROM FORT GREY

After the funeral on 18 July, Piesse, Turpin, Foulkes, Sullivan, Kirby and Tampawang (the Aboriginal man) set out on their return journey to Laidley's Ponds and to Adelaide. Sturt, Browne, Brock, Flood, Morgan, Mack, Cowley (who had been Poole's servant), Davenport, Jones and Lewis set off a few days later towards the north-west. Stuart and Piesse had already 'chained' the route for 48 kilometres (30 miles) before Poole's death, and the chaining was continued for a further 50 kilometres (31 miles) until they reached Lake Pinnaroo – where Sturt established another base camp. It was first called 'the Park', but later, after the stockade had been completed, it became 'Fort Grey' – after the governor. The chaining party was sent off to the west, and Sturt and Flood rode off to overtake them – leaving Davenport, Mack, Lewis and Jones at 'the Park' with orders to build a stockyard for protection from any Aboriginal people who might covet one or two of the remaining sixty-eight sheep. Sturt and Flood overtook the chaining party. They crossed Strzelecki Creek and arrived at Lake Blanche – only to find it almost completely dry.[71] There was no alternative but to return to 'the Park'.

Sturt now decided to make a major thrust to the north-west and chose Browne, Flood, Cowley and Lewis to accompany him. Stuart was left in charge of the camp and was instructed to build a stockade within the stockyard as additional protection for the arms and ammunition. Sturt and his party left on 14 August with ten horses, a light cart and provisions for fifteen weeks. They would each live on 2.3 kilograms (five pounds) of flour (made into damper), 57 grams (two ounces) of tea, and bacon – but Sturt and Browne both decided to abstain from salt meat as a precaution against scurvy. The tea was helpful if only because they had to boil the water before drinking it!

Sturt set a course about 25 degrees west of north. They crossed Strzelecki Creek a few kilometres upstream from his earlier crossing. They crossed a creek that, some time later, he was to name Cooper Creek – in honour of his friend Judge Cooper, in Adelaide. Sturt recorded that Browne had caught thirteen 'nice little fish' in one of its branches using a hook made from a pin.[72] Not surprisingly, Sturt posed the question: 'How these fish came in that clear and isolated hole it is difficult to say ... They are most likely the product of Spawn left after the subsidence of Floods.'[73]

It is certainly an interesting problem. Studies on the ecology of the Agamid Lizard, *Amphibolurus maculosus*, have shown that they seek refuge in the permanently damp sediments that occur below the salt crust of dry lakes – where they hibernate for three or four months.[74] Moreover, the salamander-fish, *Legidogaxias salamandroides*, also burrows into deep sand to avoid the desiccation of its habitat, and can emerge after an overnight rain.[75] Attempts have been made to locate fish in dry pools and riverbeds, but without success. Nevertheless:[76]

The breaking of droughts are usually spectacular with quantities of rain falling in short periods of time. When this happens a very large area is, for a short time, covered with water and fish swim through this 'film' from permanent refuges to other locations. When the rain stops and water filters into the soil, fish are stranded ...

After kilometres of sandhills, Sturt arrived at Goyder's Lagoon – but there was no water in it and Sturt did not realise that it is connected with the Diamantina River. He then came to the gibber plains, which he called the Stony Desert. It is now usually known as Sturt's Stony Desert. A later explorer, Madigan, wrote:[77]

Gibbers are flat, roundish and flinty pebbles of all sizes from an inch or two across up to six inches or more. They are dark red to yellow in colour and are smoothed by sand blast and even quite polished through a coating of 'desert varnish', a deposit of colloidal silica or oxide of iron, or both, which is a characteristic superficial process in hot and arid regions.

Gibbers are found in other countries also, and 'desert varnish' has been found to consist of a complex aluminium silicate mineral containing 7 per cent of iron and 3 per cent of manganese. The red colour of many desert sands (for example in the Simpson Desert) is caused by the same material.[78]

Sturt continued into what is now called the Simpson Desert. He desperately wanted to be the first to reach the centre of the continent but, on 8 September, he decided that there was no inland sea in this locality and that the absence of water made it too dangerous for his party to proceed further. According to his *Daily Journal* he reached 24° 40' S, 138° 05' E, but Bonython's examination of the country led him to suggest that Sturt's longitude was nearer 138° 20' E. Moreover, Stokes has found that Sturt's 'verifiable longitudes all have a consistent error of about 15' to 20' too far west', presumably due to an error in his chronometer.[79] This would give 138° 20' or 138° 25' E in agreement with Bonython.

Gibber plain near Bedourie, south-west Queensland (C.R. Twidale)

Sturt's disappointment is made crystal clear in his journals. In his *Weekly Journal*, for example, he wrote that 'We saw the great stony desert stretching out before us like the ocean, apparently as boundless in its extent, and without a single object on the visible horizon to guide us over it.' In his *Daily Journal* he wrote: 'I may with truth affirm that man never wandered in a more gloomy and hopeless desert.' In his *Narrative* he wrote:[80]

We have now penetrated direct into the interior from the Depot 347 miles [560 kilometres], but we have seen no change in this fearful and unparalled desert. I have now lost all hope of finding any body of water or of making any discovery, and feel that I am subjecting myself and others to all this exposure and privation solely to discharge my duty conscientiously.

Sturt and his companions returned safely to the depot on 2 October and found everything in good order. Indeed, as the stockade had been completed, it now justified the name 'Fort Grey'. Men and horses alike were exhausted and needed rest and recuperation. The horses' hooves (which were unshod) were 'down to the level with their quicks'.[81]

Sturt had been searching for an inland sea but had discovered a sand ridge or dune desert that Cecil Madigan later named the Simpson Desert – after A. A. Simpson, the then president of the Royal Geographical Society of Australasia, SA Branch. As Twidale has written:[82]

The dunefield occupies the driest and lowest part of the continent. Though sand ridges dominate the landscape, there are within the confines of the Simpson (which in modern terminology embraces the Tirari, Sturt's Stony and Strzelecki deserts) many salinas and claypans, extensive areas of gibber or stony desert and river channels and associated alluvial flats as well as remnants of ridges and plateaux.

Over most of the Simpson Desert the sand ridges trend SSE–NNW and run essentially in parallel and unbroken for scores, and even hundreds, of kilometres. The sand ridges vary in height between 10 m and 18 m.

The sand of which the dunes are built is a quartz sand. It is rounded to subrounded 0.05 to 1.2 mm diameter and characteristically with a skin of iron oxide (which imparts the characteristic red colour to the dunes).

Cecil Madigan carried out an aerial exploration of the Simpson Desert in 1929 in what was the first recorded application of aerial photography to geological mapping in Australia. Later, in 1939, he led a party of nine men and nineteen camels across the Simpson Desert from Charlotte Waters to Birdsville – but the results of this expedition remained unpublished until the end of World War II.[83]

Sturt soon recovered his spirit and his energy, and decided to make another reconnaissance to the north – but to the east of his last trail. He was to take a new team of men. At the same time he was worried about Browne's health and wanted him to lead all those who would not be travelling on this new expedition back to Adelaide. Browne took the view that he had promised Sturt's wife that he would not leave Sturt and therefore refused to go. In the end Sturt agreed that Browne and the others would remain at Fort Grey, and that Browne would be in command.

For the new reconnaissance Sturt took John McDouall Stuart, Morgan and Mack, with eight horses and provisions for ten weeks. They left Fort Grey on 9 October and followed the previous route as far as Strzelecki Creek, and then followed that creek to its junction with Cooper Creek. They crossed Cooper Creek and travelled a little west of north until they arrived in the vicinity of present-day Birdsville. It was the same awful desert. So Sturt turned back to Cooper Creek and followed that waterway towards the east – beyond present-day Innamincka. There was no encouragement to proceed any further so Sturt returned down the Cooper and began his return journey towards Fort Grey.

Sturt returned to Fort Grey on 13 November

and found it deserted. Browne had decided to abandon it when the water became unfit to drink and caused dysentery. They had departed on 6 November, and moved to Depot Glen. Sturt and his party reached Depot Glen on 17 November. There was nothing to detain them there. It was fast approaching summer and water was becoming even scarcer. Sturt himself had scurvy and this had progressed to the stage when he had muscular cramp. They had a journey of 434 kilometres (270 miles) before they could reach Menindee (where Piesse was waiting for them with additional food supplies), and it seemed that Sturt would have to be carried on a litter for most of the distance. It was a continuing struggle, but Sturt gradually improved. Browne had observed a number of natives eating some of the small acid berries – and had collected a large tureen full for Sturt to eat. Sturt thought that they were of great benefit to him and he attributed his recovery from the scurvy to these berries. It seems likely that these berries were from *Solanum ellipticum* – as suggested by Frank Badman, botanist, of Roxby Downs.[84] The returning party reached Lake Victoria on 8 December where Sturt learnt that his former Aboriginal guide, Nadbuck, had been wounded by another Aboriginal man. Somehow or other Nadbuck learnt of Sturt's safe return and he:[85]

> ... made a successful effort to get to us, and tears chased each other down the old man's cheeks when he saw us again. Assuredly these poor people of the desert have the most kindly feelings; for not only was his reception of us such as I have described, but the natives one and all exhibited the utmost joy at our safety, and cheered us on every part of the river.

On 13 January Sturt decided to leave Piesse in charge of the returning expedition and pushed on to Moorundie where he was warmly welcomed. A few days later he mounted his horse for the first time since he became ill. This was short-lived, however, because he met some friends who had a carriage and they conveyed him to Adelaide. He arrived home at midnight on 19 January. His wife was so astonished by his arrival at the door that she fainted.

There is no doubt that Sturt was bitterly disappointed. He had failed to find an inland sea and he had failed to reach the geographical centre of the continent. It is equally certain, however, that he was regarded by everyone as a 'great' explorer. Indeed, it can be truly said:[86] 'Never on any other occasion in Australian History has such persistent daring met with such ill-success.'

A special dinner was organised for 10 February 1846 to celebrate the return of the expedition, and there were speeches praising the exploits of Sturt and his companions. In reply, Sturt said:[87]

> You welcome me with as much kindness as if my long and arduous journey had been most successful. But since we last met I have travelled over a fearful desert ... In that barren country, where only surface water is found, the danger of advance is great, and beyond the Darling you may well believe I have not had an hour without anxiety.

Sturt applied for some well-deserved leave and preparations were made for the whole family to sail to England. A public breakfast was organised to farewell him and to enable the colonists to express their feelings of respect and esteem before his departure. As Judge Cooper put it: 'Anyone who was then present can testify that the expression of those feelings was unanimous and unequivocal'.[88] There was an external recognition of his work which must have pleased him enormously. In 1847 the Royal Geographical Society, in London, awarded him their highest award – the Founder's Medal – 'for explorations in Australia, and especially for his journey fixing the limit of Lake Torrens and penetrating into the heart of the continent to latitude 24° 30' S, longitude 138° 00' E'. Sturt was still at sea when the medal was to be presented and it was received on his behalf by his friend John Morphett.

Sturt busied himself writing his account of his expedition to the centre of Australia. This was published in 1849.[89] In the meantime, however, Sturt had returned to Adelaide following his leave, and was now the colonial secretary. His eyesight was still poor, and he eventually decided to retire and return to England. He arrived in Plymouth, with his family, in July 1853. He still wanted to return again to Adelaide – but it was not to be. In his declining years he continued to take an interest in exploration, especially in the exploration of Australia, and he died peacefully on 16 June 1869.

STURT'S ACHIEVEMENTS

Sturt was a rather special explorer. He was a dedicated leader, and an artist of some merit. He painted watercolour sketches of some of the birds observed during his last expedition. He painted a picture – now in Canberra – of Depot Glen, and he made an excellent sketch of some Aboriginal huts. He also made a fine pencil drawing of a dusky hopping-mouse, *Notomys fuscus* – which he referred to as a Jerboa.[90] He thought it was of the same species as that which had been described by Major Mitchell. Sturt wrote to his wife:[91]

> We have captured one of those little animals called the Jerboa about which Major Mitchell makes such a fuss in his book and I have it alive and well. It is a beautiful little animal, something between the mouse and the kangaroo in shape with a very long tail having a bush at the end of it. It is very elegant in its movements, and Major Mitchell's plate is as like it as it is like the Hotentot Venus, a most absurd resemblance to the little animal altogether'.

It is now known, however, that Mitchell had observed a different but very similar species – Mitchell's hopping-mouse, *Notomys mitchelli*.

In the Appendix to his *Narrative*, Sturt gave the following description of the dusky hopping-mouse: 'They are not much larger than a mouse, have a beautiful full black eye, long ears, and tail feathered towards the end. The colour of the fur is light red, in rising they hop on their hind legs, and when tired go on all four, holding their tail perfectly horizontal ... They are taken by the natives in hundreds'.[92] On one occasion three Aborigines arrived at Sturt's camp with 'their bags full of Jerboas which they had captured on the hills. They could not indeed have had less than from 150 to 200 of these little animals.' In his letter to his wife Sturt said that they had counted them and there were 288![93] Sturt added that 'Our friends cooked all they had in the hot sand, and devoured them entire, fur, skin, entrails and all, only breaking away the under jaw and nipping off the tail with their teeth'.[94] The rats observed by Sturt, and also by Burke and Wills, were of the species known as the long-haired rat, *Rattus villosissius*, which, following a run of good seasons, often occurs in plague proportions from the Barkly Tableland south to Sturt's Stony Desert, and occasionally south to Marree.

Of the birds collected and described by Sturt in the Appendix to his *Narrative*, only one – the cinnamon-coloured ground thrush *Cinclosoma cinnamoneus* – was found to be a new species. This thrush was observed in considerable numbers at Depot Glen during the winter months. Sturt included a colour plate of this bird in his account of the expedition. J. Gould and H. C. Richter were the artists – but much of the work was probably done by Gould's wife, Elizabeth. It was lithographed by Hullmandel and Walton. Another plate by the same people was included in Gould's *The Birds of Australia*, published in 1848. Gould added that the specimen from which the plate was drawn 'now forms part of the collection at the British Museum and we learn from Captain Sturt that it was the only one procured during his lengthened sojourn at the Depot in that sterile and inhospitable country, the Interior of Australia'.[95] In general, Sturt wrote his own descriptions of the birds and animals observed during the expedition, and these were all included in the Appendix to his *Narrative*. The

Sturt used a sketchbook during his expedition to central Australia; this drawing, dated March 1845, must have been prepared when the expedition was at Depot Glen. (provided by Anthony Sturt, a great-grandson of Charles Sturt)

Sturt's pencil drawing of a 'Dusky Hopping-Mouse', *Notomys fuscus*, which he referrred to as a Jerboa. (reproduced with permission of the Sturt family)

descriptions of the plants were provided by Robert Brown.[96]

Sturt had been the leader of three expeditions – all of which added significantly to knowledge of the Australian continent. He is now widely regarded by Australians (and with considerable justification) as a hero. For many years this assessment was based almost solely on his own published accounts of his expeditions. Those who write their autobiographies, or their own accounts of their expeditions, have an opportunity to exaggerate their achievements or, at least, to put the best possible construction on their actions. Moreover, they may be inclined to omit details of which they are not particularly proud. The first full-length biography of Sturt was written by his daughter-in-law, Beatrix Sturt – who was the wife of Colonel Napier George Sturt, Charles Sturt's son. Beatrix Sturt regarded Charles Sturt as a 'hero' and doubtless contributed to the favourable perception of Sturt over the years.[97]

In recent times, Sturt's published accounts of his expeditions have been augmented by additional, but previously unpublished, material written by Sturt. Sturt wrote a *Daily Journal*, which has not yet been published *in toto*; but substantial portions have been published by Stokes.[98] The National Library of Australia has a microfilm copy of the *Daily Journal* – which was used by Stokes. Stokes provided a typewritten copy to the Royal Geographical Society of South Australia; and the present author has had an opportunity to read it. Sturt also wrote a *Weekly Journal* – which was written on Sundays and which was intended for his wife Charlotte. This was sent to Adelaide whenever a courier was available. The *Weekly Journal* has been published in recent times and is a valuable addition to the information previously available concerning Sturt's third expedition.[99]

Cumpston has written two sympathetic accounts of Sturt's expeditions, and Langley has written a biography of Sturt.[100] In addition there are two other first-hand accounts of Sturt's expedition into central Australia. The first was a journal written by John Harris Browne – the medical officer on the expedition. The second journal, which is much more critical of Sturt, was written by Daniel George Brock – the 'bird-skinner' and armourer to the expedition into central Australia.[101] The most critical account of Sturt is that by Edgar Beale in his book *Sturt: The Chipped Idol*, published in 1979.[102]

Because we now know that there is no inland sea, it is easy to be critical of Sturt, and of many of the other early explorers – including Oxley and Cunningham – for their continuing belief in the probable existence of an inland sea. It must be remembered, however, that although Lake Eyre (the southern arm of which was discovered by Eyre in 1840) is often a completely dry salt lake, it is occasionally a 'real' lake. When it is flooded with water it could well be regarded as an inland sea. For example, 'phenomenally heavy' rains fell in northern and eastern Australia in 1949–50, 'and many of the inland rivers came down in flood, inundating vast areas of plain, flooding homesteads and even isolating whole communities' – the two major water channels to the Lake being Cooper Creek and the Warburton River.[103] On this occasion the whole of the 7770 square kilometres or so of Lake Eyre North was submerged but, by 1953, the lake was again dry. Moreover, in July 1964, the lake was so completely dry that Donald Campbell was able to break the world land-speed record on the salt bed of the lake by travelling at 648.6 kilometres per hour. The salt has been found to be 96 per cent sodium chloride – with small quantities of other salts.

It has since been established that Lake Eyre contained substantial quantities of water in 1891, 1906, 1941, 1949, 1950, 1951, 1953, 1955, 1956, 1957, 1958, 1959, 1963, 1974, 1984 and 2000.[104] The *largest* flooding of Lake Eyre in recent times was in 1974 – but evidence has been found that at least three prehistoric fillings, above that of the 1974 filling, occurred about 3000, 1500, and 500 years

Lake Eyre is often completely dry, with a flat surface of salt but, every few years, it becomes a substantial body of water; in 1976 there was enough water to mount a yachting regatta *(Advertiser* Adelaide, 12 May 1975)

ago.[105] If Sturt, or any other explorer, had visited Lake Eyre in 1974, instead of in 1840, he would have discovered an inland sea. In 1976 there was even a yachting regatta there – in what was described as the first yachting regatta in the Lake's ten–million–year history.[106]

In further defence of Sturt it might also be mentioned that, although there is no 'permanent' inland sea, as Sturt hoped to find, there is a vast *underground* inland sea in central Australia. It is known as the Great Artesian Basin. It occupies about 1 700 000 square kilometres – about one-fifth of Australia. It extends across parts of Queensland, New South Wales, South Australia and the Northern Territory. It underlies many of the arid and semi-arid regions, and is of great importance to the pastoral industry. It holds an immense amount of

water and, in places, is 3 kilometres thick. From time to time the level of water falls, but it is recharged mainly from the north–east. The basin was discovered in about 1880.[107] The bore at Goyder's Lagoon was 'put down in 1905 to a depth of 4850 feet [1478 metres]. It delivered when first completed 600 000 gallons [more than two million litres] a day at a temperature of 208°F [316°C]'.[108]

Sturt has also been criticised for the fact that his own accounts of his expeditions seldom mention the individual men who accompanied him – despite his frequent praise of them in general.[109] The individuals do not 'come to life' – so he must not have been interested in them as men. It should be remembered, however, that Sturt was an army officer, and in the British Army of the nineteenth century (and in most armies today) officers were (and still are) instructed not to fraternise with the enlisted men. Officers were (and are) required to live in quarters separate from the men and to dine separately from the men. These arrangements were designed to avoid fraternisation and to ensure instant obedience to orders given by officers. Sturt was not perfect – no heroes are perfect. But he remains a hero. As Elizabeth Barrett Browning wrote 'All actual heroes are essential men, And all men possible heroes.'[110] Take Horatio Nelson, for example. Nelson is arguably the most admired and revered hero in British history. When the news of the Battle of Trafalgar reached London, an editorial in the *Times* described the action as 'the most decisive victory that has ever been achieved by British skill and gallantry'.[111] But Nelson was extremely vain and ambitious. He was not perfect.

So it was with Charles Sturt. He too was vain and ambitious. He too was dissatisfied with the level of his recognition. His knighthood (in the Order of St Michael and St George) was eventually approved, but was not gazetted until after his death. Charlotte, his widow, was given the right to be called Lady Sturt. He pandered to the titled 'great' (such as the Earl of Ripon) and sought favour by naming 'the great river' after the secretary of state for the Colonies, Sir George Murray, who, despite a distinguished army career was also 'perhaps the most ineffectual and inefficient minister to hold that office throughout the nineteenth century'.[112]

Charles Sturt was not perfect either. Nevertheless, the various criticisms of Sturt do not reduce his stature as an explorer:[113]

> Nothing that has been said has detracted, nor should it detract, from his heroism, his sureness of judgement, his perseverance, his patience, tolerance and understanding of the Aborigines, his keen observation and the constancy of his application to the totality of the venture. His achievement remains.

Daniel Brock, who journeyed with him into the heart of central Australia, often criticised Sturt in his personal journal, and some of these criticisms might well have been justified. Years later, on 9 August 1858, Brock made a public speech about Sturt:[114]

> Nobody but those who had been with him on his journies [sic] have known his courage and coolness. Often when the safety of the whole party hung upon his next movement, they knew that he would do all that was possible for man to do, and they trusted him.

They trusted him. That is the mark of a great commander.

14

AUSTRALIA FELIX
AND TROPICAL AUSTRALIA

Thomas Mitchell had established himself as one of Australia's most successful explorers – but there was more to be done. He returned to Sydney towards the end of September 1835 and, within a few days, the governor, Sir Richard Bourke, wrote to Lord Glenelg, the secretary of state for the Colonies:[1]

> It seems probable that the River Darling flows into the Murray at the point indicated by Captain Sturt, but the fact had not been determined when Major Mitchell found it necessary to retrace his steps towards the Colony.

Bourke believed that it was essential for this junction to be confirmed and, a couple of months later, he again wrote to Glenelg to say that he had decided to send Mitchell on another expedition to determine this matter and to 'return to the Colony through the country lying between the left bank of the Murray and Morumbidgee [sic] and the Snowy Range'. He added that the 'Surveyor-General is a difficult man to manage, and I fear I am rather *en mauvaise odeur* with him at present. But I do my best to keep him and others in good humour, yet within decent bounds.'[2]

Mitchell set about the organisation of this new expedition with his usual enthusiasm. Stores were purchased, and men were selected. Some of these were convicts, and others were emancipists, or men who had been given provisional pardons for past services. Eleven men had been on at least one of his previous expeditions and had agreed to join

him again. As second-in-command Mitchell chose William Darke, who was a draughtsman in his department. Before very long, however, Mitchell decided that Darke was 'a fool'. When they reached Buree (Boree), Darke was sent back to Sydney and Granville Chetwynd Stapylton, an assistant surveyor, was required to make all haste to join the expedition.[3]

In the event, therefore, this expedition had two officers, Mitchell and Stapylton – the latter being an assistant rather than a senior colleague. In addition, there were twenty-three men. On this expedition each man was to be armed – some with a carabine (carbine), some with a carabine and pistol, some with a musket. Mitchell himself had a rifle and pistols. The expedition set off and Mitchell joined them on 15 March 1836 'in a valley near the Canobolas', which he had chosen as the rendezvous.[4]

The governor was irritated by the fact that Mitchell had not completed a fair copy of the journal of his earlier expedition, and Bourke wrote to the secretary of state:[5]

> To this neglect, he has added the strange indiscretion of taking his original memoranda with him on this second expedition [to the Darling], thus risking the fruits of the labors of the first.

Mitchell was pleased that so many men who had been with him on his earlier expedition, and who had obtained their emancipation, were willing to follow him again. He obtained a promise from the governor that, if the expedition were successful, their conditional pardons might be converted into absolute pardons.[6]

Several Aboriginal people visited the camp before they departed. One, 'who called himself John Piper', agreed to join the expedition 'provided he was allowed a horse, and was clothed, fed, &c, all of which' Mitchell agreed. John Piper was to prove a valuable addition to the team. Soon afterwards, for example, Piper persuaded another Aborigine to be a guide 'as far as he knew the country'.

A few days later they came to a cattle station on the banks of the Lachlan which Mitchell thought was similar to the Darling, but on a smaller scale – 'but its waters were gone, except in a few small ponds'. He followed the general course of the Lachlan 'as laid down by Mr. Oxley'. Oxley, a

lieutenant in the Royal Navy, had been appointed the first surveyor-general on 1 January 1812, and had arrived in Sydney Cove on 25 October of the same year. They halted on Sunday, because Mitchell wished to take sights 'for the purpose of ascertaining the rate of my chronometer and to lay down my surveys'. He found that Oxley's points on this river 'were much too far to the westward' – that is, his longitudes were inaccurate. Mitchell added, however, that this was to be expected as, at that early stage of the colony, Oxley's survey could not 'be connected with Paramatta [Parramatta] by actual measurement, as mine was' and he added that their latitudes 'agreed very exactly'.[7] Three days later they came upon the tree in the trunk of which Oxley and Evans had carved their names and the date 'May 17' (1817). Mitchell found the longitude 'as now ascertained by trigonometrical measurement

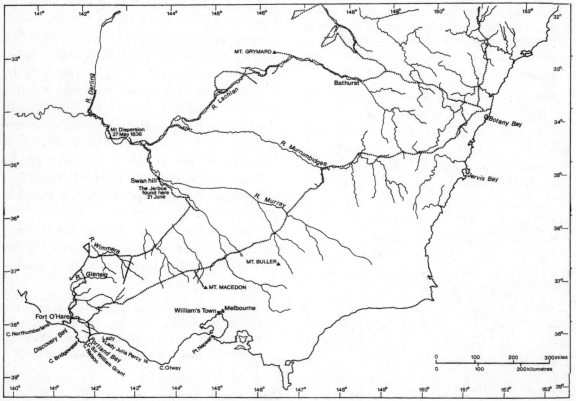

Map of south-eastern mainland Australia showing the route taken by Mitchell

from Paramatta' to be 147° 33' 50" E, just over 27 kilometres (17 miles) nearer to Sydney than that found by Oxley.[8]

As they proceeded, they met two Aborigines from the Bogan River – one of whom was carrying a tomahawk that had been given to him by Mitchell on an earlier expedition. This was on 9 April, and it was on 11 April that Stapylton joined the expedition 'having travelled in great haste from Sydney'.[9] He was soon at work surveying Lake Cargelligo ('Cudjallagong' on Mitchell's map) – which, at that time, was almost dry. Piper had previously visited this lake, with the object of obtaining a gin (wife). When he returned, Mitchell wrote that 'a good strong woman marched behind him into our camp, loaded with a new opossum-skin cloak, and various presents, that had been given to Piper with her'.[10] Mitchell had to be careful not to add too many additional mouths to feed to his party; but he did add some – including an Aboriginal widow, Turandurey (who proved to be an excellent guide), with her young daughter, Ballandella.

Two intelligent Aboriginal boys also attached themselves to the party. Both were called 'Tommy'. To distinguish them, one was called 'Tommy Came-first' and the other 'Tommy Came-last'. The Aboriginal people were helpful in various ways. On one occasion the explorers noticed that the Aborigines were eating the leaves of a plant that grew in the hollows. With this proof that it was not poisonous, a quantity was boiled and used as a vegetable. It seems likely that it contained vitamin C. Again, Mitchell received help in tracing the Oxley expedition. The Aborigines took him to a tree that Oxley had marked – and they made it clear that this indicated the furthest point reached by that explorer. Mitchell promptly determined its position as 33° 45' 10" S, 144° 56' E.[11] Then, a few days later, six of the bullocks wandered off – but Piper was able to track them and bring them back to the camp.

Mitchell and his party continued until 'suddenly' and 'at last' he stood on the banks of the Murrumbidgee – which he described as a 'magnificent stream' far surpassing the Darling. There was a group of Aboriginal people on the other bank, and Mitchell's female guide, Turandurey, was able to interpret their language. Mitchell wrote:[12]

Our female guide, who had scarcely before ventured to look up, stood now boldly forward, and addressed the strange tribe in a very animated and apparently eloquent manner; and when her countenance was thus lighted up, displaying fine teeth, and great earnestness of manner, I was delighted to perceive what soul the woman possessed, and could not but consider our party fortunate in having met with such an interpreter.

As they approached the Murray River, Mitchell found a good site for a depot. An adjacent small lake was named Lake Stapylton. Most of the heavy equipment, drays, boats, most of the cattle, and the bulk provisions were to remain here under the charge of Stapylton with eight 'trusty' men – while Mitchell and the remainder of the men were to follow the Murray as far as the Darling River, and then travel up the Darling to complete its exploration.[13] The Aboriginal widow and her child, Balaudella (now suffering from a broken thigh that had been set by Souter) were to remain at the depot – but Piper would travel with Mitchell's party. Stapylton was not too happy about the prospect of a month of dreary inactivity, and nor were the other men who had to stay behind.

Nevertheless, Mitchell set off and reached the Murray – which he estimated to have a width of a 150 metres. The next day they reached Lake Benanee and, soon afterwards, met a substantial body of warlike Aboriginal people.[14]

It will, however, be readily understood with what caution we followed these natives, when we discovered, almost as soon as we fell in with them, that they were actually our old enemies from the Darling! I had certainly heard, when still far up on the Lachlan, that these people were coming down to fight us; but I little expected, they were to be the first natives we should meet with on the Murray, at a distance of nearly two hundred miles from the scene of our former encounter.

On the next night the Aborigines made five large fires, 'which formed a cordon around our camp', and all the Aboriginal women withdrew. There was a brief attempt to obtain articles from the carts, but Mitchell drew up the men in line and sent up a rocket, at which all the Aboriginal people ran off. Next morning, however, the Aborigines set fire to a fallen tree near the tents and it was apparent that the camp would soon be enveloped in smoke. At this stage Mitchell called all his men to arms and they advanced towards the Aborigines showing their muskets – 'The savages took to their heels before these men.'[15] On the next morning, Mitchell's party continued on its way – but they were followed by Aborigines. Mitchell was assured by Piper 'and the other young natives, that we should soon lose some of the men in charge of the cattle'. The harassment continued on the next day and it became necessary for Mitchell to determine 'whether I was to allow the party, under my charge, to be perpetually subject to be cut off in detail, by waiting until these natives had again actually attacked, and slain some of my people, or whether it was not my duty ... to anticipate the intended blow'.[16] In the end, one of the party, in his excitement, discharged his carbine, without orders, and the Aboriginal people ran off as other guns were also discharged. According to Piper, seven of the Aborigines had been shot while crossing the river. According to Mitchell's notes:[17]

Numbers were shot in swimming across the Murray (and more as they got to land on the opposite bank) and some even after they had reached the opposite shore, as they ascended the bank. Amongst those shot in the water was the chief (recognised by a particular kind of cloak he wore which floated after he went down).

As Mitchell wrote in his published book: 'the result was a permanent deliverance of the party from imminent danger.'[18] Mitchell gave 'to the little hill which witnessed this overthrow of our enemies, and was to us the harbinger of peace and tranquility', the name of Mt Dispersion.[19] Nevertheless, as the explorers proceeded, they came across another group of Aboriginal people and Mitchell believed that he could recognise two from the previous year on the Darling. They wanted tomahawks; but Mitchell had now learnt a lesson and refused their requests. They also met four other Aborigines. 'Their hair was of a reddish hue, and they were altogether men of a different make from the tribe of the Darling.'[20]

Mitchell allowed them to remain in his camp. Another large group of Aborigines seemed more aggressive. Mitchell was on the alert and he pushed on to the junction of the Murray and Darling rivers. When they arrived there Mitchell decided to leave a message in a bottle. He marked a tree 'Dig Under' and pushed the bottle into the soft ground. This bottle contained a brief statement of their circumstances and the names of all the men with him. It was found less than two years later by Joseph Hawdon and Charles Bonney during their overlanding of cattle to South Australia.[21]

Hawdon and Bonney crossed the Murray on 28 February 1838, and wrote:[22]

We had travelled only three miles, when we came upon the 'River Darling', just at the point where it joins the Murray. On the trunk of a tree that stands on the neck of land forming the junction, I read the words cut in large letters 'Dig Under'. The direction was instantly obeyed, when we dug up a small phial in which was deposited a slip of paper written by Major Mitchell, dated 3rd January 1836, and stating that from this point he commenced his return from the Darling; that he was surrounded by hostile tribes, and was anxious about the safety of his party at the depot near the junction of the Murrumbidgee, and giving the names of eleven persons then with him. I again buried the phial in the same spot, after taking a copy of the Major's memorandum, and adding to it another of my own.

The 'dispersion' of the Aborigines occurred on 27 May. On 30 May Mitchell and his men camped on the banks of the Murray River – before proceeding to examine the Darling River. Mitchell was immediately disappointed – the river was, at that time, little more than a series of ponds. His entry for 1 June was:[23]

While I stood on the adverse side or right bank of this hopeless river, I began to think, I had pursued its course far enough. The identity was no longer a question. The country on its banks in this part presented also the same unvaried desert features that it did in the districts examined by us during the preceding year. The Murray, unlike the Darling, was a permanent river, and I thought it advisable to exhaust no more of my means in the survey of deserts ... I had already reached a point far above where any boat could be taken, or even any heavy carts; and nothing was to be gained by following the river further.

Mitchell, with all his troubles with the Aboriginal people, was concerned for the men he had left with Stapylton at the depot. On 10 June, as Mitchell and his party approached the depot, they heard a shot – which must have worried them – but it transpired that it had been fired at a duck. Stapylton and his men were found to be well. Indeed, during the whole of the time that Mitchell had been absent, the Aborigines had never approached the depot. The party was once more united. Mitchell was also pleased to find that the little native girl, Ballandella, was fast recovering.

They discovered the junction of the Murrumbidgee and Murray rivers on 13 June, and a short distance to the west of this junction they crossed the Murray River with the loss of one bullock, which drowned. They then followed the southern bank towards the south-east, but found difficulty with the anabranches. Then, on 20 June, they reached the junction of the Murray River and the

Little Murray River – which happens to be the lower reaches of the Loddon River. Mitchell determined the latitude of this junction to be 35° 19' 43" S.[24] On 21 June Mitchell wrote:[25]

Among the reeds on the point of ground between the two rivers [the Murray River and the Little Murray River], was a shallow lagoon, where swans and other wild fowl so abounded that, although half a mile from our camp, their noise disturbed us throughout the night. I, therefore, named this somewhat remarkable and isolated feature, Swanhill [now Swan Hill].

Some of the Aboriginal people in this area resented the presence of White men on their land and blamed Piper for bringing them. An argument ensued, during which Piper shot and killed one of the local Aborigines – a fact that greatly distressed Mitchell. The Aboriginal people in this area used spears made of reeds, pointed with bones from emus. These Aborigines 'wore cloaks made of kangaroo skins'.

The period spent travelling up the Murray River was also of interest because two very unusual animals were discovered. On 16 June they had discovered (and captured) a 'Pig-footed bandicoot'. It was the size of a 'young wild rabbit, and of nearly the same colour, but had a broad head, terminating in a long very slender snout'.[26] This animal, now named *Chaeropus ecaudatus*, was rare even at that time (the Aboriginal people who caught it declared that they had never seen one before), and it is now believed to be extinct. Mitchell wrote that he had seen the skull of such an animal in the caves in Wellington Valley. The specimen captured by the Aborigines was given to the Sydney Museum. On 21 June Mitchell recorded:[27]

A very curious and rare little quadruped, was this day found by the two Tommies, who had never before seen such an animal. Its fore and hind legs resembled in proportion those of the kangaroo; and it used the latter by leaping on its hind quarters in the same manner as that animal. It was not much

Mitchell's hopping mouse (*Notomys mitchellii*) was discovered at Reedy Plains on 21 June 1936; Mitchell called it a 'kangaroo mouse'. (Dixson Library, State Library of NSW)

larger than a common field-mouse, but the tail was longer in proportion to the rest of the body, even than that of a kangaroo, and terminated in a hairy brush about two inches long.

Mitchell made a pencil drawing of this 'mouse' and a modified version of this appeared as plate 29 in volume 2 of his *Three Expeditions*. It became known as 'Mitchell's Hopping Mouse', and its scientific name is now *Notomys mitchellii*.

Mitchell was beginning to realise that they had found some excellent pastoral country. On 25 June, for example, he wrote:[28]

> The country, we passed over this day, was upon the whole richer in point of grass, than any we had seen since we left Sydney ... We had discovered no similar country during either of the two former journeys.
>
> There were none of the acacia trees we had seen on the lower Bogan; while the grasses were also different from any of those on the Darling.

On the previous day Burnett had climbed a tree and had noted a substantial hill about 35 kilometres (22 miles) away. Mitchell first thought of naming it

'Burnett's Hill' but, in his published account, he named it Mount Hope.[29] A few days later they reached the mountain. Mitchell climbed it and was fascinated by another 'remarkable hill' that he could see. 'It was a triangular pyramid, and, being quite isolated, it closely resembled the monuments of Egypt.' So it was named Pyramid Hill. Moreover, as Mitchell explained:[30]

> The country which I had seen this day beyond Mount Hope, was too inviting to be left behind us unexplored; and I, therefore, determined to turn into it without further delay.

Later he added:[31]

> A land so inviting, and still without inhabitants! As I stood, the first European intruder on the sublime solitude of these verdant plains, as yet untouched by flocks or herds; I felt concious of being the harbinger of mighty changes; and that our steps would soon be followed by the men and the animals for which it seemed to have been prepared.

He determined to explore this very encouraging country – despite the fact that he had been ordered to return to Sydney via the Murray River.

As they proceeded in a south-westerly direction, they came to a river with steep banks – such that they had to build a makeshift bridge to enable the carts and stock to cross. Mitchell transcribed the Aboriginal name for this river as the 'Yarrayne', but it is now known as the Loddon River – a name that Mitchell used for another river a few days later. Mitchell found the water in the Yarrayne rose so much overnight that their bridge was underwater by morning. The river continued to rise and the completion of their crossing was possible only by using the boats.[32]

On 8 July they came to the little stream that Mitchell named the Loddon 'from its resemblance in some respects to the little stream in England' – but this stream is now named the Avoca River. Mitchell recorded the position of his camp on the bank of this stream as 36° 36' 49" S, 143° 35' 30" E.[33] Continuing, they came to a creek that Mitchell named the Avoca after a river of this name in Ireland – but this is now known as Sandy Creek. It is a tributary of the present-day Avoca River.[34] Mitchell was ecstatic about this country, and wrote:[35]

We had at length discovered a country ready for the immediate reception of civilized man; and destined perhaps to become eventually a portion of a great empire. Unencumbered by too much wood, it yet possessed enough for all purposes; its soil was exuberant, and its climate temperate; it was bounded on three sides by the ocean; and it was traversed by mighty rivers, and watered by streams innumerable. Of this Eden I was the first European to explore its mountains and streams ... The lofty mountain range, which I had seen on the 11th [July], was now before us, but still distant between thirty and forty miles.

Mitchell was anxious to inspect the mountain range and to take bearings for his survey. On 13 July, with six men on horseback, he set off, leaving Stapylton and the others to plan how to cross the Richardson River (which had been named after the expedition's botanist). Mitchell came to a substantial river which Piper learnt was known to

the local Aboriginal people as the Wimmera – and this name was adopted. Soon afterwards they began to climb the mountain and reached the summit – but realised that they could not hope to make the return journey before dark. They had to spend the night on the mountain in freezing weather. It was a long night of misery as they awaited the dawn. When the horizon became clear Mitchell 'took what angles I could obtain'. Their descent was as difficult as the ascent, but they managed it. Mitchell's next problem was to choose a suitable name for the mountain that they had climbed, and for the range. Normally, he favoured retaining the name used by the Aborigines – if this could be determined. On this occasion, however, he 'ventured to connect this summit with the name of the sovereign in whose reign' the exploration had been carried out.[36] So it became Mt William. He named the mountain range 'The Grampians'.[37]

Mitchell recorded that he now had 'several men on the sick list' but that they soon recovered under the treatment provided by Drysdale, their medical attendant. Stapylton recorded in his journal on 15 July that the surveyor-general was still absent – but added 'no joke these cold nights with only a military Cloak for a covering they must also be hard up for Grub this being the third night & with provisions for one day only at starting'. On the following day he wrote that the party returned that morning. He added that:[38]

[Mitchell's] constitution must be as hard as iron to stand three days of it without food wet thro the whole time a bitter wind from the Southward on the summit chilling the frame violently heated with perspiration from the fatigue of the ascent ... but he appears not at all the worse for it at present but positively in better health.

On the next day they all set off again. They were able to cross the little river by means of the passage that Stapylton had prepared during Mitchell's excursion to Mt William. They were also able to cross the Wimmera. Mitchell asked Stapylton to lead most of the party across the plains to the west-south-west, while he went to Mt Zero – the most western extremity of the mountain range. He set up his theodolite there and took bearings of all the prominent features. On 22 July he set off to examine the 'isolated mass' that he had observed from Mt Zero. On the following day he decided to name it Mt Arapiles – because he had climbed it on the anniversary of his brother's death at the Battle of Salamanca, which had taken place over two hills, known as Los Arapiles, some distance from Salamanca, in Spain, in 1812. From the summit Mitchell was able to see twenty-seven circular lakes, and he could see a curious rock that he named Mitre Rock. A lake to the north of the rock was named Mitre Lake. He spent some time surveying these lakes and examining their salinity.[39]

Mitchell continued to be delighted with the country and compared it with the country he had seen along the Darling:[40]

Indeed, the two regions were as different in character as the manners of their respective inhabitants. Every day we passed over land, which, for natural fertility and beauty, could scarcely be surpassed; over streams of unfailing abundance, and plains covered with the richest pasturage.

They continued to move 'merrily over hill and dale' and, on 31 July, discovered a fine river, about 36 metres wide and about 4 metres deep. He named this river after Lord Glenelg, the secretary of state for the Colonies – 'according to the usual custom'.[41] The next day, Mitchell embarked in the boats with some of the men – leaving Stapylton 'in a strong position' with nine men, the stores and the cattle. At first, all was plain sailing, but the river divided in several channels and was overgrown. It was apparent that it would be easier to follow the river by land – land which Mitchell thought was good, beautiful and verdant.

They proceeded and, a little later, came to the tributary that Stapylton 'had explored ... at considerable risk'. Mitchell named it the Chetwynd.

Another tributary was named Stokes River 'in memory of a brother officer, who fell at Bajadoz'. On 18 August, Mitchell again embarked in the boats, leaving Stapylton and the remainder of the party to move to occupy 'the round point of the hill' which was named Fort O'Hare – 'in memory of a truly brave soldier, my commanding officer, who fell at Badajoz in leading the forlorn hope of the Light Division to the storm'.[42] Mitchell took sixteen men with him, leaving Stapylton with eight.

Mitchell's main surveying method was by triangulation but, as he himself admitted, it was also desirable to determine latitude as often and as accurately as possible. The next morning he got up at three o'clock in the morning to determine the altitude of certain stars that were then approaching the meridian. He was able to use a placid stream as an artificial horizon and obtained their altitude below the pole.[43] On the next day the boats reached two basins – the water in which was scarcely sufficient to float the boats. This was a great disappointment because it meant that there was no possibility of a port 'at the mouth of this fine river'. The sea broke on a sandy beach and, from a sandhill, Mitchell was able to obtain bearings of Cape Northumberland Cape Bridgewater and Mt Gambier. The coastline was one grand curve, and Mitchell named it Discovery Bay. Near the beach, they observed holes (soakages) – presumably dug by Aborigines – in which the water was sweet. The latitude, from the Sun's meridian altitude, was found to be 38° 02' 58" S. The present-day town of Nelson, at the mouth of the Glenelg River, is reckoned to be at 38° 03" S, 141° 01' E.[44]

Discovery Bay was well known to the Aboriginal people, who used the shellfish there as an important food resource. Examination of shell middens on the coast has shown that the Aborigines had been gathering shellfish there for at least 10 000 years. It seems that they visited the bay for this purpose mainly in the summer – probably because they could also obtain the fruit of the native apple,

Kunzea pomifera.[45] As Dawson has pointed out: 'The southern portions of Australia are remarkably deficient in native fruits, and the only kind deserving the name is the berry which the Aboriginal people of the locality call "nurt" – resembling a red-cheeked cherry without the pip, which grows abundantly on a creeper amongst the sand on the hummocks near the mouth of the River Glenelg.'[46]

Mitchell 'laid down' his survey of the estuary of the Glenelg River and he:[47]

> ... found a considerable difference between the result of my survey and the Admiralty charts, not only in the longitude, but also in the relative position of the two capes with respect to Mount Gambier, a solitary hill easily recognised.

The Admiralty charts had, of course, been prepared from the data provided by ships captains, whose chronometers might have been in error and whose magnetic compass bearings could have been affected by the iron in the ship. Mitchell's account for 22 August carries a footnote:[48]

> At that time, I supposed the difference had arisen from some error or omission in my map, and took much pains to discover it; but not having succeeded, my work having also closed to a mile and three-quarters, on my return to the country connected by trigonometrical survey with Sydney – I have been obliged to represent these parts of the coast according to this land survey.

Mitchell's trigonometrical survey – with an error of less than 3 kilometres after having travelled from Sydney to the south coast of western Victoria and back again by a more easterly route – was a remarkable achievement of which he could well be proud.

When he had completed his survey, Mitchell and his men re-entered the river from the sea. He gave the men a bottle of whisky to celebrate the discovery. Two days later the party arrived back at Fort O'Hare and were pleased to learn that Stapylton and the others had not been troubled by Aborigines during their separation.

Mitchell then set off to examine the country to the east, and soon observed some very large trees on the ranges. These were stringy barks. Many of them were 25 metres in height, and one was found to have a circumference of 4.5 metres. As they moved forwards they were troubled by the boggy or swampy ground, and Mitchell changed his course further to the south. He discovered and named Mt Eckersley (after another soldier in the Peninsular War), Mt Napier and the Fitzroy River. He then arrived at the shores of Portland Bay – which Lieutenant James Grant, in the *Lady Nelson*, had named after the Duke of Portland. Mitchell was able to identify Laurence Rocks and Lady Julia Percy Island (in the singular, although the coastal chart referred to Lady Julia Percy Isles). This island had been named by Grant after a member of the family of the Duke of Northumberland.

Tommy Came-last showed no surprise when he saw the ocean for the first time in his life, but Mitchell was certainly surprised when the Aboriginal man told him that he had seen fresh tracks of cattle and 'the shoe marks of a white man' on the beach.[49] Mitchell had observed many signs that whalers often visited this shore, 'but how cattle could have been brought there' he could not understand. He walked in the direction of Cape Bridgewater and was further astonished to observe a number of wooden houses, and a ship at anchor in the bay. A man came towards them and told them that 'just round the point there was a considerable farming establishment.'[50] The farm belonged to the Henty brothers – as did the ship, the *Elizabeth* of Launceston.

The Henty brothers were the sons of Thomas Henty, who had sold his property in Sussex and had emigrated with his wife and seven sons to Australia. Thomas Henty was determined to establish his 'seven strong and enterprising sons on properties of their own in Australia'.[51] They had settled on land near the Swan River in Western Australia, but this had not been a success, and most members of the family departed for Van Diemen's Land. One brother, Edward, then decided to cruise along the southern shore of the continent and was immediately attracted by the environment of Portland Bay. Thomas Henty himself then went to examine the proposed site for a farm and confirmed Edward's choice. In November 1834 they chartered a vessel, which was loaded with everything needed to set up a farm, engaged labourers and sailed from Launceston to Portland Bay. Edward Henty established the first settlement in what was later to be called Victoria, and he was soon joined by three brothers – Francis, Stephen and John.[52] The four brothers became partners in 'whaling, sheep-farming and cattle-raising'. They were known as 'the Henty Brothers'; but some people referred to them as the 'Messrs Henty'. By the time of Mitchell's visit the farm was well established. They already had a good garden and:[53]

> Messrs. Henty were importing sheep and cattle as fast as vessels could be found to bring them over, and the numerous whalers touching at or fishing on the coast, were found to be good customers for farm produce and whatever else could be spared from the establishment.

Mitchell was able to obtain a small supply of flour from the Henty brothers to supplement that which the expedition had carried from Sydney – but he could not obtain a large quantity because the Henty brothers themselves were awaiting a shipment. Mitchell succeeded, however, in obtaining as many vegetables as each man could carry on horseback. Mitchell was able to obtain a number of useful bearings in the Portland Bay area. He visited and named Mt Kincaid 'after my old and esteemed friend of Peninsular recollections' and, at Henty's request, named the small river entering Portland Bay, Surry River.[54] He climbed a hill adjacent to the Surry and named it Mt Clay.

As the expedition moved forwards they had to cross the Fitzroy River. The men had to wade across with the bags of flour on their heads. The weather was now rather wet, and the ground was soft, and even boggy. It was difficult to move the carts and the boat carriage. Mitchell eventually decided to abandon the larger boat, to retain the small one, and to shorten the boat carriage. While this was being done Mitchell set off to examine Mt Napier. It was recognised as an extinct volcano. 'The surface consisted wholly of ... stone,' he wrote, 'without any intermediate soil to soften its asperity under the feet of our horses, and yet it was covered with a wood of *eucalyptus* and *mimosa*, growing there as on the open forest land.'[55] This mountain has a height of 438 metres.

A few days later he set off again for Mt Napier with a party of men with axes to clear the summit of trees – so that he could take bearings of all the visible features. On this occasion the haze made it difficult for him to see peaks in the distance. So, next morning, he again climbed the mountain and 'perceived two very extensive lakes in the low country between Mt Napier and the south-eastern portion of the Grampian range, which terminated in the hill, that I had previously named Mount Abrupt'. Mitchell was, of course, trying to select the best route for his journey to the north-east and, eventually, to Sydney. The next morning he climbed the mountain for the third time. On this occasion he reported that he could see an isolated hill on the sea shore – not far from Lady Julia Percy Island. This hill resembled a haystack and Mitchell named it Mt Hotspur; but it is now known as Tower Hill.[56] The largest lake in sight was named Lake Linlithgow and it still bears this name.

They set off to the north-east – avoiding the swamps as much as possible – and arrived near Mt Abrupt. Mitchell was anxious to climb the mountain to complete his triangulation and was delighted when the weather turned out better than he had expected. He did climb it and he:[57]

> ... beheld a truly sublime scene; the whole of the mountains, quite clear of clouds, the grand outline of the more distant masses blended with the sky,

and forming a blue and purple background for the numerous peaks of the range ... which consisted of sharp cones and perpendicular cliffs.

Their troubles were not over, however. They were still having difficulty with boggy ground, and many of the cattle were exhausted and would have to be rested before they could continue. There was another factor – the shortage of provisions – that precluded a delay of a couple of weeks to allow them to recuperate. In these circumstances, Mitchell decided to divide the party. He was to push on with the freshest cattle and with some of the men, and with rations for a month. The remainder were to rest the cattle, and were then to proceed. This group was to have rations for two months, and were to be under the command of Stapylton. The Aboriginal members of the expedition arranged their division themselves. Tommy Came-first and the widow (Turandurey) 'who most required a rest, having sore feet', were to remain with Stapylton. Piper and Tommy Came-last were to accompany Mitchell.[58]

The camp where Stapylton was to remain with his party was a good one. It was 'thickly clothed with fresh verdure' which 'extended northward into a lake of fresh water'. Mitchell named it Lake Repose. The mountains 'and especially Mount Abrupt, were landmarks which secured the men from even the possibility of losing their way in looking after the cattle'. Mitchell set off the next day but not before Turandurey had asked him to look after her daughter – a duty he accepted. He later arranged for the child's education. Stapylton, and his party of nine, remained in the camp for two weeks before proceeding.

Mitchell moved forward in a north-easterly direction. He named a hill Mt Cole and, further on, he named Mt Beckwith – but this is now Mt Misery.[59] As they proceeded they 'entered on a very level and extensive flat, exceedingly green, and resembling an English park'.[60] To the east there was a small stream that Mitchell thought was his

'Loddon'– but it was the Yarrayne, which Mitchell had seen nearly three months before. Nevertheless, the first settlers accepted the name Loddon and, consequently:[61]

> ... Mitchell's Yarrayne became the Loddon, and by a domino effect, his Loddon became the Avoca, his Avoca River became Sandy Creek (a tributary or the Avon River) and his Avon Water became Anderson Creek.

On the next day Mitchell climbed Mt Alexander – the peak that he had used as a guide when moving from Mt Cole. The view reminded him of the 'lower Pyrenees and the pass of Orbaicetta [Orbaiceta]' near which Lord Byng had fought a battle during the Peninsular War. So Mitchell named it Mt Byng, but later changed it to Mt Alexander. By this time the sun was setting and Mitchell was happy to be guided back to the camp by Tommy Came-last.[62]

From the summit of Mt Alexander Mitchell had seen another mountain to the south-east, and determined to visit it while some repairs were being made to the boat carriage. Mitchell was anxious to include this mountain in his triangulation – in order to encompass Port Phillip. The party saw a great many kangaroos and emus on the way. On arrival at the mountain they were able to reach the summit on horseback and found that it was full of wombat holes. Mitchell named the mountain Mount Macedon – after King Philip of Macedonia, a warrior King. King Philip and Olympias (the daughter of King Neoptolemus of Epirus) were the parents of Alexander the Great. Mitchell was still commemorating soldiers – but it was a change from the names of soldiers that he had known in the Peninsular War! [63] In more recent times a giant cross has been erected on the summit to commemorate Victorians who died in World War I. A few days later Mitchell named the Campaspe River – after Alexander the Great's mistress – and this might explain his decision to change the name of Mt Byng to Mt Alexander.

Continuing to travel east-nor'-east, Mitchell

came to the Goulburn River – which had been so named by Hume and Hovell. He crossed the river in his boat, and the cattle were encouraged to swim across. All reached the opposite bank in safety. Mitchell recorded that the Goulburn was 'somewhat larger than the Murrumbidgee' – about 50 metres wide. When Stapylton arrived at the site two weeks later he had to camp there until he could cross the river.[64]

Continuing to the north-east, Mitchell came to the Ovens River – a river that had been discovered and named by Hume and Hovell. They had named it after John Ovens who, at that time, was secretary to Governor Brisbane. Two days later Mitchell could see a 'lofty mass' to the south-east, and he named it Mt Aberdeen. However, Hume and Hovell had already named it Mt Buffalo – apparently because its shape resembled a buffalo – and this name has survived. A few days later they came to the Murray River and found a suitable site to transfer the cattle to the other side.

The intention had been for the boat to be taken back to Stapylton, but the carpenter, Archibald McKean, offered to build rafts using empty casks – and to return to the Goulburn River with two of the men plus Tommy Came-last. They would help Stapylton and his party to cross the Goulburn, the Ovens, and bring them to the Murray. This seemed to be a good idea and meant that the boat would not have to be sent back to the Goulburn – as originally intended.[65] In the event, Stapylton was later able to report to Mitchell that the three men, plus Tommy Came-last, duly arrived at the Goulburn and 'that the passage was effected across it, without an accident of any kind whatever'.[66] Mitchell crossed the Murray River and, on 21 October, noticed a pointed hill – which he ascended. With his mind always on the Napoleonic wars he named it Mt Trafalgar 'in honour of that memorable day' – but it is now known as Soldiers Hill.[67]

They continued towards Sydney and it was not long before their provisions were exhausted. One of their 'poor working animals' was shot for food. However, they came to 'a small house or station, and a stock-yard', and an old man named Billy Buckley came to the door. 'The poor fellow received us with the most cordial welcome, supplying us at once with two days' provisions.'[68] Just then:[69]

> ... several drays appeared on the opposite side, coming along the *road* from Sydney, and these drays contained a supply, from which Mr. Tompson the owner, accommodated me with enough to send back to meet Mr Stapylton, on the banks of the Murray.

It was seven months since Mitchell had seen a road or a bridge and, during that time, they had travelled over 4000 kilometres (2500 thousand miles). They passed Liverpool (with a population of 600) and, soon afterwards, came to Lansdowne Bridge over Prospect Creek – a bridge that had been built by Mr Lennox, with convict labour:[70]

> The bridge is wholly the work of men in irons who must have been fed, and must consequently have cost the public just as much, if they had done nothing all the while; and it may be held up, as a fair specimen of the great advantage of convict labour, in such a country, when applied to public works.

Mitchell was proud of the work that had been carried out by his department. He had 'employed Mr. Lennox on a smaller bridge, in the new pass, in the ascent to the Blue Mountains' and this had been carried out so well 'as to justify the confidence with which I suggested to the government, this larger undertaking'.

Mitchell reached Sydney on 3 November, and wrote that they had traversed the country in two directions:[71]

> ... with heavy carts, meeting no other obstruction than the softness of the soft soil; and, in returning, over flowery plains and green hills, fanned by the breezes of early spring, I named the region Australia

Felix, the better to distinguish it from the parched deserts of the interior country.

Stapylton reported that the widow Turandurey had married Joey, the 'king of the Murrumbidgee'. Her daughter, Ballandella, became 'a welcome stranger' to Mitchell's children. Mitchell's men were rewarded 'according to the standing and condition of each'. Four were given absolute pardons, and tickets of leave were awarded to the rest 'with two exceptions'. Piper was given many presents and returned to his own country, and the two Tommies likewise received gifts and returned to their own lands.[72]

Mitchell wrote an official report on his expedition for the attention of the governor. He was proud of his surveying, writing:[73]

> I have succeeded in working a continued chain of triangles along the heights between Cape Nelson and banks of this river [Murrumbidgee], thereby connecting my work on that Coast with the survey of the colony.

He added that he had been 'well satisfied with the zeal and perserverance of Mr. Stapylton on all occasions'; and: 'All the men of the party behaved well.'

All returned safely – except James Taylor, who had been drowned while endeavouring to swim a horse across a swampy river. There is no doubt that Stapylton felt aggrieved that, so often, he had been left in charge of the depot and unable to experience the exultation of discovery. His journal contains many comments adverse to Mitchell.

Mitchell's report was delivered to the governor. Bourke was distressed to learn of the conflict with the Aboriginal people at Mt Dispersion. After all, Mitchell's instructions had required him to endeavour to conciliate the Aborigines and that 'the utmost forbearance' should be shown. Moreover 'the use of firearms or force of any kind' should not be used 'unless the safety of the party should absolutely require it'.[74] The matter was referred to the Executive Council to enquire into the circumstances. The Inquiry began in December after Stapylton and the men of the follow-up party arrived in Sydney. The council consisted of the governor, the bishop of Australia (William Grant Broughton) and the colonial secretary (Alexander Macleay). They:[75]

> ... interviewed a number of members of the expedition, including Piper. The Council was convinced that the situation the party faced was extremely threatening; but at the same time, they were distressed that Mitchell should have exhibited a spirit more of exultation than regret.

Mitchell had applied for leave to visit England and this was apparently approved by December 1836 – after his return from the Australia Felix expedition. He was granted eighteen months leave on half-pay (he was also entitled to half-pay from the army). His main object in seeking leave was to arrange for the publication of the accounts of his three expeditions – but he also hoped to be able to continue his work on the maps of the Peninsular War.

He sailed, with his wife, eight children and his servant, from Sydney in the *Duchess of Northumberland* on 19 March 1837. He took with him the original copy of the journal of his second expedition for presentation to Lord Glenelg. He also took the manuscript of his accounts of his three expeditions – the publication of which he hoped would bring him fame. He doubtless took the opportunity to revise these accounts during the long voyage to England.

They arrived in London on 20 July 1837 and Mitchell soon obtained the necessary permission to publish his manuscript, together with illustrations – many prepared by himself. T. & W. Boone, of New Bond Street, agreed to publish the book, and it was released in September 1838 with the title: *Three Expeditions into the Interior of Eastern Australia; with Descriptions of the Recently Explored Region of Australia Felix and of the Colony of New South Wales.*

The book attracted excellent reviews and a second edition was published in 1839. It might be noted that Mitchell had earlier written an 'Account of the recent exploring Expedition to the Interior of Australia' – and this had been published as a supplement to the New South Wales *Government Gazette* on 5 November 1836. This paper was submitted to the Royal Geographical Society and was published in the society's journal in 1837.[76]

In the meantime, indeed only a month after his arrival in London, Mitchell wrote to Glenelg to persuade him to nominate him, Mitchell, for a knighthood. He wrote:[77]

> After the important duties on which I have been engaged for the past ten years Your Excellency will not be surprised that now relieved for a short time by your indulgence from the fatigues attendant upon such uninterrupted labours, I should feel ambitious of a mark of Royal approbation, not only to gratify my personal feelings, but, at the same time, to convey to my friends here, and to the distant Colony in which I have been employed, an unquestionable testimony that it has pleased my Sovereign to view my services favourably.

He went on to say that he had given seventeen years' previous uninterrupted service 'embracing a principal portion of the Peninsular War' – the importance of which would 'be readily attested' by Sir George Murray and the present quartermaster-general.

However, Glenelg was not willing to make a hasty decision. He wished to consult the governor of the colony, and Mitchell waited impatiently. Glenelg resigned as secretary of state on 8 February 1839 but, on the following day, left a memorandum at the Colonial Office stating: 'I was prepared to recommend Major Mitchell for knighthood. I hope my successor may do so.'[78] Mitchell was created a knight bachelor on 3 August 1846. Mitchell's *Three Expeditions* had also been greeted with acclaim by the dons at the University of Oxford – who decided to confer on him the honorary degree of doctor of civil law. The ceremony took place on 12 June 1839.[79]

Mitchell had had several extensions of his leave of absence from the Survey Department. Originally set at eighteen months, it was extended to an incredible four years. He was eventually informed that he had to leave England to return to Sydney before 18 June 1840. He sailed, with his family, in the *Mary Bannatyne* and arrived on 4 February 1841. He resumed duty a few days later. General Sir George Gipps was now the governor of the colony, and it seems that he was prepared to dislike Mitchell even before they met. On 28 September 1840, months before Mitchell's return, he had written to the secretary of state for the Colonies, Lord John Russell:[80]

> The long and expensive journies of Sir Thomas Mitchell in the years 1835 and 1836, though highly interesting, led to no discoveries which could be turned to profit, with the exception perhaps of the fertile land of Australia Felix, which would surely have been reached by the ordinary advance of our graziers, even though he had never visited it.

Gipps was unwell when Mitchell returned to Sydney, the colony was in a state of depression and he was under pressure from London. As Foster has written:[81]

> The stage was set for bitter clashes between Governor Sir George Gipps and the stubborn and self opinionated Sir Thomas Mitchell, whose sense of self-importance had been increased by two recent events: the War Office had promoted him to the rank of Lieutenant-Colonel as from 23 November 1841, and James Wyld had published [Mitchell's] monumental *Maps and Plans showing the Principal Movements, Battles and Sieges in which the British Army was engaged from 1808 to 1814 in the Spanish Peninsula and the South of France*. This was the result of 'more than ten years' persistent labour'.

Mitchell busied himself in re-invigorating the Survey Department, but continued to argue with the governor. 'I oppose your land policy because it is ruining the Colony,' he said bluntly; and 'if I thought that you [Gipps] would have stayed here longer than six years I would never have remained so long in New South Wales.'[82] In fact, Gipps retired because of ill-health on 11 July 1846, and Lieutenant Colonel Sir Maurice O'Connell, the commander of the military forces, became acting governor of the colony. He was succeeded by Sir Charles FitzRoy on 3 August 1846.

MITCHELL'S FOURTH EXPEDITION

Many people in the colony were anxious to improve communications with India, with British possessions in the Far East, and with the British Isles. After all, most of the produce from Australian farming went to Britain, and the colony was still dependent on Britain for its requirements of manufactured goods. It would clearly help if the time taken for goods to travel from Sydney to Britain, and vice versa, could be reduced. Moreover, as Mitchell recorded: 'A trade in horses required to remount the Indian cavalry had commenced, and the disadvantageous navigation of Torres Straits had been injurious to it.'[83]

It was clear that an overland route from Sydney to the Indian Ocean would solve many problems – especially because the Indian Ocean was 'already connected to England by steam navigation'. There were two main possibilities – a route from Sydney to the Gulf of Carpentaria and a route to Port Essington (which was further to the west and on the northern coast of Arnhem Land). Port Essington had been surveyed by Phillip Parker King in 1818 and had been named by him in honour of Vice-Admiral Sir William Essington. This port (just north of Van Diemen Gulf) seemed suitable for settlement and, after 1838, when a good supply of water was found, it did become occupied by a few settlers. It was named 'Victoria', and Captain John McArthur was appointed as the commandant. McArthur,

'during the 11 years of the station's fantastic existence' addressed his dispatches from 'Government House, Victoria, North Australia'.[84] However, the settlement did not thrive and, when John Lewis visited the area in 1873, nothing remained except for 'a number of graves and an old aboriginal woman'. He later named one of his sons Essington. Essington Lewis became an able 'captain of industry' and was a tower of strength in furthering Australia's war effort in the 1940s.[85]

The governor, Sir George Gipps, was a firm believer in the need to find an overland route to the Indian Ocean – and had supported the idea in his dispatch to the secretary of state on 28 September 1840. Not long afterwards, Sturt and Eyre had indicated their willingness to undertake an expedition. They proposed to proceed to Moreton Bay (Brisbane) and move to Halifax Bay (Townsville). From there they proposed to proceed to the Gulf of Carpentaria, and then to Port Essington.[86] However, there was also strong support for a direct overland route – from Sydney to Fort Bourke and then to Port Essington. Indeed, this was the route supported by the committee of the Legislative Council that had been appointed to 'enquire into the practicability of a design for an overland route to Port Essington'.[87] The governor's dispatch on this matter stated that Mitchell 'not only considers the project a practicable one, but is himself ready to lead the Expedition'. Lord Stanley wrote that he would not withhold his assent 'whenever you shall be of opinion that the funds of the Colony can properly bear such an expense'.[88]

Charles Sturt disagreed. In a private letter to Captain (afterwards Admiral) King, dated 5 December 1843, Sturt wrote:[89]

The conclusions at which the Committee of the Legislative Council has arrived at are in my judgement erroneous, and I think it is to be regretted that they did not refer to you [King] and to Mr. Hume for better information than they would probably obtain from Sir Thomas Mitchell, whose opinions I assure you I hold in the most sovereign contempt.

Mitchell initiated discussions with some of those whom he hoped would be willing to accompany him on a direct overland expedition in 1844. He discussed the project with the German naturalist Friedrich Wilhelm Ludwig Leichhardt – who was clearly interested. However, the long delay in approving the expenditure for Mitchell's proposal led Leichhardt and a number of companions to set out on their own privately funded expedition. On 13 August 1844, Leichhardt and his companions sailed for Moreton Bay – and then set off to the north-west. They arrived safely at Port Essington on 17 December 1845, and obtained a passage back to Sydney in the schooner *Heroine* – arriving on 25 March 1846. Mitchell was later to record that 'the journal of his [Leichhardt's] journey, recently published, shows what difficulties may be surmounted by energy and perseverance.'[90]

Lord Stanley's approval of the Mitchell proposal was dated 12 May 1844, but this did not reach Sydney until 13 October 1844.[91] Even so, Gipps delayed his approval until he was satisfied that the colony's funds were adequate. It was not until 11 November 1845 that he wrote to Stanley to say that the colony's funds were now able to fund Mitchell's proposed expedition.

Mitchell selected the 27-year-old assistant surveyor, Edmund B. Kennedy, to be second-in-command of the expedition, and W. Stephenson as the medical officer and botanical collector. Mitchell's servant, Anthony Brown, was asked to join the expedition, and he became the only man (apart from Mitchell himself) to be a member of all four expeditions. On this occasion, however, he was described as a 'tent-keeper'. Three others were 'free' men – one of whom, William Baldock, had been a member of Mitchell's second expedition. The remainder were convicts, and two of these had been members of the Australia Felix expedition. One of the convicts was described as a 'Sailor and Chainman' (Isaac Reid) and another as 'Chainman' (Andrew Higgs). This employment was no sinecure, for Mitchell recorded that the entire route was 'chained'.

The main party set off from Parramatta on 17 November 1845. Mitchell left Sydney on 8 December and joined the party encamped at Boree on 13 December 'having rode there from Sydney in four and a half days'. Piper, the Aboriginal guide who had been so helpful during the Australia Felix expedition, also joined the group at Boree. The expedition was well equipped. They had eight drays, three light carts, two iron boats, thirteen horses (plus four 'private horses'), 112 bullocks and 250 sheep. The sheep constituted the 'chief part of the animal food' – 'the rest consisted of gelatine, and a small quantity of pork'. Mitchell recorded that 'many experienced persons [had] suggested that bullocks, though slow, were more enduring than horses'; but he added in a footnote that the '...results of this journey proved quite the reverse'.[92] They set off 'towards the interior' on Monday 15 December 1845.

Two weeks later they approached the scene of Cunningham's murder. When 'on the Goobang Creek' Mitchell recognised the hill he that had named Mt Juson at Cunningham's request. It had been the maiden name of Cunningham's mother.[93]

Mitchell had managed to recruit a young Aboriginal man named Yuranigh, and a boy named Dicky (who was ten years old) to help the expedition – and they were both proving helpful. This was fortunate because it seemed that Piper had been spoiled by the attention he had received after his efforts during the Australia Felix expedition. He had become lazy and self-important. He was always making unreasonable demands. In addition, Mitchell learnt that Piper was planning to leave the expedition and take the two younger Aborigines with him. Mitchell decided to dismiss him and sent him back, escorted by Corporal Graham. Not long afterwards the young Aboriginal people caught 'an animal apparently of the same genus as the *Dipus mitchellii* 'and which seemed to live solely on vegetables'. On 24 January Mitchell wrote:[94]

> This morning I woke completely blind, from ophthalmia, and was obliged to have poultices laid on my eyes; several of the men were also affected in the same manner. The exciting cause of this malady in an organ presenting a moist surface was, obviously, the warm air wholly devoid of moisture, and likely to produce the same effect until the weather changed.

Stephenson, the medical officer, recommended the application of leeches – so Mitchell sent William Baldock and Yuranigh in search of some 'and they brought back enough. Fourteen were applied to my eyes the same afternoon.'[95] Mitchell's eyes soon recovered, but whether from the leeches, or from poultices applied, or from an increase in atmospheric moisture content, is not stated.

Mitchell had decided to follow the Bogan River, but the summer weather was extremely hot, and there was little water. They crossed to the Macquarie River and they laboured on until they reached the junction of the Macquarie and Darling rivers. The latter was found to have 'a good current of muddy water in it, of considerable width, and really like a river'.[96] Mitchell determined the longitude of the junction at their camp to be 147° 33' 45" E 'by actual measurements connected with my former surveys of the colony'. He added that Kennedy had 'chained the whole of the route from Bellaringa, and I had connected his work with latitudes observed at almost every encampment, which appeared to be very steady'. The latitude of the camp was found to be 30° 06' 11" S.[97]

When he reached the Darling, Mitchell learnt that his son, Commissioner Roderick Mitchell, had recently passed down the river – preparing plans of the various stations that had become established. Soon afterwards Mitchell received a dispatch from his son giving details of the various rivers that the expedition would encounter as it moved north-

wards. On 12 March, for example, Mitchell recorded: 'This day I received letters from Commissioner Mitchell, in which he strongly recommended to my attention the rivers Biree, Bokhara and Narran, as waters emanating from and leading to the Balonne.'[98] The expedition then followed the Narran River and arrived at its junction with the Balonne River on 1 April. They followed the Balonne through scrub and open forest and, on 11 April, Mitchell recorded that he 'saw an immense sheet of water before us, with islands in it'. He added that this '... was also a lagoon supplied by floods in the Balonne. It was covered with ducks, pelicans, &c. I called it Lake Parachute, no natives being near to give me their name for it.'[99] On 12 April they arrived at a natural bridge 'affording easy and permanent access to the opposite bank'. Mitchell 'at once selected the spot for a depot camp'.[100] He decided to reconnoitre to the north-west and, for this purpose he set off on 16 April – with two horses 'drawing a cart loaded chiefly with water' and with 'six trusty men, almost all old soldiers'.[101]

The country was most discouraging, however. There was no water. After two days travelling north-west, he wrote:[102]

> I had just quitted my horse's back, and had resolved to return, when two horsemen were seen approaching along our track. They were two of the party come from the depot to bring me a despatch, which had been forwarded by Commissioner Wright, communicating the news of Dr. Leichhardt's return from Port Essington, and enclosing the Gazette with his own account of his journey. Thus it became known to us that we could no longer hope to be the first to reach the shores of the Indian Ocean by land.

They returned to the depot, and Mitchell decided to follow the Balonne further. So, on 23 April, they set off across the 'natural bridge'. This day (23 April) is St George's Day – in honour of the patron saint of England – so he named it St

George's Bridge, and it appears as such on his map of the route. Today, St George is the administrative centre of the Balonne Shire and has a population of about 2500.[103]

Kennedy, and the main party, were instructed to remain at the depot at St George Bridge until 4 May 'when the cattle would have had three weeks' rest'. Kennedy was then to lead the main party along Mitchell's tracks.[104] In the meantime, Mitchell followed the Balonne River until its conjunction with the Cogoon River, and then the Narran River, and followed this northwards.

On 3 May Mitchell was pleased when three Aboriginal people were attracted to his camp. 'They were entirely naked,' he wrote, 'and without any kind of ornament or weapon, offensive or defensive.' He added that they '… had never before seen white men, and behaved as properly as it was possible for men in their situation to do'.[105] Mitchell was even more pleased with the view. He could see blue peaks at a great distance to the north-west, 'the object of all my dreams of discovery for years. No white man had before seen these.' He added that there '… we might hope to find the *divisa aquarum*, still undiscovered; the pass to Carpentaria, still un-explored.' He climbed one peak and 'called this hill Mount First View, and descended', delighted with what he had seen from 'its rocky crest'.[106] He also climbed and named Mt Redcap, Mt Abundance and Mt Bindango. Mt Bindango and Mt Bindyego are almost due east of the modern town of Mitchell – which is on the Maranoa River and has a population of a little more than 1000.

Mitchell was enchanted with the surrounding country, and named the area FitzRoy Downs. It is often thought that this was a late addition to his journal, and that he wished to name it after the new governor, Sir Charles FitzRoy, who had been appointed after Mitchell's departure from Sydney. However, Foster has suggested that Mitchell named it after General Henry FitzRoy – who served with distinction in the Peninsular War, and who later became the fifth Duke of Grafton.[107] It might be significant that Mitchell gave the name Grafton Range 'to the fine mass in the midst of it' (FitzRoy Downs). However, the governor, Sir Charles FitzRoy, was a member of the same family – being the second son of the third Duke of Grafton!

It was on Mt Abundance that he first saw the 'bottle trees' – known as boabs or baobabs – the thick-trunked trees of the genus *Adansomia*. When he returned to his camp he found eight Aboriginal people there. 'I was very glad to see them,' he wrote, 'and gave to an old man, a tomahawk to express my sentiments, and welcome the strangers.' It was from these 'strangers' that he learnt the Aboriginal names for Mt Bindango and for 'its lesser brother to the westward of it, Bindyego'. They 'were merry as larks, and their white teeth, constantly visible, shone whiter than even the cockatoo's feathers on their brows and chins'.[108]

On 12 May, Mitchell carried out a reconnaissance to the north-west, and found water in a creek. Two days later he again mentioned the old Aborigine to whom he had given the tomahawk:[109]

> We bade him adieu as civilly as we could, but he hung upon our rear for a mile or two, and I perceived that he had brought with him his whole tribe after us. Nothing more unfortunate can befall an explorer, than to be followed by a wild tribe like this, as I had experienced in former journies. The gift of the tomahawk had done all this mischief … The tall savage had set his heart upon our goods and chattels.

From Mt Bindango they travelled towards the north-west and then slightly north of east, and reached the Maranoa River – where Mitchell decided to set up his second depot. Then, on 1 June, they heard the sound of a distant shot ('which proceeded from the Doctor firing at a bird'). This was the first indication of the approach of the main party under Kennedy. 'Soon after Mr. Kennedy came in, measuring the line; and subsequently, the drays and the whole of the men in good health.'[110]

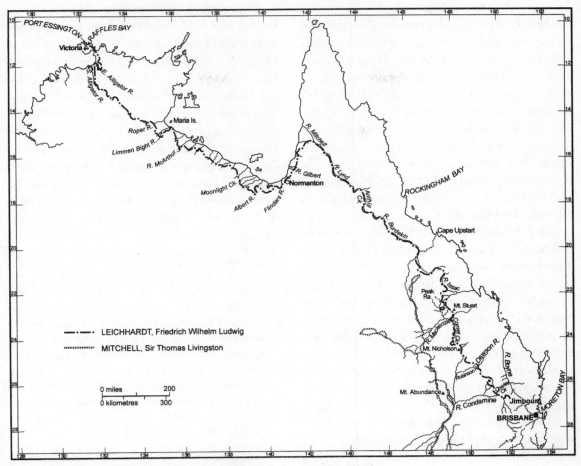

Map showing part of the route taken by Mitchell and the route of Leichhardt

They set about building a stockade, establishing a garden for vegetables, and securing the cattle. On 4 June Mitchell and his advance party – augmented by the medical officer and a shepherd to look after the sheep that they proposed to take with them – bade Kennedy adieu for at least four months 'and crossed the Maranoa'. Fortunately, the hostile Aborigines had dispersed.

They followed the Maranoa River northwards and crossed Possession Creek. Mitchell then decided to reconnoitre to the north-west; but he was soon discouraged by the absence of water in this direction. Indeed, the bullocks had to spend two nights without water to drink.[111] Mitchell then decided to return to the Maranoa and, as they

continued northwards, they were able to see a number of mountains. In the absence of Aboriginal people who could tell him their names for the peaks, he decided to name them after 'such individuals of our own race as had been most distinguished or zealous in the advancement of science, and the pursuit of knowledge'.[112] Mt Owen, for example, was named after Sir Richard Owen, the professor of comparative anatomy at the Hunterian Museum in London. Mitchell, accompanied by Yuranigh, climbed Mt Owen and, from the summit, took bearings of all the prominent peaks in view. A peak to the south-south-east was named Mt Kennedy after his second-in-command; Mt Faraday was named after Michael Faraday, the English physicist and chemist; Mt Phillip Parker King after the naval captain who had explored much of the northern and north-western coast; and Mt Clift after William Clift, the naturalist at the Hunterian Museum.[113] Further north he named Mt Salvator after Salvator Rosa, the Italian artist – famous for his landscapes. He did not follow his rule without exception, however. A mountain to the south-west of Mt Phillip Parker King was named Mt Aquarius – because Mitchell had obtained water there. He had established another depot, the 'Pyramids Depot' to the west of Mt Salvator. Many of these features had been named during the reconnaissance to the north which he commenced on 20 June. He took with him two men in addition to Yuranigh. He carried his pocket sextant and determined the latitude almost every day as he moved northwards. On 10 July, for example, his latitude was 24° 33' 25" S; on 25 July it was 23° 25' 26" S; and on 5 August it was 22° 10' 15" S.

He had had no trouble so far with the Aboriginal inhabitants but, on 10 August, he recorded that his camp had been visited 'by seventeen natives, apparently bent on hostile purposes, all very strong, several of them upwards of six feet high. Each of them carried three or four missile clubs ... They said, by signs, that the whole country belonged to the old man.'[114] However, no conflict developed, and the Aborigines were persuaded to leave without hostilities.

He had been following the Belyando River, and he himself rode as far north as 21° 30' S; but there was no river leading to the north-west. He was not far from Mt Douglas (which is at 21° 31' S, 146° 52' E).[115] On 11 August he came to the conclusion that he should be exploring the country further to the west. He therefore returned to the Pyramids depot by following their outward tracks for most of the time. All was well at the depot and, on 10 September, he again set off with two men and Yuranigh, all mounted, and with two pack-horses carrying his instruments and a month's provisions.[116]

They set off to the south-west, but soon changed to the north-west. They came to a river, and Mitchell was optimistic.'I verily believed,'he wrote, 'that *this* river would run to Carpentaria, and I called it the Nive ... in commemoration of Lord Wellington's action on the river of that name; and, to the tributary from the north, I gave the name of Nivelle.'[117] But this river system did not flow to the gulf – it changed direction. His disappointment was short-lived, however. On 15 September he found a river 'falling to the N.W. in the heart of an open country extending also in that direction'. He added:[118]

> Ulloa's [Balboa's] delight at the first view of the Pacific could not have surpassed mine on this occasion, nor could the fervour with which he was impressed at the moment have exceeded my sense of gratitude, for being allowed to make such a discovery ... the scene was so extensive as to leave no room for doubt as to the course of the river, which, thus and there revealed to me alone, seemed like a reward direct from Heaven for perseverance, and as a compensation for the many sacrifices I had made, in order to solve the question as to the interior rivers of Tropical Australia.

Mitchell named it the Victoria River – after the Queen – and hoped that it would be shown to flow into the gulf. For the time being, however, this remained undetermined. His horses were weary, and the provisions were low. Moreover, there was always a possibility that they would be troubled by the local Aboriginal people. On 25 September he wrote that 'I saw the course of the river running nearly northward. Here, then, I turned towards the east to travel home.'[119] That night they camped by some ponds that Mitchell named Yuranigh Lagoon on his map, but Yuranigh's Ponds in his book.

After they had returned to Sydney, Mitchell instructed Kennedy to return to the Victoria River and to follow its course. It was hoped that this would be to the coast, but Kennedy found that it flows to the south-west. He also expressed the view –

without definite proof – that the Victoria River of Mitchell is the same stream as Sturt's Cooper Creek. In 1858, Gregory, in search of Leichhardt, followed the Victoria and proved that it became Cooper Creek.[120] Kennedy had also discovered that Mitchell's Victoria River was known to the Aborigines as the Barcoo River. However, as Parker and Somerville have pointed out, it is unlikely that the Aboriginal people living near Sturt's Cooper Creek used the same name for it. The current practice seems to refer to the river as the Barcoo in the vicinity of Mitchell's exploration, and as Cooper Creek where Sturt discovered it. Most maps use the two names in this way. The name 'Victoria' is now applied to another river.

In this connection it is of some interest that, on 25 September, Mitchell came across a group of Aboriginal people who spoke a language unknown to Yuranigh. But the important point was that one of them carried a tomahawk. As Mitchell recorded: 'Even here, in the heart of the interior, on a river utterly unheard of by white men, an iron tomahawk glittered on high in the hand of a chief, having a very long handle to it.'[121] It is possible, as Cumpston has suggested, that this was the same tomahawk that Sturt had given to an Aboriginal man on Cooper Creek on 31 October 1845.[122]

On 23 September, Mitchell had written that 'Our only care now, was the duration of our provisions.' It would be folly to continue. Two days later he wrote: 'I saw the course of the river running northward'. He hoped that it was flowing to the coast. 'Here, then,' he added, 'I turned towards the east to travel home.'[123] At this time they were not far from the present-day township of Isisford, with Longreach further to the north.

They returned to the Pyramid depot and found all well, and Mitchell noted that the Aboriginal boy, Dicky, had grown very much 'and seemed a very intelligent boy'.[124] Continuing, the whole party crossed the Balonne at St George Bridge. Mitchell went on ahead and arrived in Sydney on 29 Dec-

ember 1846. The others, under Kennedy, arrived on 20 January 1847. It had been a disappointing expedition in some ways. They had failed to reach the coast, but they had discovered 'the finest and most extensive pastoral regions' that Mitchell had ever seen.[125] It had been a long journey – fourteen months in all – and many of the men deserved to be rewarded. Mitchell wrote:[126]

> The new Governor, Sir Charles FitzRoy, kindly granted such gratuities to the most deserving of my men as I had recommended, and also sent the names to England of such prisoners as His Excellency thought deserving of Her Majesty's gracious pardon.

Mitchell went on to praise Yuranigh, who had been his 'guide, companion, counsellor and friend ... His intelligence and his judgement rendered him so necessary to me that he was ever at my elbow ... Confidence in him was never misplaced ... Dicky became a favourite in my family.'[127] The governor granted Yuranigh 'a small gratuity'. Sadly, Yuranigh died only a few years later. Mitchell was instrumental in arranging for Yuranigh's grave to have an engraved headstone. The inscription was as follows:[128]

> To Native Courage Honesty and Fidelity YURANIGH who accompanied the Expedition of Discovery Into Tropical Australia in 1846 lies buried here According to the Rites Of his countrymen and this spot was dedicated and enclosed by the Governor General's Authority in 1852.

MITCHELL THE MAN

Mitchell was supremely self-confident. Indeed, Couch has written that 'his colossal pride is almost sickening'.[129] As such, he was a 'difficult' man. He argued with every single governor of the colony, and he maintained a private correspondence with the under-secretary of the Colonial Office, Robert Hay, detailing his opinions of his superiors. It is not surprising that the governors did not like him. Darling, for example, claimed that 'a great part of his [Mitchell's] time is taken up in squabbling with the departments and individuals with whom he has to act or communicate'.[130] Mitchell was obsequious to the 'titled great' and, to quote Couch again: 'Mitchell was a social climber and a snob, a point that was obvious later in his exultation at having a son-in-law who was a Lord, Lord Audley.'[131] Moreover, he actively sought a knighthood after his Australia Felix expedition. Many of the men he took with him were willing to join a second expedition; but he seems to have treated his officers with little consideration. Stapylton, his second-in-command during the Australia Felix expedition, certainly felt ill-used. In his journal, Stapylton wrote that Mitchell was:[132]

> A man whom no subordinate officer can like or esteem ... he displays an overweening vanity of character, an austerity of deportment a slow dictatorial manner in conversation ... a fondness of alluding to the intercourse he has had with persons of distinction in the course of his career ... All these bad qualities continually render him a most disagreeable person ... I hear nothing but his own views and Sir George Murray.

However, towards the end of the expedition, Stapylton wrote: 'Chef [Chief] I am informed by Burnett has spoken highly of me in his despatch if so some of my invective must be erased from this journal. I don't like him notwithstanding.[133]

It might also be added that Mitchell gained the support and friendship of his Aboriginal guides – Piper in the Australia Felix expedition, and Yuranigh in his Tropical Australia expedition. And, despite his worries about some hostile tribes, Mitchell endeavoured to treat the Aborigines fairly and with consideration. There is little doubt that the driving force in Mitchell's work was the desire for fame – and, in good measure, he achieved it.

There is no reason that he should not have sought fame. Many well-known men have done so in their service to King and empire. Mitchell also achieved fame – partly for his four expeditions as an explorer, but especially for his undoubted success as a surveyor of the highest calibre. There is no doubt that Mitchell's skill as a surveyor far surpassed that of all the other explorers of Australia. He concentrated on triangulation and, as Eccleston has pointed out:[134]

> A survey should always be closed. If it is closed on itself, then, providing the misclosure is within a defined tolerance, the misclosure may be apportioned throughout the survey. The amazingly small misclosure of 1¾ miles [about 2.8 km] for a traverse commencing near Molong, extending to the south-west of the Grampians, and finishing near Gundagai, is a little short of miraculous, not withstanding the almost inevitability of a number of compensatory errors and mistakes. The certainty with which features on the ground connected to by Mitchell can be identified on modern large-scale maps from his survey fieldnotes attests to the fact that his work was generally accurate positionally to within 100 or 200 metres on the ground.

Although much of his work was carried out by triangulation, he also determined latitude by astronomical observation at frequent intervals. In his *Three Expeditions* he quoted the results of ten latitude determinations during the Australia Felix expedition, and the error (in comparison with modern determinations) averaged 3 kilometres – some too far north, others too far south.[135] Longitude was more difficult to determine. It required the use of an accurate chronometer and of the tables in the current edition of the *Nautical Almanac*. Chronometers were fragile instruments and 'the difficulty in maintaining reliable chronometers pre-set in England and shipped out to New South Wales militated against confident and consistent determinations of longitude'.[136] Moreover, on overland expeditions, chronometers were subject to much more violent movement than those mounted on gymbols and used on board ship. Alternatively, it was possible to determine longitude by observation (with a sextant) of the angle between the Moon and the Sun, or between the Moon and one of the prominent stars. This method was known as the method of lunar distances.

Mitchell published the results of seven longitude determinations in his *Three Expeditions*. All seven gave a position too far to the east, and the average error of these (in comparison with modern determinations) was 17.6 kilometres. It is of some interest to compare these results with those obtained by Sturt on his exploration of the Murray River. Sturt determined the latitude of the junction between the Murray and Darling rivers to be 34° 03' S — which is 5.5 kilometres too far north. Two other latitudes have been estimated from the map that Arrowsmith prepared using Sturt's data. One had a northerly error of 1.8 kilometres; the other had a northerly error of 7.3 kilometres.[137] Sturt published the result of his determination of the longitude of the Murray–Darling junction as 141° 00' 58" E, and the modern value is 141° 54' 24" E — so Sturt's figure was 82.2 kilometres too far to the west. The longitudes of the other two river junctions as obtained from Arrowsmith's map also had a westerly error. The one published longitude had been determined by the method of lunar distances and Sturt admitted that the observations 'were not satisfactory, and that there is, probably, an error, though not a material one, in the calculations'.[138] However, if these comparisons are to be taken seriously, it should be pointed out that Mitchell's sextant was greatly superior to the small hand-held one used by Sturt. Moreover the spring in Sturt's chronometer was accidentally broken when being wound by his second-in-command.

15

LEICHHARDT – ACROSS THE CONTINENT TO PORT ESSINGTON

Friedrich Wilhelm Ludwig Leichhardt was born on 23 October 1813 at Trebatsch, in Prussia. He had a good education, first under a private tutor, then at the gymnasium (high school) at Cottbus, and later in the faculty of philosophy at the Friedrich-Wilhelm-Universität (now the Humboldt Universität) in Berlin. It seems that he had no ambition to obtain a degree, but was concerned to broaden his mind. In Berlin, he became friendly with a young Englishman, John Nicholson. When Nicholson decided to move to Göttingen, Leichhardt did likewise. Indeed, in a letter to his brother-in-law, Carl Schmalfuss, Leichhardt wrote: 'I have only one friend, the Englishman John Nicholson.'[1] It seems that it was Nicholson who awakened Leichhardt's interest in the natural sciences and, as a result, Leichhardt returned to Berlin and entered the faculty of medicine – which provided teaching in botany, and in geology and mineralogy. It was there that Leichhardt met William Nicholson, John's brother, who was studying medicine and who later assisted Leichhardt's travel to Australia.

Aurousseau has described Leichhardt as 'precocious, talented and versatile', and there is no doubt that this is a fair description of him.[2] He did not complete a medical degree but, during his time in Australia, Leichhardt often attracted the courtesy title of 'Doctor'. The University of Bologna was the first university to award doctoral degrees in any

field of learning and such degrees became a 'qualification to teach'. The prefix 'Doctor' was regarded as a sign that the recipient was 'a learned man'. Dictionaries still give 'a man of great learning' as one of the meanings of 'doctor'.[3] Nowadays,

Ludwig Leichhardt Strasse in Trebatsch – birthplace of Leichhardt; the village school has a memorial with the inscription 'Dem Australienforscher Ludwig Leichhardt 1813–1848' ('Dedicated to Ludwig Leichhardt who did research on Australia'). (Dr Hannelore Landsberg)

almost all universities award doctoral degrees to scholars who have carried out advanced studies and research in any field of learning. Only in recent years has it become customary for medical practitioners, dentists and veterinary surgeons to be given the courtesy title of 'Doctor' – a practice that was forbidden by their professional bodies until the twentieth century. In the bush, in the absence of a qualified medical practitioner, Leichhardt used his general knowledge of natural science to treat anyone who was sick or injured. It seems that Leichhardt was addressed as 'Doctor' not because he was a qualified physician, but because he was regarded as 'a learned man' – a conclusion with which anyone who reads his published letters can agree.

Leichhardt was a Prussian citizen and, as such, he was required to undertake a period of compulsory military service. However, he was anxious to begin his travels, and his studies in the natural sciences, and he managed to convince the Prussian authorities to allow him to postpone his service for three years. He never did carry out his military service. In fact, he deliberately avoided it. But, after his great feats of exploration in the years 1844 and 1845, he was granted a pardon by the King of Prussia.

Leichhardt first thought of going to Africa, or to the West Indies, but he finally decided to go to Australia and to undertake his studies of natural history in this relatively new British colony.[4] Having decided this, Leichhardt went to London. He wrote to the secretary of the Royal Geographical Society to let the society know that he planned to explore 'the interior of Australia'. He explained that he had turned to the study of the natural sciences and wished 'to become a scientific traveller' – like Alexander von Humboldt.[5] He visited the Royal Botanic Gardens. He went to the Zoological Gardens – where he met the anatomist William Little. He visited the Royal College of Surgeons – where he was able to talk with the Hunterian professor of anatomy, Richard Owen, who gave

Leichhardt a letter of introduction to Sir Thomas Mitchell, in Sydney.[6]

Leichhardt booked his passage to Sydney on the *Sir Edward Paget*. William Nicholson paid his fare of £45, and also gave him £200 as a contribution to his project, and to put him on his feet in Sydney. Nicholson was generous in supporting the impoverished Leichhardt. The latter, however, felt that although 'he pays my way … he has no feeling for me'.[7] Nonetheless, in July 1838, William Nicholson named Leichhardt as his heir.[8]

A few days before his departure, Leichhardt wrote a long letter to Carl Schmalfuss, his brother-in-law, outlining his plans for the future. He concluded with 'Don't grieve for me but rejoice with me, for I feel as if my dreams were gradually beginning to come true.'[9]

The *Sir Edward Paget* sailed from Gravesend, London, on 1 October 1841, and made for Cork, in Ireland – where it was scheduled to embark 150 Irish migrants who were suffering because of the poor potato crops over the last few years, and who were seeking a better life in the new colony. These migrants, together with ninety-eight from England, made up the list of steerage passengers. There were, in addition, the twenty saloon passengers – including Leichhardt. The *Sir Edward Paget* sailed from Cork on 24 October 1841 and arrived at Sydney Cove on 14 February 1842. Leichhardt made good use of his time. During the voyage he learnt how to determine latitude and longitude.

A little more than a month after arriving at Sydney Cove, Leichhardt wrote again to Carl Schmalfuss to give the family some news about his life in Australia – or New Holland, as he often called Australia. 'Since I left my native land and left you all behind,' he wrote, 'I have never felt so much at home as I do here.' He went on to explain that one of his fellow passengers, Stephen Marsh, was a harpist who had now settled down at Sydney Cove with his wife. And, as they had a spare room they offered it to Leichhardt. As Leichhardt explained:

'He asked me to lodge with him to help him to meet his expenses.'[10]

Leichhardt soon became known to many of the leading citizens, and especially to those with an interest in natural science and exploration. He also met the Anglican priest, William Branwhite Clarke, who had graduated from Cambridge University in 1821. During his time at Cambridge, Clarke had come under the influence of Professor Adam Sedgwick, who had inspired his interest in the earth sciences. Clarke was enthusiastic about exploration and natural science, and he and Leichhardt soon became great friends. Clarke had actually visited the Illawarra region, south of Sydney, in company with James Dwight Dana — one of the scientific members of the United States Exploring Expedition that was visiting the Pacific region, and the Antarctic, during the years 1838–42. This expedition was under the command of Charles Wilkes, and had arrived at Sydney on 29 November 1839.

Leichhardt was anxious to begin exploration and, in September 1842, he set off from Sydney to go to the Newcastle area — about 160 kilometres (a hundred miles) to the north. He became extremely interested in the coal seams in that district. He drew vertical sections of the deposits. He also obtained specimens of the plants associated with the coal seams and sent some of these to Adolphe Brongniart at the Jardin des Plantes in Paris.[11] Then, in November, Leichhardt went south from Newcastle to examine the 'fossil forest' at Awaaba. The Rev. W. B. Clarke published an account of this 'forest' in 1843.[12] Leichhardt also went to the Hunter Valley and visited the Australian Agricultural Company's coal mine, which was then in the charge of Phillip Parker King 'who became a good friend' and who, a few years later, 'edited' Leichhardt's account of his expedition from the Darling Downs to Port Essington.[13]

At this time, many of the squatters were discussing the need for an overland route from Sydney to the northern coast of Australia — to facilitate trade with India and the East Indies. It might be noted that Australians are *still* discussing the need for such an overland route today — but a railway line is now thought to be the answer, possibly from Adelaide to Darwin! In the 1840s, a route from Sydney to Port Essington would have required the exploration of the intervening country — to find a suitable route. The governor of New South Wales, Sir George Gipps, supported the proposal and, in his dispatch to the secretary of state for the Colonies in September 1840, he sought approval for the expenditure of the money needed. Sir Thomas Mitchell returned to Sydney in February 1841 after his 'home leave', and soon indicated that he would be willing to lead an expedition across the country to the north-west. He also took an opportunity to discuss his proposed expedition with a number of local people — including Ludwig Leichhardt. Leichhardt indicated his desire to be a member of Mitchell's team. Month followed month, however, without the approval from London for the expedition to proceed, and it seemed likely that the Colonial Office was lukewarm about the proposal. Leichhardt 'had no faith that Sir Thomas Mitchell's northern journey would ever eventuate'.[14] However, during a visit to a number of stations in the Darling Downs (where he was making a study of the natural history) he met Henry Stuart Russell and his younger brother, Sydenham Russell, who occupied a station known as Cecil Plains. It seems that these three men discussed the possibility of organising a private expedition to Port Essington. Leichhardt thought that the two Russells would be prepared to join such an expedition. They might well have intended to join but, when it came to the point, they declined — citing the large amount of work necessary to develop their property.[15]

Nevertheless, Leichhardt decided to go ahead and to organise an expedition under his own leadership. However, he did not make this decision without proper consideration. As his efforts became known 'private persons came forward' to support him and, with their financial help, and his own 'slender resources' he completed his preparations.[16] When he returned to Sydney, he wrote to Mitchell, on 24 July 1844: 'I called on you twice, without finding you at the office and only my increasing and pressing work prevented me from calling again.' He went on to say that he did not like 'the confined life of Sydney' and that he proposed 'to explore the country in the direction of the North-West'. He added:[17]

> Should the consent of Home government to your intended expedition come – may we meet in the Interior, which I consider my home, as I have no other one.

Leichhardt was given financial donations by many squatters – most of whom were always keen to acquire additional grazing land – and he went ahead acquiring equipment, foodstuffs and scientific instruments. He was anxious to ensure that his expedition would remain as mobile as possible, and he did not want to take an excess of equipment or foodstuffs. In the event, however, he grossly under-estimated the amount of food he should take. He was also sorry, later, that he was not better equipped with scientific instruments. He had a sextant and an artificial horizon, a hand-held compass, a watch (but not a chronometer), a thermometer and 'Arrowsmith's Map of the Continent of New Holland'. He wrote in his diary that if 'I go to Parramatta [where the observatory was situated] it will be to practice with the sextant to find latitude and longitude.'[18] On the other hand he did not have a barometer, or a boiling water apparatus – to find the elevation 'of the country and ranges we had to travel over'.

Leichhardt had chosen five companions to join him on his expedition. First and foremost there was James Calvert – who was nineteen years of age. He had been a passenger on the *Sir Edward Paget* and had met Leichhardt during the voyage. Aurousseau has commented:[19]

Of all Leichhardt's companions on his expeditions James Calvert was the only one who fully appreciated what Leichhardt was attempting to do, and who became his scientific disciple. James Calvert eventually contributed to the knowledge of Australian botany. He remained unswervingly loyal to Leichhardt and his few letters to the press are of more importance as testimony than a whole flood of journalistic writings except those of [the Rev. W. B.] Clarke.

His other companions were John Roper, aged twenty, who had an 'inflated opinion of himself', John Murphy, aged sixteen, 'who had some talent with the pencil', and William Phillips, aged forty-four, who was a convict, having been transported for forgery.[20] Then there was Harry Brown, a young 'aboriginal of the Newcastle tribe'.[21] These six men, and thirteen horses, had been given free passages to Moreton Bay on the *Sovereign* by her owners – the Hunter River Steam Navigation Company.

At Brisbane, which had been established a few miles up the Brisbane River, Leichhardt was welcomed by a group of squatters – many of whom showered him with contributions of money and stock. They also pressed him to add four men to his party. These were Pemberton Hodgson, who 'was fond of botanical pursuits'; John Gilbert, a collector for John Gould; Caleb, an American Negro; and Charley Fisher, an Aboriginal man of the Bathurst tribe. The last was always referred to as 'Charley', but the other Aboriginal member, Harry Brown, was always 'Brown'.[22] These increased the party to ten. They took 545 kilograms (1200 pounds) of flour, 90 kilograms (200 pounds) of sugar, 36 kilograms (80 pounds) of tea, 9 kilograms (20 pounds) of gelatine, 'and other articles of less consideration'. They did not forget the ammunition. They took 14 kilograms (30 pounds) of powder, and eight bags of shot of different sizes. Leichhardt thought that 'we were well provided for seven months, which I was sanguine enough to think would be a sufficient time for our journey.'[23] In a letter to his brother-in-law, Leichhardt wrote that the 'provisions were presented, and so were the arms and ammunition. My only heavy expenditure, apart from the horses, was on my instruments.' In the same letter, he wrote that it 'will take me 5 or 6 months to make the journey and five months to return'.[24] In the event, although they returned from Port Essington by *ship*, they took fourteen and a half months (see map on page 199).

Leichhardt and his companions first made for the Darling Downs – the area of good agricultural land that had been discovered by Allan Cunningham in 1827. In Leichhardt's time the Darling Downs were already dotted with thriving stations, and the exploration party made for the Westbrook Station which was owned by John Campbell and his partner, Stephens. Some time was spent at this station to accustom the bullocks to carrying loads, and they took the opportunity to purchase a few more. They now had sixteen bullocks, seventeen horses and ten men! There is no doubt that Campbell and Stephens were extremely helpful to the members of the expedition, and Leichhardt later named Campbell Creek and Stephens Creek after them.[25]

They set off again at the end of September and passed two other stations before arriving at that known as Jimbour – apparently named after the Aboriginal word, Jimba, for 'bush grass'. This station is about 27 kilometres to the north of Dalby, a present-day township on Myall Creek, a creek which flows into the Condamine River. Jimbour Creek likewise flows into the Condamine. At that time Jimbour Station was the last settlement before the unexplored country. Leichhardt's expedition left Jimbour on 1 October 1844 'and launched, buoyant with hope, into the wilderness of Australia'. They sang 'a full chorus of God Save the Queen ... which has inspired many a British soldier – aye, and many a Prussian too – with courage in the time of danger'.[26] It was exactly three years since Leichhardt had sailed from London.

A few days later they were able to follow a chain

of lagoons to the westward, and came to the Condamine River – which had also been discovered and named by Allan Cunningham in 1827. This river flows across the Darling Downs to join the Darling River. During this time Leichhardt continued to make extensive comments in his journal about the vegetation and the wildlife, and especially about the numerous sandflies and the mosquitoes. There were other problems, also. When, on 11 October, the bullocks had to force their way through a thicket, the flour bags that they were carrying were torn – causing a loss of 65 kilograms (143 pounds) of the precious staple, and the brigalow scrub was thereafter referred to as 'Flourspill Scrub'. Also, 'Mr. Gilbert lost his tent and injured the stock of his gun.'[27] In short, the experience severely tried the patience of the explorers. There were some compensations, however. On the previous day they had come upon a fine creek flowing from the north-east. They were able to cross this creek without difficulty in the vicinity of present-day Chinchilla – which Leichhardt named a couple of years later.[28]

On 17 October – just more than two weeks since they had left Jimbour – Leichhardt wrote in his journal that Charley Fisher 'had been insolent several times' and that he had 'even threatened to shoot Mr. Gilbert'. Leichhardt 'dismissed him from our service'. However, on the next day, Charley apologised to Leichhardt and to Gilbert – and was allowed to rejoin the expedition. He soon proved his worth. The young John Murphy, with Caleb, had strayed from the camp and had become lost. Hodgson and Charley, and then Hodgson, Charley and Roper, were sent to look for them. They rode more than 110 kilometres (70 miles) following the tracks of the missing men. They were eventually located, and all five returned safely to the camp. As Leichhardt wrote: 'They would certainly have perished had not Charley been able to track them.'[29] This could well have influenced Leichhardt to refer, in his journal, to the creek which they had crossed on 10 October as 'Charley's Creek'. It retains this name today.

On 3 November, a little more than a month after setting out from Jimbour, Leichhardt realised that he had been 'too sanguine' in his expectation of being able to live off the land, and that the provisions he had brought with him were diminishing too rapidly. He decided to reduce the number of men in his party and – apparently on the principle that the last to join should be the first to go – Hodgson and Caleb were sent back to Moreton Bay. Leichhardt wrote a letter 'To the Public' explaining this situation.[30] He also made it clear that the other members of the expedition were all determined to continue. At this time they had progressed only about 110 kilometres (70 miles) and Leichhardt thought that their slow progress was due to an insufficient quantity of animal food in their diet. 'The want of it,' he wrote, 'was impairing our strength.' He therefore arranged for one of the bullocks to be killed and the meat cut into thin slices and dried in the sun. This practice was adopted throughout the remainder of their journey.

As they proceeded, Leichhardt named Calvert Plains after James Calvert, who had already proved his worth, and the Dawson River after Robert Dawson, a settler who had given the expedition great support. They crossed the river and set a course to the north-west.[31] A few days later, Charley was successful in shooting an emu, and their 'kangaroo dogs' killed a kangaroo. Much of the meat so obtained was also cut into thin slices and dried in the sun. Leichhardt then decided to undertake a reconnaissance to see if he could find a route other than through the scrub, and was successful. He discovered and named Gilbert Range (after John Gilbert), Lynd Range (after Lieutenant Robert Lynd, 'an efficient officer with plenty of time on his hands', and who was also a keen naturalist) and Palm Tree Creek.[32]

They travelled up the valley of Palm Tree Creek. 'The water-holes,' wrote Leichhardt, 'abounded with jew-fish and eels; of the latter we obtained a good supply, and dried two of them, which kept very well.' Leichhardt also noted that the wild vegetable known as 'fat-hen' was growing well there and considered that 'when young, as we gratefully experienced, an excellent vegetable'.[33] It is well known nowadays as an anti-scorbutic. He also named Robinson Creek – after the Quaker, Joseph Phelps Robinson, who had contributed to the expedition. It flows through what is now the Expedition National Park. He named Murphy Range and Lake Murphy – after his teenaged companion. Further to the north they could see a 'particularly striking and imposing' range. This was named Expedition Range. The bell-shaped mountain (770 metres) at its southern end was named Mt Nicholson after Dr Charles Nicholson – who had 'first introduced into the Legislative Council of New South Wales, the subject of an overland expedition to Port Essington'.[34] On 1 December, Leichhardt carried out his usual reconnaissance – this time to the east – but was disappointed. At the same time Roper and Murphy had been to the north-west and had 'seen an open country before them'. Leichhardt and Gilbert wanted to see for themselves, and Leichhardt wrote that 'our admiration of the valley increased at every step. The whole system of creeks and glens ... would form a most excellent cattle station.'[35]

A few days later, just over two months since they had left Jimbour, Leichhardt recorded that their 'allowance of flour was now reduced from six pounds to five'.[36] Troubles of different kinds continued. Roper went to cut tent poles and became bushed. He wandered for about 8 kilometres (5 miles) 'before we were able to make him hear our cooees'.[37] Leichhardt himself had a similar problem. He had set out, with Charley, to examine the Christmas Ranges – so called because he 'hoped to reach them by Christmas time'. They had to retrace their steps, but Charley 'lost the track'. It was not really a major problem, however, because

Leichhardt's horse 'guided us back to camp'.[38] On Christmas Day they had 'suet pudding and stewed cockatoos'. On 28 December they observed a comet and the opportunity was taken to name a watercourse 'Comet Creek' (now Comet River).

On 10 January, Leichhardt set off on another reconnaissance with the two Aborigines – two, so that one of them could be sent back to bring the party on. When they had proceeded for about 11 kilometres (7 miles), Leichhardt sent back Charley, and went on with Brown. After a few more kilometres, 'to my inexpressible delight' the creek that they were following 'joined a river coming from the west and north-west, and flowing to the east and north-east'. Leichhardt named it the Mackenzie River – after Sir Evan Mackenzie – 'as a small acknowledgement of my gratitude for the very great assistance which he rendered me in the preparations for my expedition'.[39]

Exploration was not meant to be easy, however. They ate some of 'the long-podded cassia', but these 'considerably affected the bowels'. Moreover, small 'black ants, and little flies with wings crossing each other, annoy us very much, the one creeping all over our bodies and biting us severely, and the other falling into our soup and tea, and covering our meat; but the strong night-breeze protects us from the mosquitoes'.[40] A few days before this he had written that the 'mosquitoes were a little troublesome after sunset and in the early part of the night ... The flies were a much greater nuisance; at times absolutely intolerable.' Worse still, however, their 'daily allowance of flour was now reduced to three pounds. Our provisions disappear rapidly, and the wear and tear of our clothes and harness is very great.'[41]

From time to time they met a few of the local Aboriginal people. Brown met one Aboriginal man, for example, who was soon joined by his wife and their two children. Leichhardt also joined them and he thought that the father was 'a fine old man', but that they were all 'excessively frightened'. Some

days later Leichhardt recorded that he heard the cooee of an Aborigine, and 'in a short time two men were seen approaching and apparently desirous of having a parley.' Leichhardt went up to them. He described the elder one as 'a well made man' who 'had his left front tooth out'; the younger one 'had all his teeth perfect'. Their language was 'entirely different from that of the natives of Darling Downs'; but 'yarrai' meant water in both languages. Leichhardt added that 'Charley, who conversed with them for some time', had told him that, as far as he could understand them, the Mackenzie River flowed to the north-east, as Leichhardt had deduced.[42]

On 18 January, Leichhardt, Charley and Harry Brown set out on a reconnaissance to the north-west, while the other members of the expedition were preparing the charqui – the slices of dried beef. They had to ride through scrub for most of the day, and decided to camp for the night near a dry creek – with water holes not far distant. Charley was then sent back to bring up the other members of the expedition. In the meantime, Leichhardt and Brown continued to explore to the north-west. They obtained a good view of the surrounding country from the summit of a hill which was named Mt Stewart. However, it appears as Mt Stuart on Arrowsmith's map of 1847, and it remains Mt Stuart today. Stewart was a veterinary surgeon friend of Leichhardt, back in Sydney. Leichhardt and Brown continued to ride towards the north-west for some time and, because rain obliterated their tracks, they very nearly became lost on their return journey. They were also short of food; and Brown, in particular, became distressed. On the next morning, however, they continued their return journey and joined the others early the following afternoon.[43]

Leichhardt and Brown rested for a day, and the whole party then set out over the country that had been reconnoitred. On 26 January, Leichhardt planted the last of the peach stones that had been given to him by Francis Newman of the Botanic

Garden in Hobart – and named the creek where they camped Newman Creek. Leichhardt, Calvert and Charley set out again to reconnoitre and, on 27 January, Charley was sent back to bring on the others, and Leichhardt and Calvert went towards the range of peaks which was to become Peak Range. One of the peaks was named Roper Peak, another was called Scott Peak (after Helenus Scott of Hunter River 'who had kindly assisted me in my expedition') and a third was named Macarthur Peak (after William Macarthur). Leichhardt and Calvert were unable to find any water and Calvert, in particular, suffered from thirst on the night of 27 January. Leichhardt himself had laboured 'under a most painful diarrhoea'. Moreover, the horses had strayed, looking for water, and Calvert walked for four hours to retrieve them. There was another 'very remarkable cone' that Leichhardt named Calvert Peak 'in consequence of his having suffered severely in its neighbourhood'.[44]

The expedition continued to move forward slowly but steadily – between interruptions for reconnaissance; searches for water; searches for pigeons, cockatoos and emus for food; and the recovery of strayed horses and bullocks. The ration of flour had been about 1.5 kilograms (about three pounds) a day for some time but, 'by general consent of my companions,' wrote Leichhardt, it was, on 6 February, 'reduced to a pound and a half per diem for the six'. With this ration 'a damper mixed with fat was made every day, as soon as we reached our encampment.'[45]

The size of the daily ration was not the only problem, however. On 12 February, Leichhardt recorded that he had had trouble with the two Aboriginal members of the expedition. During one of Leichhardt's reconnaissances, they had deserted him – taking the provisions with them. Some time later, 'having filled their bellies and had their sulk out', they made their appearance at the camp 'considerably alarmed as to the consequences of their ill-behaviour'. Charley had brought 'about a pint of honey as a peace-offering; and both were unusually obliging and attentive to my companions'. Their conduct met with the general indignation of the other members of the expedition.[46]

Food was a continuing problem. It was necessary to 'live off the land' as much as possible, and every success in doing so was thus worthy of comment. Leichhardt noted, for example, that a crow shot and roasted was 'found to be exceedingly tender, which we considered a great discovery'.[47] Thereafter they shot as many as possible – to lessen the consumption of their dried meat. Portulaca proved to be a useful vegetable, and every opportunity was taken to taste the wild fruit. Another great problem was their relatively slow progress towards the west. Gilbert wrote in his diary that 'instead of being nearly a third of the distance [towards Port Essington] we find ourselves about one fourth only after 4 months travelling.' He thought that Leichhardt should determine the longitude by observation 'and shew us our positive position on the map, instead of trusting as hitherto to the uncertainty of what may be termed dead reconing [reckoning]'.[48] In fact, although Leichhardt's latitude determinations were usually fairly accurate, he made relatively few observations to determine the longitude and there is no doubt that these were often in error by an unacceptable amount. Aurousseau has published a map showing the results of observations for latitude and longitude which showed that the longitude observations were clearly in error.[49] Leichhardt himself doubted the accuracy of his longitude determinations. On one occasion, for example, he recorded that his observations gave a longitude of 148° 56' E; but he added, 'my bearings make it more to the westward.'[50]

Despite their slow progress there was no agitation to abandon the expedition. Leichhardt named Mt Phillips – after William Phillips, the convict member of their party – and they came to a river that was named the Isaac River, after Fred Isaac of Darling Downs. They followed it northwards and came to a creek that was named after William Suttor, a pastoralist, 'who had made me [Leichhardt] a present of four bullocks when I started the expedition'. This creek flowed into a river which became the Suttor River. They followed this to the northward and reached the junction of this river with another, very large, river, that Leichhardt named the Burdekin River after Mary Ann Burdekin – the widow of the Sydney merchant Samuel Burdekin. Mrs Burdekin had given 'liberal assistance' on the outfit of the expedition.[51] The river flows into the sea near Cape Upstart, as Leichhardt predicted.

They followed the Burdekin River to the northwest and, on 25 April, Leichhardt carried out two observations to obtain the longitude. One gave 144° 04' E and the other, 144° 14' E. As Roderick has pointed out these longitudes were about 1 degree too far west.[52] On 11 May they celebrated Whit Sunday 'with a double allowance of fat cake and sweetened tea'. Leichhardt and Charley then set out to reconnoitre the country to the westward. Leichhardt was fascinated by the large ant-hills and called a creek in the vicinity the 'Big Ant-hill Creek', now called Anthill Creek.[53] Leichhardt decided to rest for a time, and Charley went off on his own to explore. When Leichhardt woke up he returned to the vicinity of Anthill Creek on the evening of 14 May. 'At the sight of water, which we had been without full fifty hours,' he wrote, 'my horse and I rushed simultaneously into it, and we drank, and drank again, before I could induce myself to light a fire and make some tea, which was always found to be much more wholesome, and allay thirst sooner than water alone.'[54] That evening, he saw 'Charley and his wearied horse descending from the opposite range. He had not had anything to eat since the morning of the previous day, and was therefore exceedingly pleased to meet me.'[55] Leichhardt and Charley returned to the expedition's camp to find a party of Aboriginal people there, and soon learnt that their visitors had 'behaved very amicably' towards the explorers. Later, when the Aborigines

were getting ready to depart, they indicated that they were going to join the other members of their tribe at Rockingham Bay.

On 24 May, Leichhardt and his companions celebrated the Queen's birthday with their 'only remaining luxury' – a fat cake, made from four pounds of flour – and some suet that they had saved for this express purpose.[56] They also made a pot of sweetened tea.

On the previous day they had discovered a river that Leichhardt named the Lynd – after another keen naturalist, Robert Lynd. Leichhardt now decided to move down this river to the north-west, and it was during this time that they discovered a small tree 'the branches of which were thickly covered with bright green leaves'. It had small round fruit which were full of seeds. Leichhardt ate 'handfulls of this fruit without the slightest inconvenience'. They reminded him of coarse German rye bread, and he called it 'the bread tree of the Lynd'.[57]

They followed the Lynd for several days and found that it joined another river that Leichhardt 'took the liberty of naming after Sir Thomas Mitchell, the talented surveyor-general of New South Wales'.[58] At first, Leichhardt thought it might be the Nassau River, which had been discovered by the early maritime explorers and which had been shown on Arrowsmith's map of 1838. However, when the river continued to the north-west beyond the latitude of the Nassau, it was clear that the Mitchell River was a new discovery. Leichhardt now decided to set a course to round the south-eastern corner of the Gulf of Carpentaria. As Roderick has written: 'To represent his course of action as that of an aimless wanderer who did not know where he was or where he was going is far from the truth, as the entries in his fieldbook testify.'[59] It might be added that Leichhardt wrote that he felt 'compelled to reconnoitre every day for water to which we could move on the following day'.[60]

On the evening of the second day Charley and

Brown saw an Aboriginal man 'sneaking up to our bullocks' – apparently intending to drive them towards the camp of the Aboriginal people. Charley fired his gun and the Aborigines took to their heels. Real trouble erupted, however, on the evening of the next day, as Leichhardt recorded:[61]

I stretched myself upon the ground as usual, at a little distance from the fire, and fell into a dose [doze], from which I was suddenly roused by a loud noise, and a call for help from Calvert and Roper. Natives had suddenly attacked us. They had doubtless watched our movements during the afternoon, and marked the position of the different tents; and, as soon as it was dark, sneaked upon us, and threw a shower of spears at the tents of Calvert, Roper and Gilbert, and a few at that of Phillips, and also one or two towards the fire. Charley and Brown called for caps, which I hastened to find, and, as soon as they were provided, they discharged their guns into the crowd of the natives, who instantly fled, leaving Roper and Calvert pierced with several spears, and severely beaten by their waddies. Several of these spears were barbed, and could not be extracted without difficulty. I had to force one through the arm of Roper, to break off the barb; and cut another out of the groin of Mr. Calvert. John Murphy had succeeded in getting out of the tent, and concealing himself behind a tree, whence he fired at the natives, and severely wounded one of them, before Brown had discharged his gun. Not seeing Mr. Gilbert, I asked for him, when Charley told me that our unfortunate companion was no more! He had come out of his tent with his gun, shot and powder, and handed them to him, when he instantly dropped down dead.

It seems likely, as Roderick has suggested, that Leichhardt and his companions had inadvertently camped on a 'sacred site'.[62]

Gilbert had been speared through the heart; Roper had several spear wounds on the scalp, one spear had passed through his left arm, another had penetrated his cheek, and yet another entered his loins. Calvert had been hit several times with a waddy and his nose was broken. In addition, he had been hit with two spears. In the absence of a medical practitioner they were treated by Leichhardt, and both recovered in due course.

On 1 July they began their journey to the south-west and, on 5 July, they were rewarded by their first sight of the salt water of the Gulf of Carpentaria, 'which was hailed by all with feelings of indescribable pleasure'. As Leichhardt wrote, they had now 'discovered a line of communication by land, between the eastern coast of Australia, and the Gulf of Carpentaria; we had travelled along never failing, and, for the greater part, running waters; and over an excellent country, available, almost in its whole extent, for pastoral purposes'.[63] A few days later they killed their 'little steer', and on the following day, cut the meat into slices that were then hung out to dry. On 12 July, Leichhardt crossed a small river flowing to the north-west, and into the Gulf of Carpentaria. He named it the Gilbert River 'after my unfortunate companion'.

On 19 July they travelled almost due south, crossed a salt creek (now known as the Carron River), and came to 'a fine river with salt water about two hundred and fifty or three hundred yards broad, with low banks fringed with stunted mangroves'.[64] The Aboriginal people apparently called it the Yappar. Leichhardt did not name it. It was subsequently named the Norman River – after Commander W. H. Norman who, in command of HMCS *Victoria*, searched this area in 1861 while looking for Burke and Wills and their companions. Normanton, a town 80 kilometres upstream from the mouth of the river, was also named after the commander. The Norman River flows into the gulf and, at the mouth of the river, there is a busy fishing port that is named Karumba – after the local Aboriginal tribe.

By 21 July, Calvert had recovered from his injuries sufficiently to resume normal duties, but Roper was not yet fit enough to work. Leichhardt was leading his party further west and they came upon a river that had been named the Flinders River by John Lort Stokes in 1841 – but the details had not been published by the time Leichhardt and his companions set off from Jimbour. Stokes had made an excursion up the river and, when the Leichhardt expedition was in the vicinity, Calvert found what must have been a relic of the Stokes visit. It was 'a piece of pack canvas, rolled round some utensils of the natives'.[65]

Leichhardt now followed a route roughly parallel to the southern coast of the Gulf of Carpentaria – but about 25 to 50 kilometres from it. It was necessary to travel a reasonable distance from the coast to avoid the swampy mudflats traversed by many channels which intervene between the dry land and the shallow sea. During their progress they had to cross a number of rivers flowing into the gulf, and it was difficult to identify those that had been discovered and named by the early Dutch and English maritime explorers. The Dutch had reported the discovery of a river that they named the Maatsuyer (or Maet Suyker). Stokes had discovered and named the Flinders River, after Matthew Flinders, in 1841, and had also discovered and named the Albert River after Prince Albert, the consort of Queen Victoria. But which river was the Maet Suyker of the Dutch explorers? Leichhardt was not sure because both he and the Dutch were unable to determine the longitude. Leichhardt wrote that the '... river I am inclined to think, is the Albert of Captain Stokes, and the Maet Suyker of the Dutch Navigators, and the general course is from south-south-west, to north-north-east'.[66]

Leichhardt had crossed what he thought was the Flinders River and, further to the west had found another river – that he thought might be the Albert, or perhaps the Maet Suyker. In these circumstances he did not name it, and it was left to another explorer, A. C. Gregory, to name it the Leichhardt River.

(Thus, in September 1856, on crossing this large river, Gregory was to observe that 'it is evidently the river taken by Dr. Leichhardt for the Albert'

and 'as it was unnamed I called it the Leichhardt'. The Albert River is further to the west.[67] A. C. Gregory was assistant surveyor of Western Australia, and he was chosen to lead the North Australian Expedition, sponsored by the Royal Geographical Society of London, primarily to search for Leichhardt. He and his party – which included his brother H. C. Gregory as second-in-command, the noted botanist Ferdinand von Mueller, and fifteen others – was to establish a base camp near the mouth of the Victoria River, near the present border between Western Australia and the Northern Territory and, in June of 1856, were to push eastwards across what is now the 'Top End' to and beyond the Albert River – a journey of more than 1600 kilometres. He was to find four traces of Europeans – such as names cut on tree trunks, and European artefacts in the hands of Aboriginal people – but nothing certainly related to Leichhardt.[68])

But the Gregory expedition was still in the future as Leichhardt reached the Albert River in mid August. A few days later they came to another river that Leichhardt named the Nicholson River – after William Alleyne Nicholson, 'whose generous friendship had not only enabled me to devote my time to the study of the natural sciences, but to come out to Australia'.[69] He also crossed and named Moonlight Creek 'as it had been found and explored during moonlight'. They spent a day at this creek and collected a great quantity of terminal gum. 'It dissolved with difficulty in water: added to gelatine soup, it was a great improvement; a little ginger, which John had still kept, and a little salt, would improve it very much. But it acted as a good lenient purgative on all of us.'[70]

Except for the dried beef, they were now living almost entirely 'off the land'. They were able to shoot a few emus, cockatoos and other birds, and they ate wild fruits with caution. Leichhardt wrote that he frequently tasted the fruit of the Pandanus but every time was 'severely punished with sore lips and a blistered tongue; and the first time I ate it, I was attacked by a violent diarrhoea'.[71] The Aboriginal people, however, used this fruit, and Leichhardt experimented to find a method of treating it. He concluded that the fruit had to be really ripe, and washed and then boiled. He noted: 'We have not felt the slightest inconvenience from the want of flour.' They were, for some time, without salt, and became constipated; but 'when we began to use it again, almost every one of us had a slight attack of diarrhoea.' Tea was 'unquestionably one of the most important provisions', but sugar was 'of very little consequence'.[72] It should be noted, however, that Leichhardt's expedition was almost unique among the early explorations of Australia in that none of the party contracted scurvy. This can be attributed only to his use of wild fruit and vegetables whenever these could be obtained.

The expedition was still moving towards the north-west, roughly parallel to the coast of the gulf. They arrived at the largest salt-water creek that they had seen so far. Leichhardt named it the Macarthur River – after James and William Macarthur in acknowledgement of the liberal support that they had given; but it is now written as the McArthur River.[73]

On the same day, Leichhardt heard the calls of some Aboriginal people. The expedition stopped and Leichhardt dismounted and advanced slowly to have a parley. He was met by an old man with three or four young men behind him. 'As soon as he saw that I intended to make him a present,' Leichhardt wrote, 'he prepared one in return.' He gave the old man some rings and buckles, and received in return a few 'of the ornaments he wore on his person'. Leichhardt went on to say: 'All of them seemed to have been circumcised.'[74] Leichhardt thought that these Aboriginal people must have had contact with Europeans, or with Malays – because they appeared to know the use of a knife and of a firearm. We now know that they must have been Macassans, who came annually to the north coast of Australia, fishing for trepang.

Leichhardt even speculated that a few Aborigines might have accompanied the Macassans back to the East Indies at the completion of the trepang fishing season, and returned to the Australian coast in the following year.[75]

As Leichhardt moved forward they came to a river, flowing into the gulf. Leichhardt named it the Red Kangaroo River, because he saw so many of the 'Red Forester of Port Essington' in its vicinity. He identified this kangaroo as *Osphranter antilopinus*, Gould; but it is now known as *Macropus antilopinus*.[76] Unfortunately, Leichhardt's 'Red Kangaroo River' is now Rosie Creek.[77] It reaches the gulf at 15° 24' S, 136° 12' E. Then, further to the north-west, they came to a more substantial river, and this was named the Limmen Bight River – because the Dutch explorers had named this section of the gulf 'Limmen Bight'. Charley and Brown, who had been sent out on a scouting expedition, reported that, from the summit of a hill, they had seen an island. Abel Tasman had sighted this island in 1642, but did not recognise it as an island and named it *Cape Maria* – after the wife of the then governor-in-chief of the Dutch East India Company (Anthony Van Diemen) in Djakarta (then called Batavia). It is now Maria Island.

One of the bullocks was now so weak that he was unable to carry his load. Leichhardt had no alternative but to end its life and to cut the meat into slices and put them out to dry. While this was in progress Leichhardt examined all the packs to determine what could be dispensed with because the remaining animals could not carry it all – bearing in mind that, with one less bullock, there would be 60 kilograms (130 pounds) of additional dried meat to be transported. He discarded the paper that he used for drying the plant specimens. He parted with the collection of rocks made by Gilbert, and with all the duplicates of their zoological specimens. He wrote that 'necessity alone compelled me to take this step' and 'reconciled me to the loss'.[78]

They were now in difficult dissected country – with many lagoons and salt-water creeks; but there were swarms of ducks and geese, and many other water fowl. Several geese were shot, and they roasted four of them for dinner, and 'they formed by far the most delicious dish our expedition had offered: the others were stewed for the next breakfast; and they were equally good.'[79] They followed the Limmen Bight River upstream and found a place to cross. There were numerous wallabies to be seen and they 'started a flock of red foresters'.

On 17 October, Roper ascended one of the hills in the vicinity and saw a green valley 'with a rich vegetation about three miles to the northward'. Two days later Leichhardt wrote that he 'observed a green belt of trees scarcely 300 yards to the northward; and on riding towards it, I found myself on the banks of a large fresh water river from 500 to 800 yards broad'. It was the river that Roper had seen from the hill. Leichhardt named it after Roper as he had promised to do.[80] It was a very happy day for the expedition. They had discovered the Roper River and, on the same day Charley, Brown and John Murphy had visited the nearby lagoon to shoot waterfowl and returned with twenty ducks for luncheon. They went there again during the afternoon and succeeded in shooting thirty-one ducks and two geese. So they had fifty-one ducks and two geese for the three meals – luncheon, dinner and breakfast; and 'they were all eaten, with the exception of a few bony remains.'[81]

It was not all good luck, however. On 21 October, Charley was sent to the junction of the creek and the river to retrieve three of their horses, and returned to say that they had been drowned. Roderick 'wonders what part crocodiles played in this disaster, for disaster it was'. There were fewer horses to carry the goods, chattles and specimens. Leichhardt had to abandon his botanical collection, and Gilbert's collection of plants was also abandoned at this time.[82]

Two days later there was another disaster. Another horse, this one named Macarthur, slipped down the banks of the Roper River, and all efforts to get him out were in vain. Leichhardt himself, who was the only member of the expedition who could swim, went into the water to try to rescue him. He had to wait until high tide, and succeeded 'in getting him out of the water; but he began to plunge again, and unfortunately broke the tether which kept his forequarters up, and fell back into the river'. Leichhardt found a 'tolerable landing place about fifty yards higher up', but while he was swimming with it the horse became entangled in the tether rope, rolled over and drowned.[83] In the meantime, however, they had made friends with a neighbouring tribe of Aboriginal people, and exchanged presents. The explorers could not visit the camp of the Aborigines, however, because they would have to swim across the river and, as already mentioned, Leichhardt was the only one who could swim. Leichhardt noted: 'They were circumcised, and two front teeth had been knocked out; they had horizontal scars on their chests.'[84]

It was difficult to find any vegetable matter to eat. Leichhardt gathered some vine-beans that had thick pods containing one to five seeds. Their hard covering became brittle on roasting, and the seeds were boiled for several hours. 'This softened them, and made a sort of porridge, which, at all events, was very satisfying.' They also experimented with ways to make a substitute for tea or coffee. Phillips was always seeking ways to find a suitable substitute for coffee. Indeed, it was he who discovered the use of the river-bean of the Mackenzie River. In this new locality he collected some seeds and pounded and boiled them. Leichhardt found the liquid too bitter to drink; but Phillips drank about a pint of it and he became very sick. It 'produced violent vomiting and purging during the whole afternoon and night'.[85] Animal food was less likely to be poisonous, Murphy and Charley were able to shoot twenty-nine flying foxes, for example.[86]

The bullocks and horses were having a tough

time. They were very footsore, the weather was very hot and, despite the fact that there was plenty of grass and water, they suffered. One of the bullocks, the one carrying the remainder of Leichhardt's botanical collection, 'watched his opportunity, and plunged into a deep pond, where he was quietly swimming about and enjoying himself', while Leichhardt was almost crying at seeing all his 'plants thoroughly soaked'.[87] A few days later they had to kill another bullock – this time it was the one nicknamed 'Snowdrop'. The creek they were following was named Snowdrop Creek, and it still bears this name.[88]

They came to what is now known as Jim Jim Creek and 'with great difficulty' Leichhardt and his companions made their way down this creek until they came to salt water. On 24 November Leichhardt determined the latitude, by the meridian altitude of Castor, to be 13° 05' 49" S. He concluded that 'according to my latitude, and to my course' that they were at the South Alligator River 'about sixty miles from its mouth, and about one hundred and forty miles from Port Essington'.[89] They then turned northwards towards the East Alligator River. Their time near the South Alligator River was not easily forgotten because, as Leichhardt wrote to his brother-in-law, Carl Schmalfuss:[90]

It was on the South Alligator River that we encountered the first blacks who knew about white settlement to the North-west. One had a piece of cloth. Another had an iron hatchet. On the East Alligator River they knew a few words of English, and we were delighted to hear that one of them was asking us our names.

There were other signs that they were approaching their destination. Only two days later a whole

Leichhardt's grasshopper (*Petasida ephippigera*); on his way to Port Essington, Leichhardt observed a highly coloured grasshopper at what is now Kakadu National Park. (Reg Morrison)

tribe of friendly Aboriginal people visited them, and Leichhardt noted: 'One of them had a shawl and neckerchief of English manufacture; and another carried an iron tomahawk.' It was apparent that they were familiar with European people and with firearms. On 2 December, Leichhardt wrote:[91]

Whilst we were waiting for our bullock, which had returned to the running brook, a fine native stepped out of the forest with the ease and grace of an Apollo, with a smiling countenance, and with the confidence of a man to whom the white face was perfectly familiar. He was unarmed, but a great number of his companions were keeping back to watch the reception he should meet with. We received him, of course, most cordially; and upon being joined by another good-looking little man, we heard him utter distinctly the words. 'commandant', 'come here', 'very good', 'what's your name?'

Leichhardt went on:

If my readers have at all identified themselves with my feelings throughout this trying journey; if they have only imagined a tithe of the difficulties we have encountered, they will readily imagine the startling effect which these, as it were, magic words produced – we were electrified – our joy knew no limits, and I was ready to embrace the fellows, who seeing the happiness with which they inspired us, joined with a most merry grin, in the loud expressions of our feelings.

It was clear that they knew the Europeans at Victoria – the settlement on the shore of Port Essington. They called them Balanda, which meant 'Hollanders' – the name used by the Macassans.

Leichhardt continued to lead the party towards the north, but choosing a route according to the nature of the country. In the same letter to his brother-in-law, he explained that he 'encountered the East Alligator River not far from its mouth, and, as it's broad and deep there, I found myself obliged to follow it upstream until I found a crossing-place. After I succeeded in crossing it I continued on my northward line of march.'[92] They

were now out of shot and were using ironstone pellets. Even so they managed to kill a wild buffalo and shared the meat with their Aboriginal friends. The wild buffaloes had been introduced by the Macassans.

On 16 December they were at Raffles Bay, and were visited by a group of friendly Aborigines. Their chief, who was known as 'Bill White' (indicating that he had been associating with Europeans), agreed to guide them to the settlement at Victoria on the shore of Port Essington. As Leichhardt himself wrote:[93]

Friendly blacks helped me find the narrow tongue of land that forms the Coburg [Cobourg] Peninsula, and at last I arrived at Victoria, the English settlement at Port Essington, on 17th of December, 1845 … I had completed a journey of 14½ months through the wilderness.

Leichhardt had never expected the journey to take as long as it did, and their provisions did not last. 'We went for 7 months without flour,' he wrote, 'much longer without sugar, several months without salt, and finally ran out of tea, so that we were reduced to nothing but dried beef. It was the dried beef that enabled me to complete the journey.'[94] He had begun the journey with sixteen bullocks and fifteen horses, and had 'broken in' nine of the bullocks as pack animals. By the time they reached Port Essington they had killed all the bullocks except one, and they had lost six horses. They were never reduced to walking – every member of the expedition was able to travel on horseback. However, their clothes were in tatters and, on the day of their arrival at Port Essington, Leichhardt wrote an official letter to the commandant 'to supply us with the necessary provisions during our stay at Port Essington, and to furnish us with the following articles of clothing'.[95] He asked for two pairs of trousers and two shirts for each member of his party. He also asked for two jackets each for three members; but did not ask for jackets for the two Aborigines or for the 'Crown Prisoner'.

Leichhardt and his companions were warmly welcomed by the commandant, Captain John McArthur of the Royal Marines, and by the other officers. McArthur, who was a cousin of the New South Wales pastoralists William and James McArthur, had been in charge of the settlement 'for most of its existence, outlasting all its trials'. McArthur and Leichhardt became very fond of each other. Indeed, as Webster has written:[96]

Leichhardt probably came nearer than any other visitor to discovering what sustained Captain McArthur. Where others left passing remarks on a conscientious but pedestrian officer or a dogmatic old fogy, Leichhardt felt that he had been privileged to know a rare spirit. And their encounter apparently made a difference to his host, for the Commandant felt especially solitary on the eve of Leichhardt's departure.

Leichhardt was delighted with the settlement itself. 'Victoria,' he wrote, 'is a small spot of cleared forest land elevated above the level of the sea ... The snug little cottages of the marines have all their gardens behind them, in which the Coconut palm and Banana grow. The hospital, the storehouses, the house of the Commandant and of the officers are larger buildings.' He added that the '... white ant is an unceasing dangerous enemy and only the greatest attention can keep it at bay'.[97]

In planning his expedition, Leichhardt believed that he and his companions would have to return to the settled districts by an overland route. Fortunately, however, he now learnt that supply ships visited Port Essington and Victoria from time to time. On 9 January the *Flower of Singapore* and the *Heroine* arrived at Victoria. The *Heroine* was owned and operated by Captain Martin Mackenzie and was en route to Sydney. He agreed to take Leichhardt and his companions and they all embarked on 17 January for the homeward voyage.

In the meantime, Leichhardt was busy completing his notes and maps, and there were a few additional pleasures. He did not have to kill the remaining bullock! Indeed, the thought of having to kill him 'was enough to put' Leichhardt 'out of temper'. He was Leichhardt's pet 'and throughout the journey' Leichhardt used to load him himself. In his letter to his brother-in-law, written on board the *Heroine* on 24 January 1846, Leichhardt added: 'He's still at Port Essington, as my legacy to Capt. Macarthur [McArthur] ... who promised to look after him'.[98]

Leichhardt was delighted to rest on the journey back to Sydney, but took an interest in everything. They sailed eastwards through Torres Strait, and the *Heroine* was one of the first to attempt the passage in this direction. In this direction it is much more dangerous than from east to west. According to Leichhardt: 'The skill and energy of this gentleman, in conducting his vessel through a channel so recently attempted, is beyond any praise that I can bestow.'[99]

The *Heroine* arrived at Sydney on 25 March 1846 and, as soon as Leichhardt was recognised, the joy was unrestrained. The citizens of Sydney had long given Leichhardt and his companions up for lost – they were presumed to have died of thirst, or starved, or been killed by hostile Aborigines. The fact that he (and most of his companions) were alive, and that they had reached Port Essington, was almost unbelievable. When Leichhardt went to the barracks, Lynd took him off to the newspapers 'and next morning all Sydney knew that Leichhardt was back.'[100] Leichhardt wrote a letter, dated 27 March, that was published in the *Sydney Morning Herald*. In this letter he expressed his gratitude to John McArthur (now a major) and 'his little garrison' at Port Essington for all that he had done to help the expedition. He also made a point of thanking the skipper of the *Heroine*, who had brought them safely back to Sydney.[101] Leichhardt was overwhelmed by his reception, and was dubbed the 'Prince of Explorers'. He wrote that 'no king could have been welcomed with greater gladness and deeper interest by a whole people than I was myself. As it had long been presumed that I had either died or been killed by the blacks, my good friend Mr Lynd had written my funeral dirge.' [102]

Leichhardt enjoyed this interest in himself and his successful expedition, but he had other things on his mind, too. First, he must complete the account of his journey – ready for publication in England. For this purpose he asked his friend Phillip Parker King to edit his manuscript. When complete, he sent it to Dr William Nicholson who would arrange publication and keep the royalties in payment for the monies he had advanced to Leichhardt over the years. Second, he had long held another ambition: to be the first to lead an expedition from the east coast, across the continent, to the settlement at Swan River. In his letter of 18 April 1846 to his brother-in-law, he wrote:[103]

> I'm hoping to set out on a new journey at the end of October, which, though longer, will be more interesting than the last. I hope to be on my way back from Swan River in two years' time. What I have in mind is to go up to the Tropics, to make my way thence right across to the west coast of Australia in 22° or 23° of latitude, and then to follow the coast southwards to the Swan River ... I've written to India for camels, and shall at least try to get the two that are already in the colony.

The popular enthusiasm for Leichhardt's Port Essington expedition was enormous. Charles Sturt had been defeated by the desert in the centre, but Leichhardt and his companions had discovered several important rivers and a considerable area of good grazing land. The government provided a gratuity of £1000 to reward the explorers and this was divided as follows:

Dr Leichhardt	£600
Mr Calvert	£125
Mr Roper	£125
John Murphy	£70
W. Phillips	£30
Charley Fisher	£25
Harry Brown	£25

John Murphy did not rate as 'Mr' – presumably because he was still a minor. Phillips also did not rate a 'Mr' – because he was a convict.

The general public raised a further sum – nearly £1519 – to reward the explorers. Of this, £40 was set aside to provide a memorial to John Gilbert, who had been killed by hostile Aborigines. The remainder was distributed to the members of the expedition in the same proportions as the government grant. Leichhardt received a further £854. These grants made it possible for him to provide the basic funding for his proposed expedition to the Swan River colony.[104]

LEICHHARDT'S GRAND PLAN – TO CROSS THE CONTINENT FROM EAST TO WEST

On 25 March 1846, Leichhardt returned to Sydney after his successful expedition to Port Essington and, almost immediately, he announced that he proposed to lead another expedition – this time from the east coast across the continent to the Swan River colony (where Perth now stands).

Daniel Bunce – a gardener–botanist who had emigrated from England to Hobart Town (as it was then called) in 1833, and who had later moved to Launceston and then to the Port Phillip District (later called Melbourne) – learnt of this proposal and wrote to Leichhardt to request a place in this new venture. Bunce was anxious to pursue his interest in the natural history of Australia; but Leichhardt made it clear that every member of his expedition would have to take his fair share of *all* the work. On this understanding, Bunce was accepted as a member. The other senior member of the proposed expedition was to be John Mann, whose main duties were to be surveyor, draughtsman, and storekeeper. Mann had also emigrated from England. His father was an army officer, and both of his grandfathers were generals. Early in 1846 Mann had offered to lead an expedition to search for Leichhardt and his companions – who were long overdue from the Port Essington expedition. Mann was amazed, like everyone else, when Leichhardt and his companions arrived safely in Sydney. It might be added that Mann later married Camilia Victoria Mitchell – the daughter of Sir Thomas and Lady Mitchell.

The other men selected by Leichhardt to be members of his new expedition were Hovenden Hely, a squatter; James Perry, a saddler; Henry Boecking as the cook Henry Turnbull as assistant stock-keeper; and two Aboriginal men, Wommai, alias Jimmy, and Harry Brown. Both of the Aborigines were members of the Port Stephens tribe. Harry Brown had been a member of Leichhardt's expedition to Port Essington and was the only member of the proposed expedition who had travelled with Leichhardt before.[105]

It was clear that Leichhardt's proposed new expedition would be a lengthy one – two and a half years was thought to be likely. They would therefore require provisions for about that long period. Leichhardt decided to take a large number of sheep, goats and bullocks, with horses to ride, and mules as the 'beasts of burden'. According to Sprod, the number of animals on setting out was fourteen horses, sixteen mules, forty cattle, 270 goats, between 900 and 1000 sheep, and four dogs – but Bunce gives slightly different figures.[106] There is no doubt, however, that the numbers were large and, consequently, they were hard to handle – especially with only four dogs. Leichhardt knew that the stock would be hard to control, and had mentioned this to Bunce. It was expected that the goats would also cause problems.[107] Leichhardt had purchased them from William Charles Wentworth for five shillings a head. They were found to be wretchedly poor and 'in an unfit state to commence the journey'. Hely was later to write that Leichhardt 'heartily repents having bought them and so do we!' Hely himself described them as a 'most useless encumbrance to us'.[108]

Nevertheless, the explorers made their way to the Darling Downs and, on 7 December 1846, they set off and made their way towards Charley's Creek – at which they arrived on 11 December. The difficulties were not confined to the goats, however. The weather was far wetter than that experienced during Leichhardt's expedition to Port Essington, and the men and animals were tired of walking through swamps mud and similar obstacles. Sheep had to be manhandled across creeks and rivers, and stock wandered off during the night and had to be rounded up. Horses strayed and had to be found and brought back to camp. Then there were the mosquitoes and other pests, and the expedition's extremely slow progress. There was great dissatisfaction with the food and especially with the lack of flour. The whole expedition became very distressed with the conditions, and morale was extremely poor. Almost everyone felt 'sick' although no one knew why.

Sprod has pointed that nobody 'thought to blame the swarms of insects so graphically described in the expeditioners' journals, and which had been generated by heavy rains and the stagnant billabongs. These insects were largely flies, sandflies, and mosquitoes.'[109] The 'flies' were the notorious Australian 'bush flies', which are to be found in great numbers in the non-urban areas – less so in towns. They are a very great nuisance. They settle on the face, the hands, and other parts of the human anatomy. One hand has to be used almost continuously to brush them away. Then there were the sandflies, which are tiny blood-sucking flies which attack exposed skin, and cause weals which burn and itch. It is not uncommon for men, wearing shorts and short-sleeved shirts in tropical and semi-tropical country, to have scores of weals as a result of attack by sandflies. Mosquitoes are also found in many parts of Australia – especially in humid conditions. Their 'buzzing' is a signal to take steps to avoid them. Female mosquitoes have a long proboscis, which is used to puncture the skin of humans and other animals to draw blood. The resulting weals itch and are painful.

These symptoms are annoying in themselves – but it seems likely (as Sprod has suggested) that the mosquitoes that attacked the Leichhardt expedition also carried the virus *Aedes aegyptii*, which produces dengue fever. This virus produces severe head, back and muscle pain as well as rashes and fever. It is an influenza-like fever that is often found in many humid tropical and subtropical areas. Many members of the expedition became ill and dispirited, and Sprod's suggestion that they had dengue fever seems likely. It is not surprising that Leichhardt was criticised by his men for not including a larger variety of medicines among the expedition's stores but, as Sprod concludes: 'even if more were taken, it is likely that they would have been ineffective' against this disease. Moreover, Leichhardt had travelled this country before and had had no such trouble. He was inclined to think that the men should show more fortitude.[110]

Leichhardt discussed the future with every member of the expedition, and it was clear that they wanted to abandon the attempt to reach the Swan River. Leichhardt had no alternative but to agree and, as a result, Leichhardt's second expedition returned to the Darling Downs in July 1847. Sprod has summed up the situation:[111]

His party sick, defeated, dispirited and divided in their loyalties, their provisions largely abandoned, their stock all but dispersed and Leichhardt's 'Grand Plan' in tatters. Moreover, the achievements of this, his second expedition, were negligible – in nearly nine months the party had succeeded in travelling only 800 km, and this following very closely the route taken on the outward journey of his successful first expedition of 1844–45, even on many occasions, using the same campsites as the earlier journey. The farthest point reached was the Peak Ranges.

Back in Sydney, Leichhardt wrote to William Macarthur on 10 October 1847 that 'I have made a serious blunder in the choice of my companions and I have been severely punished for it.' He added that 'I shall soon commence to prepare for a new start ... My party is nearly made up and I hope I shall be better of [off] this time.'[112] A few days later he unburdened his mind to his friend Phillip Parker King:[113]

The most difficult part of my Expedition is without comparison the choice of my companions. On my trip to FitzRoy downs the other members of my party told me circumstances, of which I had not the slightest idea. It seems evident that Mr Hely and Mr Mann did me by far the greatest harm; that they started with distrust even in my honesty and from the beginning, from the first stage, they endeavoured to estrange the party from me. They were offended that I did not become familiar with them; but it was their own fault, for I got disgusted with their bawdy filthy conversations or with their continual harping on fine eating and drinking. (My other companions Mr Bunce Perry and Boecking go so far as to believe that these young men were the real cause of my return and their arguments are very plausible indeed.) There is no doubt that Turnbulls croaking on the want of medicine was equally foolish and tended to upset the resolution of men, who were suffering from constant relapses of a weakening disease.

Bunce made it clear that he would like to be selected to be a member of Leichhardt's new team to cross the continent and, at first, Leichhardt was inclined to appoint him. However, Leichhardt discussed the membership of his party 'with many gentlemen, who were capable of giving advice', and eventually came to the conclusion that it would be preferable to form an entirely new party – a party in which 'all my companions will be accustomed to bushlife good horse men and able to tend to my stock.'[114] Earlier, Bunce had also recommended a young friend of his as a man 'well adapted to the purpose'; but he too failed to be chosen.[115]

Leichhardt selected August Classen, aged thirty-four, to be one of his companions on his next attempt to cross the continent. Classen was a distant relative of Leichhardt (his sister had married one of Leichhardt's brothers) and he had arrived in Sydney in January 1847. Leichhardt described him as 'a very well educated young man who has been crossing the seas to most parts of the world for 12 years. His experiences had prepared him for a journey such as mine.' [116] It must be admitted, however, that Classen had had precious little experience with horses and bullocks, or even with men other than seamen, and he proved to be less than successful as a senior member of Leichhardt's team. Fortunately, Leichhardt was able to appoint Arthur Hentig, a station manager. In January 1848 Leichhardt wrote to John Mackay, in Sydney, saying that Hentig 'is gaining every day in my esteem' and he added: 'Everything is new to Classen and though he likes the life he scarcely feels at home amongst the people of the bush of Australia.' [117] Five weeks later Leichhardt wrote to another friend: 'Mr Hentig will be of great service to me and has been so allready [sic], for he knows the management of cattle and horses better than I myself and I willingly submit to his judgment, which I have never dared to do to any of my former companions.' [118] To another friend he wrote that 'Mr Hentig gains every day in my esteem; he is modest unassuming and yet experienced man. Classen still had his head too full of the 'Rope's End' and thinks he can put down everything by main force as on board of ship. But he is extremely handy and useful and a really good man.' [119]

Leichhardt also engaged two 'working men'. One was named Kelly but, apart from the fact that he was employed by 'a gentleman on the Logan', nothing is known. The other was named Donald Stuart (or Stewart), a ticket-of-leave man who had been assigned to George Leslie of Darling Downs. Leichhardt wrote to the colonial secretary on 24 February requesting the governor's permission for Donald Stuart to accompany him. In mid March he again wrote to the colonial secretary to request

permission to take another ticket-of-leave man, Thomas Hands, who was employed on the station belonging to St George Gore. The requisite approval was given on 18 April, but Leichhardt could not have received it because he was already on his way. It seems likely that Leichhardt believed that approval would be given and that he took Hands with him – but it is not known for certain whether Hands did travel with Leichhardt. Two Aboriginal men also joined the expedition – Wommai, otherwise known as 'Jimmy' (who had been with Leichhardt on his previous expedition), and a second man known as 'Billy'. If Hands did join the expedition, there were eight men all told – but if he did not, there were only seven.

Leichhardt had written to his friend, the Rev. W. B. Clarke from Canning Downs, on 26 February 1848. He mentioned that he had fifty bullocks – thirty from the government and twenty from Joseph Phelps Robinson, a wealthy man who greatly admired Leichhardt. Leichhardt added that his principal provisions were 363 kilograms (800 pounds) of flour, 54 kilograms (120 pounds) of tea and 45 kilograms (100 pounds) of salt – but no sugar 'which is difficult and inconvenient to carry'. [120]

Leichhardt and his companions spent a few days at Allan Macpherson's sheep station at Mt Abundance, FitzRoy Downs. His last communication to those who wished him well was an open letter to the *Sydney Morning Herald*, dated 4 April 1848. The next day, 5 April, they set off. Nothing further was ever heard from them. They disappeared.

Several search parties failed to find any clear evidence of their fate. As Grenfell Price has written: [121]

The story of Leichhardt's disappearance forms the great unsolved mystery of Australian exploration. It is amazing that so large a party of men and animals should have been lost completely without leaving a single authentic clue. Numerous expeditions have been dispatched at heavy cost to widely separated parts of Australia, rewards of thousands of pounds have been offered and several lives have been sacrificed without success, relics and spurious relics have appeared in various places, but the fact remains that there is no definitive proof of where or how Leichhardt perished.

We do not know for certain the route that the expedition followed. Nor can we determine for certain what became of its members. The best we can do is to outline some probabilities and some possibilities.

It is known that Leichhardt had no intention of travelling in a south-westerly direction from

Macpherson's station to reach the Swan River colony. He had outlined what he intended to do in his letter to the Rev. W. B. Clarke on 26 February 1848:[122]

> We shall sail down the Condamine, go up to Colgoon [Cogoon River], and follow Mitchell's outward track to the most northern bend of the Victoria [so named by Mitchell, but earlier named the Barcoo River]. I shall then proceed to the northward until I come in decided water of the gulf, and after that resume my original course to the westward.

In another letter, this time to Helenus Scott, he

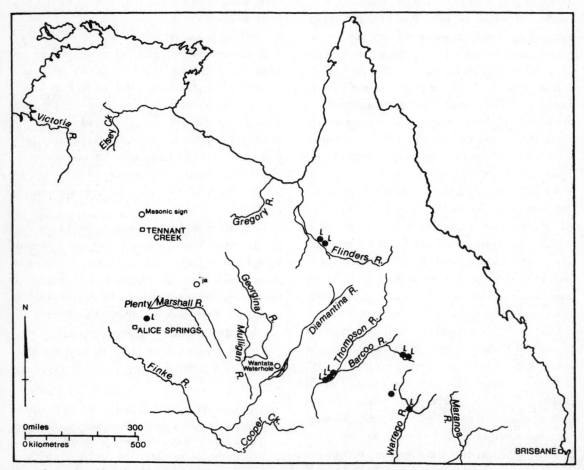

Map of areas possibly visited by Leichhardt and showing trees marked with an 'L' by Leichhardt

wrote:'I intend to follow down the Condamine to go up to the Colgoon [Cogoon] (FitzRoy Downs) and to cross over to the Victoria [the Barcoo].' It might be accepted that this was his clear intention. He then proposed to travel westwards, but using a route to the north of the known desert in central Australia. He would move to the north as far as the Flinders River and:[123]

> Should the country be sufficiently well watered, I should, of course proceed to the westward, keeping the same latitude and try to reach the waters of the northwest coast in about Lat. 17 deg. 18'. Should I succeed in this I will turn to the southward and work my way parallel to the northwest and west coast until I reach the Swan River. This journey I hope to accomplish in two years, although I am aware unforseen difficulties may retard my progress.'

In accordance with established practice at that time Leichhardt arranged for a large 'L' to be cut into occasional trees along their route. Many of these markers were discovered by search parties over the years. Such markers have been located on the banks of the Warrego River, and along the Barcoo River which becomes Sturt's 'Cooper Creek'. It seems that they returned up the river and then, judging by some very old tracks and the presence of a couple of iron tomahawks, they must have travelled up the Thomson River. It seems that Leichhardt's party then turned to the north-west, because large 'L' signs have been reported on trees adjacent to the Flinders River and then possibly southwards because an 'L' has been discovered in a tree near Arltunga – which is about 200 kilometres to the east of Alice Springs. Yet another tree marked with an 'L' has been discovered at Glenormiston, on the Georgina River. Leichhardt could well have skirted the northern edge of the Simpson Desert to reach this site.[124] Many years later three skeletons were discovered at the Wantata Waterhole in 25° 29' S, 140° 13' E.[125]

Wantata Waterhole is one of several billabongs in a complex of braided river channels belonging to the Diamantina River system. The braided river is bordered by flat black soil plains, and sand ridges up to 20 metres high are built of sand derived from the river channels. Plateaux capped by silcrete are prominent 30 kilometres to the south, but the combination of waterholes, timber, shelter and sandhills – which, though low, provide lookout points for the area to the north and west – would have made the Wantata site an attractive one amid the otherwise flat and featureless plains. A fourth skeleton, and the fragments of a skull, were found further north from the waterhole. These remains have all been shown, by pathological examination, to be those of Europeans, and probably belonged to members of Leichhardt's expedition. The remains of the one (or two?) other Europeans, and the remains of the two Aborigines, have never been found.

In 1938 the Grenfell Price expedition found an 1817 half-sovereign and an 1841 Maundy coin,[126] near the western border of the Simpson Desert. These coins might have belonged to Leichhardt himself – because he was in England in 1841. However, as Roderick has pointed out, they were found at an old campsite on the western border of the Simpson Desert, 'but the camp was Aboriginal, and the presence of these portable objects does not prove that Leichhardt's party either camped or perished there'.[127]

WAS THERE A SURVIVOR?

There is some evidence that suggests that at least one European might have separated from the main party – either by his own choice or by misadventure. First, on 5 April 1861, during his fifth expedition, John McDouall Stuart wrote:[128]

> About five miles back we passed a freshly-built worley [wurley].[129] I observed a peculiarity in it which I never noticed in any before – namely, that it was constructed with greater care than usual. It was thatched with grass down to the ground. Inside

the worley there was a quantity of grass laid regularly for a bed, on which some one had been lying. Round about the front was collected a large quantity of firewood, as much as would have done us for a night. Lat., 22° 5' 30" bearing to Central Mount Stuart, 25°.

It is difficult to avoid the speculation that this wurley had been built and used by a European. Perhaps it had been built for John McDouall Stuart? Perhaps it had been built and used by one of Leichhardt's companions after he had separated from the main party? Even stranger was McDouall Stuart's note that, during his fourth expedition, one of the Aborigines had made a Masonic sign. He wrote:[130]

One was an old man, and seemed to be the father of these two fine young men. He was very talkative, but I could make nothing of him. I have endeavoured, by signs, to get information from him as to where the next water is, but we cannot understand each other. After some time, and having conferred with his two sons, he turned round, and surprised me by giving me one of his Masonic signs. I looked at him steadily; he repeated it, and so did his two sons. I then returned it, which seemed to please them much, the old man patting me on the shoulder and stroking down my beard.

Someone must have taught the old man how to give the Masonic sign – who else but a member of the Leichhardt expedition? It is sometimes claimed that Leichhardt himself was a Freemason; but this is extremely doubtful. Some members of his family back home in Prussia were Freemasons, and evidently tried to persuade him to become a member 'but although Leichhardt writes airily several times about freemasonry as practised in England, France and Germany, no evidence has come to light to prove that he ever saw a degree conferred in any lodge or was ever initiated – although both are possible.'[131] Nevertheless he must have learnt about freemasonry from his family. By the same token, August Classen, who was a brother of Hermann Leichhardt's wife Doris, might also

have learnt about freemasonry from Leichhardt's family, and might even have become a Freemason. This is speculation, but Classen might well have been the man who taught the old Aboriginal man how to make a Masonic sign.[132]

John McDouall Stuart, in August 1861, when at Sturt Plains, recorded:[133]

A short time before we arrived a number of natives were observed following at a distance behind the rear of the party. They followed us on to our old camp ... They were seventeen in number; four of them were boys, one of them much lighter than the others, nearly a light yellow.

It seems likely that this boy was a half-caste – the result of a union between a White man (possibly a member of the Leichhardt expedition) and an Aboriginal woman. If this did occur, the Aboriginal boy with the light skin would have been twelve years old.

Another aspect of the saga was outlined by Andrew Hume in 1866. Hume had spent many years in outback Australia and had acquired an intimate knowledge of the Aboriginal people who lived in areas far from European settlement. He later claimed that, on his travels, he had come across a White man, August Classen, who was living with an Aboriginal tribe. According to his own account, Hume decided to ride to Sydney to report to the authorities that he had found a survivor of the Leichhardt expedition – together with some relics and journals. However, when he reached Baradine, in north-western New South Wales, in company with a man named John Smith, he apparently took part, while in a drunken condition, in a robbery under arms. Both men were arrested and came before Judge Cary in June 1866. Hume vigorously denied the charge, but both men were found guilty. Hume was sentenced to ten years with hard labour; Smith's sentence was for three years. Both went to jail. For several years Hume remained silent about his claim to have seen and talked with a survivor, Classen, of the Leichhardt expedition. He later explained that he had remained silent because the authorities would think that he had invented the story to enhance his chances of gaining his release from prison.

During his years in prison he learnt to read and write to a limited extent and, eventually, he decided to tell his story about the White man who was living with a tribe of Aboriginal people. His story seems to have been accepted by some – notably by the Rev. John Dunmore Lang, the Presbyterian minister and social worker. A Committee of Inquiry was formed to question Hume and, after close examination, it decided to recommend the release of the prisoner to enable him to carry out a search for the survivor. He was released on 31 October 1871.

A few weeks later Hume sailed from Newcastle to Darwin to begin his search for the lone survivor. As Perrin has pointed out:[134]

> There was still much doubt about the truth of his story, but public opinion was such that neither Government [New South Wales and South Australia – which included what is now the Northern Territory] wanted to be held responsible for not giving him the chance to solve the Leichhardt mystery.

Hume arrived back in Sydney on 18 February 1874 and went to the minister of Lands to hand over the relics – but he had to report that, when checking his luggage that morning, he had found that all the relics had been stolen! Notwithstanding this, private citizens were willing to support a further expedition to find the wild White man again. This new expedition included Lewis Thompson, Timothy O'Hea, VC, and Hume. They set off but, within a few days, they were in great distress from lack of water. Hume died and was later buried by a search party. O'Hea was also presumed dead, but his body has never been found. Thompson survived. This was not the end, however. There were repeated attempts by others – notably von Mueller – to determine the fate of Leichhardt. But all failed.

LEICHHARDT THE MAN

There is no doubt that Leichhardt was an unusual, but scholarly, man, and a very unusual explorer. He had a passion to learn – to understand the reasons for geological formations, and to understand the variations in plants and animals. He did not want to learn from books or articles – he wanted to learn and to understand from his own observations. He seems to have had no desire for financial rewards – he sought money only to finance his studies of the environment, and his explorations. He did not carry out his obligation to undertake a period of military service – he thought his scientific work and his explorations would be of greater service to humanity and, in due course, the King of Prussia 'forgave' him for his failure to carry out military service.

When Leichhardt returned to Sydney after his successful expedition to Port Essington, he was dubbed the 'Prince of Explorers'. His success in leading this expedition was regarded as almost a miracle. He had conquered all the difficulties, he had established good relations with the Aboriginal people – with one notable exception (which was probably due to his inadvertent selection of a camp site which had special significance for the local people). The failure of his second expedition came as a shock, but it was due to serious sickness – probably dengue fever – among his companions. Although he could not cure the dengue fever in his men he will always be regarded as one of the explorers who conquered scurvy. At that time vitamins were unknown, but Leichhardt (during his first expedition) made a point of collecting, and eating, and persuading his men to eat, wild fruit and any wild plants that seemed to resemble a vegetable.

Leichhardt was not a skilled surveyor – as Mitchell was. His instruments were never of high quality. He did make the observations necessary for the determination of latitude, but most of his longitudes were determined from his estimates for distance travelled in a given direction. Mitchell was clearly the most scientific navigator and surveyor of all the early overland explorers.

Leichhardt always seemed to assume that everyone was as keen as he was himself to undergo hardship to carry out the exploration. His selection of his companions left something to be desired. The failure of his second expedition was undoubtedly due to the lack of fortitude among some of his companions – and he had chosen the men himself! He could not endure the foul language of some of his companions – but was generally willing to forgive. In September 1846 Leichhardt wrote to John Roper (who had been with him on his first expedition):[135]

> You know well Mr Roper how little satisfied I was with your behaviour and you will remember that I expressed even two days before arriving at Pt Essington my ardent wish, not so much of being at the end of my journey, as being rid of companions who did take so little trouble to please.

He went on to write:

> Every one will be ready to make a fair allowance for the trying circumstances under which you were placed, even more so than I myself who is still involuntarily labouring under disagreeable recollections, which I shall however never allow to interfere with my best wishes for your welfare (and to farther your views).

Through his endeavours Leichhardt opened up huge areas of the interior and north of Australia. The disappearance of the explorer and his companions stimulated search parties which added further to our knowledge of the continent and remains the most intriguing unsolved mystery in the history of Australian exploration.

16

TRIUMPH AND DISASTER – THE BURKE AND WILLS EXPEDITION

In May 1835 John Batman, a resident of Van Diemen's Land, with a few companions – three servants and seven Aborigines – explored the country to the west and north of Port Phillip Bay on the southern coast of the colony of New South Wales. However, Batman was not the first European to visit this area. It had been visited by Charles Grimes – the surveyor-general of New South Wales – thirty years before, and he had discovered the Yarra River. Batman decided that the land adjacent to the River would 'be the place for a village'. Shortly afterwards, John Pascoe Fawkner, also from Van Diemen's Land, likewise decided to establish a settlement there – and did so. Batman and his associates in the 'Port Phillip Association' began to establish the 'village' soon afterwards.

The governor of New South Wales, Sir Richard Bourke, visited the settlement in 1837 and it was named Melbourne – after the British prime minister of the day. Within a few years Melbourne became a thriving, if small, township, and land for hundreds of kilometres was being explored for agricultural and other purposes. By the mid century there were six million sheep in what was at first called the 'Port Phillip District'. The district had a population of about 80 000 persons – 40 000 of whom lived in Melbourne. In July 1851 the Port Phillip District became the Colony of Victoria. That year was made even more notable by the discovery of gold in the colony and, before the end of that year, the Bendigo

field alone was producing gold to the value of about £200 000 every week. Gold had also been found at other sites – including Clunes, Ballarat, Castlemaine and other districts – and, in 1856, the annual production of gold exceeded three million ounces.

The discovery of gold triggered a massive increase in the number of immigrants and in the prosperity of the new colony. The increase in confidence was immediate. The planning for a substantial building for the Victorian parliament began in 1854, and the foundation stone was laid in 1856. The foundation stones for the State Library of Victoria, and for the University of Melbourne, were laid on the same day – 4 July 1854. Most of the immigrants were men and women hoping to earn enough money to improve their living standards, but many professionally qualified people arrived at this time and made important contributions to the intellectual life of the colony. Learned societies were established. The Philosophical Institute of Victoria, for example – a society for the study of scientific and related matters – was established in Melbourne in 1855, and many of the most prominent citizens became members.

In November 1857 the Philosophical Institute decided to establish an Exploration Committee, with thirty-two members, to consider what should be done to promote the scientific exploration of Australia, and to study the fauna and flora, the geology, and other scientific matters. Ferdinand von Mueller, one of Australia's most distinguished nineteenth-century botanists, had served under Gregory on the northern Australian expedition in 1855–56, and was a member of the institute's Exploration Committee. Another member, Wilhelm Blandowski, a Pole, was an ardent naturalist who had been on an expedition to the junction of the Murray and Darling rivers – but the other members had little knowledge or understanding of exploration.

The Philosophical Institute obtained a royal charter in 1859 and became the 'Royal Society of Victoria'. The Exploration Committee was reconstituted – this time with only seventeen members. Mueller was still a member, but Blandowski had returned to Germany. Another German-born scientist, Professor Georg von Neumayer, a recent arrival, was now a member.[1] The Exploration Committee, and the Royal Society itself, decided that it would send a team of explorers from Melbourne to the northern coast of Australia and, in particular, to the Gulf of Carpentaria. Their ambitions had been greatly influenced by the writings of the distinguished German scientist and philosopher, Alexander von Humboldt. It was to be a scientific expedition and it was expected that many specimens of the fauna and flora would be collected and preserved for study by scientists in Melbourne. The geological formations would be studied. Meteorological, magnetic and astronomical observations would be taken. Possible practical applications would not be ignored. Good agricultural land was always in demand – but there were other possible practical applications. After all, European scientists were finding plants useful in treating a wide range of human ailments, and the Australian plants deserved detailed study from this point of view.

Nevertheless, the emphasis of the proposed expeditions were not clear or agreed. Some wanted the society to concentrate on the advancement of science. Others were mainly interested in the possibility of discoveries with practical applications. There were also many who believed that Victoria should be seen to be exploring the continent for the benefit of all. Mueller held this view, but he was also anxious, as were many others, to find some solution to the unknown fate of that 'prince of explorers' – Ludwig Leichhardt.[2] Uppermost in many minds, however, was the desire to see a Victorian expedition as the first to cross the continent from south to north.

Money was a problem, of course. In 1857 there had been an anonymous donation of £1000 to assist exploration – but additional donations were few and far between. The Victorian government eventually decided to provide some financial support – but wanted the society's Exploration Committee to undertake the management of the proposed 'Victorian Exploring Expedition'. The Exploration Committee would have to choose the man to lead the expedition, choose all the other members, choose and purchase the foodstuffs and equipment to be taken, and decide how this mass of stores was to be transported. The Exploration Committee, and the society, would also be responsible for choosing the route to be followed by the explorers.

At an early stage Ludwig Becker, a member of the Royal Society of Victoria, but not a member of the Exploration Committee, suggested that a number of camels be imported to facilitate travel in the arid areas through which the explorers would have to travel.[3] Mueller was opposed to the use of camels because it was thought that the route to be taken by the explorers would involve stony ground – at least in some areas – and camels would not be ideal. Augustus Gregory supported this view. Nevertheless the suggestion that camels be imported for the use of the expedition was accepted by the government. George Landells was commissioned to select and purchase two dozen camels during his proposed visit to India; and this he did. These camels became an important part of the expedition;

but they caused many problems.[4] It has often been suggested that these were the first camels to be brought to Australia, but John Horrocks had used a camel in an expedition to the north of Port Augusta, in South Australia, in 1846.[5] This camel had arrived at Port Adelaide in October 1840. Horrocks was fatally shot during his expedition – when his camel lurched while he was loading his gun.[6]

Ludwig Becker was an interesting man. He was another immigrant, and another scholar of distinction. He had visited Tasmania, and had called on the governor, Sir William Denison, in 1851. Some years later Denison wrote his memoirs, and described Becker as having a large red beard. Moreover, he added:[7]

> He is a most amusing person, talks English badly, but very energetically. I have sometimes great difficulty in keeping my countenance when I see him struggling between the rapidity of his ideas and the difficulty of giving them utterance, repeating to himself in a very audible soliloquy, the German words he wishes to translate into English, and helping all out with an abundance of most expressive gesticulation ... He is one of those universal geniuses who can do anything; is a very good naturalist, geologist, &c., draws and plays and sings, conjures and ventriloquises, and imitates the notes of birds so accurately that the wild birds will come to him at the sound of the call.

The next step in organising the expedition was to select the men who would take part and, most importantly, to select the leader. The position of leader was advertised and Robert O'Hara Burke was chosen by the Exploration Committee. The decision was not unanimous, however. Mueller had advised the committee that the man to lead the expedition should have had some experience in areas distant from European habitation, and Burke had not had any such experience. Mueller knew the importance of such background experience; but the committee ignored his advice and Mueller resigned from the committee. It has sometimes been said that 'a camel is a horse designed by a committee'. Many of the actions and decisions of the Exploration Committee would seem to be in the horse–camel category.

Burke had been born in Ireland in 1820 and, in 1840, had joined the Austrian Army as a cadet. He was commissioned two years later. During this time he became a fluent speaker in German. He resigned his commission in 1848 and became an officer in the Irish police force. A couple of years later he emigrated to Melbourne where he accepted a position with the Victorian police. In 1860, when he applied for the position of leader of the proposed expedition, he was the senior police officer in Castlemaine. There is no doubt that Burke had a taste for adventure – and even glory. His younger brother, a British army officer, had been killed after an heroic struggle in the Crimean War. Burke was moved by 'the glory of his death',[8] and it has sometimes been suggested that Burke sought 'glory or death'.

Burke certainly had charm. However, he had 'no practice whatever as a bushman, never having camped in the bush, and never been in any part of Australia where there are no roads'. He could not 'construct a map of his course', he was 'altogether ignorant of the physical sciences', his literary ability was 'so small that he could not write an intelligent account of the journey', and he was unable to 'take even the sun's elevation to find his latitude'.[9] Moreover, he failed to learn how to determine latitude and longitude in the time available before the expedition began its journey.

The Exploration Committee chose George Landells to be in charge of the camels and to be second-in-charge of the expedition under Burke. Landells certainly knew more about camels than anyone else in Melbourne, but 'he had spent less than two years in Australia' and 'was even less familiar with the bush than Burke and similarly incapable of determining latitude and longitude'.[10]

William John Wills was appointed third-in-charge and 'Surveyor and Astronomical Observer'.

William John Wills (Illustrated London news, February 1862; National Library of Australia)

Wills had been born in Devonshire, England, in January 1834, and had attended a school at Ashburton before becoming articled to his father, who was a surgeon. In 1852, however, he emigrated to Australia and, initially, obtained employment on a sheep station. He later moved to Ballarat, a thriving gold-mining town, where his father had established a medical practice. It was here that Wills began to learn surveying and, by 1857, he was ordering surveying and navigational instruments, and copies of the *Nautical Almanac*, from London, for his own use.[11]

Wills became fascinated with scientific work and, in November 1858, he went to Melbourne to work with Georg Balthaser von Neumayer – who had come to Melbourne in January 1857 to undertake a magnetic survey of Victoria. Neumayer was of German birth and, indeed, many of his instruments had been purchased for him by the King of Bavaria. Wills accepted Neumayer as his mentor and quickly became skilled at astronomical, magnetic and meteorological observations. It was Neumayer (who was a member of the Exploration Committee) who recommended Wills for the position of 'Surveyor and Astronomical Observer' with the expedition.

The Exploration Committee set out instructions for all the senior members of the expedition. The surveyor and astronomical observer was required to fix the position of mountains and the junctions of rivers by astronomical observation, as well as by dead reckoning. The longitude was to be determined by the method of lunar distances and, whenever possible, by occultation of stars, and by eclipses of the Sun, Moon, and of Jupiter's satellites. The variation of the magnetic compass – that is, the angle between true north and magnetic north – was also to be determined 'as often as circumstances permit'.[12] Wills was competent to carry out these instructions – but it was a lot to expect of one observer travelling in some discomfort for many kilometres a day.

Two other 'officers' were appointed. Ludwig Becker was appointed as 'Artist, Naturalist and Geologist'. The other was Hermann Beckler, who was appointed 'Medical Officer and Botanist'. Beckler later wrote an account (in German) of the expedition as he saw it and this has, only recently, been translated into English and published.[13] The five 'officers' were all addressed as 'Mister'.

The Exploration Committee also appointed a foreman, Charles Ferguson – an American-born man with a knowledge of gold and of horses. He had spent two years on the Californian goldfields and had come to Victoria to seek his fortune from gold. He does not seem to have been regarded as an 'officer'. His salary was fixed at £200 a year – compared with £300 a year for Wills, Becker and Beckler. The assistant foreman, Thomas McDonough, was to receive £120 a year.[14] Apart from the five 'officers', the foreman and assistant foreman, there were twelve men. These included four who had arrived from India with the camels and were engaged for their knowledge of camel-handling. Several of the original twelve were discharged fairly early in the expedition – some at their own request. One of the Indians, for example, was a Hindu and could not eat meat other than mutton. The other three Indians were Muslims.

It was an enormous task to select and purchase the various foodstuffs and other items required for the expedition, and then to decide how to pack and transport it. Major items of foodstuffs included 270 kilograms (600 pounds) of salt pork, 180 kilograms (400 pounds) of bacon and 90 kilograms (400 pounds) of pemmican (a preparation of dried meat that had been pulverised and then mixed with melted fat).[15] Mueller had advised against the use of pemmican, but his advice had been ignored. As a matter of fact Mueller had recommended that 'a small flock of sheep might be purchased on the Darling and driven to the Depot on Cooper's Creek' but this suggestion had not been accepted by the Exploration Committee.[16] The foodstuffs included flour, rice, sugar, tea and coffee. Attention was also given to the possibility that members of the expedition, having no access to fresh fruit and vegetables, might contract scurvy. It was now known, however, that citrus juice would prevent and cure scurvy, and a quantity of lime juice – 75 litres (20 gallons), that cost £4 – was included among the foodstuffs to be carried. Even so, scurvy was a very mysterious disease. Hermann Beckler had seen examples of scurvy in Germany and wrote in his account of the expedition that it '... was well known that that most feared guest on such trips, scurvy, could be held off for a long time, if not for ever, by the frequent consumption of fresh meat'.[17] True or false, this was not likely to help. Members of the expedition would be unable to enjoy 'the frequent consumption of fresh meat'.

The general stores included blankets, socks and boots. There were nineteen revolvers, ten double-barrelled guns and eight rifles. Two hundred fish-hooks were included, and 227 litres (60 gallons) of rum (for the camels), 15 litres (4 gallons) of brandy (for medicinal purposes), and 113 kilograms (250 pounds) of tobacco. The rum was supposed (erroneously) to prevent the camels getting scurvy. It was also decided to include about a kilogram (two pounds) of beads – at a shilling a pound – for presents to 'the natives', and four dozen mirrors ('looking glasses') for the same purpose. Some of these items were relatively inexpensive; but the instruments for use by the 'Surveyer and Astronomical Observer' cost just under £133. The 'chronometer-watch', for the same purpose, cost £42. Books, presumably the *Nautical Almanac*, and other navigational tables, cost just under £1.[18]

It seems that the Exploration Committee purchased every item which someone or other suggested 'might come in useful'. The stores grew and grew, and it was not long before it was recognised that the transport of this mass of foodstuffs and other stores would cause serious problems. The camels and horses would be able to carry some, but it was decided to use a number of wagons – including a couple of large American wagons. Mueller had also advised against the use of wagons on the grounds that they would be difficult to move in sandy country. He was right. The wagons were to prove very impracticable. The camels also caused serious problems and, as Tipping has remarked: 'Becker was certainly to regret that he had ever thought of them and that the Society had recommended them.'[19]

The route to be followed by the expedition was determined by the Exploration Committee. The explorers were instructed to proceed:[20]

Across the country by the most direct route to Cooper's Creek, in lat. 27° 37' 8" S, long. 141° 5' E, where the party would be on the verge of the unexplored country, and on a spot where permanent water could be had, and a depot formed, whence excursions could be made to the north or north-west as might be deemed desirable, and upon which the party could at any time fall back for supplies in case of necessity.

On 18 August 1860, the society held its last meeting before the departure of the expedition – with Dr Richard Eades, vice-president, in the chair (the president being Sir Henry Barkly, the governor of Victoria). Dr Eades, who was also the mayor of Melbourne, 'bid the party God speed, and after a short speech, passed round the party, shaking each man heartily by the hand and wishing him a prosperous journey'.[21] The German influence on the expedition was considerable and Melbourne's 'Deutscher Verein' also hosted a reception for the officers immediately before the departure. Ferdinand von Mueller had played a considerable part in reaching the decision to mount the expedition. Professor Georg von Neumayer had likewise played an important part, and he was later to join the expedition for a brief period. Burke spoke fluent German, and Beckler and Becker were immigrants from Germany. Alexander von Humboldt and the King of Bavaria must surely have been present in spirit.

The expedition was mustered in Melbourne's Royal Park and was scheduled to depart on Monday 20 August 1860 at 1 p.m. However, the loading was not complete by that time – partly because of the many thousands of people who had gathered in the park to witness the departure, examine the camels, and give their farewell good wishes to the explorers. Many of the leading citizens, including the mayor, were there. When, at last, the expedition set off at 4 p.m., it was led by Burke on horseback with Landells close at hand riding a camel. Becker, the artist, was also riding a camel. The scene was recorded on canvas by Nicholas Chevalier, and in a

The start of the exploring expedition, Nicholas Chevalier; Burke, on horseback, leads the expedition out of Royal Park, followed by Landells, the central dominant figure in the picture, on his camel; Becker is at left, also on a camel; Richard Eades, in front of the crowd at right, waves his hat in farewell to Burke. (M. J. M. Carter Collection, Art Gallery of South Australia)

watercolour by William Strutt. The expedition made its first camp at Essendon, then a village, now a suburb of Melbourne, where it was possible to achieve some sort of order out of the apparent chaos.[22]

From Essendon, Burke led the expedition northwards and, on 29 August 1860, crossed the Terrick-Terrick plains (to the north of present-day Bendigo). The method of crossing was recorded by Ludwig Becker in a watercolour and pen-and-ink sketch. It shows Burke on horseback, with a line of camels (headed by Landells, followed by Becker himself) on his right, and a line of horses and a wagon on his left. Then, as later, it was found necessary to separate the camels from the horses.[23] In this way they made an average of about 16 kilometres (10 miles) a day, and arrived at Swan Hill – then a village with twelve buildings – on 8 September, but it was three days before all the

wagons arrived.[24] Burke realised that, before long, he would need to reduce the quantity of stores if they were to make satisfactory progress. He discarded some ironware here.

Professor Neumayer arrived at Swan Hill to join the expedition on the understanding that he would continue only as far as the Darling River and then return to Melbourne. Some members of the expedition were discharged by Burke at Swan Hill, and others were engaged. These were: Alexander MacPherson, a saddler; Charles Gray, a Scot who was a good bushman; Robert Bowman, who had had experience of exploration with Gregory; and William Hodgkinson, a man who was already known to Burke. There was still no assistant surveyor to support Wills and, if Wills were to die, the expedition might quickly become lost. Moreover only two Indians remained to look after the camels – Dost Mahomet and Belooch.[25] Burke obtained some local advice at Swan Hill on the best route to follow to the north. This involved making for Balranald (on the Murrumbidgee River) and then for Menindee on the Darling River – about 160 kilometres (100 miles) to the north of the junction of the Darling and Murray rivers. The expedition accordingly left Swan Hill on 12 September and, three days later, arrived at Balranald. The problems with the wagons had become increasingly more serious, and there was now no doubt that Mueller had been correct in advising against their use. As Beckler wrote in his journal:[26]

Mr Burke felt only too strongly the burden of travelling with hired wagons. He wanted very much to rid himself of some of them, that is he wanted to leave a part of our extensive and diverse equipment behind because the further inland we came the more dispensable some of the articles seemed.

Beckler's further comment explained the problem in more detail:[27]

The horses were required to draw their wagons not only through wild desert and through deep, loose sand and pathless mallee scrub; they were also required to draw them through land where there was no water.

The expedition arrived at Balranald on 15 and 16 September and, by this time, Burke was under considerable stress. He had to abide by the decisions made by the Exploration Committee back in Melbourne, but he became more and more frustrated by their slow progress – and by the number of personality clashes. He had little time for either Becker or Beckler; and they disliked him. Burke was irritated by Landells who, in addition to being deputy leader, was in charge of the camels – and the camels were far more trouble than Burke had ever expected. He had difficulties with the foreman, Charles Ferguson, and he dismissed him. He also dismissed two more men. Burke also decided to abandon a considerable quantity of heavy

equipment – some rifles and revolvers, and even some foodstuffs, including some of the sugar and rice and all of the lime juice.[28]

The disputes continued during the journey from Balranald to Menindee, and the wagons continued to be a great hindrance. The camels were causing many problems, as usual. There were also problems regarding the drinking water. Wills recorded in his 'Field Notes':[29]

Mr Burke decided on camping here and going to the Darling tomorrow, said to be distant 30 miles. There is very good feed here for the Cattle but the water is not at all good it both looks and tastes very like what one would suppose would be the taste of chalk and water with a little ink in it.

Burke was always looking for ways to reduce the stores and hence improve their rate of progress. He was especially angry at having to transport the 270 litres (60 gallons) of rum for the use of the camels, and proposed to abandon it – against the advice of Landells. The difficulties between Burke and his deputy leader became so great that Landells resigned, and Beckler resigned in sympathy with Landells.[30] Fortunately, the two Indian camel-drivers, Dost Mahomet and Belooch, remained with the expedition and did not resign with Landells. Soon afterwards, John Drakeford (the cook), was discharged having been found drunk. It was not a happy situation. As Bonyhady has pointed out, after only eight weeks, Burke had lost two of his four officers, four of his nine men and two of his camel-drivers.[31]

Burke arrived at Menindee on 15 October 1860, and it was here that Neumayer left (as originally planned) to return to Melbourne. He had become convinced that it would be impossible for the expedition to carry out the magnetic observations he sought – and he carried the instruments for this purpose back to Melbourne.

Burke now decided to divide the expedition. He would leave a back-up or supply party on the Darling. An advance party would then proceed as

River Darling and the mouth of Pamamaroo Creek; Ludwig Becker. (*La Trobe Collection*, State Library of Victoria)

rapidly as possible to Cooper's Creek, where the Exploration Committee had decided a depot should be established – prior to the trek to the Gulf of Carpentaria. In order to facilitate this, Burke engaged William Wright at Menindee. Wright had served for a time as manager of the nearby Kinchega station, and he had travelled some distance towards Cooper's Creek on an earlier occasion. His knowledge of the country would be invaluable.

The advance party consisted of Burke, Wills and Wright – with William Brahé, William Patten, John King, Charles Gray, Thomas McDonough and Dost Mahomet. The remaining members of the expedition were to establish a depot a few kilometres from Menindee at the junction of the Darling River and Pamamaroo Creek. Burke asked Beckler to remain and to take charge of this depot, and he agreed. Those remaining at the Darling–Pamamaroo depot were Beckler, Becker, Hodgkinson, MacPherson and Belooch.[32]

Burke and the other members of the advance party, and 'two blacks from here' left Menindee on 19 October 1860, with nineteen horses and sixteen camels, 'leaving behind 9 camels and 3 horses with the stores in charge of Dr Beckler'.[33] The weather was good and there was plenty of grass for the animals so they made excellent progress. Burke was very satisfied with Wright and, when they reached Torowotto Swamp he asked him to return to the Darling and to take charge of the camp there and relieve Beckler.[34] He also asked him to send the saddler, MacPherson, to join the advance party. Wright set off and Burke continued towards Cooper's Creek. It took twenty-three days for Burke to reach Cooper's Creek, and a further few days to select a suitable site for the depot, Camp 65.[35]

Wright arrived back at the depot on the Darling and, within a short time, he arranged for Mac-Pherson to set off, accompanied by a trooper named Lyons (who had arrived from Melbourne with dispatches) and a young Aboriginal man named

Cooper Creek at Innamincka. (Geoffrey Badger)

Dick (Mountain) as a guide. It appears that Dick was a member of the Barkindji tribe, and that he was an employee of Wright.[36] The three men, with four horses, left the Darling depot on 10 November. They had completed a significant part of their journey to join Burke when they lost the tracks of the advance party. The country had now become very dry and there was a serious shortage of water. It was not long before they were suffering from severe dehydration, and three of the horses died. In desperation, Dick, with the one surviving horse, set off to return to the Darling depot to seek help. The sole surviving horse also died and Dick had to continue on foot for eight more days. He arrived at the depot on 19 December in great distress:[37]

> His previously full face was sunken, his tottering legs could hardly carry him, his feet were raw, his voice was hoarse and whispering. He was a shadow of a man.

Clearly, as Beckler states, 'there was no time to lose in coming to the aid of our companions stranded in the wilderness'.[38] He immediately offered to set out to rescue them in company with the Indian, Belooch, and Peter, a young Aboriginal man who had been briefed by Dick (who was too sick to travel). They set off with three camels and a horse. This was on 21 December. On 27 December Beckler and his two companions found Mac-Pherson and Lyons. About MacPherson, Beckler wrote:[39]

> This man had left our camp on the Darling seven weeks before in the most blooming health, well built and with exuberant strength. He was now shrunken to a skeleton and a picture of total despair. His eyes were hollow ... His voice was broken and scarcely audible.

Lyons was not so affected 'but by his own confession was more depressed'.

Portrait of Dick, the brave and gallant native guide; Ludwig Becker. (*La Trobe Collection*, State Library of Victoria)

They had survived only because the local Aboriginal people had introduced them to nardoo, *Marsilea drummondii*, and taught them how to prepare it. However, as MacPherson explained, 'the new rough fare affected our intestines and we both became ill with diarrhoea.' Nevertheless 'we now live in the firm conviction that without this providential nourishment that party would never have found us alive.'[40]

The two men, and the three men of the rescue party, began their return journey to Menindee on 28 December. Beckler was enchanted with the countryside now that his colleagues had been found alive. On the next day he took an opportunity to make a side trip to the nearby Goningberri Mountains. He wrote:[41]

I myself was the only person from the entire expedition party, the only European ever to have had the good fortune to see and admire this small paradise which still slumbered in the state in which it had been created. Even from a distance its pleasing contours drew our eyes to it, and its noticeably pink colouring made it yet more eye-catching.

On the following day he was equally excited with the countryside and its flora:[42]

It is no exaggeration at all to say that during this afternoon and on the following morning I collected a much larger number of prettier, more interesting plants with flowers or fruits or both (a number of which were new) than would be possible in the next two months of our expedition. On the smaller rises that lay to the south between the plain and the main peaks of the range I found nearly all of the various acacias and cassias that I had found to date on our journey from the Darling.

Beckler, Belooch and Peter – with MacPherson and Lyons – reached the supply depot near Menindee safely, after midnight on 4 January 1861.

THE DASH TO THE GULF

Burke established the expedition's depot at Cooper's Creek – as required by the Exploration Committee – on 20 November 1860. MacPherson, the saddler, had not joined him and Burke had no knowledge of his whereabouts. No message from Wright had been received. Burke was anxious to proceed to the north as quickly as possible because he desperately wanted to be the leader of the first successful crossing of the continent from south to north. He did not want to wait any longer. He decided to divide his party yet again and, with a small group, he was to set off for the Gulf of Carpentaria. The party to go to the gulf would be Burke, Wills, Gray ('Charley') and King. Brahé could not be included. He had to 'remain behind as he was the only member of the advance party, other than Wills, who could travel by compass and hence

could, if necessary, lead the other three men back to Menindee'.[43] Those to remain at Cooper's Creek would therefore be Brahé, McDonough, Patten and Dost Mahomet. Brahé was promoted to officer rank and was to be 'in charge' at the depot.

Burke and his three colleagues, with six camels and a horse, loaded with three months' provisions, left the Cooper's Creek depot at forty minutes past six in the morning of 16 December 1860. Burke had instructed Brahé to remain at the Cooper's Creek depot for 'three months and longer if he could', and Wills had suggested that he remain there for four months if possible.[44] Nevertheless, Wills subsequently wrote that 'the party we left here had special instructions not to leave until our return unless from absolute necessity.'[45]

It was summer, and it was hot. The temperature in the middle of the day was often over 37.8 degrees Celsius (100 degrees Fahrenheit) and, on most days,

Georgina River floodplain, Bedourie, south-west Queensland. This landscape devoid of shade or fuel is typical of the country through which the Burke and Wills party passed on their journey to the Gulf and back. (C. R. Twidale)

the party started at about 5 a.m. or even earlier. Preliminary excursions from Cooper's Creek had suggested that water would be hard to find and Burke had made arrangements for the horse, each camel, and each man, to carry as much water as possible. In the event the availability of water, at this time of the year, was not a serious problem because there had been some good rains. Burke had also expected that they might meet groups of hostile Aborigines – but this was not a serious problem either. In fact, they were too friendly. Wills recorded that 'a large tribe of blacks came pestering us to go to their camp to have a dance, which we declined.'[46]

Most of the provisions were carried by the horses and the camels, and the four men therefore had to walk. Burke thought that it would be possible to supplement their food supplies by shooting birds and indigenous animals, and by killing one or more of the camels if this became necessary. They travelled via the Stony Desert and the Diamantina River, and then northwards – thereby avoiding the Simpson Desert. Wills took pains to write up his journal, and this provides the most detailed account of their progress to the gulf. On the evening of 19 December they came to a creek 'which looked so well that we followed it for a short distance, and finding two or three waterholes of good milky water, we camped for the night'.[47] Wills took an opportunity to determine the latitude, using the reflection in the water as the artificial horizon – but he added that it is more satisfactory to use mercury as the artificial horizon. He also determined the longitude by an observation of an eclipse of Jupiter's satellite Io.

On 24 December they had a day of rest to celebrate Christmas but, on the morning of Christmas Day, they left their camp at half past four to continue their journey. A couple of weeks later there was a tremendous gale that prevented Wills from determining the latitude. However:[48]

My reckoning cannot be far out … I found on taking out my instruments one of my spare thermo-meters was broken, and the glass of my aneroid barometer cracked – the latter, I believe, not otherwise injured. This was done by the camel having taken it into its head to roll while the pack was on his back.

Early in February, while still some distance from the coast, they reached the Flinders River – which flows into the Gulf of Carpentaria. The water was saline and tidal – so the coast could not be far away. Taking the horse, Burke and Wills set out to try to reach the coast – leaving Gray and King with the camels. They did approach the coast, but were defeated by the mangroves and the mud. A sight of the coast was denied them. Burke did not keep an extensive diary or journal but, some weeks later, on 28 March 1861, he wrote: 'At the conclusion of report, it would be well to say that we reached the sea, but that we could not obtain a view of the open ocean, although we made every endeavour to do so.'[49] In this context it might be noted that, following the disastrous conclusion of the expedition, Dr William Wills, the father of William John Wills, published an account with the title: *A Successful Exploration through the Interior of Australia.*[50] He had good reason to be proud of his son. Without his navigational skills they would never have made it.

To carry out his determinations of latitude and longitude, Wills had an 18 centimetre (seven-inch) sextant that had been made in Hamburg, and thoroughly tested in Professor Neumayer's Flagstaff Laboratory. Wills also had three chronometers – or 'watches' as he called them – for the use in the determination of longitude. Two had been manufactured by Murray. The first, numbered 5094, was rated as 'very good' by Wills; the second, numbered 5243, was rated as 'a good watch but not equal to the former'. The third was 'of an inferior quality by Russell and has been used as a hack watch sometimes but is only fit for rough determinations'.[51]

Some time later, the government astronomer

(Ellery) prepared a commentary on the observations that had been made by Wills:[52]

> These observations consist of a series of sextant measures for latitude, chronometer errors and Lunar Distances [for the determination of longitude] with two observations of Jupiter's satellites [for longitude]. The latitudes I think were all computed by himself for the positions of the camps as laid down on his chart correspond very closely in that respect with those that have been since computed from his observations. But as regards his longitude, his chart positions I believe to be 'by account' or dead reckoning. As [to] the longitude at which the Expedition reached the northern part of the Continent is a matter of considerable interest and importance, the few observations available for the determination have been rigorously computed, more especially as although the[y] appear to have been made with every care possible, their results differ from the plotted track at the northern portion of the journey and appear somewhat anomalous ...

Ellery gives the latitude of the northernmost camp (CXIX) as 17° 53' 38" S, with no longitude observation.

It had taken them two months of hard travelling to reach the gulf, and men and animals alike were very weary. They were now faced with a return journey to Cooper's Creek. Three-quarters of the provisions with which they had departed from Cooper's Creek had already been consumed. As Bergin summarised the situation, they:[53]

> ... had only twenty-seven days' provisions left and had taken fifty-seven days to reach the Gulf. One camel was already lost and the others were 'leg weary' and in need of rest, and on top of it all they were caught in the wet on the black soil plains.

It should be remembered that, in the tropical north of Australia, there are only two seasons – the 'wet' in the summer, and the 'dry' in the remainder of the year. As far as Burke and Wills were concerned it was not only wet, but hot.

They made slow progress over the next few days, largely due to the wet conditions – in which camels

are gravely disadvantaged. The explorers began to eat the stems of portulaca (pigweed, *Portulacae oleracea*) – a food used by the Aborigines as a substitute for European-style 'greens'.[54] This was found to be a useful addition to their diet. Indeed, Wills wrote: 'I am inclined to think that but for the abundance of portulac that we obtained on our journey, we should scarcely have returned to Cooper's Creek at all'.[55]

Nevertheless they all became weaker and weaker as their rations diminished. Burke decided to eat a snake that they had killed, and he became very unwell. He developed dysentery and 'felt giddy and unable to keep his seat'.[56] On 20 March, to lighten their loads, they abandoned nearly 27 kilograms (sixty pounds) of their equipment.[57] King later told the Burke and Wills Commission that Wills 'buried his instruments where we left the last camel' – about fourteen days before reaching Cooper's Creek.[58] In fact, Wills wrote in his notebook, immediately after the entry for 3 April:[59]

> Another of the camels having given up today and been left on the road or rather on the plain, order has been given for leaving everything behind but the grub and just what we carry on our backs, so the instruments being planted no more observations can be made.

Wills later recorded that the only instruments he had left were his watch, the prismatic compass, the pocket compass and one thermometer.[60]

Gray seems to have been the first to become sick – but his illness was not recognised at first. On 25 March, Wills had written in his journal: 'I found Gray behind a tree eating skilligolee [a kind of porridge]. He explained that he was suffering from dysentery, and had taken the flour without leave. Sent him to report to Mr. Burke.'[61] Two weeks later, Wills had recorded that 'they halted fifteen minutes to send back for Gray who gammoned [pretended] he could not walk.'[62] Nine days later, Wills wrote in his journal: 'This morning, about sunrise, Gray died. He had not spoken a word distinctly since his first attack, which was just as we were about to start.'[63]

The three remaining members of the gulf party lost another camel a few days later, on 3 April, and continued on their way. They arrived back at the Cooper's Creek depot on the evening of Sunday 21 April. As the elder Wills, Dr Wills, wrote in his account of the expedition: 'There was no one there.'[64] Brahé and his party had left the depot on that morning to return to the Darling with 'their camels and horses all well and in good condition'. The three explorers were in a completely exhausted state and there was no chance that they could overtake Brahé and his men. Wills described their condition in the following words:[65]

> After four months of the severest travelling and privation our legs almost paralysed, so that each of us found it a most trying task only to walk a few yards. Such leg-bound feeling I never before experienced, and hope I never shall again. The exertion required to get up a slight piece of rising ground, even without any load, induces an indescribable sensation of pain and helplessness, and the general lassitude makes one unfit for anything. Poor Gray must have suffered very much many times when we thought him shamming. It is most fortunate for us that these symptoms, which so early affected him, did not come on us until we were reduced to an exclusively animal diet of such inferior description as that offered by the flesh of a worn out and exhausted horse.

Brahé and the other members of the depot party had given up hope that the gulf party would return safely to the Cooper's Creek depot. At the same time, Brahé was worried about Patten's health; and Thomas McDonough was also becoming ill. Patten had been unable to walk for the last eighteen days because his leg had been severely hurt when he was thrown from his horse.[66] Nevertheless, Brahé decided to leave a cache of food for the gulf party – just in case they did return to the depot. It was buried near the camp at the foot of a large coolabah tree into the trunk of which was carved the message:

DIG
3 FT   NW
APR 21   1861

The cache contained 23 kilograms (50 pounds) of flour, 9 kilograms (20 pounds) of rice, 27 kilograms (60 pounds) of oatmeal, 27 kilograms (60 pounds) of sugar, and 7 kilograms (16 pounds) of dried meat – together with a few horseshoes, some nails and 'some odds and ends'. It was not much, but it was some help, and Burke and Wills both remarked on 'a most decided relief and a strength in the legs greater than we had had for several days'.[67]

THE ADVANCE OF THE SUPPLY PARTY

In the meantime the 'supply party' at Menindee had been engaged in putting the provisions and other stores in order – ready to transport to Cooper's Creek. They also took the opportunity to prepare a further supply of dried meat to take to the north because the pemmican originally supplied to the expedition had become unfit for use – as Mueller had said that it would. The method for the preparation of the dried meat was recorded by Beckler:[68]

> Four fat oxen were purchased and killed, drawn and quartered. The meat was cut in long thin strips, mostly following the direction of the muscles ... Then it was hung up to dry on long ropes stretched between two trees. In four or five days the strips of meat were dry and in a week they were suitable for packing. The parts with high fat content ... were salted and then buried in the ground, wrapped in the fresh skin of the slaughtered beast. After four to five days they were taken out and hung for a longer time so that they retained the greater part of the fat. The meat dried immediately after slaughter kept quite well, although we had to check every single piece of it every second or third day and remove the insects that infested it.

Hermann Beckler had resigned from the expedition. He had little or no confidence in Burke as a leader, and he sympathised with Landells in his disagreements with Burke over the control of the camels. However, when Wright was put in charge of the 'supply party', things were different. He had confidence in Wright. Moreover, he 'had not yet quenched' his 'enthusiasm for travel'.[69] He therefore volunteered, and was accepted, as a member of the party, under Wright, that was about to set off for Cooper's Creek.

Wright did not want to proceed from Menindee to Cooper's Creek until he had received confirmation of his appointment from the Exploration Committee back in Melbourne. This confirmation was received at Menindee on 10 or 11 January 1861. However, Wright did not immediately set off – because he felt that he now had to await the return of Beckler, Belooch and Peter, with Lyons and MacPherson. Beckler and his companions had arrived back after midnight on 4 January 1861, and Wright's 'supply party' set off for Cooper's Creek on 26 January.[70]

In addition to Wright and Beckler the supply party included Ludwig Becker, Charles Stone (an experienced bushman who had been engaged in place of MacPherson, who was too ill to continue), William Hodgkinson, William Purcell (the cook), John Smith (a bushman of mixed European and Aboriginal blood) and Belooch (the Indian camel-handler). Dick, the Aborigine, agreed to accompany the party only on the first day of their journey. They had thirteen horses and ten camels. It was a reasonably well-qualified party; but no one was able 'to make astronomical observations' to determine their position.[71]

Near Mootwingee they camped for a night in a 'natural roomy cave' that is now called Burke's Cave – but which is named Kokriega by the Aboriginal people. It is in the Bynguano Range (where Mt Wright is named after the leader of the supply party). The walls and ceiling of this cave were found to be covered with paintings by Aboriginal artists. They 'were covered with the impressions of outstretched human hands in the most varied

colours', and other paintings. Beckler was fascinated and regarded the whole area as 'a small paradise'.[72] Unfortunately Wright took the opportunity to paint his own initials all over one of the paintings![73]

The supply party suffered every sort of problem as it struggled to reach Cooper's Creek. It was summer, of course, and there was a continuing need to find drinking water – not only for the camels and horses, but also for the men themselves. The shortage of water was such that the horses and camels, although hobbled, wandered off in the night to search for water and had to be rounded up in the morning – a task that often required several hours. There were several incidents with some of the Aboriginal inhabitants who often resented the appearance of strangers on their land – strangers who sometimes disturbed their hunting. Somehow or other Beckler lost his blankets on this journey, a problem which he described as 'a major incident for me, a calamity'.[74] They were also greatly troubled by the mosquitoes, and by the long-haired rats, *Rattus villosissius*. According to Beckler, however:[74]

> The two greatest obstacles to the successful and uninterrupted continuation of our journey were sickness and shortage of water. Nonetheless the latter would not have prevented our eventual arrival in Cooper's Creek, however delayed.

Ludwig Becker was the first to become sick. Within a month after leaving Menindee he was complaining of sore gums, swelling painful hands, and of loss of appetite. It was not long before other members of the party – including Purcell (the cook) and Belooch (the Indian camel-handler) – were also visibly sick.[76] Soon afterwards, Beckler wrote:[77]

> The cook became more ill and more weak every day and Beludsch [Belooch] was in a very unstable state. Hodgkinson was well, as I was, but gradually I was overcome by such headaches that I became quite concerned for the continuation of my good health. I was hardly able to turn myself over during the night ...

Beckler wrote a series of medical reports on the

condition of the members of the supply party for the attention of the Exploration Committee in Melbourne.[78] On one occasion he wrote: 'We used preserved vegetables every day and a large quantity of meat biscuit, yet our patients seemed to go down irresistably.' He also mentioned that he had been treating his patients with citric acid. He commented: 'It was certain that there was a deficiency of some important chemical in the blood.'

Charles Stone had also become ill. He 'complained of exhaustion, a loss of appetite and a generally disturbed state of health'. He became worse and 'was becoming more and more a companion in suffering'. He 'was most wretched and during the night he had such pains in both his knee joints that he screamed aloud'.[79] He died on 22 April and was buried 'amidst a group of charming acacias'.[80]

Purcell had also become very ill. He 'was eating nothing at all and fainted if he so much as lifted his head from his pillow to have a drink of water'. He too died, and was buried next to Stone on 24 April.[81]

Ludwig Becker, who had been the first to become ill, was on the verge of death for several days. He had had a particularly difficult time. He was unable to walk and suffered 'from very frequent diarrhoea'.[82]

By this time the supply party had reached Bulloo, where there are scattered waterholes – but it was still 240 kilometres (150 miles) east of the Cooper's Creek depot.[83] On 29 April, the 'supply party' was astonished to see William Brahé, and other members of the Cooper's Creek depot party, arrive in their camp at Bulloo. Brahé and his men had evacuated the depot at Cooper's Creek five weeks after the time limit that had been set by Burke. In fact, as already mentioned, Burke, Wills and King had arrived back at the Cooper's Creek depot late on the same day (21 April) that Brahé and his colleagues had left. Ludwig Becker was so ill that he did not recognise Brahé and he died the day after

Brahé had arrived. 'That night', wrote Beckler, 'we dug a third grave and laid Becker with his travelling companions.'[84]

This was not the end of the suffering, however, because John Smith and Belooch were now on the sick list, and so were William Patten (who had swollen gums) and Thomas McDonough. Patten and McDonough also had physical injuries.

On 1 May the combined party retreated to their earlier camp at Koolialto Creek – where they remained for a few days while Brahé and Wright made a brief excursion back to the site of the Cooper's Creek depot to check whether Burke and his colleagues had succeeded in returning there. They did not find them and saw no evidence that they had arrived there. Brahé and Wright then returned to the Koolialto Creek camp. Wright was therefore the only member of the supply party to reach the Cooper's Creek depot.

Brahé's and Wright's combined group began their retreat on 22 May – with Patten and McDonough so weak that they fainted on several occasions. Belooch was also very ill. Patten became weaker and weaker, lost consciousness, and died. 'Wright and Brahé dug a fine grave for him and shortly after sunrise we buried him in the desert, the most peaceful resting place there can be.'[85] It was 5 June. They reached their old depot at Menindee on 19 June.

Back in Melbourne, during the early planning of the expedition, the Exploration Committee thought that scurvy might be a problem. A quantity of lime juice had been provided – but Burke discarded this at Balranald. The medical officer, Beckler, had also been provided with a quantity of citric acid – doubtless in the (mistaken) belief that this might prevent or cure scurvy. At best, it improved the palatability of the drinking water.[86] In a further attempt to counter scurvy, the men were to be given 'preserved vegetables'.

It is possible that the 'preserved vegetables' contained some vitamin C, but it is difficult to judge without a knowledge of the method used to preserve the vegetables. At one stage they used preserved vegetables every day and it does not seem likely that they had any beneficial effect – because more and more men became ill.[87] When so many became ill, the use of the preserved vegetables seems to have ceased. Beckler gave evidence to the commission: 'We had no time to prepare these preserved vegetables which we had with us; they are quite hard and require dissolving or being kept in water for some time.'[88] In any case, by this time, the preserved vegetables would have to be regarded as 'old stock', and any initial content of vitamin C would have been greatly reduced. Moreover, the preparation of the preserved vegetables in metal cooking vessels (especially if these were of copper) would have destroyed any last trace of the vitamin.[89] The list of stores (as sent to Mueller for comment) refers to 'Condensed French vegetables', and this item could be equivalent to 'preserved vegetables'.[90]

In the reports that Beckler wrote for the information of the Exploration Committee, he mentioned that his patients had 'a bluish flabby appearance of their gums with inability of masticating solid articles of food properly or without pain', 'a want of appetite, indigestion' – and similar comments. However, although he diagnosed their illness as scurvy he added that 'all our cases of sickness were different from those cases of scurvy' that he had previously seen.[91] Vitamins were unknown in 1861, and so were micro-organisms. The need to boil the water found in stagnant pools was not yet appreciated, and many members of the two parties – Wright, Becker, Smith, Stone, Purcell, Belooch, Patten and McDonough – all suffered from diarrhoea. 'Gastroenteritis and scurvy would account for their bouts of weakness, oedema, sore gums and loose teeth, dysentery, rheumatic aches and fever.' The water was probably contaminated with cyanobacterial toxins, and it seems likely that they died of inanition – that is, exhaustion from lack of nourishment.[92]

APPROACHING DISASTER

Brahé and the other members of the Cooper's Creek depot party had left the depot on the morning of 21 April with their horses and camels in good condition – but with some severe sicknesses among the members of the party. Burke, Wills and King had arrived at the depot on the evening of the same day in an extremely exhausted condition. It seemed pointless for them to try to catch up Brahé, and it seemed impossible for them to travel independently to Menindee with the provisions that they had available. They had arrived at the depot with only just over half a kilogram (1.5 pounds) of dried meat between them – and the provisions left for them at the depot were insufficient for a prolonged journey even if they were in good health.[93] Nevertheless, Wills and King both wished to 'go down our old track' – but Burke decided that they should go down the creek via Mt Hopeless in the expectation that they would reach a cattle station.

They set off on the morning of 23 April – but they were able to go only about 8 kilometres (five miles). On the following day, they were fortunate in being able to obtain some fish from a party of Aborigines whom they met. The Aborigines then proceeded in the opposite direction – but they returned the following day with more fish. They were given some sugar in return. The land was uninviting and there seemed little chance of finding sufficient water. They began to retreat and reconnoitre. They came across another group of Aborigines who gave them 'a lot of fish and bread, which they call nardoo ... until we were positively unable to eat any more'. They also introduced them to pituri. As Wills wrote: 'It has a highly intoxicating effect, when chewed even in small quantities. It appears to be the dried stems and leaves of some shrub.'[94]

The nardoo used by the Aboriginal people is obtained from a fern-like plant, *Marsilea drummondii*

– which is found in many parts of Australia but particularly at the edges of lakes, either at the surface or in the adjacent dry ground. It produces sporocarps about the size of a pea. The Aborigines collected these sporocarps – which they ground into a thin paste with water. This thin paste was then 'spooned up' with a shell.[95]

Burke, Wills and King all found the nardoo of considerable value in alleviating hunger – and they tried to locate the sporocarps themselves. Unfortunately, they could not make the Aboriginal people understand that they would like 'to be shown how to find the seed themselves'.[96] Their initial failure to find nardoo was because they assumed that the 'seeds' were from a tree. As Wills reported, he was unable 'to find a single tree of it in the neighbourhood of the camp'.[97] It was King who first found it growing on a plant 'which I took to be clover'. He added:'They were very glad when I found it.'[98]

From that time on Burke, Wills and King took it in turns to collect nardoo while the one not collecting was engaged in the laborious task of pounding the sporocarps into a flour. This became the principal component of their diet. King seemed to be satisfied with the nardoo, but Wills wrote:[99]

I cannot understand this nardoo at all; it certainly will not agree with me in any form. We are now reduced to it alone, and we manage to get from four to five pounds a day between us. The stools it causes are enormous, and seem greatly to exceed the quantity of bread consumed, and is very slightly altered in appearance from what it was when eaten.

A few days later, in some despair, Wills wrote:[100]

Mr. Burke suffers greatly from the cold, and is getting extremely weak; he and King start tomorrow up the creek, to look for the blacks – it is the only chance we have of being saved from starvation. I am weaker than ever although I have a good appetite, and relish the nardoo much, but it seems to give us no nutriment, and the birds here are so shy as not to be got at. Even if we had a good supply of fish, I doubt whether we could do much work on them and the nardoo alone. Nothing now but the greatest good luck can now save any of us; and as for myself, I may live four or five days if the weather continues warm. My pulse is at forty-eight, and very weak, and my legs and arms are nearly skin and bone. I can only look out, like Mr. Micawber, 'for something to turn up', but starvation on nardoo is by no means very unpleasant, but for the weakness one feels, and the utter inability to move oneself, for as far as appetite is concerned, it gives me the greatest satisfaction. Certainly, fat and sugar would be more to one's taste, in fact, those seem to me to be the great stand by for one in this extraordinary continent; not that I mean to depreciate the farinaceous food, but the want of sugar and fat in all substances obtainable here is so great that they become almost valueless to us as articles of food, without the addition of something else.

All three men were in an extremely weak condition – although King was better than either Burke or Wills. The only chance seemed to be to seek the help of the local Aboriginal people. Burke and King set out with this purpose, leaving Wills with 'some nardoo, wood and water, with which I must do the best I can until they return'.[101]

Burke and King failed to find the Aborigines and, on the second day, Burke was so weak that he could go no further and, 'although he ate his supper', it was clear that he would soon die. He then said to King: 'I hope you will remain with me till I am quite dead – it is a comfort to know that someone is by; but when I am dying, it is my wish that you should place the pistol in my right hand, and that you leave me unburied as I lie.' The following morning he was speechless and at 'about eight o'clock he expired.'[102]

A few days later King managed to return to Wills – but found him dead. King later reported that 'the natives had been there and had taken away some of his clothes.' King buried Wills in the sand.

King eventually located the Aboriginal people,

and they allowed him to stay. He shared their food and, by shooting a few birds, he contributed to their food supply. King was found by one of the rescue teams on 15 September 1861.

It was originally believed that Burke, Wills and Gray must have died of starvation and of scurvy. The extensive notes left by Wills, however, make no mention of swollen, sore or bleeding gums – and scurvy does not seem to have been a serious factor in their illness and death. It is possible that their frequent use of portulaca might have prevented the onset of scurvy. In recent times, it has been shown that they were suffering from another vitamin-deficiency disease – beri-beri.

The Exploration Committee in Melbourne had not considered the possibility that the members of the expedition might develop beri-beri. In the mid nineteenth century this was regarded as a disease confined to the rice-eating peoples of the East, and its cause was unknown. It was first recognised as a nutritional disease by a Japanese naval surgeon named Takaki – who recommended adding meat, vegetables and condensed milk to the diet of Japanese sailors. It was some years, however, before it was shown that beri-beri develops when the diet contains an inadequate amount of a specific vitamin – vitamin B_1 (thiamine). This vitamin occurs in yeast, and in the husks of various grains. It was first obtained on a reasonably large scale in 1934.

The symptoms of beri-beri have been described in *Human Nutrition and Dietetics* as follows:[103]

At first there is anorexia and ill-defined malaise associated with heaviness and weakness of the legs. This may cause some difficulty in walking ... the pulse is usually full and moderately increased in rate. There may be tenderness of the calf muscles on pressure, and complaints of 'pins and needles' and numbness in the legs ... The essential feature [of 'dry' beri-beri] is polyneuropathy ... The muscles become progressively more wasted and weak, and walking becomes increasingly more difficult ... Bedridden patients and those with severe cachexia are very susceptible to infections.

There is little doubt that the members of the gulf party suffered from a deficiency of thiamine in their diet (especially after arriving at Cooper's Creek), that they developed beri-beri, and that this eventually led to the death of three of the four men. Nevertheless their illness had a few puzzling features. Wills recorded that he had a slow heartbeat (bradycardia, when tachycardia would have been expected if as is reasonably assumed he was suffering from beri-beri).[104]

When Burke and his three companions began their 'dash to the Gulf' their diet included oatmeal and flour – which contain sufficient thiamine to avoid the development of thiamine deficiency. As their supplies of oatmeal and flour diminished (on their return journey) they did develop a deficiency of this vitamin – which was not sufficiently relieved when they consumed the horseflesh. Gray was the first to develop a serious state of deficiency and this led to his taking some of their diminishing stock of flour 'without leave'. By the time that Burke, Wills and King reached the Cooper's Creek depot, they were all showing symptoms of thiamine deficiency. They improved for a time when they consumed the supplies that Brahé had left for them at the depot but, when these stores were exhausted, they began to live on freshwater mussels and nardoo. It has since been shown that freshwater mussels and nardoo contain an enzyme, thiaminase, which destroys thiamine – so their diet during their time in the Cooper's Creek area soon further lowered their thiamine reserves, and hastened the development of beri-beri.[105]

However, the Aboriginal people in the Cooper's Creek area did not develop beri-beri. Why? Earl and McCleary have pointed out that Burke, Wills and King prepared their nardoo in the usual European manner of preparing food from grain – namely, grinding, and then cooking 'cakes'. This treatment does not destroy thiaminase. In contrast, the Aboriginal people prepared their nardoo, as already mentioned, by grinding it into a paste with water and then spooning it into their mouths with a shell. Earl and McCleary have shown that dilution with water rapidly diminishes the enzyme's activity.[106]

Back in Melbourne, and in the other centres of population, there was increasing anxiety about the explorers. Had they disappeared or perished – like Leichhardt? Had they reached the gulf and failed to survive the return journey? Had they been attacked by Aborigines? When Brahé arrived back in Melbourne, it was abundantly clear – rescue operations had to be organised as rapidly as possible. A ship was to be sent to the gulf. Alfred William Howitt, an experienced bushman, was chosen to lead an expedition to search for Burke and Wills – and Brahé was to accompany them. An expedition from New South Wales was to be led by William Landsborough; an expedition from Queensland was to set off under the leadership of Frederick Walker. John McKinlay was to lead a party from Adelaide.[107]

John McKinlay and the 'Burke Relief Party' left Adelaide on 16 August 1861. They located Charley Gray's grave and exhumed the body – which was found to be enveloped in a flannel shirt with short sleeves.[108] The Victorian Rescue Expedition also had limited success. Howitt and his companions left Melbourne on 4 July 1861 and made for Swan Hill where three members had already arrived and were waiting for Howitt. They departed a few days later and followed Burke's route to Menindee, and then to Cooper's Creek. Within a few days they were lucky to find John King alive, but very frail. With King's help they then found the graves of both Burke and Wills – and retrieved the notebooks and letters that had been buried near the 'Dig Tree'.

The bodies were taken back to Melbourne where an elaborate funeral was arranged and held on 21 January 1863. It seems that 'everyone' attended. The funeral car was a replica of the one that had been used to convey the Duke of Wellington to St Paul's Cathedral, in London, some years before.

17

JOHN MCDOUALL STUART – ACROSS THE CONTINENT FROM SOUTH TO NORTH

John McDouall Stuart was born on 7 September 1815 at Dysart – a small town (now merged with Kirkaldy) on the northern shore of the Firth of Forth, in Scotland. His father, William Stuart, had served as a captain in the army, but had been released following the Peace of Amiens in 1802. His mother had been born Mary McDouall.

Little is known about his childhood. It seems likely that he attended a local private school for a time, but both his parents died when he was about eleven years old and he was then enrolled at the Scottish Naval and Military Academy in Edinburgh and was cared for by an old family retainer. The academy was intended for the education of the sons of naval and military officers. As such, it doubtless included surveying and navigation in the curriculum. He later joined his brother, Samuel, in Glasgow, and it seems likely that it was there that he obtained some knowledge of civil engineering – but little has been established with certainty.[1]

In 1838 John McDouall Stuart decided to emigrate to South Australia. Mudie has claimed that Stuart had read a book about South Australia entitled *Land of Promise*, 'By one who is going'. But this book was not published until 1839 and the preface was dated 7 December 1838. It seems likely that Stuart was induced to emigrate (as many others were) by the publicity afforded to this new colony which would not be a penal settlement. This publicity was so effective that thirty-four ships were required to transport the migrants (including many from Scotland) to Adelaide in 1838. Stuart sailed from Dundee on 13 September 1838 as a passenger in the *Indus*, a barque of 429 tonnes (422 tons) – which was on her maiden voyage. He was listed as John Stewart on the manifest. Many other emigrants were also passengers on this ship, and one, James Sinclair, from the Isle of Arran, became a life-long friend of Stuart. Stuart disembarked at the Port River, Adelaide, on 21 January 1839.

Stuart obtained work as a surveyor's assistant, and later joined the government's Survey Department – to the management of which Charles Sturt had been appointed by the colonial government in March 1839. The position of surveyor-general was, however, taken over in October 1839 by Captain Edward Charles Frome – who had been appointed to this position by the authorities in London without reference to the governor of South Australia, Colonel George Gawler.

When Charles Sturt was planning his expedition to central Australia to search for an inland sea, he appointed John McDouall Stuart as the draughts-man. Sturt's expedition left Adelaide on 18 August 1844, and returned on 19 January 1846 – by which time John McDouall Stuart had become an experienced bushman and a devoted friend to Sturt. Sturt acknowledged and praised the endeavours of Stuart on this expedition. Indeed, when Poole (the

This photograph of John McDouall Stuart was donated to the John McDouall Stuart Society by Mr Keith Borrow in 1998; it might have been taken at the time Stuart was presented with a gold watch by Governor MacDonnell in October 1860, or the Patron's Medal in September 1861 – both awarded to him by the Royal Geographical Society, London.

second-in-command of the party) died, Stuart appointed Stuart to that position.

After his return to Adelaide, Stuart continued to work as a surveyor. He moved to the Port Lincoln district, worked for James Sinclair, and even tutored Sinclair's children – as well as carrying out surveys for various people. Then, towards the end of 1853 or early 1854,[2] Stuart became associated with William Finke who had made a modest fortune from copper mining and from the sale of the land (near present-day Glenelg) – which he had purchased for £1 an acre (0.4 hectares).[3] In 1854

Finke and Stuart left Port Lincoln to go prospecting and exploring in the North Flinders Ranges. It seems likely that Stuart met James and John Chambers about this time because Finke was a friend of the Chambers brothers. James Chambers (1811–62) arrived in the *Coromandel* in January 1837, and John Chambers (1815–89) in the *John Renwick* in February 1837. James Chambers became well known in Adelaide as 'the first man to drive a team of bullocks from Port Adelaide to the town, so marking the track which afterwards became the Port Road'.[4] The Chambers brothers became wealthy, and developed substantial pastoral leases. Indeed, by September 1857, James Chambers was holding leases for 'more than double the amount listed for any other pastoralist'. He had established a station at Oratunga, in the 'Far North' – that is, in the North Flinders Ranges.[5] The head station of the Chambers brothers was established at Moolooloo – also in the Far North.

FIRST EXPEDITION

It seems that William Finke was the first to suggest that Stuart carry out an exploration in search of further good pastoral country and, perhaps, find the long-hoped-for 'inland sea'. Stuart accepted the suggestion with enthusiasm. It was to be a small but important expedition. Stuart was accompanied by a man named Forster,[6] and a young Aboriginal man, and they took provisions for six weeks. They left the Chambers station at Oratunga on 14 May 1858, with five horses. For some time they were accompanied by Alfred Barker, a brother-in-law of the Chambers, who then returned to the station.[7] They travelled to the south-west, turned northwards from the southern end of Lake Torrens and, at the northern boundary of the lake, turned to the north-west. On 26 June they came to 'a large gum creek' (a watercourse with gum trees) – that Stuart named Chambers Creek. It was later rediscovered by Babbage, who named it Stuart Creek – and both names are still used. It was an important discovery because Stuart was to use Chambers Creek as an advanced depot on all his later expeditions. Stuart and his companions took a north-westerly route from Chambers Creek as far as present-day Coober Pedy. They then turned towards the south and the two Europeans arrived at the south coast near Denial Bay on 17 August.

They were both in a sorry state and in need of rest and good food. It had been a gruelling experience. The young Aboriginal man had deserted on 3 August, and Forster had often despaired of reaching a settlement. They had been without food and water for a dangerous period. Stuart wrote:[8]

> For upwards of a month we have been existing upon two pounds and a half of flour cake daily, without animal food. Since we commenced the journey, all the animal food we have been able to obtain has been four wallabies, one opossum, one small duck, one pigeon, and latterly a few kangaroo mice, which were very welcome ... These kangaroo mice are elegant little animals about four inches in length resembling the kangaroo in shape, with a long tail terminating with a sort of brush. Their habitations are of a conical form, built with twigs and rotten wood, about six feet in diameter at the base, and rising to a height of three or four feet.

They were probably *Notomys fuscus* – the same species as those seen by Sturt during his expedition in search of an inland sea.[9] On 17 August Stuart had recorded: 'We have only two meals left to take us to Streaky Bay which is distant from this place one hundred miles'.[10] They reached Streaky Bay on Sunday 22 August, and Gibson's station on the following day – where they were 'received and treated with great kindness, for which we were very thankful. We enjoyed a good supper, which, after three days' fasting as may readily be imagined, was quite a treat.' It had been a remarkable expedition. Stuart's only instruments had been a pocket compass and a watch!

On 1 September 1858, while he rested at Gibson's station, Stuart wrote to his friend James Sinclair:[11]

> I have just arrived from a long exploring excursion into the interior which has occupied me for the last three months, in that time I have travelled upwards of 1500 miles. I went north on the west side of Lake Torrens, then north-west to near the west boundary of this colony, then down towards Fowler's Bay, and along the coast to this place. I had a very severe journey of it from want of sufficient provisions; not intending to be out more than six weeks at furthest I only took 4 weeks

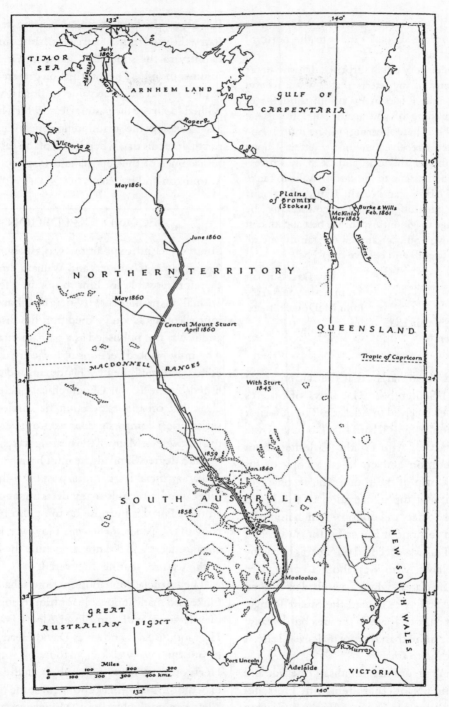

Map showing the route taken by John McDouall Stuart on his expeditions to central Australia and across the continent from 1845 to 1862. (reproduced from a book about her great-great-uncle by Mona Stuart Webster (1958), with permission of her family)

provisions. I was obliged to leave a very valuable mare behind me about 70 miles to the north of Hack's West run.

I have been very much surprised that you never answered any of my letters that I wrote to you from Adelaide. I had given up all thoughts of hearing anything of you again, but I have seen Darling who is here shearing, and he informs me that you never received any of my letters. I hope you will answer this one and keep up correspondence, address me to the care of William Finke Oratunga Mine Far North. I intend to start tomorrow morning across the country by the Gawler range to Mount Arden. My best and kindest regards to Mrs Sinclair and all the family and all enquiring friends and believe me to be

My Dear Sinclair
in haste yours truly
John McDouall Stuart.

To James Sinclair Esq.
Green Patch
Port Lincoln

Stuart and Forster arrived at the station at Mt Arden on 11 September. The news of Stuart's success was well received in Adelaide. The governor of South Australia, Sir Richard MacDonnell, wrote to the secretary of state for the Colonies about Stuart's expedition and enclosed a copy of his journal and a map of the route. The secretary of state, in turn, sent the information to the Royal Geographical Society in London – which immediately decided to honour Stuart by the award of a gold watch. This was accepted on Stuart's behalf by Count Strzelecki, who was about to return to Australia.[12] The plateau which Stuart had discovered near Coober Pedy was named the Stuart Range. Stuart sought pastoral leases in the area but, because he applied for more than the normal-sized lease, it took a long time to finalise.[13]

Stuart spent the summer months in Adelaide and it was in this period that Benjamin Herschel Babbage, and later Major Peter Warburton, were exploring in the vicinity of Chambers Creek. Warburton discovered and named Davenport Range, and its highest peak, Mt Margaret. Samuel Parry, the government surveyor, had examined the country to the south of Chambers Creek in the summer months. The information gathered by these explorers was of great value to Stuart, who now wished to survey the pastoral lease which he sought, and to explore the surrounding country and further north. It seems that when he set off he carried with him copies of the reports and maps prepared by Warburton and by Parry.[14]

SECOND EXPEDITION

Stuart's second expedition was financed by his friends James Chambers and William Finke. It was therefore possible for him to obtain a few navigational instruments. His original handwritten journal of his second expedition has disappeared, and it was not published as a parliamentary paper. The only printed versions of his journal are those edited and published by Hardman, and that published by the Royal Geographical Society.[15] It is clear that on this expedition he carried a good (prismatic?) compass graduated from zero degrees to 360 degrees. Many of the bearings taken are given to half a degree. Similarly, he must have had a sextant and an artificial horizon (or possibly a theodolite) – because he records many determinations of the latitude. For this purpose he must also have had a copy of the Nautical Almanac. However, he had no chronometer, and did not determine the longitude of the features that he discovered.

The financial contributions from Chambers and Finke also made it possible for him to engage three men to travel with him. Josef Albert Franz David Herrgott, usually known as David Herrgott, was a botanist and was well known to Baron von Mueller. Herrgott had been a member of the Babbage expedition, and he had also spent some time at the Victorian goldfields. Louis Müller was apparently a miner who had also been to the Victorian diggings. The third man was a stockman named Campbell –

but nothing seems to be known about his background.

Stuart's party began their journey at the Chambers station at Oratunga and then moved forward to a station, centred on Leigh Creek, which was known as Glen's – because it was managed by Alexander Glen, a former naval officer. At that time this property was the furthest north from Adelaide. They set off from Glen's station on 2 April 1859 and reached St a'Becket's Pool – which had been named by Samuel Parry. Stuart thought the country was good: 'a large salt bush and grassy plain, with upwards of 300 cattle feeding upon it'. He added that they 'found the native cucumber growing'. Mudie identifies this as *Cucumis melo* var. *agrestis* – a cucumber-like plant often used by the Aboriginal people. It has been shown to contain a small amount of vitamin C.[16] Soon afterwards, Herrgott found a group of springs with a good flow of water and these became Herrgott Springs – now, however, the settlement is known as Marree.[17] On 19 April, a 'gum creek' was examined. They found 'seven small hillocks from which flow the springs; their height above the plain is about eight feet [2.4 metres], and they are surrounded with a cake of salt-petre but the water is very good indeed and there is an unlimited supply'.[18] Two days later they saw Warburton's tracks which they followed to Finniss Springs – so named by Warburton.[19] From here they obtained a good view of what they thought to be Eyre's horseshoe-shaped Lake Torrens – in the vicinity of Lake Eyre South. Babbage had named it Lake Gregory (and had also named Gregory Creek). They then came to Chambers Creek and Stuart wrote that 'I am sorry I did not name it a river in my former Journal.' They moved on to Hamilton Hill – which had been named Mt Hamilton by Warburton – where Stuart determined the latitude to be 29° 27' 37" S (which is essentially correct) and rebuilt Warburton's cone of stones to be used for surveying purposes.[20]

Stuart continued to look for known and un-

known springs. On 10 May, for example, he set out from Hamilton Hill in the direction of Mount Hugh [Kewson Hill] where he 'found a splendid number of springs; they give out a fine stream of water, not the least brackish'. He added that the 'hill from which this stream issues is one hundred feet [30 metres] above the level of the plain, the water coming from the very top'. He named it Elizabeth Springs. A few kilometres further on he came to Beresford Springs but he considered that these 'are nothing in comparison with the others; there are only two that are running, but they are very good.'[21] He continued to look for springs and to assess their value for stock. Two weeks later, he found twelve springs with first-rate water, and he named these Hawker Springs after the speaker of the House of Assembly in Adelaide. He continued to name new features after members of parliament – although they might have been selected by Chambers or Finke after his return. However, J. B. Neales was a friend as well as a member of parliament and commissioner of Crown Lands, and it seems likely that Stuart himself was responsible for naming the 'River Neales'. This multi-channel river (Stuart referred to it as a 'gum creek')[22] flows near present-day Oodnadatta into Lake Eyre North. Stuart added: 'No person could wish for a better country for feed than that we have passed over to-day [6 June]; it resembles the country about Chambers Creek'.[23] A few days later, on 12 June, he named 'a large dark-coloured hill ... from fifteen to twenty miles [24–32 kilometres] distant' Mount Browne – after J. H. Browne, of Port Gawler, who was the medical officer on Captain Sturt's expedition to the inland and on which Stuart was the draughtsman.[24] It was also on this day, 12 June, that Stuart wrote: 'We are now come to our last set of shoes for the horses, and having experienced the misery of being without them in my previous journey I am, though with great reluctance, forced to turn back.'[25] They managed to find a few more springs. On 23 June, for example, they 'came upon a hill of springs surrounded by a number of smaller ones with an ample supply of first-rate water'.[26] They were named the Loudon Springs – after the manager of Mt Arden station.

Stuart continued to move southwards and reached Glen's station on 3 July. He reported to the governor on 18 July 1859. Stuart had terminated his expedition earlier than expected because he feared for the well-being of his horses. Nevertheless, he had observed and named a number of prominent features. The great value of the expedition, however, had been his discovery of so many 'mound springs'.

Benjamin Babbage had made the first discovery of some mound springs on 22 October 1858, and he had named Emerald Springs. On 11 May 1859 Stuart determined the latitude of these springs to be 29° 17' 43" S.[27] Not long after Babbage had made this discovery, Major Peter Warburton discovered and named Blanche Cup[28] (near Hamilton Hill and at 29° 27' S), Strangways Springs (at 29° 09' S) and Coward Springs (at 29° 24' S). Warburton named the last 'in token of my approval of the zeal and intelligence with which Corporal Coward had assisted me'.[29]

These mound springs, and those discovered by Stuart, were of great value during Stuart's second and later expeditions to the north, and were to be of importance in the development of the pastoral industry. The head stations of the pioneer pastoralists were conveniently established close to good mound springs. Unfortunately, the cattle tended to degrade the environment near the springs and the governor indicated that all useful mound springs be fenced.

Mound springs are of great geological interest. The naturalist, Frederick George Waterhouse – who travelled with Stuart on his sixth expedition – believed that they must be of volcanic origin. But this is not so. They exist in an arc along the south-western edge of the Great Artesian Basin. The water that flows from the springs is artesian. According to Thomson and Barnett: 'Springs can be defined as naturally occurring outlets for ground water

discharges'; and 'Mound springs are those outlets which possess an accretion of sediment around the outlet.'[30] These mounds are usually between 1 metre and 10 metres high.[31]

The governor had been impressed by Stuart's account of his discoveries. He reported to London that they formed 'another decided step in advance through available country towards the Victoria River' – which had been discovered and named by John Lort Stokes, and which flows into the Joseph Bonaparte Gulf, in the north. He also thought that Stuart's discoveries were encouraging as a first step in determining 'the most practicable route for the Electric wire intended to unite this continent with India and Europe'.[32]

The South Australian government was also keen to see a telegraph wire from Adelaide to the north coast for connection to an overseas cable. Indeed, it offered a reward of £1000, soon increased to £2000, to 'the person who shall succeed in crossing through the country lately discovered by Mr. Stuart either to the North or North-western shores of the Australian Continent'.[33]

THIRD EXPEDITION

James Chambers had also been impressed by the discoveries that had been made by Stuart – and was more than willing to finance a further expedition.[34] Moreover, Stuart needed to return to Chambers Creek to resurvey the area that he desired to lease. Additional land would be welcome to the Chambers, and there was also the possibility of mineral discoveries – especially of gold. Chambers engaged William Darton Kekwick, a former miner and an amateur botanist, to be second-in-command of Stuart's third expedition, and three others, Louis Müller, Strong and Smith, to accompany Stuart. Stuart's party left Adelaide on 22 August and arrived at Oratunga and then at Moolooloo – which had become the Chambers head station. From there they went to Mount Stuart, which was the most northerly of the Chambers stations. During this time the stores were collected, and a quantity of beef was prepared and dried. An Aboriginal guide named Cowlingh was engaged – but he deserted within a few days.

Stuart, Kekwick and the three men left Mt Stuart Station on Tuesday 4 October with twelve horses and provisions for three months. They called at Glen's station and met a man named Humphrey (or Humphries) who accompanied them to Chambers Creek – apparently to learn the route. On 18 October, en route to Chambers Creek, they arrived at Finniss Springs. A few days later Stuart discovered and named Priscilla Springs – after the daughter of John Chambers.[35] It was here that Cowlingh left the party. The next day they arrived at Chambers Creek and, soon afterwards, Stuart wrote that they would 'chain a base line' – so it seems that he was better equipped for the task of surveying than on his earlier expeditions. He also had a thermometer – but it was soon broken.[36] Humphrey set off on his return journey to Glen's station on 3 November taking survey maps relating to Stuart's pastoral lease application. Stuart's party then made its way to Emerald Springs, where he noted with surprise that 'there are fish in this Spring about three inches long.'[37] He then set out for what was then known as the North Lake Torrens – one section of Eyre's horseshoe lake. Stuart and Kekwick arrived at what is now known as the Hunt Peninsula (which Babbage had seen), and where the Elliott Price Conservation Park is situated.

Early in November 1859 Stuart became concerned about the dried beef that was the chief component of their diet. 'The weevil is at work in my dried beef,' he wrote, and he had to spend some time correcting this.[38]

They travelled from hill to hill, from creek to creek, and from springs to springs – taking bearings, observing the latitude, and drawing the maps. They determined the positions of Beresford Springs, Strangways Springs, William Springs (named after

the youngest son of John Chambers), Hawker Springs (at the foot of Mt Margaret, where a cone of stones was built for surveying purposes) and Fanny Springs. That night, while Stuart was busy taking star sights, Smith deserted – taking a good mare, harness and provisions with him. Stuart learnt of this when he returned to the camp the following morning. He was very angry, but was not particularly sorry to lose him – Smith 'being a lazy indolent, good-for-nothing man and, worse than all, an incorrigible liar. I could place no dependence upon him.'[39]

The surveys continued, and they also spent some time looking for gold in some quartz reefs – but without success. On 23 December there was a heavy thunderstorm, but very little rain. Stuart wrote: 'The wind blew my tent in two' – the first indication that they were using tents.[40] Not long afterwards, on Friday 6 January, he decided that he 'must sound a retreat' to obtain further provisions. In any case Müller and Strong were anxious to return. Stuart observed:[41]

I am sorry to say that I have lost confidence in all except Kekwick ... [Müller and Strong] have been a constant source of annoyance to me from the very beginning of my journey. The man that I had out with me on my last journey [Müller] has been the worst of the two. They seem to have made up their minds to do as little as possible, and that in the most slovenly and lazy manner imaginable ... I am surprised that I have endured it so long.

They returned to Chambers Creek on 21 January, and found provisions waiting for them, but 'the two men still exhibit a spirit of non-compliance, and refuse to proceed again to the north-west; they are bent on leaving me and returning to Adelaide,' wrote Stuart.[42] On the other hand, 'Kekwick is everything I could wish a man to be. He is active, pushing and persevering'.[43] Müller and Strong were discharged without their wages. Kekwick was sent back to Moolooloo with despatches and to endeavour to find other men to join the expedition –

leaving Stuart at Chambers Creek to pack up the stores. Stuart received news of Smith (one of the original members of this expedition) while he was at Chambers Creek. It seems that he 'left the mare, whether dead or alive we know not at present. He was lost for four days without water (according to his account) and, after various adventures ... reached the settled districts in a most forlorn condition.'[44]

Stuart's third expedition had not found any gold or mineral deposits; but it had pushed further north than before, and had found some useful land. It had added to the map and had improved its accuracy. Moreover, they had 'surveyed and laid off in runs nearly 8000 square miles [20 700 square kilometres] of country', which was 'a considerable amount of work for so small a party to have achieved in the time'.[45]

FOURTH EXPEDITION

Because there was a shortage of labour – owing to the booming pastoral industry – Kekwick found it very difficult to recruit men to continue the expedition to the north. In the end, he engaged a young man of eighteen years named Benjamin Head – who had been with Babbage in 1858. He was thus not inexperienced – but he was grossly overweight. Stuart was determined to proceed and, on Friday 2 March 1860, the three men – Stuart, Kekwick and Head – left Chambers Creek, with thirteen horses, to begin Stuart's fourth expedition.[46] The third expedition had returned to Chambers Creek on Saturday 21 January – so Stuart and Kekwick had had little time for rest and recreation.

They proceeded from spring to spring. On 15 March the expedition had its first accident. The horse carrying Stuart's instruments broke away and threw the saddle-bags to the ground. The sextant was put out of adjustment and it took Stuart 'all day to repair it'. Even then he was 'not sure now whether it is correct or not'.[47] The next day they had an accident of another kind. They were about to cross Peake Creek 'but had a fearful job in doing so' – because the banks were so boggy and the current so strong. One of the horses became stuck in the mud and they were unable to get him out – although they tried for hours. Stuart decided that he could not proceed further that day but camped on the west side of the springs that he had seen from the last camp, and which he named Kekwick Springs. Next morning they tried again to get the horse on shore but 'the more we try to extricate him, the worse he gets'. So they had to leave him, expecting that he would not survive the night.

Stuart pushed on. They were further west than on his earlier expedition. Then, on 1 April, Stuart wrote:[48]

> I find to-day that my right eye, from the long continuation of bad eyes, is now become useless to me for taking observations [with the sextant]. I can now see two suns instead of one, which has led me into an error of a few miles.

Two days later, however, he recorded the results of a noon observation of the altitude of the Sun. He also observed and named a large gum creek Finke Creek (now Finke River) – after William Finke 'my sincere and tried friend, and one of the liberal supporters of the different explorations I have had the honour to lead'.[49] They crossed the Finke and saw a most remarkable sandstone pillar that he estimated to be about 46 metres (150 feet) high, 6 metres (20 feet) wide, and 3 metres (10 feet) deep. Stuart named this 'Chambers Pillar' – in honour of James Chambers 'who, with William Finke, Esq., has been my great supporter in all my explorations'.[50] It is now known to be somewhat higher than Stuart estimated – namely 51 metres (167 feet) from base to summit.[51] Continuing on a 330-degree course he soon discovered and named a number of features including the Hugh Creek, a large gum creek, and the James Range (just south of the MacDonnell Ranges) – both named after sons of James Chambers. He named the MacDonnell

Ranges after the governor, Brinkley Bluff after the governor's ADC, and Waterhouse Range after the colonial secretary.[52] It was on his return journey that he named Mt Freeling after Colonel Freeling, the surveyor-general.

Captain Sturt, Stuart's former leader, had been anxious to reach the 'centre' of Australia; but the continuing dry weather at that period had compelled him to retreat. It was natural for John McDouall Stuart to have the same desire; but how does one define the 'centre'? Webster has reasoned in the following way:[53]

> The position in his [Stuart's] map of his camp on 22 April gives a longitude of approximately 133° 27' E. Taking Shark Bay and Brisbane as the extreme west and east points of the continent of Australia, the central meridian between these points is 133° 30' E, so Stuart's camp was probably a small distance west of this meridian, which cuts the northern coast in latitude 11° 53' S., and the southern coast in latitude 32° 07' S. This gives a latitude of 22° S as the point half-way along the line between the seas. These are round figures only, but it is obvious that Stuart regarded the Centre as the point half-way from sea to sea along the central meridian.

Stuart succeeded in reaching the 'centre' on Sunday 22 April 1860. Using an artificial horizon, he found the double altitude of the Sun's Lower Limb to be 111° 00' 30". He did not explain the meaning of this observation in his journal and it was not explained in the Hardman edition of his published account of his expeditions. The latitude of his place of observation was calculated as follows:[54]

Observed double altitude	111° 00' 30"
Observed altitude (half the above)	55° 30' 15"
Subtract correction for refraction (39"), and add correction for parallax (5") and for the Sun's semi-diameter (15' 55") to give meridian altitude of Sun's centre	55° 45' 36"
Subtract from 90° to obtain zenith distance	34° 14' 24"
Subtract Sun's declination at the time of observation and at place of observation using data from *Nautical Almanac*	12° 14' 39" N
Latitude	21° 59' 45" S

Stuart took his latitude to be 22° S, and his estimated longitude to be 133° E, and decided that he was midway between the eastern and western coasts of Australia, and midway between the northern and southern coasts. He wrote in his journal:[55]

> I am now camped in the centre of Australia I have marked a tree and planted the British flag in the centre, there is a high mount about two and one-half miles to the NNE [4 kilometres] which I hoped would be in the centre but on it tomorrow I will raise a cone of stone & plant the flag there and will name it Mt Sturt after my excellent and esteemed commander of the expedition in 1844 & 45 Capt Sturt, as a mark of gratitude for the great kindness I received from him during that journey.

On the Monday, Stuart wrote that he:

> Took Kekwick and the flag and went to the top of the mount but found it to be much higher and more difficult of ascent than I supposed it to be, after a deal of labour slips and knocks we at last arrived on the top, it is quite as high as Mt Serle if not higher ...

On the summit he:[56]

> ... built a large cone of stones, in the centre of which placed a pole with the British flag nailed upon it also near the top of the cone I placed a small bottle in which is a slip of paper stating by whom it was raised, with our signatures to it, on finishing it we gave three cheers for the flag the emblem of civil and religious liberty, and it may be a sign to the Natives that the dawn of liberty civilization and Christianity is about to brake upon them. I then named the mount Mt Sturt the Father of Australian Exploration, for whom we also gave three hearty cheers, and one more for Mrs Sturt and family.

Modern determinations give the position of the mountain as 21° 55' S, 133° 27' E, and its height as 846 metres. Mt Serle has a height of 912 metres.[57]

Stuart's journal account of his fourth expedition was 'read' at the Royal Geographical Society on 11 February 1861, and was published in the same year.[58] In this account, and in the edited version of the journals of all his expeditions, all mention of Mount Sturt[59] on 22 April have been replaced by: 'I will raise a cone of stones and plant the flag there, and name it Central Mount Stuart'.[60] There are several other references to Central Mount Stuart in the entries for 24 April and 25 April 1860. The same change was made in the printed version of his journal and published as a parliamentary paper in 1861.

Why the change from Sturt to Stuart? There is persistent legend that the man commissioned to engrave the plates for the maps thought that Stuart must have made a mistake in writing his own name, and that he meant to write 'Stuart' and not 'Sturt' on his draft of the map showing his route to the north. This legend suggests that it was not possible to change the engraved plate and that it became 'Stuart' for all time. Another suggestion was that the name was changed by Stuart's 'sponsor', James Chambers. This suggestion is favoured by Webster, and by Mudie, in their books about Stuart.[61] Stuart himself wrote, however: 'I had named this grand centre point after my esteemed commander Captain Sturt, but the Governor-in-Chief, on my return to Adelaide, observing it on my map, said, "Not so, it shall be named Mount Stuart".'[62] It is now 'Central Mount Stuart' on all modern maps. This name was not immediately accepted, however. Alfred Giles, a member of the party led by John Ross, kept a daily journal during their expedition to pave the way for a telegraph wire to be laid right across the continent from Adelaide to Darwin. They reached what Stuart had named Central Mount Sturt in January 1871 and Giles continued to refer to it by that name in his journal. He records that Harvey, the party's surveyor, remarked:[63]

Well comrades, you see yonder mountain. That is Central Mount Sturt, discovered and named by John McDouall Stuart, who led the first exploring party across Australia from south to north and back again. Our party is the second to sight it since he named it 10 years ago.

Harvey then produced a bottle of 'O.P.' (over-proof) rum and they drank Ross's health, and the health of each other. 'It certainly must have been the first rum to reach Central Australia.' On 4 January Ross and two others climbed the mountain and found the bottle (which had 'apparently been used for preserving French capers') containing Stuart's historic document:[64]

John McDouall Stuart and party, consisting of two men and himself, arrived from Adelaide in the Centre of Australia on Saturday evening, the twenty-first day of April, 1860, and have built this cairn of stones and raised the flag, to commemorate the event, on the top of Mount Sturt. The Centre is about two miles [3 kilometres] south-south-west, at a small gum creek, where there is a tree marked, facing the south. John McDouall Stuart (leader), William Darton Kekwick, Benjamin Head.

In view of the fact that Stuart suffered greatly from scurvy during the last stages of his expedition, it is of interest that Giles recorded: 'We discovered some new wild fruit here, about the size of a pear. We ate six or seven and found no ill-effects from doing so.'[65] Fruit of this nature would, almost certainly, have cured Stuart's scurvy. It seems likely that this fruit was the 'native pear' or 'doubah', *Marsdenia australis* — also known as *Leichhardtia australis*.[66]

A small hill to the north of Central Mount Stuart was named Mt Esther — after Esther Knowles who was employed at Moolooloo and who had made the flag that Stuart had raised;[67] but this name does not seem to have survived.

Stuart was hoping to make for the Victoria River

– which is more to the west – and he set off again 'a little to the north of west' towards a high peak, thinking that this direction was more likely to provide water. The 'remarkable hill' was named Mt Leichhardt, and water was indeed found in the vicinity. Two other mountains were discovered – one was named Mt Denison after the governor of New South Wales, and the other was called Mt Barkly after the governor of Victoria. It was necessary to change course from time to time to try to find water; but it was becoming increasingly difficult, and the time came when he could no longer see any prospect of finding water. He decided to retreat. By that time he was approaching the Tanami Desert, and he wrote:[68]

> I intended to have turned back sooner but I was expecting every moment to meet with a creek ... I am almost afraid that I have allowed myself to come too far. I am doubtful if all my horses will be able to get back to water ... There is no chance of getting to the north-west in this direction unless this plain soon terminates.

They began their retreat to the east on 4 May and were fortunate to find two native wells – one of which proved to be very satisfactory, especially for the horses. Stuart wrote: 'They had as much water last night and morning as they could drink and the quantity some of them drank was enormous. I had no idea that a horse could hold so much, and still want more.' [69] A few days later, still moving to the east, he named Mt Browne after the medical officer on Captain Sturt's expedition to central Australia.[70]

Stuart had now developed scurvy. He had a series of 'dreadful nights', and the 'medicines that I brought with me are all bad and of no effect'.[71] The pain was so great that he 'almost wished that death would come' and relieve him of the pain. His mouth and gums were so bad that he was obliged to 'eat flour and water boiled'.[72] Kekwick was also showing early signs of the disease. Stuart's illness continued – some days being worse than others. His diet seems to have been deficient in vitamin C, but on 17 June

he wrote: 'Although I am much better I am still very weak; the pains in my limbs are not so constant. I attribute the relief to eating a number of native cucumbers which are in quantities on this creek.' [73] The value of this vegetable has been mentioned previously.

Stuart still had to find a route to the north and this could only be done by trying one direction after another. He went to the creek to the east of Mt Denison, set off on a 028-degrees course, later changed to a more easterly course, and so on – as the nature of the country and the availability of water dictated. He named Mt Strzelecki and Mt Porphett and, further north, named Mt Samuel after his brother. He named McDouall Ranges after Colonel James McDouall of the Life Guards, who was a half-brother of his mother.[74] He also named Tennant Creek after John Tennant, and Tennant Creek was adopted as the name for the modern town. Short Range, a little to the north, was named after Bishop Short of Adelaide, and a gum creek was named Bishop Creek.

He continued on a course of 315 degrees and became increasingly worried about the nature of the country. He climbed a tree and found that if they continued it would be the same terrible scrub with no creeks. He turned to the south, but he soon regretted his decision, and made for the water of Bishop Creek. Several of the horses, including Stuart's mare Polly, had been severely 'knocked up'. Stuart wrote that they had been 101 hours without a drop of water and had 'accomplished a journey of one hundred and twelve miles' [180 kilometres]. Two days later they were visited by several Aborigines who demonstrated their hostility and made signs that seemed to indicate that Stuart and his companions should leave. They were on the opposite side of the creek and would not cross, so Stuart did so, carrying a branch of green leaves as a sign of peace. The Aborigines left. A few days later an old man, with his two sons ('two fine young men' as Stuart described them) approached – but they could not understand one another. Stuart recorded:[75]

> After some time, and having conferred with his two sons, he turned round, and surprised me by giving me one of the Masonic signs. I looked at him steadily; he repeated it, and so did his two sons. I then returned it, which seemed to please them much, the old man patting me on the shoulder and stroking down my beard.

Webster has recorded that 'Stuart was a Freemason, but the sign, of course, had unknown significance for the natives.'[76] In any case it is doubtful that Stuart was a Freemason (see also Chapter 15, page 226). Two days later Stuart's small party moved off to the north and it was not long before a large group of angry Aborigines indicated their displeasure. Stuart wrote:[77]

> I then faced them, making every sign of friendship I could think of. They seemed to be in a great fury, moving their boomerangs above their head, bawling at the top of their voices, and performing some sort of dance.

By this time there were 'upwards of thirty'. Stuart's men remained calm even when they 'received a shower of boomerangs, accompanied by a fearful yell', and even when the Aborigines 'set fire to the grass, and commenced jumping, dancing, yelling, and throwing their arms into all sorts of postures, like so many fiends'.[77] Stuart decided to retire to his previous night's camp, and beyond. The creek became known as Attack Creek, and there is a memorial near the site near where the Stuart Highway crosses the creek.

Stuart thought that the odds of at least ten to one were too great, and that open conflict should be avoided. He wrote that 'after considering the matter over the whole night, I have reluctantly come to the determination to abandon the attempt to make the Gulf of Carpentaria.'[78] It was a sensible decision. Three men could hardly expect to be able to defend themselves against so many. Moreover, he had another 'enemy' in his own camp. Ben Head

had been stealing food from the communal rations for some time, and Stuart and Kekwick were feeling the loss.[79] On 21 July, Stuart wrote:[80]

> For the last 14 days we have been getting a quantity of native cucumber and other vegetables which has done me a very great deal of good. The pains in my limbs and back are much relieved and I trust will soon go away altogether and have not the least doubt will if the vegetable and cucumber continue. We boil and eat them with a little sugar; in this way they are very good, in taste resembling the gooseberry.

Kekwick and Hall also seem to have developed scurvy. However, they had been forbidden to keep a diary of their daily experiences – apparently as a result of a government rule that there be only one account – so we have no first-hand accounts from them. On 7 August, Stuart wrote: 'Kekwick was unwell last night, but I cannot stop on his account ... He is completely done up.' He added: 'I hope and trust he will soon get better again ... He has been a most valuable man to me. I place entire confidence in him.'[81]

They came to the Finke, then the Neales, Freeling Springs, Loudon Springs, William Springs and Paisley Ponds, and arrived at Hamilton Springs on Sunday 26 August 1860 – where they rested before proceeding to Chambers Creek, which they reached on 3 September. Stuart's journal ends on that day.[82]

They found George Goyder, then the assistant surveyor-general, at Chambers Creek – where he was busy with his surveys. Stuart and his companions left Chambers Creek on 13 September 1860 to return to Adelaide by ship from Port Augusta. Goyder's letter stating this was read to parliament by the chief minister on 29 September:[83]

> Mr. Stuart left here today for the south. He and his party are ill with scurvy; they have been in latitude 18° 47' S, longitude 133° E when they were compelled to return, their party being unable to cope with the natives who attacked them.

Stuart reached Adelaide on Sunday 7 October 1860 and was enthusiastically welcomed. It was immediately agreed that a further, larger and better-equipped, expedition should be mounted as soon as possible, and that this new expedition should endeavour to reach the north coast. According to a local newspaper: 'the importance of crossing this continent from south to north [is] ... scarcely inferior to the discovery of the north west passage.'[84] Moreover, in Victoria, an expedition under the leadership of Robert O'Hara Bourke had left Melbourne on 20 August 1860 – with the object of being the first to travel from the south coast to the northern shores. Local pride demanded that South Australia should achieve this before Victoria. Further, there was an increasing need for a route by which horses and cattle could be sent to the north for shipment, by the shortest possible sea route, to India. Furthermore, there was the need to establish a route for the construction of an overland telegraph line to connect with the overseas cable.[85] Stuart had arrived back on a Sunday. On the following Wednesday, the South Australian parliament authorised an expenditure of £2500 'to enable Mr. Stuart to complete the discovery of an available route across the continent'.[86]

FIFTH EXPEDITION

Men were selected, and an advance party of six men set off for the north on 20 October – two weeks after Stuart's return. The second party, of five men, left Adelaide on 31 October 1860. Stuart himself left Adelaide by train on 2 November and joined the second party at Clare. But, because of illness, he had to delay his further advance. The whole expedition was united at Chambers Creek on 12 December. There were forty-nine horses, but many of these were 'town' horses which proved to be far too weak for the conditions. The only satisfactory horses were those that had been bred by James Chambers at his Cobdogla station.

There is some uncertainty about the names of all the members of the expedition which left Chambers Creek on 1 January 1861; but the following is thought to be correct, or nearly correct:

John McDouall Stuart	leader
William Kekwick	second-in-command
Patrick Thring	third-in-command
J. Wall	
J. N. Ewart	storekeeper
J. Woodforde	
A. J. Lawrence	
W. Masters	
D. Thompson	saddler
?. Sullivan	shoeing smith

There were now ten men and forty horses – with provisions for thirty weeks. They advanced, using the known springs whenever possible. On 5 April they found a wurley fitted with a layer of grass for use as a bed, and speculated whether this could have been constructed by a survivor from Leichhardt's expedition (see page 226).[87] Then, on 6 April, after three months of travelling, they crossed the 22° S latitude. On 18 April Stuart named Anne Creek after Thring's sister and, a few days later, reached Tennant Creek. He determined its position to be 19° 34' 45" S, 134° 45' 09" E.[88] This was the first record of a longitude observation on this expedition, and indicated that Stuart now had the appropriate instruments. Even so, most of his later determinations were of latitude only.

On 25 April 1861, they arrived at Attack Creek. On this occasion, however, he passed by without incident. As Stuart progressed to the north they observed 'many new plants, flowers and some new trees; one grows to a large size, the fruit has the appearance of plums, the foliage dark green ... A few days later he wrote: 'I believe this plain to be a continuation of the one from the Centre [the Tanami Desert] and may continue to the banks of the Victoria [River]. The absence of all birds has a bad appearance.'[89]

Stuart named these plains the 'Plains of Sturtia' 'after the venerable father of Australian exploration and my respected commander of the expedition of 1845'.[90] In the printed version, however, these became 'Sturt Plains' (now Sturt Plain). Stuart was greatly depressed by the sight of this plain – 'nothing to be seen all round but sand hills,'[91] he wrote, and 'I can see no hope of succeeding in reaching the Victoria [River] on this course'.[92] Ten days later he wrote:[93]

I think I must have seen for at least 60 miles through the telescope and I could not see the least appearance of the lowest rise nor of any water, nor can we see any tracks of natives nor their smoke in any direction ... The sun in the plains is very hot.

On 23 May 1861 they noted a flock of pelicans – indicating the presence of water not far away – and they came to a chain of ponds that Stuart named 'Glandfield Lagoon' (now Newcastle Waters) after the Duke of Newcastle, who was the secretary of state for the Colonies.[94] This was a happy discovery. They even caught a few fish – but it was a short-lived pleasure. On 12 June he wrote:[95]

This is the third time that I have tried to make the Victoria in this latitude but have been turned back every time by the same description of country ... Thus end my hopes of making the Victoria in this latitude, which is a very great disappointment.

A few days later he wrote: 'I shall now proceed to the south and try once more to round that horrid thick forest to the west.'[96] Indeed, as Webster has pointed out, Stuart made eleven different attempts 'to penetrate the barrier of waterless plain and dense scrub that lay between him and the Victoria River on the west, and the Gulf of Carpentaria on the east'.[97] Stuart did not give up easily, but men and horses alike were worn out. Their clothes were in tatters and their provisions were seriously depleted. Stuart had commented about this in his journal as early as 13 June, and had written that they were then reduced to 1.8 kilograms (4 pounds) of flour and 0.5 kilograms (1 pound) of dried meat per week for each man.[98] So, on 12 July, Stuart began his retreat.[99]

On 7 September they arrived at Chambers Creek where they spent a few days – before moving on to Moolooloo. On 16 September Stuart and Woodforde set off from Moolooloo for Port Augusta – leaving Kekwick to lead the others back to Adelaide. Stuart and Woodforde boarded the *Lubra* at Port Augusta and arrived in Adelaide early on the morning of Sunday 22 September 1861.

On Monday morning Stuart called on the governor, Sir Richard MacDonnell, and reported the results of his fifth expedition and indicated that he was more than willing to set off again in yet another attempt to reach the north coast.

Chambers had sent a copy of Stuart's journal of his fourth expedition – in which he had reached Central Mount Stuart and beyond – to Sir Roderick Murchison, the president of the Royal Geographical Society in London. This was read at a meeting of the society on 14 January 1861. Both the president and the vice-president spoke on Stuart's achievements.[100] Charles Sturt had learnt of Stuart's success – but was too sick to attend. However, Charles Bonney, who had overlanded cattle from Melbourne to Adelaide with Sturt, and who was now on a visit to London, also spoke and read a letter from Sturt:[101]

I am not at all surprised at Stuart's success, for I know him to be a plucky little fellow – cool, persevering and intelligent, as well as an excellent bushman ... He is entitled to all praise for his exertions, and it is really a matter of pride to me that it has fallen to one of my oldest and best followers to have achieved so very creditable an enterprise and to have shown such zeal and energy. He has fairly passed, or I should say, surpassed me, and may justly claim the laurels.

The society decided to award Stuart its highest honour – the Patron's Medal – and this was done on 27 May 1861. The Duke of Newcastle received the medal on Stuart's behalf and forwarded it to the governor – who presented it to Stuart himself.[102]

SIXTH EXPEDITION

Preparations for Stuart's next expedition to the north began immediately. Provisions were purchased and sent on to Chambers Creek, and Kekwick and Woodforde went there to organise the stores for a ready departure. The South Australian parliament voted to provide £2000 for expenses. Members of the party were selected by Chambers and Stuart – except for Waterhouse, the naturalist, who was added to the party by order of the government, but against the wishes of Stuart. Stuart and Kekwick were to be paid by Chambers. In the end, the party consisted of:

John McDouall Stuart	leader
William Darton Kekwick	second-in-command
Francis W. Thring	third-in-command
W. Patrick Auld	assistant
James Frew	
Stephen King	
Heath Nash	acting cook
John McGorrerey	shoeing smith
Frederick G. Waterhouse	naturalist
John Billiatt	

Jeffries (who had been added at Chambers Creek) and Woodforde were on the original list – but both were later dismissed for insubordination. John Billiatt, who accompanied the party in its early stages as a volunteer, then became an official member of the expedition. Several members were rather young. Frew, for example was aged eighteen, and Stephen King was twenty. Stuart went to the Chambers property at Cobdogla to select the horses required for the expedition, and fifty-five were selected – fifteen of which were to be for the personal use of Stuart and Kekwick. The twenty-six horses brought back from the fifth expedition (and which had been resting at Clare) were again included. Stuart's mare, Polly, was one of these. With the approval of the government, the commissioner of Crown Lands, H. B. T. Strangways, wrote a letter to Stuart setting out the aims and objects of the expedition as seen by the government. This letter concluded as follows:[103]

> The Government rely with confidence on your prudence and the abilities you have exhibited as an explorer for the carrying out of the objects shadowed forth in this letter and you are specially requested not to regard this letter as giving positive instructions but merely as setting forth the views of the Government – and you are of course at full liberty to act as circumstances may require or your mature judgement indicate as expedient.

The government did not advocate a change of route – for example to make for the Gulf of Carpentaria rather than for the Victoria River – but an important letter was received by the Lands Department which led Stuart to decide to make for the Adelaide River rather than the Victoria. This required a more easterly route for the final section than that necessary to make for the Victoria River. The letter was written by Lieutenant Frank Helpman who had served in the *Beagle* – first under Captain John Wickham and then with Captain John Lort Stokes. He wrote from Warrnambool on 5 October 1861, and pointed out that, with Captain Wickham, he had travelled up the Adelaide River for about 112 kilometres (70 miles) – the water never being less than about 4 metres (2 fathoms) deep. He regarded the Adelaide as 'a river formed by nature for some grand purpose. It is easy to access in all monsoons.' In contrast, the Victoria River 'is filled with most dangerous sand banks at its approaches and all the way up'.[104] Stuart took note of these comments by an experienced observer and decided that, this time, his expedition would make for the Adelaide River.

The main party left Adelaide on 25 October 1861 for Moolooloo, and then for Chambers Creek. Stuart had had an accident and was unfit to travel. A horse had reared and knocked him unconscious, and had badly damaged his right hand. He remained in Adelaide for a further six weeks and then travelled north accompanied by Waterhouse. They reached Moolooloo on 9 December and, after spending a few days there, proceeded to Chambers Creek, where the men had been busy preparing the stock of dried or 'jerked' meat.[105] Stuart arrived at Chambers Creek on 31 December 1861, and all members of the expedition were together. When they left Chambers Creek, Stuart had nine men and seventy-two horses. They proceeded – taking full advantage of the mound springs that had already been discovered. They had some trouble with a few warlike Aborigines, and Thring 'was obliged to use his revolver in self defence' on 17 February 1862.[106] A few days later, on 25 February 1862, the party was harassed by a number of Aborigines who set fire to the grass and appeared ready to use their spears. Stuart asked Auld to fire at a rock not far from the angry tribesmen and this 'had the effect of sending them all off at full speed'.[107] However, they again encountered no trouble at Attack Creek.

Stuart was taking particular care of the navigation and, on Saturday 19 April 1862, when they were at the north end of Newcastle Waters, he wrote: 'I shall remain here till Monday in order to take some lunar observations as I am not quite certain that my longitude is correct.'[108] Then, on 23 April, he recorded the details of his courses and distances, for transfer to his map:[109]

> I started with Thring and Frew at 8.5 a.m. [sic] on a course of 284°. At 9.55 a.m. (7 miles) changed to 320°. At 11.20 a.m. (4½ miles) crossed the open plain, changed to 40° to avoid the scrub. At 1½ miles changed to west. At 1 mile changed to north-west (12¼ miles) at 2.20 p.m. (5 miles) changed to 45°. At 3 o'clock (2 miles) changed to north, at 3.25 (1½ miles) changed to north-west. At 3.45 (1 mile) camped without water.

As if to reinforce his decision to make for the Adelaide River he wrote: 'With such hot weather as this I dare not attempt to make the Victoria. The horses could not go 140 miles [220 kilometres] without water.'[110] Stuart was now scouting about

in order to find a suitable course. On 29 April they 'Started on an easterly course, following the flight of the birds'; but they encountered thick forest. They changed course again and again but 'without seeing a drop of water'.[111] On 2 May, however, they came to a chain of ponds that Stuart decided to name King's Ponds 'in token of my approbation of his care and attention towards the horses and his readiness and care in executing all my orders'.[112] A few days later they were visited by some Aboriginal people who appeared to be friendly. But after they left, they set fire to the grass presumably in an endeavour to persuade Stuart to leave their area. On 8 May 1862 Stuart found many tracks leading to a spring and he named this Nash Spring after Heath Nash 'in token of my approbation'.[113] It was a constant struggle to find water. One horse died on 11 May and another was 'completely knocked up'. Stuart wrote that 'I must now endeavour to the northward and make the Roper.'[114]

On 19 May he took 'a lunar observation' but did not record the longitude. On 20 May he named Auld's Ponds 'in token of my approbation of his conduct', and the following day he named McGorrerey Ponds. The next day, having returned to McGorrerey Ponds, he wrote: 'Day very hot and the horses much distressed for the want of water – they have the appearance of being half starved for a month and have drunk an immense quantity of water, having gone to the water about 4 or 5 times in an hour.'[115] They continued on a course a little to the east of north and came to a number of ponds surrounded by gum trees. 'I have named this Daly Waters,' he wrote, 'in honour of his Excellency the Governor in Chief.' But, as Webster has pointed out, this name must have been inserted later – because Sir Dominick Daly did not take office until 4 March 1862, long after Stuart had left Adelaide.[116]

Stuart always had to go 'where the water leads me'. They came to Purdie's Ponds and, on 11 June, came to a creek, apparently flowing to the north, that Stuart named Strangways River after the commissioner of Crown Lands. He later named Mt Mueller, after the botanist. He came to a branch of the Roper River and followed it for a time. On 26 June 1862, however, he wrote:[117]

> My journeys have been very short last week in consequence of my being weak from the effects of scurvy and a severe attack of dysentery ... but having lately obtained some native cucumbers I find they are doing me a deal of good and hope by next week to be all right again.

Many of the horses were now in a very sorry state. One died and was soon cut up – partly for use as fresh meat and partly for drying. They enjoyed a 'delightful change of fresh meat from dry'. Stuart added 'the horse eats remarkably well although not quite as good as bullock.'[118]

On 30 June they came to another river and Stuart wrote: 'As this is a different branch [of the Roper River] to those previously discovered I have named it the River Chambers, after my late lamented friend James Chambers, Esq., whose zeal in the cause of Australian exploration is already well known.'[119] This must have been added after his return to Adelaide. He also named a river after Frederick George Waterhouse, the naturalist with the expedition, and curator at the South Australian Museum.[120] As they moved forwards another stream was named the 'Fanny' after the eldest daughter of James Chambers, and another the 'Catherine' after his second daughter. It is now the 'Katherine'.[121] Beyond the Katherine they came to some springs having an excellent flow of water; these were named Kekwick Springs 'in honour of my Chief Officer'.[122] Other springs were named Billiatt Springs 'in token of my approbation of Billiatt's thoughtful, generous, and unselfish conduct throughout the expedition'.[123]

Stuart sought to follow the river he thought to be the Adelaide River. However, he was, in fact, further east – near the Mary River. He determined his longitude only rarely – but in any case the Admiralty chart of the coastline and rivers was not accurate. As they neared the coast, the river deteriorated to a swamp. Stuart led them about 10 kilometres (6 miles) to the east where they discovered another creek – which was named Thring Creek. From there, further east and then north for about 15 kilometres (9 miles), they were still unable to avoid the marsh. However, on 24 July, they succeeded in finding a way through the marshy country. 'I have taken this course,' Stuart wrote, 'in order to make the seacoast, which I suppose to be distant about 8½ miles [14 kilometres], as soon as possible; by this I hope to avoid the swamps.'[124] He added: 'I did not inform any of the party, except Thring and Auld, that I was now so near to the sea, as I wished to give them a surprise on reaching it.'[125] He crossed a valley, entered the scrub, and stopped the horses. He 'advanced a few yards on to the beach' and was 'delighted and gratified at the sight of the sea'. Thring called out 'The Sea', and they all gave three long and hearty cheers.[126] Stuart dipped his feet in the waters of the Arafura Sea (Van Diemen Gulf) and washed his face and hands in it. He found it was impossible to take the horses along the beach to the mouth of the Adelaide River. It was covered with a 'soft bluish mud in which my horse sank up to his knees'. He left the beach and, finding a large tree some distance from the beach, had his initials, 'J. M. D. S.', carved in the bark.[127]

He hoped to be able to travel to the mouth of the Adelaide River – some distance behind the beach – and he made a little progress in this direction. He came across a stream that was named Charles Creek – after the eldest son of John Chambers. Further progress was more and more difficult, and he decided that the mouth of the Adelaide River could not be reached without the loss of several horses. He therefore abandoned the idea of raising the flag at the mouth of the river and to carry out the ceremony at a site to the west of their first sight of the sea. An open space was cleared of mangroves, a tall tree was stripped of its lower branches, and the Union Jack, with his name sewn

Stuart's Marked Tree was found in 1883 by a party including G. R. McMinn (left), and J. R. Parsons (right); photograph by Paul Foelsche – also a member of the party. (Royal Geographical Society of South Australia)

in the centre of the flag, was raised. They then gave three cheers. Kekwick made a speech and Stuart replied. Waterhouse also said a few words. There were then three cheers for the Queen, and another three for the Prince of Wales. It was exactly nine months since the party had left North Adelaide.

At the foot of the tree which had served as a mast they buried an airtight tin containing the following message:[128]

The exploring party under the command of John McDouall Stuart arrived at this spot on the 25th day of July, 1862, having crossed the entire Continent of Australia from the Southern to the Indian Ocean passing through the centre. They left the City of Adelaide on the 26th [actually the 25th] day of October 1861 and the most northern station of the colony on 21st day of January 1862. To commemorate this happy event, they have raised the flag bearing his name. All well. God save the Queen!

The flag had been made by Miss Elizabeth Chambers. Stuart named the bay where it had been raised 'Elizabeth Bay' – but it was later changed to Chambers Bay. The bay to the east, where they had first seen the sea, was named Finke Bay, and the point between the two bays was later named Point Stuart. The tin in which the message was placed has never been found. It is thought that it must have been destroyed by sea water.

Stuart was disappointed that he had not been able to reach the mouth of the Adelaide River – but the horses were a continuing concern. Many of the 'town' horses were now so weak that he was compelled to use the Cobdogla horses for more and more of the work. He noted that 'not one of them had failed.' He also noted:[129]

The sea has been reached which was the great object of the expedition and a practicable route found through a splendid country from Newcastle Waters to it, abounding for a great part of the way in running streams well stocked with fish.

Stuart commenced his return journey to the south on Saturday 26 July and, a few days later, one of the Cobdogla horses did fail. But he had been overloaded.[130] As they progressed they often camped at the sites that had been used on the forward journey. Stuart kept a sharp eye on any Aboriginal people who were seen. Within a few days, for example, they were visited by some of the native people who appeared friendly – but the Aborigines set fire to the grass as they departed. Stuart thought they were 'certainly the smallest and most miserable-looking race of men that I have ever seen'.[131] Burning grass continued to be a problem on other occasions.

The horses were the biggest problem, however – especially because 'knocked-up' horses often had to be abandoned. Stuart himself was also 'knocked up'. On 20 August he noted that his teeth and gums were so bad that it was extremely painful for him to eat anything. His scurvy was becoming worse. Furthermore, his sight was now 'very much impaired'. After sundown he was 'in total darkness' and incapable of taking observations at night.[132] On 27 August, a month after he began his return journey, he wrote: 'I cannot now see a single star, everything to me at night is total darkness.'[133] It seems likely that he was suffering from a deficiency of several vitamins. Night blindness is now known to be caused by a deficiency of vitamin A. However he believed that he 'must submit to the will of Divine Providence'. Surprisingly, he seems to have been the only member of the party who was seriously troubled by scurvy.

Water became difficult to find as they moved further south, and the Aboriginal people also changed. One group he thought were 'a fine race of men, stout, tall and muscular', and 'very quiet'.[134] He decided to 'push through to Attack Creek where I am almost sure of there being water'.[135] He did

find water at Attack Creek – but it was much reduced. Fortunately, the Aborigines were friendly on this occasion.

On 25 September 1862 their rations were reduced to 2.5 kilograms (5 pounds) of flour and 0.5 kilograms (1 pound) of dried meat per man per week. The next 'knocked-up' horse was shot and used for meat. Stuart was becoming very irritable from the increasing pain of scurvy. It was impossible for him to remain for a long time in the saddle. A stretcher was constructed and suspended between two horses and Stuart began to travel on this device. He was certainly very unwell. Auld even remarked, on one occasion, that Stuart's breath 'smelt the same as the atmosphere of a room in which a dead body had been kept for some days'.[136] Still, with the help of his companions, he arrived at Chambers Creek on 4 December.[137] They pushed on to Glen's station on 9 December, and to Mt Stuart station – where they were met by John Chambers and learnt of the death of James Chambers. Stuart, Auld and Chambers rode to Kooringa station, or Burra, and sent a telegram to the commissioner of Crown Lands in Adelaide.[138]

Kooringa Station
December 16th 1862

John McDouall Stuart,
Commander of the South Australian Great Northern Exploration Expedition.

To Hon. Commissioner of Crown Lands.

Through you I beg to inform His Excellency the Governor-in-Chief and the Government that I have accomplished the object of expedition party behind all well I will be in by the evening train tomorrow.

Stuart, Auld and Chambers travelled by stage coach to Kapunda – where they caught the train into Adelaide. It was 17 December 1862. They were given a grand welcome. Kekwick and the remainder of the party had remained at Mt Margaret to allow the horses to recover. They set out again on

8 December and arrived at Gawler on 18 December. A public procession was arranged for 21 January to allow the citizens to cheer and congratulate the explorers who 'by perseverance and courage had accomplished a great national undertaking'.[139] On the same day, the remains of Burke and Wills were carried through the streets of Melbourne.

Stuart and his companions were the heroes of the hour. They had made discoveries enabling further expansion of the settled districts, and had discovered a route suitable for building the projected overland telegraph line. However, Stuart was now a sick man – and he was never to recover his health. In the past he had frequently lived in the home of his best friend, James Chambers. But Chambers was now dead, and Stuart could hardly intrude on the widow's sorrow. Stuart had no home and few friends. He went to stay in the Seaside Family Hotel at Brighton – a suburb of Adelaide – hoping that the sea air would be beneficial. He was lonely and dispirited. He was reduced to petitioning for a government pension from the colonial government, or from the United Kingdom, and to requesting friends (such as Charles Sturt) to support his application for financial help. Some such assistance was necessary because he was no longer able to pursue his former profession as a surveyor. In all this he had only moderate and inadequate success.

In 1863 Stuart visited Cobdogla, Moolooloo and Chambers Creek. He sold his lease of the Chambers Creek station – partly to John Chambers, and the remainder to Alfred Barker. On 25 April 1864 he sailed for England in the *Indus*. Stuart wanted to publish his journal accounts of his various expeditions, and they had been submitted to the London publishers Saunders, Otley & Co. The journals clearly required rewriting in a more narrative style – but this was beyond the capacity of Stuart in his state of health. Sir William Hardman, an experienced editor, was given the task. Hardman had had no experience of Australia, and little sympathy with Stuart. He wrote that he was to 'be allowed full latitude to add, curtail, or dish up as I may fancy best for Stuart and the public at large'. He later wrote:[140]

> I have cut a good deal of his *earlier* explorations, and have remodelled multitudes of passages everywhere, for the Journal in its untouched form is frequently little better than a collection of *rough* jottings, without the slightest regard for literary composition.

He also wrote: 'I hope Stuart may recognize his journals after they leave my hands, pared and trimmed as they will be to a fearful extent.' Webster has pointed out: 'As examples of editorial ineptitude these would be difficult to equal.' Hardman also persuaded the artist to embellish the illustrations by adding a few Aborigines and suitable – or unsuitable – vegetation.[140] Stuart's journals were also published as parliamentary papers – but these too were edited, this time by an unknown hand.

It might be true, as Strehlow has written, that 'Stuart lacked the literary style of Ernest Giles … and hence the Journals recording his three great journeys of 1860, 1861 and 1862 across the continent from south to north are rarely read and even more rarely appreciated.'[141] It must be remembered, however, that Stuart's journals were written in the field and that most explorers, Charles Sturt for example, had an opportunity to rewrite their accounts before publication. Stuart was too ill to undertake this task and his reputation has suffered. It is hoped that, one day, a new, well-edited account of Stuart's journals will be published. Such a work, in typescript, has been prepared by the late Mona Stuart Webster, and is in the Mortlock Library in Adelaide. Her manuscript was prepared using the original handwritten journals which have survived (some have been lost), the relevant parliamentary papers, and the Hardman edition.

Stuart's reputation also suffered from other problems. He and his companions had reached the north coast, but where exactly? He had thought that the Mary River was a branch of the Adelaide

River – but he was incorrect in this belief. He had been further to the east than he thought. When subsequent explorers and surveying parties visited the area to the east of the Adelaide River, they failed to find any evidence that Stuart's party had been there. In particular, they failed to find the great tree in which Stuart had reported that his initials had been cut. Stuart's marked tree was not found until 1883 – largely owing to the perseverence of G. R. McMinn, a senior government surveyor. McMinn visited the site himself, in company with Police Inspector Paul Foelsche – who took a photograph of the tree in which Stuart's initials are plainly visible. Since then, however, the tree has been completely destroyed by fire.[142]

In the meantime, however, John McDouall Stuart died on 4 June 1866, aged fifty, at a house in Notting Hill Square (later Campden Hill Square), London. He was buried at the Kensal Green Cemetery, and a funeral notice was published in the *Times*. The funeral service was attended by a total of seven people – four relatives, Alexander Hay (an Australian pastoralist and politician), and John Arrowsmith and A. G. Findlay (both representing the Royal Geographical Society).

Statue of John McDouall Stuart in Victoria Square in Adelaide. (Geoffrey Badger)

STUART THE MAN

Stuart's biographer, Mona Stuart Webster, has described him as a 'somewhat shy, reserved and unassuming man' with a 'capacity for loyal friendship and an ability to inspire the same feeling in others'.[143] There is no doubt that he was a born leader and no doubt that his friendships with James Sinclair, James Chambers, John Chambers and William Finke were real and lasting. He showed 'the greatest loyalty and affection' for Charles Sturt – his leader on the 1844–46 expedition that attempted to find an inland sea. He wanted to name the mountain at the centre, Central Mount Sturt in honour of Charles Sturt, but was thwarted by the governor. He always placed on record his appreciation of the services of his officers – particularly William Kekwick, Francis Thring and Patrick Auld. He also recorded his appreciation of his men, and several geographical features were named after the best of them.

Many writers have praised Stuart's own qualities. Strehlow, for example, wrote that Stuart was 'a man whose amazing persistence, indomitable courage, and unfailing common sense enabled him to succeed on a mighty task in which others would have failed'; and:[144]

Compared with him Leichhardt was an ill-advised, impetuous, and unlucky adventurer, and Burke a hot-headed newchum who muffed a relatively easy assignment by his incredible incompetence, thus snatching defeat and death out of an expedition of which victory had originally seemed the only possible outcome.

Another important testimony to Stuart was written by Aeneas Gunn and published in the Melbourne *Leader* in 1903. It was quoted by Mona Stuart Webster in 1961:[145]

> Stuart was the last of the great explorers, if not the greatest of them all. Others may have undergone greater privations and encountered more considerable hard-ships, but Stuart had qualities that enabled him to avert calamities that befell the most intrepid and zealous of his compeers. His expeditions were undertaken without ostentation. He took no theatrical risks nor hazardous shortcuts and he came through his journeys without tragic failures or dramatic incidents to mark them for public concern. Stuart had an especial genius for organization and command, a wonderful instinct in bushcraft, an indomitable perseverance and an invincible determination, allied with a scrupulous regard for the welfare of his party and a constant care for his resources in horseflesh. His longest and most important journey, from Adelaide to Van Diemen Gulf and back across what were then believed to be the hopeless wastes of the centre, occupied precisely twelve months, for the whole of which distance and time he had to carry provisions and plant, yet he never lost a life, and his loss of horses was infinitesimal.
>
> The value of his work is demonstrated by the fact that the Overland Telegraph Line built ten years later, practically follows the route of his march; that prosperous cattle, horse and sheep stations are established on all the principal waters discovered by him; and that it is highly probable the transcontinental railway projected by the South Australian Government will, if ever constructed, follow broadly in the track of the last of the great Australian explorers – John McDouall Stuart.

With the progress of modern technology the overland telegraph is no longer used and the repeater stations have fallen into decay. But, at the time, it was of enormous importance. Today, the Stuart Highway practically follows Stuart's route and continues to provide a valuable service – especially as the north–south transcontinental railway has not yet been constructed.

NOTES

PREFACE

1. Beaglehole 1968, vol. 1, p. 381; Abbot 1995 p. 4; Abbot & Leech 1996, p. 51.
2. James 1994.
3. *Time Magazine*, 28 July 1997, p. 9.

– 1 –
THE OPENING OF THE WORLD

1. Latham 1958, p. 125.
2. ibid., p. 130.
3. ibid., p. 156.
4. Waugh 1984, p. 10. This edition is extensively illustrated.
5. 'Letter to the King and Queen of Spain in 1501' in Varela 1992, pp 444–5; Rienits & Rienits 1970, p. 15; Phillips & Phillips 1992, p. 92; Columbus 1959.
6. Ferdinand inherited the Crown of Aragón and Sicily; Isabella inherited the Crown of Castilla and León.
7. Phillips & Phillips 1992; Granzotto 1986.
8. Judge & Stanfield 1986.
9. Jane 1968.
10. Jane 1968, p. 39.
11. Phillips & Phillips 1992.
12. ibid., p. 241.
13. Dor-Ner & Scheller 1992, p. 234.
14. Cox 1995, p. 618; Roizman 1995.
15. Dor-Ner & Scheller 1992, p. 217.
16. Henneberg & Henneberg 1994.
17. Phillips & Phillips 1992, p. 188.
18. Bell 1974, pp 150–3; Wallis 1986, p. 27.
19. Bell 1974, pp 201–17; Hart 1952, pp 136 et seq.
20. Innes 1986, p. 135; Kirkpatrick 1934, pp 49–53.
21. Devine 1973. David Devine has written an interesting volume entitled *The Opening of the World*.

22. Roditi 1972, p. 85.
23. Quoted by Hart 1952, p. 242.
24. Guillemard 1890, pp 329–36.
25. Villiers 1976.
26. Pigafetta 1969.
27. ibid., vol. 1, p. 51.
28. Guillemard 1890, p. 222.
29. His name is often given as Juan Sebastian d' Elcano; however, he himself signed his name as Sebastian del Cano. See Guillemard 1890, p. 303.
30. Devine 1973, p. 178.
31. Roditi 1972, p. 257.
32. See, for example, the novel *Manila Galleon* by van Wyck Mason 1961.

– 2 –
NAVIGATION AT SEA AND ON LAND

1. Bennett 1987, p. 29; Waters 1958, pp 20 et seq.; Williams 1994, pp 22 et seq.
2. Williams 1994, p. 13.
3. This map is reproduced on the end papers of Badger 1988.
4. Williams 1994, p. 81.
5. Waters 1958, p. 136.
6. Brown 1978, pp 6, 49.
7. Jane 1968, p. 11.
8. Columbus 1959, p. 74.
9. Taylor & Richey 1962, p. 28.
10. North 1974, p. 96.
11. Taylor & Richey 1962, p. 37.
12. ibid., pp 53, 57.
13. ibid., loc. cit.
14. Guillemard 1890, pp 334–5.
15. Day 1967, pp 15, 33.
16. Sobel 1995.
17. Bennett 1987, p. 203.
18. Queensland Department of Mapping and Surveying 1987.

19. McMinn 1970, pp 18, 78; see also Cunningham 1828, p. 65.
20. Andrews 1992, p. 358; Johnston 1962, p. 97.
21. Sturt 1849, Vol. 1, p. 345.
22. Bennett 1987, p. 153.
23. W. J. Wills, Astronomical Observations, 31 August–4 October 1860, *La Trobe Manuscripts Collection*, State Library of Victoria, box 2083/1c.
24. Barratt 1988, p. 154.

– 3 –

THE FIRST SIGHTINGS OF AUSTRALIA

1. Thorne et al. 1999.
2. Williams et al. 1993, p. 81.
3. Flood 1995, pp 28–9.
4. Serjeantson 1989, p. 120.
5. Flood 1995, p. 34; Thorne & Raymond 1989, pp 39–45.
6. Corbett 1995, p. 17. The oldest carbon-dated skeleton of a dingo in Australia was 3450±95 years BP; O'Neill 1997; Holden, 1991.
7. Flood 1995, p. 200.
8. Blainey 1994, p. 12.
9. Fernández-Armesto 1991, p. 23.
10. Latham 1958, pp 43–5.
11. Rolls 1990.
12. Wade 1977.
13. Davidson 1939; Tindale 1928; Tindale 1940; Fitzgerald 1953.
14. Terence Measham, Director of the Powerhouse Museum, pers. comm.
15. Warner 1932.
16. Flinders 1814, vol. 2, p. 172.
17. ibid., pp 228–33.
18. Dumont d'Urville 1987, vol. 2, pp 392–3.
19. Tindale 1926.
20. Davidson 1935. The South Australian Museum has a dug-out canoe which was made by Australian Aboriginal people after instruction by Macassans.
21. Macknight 1972; Macknight 1976, p. 97.
22. Archibald 1891; McCrae 1910–11.
23. McKiggan 1987, p. 61.
24. Sharp 1963, p. 55; McIntyre 1977, p. 263; FitzGerald 1984, p. 127.
25. Hervé 1983.
26. Langdon 1975.
27. FitzGerald 1984, p. viii.
28. Richardson 1995a, p. 90.
29. FitzGerald 1984, p. viii.
30. Spate 1982.
31. Collingridge 1895.
32. ibid., p. viii.
33. Richardson 1995a, pp 83–107.
34. Richardson 1989, p. 6.
35. McIntyre 1977; FitzGerald 1984; Wallis 1986; Duncan 1997.
36. Beaglehole 1968, vol. 1, p. 310.
37. Richardson 1989, p. 8.
38. FitzGerald 1984, p. 134.
39. Richardson 1988; W. A. R. Richardson, pers. comm., 1995.
40. Richardson 1995b, p. 136.
41. Collingridge 1895, p. 324; McIntyre 1977, p. 114; FitzGerald 1984, pp 84, 113. He also equates it with 'ap quieta' on the Descelliers Map.
42. Richardson 1995b, pp 141–2.
43. I am indebted to Kenneth Price for drawing my intention to these paintings. E. B. White-house (1995, p. 19) 'identifies' them as Arab dhows!
44. Bambrick 1994, p. 83.
45. Sharp 1963, pp 89–91.
46. ibid., pp 15-20.
47. ibid., pp 22–30; Stevens 1930; Bayldon 1926, 1930.
48. Austrialia, not Australia. According to J. C. Beaglehole (1947, p. 94) the name was in honour of Phillip III who was also Archduke of Austria.
49. Stevens 1930; Bayldon 1926, 1930; Sharp 1963, pp 22 et seq.; Hilder 1980.
50. Chisholm 1958, vol. 9, pp 132–4; Sharp 1963, p. 32; Heeres 1898, pp 93–6.
51. The Mary Rose Trust 1994, p. 20.
52. Sharp 1963, p. 41.
53. Schilder 1976, p. 96.
54. Sharp 1963, p. 55; Heeres 1898, pp 51, 97.
55. Heeres 1898, quoted by Sharp 1963, pp 39–40.
56. W. A. R. Richardson, pers. comm., 1995.
57. Drake-Brockman 1963; Sharp 1963, pp 59–64; Godard 1993.
58. Playford 1996, p. 19; Leyland & Leyland 1967, pp 30, 37–8, 47.

59. Dickman, C., *Rottnest Island: the Quokka* – A pamphlet published by the Rottnest Island Authority, Western Australia.
60. Chisholm 1958, vol. 9, pp 132–4.
61. Dunmore 1969, vol. 2, p. 73; Freycinet 1827–39, vol. 1, p. 449.
62. Sharp 1963, p. 72; Sharp 1968, pp 82, 88–90; Duyker 1992, p. 10.
63. Duyker 1992, p. 10.
64. Sharp 1968, p. 68; McIntyre 1977, p. 17.
65. Duyker 1992 (p. 13) identifies this with *Apium prostratum*, which Cook later used as an antiscorbutic in Tierra del Fuego and in New Zealand.
66. Flinders 1801, reprinted 1979.
67. Quoted by Sharp 1968, p. 314.
68. Marchant 1988, p. 38.
69. Both ships were privateers. Marchant 1988 was at some pains to dismiss the suggestion that Dampier was ever a pirate. The dictionary meaning of 'buccaneer' is 'a pirate'; or 'one of the piratical adventurers who raided Spanish colonies or shipping in America'; or 'to act like, or lead the life of, a buccaneer' (Delbridge 1991, p. 232).
70. Dampier 1697; republished 1937, p. 254.
71. Karra Katta Bay has, with the help of the Royal Australian Navy, been identified as the site of the careening (Marchant 1988, p. 114). See also Dampier 1937, p. 311; Sharp 1963, p. 96.
72. Quoted by Marchant 1988, p. 121.
73. Dampier 1729; facsimile edition 1981, p. 46. This edition was edited, and is provided with an introduction by James Spencer.
74. Dampier 1729 (1981), p. 65.
75. ibid., p. 79.
76. ibid., p. 81.
77. ibid., p. 87.
78. ibid., p. 107.
79. ibid., p. 110.
80. Marchant 1988, pp 138–142.
81. Dampier 1729 (1981), p. 117.
82. ibid., p. 125.
83. Badger 1988, p. 40.
84. Dampier 1729 (1981), p. 150.
85. Spencer 1981.

– 4 –

THE MARITIME EXPLORATION.

1. Scott 1912, p. 146.
2. Beaglehole 1968, vol. 1, p. 304.
3. ibid., p. 305.
4. ibid., p. 310.
5. ibid., p. 312.
6. ibid., p. 343.
7. ibid., p. 346.
8. Badger 1970, p. 30.
9. Banks 1980.
10. Prof. G. B. Sharman, pers. comm.
11. Beaglehole 1968, vol. 1, p. 387.
12. ibid., p. 388.
13. Scott 1912, pp 151, 158.
14. Green & Cook 1771; Skelton 1954.
15. Green & Cook 1771.
16. Beaglehole 1968, vol. 1, p. 119.
17. Woolley 1970, p. 118.
18. Admiralty Instructions to Cook, *Canberra Letter Book*, National Library of Australia, Canberra; White 1970, p. 50.
19. Walter 1911; Pack 1960; Emsley 1995.
20. J. Banks in Beaglehole 1962, vol. 1, p. 393.
21. Lind 1953.
22. Kodicek & Young 1969.
23. Cook 1776.
24. Beaglehole 1967, vol. 3, pt 2, p. 1456.
25. Beaglehole 1969, Appendix 6, p. 871.
26. Cook 1776, p. 402.
27. Hatt 1949.
28. Chick 1953; Badger 1988, p. 127.
29. Ingleton 1962; author John White was surgeon-general to the First Fleet.
30. Eldershaw 1938, p. 34.
31. Tench, in Flannery 1996, p. 19.
32. Smith 1974, p. 40; Moore 1987, p. 283.
33. Tench, in Flannery 1996, p. 37.
34. ibid., p. 38.
35. King 1984, p. 11.
36. Watson 1914–25, vol. 1, p. 18.
37. Tench 1961, p. 59.
38. Tench, in Flannery 1996, p. 44.
39. ibid., p. 49.
40. ibid., p. 50.
41. ibid., p. 125.

42. White 1962, pp 133–4.
43. Tench, in Flannery 1996, p. 53.
44. ibid., p. 55.
45. ibid., p. 53.
46. Flannery 1994, p. 264.
47. Tench, in Flannery 1996, p. 103, footnote.
48. Rienits 1962, p. 18; 'Governor Phillip to Lord Sydney' in Bladen 1892–1901, vol. I (2), p. 308.
49. Watson 1914–25, vol. 1, pp 20, 32.
50. White 1962, p. 133.
51. Milford 1935, p. 33.
52. Tench, in Flannery 1996, p. 88.
53. ibid., p. 92.
54. ibid., p. 127.
55. ibid., loc. cit.
56. Milford 1935, p. 44.
57. Tench, in Flannery 1996, p. 78.
58. Watson 1914–25, vol. 1, p. 20.
59. 'Governor Phillip to Lord Sydney' in Bladen 1892–1901, vol. I (2), p. 134.
60. 'Letter from Vancouver to Grenville, 9 August 1791, from the Cape of Good Hope', in Vancouver 1984, vol. 1, p. 58.
61. Vancouver 1984, vol. 1, pp 355–6.
62. Newcombe 1923. See entries for 30 September, and 1 and 4 October 1791; Balfour 1944, p. 170; Dillon 1951, p. 151.
63. Lamb 1984.
64. Dunmore 1965, vol. 1, pp 283 et seq.
65. Rossel 1808.
66. Bowden 1952, p. 23.
67. Scott 1912, p. 155.
68. Mackaness 1979, p. 9.
69. Flinders 1979 (Flinders 1801), p. 54.
70. Grant 1803.
71. Campbell 1916, p. 489.
72. Grant 1803, p. 80.
73. ibid., p. 81.
74. ibid., p. 85.
75. Macqueen 1993.
76. Collett 1996, p. 27; Webb 1995; Wilson 1995, p. 22; Caley 1966; Andrews 1984.
77. Caley 1966, pp x, xi.
78. Beaglehole 1968, vol. 1, p. 303.
79. Grant 1803, p. 139.
80. ibid., p. 125; Scott 1912, p. 160.
81. Grant 1803, p. 173.

82. Grant wrote the name 'Schank' and, because the two men were friends, it seems likely that this is the way that Schank wanted his name written. However, many charts write the name as 'Schanck', and Flinders also used this spelling.
83. Scott 1912, p. 164.

– 5 –
A MAJOR FRENCH EXPEDITION

1. Faivre 1974.
2. Fleurieu 1791.
3. Dunmore 1969, p. 13; Baudin 1974, p. 576.
4. Baudin 1974, pp 573 et seq.
5. Horner 1987, p. 72; Péron 1809, p. 15.
6. Horner 1987, p. 81.
7. de Beer 1952, p. 257.
8. Horner 1987, p. 121.
9. Péron 1809, p. 54.
10. Wallace 1984, p. 51.
11. ibid., p. i.
12. Freycinet 1811.
13. Horner 1987, p. 178.
14. Péron 1809, p. 132; Wallace 1984, p. 67.
15. Péron 1809, pp 134–6.
16. Horner 1987, p. 190.
17. Baudin 1974, pp 301–2.
18. Horner 1987, p. 204.
19. ibid., p. 210.
20. Baudin 1974, p. 364.
21. ibid., p. 363.
22. Horner 1987, p. 214.
23. Baudin 1974, p. 379.
24. Horner 1987, pp 216 et seq.
25. Baudin 1974, p. 402.
26. ibid., p. 399.
27. ibid., p. 401.
28. ibid., p. 409.
29. Péron 1809, pp 260–7.
30. ibid., p. 261.
31. Triebel & Batt 1943, p. 47. The translated passages are from the original French edition.
32. Flinders 1814, vol. 1, p. 230.
33. Péron 1809, p. 262.
34. ibid., loc. cit.
35. Flinders 1814, vol. 1, p. 226.
36. Horner 1987, p. 242.

37. ibid., p. 249.
38. ibid., p. 250.
39. 'Contract with Bass and Bishop for the Importation of Pork, 9.10.1801', in Watson, 1921–23, pp 337–8; Maude 1968.
40. Horner 1987, p. 261.
41. Baudin 1974, p. 441.
42. ibid., loc. cit.
43. Horner 1987, p. 273.
44. ibid., pp 271–2.
45. ibid., p. 276.
46. ibid., p. 278.
47. Jouanin 1959, p.169; Baudin 1974, p. 453; Parker 1984, p.19; Badger 1988, pp 182–3.
48. Baudin 1974, p. 465.
49. Cooper 1954, p. 57.
50. Cawthorne 1926, p. 91.
51. Horner 1987, p. 282.
52. ibid., p. 286.
53. Baudin 1974, pp 484, 491; Marchant 1982, pp 189–190; Horner 1987, p. 291.
54. Horner 1987, p. 290.
55. Baudin 1974, p. 490.
56. ibid., loc. cit.
57. ibid., p. 509.
58. Horner 1987, p. 298.
59. ibid., p. 385.
60. ibid., p. 304.
61. ibid., p. 306.
62. Baudin 1974, p. 542.
63. ibid., p. 543; Horner 1987, p. 312.
64. Baudin 1974, p. 560.
65. Horner 1987, p. 333.
66. Faivre 1974, p. xii.
67. Wallace 1984, p. iii.
68. ibid., p. ii; Scott 1910, pp 75–6.
69. Horner 1987, p. 317.
70. ibid., p. 257.
71. Baudin 1974, p. 441.
72. ibid., p. 452.

– 6 –

FLINDERS AND THE *INVESTIGATOR*

1. Mack 1972, pp 43–4.
2. 'Letter from Flinders to Banks' in Mack 1972, p. 45.
3. Flinders 1814, vol. 1, p. cciv.
4. Mack 1972, p. 50; Flinders 1814, vol. 1, p. 3.
5. Flinders 1814, vol. 1, p. 5.
6. 'Nepean to Banks, 28 April 1801' in Bladen 1892–1901, vol. 4, p. 318.
7. Bladen 1892–1901, vol. 4, p. 291.
8. Austin 1974, p. 15.
9. Flinders 1814, vol. 1, Appendix, p. 256.
10. Mack 1972, pp 61–3.
11. Flinders 1814, vol. 1, pp 16, 229.
12. Mack 1972, pp 61–3.
13. ibid., p. 76.
14. Cooper 1953, p. 8.
15. Flinders 1814, vol. 1, p. 36.
16. ibid., p. 36.
17. ibid., pp 40–1.
18. ibid., p. 43.
19. ibid., pp 49, 101.
20. ibid., p. 50.
21. ibid., p. 51.
22. ibid., p. 73.
23. Mack 1972, p. 100.
24. Osborn 1958, p. 127; Edwards 1981, pp 46 et seq.; Flinders 1814, vol. 1, p. 69.
25. Flinders 1814, vol. 1, p. 66.
26. ibid., pp 79–80.
27. ibid., p. 102.
28. ibid., p. 98.
29. ibid., pp 107–9; Cooper 1953, p. 104.
30. Flinders 1814, vol. 1, p. 117. Lacy's name is given as 'Lacey' on p. 42.
31. Flinders 1814, vol. 1, pp 127–8; Cooper 1953, pp 52, 87.
32. Flinders 1814, vol. 1, pp 126, 131.
33. ibid., p. 132.
34. ibid., pp 135–7.
35. ibid., p. 139.
36. ibid., pp 144–5.
37. ibid., p. 148.
38. ibid., p. 152.
39. ibid., pp 157, 159.
40. Cooper 1953, p. 99.
41. Flinders 1814, vol. 1, p. 167.
42. ibid., pp 169–70.
43. ibid., p. 187.
44. ibid., p. 211; Austin 1974, pp 35–6.
45. Flinders 1814, vol. 1, p. 212; Austin 1974, p. 36.
46. Whitehouse 1995, p. 13.

47. Flinders 1814, vol. 1, p. 237; Reader's Digest 1994 gives the position of Sydney as 33° 53' S, 151° 13' E.
48. Howse & Hutchinson 1969.
49. Flinders 1814, vol. 2, p. 135.
50. See the chart published by Thevenot in 1663 and reproduced in Austin 1964, p. 160.
51. Flinders 1814, vol. 1, p. 375; Mack 1972, p. 135.
52. Flinders 1814, vol. 1, p. 376, 26 November 1802; Mack 1972, pp 135–7, text of full report.
53. Battle & Bachmann 1998, pp 81–107.
54. Flinders 1814, vol. 2, p. 170, December 1802.
55. ibid., p. 188.
56. ibid., loc. cit.
57. McCarthy 1955, p. 68.
58. ibid., loc. cit.
59. Flinders 1814, vol. 2, p. 229.
60. It is at 11° 55' S, 136° 27' E. see Reader's Digest 1994.
61. Quoted by Mack 1972, p. 148; Flinders 1814, vol. 2, p. 8.
62. Quoted by Mack 1972, p. 146; Flinders 1814, vol. 1, pp 479, 482.
63. Matthew Flinders, quoted by Mack 1972, p. 152; Flinders 1814, vol. 2, p. 48.
64. Mack 1972, p. 155.
65. Quoted by Edwards 1981, p. 28.
66. Mack 1972, p. 216.
67. Flinders 1814, vol. 2, p. 496.

– 7 –

PHILLIP PARKER KING

1. King 1827, vol. 1, p. xxvii.
2. King & King 1981, p. 52.
3. Hordern 1997, appendix I, p. 403.
4. Heward 1842, p. 266; McMinn 1970, p. 44.
5. McMinn 1970, p. 44.
6. O'Brian 1987, p. 295.
7. Hordern 1997, p. 405.
8. King 1827, vol. 1, p. xxxvi.
9. ibid., p. 29; Hordern 1997, p. 75.
10. King 1827, vol. 1, p. 26.
11. W. Dampier, quoted by King 1827, vol. 1, p. 55.
12. Hordern 1997, p. 82.
13. ibid., p. 89.
14. Reader's Digest 1994, p. 253.
15. Hordern 1997, p. 90.
16. ibid., p. 91.
17. Readers Digest 1994, p. 259.
18. Hordern 1997, p. 95.
19. ibid., p. 101.
20. King 1827, vol. 2, p. 555; Hordern 1997, p. 120.
21. Hordern 1997, p. 114.
22. King 1827, vol. 1, p. 104.
23. Hordern 1997, pp 122–3.
24. ibid., pp 128–9.
25. King 1827, vol. 2, p. 123.
26. ibid., p. 127.
27. King 1827, vol. 1, p. 140.
28. ibid., p. 142.
29. Hordern 1997, p. 138.
30. Powell 1980, p. 225.
31. Stokes 1846.
32. See Chapter 8.
33. King 1827, vol. 1, p. 150.
34. Now Goold Island National Park, 18° 10' S, 146° 10' E. see Reader's Digest 1994, p. 193.
35. King 1827, vol. 1, p. 202.
36. ibid., p. 202.
37. ibid., p. 203.
38. ibid., p. 209.
39. ibid., p. 211.
40. ibid., p. 212.
41. ibid., p. 219.
42. Hordern 1997, p. 180; *Hobart Gazette*, 11 May 1816.
43. King 1827, vol. 1, p. 242.
44. ibid., p. 243.
45. ibid., loc. cit.
46. See Flinders 1814, vol. 2, p. 293.
47. King 1827, vol. 1, p. 247.
48. ibid., p. 251.
49. ibid., p. 258.
50. ibid., p. 261.
51. ibid., p. 262.
52. ibid., p. 252.
53. ibid., p. 262.
54. ibid., p. 263.
55. ibid., p. 265.
56. Hordern 1997, p. 192.
57. King 1827, vol. 1, p. 308.
58. ibid., p. 272.
59. ibid., p. 275.
60. ibid., p. 306.

61. ibid., p. 310.
62. ibid., p. 324.
63. ibid., p. 325.
64. ibid., p. 327.
65. ibid., p. 342.
66. ibid., loc. cit.
67. ibid., loc. cit.
68. ibid., p. 345.
69. ibid., p. 366; Reader's Digest 1994.
70. Denoted a high-ranking naval officer in a class named for the colours hoisted by him.
71. King 1827, vol. 1, p. 413.
72. ibid., p. 415.
73. Hordern 1997, p. 250, footnote.
74. King 1827, vol. 1, p. 427.
75. ibid., p. 27.
76. Reader's Digest 1995, p. 628.
77. King 1827, vol. 2, p. 96.
78. ibid., p. 108.
79. King 1825.
80. King 1827, vol. 2, p. 163.
81. Sharp 1963, p. 94.
82. Rigby & Ward 1969.
83. King 1827, vol. 2, p. 180.
84. ibid., p. 199.
85. ibid., p. 202.
86. ibid., p. 216.
87. ibid., p. 220.
88. Ingleton 1944, pp 39, 41; Branagan 1985.
89. Powell 1980, pp 217–29.
90. King 1827, vol. 1, p. 411; Powell 1980, p. 38.
91. McMinn 1970, p. 119.
92. King 1827, vol. 2, p. 243.

– 8 –

THE BREAKOUT

1. King 1984, p. 13.
2. King 1982, p. 186.
3. Rudzki 1995, p. 287.
4. Passage in a manuscript by Matthew Flinders, quoted by Scott 1914, p. 75.
5. J. Banks in Bladen 1892–1901, vol. 3, pp 382–3; quoted by Cumpston 1964, p. 56.
6. Mackaness 1950; reprinted 1978, Part I, p. 5.
7. Oxley 1820, p. vii; Cumpston 1954, p. 41.
8. Mackaness 1950, Part I, p. 10.
9. ibid., p. 40.
10. Oxley 1820, p. 362.
11. McMinn 1970, p. 24.
12. Oxley 1820, pp 5, 73.
13. ibid., p. 19.
14. ibid., p. 175.
15. ibid., p. 10.
16. McMinn 1970, p. 27.
17. Oxley 1820, pp 243–4.
18. ibid., pp 252, 385.
19. ibid., p. 351.
20. Riviére 1996, p. 159.
21. ibid., p. 145.
22. Lee 1925, p. 529.
23. Oxley 1925.
24. ibid.
25. Nelson 1900.
26. Entry dated '11 October 1825' in Lockyer 1828; Russell 1888, pp 589–601.
27. Stephens 1936.
28. McMinn 1970, p. 47.
29. Cunningham 1828, p. 65.
30. McMinn 1970, p. 81.
31. ibid., pp 89–91.
32. O'Grady 1964, p. 347.
33. ibid., p. 348.
34. Hovell 1921.
35. Readers Digest 1995, p. 288.
36. Scott 1921.
37. Hovell 1921, p. 309.
38. O'Grady 1964, p. 350.
39. Flemming 1984, p. 57.
40. Scott 1936, p. 155.
41. ibid., p. 156.
42. Reader's Digest 1995, p. 279.
43. Heney 1967; further details of Strzelecki's early life are given in Kaluski 1985.
44. Kaluski 1985, p. 16.
45. Havard 1940.
46. Kaluski 1985, p. 16.
47. Havard 1940, p. 45.
48. ibid., loc. cit.; Strzelecki 1856, p. 9.
49. Strzelecki 1856, p. 4.
50. Parbo 1992, p. 11.
51. Havard 1940, p. 53.
52. Quoted by Havard 1940, p. 54.
53. This quotation is included on the commemorative plaque on the summit of Mount Kosciuszko; see also Clews 1973.

54. Original letter held by the Royal Geographical Society of South Australia.
55. Strzelecki 1845.
56. Heney 1967.

– 9 –
EXPANSION TO VAN DIEMEN'S LAND

1. Giblin 1928, p. 257.
2. Hordern 1997, p. 145.
3. Sharp 1963, p. 277; Burn 1955. This edition was edited, and is provided with an introduction by G. Mackaness.
4. Burn 1955, p. 5.
5. ibid., loc. cit.
6. Tench 1961, p. 62.
7. Clarke 1929, p. 176.
8. Watson 1921–23, vol. 4, p. 134; vol. 6, p. 99.
9. Butler 1989, pp 11–12.
10. *Macquarie Dictionary* 1991 (see Delbridge 1991), p. 1277.
11. Burn 1955, pp 43, 54.
12. Walker 1914, p. 106.
13. ibid., p. 110.
14. ibid., p. 118.
15. Bladen 1892–1901, vol. 6, p. 256.
16. ibid., loc. cit.
17. Pike 1967, vol. 2, pp 97–8.
18. Watson 1921–23, vol. 1, note 333; Dowd 1937.

– 10 –
CHARLES STURT –
MURRAY–DARLING BASIN

1. Langley 1972, pp 18–27.
2. ibid., p. 192.
3. ibid., p. 31.
4. Sturt 1833, vol. 1, pp xiv, xviii.
5. ibid., p. xviii.
6. Langley 1972, p. 63.
7. Quoted by Sturt 1833, Appendix 1, p. 185.
8. Langley 1972, p. 65.
9. Sturt 1833, vol. 1, p. 189.
10. ibid., p. 8; Langley 1972, p. 67; Beale 1979, p. 49.
11. Sturt 1833, vol. 1, p. 10.
12. ibid., p. 19.
13. ibid., p. 26.

14. ibid., p. 85.
15. ibid., p. 95.
16. ibid., p. 100.
17. ibid., p. 107.
18. ibid., pp 119, 133.
19. ibid., p. 139.
20. ibid., p. 148; Langley 1972, p. 76.
21. Langley 1972, p. 76.
22. Sturt 1833, vol. 2, p. 9.
23. ibid., p. 19.
24. ibid., p. 60.
25. ibid., p. 22.
26. Croker 1979.
27. Beale 1979, pp 61–2.
28. Sturt 1833, vol. 2, p. 71.
29. ibid., p. 113.
30. ibid., p. 86.
31. ibid., p. 88. Sturt, not a nautical man, wrote 'two and a half knots an hour', seemingly unaware that that means two and a half nautical miles per hour.
32. Sturt 1833, vol. 2, p. 111.
33. ibid., p. 116.
34. Beale 1979, p. 66.
35. Sturt 1833, vol. 2, p. 140.
36. ibid., p. 148.
37. Cleland 1914, p. 163.
38. ibid., p. 164.
39. Campbell 1983, 1985.
40. Campbell 1985, p. 346; Cumpston 1951, p. 185; *Sturt Papers*, Rhodes House: Oxford; held on microfilm, National Library of Australia, p. 147.
41. Dowling 1990; I am indebted to Professor Frank Fenner, AC, and to Mr Graeme Pretty for helpful comments on smallpox.
42. Gill 1905.
43. Grenfell Price 1926–7.
44. Beale 1979, p. 66.
45. Sturt 1833, vol. 2, pp 211–12.
46. Evans 1995.

– 11 –
THOMAS LIVINGSTON MITCHELL

1. Cumpston 1954, p. 1, uses 'Livingstone'; Foster 1985, p. 1; Andrews 1986, p. 259; but 'Livingstone' in *Macquarie Dictionary*, *Cambridge*

Biographical Encyclopaedia, and Australian
Dictionary of Biography.
2. Cumpston 1954, pp 7, 16.
3. Couch 1963, p. 18.
4. This paragraph, written by R. Montgomery
Martin in History of the British Colonies, 1835,
vol. 4, xii, n, pp 170–89, was quoted by
Beaglehole (1940–41, p. 184) and also by
Cumpston (1954, p. 23), but his version differs
from that of Beaglehole in having more capitals
and different punctuation.
5. Young 1961, pp 86, 263.
6. ibid., p. 87.
7. Couch 1963, p. 39.
8. Shann 1948, p. 91; Cumpston 1954, p. 41.
9. Andrews 1992, p. 5.
10. Quoted by Cumpston 1954, p. 56.
11. Foster 1985, p. 109.
12. Cumpston 1954, p. 56.
13. ibid., p. 57.
14. ibid., p. 66.
15. ibid., pp 66–7; Watson 1914–25, vol. 16, pp
219, 248, 391.
16. Cumpston 1954, p. 67; Watson 1914–25, vol.
16, p. 771.
17. Mitchell 1839, Facsimile Edition 1965, vol. 1,
p. 9.
18. Mitchell 1839, vol. 1, pp 2–3.
19. ibid., pp 4, 16.
20. ibid., pp 4–5.
21. ibid., pp 29, 39.
22. ibid., p. 19.
23. ibid., p. 26.
24. ibid., p. 43.
25. ibid., pp 68, 73, 75.
26. ibid., 27 February, p. 138; with reference to
18 January entry, p. 88.
27. Brand-Miller, James & Maggiore. 1993, p. 132;
also J. Brand-Miller, pers. comm., December
1996.
28. Frank Badman, Olympic Dam Operations,
pers. comm.
29. Mitchell 1839, vol. 1, p. 140.
30. ibid., pp 152, 155, 158.
31. Readers Digest, 1995, p. 85.
32. Mitchell 1839, vol. 1, p. 164.
33. ibid., p. 172.
34. ibid., p. 179.
35. ibid., Appendix 2, p. 353.
36. ibid., p. 209.
37. ibid., p. 215.
38. ibid., p. 220.
39. ibid., p. 230.
40. ibid., p. 241.
41. ibid., pp 245–6.
42. ibid., p. 248.
43. ibid., p. 244.
44. ibid., loc. cit.
45. ibid., p. 258.
46. ibid., p. 274.
47. ibid., p. 288.
48. ibid., pp 271, 275, 281.
49. ibid., p. 303.
50. ibid., Appendix 2, p. 353.

– 12 –
EDWARD JOHN EYRE

1. Eyre 1984, p. 1; Dutton 1967, pp 17, 403.
2. Uren & Stephens 1941, pp 37, 43; Eyre 1984,
p. xviii.
3. Waterhouse 1984b, p. xxvii.
4. Eyre 1984, p. 114.
5. Eyre 1984, p. 98.
6. Eyre 1984, p. 105.
7. Uren & Stephens 1941, p. 52.
8. Eyre 1984, p. 115.
9. ibid., p. 116.
10. ibid., p. 117.
11. ibid., pp 121, 124.
12. ibid., p. 123.
13. Dutton 1967, p. 37; Hawdon 1952, p. 6.
14. Waterhouse 1984b, p. xxii.
15. ibid., pp xxiv–xxv.
16. Eyre 1984, p. 116.
17. Dutton 1967, p. 37.
18. ibid., p. 56.
19. ibid., p. 62; Uren & Stephens 1941, p. 79.
20. Dutton 1967, p. 65.
21. Eyre 1984, p. 211; Dutton 1967, p. 67.
22. Eyre 1984, pp 195, 212.
23. Dutton 1967, p. 69.
24. Eyre 1845, vol. 1, p. 202.
25. Sturt 1849, vol. 1, p. 155; Stokes 1986, pp 58, 60.
26. Eyre 1845, vol. 1, p. 7.

27. ibid., p. vii.
28. ibid., p. 11.
29. ibid., p. 13.
30. ibid., p. 16; Dutton 1967, p. 81.
31. Eyre 1845, vol. 1, p. 16.
32. ibid., p. 21.
33. ibid., p. 28.
34. ibid., p. 25.
35. ibid., p. 26.
36. ibid., p. 66.
37. ibid., p. 99.
38. ibid., p. 109.
39. ibid., p. 110.
40. ibid., p. 116.
41. ibid., p. 118.
42. ibid., p. 125.
43. ibid., p. 127.
44. ibid., p. 128.
45. Eyre 1845, Supplement.
46. Black 1963, pp 43–50.
47. Eyre 1845, vol. 1, p. 142.
48. ibid., pp 142–3.
49. ibid., p. 147.
50. ibid., pp 149–150.
51. ibid., p. 155.
52. Dutton 1967, p. 100.
53. Eyre 1845, vol. 1, p. 191.
54. ibid., p. 208.
55. ibid., p. 210.
56. ibid., pp 213–15.
57. ibid., pp 166–7.
58. ibid., p. 228.
59. ibid., p. 231.
60. ibid., p. 235.
61. ibid., p. 239.
62. ibid., p. 241.
63. ibid., p. 244.
64. Magarey 1899, vol. 3, p. 67. This paper had been published separately in 1895. In this form it contained several illustrations. It was completely reset, without illustrations, for the *Proceedings*.
65. Magarey 1895/1899, pp 4–5.
66. ibid., p. 5.
67. Eyre 1845, vol. 1, p. 350.
68. ibid., pp 245, 248.
69. ibid., p. 251.
70. ibid., pp 253–4.

71. ibid., p. 255.
72. ibid., p. 276.
73. ibid., p. 277.
74. ibid., loc. cit.
75. ibid., p. 246.
76. ibid., p. 279; Stokes 1993, p. 65.
77. Eyre 1845, vol. 1, p. 284.
78. ibid., p. 295.
79. ibid., p. 306.
80. ibid., p. 324.
81. ibid., p. 332.
82. Dr C. R. Twidale, pers. comm.
83. Eyre 1845, vol. 1, p. 336.
84. ibid., p. 337.
85. ibid., p. 353.
86. ibid., pp 363–4.
87. ibid., p. 402.
88. ibid., p. 5; Eyre 1845, vol. 2, p. 8.
89. Dutton 1967, facing p. 80.
90. Eyre 1845, vol. 2, pp 16–17.
91. ibid., p. 55.
92. ibid., p. 59.
93. ibid., p. 62.
94. ibid., p. 75.
95. ibid., p. 110.
96. Drawing by J. Neil, in Eyre 1845, vol. 2, p. 109.
97. Reproduced in Uren and Stephens, 1941.
98. Eyre 1845, vol. 2, p. 113.
99. Eyre 1845, vol. 1, p. v.
100. Eyre 1845, vol. 2, p. 149.
101. Dutton 1967, 1982; Hume 1867.

– 13 –

STURT'S SEARCH FOR AN INLAND SEA

1. Sturt 1833, vol. 1, p. iv.
2. Noad 1979.
3. Sturt 1833.
4. Langley 1972, p. 129.
5. Hawdon 1952.
6. ibid., p. 62.
7. ibid., p. 2.
8. Langley 1972, p. 163.
9. Sturt 1849, vol. 1, pp 19–20; Eyre 1845.
10. Sturt 1849, vol. 1, pp 12–34.
11. Frakes 1987.
12. Sturt 1849, vol. 1, pp 23, 25.
13. ibid., p. 57.

14. ibid., p. 56.
15. ibid., pp 44–7; Brock 1975, p. 2.
16. Sturt 1849, vol. 1, p. 47.
17. Sturt, *Daily Journal*, 9 January 1845: see Stokes 1986, p. 106; Brock 1975, p. 84.
18. Sturt, *Weekly Journal*: see Waterhouse 1984a, pp 29, 35.
19. Brock 1975, p. 36.
20. Sturt 1849, vol. 1, p. 46.
21. ibid., p. 43.
22. Hancock 1936.
23. Sturt, *Daily Journal*, 10 August 1834: see Stokes 1986.
24. Brock 1975, pp 2–3.
25. Sturt 1849, vol. 1, p. 40; Sturt, *Daily Journal*, 15 August 1844: see Stokes 1986.
26. Sturt, *Weekly Journal*: see Waterhouse 1984a, p. 20.
27. Sturt 1849, vol. 1, p. 43.
28. ibid., p. 45; Brock 1975, p. 9; Sturt, *Daily Journal*: see Stokes 1986, pp 28, 52.
29. Ruediger 1986, p. 33.
30. Moorhouse 1846.
31. Hale & Tindale 1930; Tindale 1939.
32. Pretty et al. 1977, p. 92.
33. Lewis 1916–17.
34. ibid.; Pretty et al. 1977, p. 93.
35. Hawker 1899, First Series, p. 82.
36. Hawker 1901, Second Series, p. 15.
37. Sturt, *Weekly Journal*: see Waterhouse 1984a, pp 27, 32.
38. ibid., p. 34.
39. Sturt 1849, vol. 1, p. 108.
40. ibid., p. 114.
41. ibid., p. 116.
42. ibid., p. 127; Brock 1975, p. 29.
43. Sturt, *Weekly Journal*: see Waterhouse 1984a, p. 30.
44. ibid., p. 36.
45. Stokes 1986, p. 18.
46. ibid., loc. cit.
47. Sturt 1849, vol. 1, p. 141.
48. ibid., p. 155; Stokes 1986, pp 58, 60.
49. Boden 1985, p. 16.
50. Eyre 1845, vol. 1, p. 202.
51. Stokes 1986, p. 85.
52. Brock 1975, p. 76.
53. Sturt, *Weekly Journal*: see Waterhouse 1984a, p. 44.
54. Stokes 1986, p. 87.
55. Sturt, *Daily Journal*, 11 December 1844: see Stokes 1986, p. 90.
56. Sturt, *Daily Journal*, 14 December 1844: see Stokes 1986, p. 92; Sturt 1849, vol. 1, p. 207.
57. Sturt 1849, vol. 1, p. 263; Stokes 1986, p. 113.
58. Sturt 1849, vol. 1, p. 265.
59. ibid., p. 270.
60. ibid., p. 274.
61. ibid., p. 296.
62. ibid., p. 298.
63. Sturt, *Weekly Journal*: see Waterhouse 1984a p. 47; Sturt 1849, vol. 1, p. 288.
64. Brock 1975, pp 114, 116.
65. Sturt 1849, vol. 1, p. 270.
66. ibid., p. 306.
67. Sturt, *Weekly Journal*: see Waterhouse 1984a, p. 45; Sturt 1849, vol. 1, pp 267, 306–7.
68. Sturt 1849, vol. 1, pp 313–14.
69. Sturt, *Weekly Journal*: see Waterhouse 1984a, p. 52; Stokes 1986, p. 130.
70. Sturt 1849, vol. 1, p. 334; the initials are followed by full stops in the *Narrative*, but were not cut into the tree.
71. Stokes 1986, p. 148.
72. Sturt, *Daily Journal*, 23 August 1845: see Stokes 1986, p. 92; Sturt, *Weekly Journal*: see Waterhouse 1984a, p. 66. In this account Sturt described them as 'nice silver perch'; Stokes 1986, p. 160.
73. Sturt, *Daily Journal*, 23 August 1845: see Stokes 1986, p. 92.
74. Mitchell 1973.
75. Berra & Allen 1989.
76. T. Sim, South Australian Museum, pers. comm.; see also Glover & Sim 1978.
77. Madigan 1946a, p. 119.
78. Bonython 1980, p. 73; Engel & Sharp 1958.
79. Sturt, *Daily Journal*, 13 September 1845: see Stokes 1986, p. 92; Bonython 1980, p. 16; Stokes 1986, p. 188.
80. Sturt, *Weekly Journal*: see Waterhouse 1984a, p. 84; Sturt, *Daily Journal*, 13 September 1845: see Stokes 1986, p. 92; Sturt 1849.
81. Sturt, *Weekly Journal*: see Waterhouse 1984a, p. 86.

82. Dr C. R. Twidale, pers. comm.
83. Madigan 1930; Madigan 1936; Madigan 1946a; Madigan 1946b; Twidale, PArkin & Rudd. 1990.
84. Sturt 1849, vol. 2, p. 108; F. Badman, Roxby Downs, pers. comm.
85. Sturt 1849, vol. 2, p. 120.
86. Chisholm 1962, vol. 3, p. 440.
87. Stokes 1986, p. 235.
88. Langley 1972, p. 223.
89. Sturt 1849.
90. Some of his paintings and drawings are still in the hands of the Sturt family and are reproduced in Waterhouse 1984a.
91. Sturt, *Weekly Journal*: see Waterhouse 1984a, pp 58, 60.
92. Sturt 1849, vol. 2, Appendix, p. 6.
93. ibid., vol. 1, p. 340; Sturt, *Weekly Journal*: see Waterhouse 1984a, pp 58, 60.
94. Sturt 1849, vol. 1, p. 340; I am indebted to Dr Chris Watts for information about the dusky hopping-mouse. See also Watts & Aslin 1981, p. 114.
95. Gould 1848, vol. 4, plate 4.
96. Sturt 1849, vol. 2, appendix, pp 1–92.
97. Sturt 1899.
98. Stokes 1986.
99. Waterhouse 1984a. This includes a facsimile of Sturt's *Narrative*, vol. 2, pp 145–286.
100. Cumpston 1951, 1964; Langley 1972; see also Langley 1967.
101. Browne 1966; Brock 1975.
102. Beale 1979.
103. Bonython & Mason 1953; Grenfell Price 1955, p. 1.
104. Bonython 1962–63; Kotwicki 1986, p. 50.
105. Dulhunty 1975.
106. *Advertiser*, Adelaide, 12 May 1976.
107. Habermale 1980.
108. Madigan 1946a, p. 120.
109. Beale 1979, p. 49 and elsewhere.
110. Browning 1887, p. 186.
111. *Times*, London, 7 November 1805.
112. Langley 1972, p. 51.
113. Beale 1979, pp 72–3.
114. *South Australian Register*, 10 August 1855; Langley 1972, p. 220.

– 14 –
AUSTRALIA FELIX

1. Watson 1914–25 (1923), vol. 18, p. 157.
2. ibid., p. 286.
3. Andrews 1986, pp 13–14.
4. Mitchell 1839, vol. 2, p. 2.
5. Watson 1914–25 (1916), vol. 11, p. 151.
6. Mitchell 1839, vol. 2, p. 3.
7. ibid., p. 15.
8. ibid., p. 19.
9. ibid., p. 30.
10. ibid., p. 37.
11. ibid., p. 63.
12. ibid., p. 76.
13. ibid., p. 87.
14. ibid., p. 92.
15. ibid., p. 95.
16. ibid., pp 97, 101.
17. Quoted by Andrews 1986, p. 81.
18. Mitchell 1839, vol. 2, p. 103.
19. ibid., p. 104.
20. ibid., pp 106, 108.
21. Hawdon 1952, p. 38.
22. ibid., p. 38.
23. Mitchell 1839, vol. 2, p. 114.
24. ibid., p. 139. Recent determinations give the latitude of Swan Hill as 35° 20' S; see Reader's Digest 1994.
25. Mitchell 1839, vol. 2, p. 140.
26. ibid., p. 132.
27. ibid., p. 144.
28. ibid., p. 151.
29. Eccleston 1990, p. 27.
30. Mitchell 1839, vol. 2, p. 157.
31. ibid., p. 159.
32. ibid., p. 162.
33. ibid., p. 168; Eccleston 1990, p. 37.
34. Eccleston 1990, p. 41.
35. Mitchell 1839, vol. 2, p. 171.
36. ibid., p. 179.
37. ibid., p. 180.
38. Andrews 1986, p. 140.
39. Mitchell 1839, vol. 2, p. 189.
40. ibid., p. 195.
41. ibid., pp 200–1.
42. ibid., pp 218, 233.

43. ibid., p. 244.
44. Reader's Digest 1994, p. 276.
45. Godfrey 1996, p. 543.
46. Dawson 1881, p. 22; Gott 1982, pp 13–17.
47. Mitchell 1839, vol. 2, p. 230.
48. ibid., p. 230 footnote.
49. ibid., p. 240.
50. ibid., loc. cit.
51. Scott 1936, p. 154.
52. ibid.
53. Mitchell 1839, vol. 2, p. 241.
54. ibid., pp 242–3.
55. ibid., p. 248.
56. ibid., p. 253; Eccleston 1990, p. 83.
57. Mitchell 1839, vol. 2, p. 258.
58. ibid., p. 264.
59. Eccleston 1990, p. 95.
60. Mitchell 1839, vol. 2, p. 278.
61. Eccleston 1990, p. 99.
62. Mitchell 1839, vol. 2, p. 280; Eccleston 1990, p. 101.
63. Mitchell 1839, vol. 2, p. 285; Eccleston 1990, p. 103.
64. Mitchell 1839, vol. 2, p. 291.
65. ibid., p. 305; Eccleston 1990, pp 121–2.
66. Mitchell 1839, vol. 2, p. 335.
67. Andrews 1986, illustration 17, between pp 104 and 105; Mitchell 1839, vol. 2, p. 306.
68. Mitchell 1839, vol. 2, p. 311.
69. ibid., loc. cit.
70. ibid., pp 327–8.
71. ibid., p. 333.
72. ibid., p. 338.
73. Eccleston 1990, p. 124.
74. Cumpston 1954, p. 138.
75. Cumpston 1954, p. 140.
76. Foster 1985, p. 304; Mitchell 1837, pp 271–85.
77. Foster 1985, p. 308; Cumpston 1954, p. 149.
78. Foster 1985, p. 309.
79. Cumpston 1954, p. 150; Foster 1985, p. 315.
80. Watson 1914–25, vol. 20, p. 556; Foster 1985, p. 333.
81. Foster 1985, p. 341.
82. ibid., p. 354.
83. Mitchell 1848, p. 2.
84. Chisholm 1962, vol. 7, p. 198.
85. ibid., vol. 7, p. 199.
86. Watson 1914–25, vol. 23, p. 245.
87. ibid., loc. cit.
88. ibid., p. 599.
89. Quoted by Cumpston 1954, p. 171; Lethbridge 1944.
90. Foster 1985, p. 371.
91. ibid., loc. cit.
92. Mitchell 1848, pp 5–6.
93. ibid., p. 24.
94. ibid., p. 54.
95. ibid., pp 42–3.
96. Foster 1985, p. 382.
97. Mitchell 1848, p. 78.
98. ibid., p. 92.
99. ibid., p. 123.
100. ibid., p. 126.
101. ibid., p. 126.
102. ibid., p. 130.
103. Reader's Digest 1995, p. 493.
104. Mitchell 1848, p. 134.
105. ibid., pp 143–4.
106. ibid., p. 145.
107. ibid., p. 153; Foster 1985, p. 388.
108. Mitchell 1848, p. 160.
109. ibid., p. 163.
110. ibid., pp 184–8.
111. ibid., p. 201.
112. ibid., p. 203.
113. Foster 1985, p. 392.
114. ibid., p. 269.
115. See Readers Digest 1994; for comparison Mackay is at 21° 09' S 149° 11' E.
116. Mitchell 1848, p. 300.
117. ibid., p. 305.
118. ibid., p. 309; Foster 1985, p. 402.
119. Mitchell 1848, p. 326.
120. Parker & Somerville 1943, p. 224.
121. Mitchell 1848, p. 325.
122. Cumpston 1954, p. 190; Sturt 1849, vol. 2, pp 61, 73.
123. Mitchell 1848, pp 324–5.
124. ibid., p. 356.
125. ibid., p. 312.
126. ibid., p. 405.
127. ibid., p. 415.
128. Cumpston 1954, p. 194, see also the photograph of the headstone, facing p. 208; Foster 1985, p. 409.

129. Couch 1963, p. 215.
130. Quoted by Couch 1963, p. 125.
131. Couch 1963, p. 85.
132. Andrews 1986, p. 49.
133. ibid., p. 234.
134. Eccleston 1992, p. 81.
135. ibid., p. 88.
136. ibid., p. 22.
137. ibid., p. 88.
138. Sturt 1833.

– 15 –

LEICHHARDT

1. Aurousseau 1968, vol. 1, pp vii, 2, 9. Aurousseau was a graduate of the University of Sydney (1914), but he lived overseas for most of his life. He was more than seventy-five when he completed the translation and editing of Leichhardt's letters. He died in 1983, aged ninety-two.
2. ibid., p. vii.
3. See meaning of word 'doctor' in *Macquarie Dictionary* 1991 (under Delbridge 1991).
4. Aurousseau 1968, vol. 1, p. 385.
5. ibid., loc. cit.
6. Roderick 1988, pp 154–5.
7. ibid., p. 153.
8. Aurousseau 1968, vol. 1, p. 401.
9. ibid., p. 394.
10. Aurousseau 1968, vol. 2, p. 439.
11. Branagan 1994.
12. Clarke 1843, p. 161.
13. Branagan 1985.
14. Roderick 1988, p. 225.
15. ibid., p. 229.
16. Aurousseau 1968, vol. 2, p. 780.
17. Roderick 1988, p. 235.
18. Aurousseau 1968, vol. 2, p. 780.
19. ibid., p. 805.
20. Roderick 1988, p. 237.
21. Leichhardt 1847, p. xiv.
22. ibid., pp xiv, xx; Roderick 1988, p. 241.
23. Leichhardt 1847, p. xviii.
24. Aurousseau 1968, vol. 3, pp 827–8.
25. Leichhardt 1847, pp 138–9.
26. ibid., p. 5.
27. ibid., pp 8–13.
28. Roderick 1988, p. 249; Chinchilla is at 20° 44' S, 150° 38' E: See Readers Digest 1994, p. 240.
29. Leichhardt 1847, pp 17–18.
30. Aurousseau 1968, vol. 3, p. 828.
31. Leichhardt 1847, p. 36.
32. Roderick 1988, p. 160.
33. Leichhardt 1847, p. 40; see also Roderick 1988, p. 253.
34. Leichhardt 1847, p. 51.
35. ibid., p. 58.
36. ibid., p. 62.
37. ibid., p. 65.
38. ibid., p. 75.
39. ibid., pp 103, 105.
40. ibid., pp 105–6.
41. ibid., pp 94, 99.
42. ibid., p. 111; Roderick 1988, p. 266.
43. Leichhardt 1847, pp 116, 118; Roderick 1988, pp 267–8.
44. Leichhardt 1847, pp 124, 125, 127.
45. ibid., p. 137.
46. ibid., p. 146.
47. ibid., p. 148.
48. Roderick 1988, p. 272; Leichhardt 1847, p. 148.
49. Aurousseau 1968, Volume 3, p. 822.
50. Leichhardt 1847, p. 170.
51. ibid., pp 173, 199.
52. ibid., p. 229; Roderick 1988, p. 293.
53. Leichhardt 1847, p. 232.
54. ibid., pp 255–6.
55. ibid., p. 257.
56. ibid., p. 265.
57. ibid., p. 273.
58. ibid., p. 292.
59. Roderick 1988, p. 314.
60. Aurousseau 1968, vol. 3, p. 841.
61. Leichhardt 1847, pp 308–9.
62. Roderick 1988, p. 504.
63. Leichhardt 1847, p. 318.
64. ibid., p. 334.
65. ibid., p. 347; Roderick 1988, p. 347.
66. Leichhardt 1847, p. 358.
67. Webster 1980, p. 368; Roderick 1988, pp 342–5; Reader's Digest 1994, p. 237.
68. Connell 1980, pp 28 et seq.

69. Leichhardt 1847, p. 370.
70. Leichhardt 1847, pp 373–4.
71. ibid., p. 400.
72. ibid., p. 392.
73. ibid., p. 412.
74. ibid., p. 413.
75. ibid. loc. cit.
76. ibid., pp 423, 425; Gould 1863, vol. 2, Plate 8. Gould describes this kangaroo as 'fierce, bold and even dangerous'; Waterhouse 1846, p. 95; Frith & Calaby 1969.
77. Leichhardt 1847, p. 423; Roderick 1988, p. 356.
78. Leichhardt 1847, p. 424.
79. ibid., p. 431.
80. ibid., p. 443.
81. ibid., p. 443.
82. ibid., p. 445; Roderick 1988, p. 358.
83. Leichhardt 1847, p. 449.
84. ibid., p. 447.
85. ibid., pp 451, 459.
86. ibid., p. 464.
87. ibid., p. 469.
88. Roderick 1988, p. 362.
89. Leichhardt 1847, p. 488; letter from Leichhardt to his brother-in-law, Carl Schmalfuss, in Aurousseau 1968, vol. 3, p. 842.
90. Aurousseau 1968, vol. 3, p. 843.
91. Leichhardt 1847, p. 502.
92. Aurousseau 1968, vol. 3, p. 842.
93. Leichhardt 1847, p. 843.
94. Leichhardt 1847, p. 839.
95. Leichhardt 1847, p. 829.
96. Webster 1986, p. 5.
97. ibid., p. 23.
98. Aurousseau 1968, vol. 3, p. 844.
99. ibid., p. 847.
100. Roderick 1988, p. 390.
101. Aurousseau 1968, vol. 3, p. 846.
102. ibid., p. 860.
103. ibid., p. 861.
104. Roderick 1988, pp 397–407.
105. Bunce 1979, pp 79 et seq.; foreword to this volume written by Russel Ward; Sprod 1994; Roderick 1988, pp 396 et seq.
106. Bunce 1979, p. 92; Sprod 1994, p. 162.
107. Aurousseau 1968, vol. 3, p. 891.
108. Sprod 1994, p. 163.
109. ibid., p. 165.
110. ibid.
111. ibid., p. 150.
112. Aurousseau 1968, vol. 3, pp 941–942.
113. ibid., p. 945.
114. ibid., p. 975.
115. ibid., p. 947.
116. ibid., p. 955.
117. ibid., p. 981.
118. ibid., p. 997.
119. ibid., p. 984.
120. ibid., p. 1002.
121. Grenfell Price 1937–38.
122. Aurousseau 1968, vol. 3, p. 1004.
123. Pike 1949, p. 271.
124. Connell 1980; Roderick 1988, pp 499–505; Grenfell Price 1937–38; Pike 1949, pp 271–84.
125. Reader's Digest 1994, p. 298.
126. Coins specially minted for presentation to 'the poor' on Maundy Thursday, the day before Good Friday.
127. Roderick 1988, p. 505.
128. Hardman 1865, p. 265.
129. Defined as 'an Aboriginal hut or shelter made of boughs, leaves and plaited grass' in *Macquarie Dictionary* 1991 (see under Delbridge 1991).
130. Hardman 1865, p. 213.
131. Roderick 1988, p. 68.
132. ibid., p. 452.
133. Hardman 1865, p. 432.
134. Perrin 1990, p. 44.
135. Aurousseau 1968, vol. 3, p. 902.

– 16 –

THE BURKE AND WILLS EXPEDITION

1. Hoare 1967, p. 7; Bonyhady 1991, pp 18–25.
2. The phrase, the 'prince of explorers' was used by Colin Roderick (1988, p. 7).
3. Tipping 1979, p. 23.
4. Bonyhady 1991, p. 18.
5. Tipping 1979, p. 39, note 108.
6. Morphett 1939, p. 8.
7. Denison 1870, vol. 1, p. 170.
8. Bonyhady 1991, p. 31.
9. Quoted by Bonyhady 1991, p. 42.

10. Bonyhady 1991, p. 45.
11. Wills 1860, p. 34; from the Journals and Letters of William John Wills, edited by his father, William Wills.
12. 'Instructions ... to scientific observers attached to the Victorian Exploring Expedition' in Royal Society of Victoria Exploration Committee 1860, pp lxviii–lxxiv.
13. Beckler 1993 (trans. S. Jeffries and M. Kertesz).
14. 'Instructions to Robert O'Hara Burke, Esq., Leader, Victorian Exploring Expedition' in Royal Society of Victoria Exploration Committee 1860, p. xv.
15. 'List of Articles and Services' in Royal Society of Victoria Exploration Committee 1860, pp lxxv–lxxxiv; Bonyhady 1991, p. 72.
16. Letter dated 12 July 1860, *La Trobe Manuscripts Collection*, State Library of Victoria, Box 2077/5.
17. Beckler 1993, p. 11.
18. 'List of Articles and Services', in Royal Society of Victoria Exploration Committee 1860, pp lxxv–lxxxiv; Bonyhady 1991, p. 72.
19. Tipping 1979, p. 23.
20. 'Progress Report of Exploration Committee', in Royal Society of Victoria Exploration Committee 1860, pp xxxiii–xxxv.
21. 'Memorandum of Agreement', in Royal Society of Victoria Exploration Committee 1860, p. xv.
22. Bonyhady 1991, p. 79.
23. ibid., plate 3, facing p. 96.
24. ibid., p. 87.
25. ibid., p. 88.
26. Beckler 1993, p. 29.
27. ibid., p. 33.
28. Bonyhady 1991, p. 90; Burke and Wills Commission 1862, Q 124, 125, p. 8.
29. Surveyor's Field Notes September 1860, *La Trobe Manuscripts Collection*, State Library of Victoria, Box 2082/6b.
30. Bonyhady 1991, p. 103.
31. ibid., p. 105.
32. ibid., p. 142; Becker painted a watercolour of the site of this depot, and this is reproduced in Bonyhady 1991, facing p. 145.
33. Ludwig Becker's letter to the secretary of the Royal Society of Victoria, dated 30 October 1860, *La Trobe Manuscripts Collection*, State Library of Victoria.
34. Torowotto Swamp, latitude 30° 01' 30" S, longitude 142° 36' E. see Wills 1863, p. 153.
35. W. J. Wills determined its position as 27° 37' 08" S, 141° 06' E. See Wills 1863, p. 153.
36. Tipping 1979, p. 206.
37. Beckler 1993, p. 48.
38. ibid., p. 49.
39. ibid., pp 64–5.
40. ibid., p. 75; Isaacs 1987, pp 115, 225.
41. Beckler 1993, pp 76–7.
42. ibid., p. 78.
43. Bonyhady 1991, p. 123.
44. ibid., loc. cit.
45. W. J. Wills' last letter, dated 27 June 1861, to his father, in Wills 1861, p. 33, reprinted from *The Argus*.
46. Wills 1861, p. 15.
47. ibid., loc. cit.
48. ibid., .
49. W. O'H. Burke, in Wills 1861, p. 33; see also Bonyhady 1991, p. 130.
50. Wills 1863.
51. Wills 1860.
52. Commentary by Government Astronomer on observations made by W. J. Wills, *La Trobe Manuscripts Collection*, State Library of Victoria, Box 2082/5g.
53. Bergin 1981, p. 122.
54. Isaacs 1987, pp 123, 128; Low 1989, p. 128.
55. Wills 1861, p. 26.
56. ibid., p. 23.
57. ibid., p. 24.
58. Burke and Wills Commission 1862, 'J. King', Q 963, p. 35.
59. W. J. Wills notebook, *La Trobe Manuscripts Collection*, State Library of Victoria, box 2083/1d.
60. Wills 1861, p. 27.
61. ibid., p. 24.
62. ibid., p. 25.
63. ibid., loc. cit.
64. ibid., p. 232.
65. ibid., p. 25.
66. W. Brahé, In Wills 1861, p. 6.
67. Wills 1861, p. 26.
68. Beckler 1993, pp 47-48.

69. ibid., p. 91.
70. Burke and Wills Commission 1862, Q 601, p. 26; Beckler 1993, p. 97; Bonyhady 1991, p. 149.
71. Beckler 1993, pp 94–5, 98, 170.
72. ibid., p. 52.
73. Walsh 1988, p. 27.
74. Beckler 1993, p. 124.
75. ibid., pp 114–15.
76. ibid., pp 125, 127, 130.
77. ibid., p. 138.
78. H. Beckler, Medical Reports, *La Trobe Manuscripts Collection*, State Library of Victoria, Box 2082/4b.
79. Beckler 1993, pp 128, 147, 151.
80. ibid., p. 170.
81. ibid., p. 171.
82. ibid., pp 153, 175.
83. Bergin 1982, p. 18.
84. Beckler 1993, p. 175.
85. ibid., p. 182.
86. Burke and Wills Commission 1862, 'T. McDonough', Q 489, p. 21; Burke and Wills Commission 1862, 'H. Beckler', Q 1887, p. 73; note that the Royal Navy used lime juice because this was available from British possessions in the West Indies; oranges and lemons would have had to be obtained from the Mediterranean area; for the history of vitamin C, see Emsley 1995.
87. H. Beckler to the Exploration Committee, *La Trobe Manuscripts Collection*, State Library of Victoria, box 2082/4b.
88. Burke and Wills Commission 1862, H. Beckler, Q 1889, p. 73.
89. Clemeston 1989, vol. 1, p. 89.
90. Provisional list of stores sent to Mueller, *La Trobe Manuscripts Collection*, State Library of Victoria, box 2077/5.
91. H. Beckler, Medical Reports, *La Trobe Manuscripts Collection*, State Library of Victoria, box 2082/4b.
92. Professor John Earl, pers. comm.; Hayman 1994, p. 408.
93. J. King, in Wills 1861, p. 3.
94. Wills 1861, p. 28.
95. Isaacs 1987, p. 115; Low 1989, p. 87; Kerwin 1986, p. 37.
96. J. King, in Wills 1861, p. 3.
97. Wills 1861, p. 29.
98. J. King, in Wills 1861, p. 3.
99. Wills 1861, p. 31.
100. ibid., p. 32.
101. ibid., pp 31–2.
102. J. King, in Wills 1861, p. 5.
103. Davidson et al. 1979, pp 284–5.
104. Dr Richard Smith, pers. comm.
105. Earl & McCleary 1994, p. 683; McCleary & Chick 1977, p. 207; McCleary, Kennedy & Chick 1980, p. 40.
106. Earl & McCleary 1994, p. 683.
107. Moorehead 1965, p. 131 et seq.
108. McKinlay 1862?, p. 11; Whyte 1881, p. 14; Alexander 1961, pp 1–22; Wills 1863, pp 228–9; Madigan 1936b, p. 27.

– 17 –

JOHN MCDOUALL STUART

1. Webster 1958; Mudie 1968; Webster 1996.
2. Webster 1958, p. 55.
3. Select Committee Report on Prospectus of Great Northern Copper Mining Co., *South Australian Parliamentary Papers*, 1860, No. 83.
4. Webster 1958, p. 58.
5. ibid., p. 61.
6. ibid., p. 56, identifies Forster as William Forster (or Foster) from Port Lincoln; Mudie 1968, p. 23, refers to him as George Forster.
7. Webster 1958, p. 69, points out that the governor's despatch refers to five horses; but the editor of Stuart's journal (Hardman 1865) mentions six. The sixth horse might have been that ridden by Alfred Barker who returned to Oratunga.
8. Hardman 1865, Tuesday 17 August, p. 39; Webster 1996, First Journey, p. 33.
9. Hardman 1865, p. 40.
10. ibid., p. 42.
11. The original of this letter is in the possession of the Royal Geographical Society of South Australia and has been reproduced in facsimile in the *Proceedings of the Royal Geographical Society of South Australia*; also reproduced in Webster 1958, p. 77.

12. 'Presentation of the Royal Awards', *Journal of the Royal Geographical Society*, 1859, vol. 29, p. c: this note, on the business of the society, gave Stuart's name as John Macdougall Stuart!

13. Webster 1958, pp 84–5.

14. Report, with chart of northern explorations, *South Australian Parliamentary Papers*, 1858, no. 25.

15. Hardman 1865, p. 46; Stuart 1861a. The paper was 'Read' 12 March 1860.

16. Mudie 1968, p. 56; Brand-Miller, James & Maggiore 1993, p. 132.

17. Webster 1958, p. 97.

18. Hardman 1865, p. 52.

19. ibid., p. 54.

20. ibid., p. 60.

21. ibid., pp 60–1.

22. ibid., p. 76.

23. Webster 1996, Second Journey, p. 90.

24. Hardman 1865, p. 79.

25. ibid., loc. cit.; Webster 1996, p. 94.

26. Hardman 1865, p. 85. Incorrectly spelt 'Louden' by this author; Webster 1996, 23 June 1859, p. 102.

27. Hardman 1865, p. 61.

28. Blanche was the first name of the governor's wife.

29. Northern Explorations, *South Australian Parliamentary Papers*, 1858, No. 151, p. 15.

30. Thomson & Barnett 1985.

31. Casperson 1979; McLaren, Wiltshire & Leslie 1986; Harris 1980–81; Boyd 1990.

32. Governor's Despatch to London: quoted by Webster 1958, p. 103.

33. Quoted by Webster 1958, p. 104.

34. For the third expedition, see Stuart 1861b, p. 83.

35. Webster 1996, Third Journey, 28 October, p. 113.

36. ibid., 31 October, p. 119.

37. ibid., 7 November, p. 122.

38. The method used to prepare and dry beef at this time has been described by Stephen King, a member of Stuart's sixth expedition, in his handwritten *Account of Stuart's Expedition*, Mortlock Library, State Library of South Australia, Adelaide, PRG627, Item 297.

39. Webster 1996, Third Journey, 20 November, p. 136; Hardman 1865, p. 100.

40. Hardman 1865, p. 117.

41. ibid., 6 January, p. 123.

42. Hardman 1865, p. 130.

43. ibid., p. 124; Kekwick is buried in Blinman Cemetery.

44. ibid., p. 130; Webster 1996, Third Journey, p. 163.

45. Webster 1958, p. 122.

46. Stuart 1861c. Read 11 February 1861.

47. Hardman 1865, p. 134.

48. ibid., p. 146.

49. ibid., p. 143.

50. ibid., p. 151.

51. Mudie 1968, p. 100.

52. Hardman 1865, pp 153–63; Webster 1958, p. 288; Brinkley Bluff is at 23° 43' S, 133° 24' E, Waterhouse Range is at 23° 59' S, 133° 20' E. See Reader's Digest 1994.

53. Webster 1958, p. 136.

54. ibid., p. 289.

55. Stuart 1983, p. 34. Accurate transcription of Stuart's handwritten account during his fourth expedition, first published in *South Australian Register*, 6–11 December 1860.

56. Stuart 1983, pp 34–5.

57. Reader's Digest 1994.

58. Stuart 1861c.

59. Hardman 1865, p. 164.

60. J. M. Stuart's Exploration 1860, *South Australian Parliamentary Papers*, 1861, No. 65.

61. Webster 1958, p. 154; Mudie 1968, p. 107.

62. Stokes 1996, p. 34; Stuart 1864. 'Exploration in Australia, Epitome of the Journals', a handwritten ten-page statement held by the Royal Geographical Society, London.

63. Giles 1926; facsimile edition 1995, p. 47.

64. Giles 1926, p. 48.

65. ibid., p. 47; Dr Eric Simms, pers. comm.

66. See Cunningham et al. 1992.

67. Webster 1996, Fourth Journey, p. 202 and notes.

68. ibid., p. 210.

69. ibid., p. 212; Hardman 1865, p. 196.

70. Omitted from Hardman 1865.

71. Webster 1996, Fourth Journey, 16 May, p. 218; Hardman 1865, p. 182.

72. Hardman 1865, p. 182.

73. ibid., p. 207; Webster 1996, Fourth Journey, p. 242; Brand-Miller, James & Maggiore 1993, p. 132.

74. Webster 1958, pp 145, 291.

75. Hardman 1865, p. 213.

76. Webster 1996, Fourth Journey, p. 248.

77. Hardman 1865, pp 216–18.

78. ibid., p. 219.

79. ibid., p. 225.

80. Webster 1996, Fourth Journey, 21 July, p. 265; Hardman 1865, p. 231.

81. Hardman 1865, pp 237–8.

82. ibid., p. 243.

83. Webster 1958, p. 153.

84. Webster 1996, Fifth Journey, p. 283.

85. ibid., pp 282–3.

86. ibid., p. 283; Stuart 1862. Read 25 November 1861.

87. Webster 1996, Fifth Journey, p. 293.

88. Webster 1996, Fifth Journey, p. 300; the present-day town of Tennant Creek is a little to the south of the creek and its position is 19° 39' S, 134° 11' E. See Reader's Digest 1994.

89. Webster 1996, Fifth Journey, p. 300.

90. Webster 1958, p. 174; Stuart 1862, p. 346; Hardman 1865, p. 180.

91. Hardman 1865, p. 284; Webster 1996, Fifth Journey, p. 313.

92. Webster 1996, Fifth Journey, p. 313.

93. Hardman 1865, p. 292; Webster 1996, Fifth Journey, p. 320.

94. Hardman 1865, p. 294; Webster 1996, Fifth Journey, p. 323.

95. Hardman 1865, p. 306; Webster 1996, Fifth Journey, p. 334.

96. Hardman 1865, p. 309; Webster 1996, Fifth Journey, p. 337.

97. Webster 1958, p. 176.

98. Hardman 1865, p. 307; Webster 1996, Fifth Journey, p. 335.

99. Hardman 1865, p. 323; Webster 1958, p. 180.

100. In discussion of Stuart 1861b, p. 83. Read 14 January 1861.

101. Webster 1958, p. 158.

102. According to Webster (1958, p. 158), the governor presented it to Stuart 'in November 1861 on his return from his fifth expedition'; however, on p. 183, Webster writes that, 'when Stuart visited the Government Offices on Monday 23 September 1861, the Governor, Sir Richard MacDonnell, took the opportunity of presenting to him the gold medal of the Royal Geographical Society ...' According to Mudie (1968, p. 164), Stuart attended the governor on 23 September 1861, and 'As the Patron's Medal had arrived from London, MacDonnell, acting as representative of the Royal Geographical Society, now presented it to the explorer.'

103. Webster 1958, p. 189; This letter was dated 5 November 1861; it is a rare example of a 'non-expert' body avoiding telling the 'expert' how to carry out his work in unexpected circumstances.

104. The letter is reproduced in full in Webster 1958, p. 191.

105. ibid., p. 175.

106. Hardman 1865, p. 327.

107. Hardman 1865, p. 329; Webster 1996, Sixth Journey, p. 371.

108. Webster 1996, Sixth Journey, p. 383.

109. ibid., p. 383.

110. ibid., p. 383.

111. Hardman 1865, p. 338; Webster 1996, Sixth Journey, p. 386.

112. Hardman 1865, p. 341; Webster 1996, Sixth Journey, p. 329.

113. Hardman 1865, p. 343; Webster 1996, Sixth Journey, p. 381.

114. Webster 1996, Sixth Journey, p. 394; Hardman 1865, p. 346, records: 'I must now endeavour to find a country to the northward and make the Roper.'

115. Hardman 1865, 22 May, p. 341; Webster 1996, Sixth Journey, p. 349.

116. Hardman 1865, p. 352; Webster 1996, Sixth Journey, p. 400.

117. Hardman 1865, p. 375; Webster 1996, Sixth Journey, p. 421.

118. Webster 1996, Sixth Journey, 29 June, p. 423.

119. Hardman 1865, pp 377–8; Webster 1996, Sixth Journey, 30 June, p. 424.

120. Hardman 1865, p. 384, incorrectly gives Waterhouse the initials 'H. W. W.'

121. Hardman 1865, p. 387, refers to this river as the 'Katherine', but Webster 1996, Sixth Journey, p. 432, uses 'Catherine'.

122. Hardman 1865, p. 388; Webster 1996, Sixth Journey, p. 433.
123. Hardman 1865, 15 July, p. 393; Webster 1958, p. 271; Webster 1996, Sixth Journey, p. 438.
124. Webster 1996, Sixth Journey, p. 449.
125. Hardman 1865, p. 406.
126. ibid., pp 406–7; Webster 1996, Sixth Journey, p. 449.
127. Webster 1958, pp 230, 271–4; the tree has been identified as *Hemicyclia australasica*.
128. Hardman 1865, p. 410; Webster 1958, p. 233; Webster 1996, Sixth Journey, p. 453; Hardman 1865, p. 411, gives the latitude 12° 14' 50" S.
129. Webster 1996, Sixth Journey, p. 454.
130. ibid., 2 August, p. 457.
131. ibid., p. 459.
132. ibid., 21 August, p. 468.
133. ibid., pp 469–70.
134. ibid., p. 472.
135. ibid., 8 September, p. 476.
136. ibid., 31 October, pp 502–3.
137. ibid., p. 516.
138. Telegram to hon. commissioner of Crown Lands from John McDouall Stuart, in Webster 1958, p. 249.
139. ibid., pp 249–53.
140. ibid., pp 258–9; Ellis 1925.
141. Strehlow 1967, p. 1.
142. Webster 1958, pp 272–4; Stuart 1861c; J. M. Stuart's Exploration 1860, *South Australian Parliamentary Papers*, 1861, No. 65; Lindsay 1889.
143. Webster 1964; reproduced without change of pagination from *Proceedings of the Royal Geographical Society of South Australia*, 1961, vol. 62, pp 37–46.
144. Strehlow 1967, p. 1.
145. Webster 1961, p. 46.

BIBLIOGRAPHY

Abbot, R. 1995, 'If only Captain Cook's "my lads" had been "my LADS"', *Defence Science News*, No. 10.

Abbot, R. & Leech, J. 1996, 'Charting dangerous waters with airborne lasers', *Search*, Vol. 27.

Alexander, C. L. 1961, 'John McKinlay, Explorer, 1819–1872', *Proceedings of the Royal Geographical Society of Australasia (South Australian Branch)*, Vol. 63.

Andrews, A. E. J. (ed.) 1984, *The Devil's Wilderness: George Caley's Journey to Mount Banks: 1804*, Blubber Head Press, Hobart.

Andrews, A. E. J. 1986, *Stapylton*, Blubber Head Press, Hobart, 297 pp.

Andrews, A. E. J. 1992, *Major Mitchell's Map 1834*, Blubber Head Press, Hobart, 402 pp.

Archibald, J. 1891, 'Notes on the ancient wreck discovered near Warrnambool', *Transactions of the Royal Geographical Society of Australasia (Victorian Branch)*, Vol. 9, p. 40.

Aurousseau, M. 1968 (ed.), *The Letters of F. W. Ludwig Leichhardt* (3 vols) Hakluyt Society, Cambridge University Press, London.

Austin, K. A. 1964, *The Voyage of the Investigator*, Rigby, Adelaide.

Austin, K. A. 1974, *Matthew Flinders on the Victorian Coast April–May 1802*, Cypress, Melbourne.

Badger, G. M. 1970, 'Cook the Scientist', In G. M. Badger (ed.), *Captain Cook: Navigator and Scientist*, ANU, Canberra.

Badger, G. 1988, *The Explorers of the Pacific*, Kangaroo Press, Kenthurst, NSW.

Balfour, F. R. S. 1944, 'Archibald Menzies', *Proceedings of the Linnaean Society*, Vol. 156.

Bambrick, S. (ed.) 1994, *The Cambridge Encyclopedia of Australia*, Cambridge University Press, Cambridge.

Banks, J. 1980, *Banks' Florilegium*, Alecto Historical Editions in association with the British Museum of Natural History, London.

Barratt, G. 1988, *The Russians and Australia*. University of British Columbia Press, Vancouver.

Battle, L. & Bachmann, B. 1998, 'Rugged Outback Isle', *Australian Geographic*, (January–March), pp 81–107.

Baudin, N. 1974, *Journal de Mer: The Journal of Post-Captain Nicolas Baudin*, trans. C. Cornell, Libraries Board of South Australia, Adelaide.

Bayldon, F. J. 1926, 'Voyage of Louis Vaez de Torres', *Journal of the Royal Australian Historical Society*, Vol. 11.

Bayldon, F. J. 1930, 'Voyage of Torres', *Journal of the Royal Australian Historical Society*, Vol. 16.

Beaglehole, J. C. 1940–41, 'The Colonial Office, 1782–1854', *Historical Studies Australia and New Zealand*, Vol. 1, pp 170–89.

Beaglehole, J. C. 1947, *The Exploration of the Pacific*, Adam & Charles Black, London.

Beaglehole, J. C. (ed.) 1962, *The Endeavour Journal of Joseph Banks 1768–1771* (2 vols) Angus & Robertson, Sydney.

Beaglehole, J. C. (ed.) 1967, 'The Voyage of the *Resolution* and *Discovery* 1776–1780', in *The Journals of Captain James Cook* (4 vols), Cambridge University Press, Cambridge, Vol. 3, pt 2.

Beaglehole, J. C. (ed.) 1968, 'The voyage of the Endeavour' in *The Journals of Captain James Cook* (4 vols), Hakluyt, Cambridge, Vol. 1.

Beaglehole, J. C. (ed.) 1969, 'The Voyage of the *Resolution* and *Adventure* 1772–1775', in *The Journals of Captain James Cook* (4 vols), Cambridge University Press, Cambridge, Vol. 2.

Beale, E. 1979, *Sturt: The Chipped Idol*, Sydney University Press, Sydney.

Beckler, H. 1993, *A Journey to Cooper's Creek*, (trans. S. Jeffries & M. Kertesz), Melbourne University Press, Melbourne.

Bell, C.1974, *Portugal and the Quest for the Indies*, Barnes and Noble, New York.

Bennett, J. A. 1987, *The Divided Circle*, Phaidon-Christie's, Oxford.

Bergin, T. 1981, *In the Steps of Burke and Wills*, Australian Broadcasting Commission, Sydney.

Bergin, T. J. 1982, 'Courage and Corruption', unpublished masters thesis, University of New England, NSW.

Berra, T. M. & Allen, G. R. 1989, 'Burrowing, emergence, behaviour and functional morpholoy of the Australian Salamanderfish *Lepidogalaxias salamandroides*', *Fisheries*, Vol. 14 (5), pp 2–10.

Black, E. C. 1963, 'The Lake Torrens Hoodoo', *Proceedings of the Royal Geographical Society of Australasia (South Australian Branch)*, Vol. 64.

Bladen, F. M. (ed.) 1892–1901, *Historical Records of New South Wales* (7 vols.), Government Printer, Sydney; facsimile reprint, Lansdown Slattery & Co., Mona Vale, NSW, 1978.

Blainey, G. 1994, *A Shorter History of Australia*, Heinemann Australia, Port Melbourne.

Boden, A. 1985, *Floral Emblems of Australia*, Australian Government Publishing Service, Canberra.

Bonyhady, T. 1991, *Burke and Wills. From Melbourne to Myth*, David Ell, Balmain, NSW.

Bonython, C. W. 1962–63, 'Further light on river floods reaching Lake Eyre', *Proceedings of the Royal Geographical Society of Australasia (South Australian Branch)*, Vol. 64, pp 9–22.

Bonython, C. W. 1980, *Walking the Simpson Desert*, Rigby, Adelaide.

Bonython, C. W. & Mason, B. 1953, 'The filling and drying of Lake Eyre', *Geographical Journal*, Vol. 119.

Bowden, K. M. 1952, *George Bass*, Oxford University Press, London.

Boyd, W. E. 1990, 'Mound springs', in M. J. Tyler, C. R. Twidale, M. Davies & C. B. Wells (eds), *Natural History of the North East Deserts*, Royal Society of South Australia, Adelaide.

Branagan, D. F. 1985, 'Phillip Parker King: Colonial Anchorman', in A. Wheeler & J. H. Price (eds), *From Linnaeus to Darwin: Commentaries on the History of Biology and Geology*, Special Publication no. 3, Society for the History of Natural History, London.

Branagan, D. F. 1994, 'Ludwig Leichhardt: Geologist in Australia', in H. Lamping & M. Linke (eds), *Australia: Studies on the History of Discoveries and Exploration*, Johann Wolfgang Goethe-Universitat, Frankfurt am Main.

Brand–Miller, J., James, K. W. & Maggiore, P. M.A. 1993, *Tables of Composition of Aboriginal Foods*, Aboriginal Studies Press, Canberra.

Brock, D. G. 1975, *To the Desert with Sturt*, (ed. K. Peake-Jones) Royal Geographical Society of Australasia, South Australian Branch, Adelaide.

Brown, H. 1978, *Man and the Stars*, Oxford University Press, Oxford.

Browne, J. H. 1966, 'Journal of the Sturt Expedition 1844–1845', (ed. H. J. Finniss), *South Australiana*, Vol. 5, p. 23.

Browning, E. B. 1887, *Aurora Leigh*, Smith, Elder & Co., London.

Bunce, D. 1979, *Travels with Dr Leichhardt in Australia*, Oxford University Press, Melbourne.

Burke and Wills Commission 1862, *Report of the Commissioners appointed to enquire into and report upon circumstances connected with the sufferings and death of*

Robert O'Hara Burke and William John Wills, the Victorian explorers, Government Printer, Melbourne.

Burn, D. 1955, *Narrative of the Overland Journey of Sir John and Lady Franklin and Party from Hobart Town to Macquarie Harbour 1842*, (ed. G. Mackaness) D. S. Ford, Sydney.

Butler, R. 1989, *The Men That God Forgot*, originally published by Hutchinson, 1975; published and reprinted many times by the author; Richard Butler, Richmond, Victoria, 1989.

Caley, G. 1966, *Reflections on the Colony of New South Wales*, (ed. J. E. B. Currey), Lansdowne Press, Melbourne.

Campbell, J. 1983, 'Smallpox in Aboriginal Australia 1829–1931', *Historical Studies*, 1983, Vol. 20.

Campbell, J. 1985, 'Smallpox in Aboriginal Australia, The Early 1830s', *Historical Studies*, Vol. 21.

Campbell, W. S. 1916, 'An historical vessel: the Lady Nelson', *Journal of the Royal Australian Historical Society*, Vol. 3.

Casperson, K. 1979, *Mound Springs of South Australia*, South Australian Department of Environment, Adelaide.

Cawthorne, W. A. 1926, *The Kangaroo Islanders*, Rigby, Adelaide.

Chick, H. 1952, 'Early investigations of scurvy and of the antiscorbutic vitamin', *Proceedings of the Nutrition Society*, 1953, Vol. 12.

Chisholm, A. A. (ed.-in-chief) 1958–1962, *The Australian Encyclopaedia* (10 vols), Angus & Robertson, Sydney.

Clarke, M. 1929, *For the Term of His Natural Life*, Angus & Robertson, Sydney.

Clarke, W. B. 1843, 'On a fossil pine forest at Kurrur-Kurran, in the inlet of Awaaba, east coast of Australia', *Proceedings of the Geological Society of London*, Vol. iv.

Cleland, J. B. 1914, 'Appendix B, Commonwealth of Australia, Quarantine Service Publication No. 3',

in J. H. L. Cumpston, *The History of Smallpox in Australia, 1788–1908*, Government Printer, Melbourne.

Clemeston, C. A. B. 1989, *Vitamin C* (3 vols), CRC Press, Boca Raton, Florida.

Clews, H. P. G. 1973, *Strzelecki's Ascent of Mount Kosciusko 1840*, Australia Felix Literary Club, Melbourne.

Collett, J. 1996, 'George Caley: recognition at last for a scientific outcast', *Search*, Vol. 27.

Collingridge, G. 1895, *The Discovery of Australia: A Critical, Documentary, and Historic Investigation Concerning the Priority of Discovery in Australasia by Europeans Before the Arrival of Lieut. James Cook in the 'Endeavour', in the Year 1770*, Hayes, Sydney.

Columbus, F. 1959, *The Life of the Admiral Christopher Columbus by His Son, Ferdinand*, The Folio Society, London.

Connell, G. 1980, *The Mystery of Ludwig Leichhardt*, Melbourne University Press, Melbourne.

Cook, J. 1776, 'On the Method taken for preserving the Health of the Crew of His Majesty's Ship the *Resolution* during her late voyage round the World', *Philosophical Transactions of the Royal Society*, Vol. 66.

Cooper, H. M. 1953, *The Unknown Coast*, Advertiser Printing Office/Cooper, Adelaide.

Cooper, H. M. 1954, 'Kangaroo Island's wild pigs', *South Australian Naturalist*, Vol. 29.

Corbett, L. 1995, *The Dingo in Australia and Asia*, University of NSW Press, Sydney.

Couch, B. V. 1963, 'Thomas Livingston Mitchell 1827–1837', unpublished masters thesis, University of Sydney, Sydney.

Cox, F. 1995, 'The threat of diseases old and new', *Chemistry and Industry*.

Croker, H. 1979, *The Camp by the River*, Charles Sturt Memorial Museum Trust, Adelaide.

Cumpston, J. H. L. 1951, *Charles Sturt: His Life and Journeys of Exploration*, Georgian House, Melbourne.

Cumpston, J. H. L. 1954, *Thomas Mitchell: Surveyor General and Explorer*, Oxford University Press, London.

Cumpston, J. H. L. 1964, *The Inland Sea and the Great River*, Angus & Robertson, Sydney.

Cunningham, A. 1828, 'The late tour of A. Cunningham Esq.', in A. Hill (ed.), *Australian Quarterly Journal of Theology, Literature and Science*, Edgar, Sydney.

Cunningham, G. M., Mulham, W. E., Milthorpe, P. L. & Leigh, J. H. 1992, *The Plants of Western New South Wales*, Soil Conservation Service of New South Wales, Inkator Press, Melbourne.

Dampier, W. 1697, *A New Voyage Round the World*, James Knapton, London; republished 1937, A. & C. Black, London.

Dampier, W. 1729 (1981), *A Voyage to New Holland: the English voyage of discovery to the South Seas in 1699*, (ed. J. Spencer), Knapton, London; facsimile edition 1981, Alan Sutton Publishing, Gloucester, UK.

Davidson, D. S. 1935, 'Chronology of Australian watercraft', *Journal of the Polynesian Society*, Vol. 44.

Davidson, D. S. 1939, *Journal of the American Oriental Society*, Vol. 58.

Davidson, S., Passmore, R., Brock, J. F. & Truswell, A. S. 1979, *Human Nutrition and Dietetics*, Churchill Livingstone, Edinburgh.

Dawson, J. 1881, *Australian Aborigines*, George Robertson, Melbourne.

Day, A. 1967, *The Admiralty Hydrographic Service 1795–1919*, H. M. Stationery Office, London.

de Beer, G. R. 1952, 'The relations between Fellows', *Notes and Records of the Royal Society of London*, Vol. 9.

Delbridge, A. 1991 (ed. in chief), *The Macquarie Dictionary*, 2nd edn, Macquarie Library, McMahons Point, NSW.

Denison, W. 1870, *Varieties of Vice-Regal Life* (2 vols), Longmans, London.

Devine, D. 1973, *The Opening of the World*, G. P. Putnam's Sons, New York.

Dillon, R. H. 1951, 'Archibald Menzies trophies', *British Columbia Historical Quarterly*, Vol. 15.

Dor-Ner, Zvi & Scheller, W. G. 1992, *Columbus and the Age of Discovery*, HarperCollins, London.

Dowd, B. T. 1937, 'Charles Grimes: The Second Surveyor-General of New South Wales', *Journal of the Royal Historical Society*, Vol. 22.

Dowling, P. J. 1990, 'Violent epidemics, disease, conflict and Aboriginal population collapse as a result of European contact in the Riverland of South Australia', unpublished masters thesis, Australian National University, Canberra.

Drake-Brockman, H. 1963, *Voyage to Disaster: The Life of Francisco Pelsaert*, Angus & Robertson, Sydney.

Dulhunty, J. A. 1975, 'Shoreline shingle terraces and prehistoric fillings of Lake Eyre', *Transactions of the Royal Society of South Australia*, Vol. 99.

Dumont d'Urville, J. S. C. 1987, *Two Voyages to the South Seas*, 2 vols (trans. H. Rosenman), Melbourne University Press, Carlton, Victoria.

Duncan, S. 1997, 'The discovery of Australia: The Portuguese priority reconsidered', *Victorian Historical Journal*, Vol. 68 (1).

Dunmore, J. 1965, *French Explorers in the Pacific*, Vol. 1, Clarendon Press, Oxford.

Dunmore, J. 1969, *French Explorers in the Pacific*, Vol. 2, Oxford University Press, Oxford.

Dutton, G. 1967, *The Hero as Murderer*, Collins, Sydney/Cheshire, Melbourne.

Dutton, G. 1982, *In Search of Edward John Eyre*, Macmillan, South Melbourne.

Duyker, E. (ed.) 1992, *The Discovery of Tasmania*, St David's Park Publishing, Hobart.

Earl, J. W. & McCleary, B. V. 1994, 'Mystery of the poisoned expedition', *Nature*, Vol. 368.

Eccleston, G. C. 1990, *The Major Mitchell Trail: Exploring Australia Felix*, Department of Conservation and Environment, Melbourne.

Eccleston, G. C. 1992, 'Major Mitchell's 1836 "Australia Felix" Expedition, *Monash Publications in Geography*, Vol. 40.

Edwards, P. I. 1981, *The Journal of Peter Good*, British Museum of Natural History, London.

Eldershaw, M. S. 1938, *Phillip of Australia*, Angus & Robertson, Sydney.

Ellis, S. M. 1925 (ed.), *The Letters and Memoirs of Sir William Hardman*, Second Series, 1863–5, C. Palmer, London.

Emsley, J. 1995, 'A life on the high Cs', *Chemistry in Britain*, Vol. 31.

Engel, C. G. & Sharp, R. P. 1958, 'Chemical data on desert varnish', *Bulletin of the Geological Society of America*, Vol. 69.

Evans, W. R. 1995, 'The Murray Darling Basin: Underlying hydrogeology and broad scale changes', *ATSE Focus*, Vol. 89, p. 8.

Eyre, E. J. 1845, *Journals of Expeditions of Discovery into Central Australia, and Overland from Adelaide to King George's Sound in the years 1840–41* (2 vols), T. & W. Boone, London.

Eyre, E. J. 1984, *Autobiographical Narrative of Residence and Exploration in Australia, 1832–1839*, (ed. J. Waterhouse), Caliban Books, London.

Faivre, J-P. 1974, 'Foreword' to N. Baudin *Journal de Mer: The Journal of Post-Captain Nicolas Baudin*, (trans. by C. Cornell), Libraries Board of South Australia, Adelaide.

Fernández-Armesto, F. 1991, *The Times Atlas of World Exploration*, HarperCollins, London.

Fitzgerald, C. P. A. 1953, 'Chinese discovery of Australia', in T. Inglis Moore (ed.), *Australia Writes: An Anthology*, Cheshire, Melbourne.

FitzGerald, L. 1984, *Java La Grande*, The Publishers, Hobart.

Flannery, T. 1994, *The Future Eaters*, Reed Books, Chatswood, NSW.

Flannery, T. (ed.) 1996, *1788*, Text Publishing, Melbourne.

Flemming, J. 1984, *Journal of the Explorations of Charles Grimes*, Queensberry Hill Press, Carlton, Victoria.

Fleurieu, C-P-C., comte de 1791, *Discoveries of the French in 1768 and 1769, to the south-east of New Guinea* (trans. A. Nares), Stockdale, London.

Flinders, M. 1801, *Observations on the Coasts of Van Diemen's Land* … , Arrowsmith, London, 1801; reprinted with an introduction by G. Mackaness, 1979, Review Publications, Dubbo, NSW.

Flinders, M. 1814 (1774–1814), *A Voyage to Terra Australis* (3 vols), G. & W. Nicol, London.

Flood, J. 1995, *Archaeology of the Dreamtime*, Angus & Robertson, Sydney.

Foster, W. C. 1985, *Sir Thomas Livingston Mitchell and His World 1792–1855*, Institution of Surveyors, Sydney.

Frakes, L. A. (compiler) 1987, 'Australian Cretaceous shorelines, stage by stage', *Palaeogeology, Palaeoclimatology, Palaeoecology*, Vol. 59.

Freycinet, L. C. D. 1811, 'Atlas' in F. Péron, 1775–1810, *Voyage de découvertes aux terres australes exécute spar ordre de Sa Majeste l'empereur et roi, ur les corvettes*, Le Géographe, Le Naturaliste *et la goelette* La Casuarina … *1800–04* (2 vols), 1807–1816, Imprimerie Imperiale, Paris, Vol. 2.

Freycinet, L. C. D. 1827–39, *Voyage autour du monde entrepris par ordre du Roi* … *exécuté sur les corvettes de S.M*, L'Uranie *et* La Physicienne (5 vols), Imprimerie Imperiale, Paris.

Frith, J. H. & Calaby, J. H. 1969, *Kangaroos*, C. Hurst & Co., London.

Giblin, R. W. 1928, *The Early History of Tasmania: The Geographical Era 1642–1804*, Methuen, London.

Giles, A. 1926, *Exploring in the Seventies and the Construction of the Overland Telegraph Line*, W. K.

Thomas, Adelaide, 1926; facsimile edition 1995, Friends of the State Library of South Australia, Adelaide.

Gill, T. 1905, 'Who discovered Lake Alexandrina?', *Proceedings of the Royal Geographical Society of Australasia (South Australian Branch)*, Vol. 8.

Glover, C. J. M. & Sim, T. C. 1978, 'Studies on Central Australian fishes: A progress report', *South Australian Naturalist*, Vol. 52 (3).

Godard, P. 1993. *The First and Last Voyage of the Batavia*, Abrolhos Publishing, Perth.

Godfrey, M. C. S. 1996, 'Understanding the prehistoric diet of Aborigines in Australia', *Chemistry in Australia*, Vol. 63.

Gott, B. 1982, 'Kungea pomifera – Dawson's "nurt"', *The Artifact*, Vol. 7 (1–2).

Gould, J. 1848, *The Birds of Australia* (7 vols), John Gould, London.

Gould, J. 1863, *Mammals of Australia* (3 vols), J. Gould, London.

Grant, J. 1803, *The Narrative of a Voyage of Discovery, performed in His Majesty's Vessel The Lady Nelson*, T. Egerton, London; facsimile edition (1973), Adelaide.

Granzotto, G. 1986, *Christopher Columbus*, Guild Publishing, London.

Green, C. & Cook, J. 1771, 'Observations made ... at King George's Island [Tahiti] in the South Sea', *Philosophical Transactions of the Royal Society*, 1771, Vol. 61.

Grenfell Price, A. 1926–7, 'Sturt's voyage down the Murray: The Last Stage,' *Proceedings of the Royal Geographical Society of Australasia (South Australian Branch)*, Vol. 28.

Grenfell Price, A. 1937–38, 'The Mystery of Leichhardt. The South Australian Government Expedition of 1938, *Proceedings of the Royal Geographical Society of Australasia (South Australian Branch)*, 1937-38, Vol. 39, pp 9–48.

Grenfell Price, A. 1955, *Lake Eyre, South Australia: the great flooding of 1949–50*, Royal Geographical Society of Australasia, South Australian Branch, Adelaide.

Guillemard, F. H. H. 1890, *The Life of Ferdinand Magellan*, George Philip, London.

Habermale, M. A. 1980, 'The Great Artesian Basin, Australia', *BMR Journal of Australian Geology and Geophysics*, Vol. 5.

Hale, H. M. & Tindale, N. B. 1930, 'Notes on some human remains in the Lower Murray Valley', *Records of the South Australian Museum*, Vol. 4.

Hall, W. 1914, *Modern Navigation*, University Tutorial Press, London.

Hancock, W. K. 1936, 'Early settlement in South Australia', *Geographical Magazine*, Vol. 2.

Hardman, W. 1865 (ed.), *The Journals of John McDouall Stuart during the years 1858, 1859, 1860, 1861 and 1862*, Saunders, Otley & Co., London, 1865; facsimile edition (1975), Libraries Board of South Australia, Adelaide.

Harris, C. 1980–81, 'Oases in the desert: The mound springs of northern South Australia', *Proceedings of the Royal Geographical Society of South Australia*, Vol. 81.

Hart, H. H. 1952, *Sea Road to the Indies*, William Hodge, London.

Hatt, H. H. 1949, 'Vitamin C content of an old antiscorbutic: The Kerguelen cabbage', *Nature*, Vol. 164.

Havard, W. L. 1940, 'Sir Paul Edmund de Strzelecki', *Journal of the Royal Historical Society*, Vol. 26.

Hawdon, J. 1952, *The Journal of a Journey from New South Wales to Adelaide performed in 1838 by Mr Joseph Hawdon*, Georgian House, Melbourne.

Hawker, J. C. 1899–1901, *Early Experiences in South Australia* (2 vols), Wigg, Adelaide, facsimile edition (1975), Libraries Board of South Australia, Adelaide.

Hayman, J. 1994, 'The far Barcoo where they eat mardoo', *Nature*, Vol. 370.

Heeres, J. E. 1898, *Abel Tasman's Journal, His Life and Labours*, Muller, Amsterdam.

Heney, H. 1967, 'Strzelecki, Sir Paul Edmund de (1797–1873)', in D. Pike (ed.) *Australian Dictionary of Biography*, Melbourne University Press, Vol. 2.

Henneberg, M. & Henneberg, R. J. 1994, 'Treponematosis in an ancient Greek colony of Metaponto, southern Italy, 580–250 BCE', in O. Dutour, G. Palfi, J. Berato & J.-P. Brun (eds), *The Origin of Syphilis in Europe before or after 1493?* Centre Archeologique du Var-Editions Errance, Toulon, pp 92–8.

Hervé, R. 1983, *Chance Discovery of Australia and New Zealand by Portuguese and Spanish Navigators between 1521 and 1528*, (trans. J. Dunmore), Dunmore, Palmerston North, New Zealand.

Heward, R. 1842, 'Biographical sketch of the late Allan Cunningham', in W. J. Hooker, *Journal of Botany*, Longman Orme & Co. and Wm Pamplin, London.

Hilder, B. 1980, *The Voyage of Torres*, Queensland University Press, Brisbane.

Hoare, M. E. 1967, 'Learned societies in Australia: The foundation years in Victoria 1850–1860', *Records of the Australian Academy of Science*, Vol. 1 (2).

Holden, P. 1991, *Along the Dingo Fence*, Hodder & Stoughton, Sydney.

Hordern, M. 1997, *King of the Australian Coast*, The Milgunyah Press/Melbourne University Press, Melbourne.

Horner, F. B. 1987, *The French Reconnaissance*, Melbourne University Press, Carlton, Victoria.

Hovell, W. H. 1921, 'Journal kept on the journey from Lake George to Port Phillip, 1824–1825', *Journal of the Royal Australian Historical Society*, Vol. 7.

Howse, D. & Hutchinson, B. 1969, *The Clocks and Watches of Captain James Cook, 1768–1969*, Antiquarian Horological Society, London.

Hume, H. 1867, *The Life of Edward John Eyre, Governor of Jamaica*, Bentley, London.

Ingleton, G. C. 1944, *Charting a Continent*, Angus & Robertson, Sydney.

Ingleton, G. C. 1962, 'General Introduction' in J. White, *Journal of a Voyage to New South Wales*, (ed. A. H. Chisholm), Angus & Robertson, Sydney, p. 6.

Innes, H. 1986, *The Conquistadors*, Collins, London.

Isaacs, J. 1987, *Bush Food*, Ure Smith Press, Sydney.

James, L. 1994, *The Rise and Fall of the British Empire*, Little, Brown & Co., London.

Jane, C. 1968, *The Journal of Christopher Columbus*, (trans.; revised L. A. Vigneras), Anthony Blond, London.

Johnston, F. M. 1962, *Knights and Theodolites*, Edwards & Shaw, Sydney.

Jouanin, C. 1959, 'Les emeus de l'Expedition Baudin', *Oiseau et la Revue Française d'Ornithologie*, Vol. 29.

Judge, J. & Stanfield, J. L. 1986, 'Where Columbus found the New World', *National Geographic*, Vol. 170 (No. 5).

Kaluski, M. 1985, *Sir Paul Strzelecki*, A. E. Press, Melbourne.

Kerwin, B. 1986, 'Narrative', in L. Hercus & P. Sutton (eds), *This Is What Happened. Narratives by Aborigines*, (trans. G. Breen), Australian Institute of Aboriginal Studies, Melbourne.

King, J. 1982, *The First Fleet*, Macmillan, Melbourne.

King, J. 1984, *The First Settlement*, Macmillan, Melbourne.

King, J. & King, J. 1981, *Phillip Gidley King*, Methuen, North Ryde, NSW.

King, P. P. 1825, 'On the Maritime Geography of Australia', in B. Field (ed.) *Geographical Memoirs of New South Wales; by Various Hands*, Murray, London.

King, P. P. 1827, *Narrative of a Survey of the Intertropical and Western Coasts of Australia* (2 vols.), John Murray, London.

Kirkpatrick, E. A. 1934, *The Spanish Conquistadores*, A. & C. Black, London.

Kodicek, E. H. & Young, F. G. 1969, 'Captain Cook and scurvy', *Notes and Records of the Royal Society of London*, Vol. 24.

Kotwicki, V. 1986, *Floods on Lake Eyre*, Engineering and Water Supply Department, Adelaide.

Lamb, W. K. 1984, 'Introduction' in G. Vancouver, 1757–1798, *A Voyage of Discovery* (4 vols.), (ed. W. Kaye Lamb), Hakluyt Society, London, Vol. 1.

Langdon, R. 1975, *The Lost Caravel*, Pacific Publications, Sydney.

Langley, M. 1967, 'Charles Sturt and the Heart of Australia', *History Today*, Vol. 17.

Langley, M. 1972, *Sturt of the Murray*, originally published by Robert Hale, London, 1969; Discovery Press, Penrith, NSW.

Latham, R. (trans.) 1958, *The Travels of Marco Polo*, Penguin Books, Harmondsworth.

Lee, I. 1925, *Early Explorers in Australia*, Methuen, London.

Leichhardt, L. 1847, *Journey of an Overland Expedition in Australia from Moreton Bay to Port Essington a Distance of 3000 miles, During the Years 1844–1845*, T. & W. Boone, London; facsimile edition, Corkwood Press, North Adelaide, 1996.

Lethbridge, H. O. 1944, 'Sturt the Man' in *Souvenir of the Sturt Centenary*, Sturt Memorial Committee, Barrier Field Naturalists' Club, Broken Hill, NSW.

Lewis, J. 1916–17, 'Some Notes on the Early Navigation of the River Muray', *Proceedings of the Royal Geographical Society of Australasia (South Australian Branch)*, Vol. 18.

Leyland, M. & Leyland, M. 1967, *Where Dead Men Lie*, Lansdowne, Melbourne.

Lind, J. 1953, *Lind's Treatise on Scurvy ...* reprint of the first edition of *A Treatise of the Scurvy* by James Lind, M.D., with additional notes, Edinburgh University Press, Edinburgh.

Lindsay, D. 1889, 'An expedition across Australia from south to north between the Telegraph Line and the Queensland boundary in 1885–6 by David Lindsay', *Proceedings of the Royal Geographical Society, London*, Vol. 11 (11).

Lockyer, E. 1828, 'Journal', in A. Hill (ed.), *Australian Quarterly Journal of Theology, Literature and Science*, Edgar, Sydney.

Low, T. 1989, *Bush Tucker*, Angus & Robertson, Sydney.

Mack, J. D. 1972, *Matthew Flinders*, originally published by Collins, Australia, 1966; Discovery Press, Penrith, NSW.

Mackaness, G. (ed.) 1950, 'Introduction' to *Fourteen Journeys over the Blue Mountains of New South Wales 1813–1841* (3 vols), Ford, Sydney, 1950–1951; Reprinted by Review Publications, Dubbo, NSW, 1978, Vol. 1.

Mackaness, G. 1979, 'Introduction' in M. Flinders, 1774–1814, *Observations on the Coasts of Van Diemen's Land*, Australian Historical Monograph, 1946, Vol. 39, reprinted by Review Publications, Dubbo, NSW.

Macknight, C. C. 1972, 'Macassans and Aborigines', *Oceania*, Vol. 42 (4).

Macknight, C. C. 1976, *The Voyage to Marege: Macassan Trepangers in Northern Australia*, Melbourne University Press, Carlton, Victoria.

Macqueen, A. 1993, *The Life and Journeys of Barrallier*, Macqueen, Springwood, NSW.

Madigan, C. T. 1930, 'An aerial reconnaissance into the southeastern portion of central Australia', *Proceedings of the Royal Geographical Society of Australasia (South Australian Branch)*, Vol. 30.

Madigan, C. T. 1936a, 'The Australian sand-ridge deserts', *Geographical Review*, Vol. 26.

Madigan, C. T. 1936b, *Central Australia*, Oxford University Press, London.

Madigan, C. T. 1946a, *Crossing the Dead Heart*, Georgian House, Melbourne.

Madigan, C. T. 1946b, 'The Simpson Desert Expedition, 1939, Scientific Report No. 6. Geology – The sand formations', *Transactions of the Royal Society of South Australia*, Vol. 70.

Magarey, A. T. 1899, 'Australian aborigines water-quest', *Proceedings of the Royal Geographical Society of Australasia (South Australian Branch)*, Vol. 3.

Marchant, L. R. 1988, *France Australe*, Artlook Books, Perth.

Marchant, L. R. 1988, *An Island Unto Itself: William Dampier and New Holland*, Hesperion Press, Victoria Park, WA.

The Mary Rose Trust 1994, *The Mary Rose.*

Maude, H. E. 1968, 'The Tahitian Pork Trade: 1800–1830', in *Of Islands and Men*, Oxford University Press, Melbourne, chap. 5.

McCarthy, F. D. 1955, 'Notes on the cave paintings of Groote and Chasm islands in the Gulf of Carpentaria', *Mankind*, Vol. 5.

McCleary, B. V. & Chick, B. F. 1977, 'The purification and properties of a thiaminase I enzyme from nardoo (*Marsilea drummondi*)', *Phytochemistry*, Vol. 16.

McCleary, B. V., Kennedy, C. A. & Chick, B. F. 1980, 'Nardoo, bracken and rock ferns cause vitamin B1 deficiency in sheep', *Agricultural Gazette of New South Wales*, Vol. 91 (v).

McCrae, G. G. 1910–11, 'The ancient buried vessel at Warrnambool', *Victorian Geographical Journal*, Vol. 28.

McIntyre, K. G. 1977, *The Secret Discovery of Australia*, Souvenir Press, Menindee, South Australia.

McKiggan, I. F. 1987, 'The wreck site – historical and geographic factors', in B. Potter (ed.) *The Mahogany Ship: Relic or Legend?*, Institute Press, Warrnambool.

McKinlay, J. 1862?, *McKinlay's Journal of Exploration in the Interior of Australia*, Bailliere, Melbourne.

McLaren, N., Wiltshire, D. & Leslie, R. 1986, 'Biological Assessment of South Australian Mound Springs', in South Australian Department of Environment and Planning, *Heritage of the Mound Springs*, Government Printer, Adelaide.

McMinn, W. G. 1970, *Allan Cunningham, Botanist and Explorer*, Melbourne University Press, Carlton, Victoria.

Milford, G. D. 1935, *Governor Phillip and the Early Settlement of New South Wales*, Harbour Newspaper & Publishing, Sydney.

Mitchell, F. J. 1973, 'Studies on the ecology of the Agamid lizard *Amphibolurus maculosus* (Mitchell)', *Transactions of the Royal Society of South Australia*, Vol. 97 (1).

Mitchell, T. L. 1837, 'Account of the recent exploring expedition to the interior of Australia', *Geographical Journal*, Vol. 7.

Mitchell, T. L. 1838–39, *Three Expeditions into the Interior of Eastern Australia* (2 vols), T. & W. Boone, London, 1838; 2nd edition, T. & W. Boone, London, 1839; facsimile edition, Libraries Board of South Australia, 1965.

Mitchell, T. L. 1848, *Journal of an Expedition into the Interior of Tropical Australia, in Search of a Route from Sydney to the Gulf of Carpentaria*, Longman, Brown, Green & Longmans, London.

Moore, J. 1987, *The First Fleet Marines 1786–1792*, University of Queensland Press, St Lucia, Queensland.

Moorehead, A. 1965, *Cooper's Creek*, first published by Hamish Hamilton, London, 1963, Reprint Society, London.

Moorhouse, M. 1846, *A Vocabulary and Outline of the Grammatical Structure of the Murray River Language*, Murray, Adelaide.

Morphett, G. C. 1939, President's Address, *Proceedings of the Royal Geographical Society of Australasia (South Australian Branch)*, Vol. 40.

Mudie, I. 1968, *The Heroic Journey of John McDouall Stuart*, Angus & Robertson, Sydney.

Nelson, H. M. 1900, *Exploration Pamphlets*, Brisbane, Vol. 2.

Newcombe, C. F. (ed.) 1923, *Menzies' Journal of Vancouver's Voyage*, W. H. Cullin, Victoria, BC.

Noad, K. 1979, 'Commentary' in E. Beale, *Sturt: The Chipped Idol*, Sydney University Press, Sydney.

North, J. D. 1974, 'The astrolabe', *Scientific American*, Vol. 230 (1).

O'Brian, P. 1987, *Joseph Banks: A Life*, Collins Harvill, London.

O'Grady, F. 1964, 'Hamilton Hume', *Journal of the Royal Australian Historical Society*, Vol. 49.

O'Neill, T. 1997, 'Travelling the Australian dog fence', *National Geographic*, Vol. 191 (April).

Osborn, T. G. B. 1958, 'Robert Brown (1773–1858), *Australian Journal of Science*, Vol. 21.

Oxley, J. 1820, *Journals of Two Expeditions into the Interior of New South Wales*, Murray, London.

Oxley, J. 1925, 'Extract from the field books of Mr. John Oxley, relating to the discovery of the Brisbane River on 2 December 1823', *Journal of the Royal Historical Society of Queensland*, Vol. 2.

Pack, S. W. C. 1960, *Admiral Lord Anson: The story of Anson's voyage and naval events of his day*, Cassell, London.

Parbo, A. 1992, *Down Under: Mineral Heritage in Australasia*, Australian Institute of Mining and Metallurgy, Parkville, Victoria.

Parker, F. L. & Somerville J. D. 1943, 'The Cooper's Creek controversies', *Historical Studies Australia and New Zealand*, Vol. 2 (8).

Parker, S. A. 1984, 'The Extinct Kangaroo Island Emu', *Bulletin of the British Ornithologists' Club*, Vol. 101.

Péron, F. 1809, *A Voyage of Discovery to the Southern Hemisphere*, Richard Phillips, London.

Perrin, L. 1990, *The Mystery of the Leichhardt Survivor*, Downs Printing, Toowoomba, Queensland.

Phillips, W. D. & Phillips, C. R. 1992, *The Worlds of Christopher Columbus*, Cambridge University Press, Cambridge.

Pigafetta, A. 1969, *Magellan's Voyage: A Narrative Account of the First Circumnavigation* (2 vols), Yale University Press, New Haven, Vol. 1, 195 pp, (trans. R. A. Skelton); Vol. 2 reproduces the original version, written in French.

Pike, D. (ed.) 1967, *Australian Dictionary of Biography*, Melbourne University Press, Carlton, Victoria, Vol. 2.

Pike, G. 1949, 'Where did Leichhardt wander? A theory of his probable route and fate', *Journal of the Historical Society of Queensland*, Vol. 4.

Playford, P. 1996, *Carpet of Silver. The Wreck of the Zuytdorp*, University of Western Australia Press, Nedlands, WA.

Powell, A. P. 1980, 'P. P. King and the men of the *Mermaid* and *Bathurst*, *Journal of the Royal Australian Historical Society*, Vol. 65.

Pretty, G. et al. 1977 (Pretty, chairman, Feasibility Study Steering Committee), *Ngaiawang Folk Province*, Anthropology and Archaeology Branch, South Australian Museum, Adelaide.

Queensland Department of Mapping and Surveying 1987, 'Surveyors on horseback', *Bulletin of the Royal Geographical Society of Australasia (Queensland Branch)*, Vol. 22 (2).

Reader's Digest 1994, *Atlas of Australia*, Reader's Digest (Australia), Surry Hills, NSW.

Reader's Digest 1995, *Illustrated Guide to Australian Places*, Reader's Digest (Australia), Surry Hills, NSW.

Richardson, W. A. R. 1988, 'Piloting a toponymic course through sixteenth-century Southeast Asian waters', *Terrae Incognitae* (Journal of the Society for the History of Discoveries), Vol. 20.

Richardson, W. A. R. 1989, *The Portuguese Discovery of Australia: Fact or Fiction?*, National Library of Australia, Canberra.

Richardson, W. A. R. 1995a, 'A critique of Spanish and Portuguese claims to have discovered Australia', *The Investigator*, Vol. 30 (3).

Richardson, W. A. R. 1995b, 'A critique of Spanish and Portuguese claims to have discovered Australia – 2', *The Investigator*, Vol. 30 (4).

Rienits, R. 1962, 'Biographical Introduction', in J. White *Journal of a Voyage to New South Wales*, (ed. A. H. Chisholm), Angus & Robertson, Sydney.

Rienits, R. & Rienits, T. 1970, *The Voyages of Columbus*, Hamlyn, London.

Rigby, P. & Ward, K. 1969, *Rottnest Island Sketchbook*, Rigby, Adelaide.

Riviére, M. S. 1996, 'Discovery of the Brisbane River (from the Journal of John Uniacke)', *Journal of the Royal Historical Society of Queensland*, Vol. 16 (No 4).

Roderick, C. 1988, *Leichhardt the Dauntless Explorer*, Angus & Robertson, North Ryde, NSW.

Roditi, E. 1972, *Magellan of the Pacific*, Faber & Faber, London.

Roizman, B. (ed.) 1995, *Infectious Diseases in an Age of Change: The Impact of Human Ecology and Behaviour on Disease Transmission*, National Academy Press, Washington.

Rolls, E. C. 1990, 'The erratic communication between Australia and China', *Northern Territory Library Service, Occasional Papers*, Vol. 14.

(de) Rossel, E. P. E. 1808, *Voyage de D'Entrecasteaux, Envoyé a la Recherche de La Pérouse* (2 vols), L'Imprimerie Imperiale, Paris.

Royal Society of Victoria Exploration Committee 1860, 'Instructions ... and ... List of Articles and Services, Victorian Exploring Expedition', *Transactions and Proceedings of the Royal Society of Victoria*, Vol. 5, Appendix 1, pp lxv–lxxxiv.

Rudzki, K. 1995, 'Escaped rabbit calicivirus highlights Australia's chequered history of biological control', *Search*, Vol. 26.

Ruediger, W. J. 1986, *The Nor'west Bend Story*, Lutheran Publishing House, Adelaide.

Russell, H. S. 1888, *The Genesis of Queensland*, Turner & Henderson, Sydney, reprinted by Vintage Books, Toowoomba, Queensland.

Schilder, G. 1976, *Australia Unveiled*, Theatrvm Orbis Tarrararvm, Amsterdam.

Scott, E. 1910, *Terre Napoléon: A history of French explorations and projects in Australia*, Methuen, London.

Scott, E. 1912, 'English and French navigators on the Victorian coast, *Victorian Historical Magazine*, Vol. 2.

Scott, E. 1914, *The Life of Captain Matthew Flinders, R.N.*, Angus & Robertson, Sydney.

Scott, E. 1921, 'Hume and Hovell's journey to Port Phillip', *Journal of the Royal Australian Historical Society*, Vol. 7.

Scott, E. 1936, *A Short History of Australia*, Oxford University Press, London.

Serjeantson, S. W. 1989, 'HLA genes and antigens', in A. V. S. Hill & S. W. Serjeantson (eds), *The Colonization of the Pacific: A Genetic Trail*, Clarendon Press, Oxford.

Shann, E. O. 1948, *An Economic History of Australia*, Georgian House, Melbourne.

Sharp, A. 1963, *The Discovery of Australia*, Oxford University Press, Oxford.

Sharp, A. 1968, *The Voyages of Abel Janszoon Tasman*, Clarendon Press, London.

Skelton, R. A. 1954, 'Captain James Cook as a Hydrographer', *Mariner's Mirror*, Vol. 40.

Smith, P. C. 1974, *Per Mare Per Terram: A History of the Royal Marines*, Photo Precision, St Ives, Cambridgeshire.

Sobel, D. 1995, Longitude: *The True Story of a Lone Genius Who Solved the Greatest Scientific Problem of His Time*, Walker, New York.

Spate, O. H. K. 1982, 'George Collingridge 1847–1931: From Papal Zouave to Hermit of Berowra', in G. Collingridge *The First Discovery of Australia and New Zealand*, Pan Books, Sydney.

Spencer, J. 1981, 'Introduction', in W. Dampier *A Voyage to New Holland: The English voyage of discovery to the South Seas in 1699*, Knapton, London, 1729; facsimile edition 1981, (ed. J. Spencer), Alan Sutton Publishing, Gloucester, UK.

Sprod, D. 1994, 'Leichhardt's Second Expedition, 1846–1847; Why did it fail?', in H. Lamping & M. Linke (eds), *Australia: Studies on the History of Discoveries and Exploration*, Johann Wolfgang Goethe-Universität, Frankfurt am Main.

Stephens, R. 1936, 'Major Edmund Lockyer', *Journal of the West Australian Historical Society*, Vol. 2 (19), pp 1–9.

Stevens, H. N. (ed.) 1930, *New Light on the Discovery of Australia*, Hakluyt Society, London.

Stokes, E. 1986, *To the Inland Sea: Charles Sturt's Expedition 1844–1845*, Hutchinson of Australia, Melbourne.

Stokes, E. 1993, *The Desert Coast: Edward Eyre's Expedition 1840–41*, Five Mile Press, Knoxfield, Victoria.

Stokes, E. 1996, *Across the Centre*, Allen & Unwin, St. Leonards, NSW.

Stokes, J. L. 1846, *Discoveries in Australia: With an account of the coasts and rivers explored and surveyed during the Voyage of H.M.S. Beagle in the Years 1837–1843* (2 vols), T. & W. Boone, London.

Strehlow, T. G. H. 1967, *Comments on the Journals of John McDouall Stuart*, Libraries Board of South Australia, Adelaide.

Strzelecki, P. E. de 1845, *Physical Description of New South Wales and Van Diemen's Land*, Longman, Brown, Green & Longmans, London.

Strzelecki, P. E. de 1856, *Gold and Silver*, Longman, Brown, Green & Longmans, London.

Stuart, J. McDouall, 1861a, V, 'Journal of Australian Exploration. Second preparatory journey in the vicinity of Lake Torrens', *Journal of the Royal Geographical Society, London*, Vol. 31.

Stuart, J. McDouall 1861b, VI, 'Journal of Australian Exploration. Third preparatory journey in the vicinity of Lake Torrens', *Journal of the Royal Geographical Society, London*, 1861, Vol. 31.

Stuart, J. McDouall 1861c, VII, 'Journal of Australian Exploration. Last expedition into the Interior of Australia', *Journal of the Royal Geographical Society, London*, Vol. 31.

Stuart, J. McDouall 1862, 'Diary of Mr John McDouall Stuart's Exploration to the North of Murchison Range, in 20° S Lat., 1860–61', *Journal of the Royal Geographical Society, London*, Vol. 32.

Stuart, J. McDouall 1983 (1815–1866), *Fourth Expedition Journal March to September 1860*, Sullivan's Cove, Adelaide, 92 p.

Sturt, C. 1833, *Two Expeditions into the Interior of Southern Australia* (2 vols), Smith, Elder & Co., London.

Sturt, C. 1849, *Narrative of an Expedition into central Australia performed under the Authority of her Majesty's Government, during the years 1844, 5, and 6, together with a notice of the Province of South Australia in 1847*, (2 vols), T. & W. Boone, London.

Sturt, N. G. (Beatrix) 1899, *Life of Charles Sturt*, Smith, Elder & Co., London.

Taylor, E. G. R. & Richey, M. W. 1962, *The Geometrical Seaman*, Hollis & Carter, London.

Tench, W. 1961, *Sydney's First Four Years*, Angus & Robertson, Sydney.

Thomson, R. & Barnett, S. 1985, 'Geology, geomorphology and hydrogeology.', in J. Greenslade, C. Joseph & A. Reeves (eds), *South Australia's Mound Springs*, Nature Conservation Society of South Australia, Adelaide.

Thorne, A., Grün, R., Mortimer, G., Spooner, N. A., Simpson, J. J., McCulloch, M., Taylor, L, & Curnoe, D. 1999, 'Australia's oldest human remains: Age of the Lake Mungo 3 skeleton', *Journal of Human Evolution*, Vol. 36.

Thorne, A. & Raymond, R. 1989, *Man on the Rim*, Angus & Robertson, Sydney.

Tindale, N. B. 1926, 'Natives of Groote Eylandt and of the West Coast of the Gulf of Carpentaria', *Records of the South Australian Museum*, Vol. 3.

Tindale, N. B. 1928, 'Natives of Groote Eylandt and of the West Coast of the Gulf of Carpentaria', *Transactions of the Royal Society of South Australia*, Vol. 52, p. 6.

Tindale, N. B. 1939, 'Notes on the Ngaiawung Tribe, Murray River, South Australia', *South Australian Naturalist*, Vol. 20.

Tindale, N. B. 1940, 'Stone figure of Shou Lao', *Bulletin of the National Gallery of South Australia*, Vol. 2 (3).

Tipping, M. 1979, *Ludwig Becker: Artist and Naturalist with the Burke and Wills Expedition*, Melbourne University Press, Melbourne.

Triebel, L. A. & Batt, J. C. 1943, *The French Exploration of Australia*, University of Tasmania, Hobart.

Twidale, C. R., Parkin, L. W. & Rudd, E. A. 1990, 'C. T. Madigan's contributions to Geology in South and Central Australia', *Transactions of the Royal Society of South Australia*, Vol. 114.

Uren, M. & Stephens, R. 1941, *Waterless Horizons*, Robertson & Mullens, Melbourne.

Vancouver, G. 1984, *A Voyage of Discovery* (4 vols), (ed. W. Kaye Lamb), Hakluyt Society, London, 1757–98, Vol. 1.

van Wyck Mason, F. 1961, *Manila Galleon*, Hutchinson, London.

Varela, C. (ed.) 1992, *Cristóbal Colón, Textos y documentos completos.* Alianza Editorial SA, Madrid.

Villiers, A. 1976, 'Majellan: A voyage into the unknown changed man's understanding of his world', *National Geographic*, Vol. 149 (6).

Wade, J. 1977, 'Shou Lao: A Chinese figurine excavated at Darwin in 1879', *Australian Society for Historical Archaeology Newsletter*, Vol. 7 (no. 2, June).

Walker, J. B. 1914, *Early Tasmania*, Government Printer, Hobart.

Wallace, C. 1984, *The Lost Australia of Francois Péron*, Nottingham Court Press, London.

Wallis, H. 1986, 'The Portuguese voyages of discovery', *History Today*, Vol. 36 (June).

Walsh, G. L. 1988, *Australia's Greatest Rock Art*, Brill, Brown & Associates, Bathurst, NSW.

Walter, R. 1911, *A Voyage Round the World in the years 1740–4 [by] George Anson*, Dent, London.

Warner, W. L. 1932, 'Malay influence on the Aboriginal cultures of north-eastern Arnhem Land', *Oceania*, Vol. 2.

Waterhouse, G. R. 1846, *Natural History of Mammalia*, Vol. 1: Marsupiata, or pouched animals, Hippolyte, Baillière, London.

Waterhouse, J. 1984a (ed.), 'Charles Sturt', *Journal of the Central Australian Expedition 1844–45*, Caliban Books, London.

Waterhouse, J. 1984b, 'Introduction', in E. J. Eyre *Autobiographical Narrative of Residence and Exploration in Australia, 1832–1839*, (ed. J. Waterhouse), Caliban Books, London.

Waters, D. W. 1958, *The Art of Navigation in England in Elizabethan and Early Stuart Times*, Hollis & Carter, London.

Watson, F. (ed.) 1914–25, *Historical Records of Australia*, Series 1, 'Governors' despatches to and from England' (26 vols), Library Committee of Commonwealth Parliament, Sydney.

Watson, F. (ed.) 1921–23, *Historical Records of Australia*, Series 3, 'Despatches and papers relating to the settlement of the states' (7 vols), Library Committee of Commonwealth Parliament, Sydney

Watts, C. H. S. & Aslin, H. J. 1981, *The Rodents of Australia*, Angus & Robertson, London

Waugh, T. (trans.) 1984, *The Travels of Marco Polo*, Book Club Associates, London

Webb, J. 1995, *George Caley: 19th Century Naturalist*, Surrey Beatty & Sons, Sydney

Webster, E. M. 1980, *Whirlwinds in the Plain*, Melbourne University Press, Melbourne

Webster, E. M. 1986, *An Explorer at Rest: Ludwig Leichhardt at Port Essington*, Melbourne University Press, Melbourne

Webster, M. S. 1958, *John McDouall Stuart*, Melbourne University Press, Melbourne

Webster, M. S. 1964, 'John McDouall Stuart: His character and personal qualities', *Proceedings of the Royal Geographical Society of Australasia (South Australian Branch)*, Vol. 62; Reproduced in book form: Webster, M. S. 1964, *John McDouall Stuart: His Character and Personal Qualities*, Libraries Board of South Australia, Adelaide

Webster, M. S. 1996, 'The Journals of Journeys of Exploration in Australia by John McDouall Stuart, 1858–1862', unpublished manuscript, Mortlock Library, Adelaide

White, F. 1970, 'Cook the Navigator', in G. M. Badger (ed.), *Captain Cook: Navigator and Scientist*, ANU Press, Canberra

White, J. 1962, *Journal of a Voyage to New South Wales*, (ed. A. H. Chisholm), originally published by I. Debrett, London, 1790; Angus & Robertson, Sydney

Whitehouse, E. B. 1995, *The Northern Approaches: Australia in Old Maps 820–1770*, Boolarong Press, Brisbane

Whyte, D. 1881, *Sketch of Explorations of the late John McKinlay in the Interior of Australia 1861–2*, Aird & Coghill, Glasgow; facsimile edition, Public Libraries of South Australia, Adelaide, 1962

Williams, J. E. D. 1994, *From Sails to Satellites*, Oxford University Press, Oxford

Williams, M. A. J., Dunkerley, D. L., De Deckker, P., Kershaw, A. P. & Stokes, T. 1993, *Quaternary Environments*, Edward Arnold, London

Wills, W. (ed.) 1860, *A Successful Exploration through the Interior of Australia, from Melbourne to the Gulf of Carpentaria*, Bentley, London

Wills, W. J. 1861, *The Burke and Wills Exploring Expedition*, Wilson & MacKinnon, Melbourne

Wilson, N. 1995, 'Caley's Grevillea', *Australian Natural History*, Vol. 24 (12)

Woolley, R. 1970, 'The significance of the transit of Venus', in G. M. Badger (ed.), *Captain Cook: Navigator and Scientist*, ANU Press, Canberra

Young, D. M. 1961, *The Colonial Office in the Early Nineteenth Century*, Longmans, London

INDEX